POMPEY ELLIOTT

Previously a solicitor, archivist, and briefly a professional cricketer, Ross McMullin is one of Australia's finest historians. His books include the widely acclaimed ALP centenary history *The Light on the Hill*, the outstanding illustrated biography *Will Dyson: Australia's radical genius*, and the celebrated *So Monstrous a Travesty*, a history of the world's first national labour government.

He has written numerous chapters for multi-authored books on sport, Australian politics and history, and Australia's participation in the Great War. These publications include *Australian Prime Ministers*, edited by Michelle Grattan; *True Believers*, edited by John Faulkner and Stuart Macintyre; and *Test Team of the Century*, edited by Garrie Hutchinson.

Ross McMullin also writes frequent articles for newspapers and periodicals. He is a senior research fellow with the history department at the University of Melbourne.

Pompey Elliott

Ross McMullin

SCRIBE
Melbourne • London

Scribe Publications
18–20 Edward St, Brunswick, Victoria 3056, Australia
2 John St, Clerkenwell, London, WC1N 2ES, United Kingdom

First published by Scribe 2002
Reprinted (with minor corrections) 2002, 2006, 2007
This edition published 2008
Reprinted 2010, 2014, 2015, 2017, 2018

Edited by Catherine Magree

Indexed by Ann Philpott

Cover and text designed and typeset by Miriam Rosenbloom

Cover image: Brigadier General Harold Elliott by W B McInnes, 1921
(Australian War Memorial)

Text typeset in 11 on 14.3 pt Minion.

Printed and bound in Australia by Griffin Press.

Scribe Publications is committed to the sustainable use of natural resources and the use of paper products made responsibly from those resources.

9781921372018 (paperback)
9781921942730 (e-book)

A CiP entry for this title is available from the National Library of Australia.

scribepublications.com.au
scribepublications.co.uk

CONTENTS

Maps

Charts of formations and commanders

For three major Western Front battles of particular significance to Elliott there is, alongside the map, a chart showing the inter-relationship of the various formations and commanders engaged in that battle. The formations under Elliott's command are marked in bold.

Formations in the military hierarchy

Formations in descending order are as follows:

army
corps
division
brigade
battalion
company
platoon
section

[Photographs appear between pages 306 and 307]

Abbreviations in the text

AIF Australian Imperial Force
AIR Australian Infantry Regiment
ALP Australian Labor Party
CB Companion of the Order of the Bath
CMG Companion of the Order of St. Michael and St. George
DCM Distinguished Conduct Medal
DSO Distinguished Service Order
GHQ General Headquarters
GOC General Officer Commanding
MC Military Cross
MHR Member of the House of Representatives
MM Military Medal
MP Member of Parliament
NCO non-commissioned officer
RSSILA Returned Sailors' and Soldiers' Imperial League of Australia
VC Victoria Cross
VFL Victorian Football League
VIB Victorian Imperial Bushmen

Conversions

£1 (pound)	$2 Australian (post-1966)
1 shilling	10 cents
1 mile	1.6 kilometres
1 yard (=3 feet)	0.91 metres
1 inch	2.54 centimetres
1 acre	0.4 hectares

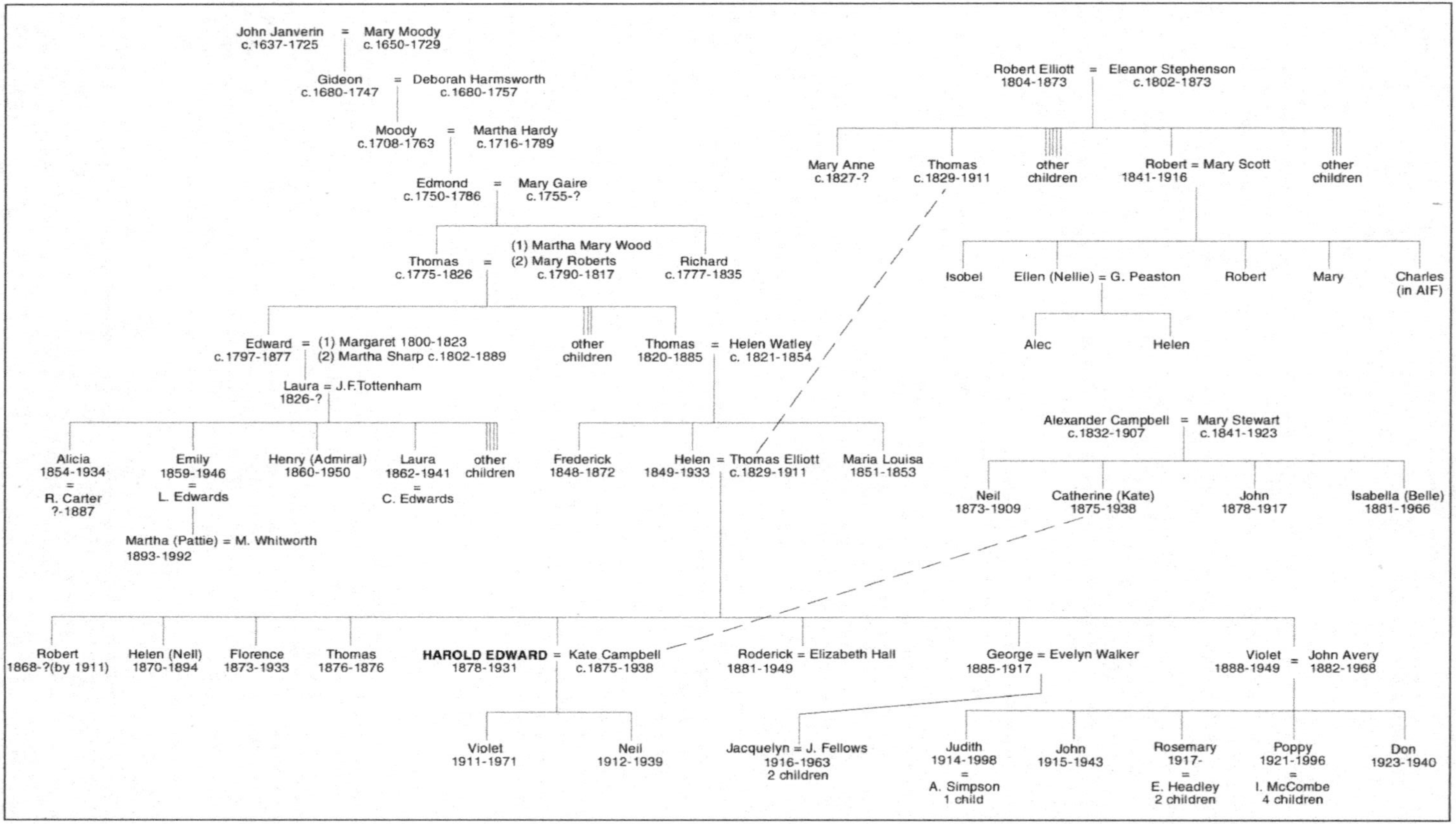
John Janverin = Mary Moody
c.1637-1725 c.1650-1729
Gideon = Deborah Harmsworth
c.1680-1747 c.1680-1757
Moody = Martha Hardy
c.1708-1763 c.1716-1789
Edmond = Mary Gaire
c.1750-1786 c.1755-?
Thomas = (1) Martha Mary Wood (2) Mary Roberts c.1790-1817
c.1775-1826
Richard
c.1777-1835
Edward = (1) Margaret 1800-1823 (2) Martha Sharp c.1802-1889
c.1797-1877
other children
Thomas = Helen Watley
1820-1885 c. 1821-1854
Laura = J.F.Tottenham
1826-?
Alicia
1854-1934
=
R. Carter
?-1887
Emily
1859-1946
=
L. Edwards
Martha (Pattie) = M. Whitworth
1893-1992
Henry (Admiral)
1860-1950
Laura
1862-1941
=
C. Edwards
other children
Frederick
1848-1872
Helen = Thomas Elliott
1849-1933 c.1829-1911
Maria Louisa
1851-1853
Robert Elliott = Eleanor Stephenson
1804-1873 c.1802-1873
Mary Anne
c.1827-?
Thomas
c.1829-1911
other children
Robert = Mary Scott
1841-1916
other children
Isobel
Ellen (Nellie) = G. Peaston
Robert
Mary
Charles
(in AIF)
Alec
Helen
Alexander Campbell = Mary Stewart
c.1832-1907 c.1841-1923
Neil
1873-1909
Catherine (Kate)
1875-1938
John
1878-1917
Isabella (Belle)
1881-1966
Robert
1868-?(by 1911)
Helen (Nell)
1870-1894
Florence
1873-1933
Thomas
1876-1876
HAROLD EDWARD = Kate Campbell
1878-1931 c.1875-1938
Roderick = Elizabeth Hall
1881-1949
George = Evelyn Walker
1885-1917
Violet = John Avery
1888-1949 1882-1968
Violet
1911-1971
Neil
1912-1939
Jacquelyn = J. Fellows
1916-1963
2 children
Judith
1914-1998
=
A. Simpson
1 child
John
1915-1943
Rosemary
1917-
=
E. Headley
2 children
Poppy
1921-1996
=
I. McCombe
4 children
Don
1923-1940

Foreword
by
Les Carlyon

'The history of the world is but the biography of great men.'
– Thomas Carlyle

IF ONE SETS OUT to write biography, best to avoid saints and villains. The first lead on to hagiography, the second to finger wagging. Better to be writing about someone of quirks and contrasts and mysteries, someone to admire but also to puzzle over because, try as one may, one can never quite solve all of the riddles. Better to be writing about a character of Shakespearean complexities. Pompey Elliott is such a man: bush kid, scholar, fabled soldier of the Great War, family man, solicitor, parliamentarian. He is tough and tender, cocksure and vulnerable, charismatic and cranky, a burly and ruddy-cheeked man who, once seen, is not to be forgotten.

First of all, though, Elliott was an outstanding fighting soldier. He went up to the frontline during the battle of Polygon Wood in 1917, past blackened tree stumps and huddled corpses, to sort out the confusion there. Welch Fusiliers were mixed up with his forward troops. One wrote: 'It was the only time during the whole of the war that I saw a brigadier with the first line of attacking troops.' Another said it was 'rare for anyone who combines authority and nous to be on the spot'. The Australians were unsurprised. Their brigadier was just being himself.

Ross McMullin's biography has already found a wide audience, for the timeless reasons that it is good to read and tells us things we didn't know. Here is a fine piece of storytelling, a journey back to an Australia that is long gone. Here is a narrative that never stalls but carries us along like a river heading for the sea. Here is Pompey Elliott, bursting out of the page, larger than life and worn down by life. And here, as a backdrop, is the story of Australia's part in the Great War, from the tawny gullies of Gallipoli to the sullen blockhouses of the Hindenburg Line.

Introduction

POMPEY ELLIOTT IS a superb subject for a biographer. He was a vibrant character, and he lived an extraordinary life.

The commander of a battalion at Gallipoli and a brigade at the Western Front, Elliott could well have risen higher still in the Australian army during the Great War; he certainly thought he should have. Vigorous and capable, volatile and controversial, he was an outstandingly successful leader. His admirers—and there were plenty of them—thought he was marvellous. But among his detractors were influential superiors wary of his idiosyncrasies, who denied him promotion to divisional command in 1918. The question of whether or not that denial was justified is thoroughly analysed for the first time in these pages.

Elliott was a household name and widely admired in his time, he was a prominent identity in the traumatic Great War era that influenced Australia profoundly, and the life he lived constitutes a remarkable story. It is surprising, then, how little has been written about him. My main aim in this book has been to remedy this gap in the Australian narrative by telling the previously untold story of his life comprehensively, accurately, and vividly.

This book also contains numerous reassessments of Great War engagements involving Elliott. The quality of Charles Bean's epic *Official History of Australia in the War of 1914–18* has tended to inhibit reappraisal of the battles he chronicled in his innovative, painstakingly researched, and unprecedentedly detailed volumes. Such was the excellence of his *History* that later writers have, in the main, concluded that re-examining Bean's interpretation of what occurred was not only difficult and time-consuming but also ultimately unnecessary. That kind of approach would have been inappropriate here. Elliott was involved in so many controversies and had such forthright views about what happened and what should feature in the historical record—some assertions being accepted by Bean and incorporated into his *History*, some not—that a biographer of Elliott would not be doing the task properly if he accepted Bean's findings with minimal scrutiny. In exploring these contentious questions I have endeavoured to immerse myself in as many of the sources that Bean used as possible (together with other sources emerging more recently that were not available to him).

This reappraisal has involved a fresh look at some of the most momentous Australian engagements of the Great War. They include the Gallipoli landing, Lone Pine, Fromelles, Polygon Wood, Villers-Bretonneux and much more, as well as episodes such as the AIF mutinies, the pursuit to the Hindenburg Line, and the British retreat of March–April 1918. Interesting reinterpretations have resulted. I have ended up disagreeing with Bean on a number of issues while remaining a firm admirer of his idealism, his priorities and objectives as a historian, and the sustained quality of his work.

Pompey Elliott justified his actions in all these controversies with verve and conviction. I have examined his vigorous accounts in personal correspondence, in publications, and in various other sources; naturally, I have quoted them freely in these pages. I have concluded that Elliott's writings, in aggregate, are more historically significant (that is, to the history of the AIF) than the writings of any of his contemporaries except Bean. Pompey is not only notable as a soldier and commander, but as a recorder and interpreter of the AIF's history.

Telling Elliott's story in his own words as much as possible enables a Bill Gammage-like evocation of the collective AIF experience based on superbly vivid diaries and correspondence. And because Elliott identified himself so strongly with the formations he commanded, this book is in some ways not unlike a combined unit history—that is, a history of the 7th Battalion at Gallipoli and the 15th Brigade at the Western

Front. Also, significant facets of Australia's collective experience during Elliott's lifetime are illuminated. This is particularly evident in connection with the sometimes under-recognised period immediately after the war, a time when Elliott used his prominence and presence in parliament to ventilate numerous controversial questions. My extensive survey of this period, culminating in Elliott's sad demise, contains considerable previously unpublished material.

Finally, for a book appearing in this millennium, this biography incorporates to a rare extent the eyewitness perspectives of Australian Great War veterans who have been consulted specifically about individuals and events featured in it. As explained in the Acknowledgments, my work on this book has not been continuous. When I began my research I gave priority to consulting and interviewing returned soldiers about Pompey Elliott, and at that time veterans were still accessible in significant numbers. Regrettably, this is no longer the case.

CHAPTER ONE

'Awkward Bush Shyness': Straitened upbringing

1878-1894

HAROLD EDWARD ELLIOTT, who was to become a household name in Australia as 'Pompey' Elliott, was born in West Charlton, Victoria, in humble circumstances on 19 June 1878. His parents, English-born immigrants Thomas and Helen Elliott, were part of the great wave of migration attracted by the marvellous gold discoveries that transformed the colony of Victoria.

Helen had been only three years old when she arrived in Melbourne with her brother, sister, and parents in December 1852. Her father, Thomas Frederick Janverin, a handsome man with a full dark beard, was a house-painter. His Janverin ancestors, many of them mariners, had been based for two centuries in and around Southhampton and previously at Jersey in the Channel Islands. The unusual name of Thomas's great-grandfather, Moody Janverin, presumably reflected a tribute to his grandmother (who was Mary Moody before she married John Janverin in 1673) rather than a grumpy disposition: Moody and his wife Martha reputedly had no fewer than nineteen children. A shipbuilder for the Royal Navy, Moody had shipyards at several coastal spots near Southhampton, and the sea and the ships that sailed in it also dominated the lives of most of his children. Two of Moody's grandsons became officers in the British navy; one, Thomas Janverin's father, served on Lord Nelson's flagship and participated at the battle of Trafalgar.

With such a nautical heritage Thomas Janverin would have felt less intimidated than most Britons in 1852 by the prospect of a daunting voyage to the other side of the world. When news of the staggering Victorian gold discoveries reached England he was residing in London, where he had married Helen Watley in January 1847. Helen was the daughter of a publican and the niece of a famous general who commanded the cavalry in the Duke of Wellington's army. Thomas and Helen became parents five months after their wedding, when their son Frederick was born. They had their second child, Helen, who was to become Harold Elliott's mother, in September 1849; another daughter, Maria Louisa, was born two years later. Whatever Janverin was managing to earn as a painter of London houses was dwarfed by the stupendous riches reportedly awaiting adventurers prepared to try their luck at Ballarat or Mount Alexander (Castlemaine). The reports that galvanised Britain in April 1852 were so euphoric that hundreds of thousands concluded that they only had to get themselves there to make a fortune. Janverin applied for financially assisted migration under a scheme designed to attract to the Port Phillip district particular types of workers whose skills were in short supply. He was successful, and the family departed on the *Bombay* in August.

Travelling from England to Australia in 1852 was a daunting undertaking, even for someone from a seafaring family. Once out on the open sea, many immigrants had misgivings about their bold venture when white-crested blue-green mountains buffeted their lonely vessel, flooding the decks, and turning the cabins into a chaotic 'shambles of broken crockery, scattered personal effects and reeling, seasick passengers'. Living conditions on board were primitive; disease was an insidious threat, and shipboard hazards were rife, especially for families such as the Janverins with toddlers and infants. Of the *Bombay*'s 798 passengers and crew, 24 did not survive the journey.

Thomas and his family reached Melbourne safely just before Christmas 1852. Some assisted migrants headed straight for the goldfields, but Thomas remained in Melbourne to do the work he had been recruited to perform. The family had settled in St Kilda by April 1853, when they had to endure the loss of little Maria Louisa who died at the age of eighteen months. Helen became pregnant again, but suffered a miscarriage in February 1854 and developed peritonitis. Thomas watched her gradually decline until life ebbed away from her altogether at the age of 33; he was present when she died. Having arrived full of hope only fourteen months earlier, he was now a desolate widower with sole responsibility for two youngsters in a land he had every reason to curse after what he had already suffered during his brief time in it.

In an attempt to retrieve his fortunes, Thomas decided to join the gold seekers. Leaving his children in the care of relatives of his wife who had also emigrated to Australia, he set off to try his luck like thousands of others. Many found the heavy physical exertion beyond them, but he remained a miner for fourteen years. As he toiled perseveringly to eke out a living on the diggings, his daughter Helen eventually joined him (Fred preferred New Zealand).

Although he moved about like most diggers, Thomas apparently spent most of his mining years in and around Maryborough. In March 1863 there was a major rush to a field five miles south-east of Maryborough named Majorca. Six men made £800 there in three weeks. There were 250 shops and stores already operating in May, and when winter turned Majorca into a sea of mud some 10,000 miners were clustered there. Twelve months later, when new leads had reinforced interest in Majorca, Janverin's presence there was confirmed by a written agreement between two diggers formally witnessed by him in July 1864. By 1867 he was based near Talbot, about eight miles south-west of Majorca, at a settlement named Cockatoo, where Helen was keeping company with a miner much closer to her father's age than her own. That miner was Thomas Elliott.

Born at Newton-by-the-Sea in the most northerly tip of England, Thomas Elliott had also crossed the world in search of the precious metal, arriving in Australia in the mid-1850s. He was the eldest son of Robert, a Northumberland colliery proprietor, and Eleanor, first cousin of the celebrated inventor of the locomotive engine, George Stephenson. Financially the Elliotts had been relatively comfortable, but a sharp decline in the profitability of his father's collieries convinced Thomas his prospects would be better in Australia.

The Elliotts, like the Janverins, were proud of their heritage. According to family lore, they were descendants of the Elliott clan who had been prominent in the fierce skirmishes along the Anglo-Scottish border. Thomas, tall and powerfully built, reputedly had five Elliott uncles, all over six feet in height, in the prestigious Life Guards. The family had also involved themselves prominently in politics. Robert was

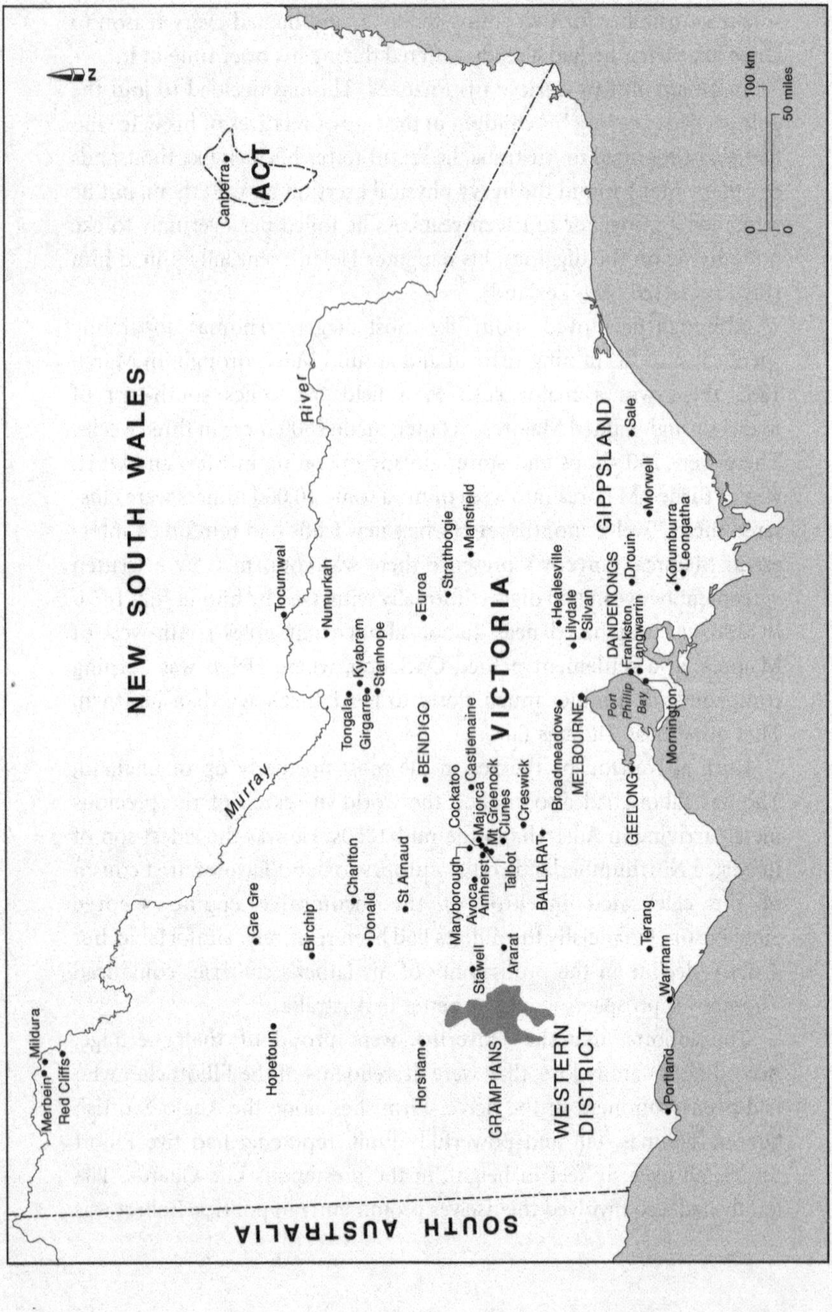

South-East Australia

a close associate of Sir George Grey, a senior minister in a number of British governments; a series of lectures in Illinois by Eleanor's brother helped Abraham Lincoln become United States President; and one of Thomas's younger brothers, Robert, became a political activist. However, what attracted Thomas Elliott more than politics—in fact, more than just about anything—was travel. The discovery of gold in such abundance in Australia was an irresistible magnet.

Just getting there was an adventure in itself, and once he adjusted to his new surroundings he found goldfields life congenial. The free-and-easy roving appealed to him, his sturdy frame could handle the heavy toil involved, and he was attracted by the elusive combination of good fortune, shrewdness, and hard work that underpinned success. Early on he fossicked at Sandhurst (Bendigo) and Ballarat. During the 1860s he apparently concentrated on the Amherst-Talbot diggings, where he became acquainted with Thomas Janverin and his daughter. Helen was very attractive. Not much over five feet in height, she had pretty features and a spirited nature, and her experiences had endowed her with a maturity beyond her years. At some of the more isolated diggings, where there were few or no other non-Aboriginal women, she acted as the field's unofficial 'doctor', dispensing rough-and-ready medical advice and treatment to all comers, including some Aboriginals (although they terrified her). With women so outnumbered in these goldfields communities, she attracted many an appreciative glance. But Thomas Elliott was the man for her, and they were married on Christmas Eve 1867 at St Michael's Church of England, Talbot. She was 18, he was 38, and perhaps some sensitivity about the difference was the reason for his age being understated by two years on the marriage certificate.

The newly-weds began married life at Cockatoo. Twelve months later they became parents, when Helen gave birth to Robert Norman Janverin Elliott. By 1870 they were ensconced in a dwelling of their own at Amherst and also had a baby daughter, Helen Margaret (Nell). Thomas, as one of a party of eight men who had registered themselves as the Talbot Gold Mining Company, was working a sixteen-acre claim at Mount Greenock, a prominent landmark near Talbot. By mid-1871 he was back at Cockatoo, working on a seven-acre claim with six new partners, but he moved on again before long. A year later he and four others, who had saluted his famous relative by registering themselves as the Sir George Stephenson Gold Mining Company, were making promising progress at the popular Talbot lead known as Rocky Flat.

However, that claim must have proved as ultimately inadequate as all the others, because Thomas decided to abandon his search for a golden fortune. Like all miners, he had dreamed that one day his persistent toil would be rewarded and he would find himself looking in wonder at a strike so rich that he would never have to work again. His reluctant decision to turn away from this dream reflected the harsh reality that its fulfilment was experienced by only a tiny minority of gold seekers; most could barely manage to make enough to live on. Also influential was the arrival of another daughter, Florence Mary. Even without pressure from Helen, wandering all over the countryside hunting for gold with little success was hardly appropriate now he had a wife and three young children to look after. It was time to settle down and provide more stability for the family, whether he felt like doing it or not.

He opted to tackle something he had never tried before: farming. Being a farmer had some similarities to gold seeking. There was the same vigorous outdoor life, wrestling with the soil to extract wealth from it, and the independence of being one's own boss. Many other miners who, like Thomas, were discouraged by their diminishing returns from goldmining, also decided that farming was more palatable than the other alternatives open to them, such as becoming a wage slave in a factory.

Miners turned to farming in large numbers because land was so freely available. For decades there had been a fierce struggle over access to rural land in Australia. On one side were the squatters, who had grabbed the best land in large quantities and were unimpressed by any suggestion that they were not entitled to keep what they had. Their opponents wanted to 'unlock the lands' to make them more available to small farmers. Previous attempts by the Victorian parliament to respond to the insistent clamour for land reform had been stymied by the squatters, but legislation in 1869 proved more successful. Under this version an aspiring farmer could select a block of up to 320 acres and live on it under licence for three years while making certain stipulated improvements to it and paying an annual rent of two shillings per acre. At the end of that three-year period the selector could either continue to pay the annual rental for seven more years until the full purchase price of £320 had been paid, or become the outright owner of the selection immediately by paying all the balance owing.

A suitable block was obviously crucial to success, and making the right choice was a tricky business. This vital decision was often made by newcomers to farming who were unfamiliar with the area they were considering and inexperienced about agriculture generally. In March 1874 Thomas Elliott chose a block five miles west of Charlton, a small township on the Avoca river about 150 miles north-west of Melbourne. This district, in which white settlement had first occurred when squatters arrived in the 1840s, was very popular among the new wave of aspiring farmers. The influx of selectors responding to the 1869 legislation led to a rapid growth in population and development in and around Charlton during the 1870s. There were 'selectors everywhere' and 'bush tracks alive with bullock drays and horse waggons loaded with household goods', reported a local newspaper in June 1874.

Among the many new settlers in the region was Thomas Janverin. Having given up gold seeking, he had returned to Melbourne; residing in Collingwood, he had resumed his old calling of house-painting. With Helen now the only survivor of the wife and three children he had brought to Australia (Fred having drowned in New Zealand), Janverin, now 54, decided to join his daughter's growing family in their new farming venture by selecting a block next to his son-in-law's. Any misgivings Janverin had about his suitability as a farmer were outweighed by the prospect of moving back to the bush alongside Helen and the grandchildren. This was much more attractive than seeing out his days on his own in the big smoke, too far away to see much of them.

The first task for selectors was to clear their land sufficiently to enable cultivation to commence. Compared to selections in some other parts of Victoria, Gippsland in particular, the Elliott and Janverin properties were only moderately timbered; but there were more than enough box and gum trees to make this task very onerous (even if it did generate plenty of timber for housing, fencing, and firewood). The family were not blessed with an easy initiation. Their first summer was a particularly bad one for bushfires, and the ensuing winter brought a damaging flood, followed by 'the most fearful gale one could imagine', which demolished mighty trees and selectors' primitive dwellings with devastating impartiality. It was not long before the Elliott-Janverin partnership began to struggle in this new environment; they lacked the sort of capital that would have enabled them to overcome their difficulties without assistance. In October 1875 Janverin wrote to the Lands minister, admitting that 'in consequence of many unforseen expenses we are not in a position to pay rent of both selections', and asking for an extension of three months for the payment then due from his son-in-law. His request was granted. It was not the last such appeal they would feel impelled to make.

Meanwhile Helen was pregnant again, and she gave birth to her fourth child early the following year. He was named Thomas Frederick in honour of his proud grandfather, who could easily hear his crying late at night in all but the wildest weather, so close were the neighbouring huts the family were building. However, after a tragic incident that left him with severe burns and scalds when he was only six months old, the child's heartrending wailing was acutely distressing. Despite medical attention, he lapsed into a coma nineteen days later and died.

Helen became pregnant again around the first anniversary of his death. When she gave birth to a son in June 1878 it was hardly surprising that she cherished and nurtured him with especially devoted attention. They decided to call the baby Harold Edward. Many years later, having become a household name in Australia as 'Pompey' Elliott, he acknowledged that his mother had been the main influence in his upbringing.

Home for baby Harold was a two-room hut made of timber, iron, and bark. His father had also built a barn of similar size and a slightly larger shed, both of wood and bark, as well as constructing a dam. The Elliott selection was rectangular in shape, with the longer sides running north-south; Thomas had just finished fencing its entire perimeter. The terrain sloped noticeably. The farm's highest point, where the hut was situated, was near the middle of the western edge; from there the ground descended gradually in every direction. That western edge coincided with the eastern boundary of Janverin's selection, with only a straight narrow track separating them.

When Harold was born his father and grandfather were in the process of completing the stipulated improvements necessary for a three-year licence to be upgraded to a lease. Each had cultivated well over the required 10 per cent minimum of their selection (Janverin cropping wheat, his son-in-law mostly wheat with oats and barley as well), but both needed extra time to complete their fencing. As Janverin explained to the Lands minister,

> my means being small I have had to expend so much time in cropping, the produce of which I have had to expend in great part on farm machinery, added to which I have had a long and severe illness which for many months rendered me incapable of the slightest exertion.

In due course both were granted leases. However, within two months of obtaining his lease, Thomas Elliott wrote to the minister seeking 'an extension of time to pay my rent as I have not got the money at present time'. During the following year Janverin was forced to make a similar appeal, while his son-in-law felt so overwhelmed by his liabilities that he arranged a mortgage on his lease through a solicitor he had known at Talbot. Both seized the opportunity provided by amendments to the Land Act—enacted because so many other selectors were in similar difficulties—to convert their leases, reducing the rental from two shillings per acre (£32 annually) by half and extending their term of repayment accordingly. Janverin cited a disappointingly low yield on his crop, owing to 'late spring frosts and early hot winds', in addition to 'heavy expense of implements and preliminary work'.

Harold grew up in a family environment dominated by endless endeavour to extract a living from the land. Life was a constant battle against the elements; bushfires, snakes, rabbits, locust plagues, and too much or too little water were just some of the difficulties. He had been born into a genuine family enterprise: his eldest brother and sister already had their allotted jobs, as Harold would in future years, and Helen's role was, of course, crucial. She had to make the farm as self-sufficient as possible, so that in carrying out her task of keeping the family fed and healthy she made minimal inroads on the limited income accruing from the farm's crops. Many selectors' wives supplemented the inadequate income from their farms'crops by selling food they had produced, such as fruit, vegetables, and dairy products. Moreover, since the nearest school during their first seven years at Charlton was too far away for her children to attend, Helen did what she could to educate them herself. And she managed to do all this while continuing to have children: Roderick Charles in 1881, George Stephenson in 1885, and Violet Alberta in 1887.

Her husband toiled away, too, striving to make the farm economically viable; but he found it heavy going and felt increasingly inclined to explore alternatives. At one stage he ventured to the Strathbogie district to evaluate the possibility of resettling there, but the toil involved in starting all over again was too discouraging for him. His growing absences became notorious. He was away so often, nearby farmers quipped, that he seemed to briefly reappear just to get Helen pregnant again before finding some excuse to take off once more. Harold received firm fatherly advice that he should definitely avoid farming as an occupation.

A shy, rosy-cheeked youngster, Harold began his formal education at an isolated one-teacher school that materialised only after persistent and vigorous lobbying. A group of West Charlton residents, including Thomas Elliott, had initially approached the government in 1879, pointing out that over 30 children in their district needed a school and the nearest one was five miles away. When their agitation had produced nothing tangible by April 1881, Thomas put his name to a joint letter calling once again for action:

> for the last two years we received different letters from the Education Department telling us we would get one but we do not see it comming, [sic] there is not a school in all West Charlton ... and some of the children will soon be past school age.

Eventually a school was built at the lobbyists' preferred site, a location east of the Elliott farm known as the Rock Tank (reputedly because a nearby dam had a sizeable rock in the bottom of it).

The Rock Tank school was a timber structure containing a solitary classroom with another room attached to serve as a teacher's residence. Facilities were extremely basic, although the farm dwellings in the vicinity were generally no different—freezing in winter, and unbearably stifling during the dusty, baking days of summer when the soil was as parched as the farming communities and everyone was desperate for rain. For teachers consigned to this isolated spot four miles away from even the modest civilising influences afforded by the Charlton township, it was a cultural desert, hardly a congenial environment where the fruits of education could flourish. The first teacher was resilient enough to last six years, but there was a rapid turnover thereafter. Her successor applied for a transfer only two months after arriving at Rock Tank; the accommodation was 'miserably small', he complained with justification, and 'altogether inadequate for the comfort of a married man'. When one of the most significant figures in the development of education in Victoria, Frank Tate, began a stint as a school inspector based at Charlton, he was amazed by 'the intellectual poverty of country life and depressed by the farmers' tolerance of their squalid living conditions'.

Harold, however, had known nothing else. Accompanied by his brothers and sisters and children from surrounding farms, he walked over a mile to and from school along rough bush tracks that were sometimes almost impassably boggy and sometimes wreathed in clouds of stinging dust. At school he grappled with the fundamentals of reading, writing, spelling, grammar, and arithmetic. He soon 'displayed a keenness of perception and enquiry which marked him out among his companions', and became a particularly 'keen student of plants and animals'; Helen encouraged his scholastic endeavours and dreamed he might develop into a naturalist. She also nurtured his growing interest in the geography and history he absorbed at school by telling him about the military and naval exploits of his Elliott and Janverin ancestors. This reinforced the admiration of all things British firmly inculcated by the education system into all but the most determinedly non-conformist Australian schoolchildren of that era. Like nearly all his contemporaries, Harold imbibed from his school years an ardent imperial patriotism, which encompassed more than a strong attachment to the British Empire; there was also an expectation that even such outposts of empire as the pupils of Rock Tank school might well be called upon to defend it.

Growing up without much in the way of amenities, the Elliotts derived most of their amusement from activities of their own creation. Life was certainly rigorous, but there was plenty of fun as well: swimming, fishing, horse-riding, and shooting all featured prominently. Terrorising some of the local animal population was part of the leisure routine. There was no squeamishness about the brutal disposal of cats considered surplus to pet requirements, and of course rabbits were a curse and considered fair game.

Harold wished he felt more at ease in non-family company. He came to sense that growing up on an impoverished, relatively isolated farm with limited personal horizons had hampered his social development. Decades later, having become a general, he felt his 'awkward bush shyness' was 'still a terrible handicap'. The Elliotts gave themselves unusual nicknames. Harold somehow acquired the label 'Harkey', which endured even after he had become famous as 'Pompey' Elliott. Other nicknames also proved lasting within the family: George was 'Jack', Florence 'Punk', and Violet 'Wick'. The games Harold played with his siblings, and the books he read, frequently involved military or 'Wild West' episodes. As he grew older Harold became increasingly engrossed in military history. Out in the paddocks, engaged on monotonous farming chores, he often imaginatively transformed the undulating landscape around him into historic battlefield scenes with himself at the centre of the action.

But the battle that dominated Harold's life at Charlton was his family's arduous and perpetual struggle to wrest a livelihood from the soil. The Elliotts' difficulties were aggravated by the senility that gradually overwhelmed Janverin, who died in May 1885 aged 64; his sad decline as he became engulfed by what was presumably Alzheimer's disease was distressing to behold. After his death his lease was formally transferred to Helen. The consequent increase in the Elliotts' holding provided them with much-needed additional flexibility in the use of their land, but the doubling of their rent was not so welcome. Five months after his father-in-law's death, Thomas felt obliged to obtain another mortgage loan, this time from the Ballarat Bank, which assisted many other impoverished selectors with loan finance.

Thomas's problems intensified in 1886 when his eldest son went off the rails. Life had not been easy for Robert since his tragic accident at the age of eleven. In May 1880, just before Harold's second birthday, Robert was helping with strenuous clearing work when a tree toppled over in an apparently unexpected direction and struck him on the head, fracturing his skull. He was taken to St Arnaud Hospital, 25 miles away, where his injuries were pronounced incurable. Robert's permanent legacies from the accident included severe scarring on the back of his head and a propensity to sporadic epileptic fits. He also emerged with a different temperament—more impulsive, less inhibited, and with a much lower ability to tolerate frustration.

Hard-pressed selectors seeking financial relief sometimes resorted to providing seasonal labour for others, and Thomas took his threshing machine to Bendigo early in 1886. Robert, now seventeen, was part of the threshing team; he took an active role in soliciting work for it, and was furious to be rejected after pursuing what would have been a lucrative assignment. Within hours of Robert discovering they had been denied this opportunity, a blazing fire caused £500 damage at the property concerned. Arson was immediately suspected. Questioned the following day by police, Robert denied any knowledge of the cause of the blaze, and headed soon afterwards to Gippsland. In July an incident involving a Drouin baker resulted in a warrant being issued for his arrest on a charge of false pretences relating to 'divers goods of the value of four pounds nine shillings'. He became a wanted man, featuring in police notices. Early in September he was arrested near Mansfield.

On 9 September 1886 Robert was convicted of the false pretences charge, and sentenced to a month's imprisonment in Sale Gaol. Meanwhile the police investigating the Bendigo blaze had become convinced Robert was the culprit; he was charged with incendiarism and transferred to Sandhurst for a Supreme Court trial. When it began, however, the defence barrister stunned the prosecution by making an issue of Robert's sanity, citing the severe head injury years earlier that 'had made him subject to silliness'. The trial judge gave Robert a reprieve, postponing the case to enable his mental health to be assessed. A medical official pronounced Robert 'of unsound mind and unfit to plead', which brought him within the ambit of the Lunacy Statute. On 8 December 1886 Alfred Deakin, as Chief Secretary of Victoria, signed the warrant of committal; Robert was conveyed to Melbourne, and admitted to Yarra Bend Lunatic Asylum.

The authorities' pursuit of further information about Robert's background resulted in an approach to Constable Steel of Charlton. Asked to comment on Robert's 'Habits of Life', the constable wrote 'Steady and Quiet when about here', though he was subject to fits. Steel described Thomas and Helen as 'respectable parents', who were (and here he put the best possible gloss on their financial situation) 'in fair circumstances'.

Eight-year-old Harold, like the rest of the family, had to make a sizeable adjustment. He had to come to terms with the fact that his big brother was a criminal and a certified lunatic. Four months later, however, Robert was released on probation from Yarra Bend, and the arson charge was formally dropped. This was a tremendous relief for Thomas and Helen. Not only did Robert's return signify he was in a better state of mind; he would also be able to resume his important contribution to the farm work.

On 16 January 1889 there was further drama involving Robert when he was bitten by a snake. His pulse was faint and his heart had almost stopped beating by the time he was examined by Dr McEniry of Charlton, whose initial assessment was that death was inevitable. But the doctor and a team of willing assistants, principally friends of Robert's from neighbouring farms, did their utmost to revive him. While McEniry kept him supplied with copious stimulants, the others exhorted and encouraged him to keep moving, in order to overcome the effects of the poison, when all he wanted to do was sleep. Their persistent efforts continued for more than 24 hours; during that time Robert reputedly drank no less than two bottles of brandy and did a great deal of enforced walking. Ultimately he pulled through.

Dr McEniry considered Robert's recovery so remarkable from a medical standpoint that he felt inspired to write an account of it for publication in medical journals. According to expert opinion a century later, however, the treatment Robert received—which had adherents in 1889 before being subsequently discredited—hindered rather than helped his recovery, and during the 24 hours after he was bitten he probably suffered brain damage.

The Elliotts' relief was short-lived. A month later they endured a terrifying ordeal when Robert embarked on a rampage of arson and murderous violence. Not content with starting substantial fires at a farm adjoining the Elliotts and almost choking one of his brothers to death, he threatened to kill one of his sisters. For some time he was prowling menacingly around the countryside with a knife looking for her while two men were looking for him. Eventually Constable Steel arrested him. His probationary release had obviously come to an abrupt end; with minimum delay he was returned to the Yarra Bend asylum.

Later in 1889 he escaped. No doubt, like everyone else, he realised it would be a long time before he was allowed out again, so he decided to take matters into his own hands. The police notice circulated in the wake of his escape described him as a 'dangerous lunatic'. What happened to him after his disappearance is a mystery. When Thomas died in 1911, the death certificate, signed by Harold as informant, recorded Robert (in the column for the deceased's children) as 'dead'.

Harold was profoundly influenced by his wayward big brother. Much of the drama surrounding Robert occurred during a highly impressionable period of Harold's life; eight years of age when Robert was first admitted to Yarra Bend, Harold was ten when he was sent back there. It is unclear whether Harold was the brother nearly strangled by Robert, although he probably was: Rod and George were younger, and from the perspective of Harold's later life it is easy to envisage him courageously trying to protect other family members and becoming the object of Robert's thwarted fury. As an adult Harold was much more like an eldest sibling in his relationships with his brothers and sisters than the fifth child in a family of eight. Admittedly, he was the eldest surviving son apart from Robert, which was inevitably significant in an era when nearly all families had vastly differing expectations of sons and daughters. Nevertheless the pronounced sense of responsibility and maturity that was characteristic of Harold well before he reached adulthood was surely shaped by Robert's delinquency; children charting their own temperamental territory often react to the characteristics they perceive in older siblings by adopting contrasting ones.

Allied to this dependability, and also accentuated by Robert's transgressions, was Harold's commitment to the widely accepted goal of respectability. Being accepted as 'respectable', as Thomas and Helen were described by Constable Steel, was immensely important to many Australians of that generation. The shame and hurt the Elliotts endured as a result of Robert's misdeeds instilled or reinforced in Harold's make-up a steely resolve not to let himself, his parents, or the rest of his family down by causing them shame or dishonour. That determination never slackened. During the 1920s there were frequent occasions when he publicly recalled aspects of his life, referring at various times to his parents or his younger brothers, but on no occasion in public (nor, very probably, in private) did he ever refer to Robert or even acknowledge, explicitly or implicitly, that he had an elder brother.

By the early 1890s Thomas Elliott had become more disenchanted with farming than ever. There was not much to show for almost two decades of hard toil at Charlton. Admittedly, he had upgraded the family's accommodation by constructing a more substantial four-roomed house—using mud bricks he had fashioned himself—and he had accumulated a considerable collection of agricultural machinery. But it was a continuous struggle to meet the family's recurring financial obligations, and they were still a depressingly long way from owning their own land. Moreover, Victoria's wheat industry was 'in crisis', with 'prices and yields per acre ... lower than they had ever been'; like many other battling selectors, the Elliotts were relying increasingly on dairying. Water remained an acute concern. And the economic tidings from the metropolis, which significantly influenced farmers' prospects, could not have been more grim. The splendour of 'Marvellous Melbourne' had attracted international acclaim during the 1880s, but after the calamitous bank crashes of 1893 the once-wondrous capital was like a pricked balloon. The ensuing profound depression affected the whole colony.

Many Victorians decided to escape this widespread gloom and hardship by venturing, like their parents and grandparents, to the latest gold discoveries. Their destination was Western Australia, which was in the process of being as dramatically transformed by its golden riches as Victoria had been during the 1850s. Even the relatively modest quantity of gold that was unearthed in the Kimberley ranges well before the catastrophic bank crashes was enough to attract to that arid, remote, and sparsely settled region plenty of adventurers from the other side of the continent. 'The Kimberley goldfields are still unsettling the minds of many farming residents of this district', reported the *East Charlton Tribune* in mid-1886. It 'is now certain', the paper added, 'that many settlers, disheartened by the miscarriage of their efforts to make a comfortable living out of their holdings, propose venturing to the new outbreak'. The rush to the Kimberleys was the prelude to further Westralian gold discoveries. Soon there were other golden tidings from newly famous places such as Pilbara, Murchison, Yilgarn, and Southern Cross to lure adventurers westwards. Late in 1892, just when Victoria's economic plight was about to become alarming, confirmation came that gold had been unearthed in dazzling quantities 120 miles east of Southern Cross at the spot that became known around the world as Coolgardie. Shortly afterwards there were spectacular discoveries at Kalgoorlie. Gold seekers poured into Western Australia.

The Charlton newspaper which described local residents as being unsettled by the rush to the Kimberleys reported in its same issue that Thomas Elliott had again been charged with breaching the Education Act. With state education compulsory, parents were liable to prosecution if their school-age children lacked a reasonable excuse for failing to attend school on a stipulated minimum number of days. For many farmers, however, the struggle to keep their heads above water took priority over everything, including education. In 1886 Thomas was fined twice for absenting his children from school. When Helen appeared on his behalf at Charlton Court in response to yet another charge, and pleaded that Harold and Rod 'had been kept at home during the pressure of harvest work', the court reiterated that such excuses were unacceptable, and imposed a further fine.

No Charlton settler was more likely to be unsettled by the Western Australian discoveries than Thomas Elliott. Advancing age had not curbed his insatiable wanderlust; gold seeking and adventurous roving remained as alluring as ever. With fabulous riches being won in the West, there was no holding him back. In July 1893 he set off on his own to join the growing Victorian exodus.

After arriving in Perth, most of his shipboard companions hurried away to get to the scene of the latest rush as soon as they could. But Thomas Elliott had other plans. He was of course no novice at gold seeking, even if his considerable experience had not produced commensurate returns, and he did not lack confidence in his own judgment. After surveying the countryside, he decided to try his luck at an isolated spot known as Dundas Hills, some 100 miles south of Coolgardie. At that stage the Dundas Hills population had not reached double figures, but Thomas was confident gold was there. Those who saw this newcomer, who was well into his sixties, single-mindedly and single-handedly digging a tunnel into the side of a hill in the middle of nowhere, reacted with a mixture of amusement and admiration. 'You must have a heart like a lion', remarked one observer; another assured him that, if he found gold, there would surely be a monument built to pay homage to him. Eventually a couple of prospectors, impressed with his purposefulness, decided to join up with him, but they ran out of water before finding any gold.

Thomas was still convinced that further exploration at Dundas Hills would pay dividends, and he liked his chances at other places he had inspected during his Westralian travels. But he felt guilty about staying any longer when Helen, Harold, and the other children had been working the farms for months without him and would soon be harvesting. At times like this he found the yoke of family responsibilities intensely irksome. Trying to quell his frustration, he reluctantly dragged himself back to Charlton.

By early 1894 he had itchy feet again. Helen was distinctly unimpressed; her husband's frequent absences had become intolerable. Though diminutive in stature, especially when compared to her husband's strapping frame, Helen had a strong personality, and there were stormy scenes. 'If you go back', she fumed, 'you'll only be taking your bones over to leave them there'. But Thomas was determined to return, and he left at the end of February. Once again Harold, now fifteen, took over as senior male of the household.

After completing the westwards journey again, Thomas had bittersweet news to digest. He found that someone had taken over his Dundas Hills site with very lucrative results—it had become the basis of a float on the English financial market worth £60,000. Although this was gratifying vindication of his judgment, he was very disappointed to have narrowly missed out on such a windfall. He decided to head for a locality halfway between Coolgardie and Dundas Hills known as Widgiemooltha, which he had regarded as particularly promising. Once there, however, it was a depressingly similar story: the area he had his eye on had been leased, profitably developed, and sold to a syndicate for £800. Fate had evidently cast him as one of those unfortunates permanently infected with gold fever, forever searching for the big bonanza but doomed never to find it.

Back in Charlton, Helen was also preoccupied with depressing news. There was a severe drought to contend with, and the Elliotts were sliding further into debt than ever. 'I cannot pay any more at present', she informed the Lands department on 29 March, 'but I hope to be able to further reduce my arrears before the end of the year'. However, instead of the 'favourable consideration' she was after, the department responded with a blunt ultimatum: if the arrears were not substantially reduced by mid-June, steps would be taken to declare the lease forfeited. The future looked bleak.

At this nadir in the family's fortunes Helen and Harold were stunned by incredible news. Thomas had hit the jackpot. He had found gold at last, and in a big way. 'SIX TIRED, DISHEARTENED DIGGERS STRIKE IT RICH' was one of no fewer than eight separate headlines above the *West Australian*'s effusive announcement of the 'most wonderful find of gold ever made in the colony', the 'marvellously rich' Londonderry reef. Helen, Harold, and his siblings remained unaware for days that Thomas was one of the lucky prospectors because the initial reports, based on an account conveyed by bicycle to Southern Cross and then telegraphed to Perth, referred to him as 'Elliot, a farmer from Avoca'. 'Up to the present all efforts in Avoca to discover the identity of the lucky young man, Elliott, who recently was one of a party to discover the richest reef in Coolgardie, have proved futile', lamented the *Avoca Mail and Pyrenees District Advertiser* on 6 July; 'whoever Mr Elliott may be we congratulate him and his mates on their good fortune'. The *Avoca Free Press and Farmers and Miners Journal*, however, was prepared to hazard a guess: 'we believe that the lucky individual is William Elliott, son of a well known bullock driver, who left Avoca for Western Australia some years ago'. It was not until a week after the Melbourne dailies first announced the fabulous discovery that the confusion about Thomas's identity was resolved. On 10 July the *Donald Times* reported that he was not an Avoca farmer at all, but a 'farmer and dairyman of Charlton' whose farm was situated close to the Avoca river.

Helen, Harold, and the other Elliotts reacted to the stunning news with jubilation and disbelief. The Londonderry discoverers had to pinch themselves even when they had the tangible proof of their good fortune staring them in the face; coming to terms with it was harder still for the Elliotts in faraway Charlton, preoccupied as they were with their perennial struggle to eke out a meagre living from the land. With their prospects looking grimmer than ever, the astonishing news from Coolgardie was like a miracle. Their expectations were instantly transformed. As they contemplated the sweeping ramifications, one that particularly gratified Helen was that their newly acquired prosperity would enable Harold to have a quality education. She was certain he had the aptitude for it; although he was already sixteen and had missed several years of formal schooling, she was confident he would be able to make up the lost ground satisfactorily.

Once Harold had adjusted to the Londonderry bombshell, his new, expanding horizons excited him. Previously his aspirations had been necessarily restricted; now, however, all sorts of congenial possibilities beckoned. Londonderry had unexpectedly given him a precious opportunity to reshape his future. He was determined to make the most of it.

CHAPTER TWO

'A Very Glutton for Work':
Striving for glittering prizes

1894-1900

THE LONDONDERRY DISCOVERERS sold the 'golden hole' to a syndicate for £180,000 (plus an interest in the company to be floated by the syndicate in London). Thomas Elliott used his share of the proceeds to move his family to Ballarat. He and Helen appreciated their financial liberation most of all when they paid off the arrears on the West Charlton farms. After years of struggle to find the wherewithal to meet their rental obligations and numerous pleas for understanding when payment was beyond them, the Elliotts managed at one stroke on 5 February 1895 to extinguish their debts and become the outright owners of their farms. That same month Thomas purchased 'Elsinore', a grand Ballarat residence near Lake Wendouree, for £2,500 from J.J. Fitzgerald J.P. For a further £4,500 he also acquired Brophy's Hotel, another noted Ballarat property previously owned by a well-known local identity. He arranged for an agent to auction the considerable stock, implements, and machinery the Elliotts had accumulated at Charlton, and leased the farms to neighbours keen to increase their holdings.

The Elliotts' new home was an extraordinary edifice after the very basic dwelling they had lived in at Charlton. A stately, two-storey bluestone-and-brick building on a spacious property, Elsinore also included a stable, a large garden and, in a paddock alongside and behind the house, an orchard and a creek. Its features included a cedar staircase and extensive first-floor balconies with attractive cast-iron decoration.

Moreover, the family could now afford to employ people to help with the household chores and the garden.

Elsinore's expansive grounds and its proximity to a range of aquatic amusements at Lake Wendouree opened up all sorts of recreational possibilities for Harold and his siblings. Many years afterwards his youngest sister Violet fondly recalled games of cowboys and Indians in the paddock behind Elsinore, where skilful use of the creek could result in a devastating ambush of the enemy. Harold was not averse to bossing his siblings around, and he exerted a commanding influence when he involved himself in these activities. This tendency was accentuated by the further prolonged absences of his father. Now that Londonderry had liberated Thomas from the burden of toiling to provide for his large family, he had the time and money to indulge his hankering for adventurous travel as never before.

Ballarat's tremendous golden riches had rapidly transformed it from a sparsely settled sheep run into a modern city. It was grand and stylish, confident and cultured, public-spirited and progressive. When the Elliotts moved to Ballarat the depression affecting nearly all of Australia had left Marvellous Melbourne looking anything but marvellous, but the Golden City was thriving. Its public buildings were impressive and attractive, and visionary measures to beautify the city had paid handsome dividends: no longer the 'howling wilderness' of the 1860s, Ballarat had become renowned for its trees, Botanical Gardens, and Lake Wendouree. Amenities and cultural facilities were also relatively advanced; monuments were so popular and prolific that Ballarat was known as the 'city of statues'.

Animating all this prosperous vitality, buoyant optimism, and cultural activity was a distinctive local spirit. Its strong democratic pulse was a feature. This did not primarily reflect an agitation for radical reform, although the Eureka Rebellion had occurred on Ballarat's goldfields. Rather, it was an expression of the satisfaction felt by people imbued with middle-class liberalism who believed that democratic freedom had enabled Ballarat citizens to shape not just a successful city, but a special place where opportunities for self-improvement were greater than anywhere else in the world. The other dominant strand in Ballarat's ethos was a fervent pride in both its past and its present. There were still plenty of pioneers around who could, like Thomas Elliott, remember what Ballarat was like four decades earlier in the first years of the gold rushes, and their achievement in developing such a distinguished city was frequently saluted.

The Elliotts were very comfortable in this environment. Thomas Elliott's experience of persevering toil leading to ultimate wealth was precisely the sort of individual success story that was widely admired in Ballarat and regarded as fundamental to its progress. Harold relished his association with Ballarat, too; although he lived there on a permanent basis for only three years, he demonstrated in later life an affectionate affiliation with it.

Harold retained his affection for Ballarat despite its association with a distressing family tragedy that had occurred prior to the family's move. Late in 1894 his eldest sister Nell visited Western Australia with her parents. For 24-year-old Nell the trip was an absorbing contrast to the laborious routine of farm chores, and she had been looking forward to seeing the West and the world-famous golden hole. But her inability to escape from the grip of a severe and tenacious influenza virus that swept through the insanitary goldfields environment left her exhausted and depressed. According to a Coolgardie doctor, she was suffering from nervous prostration arising from the influenza. Thomas was also feeling unwell—possibly the same virus had snared him, too—and the Elliotts decided to return to Victoria earlier than planned in order to obtain more sophisticated medical attention than Coolgardie could provide.

Having travelled by ship to Adelaide and then by train to Victoria, they arrived in Ballarat and stayed overnight at Reid's Coffee Palace close to the railway station. After breakfast next morning (a Sunday), Thomas and Helen decided to spend some time in the sitting room; when they returned to the bedroom and Nell was not there, they assumed she had gone out to church. It was not until several hours later, when she had not reappeared, that her parents began to feel concerned. Next morning the body of a woman was found on a railway about three miles west of Ballarat; her severed head lay between the rails, and the rest of her body was three feet away beside the track. The police conveyed her remains to the morgue, where Thomas was faced with the dreadful task of having to confirm that the deceased was his daughter.

All the circumstances, from her state of mind to the position of her severed body, pointed to suicide. This was confirmed the following day by a coronial inquiry; Nell had 'not been quite right in her mind since her illness', Thomas admitted. The first train after her disappearance to pass the spot where her body was found was a special goods train that left Ballarat early on Monday morning; its driver had not noticed anything unusual during that 'gloomy and overcast' night. It seemed, then, that Nell had been wandering around in a disturbed and distressed state for much of Sunday, before choosing to end her desperate anguish by lying across the track in the dark so the 3.15am train could rumble over her.

Nell's death was, of course, a devastating shock. This tragedy in the wake of the incredible euphoria of Londonderry made the later months of 1894 a time of extreme emotional turbulence for all the Elliotts. The upheaval left its mark on Harold. On top of having a certified lunatic with a criminal record as an elder brother, he now had to come to terms with the similarly unpalatable fact that his elder sister had taken her own life. Furthermore, he was moving to the city where this dreadful tragedy had occurred. It was a big change; life at Charlton had been full of hardships, but it was the life he knew, and there had been some good times there. He was moving from a small farm, five miles away from the nearest town, to a sizeable modern city; he was moving from a small, basic cottage to a stately residence that was palatial in comparison; and he was moving from laborious but familiar farming pursuits to an unfamiliar scholastic environment, where he would resume the formal education he had discontinued years earlier. It was a daunting transformation, even though he relished the chance to expand his horizons and make for himself a much more satisfying life than the one he had previously accepted as his lot. He was acutely aware of his reprieve, and determined to grasp this opportunity.

In January 1895 Harold was enrolled at Ballarat College, a male-only environment and one of several private schools in the Golden City. Ballarat College and other schools like it functioned as exclusive institutions for the privileged, providing an educational preparation for university and professional life that was inaccessible to even the brightest pupils in the public system unless they managed to win one of the few scholarships available. As well as providing scholarly instruction, these private schools prided themselves on instilling adherence to values such as service, discipline, morality, and loyalty. They also sought to nurture an enduring and affectionate affiliation to one's school. 'A Ballarat College boy should ever bear in mind that on his appearance and conduct depends the reputation of his College', declared its 'Rules and Regulations'. 'He ought to pay great attention to personal cleanliness, and should be unassuming, truthful, honorable, and manly'.

Harold's headmaster at Ballarat College, and an influential figure in his development, was John Garbutt. While the pursuit of academic excellence and creditable examination results were important, Garbutt regarded the school's role as being much broader. 'Great attention is paid to the formation of a modest, frank, manly character, and to the development of a high and nice sense of honour', proclaimed the college prospectus. Garbutt deplored the tendency of some parents to

> send their children to school, not to have their mental faculties educed and disciplined, not to have their moral sense developed, strengthened, and ennobled, but simply to have their minds stored, or, shall I say, stuffed, so as to pass some examination or other.

According to one of Garbutt's more notable pupils (Newton Wanliss), the headmaster's

> success was probably due to his great personality, his ability as a teacher, his knowledge of human nature, and his power of gaining the esteem of the boys, none of whom could humbug him. He was not faultless. When the old man's liver was out of order you had to look out for squalls. It was on these occasions that he made remarks to the boys and sometimes even to the masters that were uncalled for and frequently unjustified. I say this advisedly because John Garbutt made no pretence of saintliness. Sometimes, too, he indulged in bursts of egotism that were not in accord with his character, and he sometimes spoke out his mind with a freedom that showed more independence than prudence. These, however, were but the notches on the oak—the faults of a too virile temperament. When one examines the elements of his character as distinguished from occasional failings of temperament, his record is of the highest. His manly independence, his unimpeachable honesty, his sense of justice, his rectitude, his courage, and his love of truth and honour were above all praise ... His measures were drastic—his discipline severe—but it was successful.

This assessment bears an uncanny resemblance to Harold Elliott's later style as a military commander.

The college was situated in Ballarat's main thoroughfare, Sturt Street, a 'magnificent street over 100 feet wide, with a double avenue of trees down the middle, and a broad gravel walk and bicycle path in between the trees'. The Elliotts' residence, Elsinore, had been built near the eastern side of Lake Wendouree, so the journey to school for Harold, Rod, and George involved a walk or bike-ride of about a mile. In favourable weather it was a pleasant journey in picturesque surroundings, although it was another matter altogether if you were running late on a freezing morning knowing that unpunctuality meant punishment. (The college prospectus, trying to make a virtue out of necessity, asserted that Ballarat's 'bracing and invigorating climate' was 'peculiarly beneficial to growing boys'.)

Both Harold and Helen were understandably concerned about the educational ground he had to make up. Before leaving Charlton he benefited from an intensive burst of evening tuition from the obliging Rock Tank schoolteacher. He also started at Ballarat College at the beginning of the 1895 school year, although the family was not then installed in their new home and his younger brothers did not commence at the college until April. Harold was determined to do well. When he first saw the college honour board with its enduring recognition of those who had been dux of the school, he vowed to do his utmost to get his name on that list.

At the end of his first year he topped his class in geography, Latin, book-keeping, and Bible; came second in history, geometry, and French; and was satisfactorily although less highly ranked in English, arithmetic, and algebra. In 1896 his academic results were again very good; his best subjects were history, English, geography, French, and geometry. He did even better the following year, when he achieved the outstanding feat of finishing top of the class in seven of his eight subjects, having been narrowly pipped in the eighth. At the end of that year Garbutt singled him out for a special tribute in the headmaster's address that was a regular feature of the school's annual speech day:

> The dux of the college for 1897 is Harold Elliott, a very glutton for work. He has worthily won the position, and will be a credit to his predecessors and to his college.

The headmaster's high opinion did not just derive from Harold's determination to maintain his high standards in history, French, and geometry while attaining similar levels of excellence for the first time in algebra and physiology. Garbutt regarded wholehearted participation in sport as an important facet of college life; Harold, who already had a strapping physique (his Ballarat schoolmates called him 'Jumbo'), liked sport and represented the school at football. Furthermore, Garbutt, an officer in the Ballarat militia battalion, was delighted that Harold found military activities as absorbing and worthwhile as he did. Most important of all from the headmaster's perspective, Harold had a responsible temperament, conspicuous integrity, and fine leadership qualities, and was very receptive to the traditional private school values that Garbutt was seeking to instil into his charges. Honour, morality, and discipline would eventually become distinctly unfashionable precepts; however, to Harold Elliott and other upright Australians of his generation, they were not antiquated, ethereal notions but vitally meaningful concepts that provided sound guidance in how to lead one's life.

Religion also had a place in Harold's system of values. Since its inception Ballarat College had been closely associated with Presbyterianism; the initial school building was actually a superseded Presbyterian church. By the time Harold attended the college it had graduated to a two-storey brick building; the Presbyterians worshipped at the adjacent St Andrew's Kirk, and the minister there, the Rev. Dr T.R. Cairns, dispensed 'biblical instruction' at the college as an academic subject. That Harold topped his class in Bible in his first year at Ballarat suggests that the subject matter was both familiar and congenial to him. His sister Violet later told her children that there had been too much religion in her childhood, so she was not going to ram it down their throats; but Harold was more favourably disposed to the doctrines and rituals of the Presbyterian Church.

In view of the scholarly aptitude Harold displayed at Ballarat College he was clearly a candidate for tertiary education. Students aspiring to the University of Melbourne had to pass its Matriculation examination. Harold met this requirement easily: candidates matriculated by passing in six subjects, and he passed eight. He decided to study law. It suited his intellect and interests, particularly as he could pursue some of his favourite subjects, such as history and English, in the sizeable arts component that was a compulsory part of the law course.

Harold and his parents also had to decide where he would live in Melbourne, a city largely unfamiliar to him, while the rest of his family remained at Elsinore. They opted for Ormond College, one of the halls of residence located at the university. Named after the wealthy squatter who was its principal benefactor, Ormond was, like Ballarat College, affiliated to the Presbyterian Church. Ormond's initial master, John MacFarland, remained in charge from 1881 until 1914, and under his distinguished leadership the college flourished. When Harold entered Ormond in 1898 it had already become the biggest and most successful university college in Australia, renowned for its high academic standards, the calibre of the students it attracted, and the esprit de corps they developed during their years at Ormond. There was intense rivalry between Ormond and the other residential colleges, the Anglican stronghold, Trinity, and the Methodist edifice known as Queen's. Ormond enthusiasts had no doubt that their college was the best, and they felt very motivated to prove it whenever possible—academically, on the sporting field, and in other activities.

Harold became very attached to Ormond during his years there. A striking structure of Barrabool sandstone standing on the northern side of the university grounds, Ormond had grown rapidly in stature since its inception, both in physical size (thanks to the lavish generosity of its main benefactor) and in prestige. Extensions had been necessary to meet the rising demand for places. Together with more bedrooms, the facilities by 1898 included a stunning vaulted dining hall, library facilities, a common room, a billiard room, tennis courts, and a swimming pool. Each resident had his own bedroom, shared a sitting-room with another student, and had his meals provided in the dining hall, where the stodgy food was a perennial source of complaint: 'mutton, beef and sausages succeeded each other night after night with mechanical regularity, and with little or no element of variety in regard to the accompanying vegetables'.

While a significant proportion of Ormond residents hailed from Victorian rural areas and beyond, the large contingent emerging from Melbourne's most influential Presbyterian private school, Scotch College, ensured that residence at Ormond reinforced the values that Harold had willingly absorbed from John Garbutt at Ballarat College. The atmosphere at Ormond was assertively masculine, with its own bonding rituals associated with sporting and other triumphs. The few residents who privately regarded these customs as puerile were vastly outnumbered by those outside Ormond who envied its exclusive and very evident community spirit (an ingredient which, apart from the colleges, was lacking in the university generally). Both within the university and beyond, being 'an Ormond man' carried connotations of belonging to an elite. As it was, few students from disadvantaged backgrounds attended the university; but they were particularly scarce at Ormond, which was hardly a hotbed of radical thought. Harold could not have retained such an enduring regard for Ormond if he found this environment uncongenial.

MacFarland, Garbutt's equivalent at Ormond, was widely admired beyond his college and a venerated figure within it.

> For a start he was a good teacher himself and had gathered other good tutors. He was physically impressive—tallish, lean, searching eyes behind the glasses, a fast walker with gown streaming behind. Above all, however brusque and stern, he was just. In time his reputation enabled various generalizations to build a legend. 'He thought of the students as boys and treated them as men.' ... 'He has taught us to dislike all rules and regulations, but to honour the higher spirit of "noblesse oblige".' ... He would 'never allow an Ormond man to degrade himself or his College for want of a manly reproof'.

And although he was 'never inquisitorial' he was perceptive enough to know 'everything that was going on'.

Melbourne University law students then (and for many years afterwards) had to study a number of arts subjects before they could begin their law degree. From 1883 to 1896 they had even been required to complete a three-year arts degree before they could tackle a law course, but in 1898 recently altered regulations stipulated that law students now had to pass only two years of arts subjects before embarking on the customary two years of law subjects. This change was highly desirable to the overwhelming majority of aspiring lawyers who wanted to obtain a meal ticket in their chosen profession as soon as possible. Harold, however, decided to adhere to previous practice and complete an arts degree before beginning his law subjects. He had a greater intrinsic interest than many other law students in some of the arts subjects and, because of the Londonderry proceeds, he was not financially obliged to qualify in the shortest possible time.

The arts subjects Harold Elliott chose in first year were English I, Latin I, pure mathematics I, and deductive logic. With all his hour-long lectures scheduled in the morning, his term-time routine involved waking in time to have breakfast in the dining hall at around eight o'clock. If he was slow to get going on a Monday, Wednesday, or Friday he risked being late for his deductive logic class, which started at nine; Latin followed at eleven. On Tuesdays and Thursdays he had mathematics at ten and English at midday, and there was another maths lecture each Saturday at ten.

Ormond provided an equivalent amount of tuition that did not clash with the university timetable. Talented scholars recruited by MacFarland enlightened students with lectures as well as tutorials; the latter were not then part of a standard university education. The college teachers in Harold's subjects were outstanding—J.G. Latham, who had just graduated with first-class honours in logic and philosophy; MacFarland himself in mathematics; and popular vice-master Darnley Naylor in classics (assisted by another recent arts graduate, H.W. 'Barney' Allen, who was to become a legendary figure at Ormond). Apart from fitting in lunch between midday and two o'clock, and returning to the dining hall for dinner at 6.15, the rest of Harold's time was his own.

He had options aplenty. University clubs and societies offered a wide range of activities. There were also the theatres and other attractions of central Melbourne (although he was a teetotaller, and frequenting pubs was not for him). Or he could while away many a pleasurable hour in the college billiard room. He was a popular identity at Ormond, but too conscientious a student to allow these sorts of distractions to affect his academic performance.

It was a hard slog. Unimaginative teaching methods were not conducive to intellectual stimulation or nourishment, and everything depended on successful cramming for the end-of-year examination. In those days the transition from Matriculation to first-year university (especially in mathematics) proved beyond numerous students; even a former dux of Scotch College, John Monash, failed his initial arts year after succumbing to various extra-curricular diversions. But Harold, who was older and more mature than many of his first-year contemporaries (due to his late start at secondary education), did well. The gruelling hours he spent mastering the mysteries of algebra and trigonometry, the long nights devoted to Shakespeare, Milton, Euclid, and Virgil's Aeneid, were rewarded when he obtained satisfactory passes in all four subjects.

He did allow himself some recreational pursuits. During his years at Ormond he represented the college at football and athletics. He also enjoyed going back to Elsinore when studies permitted. At the 1899 Ballarat College athletics meeting he won the coveted College Cup for ex-students. One year during his holidays he and Rod rode their bikes all the way to Charlton to catch up with old friends and acquaintances.

But it was his keen interest in military affairs that dominated his leisure hours. He joined the University Officers Corps, which had been formed in 1894 to help those students who aspired to become officers attain their goal of a commission. There was a subscription payable each term of 2/6, and the uniform cost 30 shillings. 'For this small amount members may appear in gorgeous brass buttons with a large badge on the field service cap' and take part in a variety of 'pleasant outings' and 'military functions', proclaimed a Corps enthusiast seeking recruits. Harold participated purposefully in all the Corps' activities—drill parades at the university on Monday and Thursday afternoons, camps, field manoeuvres, instructional sessions, and shooting practice at Williamstown Rifle Range.

He became increasingly fascinated by military history. Visitors to his room often found him sitting near the fireplace in his armchair, alongside the mantelpiece cluttered with bric-a-brac and family photographs, intently absorbed in a book. If it was not one of the prescribed texts—and in his first year he tackled none of them with greater relish than Macaulay's *Essay on the War of Succession in Spain*—it was likely to be a volume dealing with significant battles of the past.

One treatise that Harold devoured was Colonel Henderson's acclaimed two-volume work, *Stonewall Jackson and the American Civil War*, soon after it was first published in 1898. 'Stonewall' Jackson overcame poverty and acute educational disadvantage with a combination of dedicated studying (especially of past battles), a resourceful temperament, and devout Presbyterianism. He went on to become one of America's greatest and most celebrated generals, admired for his tactical skill and revered by the men he led. He was a stern disciplinarian and a legendary 'character' who inspired his men to extraordinary deeds in the Confederate cause: they covered so much ground so rapidly in remarkable marching feats that they became known as 'foot cavalry'. Stonewall preferred unadorned shabbiness to a glittering general's uniform, made exorbitant demands of his subordinate officers, and could not contain his excitement at the height of battle. He had a bitter confrontation with another Confederate general, and was suspected of excessive individualism as a commander. In view of the way Harold Elliott later commanded soldiers himself, it is likely that this book influenced him a great deal.

In 1899 he enrolled in ancient history and history of the British Empire I together with another year of English and pure mathematics. That year's timetable gave him three hours of lectures without a break on three mornings each week, but again he applied himself diligently and was well prepared for his examinations in October. The examiners tested his familiarity with the political views of Hobbes and Locke, the rule for differentiation of a function of a function, and the early history of the *Tatler* and the *Spectator*. They asked him to outline the strengths and weaknesses of Edward I's character, to nominate who was 'king of the world of letters' in 1620, 1688, 1715, and 1770, and to discuss 'the true meaning of feudalism'. And they probed his knowledge of ancient history with questions concerning the military conquests of republican Rome and the circumstances leading to Cicero's banishment and recall. Surmounting these varied challenges, he again passed in all four subjects.

A distinctive feature of Ormond life was the role of the Students' Club. The club not only enforced its own elaborate rules and fines covering use and alleged misuse of the billiard room and tennis court; it also functioned as a forum for airing grievances of varying significance affecting the students. In May 1898, for example, one resident wanted 'more suitable soap ... in the bedrooms than yellow kitchen soap', asked for 'more variety in puddings', and urged that 'the type of college domestic servants should be improved and ... compelled to dress more tidily'. The following year another student requested that 'the mustard pots be freed from flies and other extraneous matter'. However, one issue in particular generated much more passion than any other at club meetings during Harold's first two years at Ormond—the presence in the college common room of the famous weekly, the *Bulletin*. There were several animated debates and closely contested ballots on this vital question, and the fact that so many Ormond residents found the

Bulletin's progressive vigour so repugnant underlines the extent of the social and political conservatism prevalent at the college. The minutes indicate that Harold Elliott was not a loquacious participant at general meetings of the Students' Club, although in August 1898 he and another student then doing first-year arts, George Brodie (who was one of the most persistent *Bulletin* traducers), were together appointed club auditors.

In March 1900 Harold was placed on a Students' Club subcommittee responsible for the pool and gymnasium, and at the club's first general meeting of the year he seconded a motion of Brodie's concerning an issue of greater substance than the quality of the desserts or the publications in the reading room. Brodie and Elliott wanted the Students' Club to make a donation to the 'Patriotic Fund' supporting Victoria's involvement in a war in South Africa. Harold was obviously doing a great deal of hard thinking about this conflict. A few weeks later he decided to interrupt his studies in order to participate in it himself.

CHAPTER THREE

'Your Brilliant Record':
The Boer War

1900-1902

THE WAR THAT began in South Africa in October 1899 was the culmination of escalating incompatibility between the imperial objectives of Great Britain and the aspirations of stubborn and resourceful local settlers. In 1806 strategic concerns prompted the British government to annex the Dutch East India Company's settlement at the Cape of Good Hope. The colonists of European origin it acquired as a result were descendants of the initial settlers: Dutch Calvinists in the main, together with some German Protestants and French Huguenot refugees. These Afrikaners, as they called themselves, tended to accept British rule; but a minority of them, the roving farmers known as the Boers, were unimpressed with the British policy of ending black slavery, and were much less inclined to acquiesce.

During the ensuing decades British policy varied between grudging tolerance of the Boers' defiance and ill-fated attempts to crush their resistance. In the 1850s Britain recognised the independence of Boer republics in the Transvaal and the Orange Free State, yet in 1877 annexed the Transvaal. This annexation was overturned four years later after a successful Boer rebellion culminated in a humiliating defeat for the British army at Majuba. Tremendously valuable gold and diamonds discoveries in Cape Colony and the Transvaal complicated the situation: the immigrants, mainly British, who flocked to South Africa in pursuit of quick wealth, were denied citizenship rights by the Boers. Britain's hostile intentions were confirmed by the farcical and humiliating Jameson Raid, which was effortlessly stymied by the Boers early in 1896.

Relations between Britain and the Boers deteriorated further during 1899, and war was formally declared in October. Influential manoeuvring had commenced as early as July to ensure that Australian soldiers would be involved on the British side. There was, however, a significant and vocal minority in Australia who opposed the war and Australian participation in it. 'We are now asked to send troops to the Transvaal, not because the empire is in danger, but only to show the solidarity of the empire', remarked a leading member of the embryonic Labor Party, W.M. ('Billy') Hughes, who explained his attitude in a neat analogy:

> But when it comes to a great pugilist attacking an infant, and asking his little brother to come and hold the infant while he gets at him, it savours too much of political bravado and swashbuckling to be on all-fours with the noble traditions of the British race.

Such dissent was not conspicuous at the University of Melbourne. It was very muted—perhaps completely absent—at Ormond College, where the considerable animosity shown to the *Bulletin* was partly a product of that publication's vehement condemnation of those who were intent on teaching the Boers a lesson. In September 1899 the university magazine *Alma Mater* was expressing almost universal campus complacency when it sneered at the 'childlike and pious' Boers, and contemptuously dismissed any notion that the resistance of these 'simple and guileless' farmers could result in further embarrassments for the mighty British Empire following Majuba and the Jameson Raid. 'War is diabolical, but at times a diabolical necessity', pronounced *Alma Mater* in its remarkably condescending assessment of the looming confrontation:

> The Anglo-Saxon race we are pleased to regard as the engineer of civilisation, whose duty it is to clear away all obstacles, natural and artificial ... No one can blame the Boers. They are doomed ... A determined stand by them for independence would not fail to be admired, if only it were not accompanied by such appalling and suicidal ignorance ... They are still in the stage of Old Testament darkness. Imbued with it and with its gloomy history, they imagine

> themselves the chosen people; and truly they are chosen—of dirt, and treachery, and ignorance.

The first Victorian contingent contained two Ormond representatives, Lieutenants A.J.N. Tremearne and J.C. Roberts. Tremearne (who had proceeded from Ballarat College to Ormond, like Elliott) had firm views about the motives of Australians who felt impelled to enlist:

> So much has been written about our 'wanting to help England', that it might be as well to say at once that very few of the volunteers ever thought of such a thing. A soldier does not support his regiment, an MP does not aid his Parliament, a footballer does not assist his club … each is part and parcel of the whole, and that is how we regarded the struggle with the Boers … The word 'help' gives one the notion that we were outside the quarrel; that was not so. The United Kingdom is the head, but we are one of the limbs of the Empire, and it is impossible for one part of the body to fight, and yet leave other parts entirely unconcerned and unaffected. This was certainly the main incentive, but there were, of course, others, such as the fatal fascination of war, the chance of really learning the game, the wish for adventure, and the realization that if a man wishes to wear a uniform, he ought to do something to deserve it, if fortunate to be given the chance.

On Saturday 28 October a huge crowd gave the first Victorian contingent an exhilarating farewell. Some observers estimated that as many as a quarter of a million Victorians gathered to wish them well. That military enthusiast Harold Elliott was surely among the cheering throng. Perhaps he was one of the Ormond group spotted by Tremearne waving the black-and-yellow college flag as the heroes of the hour marched through packed city streets, feeling 'proud to be chosen to represent one's country, full of the intoxication of the glory and adventure of war'.

Many Australians were so certain of the military outcome that they wondered whether the war would be over before Australian soldiers could become involved. However, these confident expectations were severely jolted before the end of 1899. During the initial fighting the Boers were ascendant, and achieved several notable successes. In

December, during what became known as 'Black Week', the British suffered disastrous reverses at Magersfontein, Stormberg, and Colenso. Realising that their opponents should no longer be underestimated, the British authorities sought further colonial contingents—Australian 'bushmen' in particular. In order to counter the unorthodox tactics of these troublesome Boers, who were mobile and frustratingly elusive, they wanted adaptable, durable men adept at riding, shooting, and 'roughing it'. Early in 1900 a bushmen's contingent containing representatives from each Australian colony was recruited and made ready for departure.

These men were still in the process of leaving when the Victorian government announced on 4 March that, pursuant to a further request from the British government, an additional contingent of bushmen from each Australian colony would be formed immediately for service in South Africa. Harold Elliott was one of about 4,000 applicants who volunteered within a week for the 626 vacancies allocated to Victoria (making it the largest contingent yet from that colony). Tests examined the volunteers' health, and exposed their shooting and riding proficiency. Harold had to show what he could do at Williamstown Rifle Range, and was summoned to the Domain for a very public display of his horseback prowess:

> This riding test seemed to be looked upon by the general public as a kind of circus, and was attended daily by thousands of spectators. The track was about half a mile round, and the test was to commence at a trot, break into a gallop, and negotiate three jumps. A man could judge fairly his chance of success by the applause or 'barracking' as he passed the crowd. There were many good horsemen among the recruits, men who could ride anything anywhere, and not a few who could rarely have seen a horse, much less have ridden it over a jump.

These tests held no terrors for Harold, a capable marksman and first-rate horseman; riding and shooting had featured prominently in his upbringing, and were recreations he greatly enjoyed. As a 21-year-old who was five inches taller than the requisite five feet five inches in height, and with a chest expansion greater than 35 inches, he also met the other stipulated requirements. He was directed to proceed to the pre-embarkation training camp.

Harold was delighted. For years much of his study and recreation had been devoted to the history, theory, and practice of military combat. Voracious reading about commanders and campaigns ancient and modern had familiarised him with the strategy and tactics, the masterstrokes and errors, that had decided great battles. Nearly all young men who grew up in Australia when he did were imbued with a strong attachment to the British Empire. They felt good about belonging to it, and wanted to contribute to what they saw as its continuing greatness. Harold Elliott felt such sentiments at least as strongly as his contemporaries, and he was gripped by a yearning to experience this phenomenon of war he had read so much about. Deep down he also nurtured an ambition to become a famous soldier himself. Here was an exciting opportunity to fulfil all these objectives. It was clear that the British forces were struggling and that this conflict was no picnic but the real thing—Ormond's representatives in the first Victorian contingent had become casualties in February when Tremearne was wounded and Roberts was killed. However, such harsh realities only increased Harold's eagerness to get involved.

Before long Harold could have been forgiven for wishing he had stayed in his Ormond study reading about his military heroes of the past instead of trying to emulate them. The pre-embarkation ordeal of the Victorian Imperial Bushmen (VIB) would have tested the resolve of the most dedicated and hardened soldier. Towards the end of March Harold went into camp 50 miles south-east of Melbourne at Langwarrin, where he and his new comrades were supposed to be undergoing beneficial training. In fact they had no uniforms, there were complaints about inadequate rations, and less than one-tenth of them could do any riding because of severe deficiencies in the supply of horses and saddles. In addition, they were given tents designed to accommodate eight people and ordered to cram ten men into them. Worst of all, the weather was appalling. Prolonged heavy rain flooded the camp. The Victorian government ruled that constructing a basic iron shelter above the cooking fires was an unjustifiable expense, so the cooks had to prepare the food in torrential downpours. The men were understandably unimpressed by lukewarm meat and soggy bread swimming on wet plates. Nor did they enjoy sliding around in ankle-deep slush doing 'outpost duty' drills without proper boots or overcoats.

Day after day most of the men seemed to spend most of their time doing little worthwhile and getting saturated, 'their teeth chattering with the cold'. The government could hardly be blamed for the weather, but its incompetent, niggardly approach was primarily responsible for what the *Argus* described as 'the extraordinary and disgraceful bungling which … marked the training and equipment and control of this contingent'. The acting governor felt impelled to apologise publicly to the bushmen for the excessive 'adversity and discomfort' they had endured at Langwarrin.

On 1 May a large crowd defied drizzling rain to watch the contingent march from Flemington to Port Melbourne, where they were farewelled with hearty cheers, heartfelt tears, and piercing 'cooees'. Harold and his comrades spent that night anchored off Williamstown. The bushmen obtained whatever sleep they could manage in their hammocks, a new experience for some of them. Early next morning their ship made its way towards the heads, and around midday they had their last glimpse of the colony of Victoria. Back in Melbourne an official inquiry was about to begin into the administrative ineptitude that had scarred the formation of the departing contingent.

The journey took three weeks. Drill, seasickness, and looking after the horses were its main features; there were also concerts, boxing contests, and shooting competitions (an empty box or fruit case discarded overboard served as the target). For much of the voyage both the weather and ocean were relatively benign, but as the ship neared South Africa the temperature rose until the heat became (according to one bushman) 'almost unbearable day and night'. While at sea the bushmen had seen no other ship; after weeks of nothing but ocean to look at, their departure seemed a long time ago. At last, however, the coast of Madagascar became visible on 20 May, and two days later they reached their destination, the unprepossessing coastal town of Beira in Portuguese East Africa.

After weeks of isolation they were anxious to obtain the latest news about the war. With Britain retrieving its fortunes, many bushmen were concerned that after all they had gone through to get to South Africa there might not be much for them to do. None was more concerned than Corporal Elliott, whose purposeful approach to the serious business of soldiering had already been rewarded with promotion. His worst fears were confirmed by rumours sweeping Beira that the war would soon be over.

The British revival had occurred under a different commander-in-chief, Lord Roberts. His predecessor, Sir Redvers Buller, had performed so ineffectively he had come to be mocked as 'Reverse' Buller, but under

Roberts's leadership the rejuvenated British forces regained the upper hand with a series of successes. The besieged towns of Kimberley, Ladysmith, and Mafeking were liberated, and the Boer capitals Bloemfontein and Pretoria were occupied. News of the relief of Colonel Baden-Powell's garrison in Mafeking produced hysteria in London and ecstatic jubilation in Australia; the VIB happened to arrive at Beira as huge crowds back in Melbourne celebrated 'Mafeking Day' with extraordinary fervour on a special public holiday. When Roberts arrived at Pretoria shortly afterwards, many observers understandably concluded that the war was basically over. In fact a new phase of the conflict, guerrilla warfare, was just beginning.

The bushmen were ordered to join the Rhodesian Field Force based at Marandellas. They were not sorry to be leaving Beira. Amenities there were primitive, streets were ankle deep in sand, flies were an acute irritation, fierce daytime heat contrasted with chilly nights, and illness was a serious problem. For eleven hours on Harold's 22nd birthday they travelled on a 'terribly rough' narrow-gauge railway through dense tropical jungle, before arriving in the middle of the night at an isolated locality known as Bamboo Creek. Having spotted plenty of discarded, broken rolling stock along the way, they felt relieved to have arrived in one piece. But hyenas and jackals howled all night disconcertingly close to their campsite, and Bamboo Creek did not seem a particularly healthy place either: 'the cemetery opposite the camp ... had been well filled from the Imperial Yeomanry who had passed through ahead of us'.

The next leg of the journey to the Rhodesian town of Umtali, 150 miles further west, involved another train ride. Travelling 'in a troop truck with open sides', wrote one of the contingent's officers, an accountant from Inglewood named Edwin Tivey, was 'very nice for admiring the scenery in the daytime but bitterly cold at night'. Umtali, over 4,000 feet above sea level and encircled by picturesque mountains, was a more attractive town with better facilities than Beira or Bamboo Creek.

From Umtali the VIB covered the hundred or so miles to Marandellas by overland trek. At least in terms of arduousness, if not danger (in the absence of enemy bullets), it was the bushmen's first taste of the mobile, 'roughing it' role in foreign surroundings that they had been recruited to perform. The novelty and attractiveness of the countryside initially helped to offset the rigours and discomfort. Coming from relatively closely settled Victoria, they were struck by the sparse settlement, the lush grass on the veldt (which ranged from three to six feet high) and the wild animals they encountered. While they saw plenty of deer, they were relieved that they glimpsed few of the lions which, the locals informed them, were also about; other predators again 'made the night hideous with weird and blood-curdling sounds'. With assistance from the local population, the bushmen utilised eight large transport wagons, each hauled by eighteen oxen. There were sometimes delays at the many river-crossings. At one ford it was touch and go, and they just managed to get one of the wagons across after attaching 54 bullocks and making a racket with whip-cracking and bullocky-style invective that was audible miles away.

The weather continued to be very hot in the daytime and freezing at night. Much of the sickness affecting soldiers on the veldt stemmed from the inability of hot, thirsty men to restrain themselves when they came across a watercourse. In the prevailing conditions it was difficult to maintain compliance with the strict orders forbidding troops from drinking unboiled water. Nevertheless, Captain Tivey assured his mother more than once, whatever their difficulties in this new environment the bushmen were better off than they had been at Langwarrin. On 11 July they reached Marandellas, where they were delighted to find a large pile of letters and newspapers awaiting them with longed-for news from home.

Since the Boers had shown no inclination (despite rumours to the contrary) to infiltrate Rhodesia, Harold was hoping the VIB would be directed to proceed further south so they could get properly involved while the fighting lasted. Some of the contingent's five squadrons were ordered south shortly afterwards but, to Harold's bitter disappointment, his was not one of them. It was acutely frustrating. Like many in his squadron, Harold was not at all mollified by assurances that they were playing an important role in protecting the British army's lines of communication. Nor was he appeased by suggestions that their presence was also needed to deter the indigenous blacks in the region from engaging in warlike activities against the British as they had only four years earlier. None of this made any difference. These bushmen had come a very long way voluntarily and at considerable inconvenience to make a meaningful contribution in the war; yet for month after tedious month they had been kept isolated, without civilised amenities and surrounded by endless veldt, in a dusty camp full of horses, mules, oxen, and vast stacks of military equipment hundreds of miles from the real action. Their main adversary was not the Boer but boredom. No wonder they were fed up.

Harold's disenchantment was aggravated by a clash with his sergeant-major. One oppressively hot day Corporal Elliott was in charge of a party unloading bags of grain, and he allowed them a short rest from their toil. They were enjoying this welcome break when, as Harold related, it was abruptly interrupted:

> Suddenly the sergeant-major, who was an old Imperial soldier, dashed up, called us a loafing lot of blackguards who had never done a day's work in their lives, and so on. He made a number of other uncomplimentary remarks ... After the men had gone away, I said to him, 'Sergeant-major, that was not a fair way to talk to these men. We came here to fight, and we have been kept for a month feeding mules. I, for one, want to get back to my university course, which I broke off to come over here and help the Empire.'

Claiming to be grievously affronted, the sergeant-major called Corporal Elliott to attention, summoned a detachment of the guard, charged him with insolence to a superior officer, and ordered him to parade before the squadron commander, Captain Joe Dallimore. The sergeant-major told Dallimore in Harold's presence that because Corporal Elliott had 'too much sympathy with the men' he was 'not fit to be a corporal', and recommended his demotion to private. Dallimore looked at the sergeant-major, and then at Harold. 'Admonished', he said. 'Corporal, don't do it again'. That was all. Fortunately for Elliott, the squadron leader had made a shrewd assessment of the incident and the two individuals involved; he had already formed a favourable impression of Harold's ability, reliability, and purposefulness. Before long, to Harold's profound satisfaction, it was the sergeant-major who found himself demoted.

Compensations at Marandellas were few. To relieve the boredom some bushmen hunted deer, an activity providing target practice and welcome variation in their repetitive army diet. They were gratified by the willingness of British administrators—in stark contrast to the Victorian government's parsimony—to furnish them with top-quality uniforms and equipment, which they accepted as proof that the imperial authorities regarded them seriously as soldiers. Furthermore, it was true that they were still alive, and some members of Squadrons A and B who had stopped a bullet were not; but they could not feel grateful for that when they would gladly have swapped the monotony of Marandellas for an opportunity to do what they had come so far to do. It was hard for Harold to resist the depressing feeling that life was passing him by.

A few days into the new century, however, his frustration was punctured when his squadron was directed to proceed to Cape Colony. As people throughout Australia planned celebrations to commemorate the day when Australia would formally become a nation, Elliott and his D Squadron comrades felt imbued with renewed purposefulness as they made their way south. Lord Roberts, mistakenly convinced the war was practically over, had returned to England; in charge of British operations now was Lord Kitchener, who was determined to use resolute methods to crush the Boers' tenacity. After two bands of Boer raiders entered Cape Colony in December, Squadrons C, D, and E of the VIB were part of the force Kitchener assembled to deal with them. For this task the three Victorian squadrons were attached to the Coldstream Guards, whose commander, Lieutenant-Colonel Henniker, also had a battery of Royal Horse Artillery at his disposal.

Harold was thrilled to learn he would be participating in genuine military operations alongside such elite British units. Boys from the bush like him would be able to scrutinise such arrestingly named Coldstream notables as Surgeon-Major Crooke-Lawless and Captain the Honourable Claud Heathcote-Drummond-Willoughby. Before the force could begin its work in earnest, however, news arrived on 23 January of the death of the seemingly indestructible Queen Victoria, who had reigned over the British Empire for 63 years. 'We all received a shock', wrote Tivey. 'This evening the band of the Coldstream Guards played the Dead March and marched past headquarters and the troops are all very sad'.

Early in February Henniker's column was rushed by train to De Aar, the site of an important railway junction in Cape Colony, in response to further Boer activity. A force of over 2,000 Boers headed by their most able remaining commander, Christiaan de Wet, was heading south with the dual aim of causing disruption to the British forces stationed in the Cape and inciting Boer sympathisers in that colony to take up arms against the British. On 11 February 55 C Squadron bushmen under

Tivey were ordered to proceed to Philipstown 25 miles away. At dawn the following morning Tivey's men encountered a detachment of 300 Boers who were in the process of completing their occupation of the town. In the ensuing skirmish Tivey's outnumbered bushmen succeeded in holding the Boers at bay for eleven hours until reinforcements arrived in the form of D and E Squadrons, who had covered the distance from De Aar in seven hours. Aware of these advancing reinforcements, the Boers decided to withdraw from Philipstown, so the fight was actually over before Harold could get there.

Nevertheless there was no doubt he was now directly involved in the grim reality of war. It was no coincidence that he started a diary of his military service with the Philipstown engagement, which began his involvement in 'The Great de Wet Hunt'. During this relentless pursuit the three VIB squadrons covered vast distances and participated in intermittent skirmishing with the enemy. On 13 February, for example, Lieutenant Code of D Squadron and Lieutenant Mason of E Squadron were wounded in separate incidents, and various troopers fighting alongside them also became casualties. And later that week, according to Harold's diary, he and the bushmen with him rode 35 miles one day and another 30 miles the next in 'very wet weather' as they strove to keep up with their elusive quarry. The stakes were high. The capture of de Wet could well end the whole conflict. On no previous occasion during the war had so many columns been assembled for a single objective.

At times Henniker's column was assigned to a larger formation commanded by Colonel Plumer, which was the most persistent and troublesome of the forces pursuing de Wet. Although de Wet used masterly evasive skills and benefited from the fresh animals and provisions he commandeered wherever he could, the dogged perseverance of the various units chasing him—Plumer's force in particular—was soon testing his renowned ingenuity to the limit. On 23 February Harold was among a group of bushmen who rode about 50 miles to catch up with their hard-pressed quarry as de Wet and his men tried to cross the swollen Orange River. The Boers retreated rapidly, but were forced to relinquish a large number of prisoners and the only two artillery pieces de Wet's force possessed. The bushmen then covered another 120 miles in four days. 'I have not had my clothes or boots off for nearly a fortnight', wrote Tivey.

On 28 February Captain Dallimore and fifteen of his D Squadron, including Harold, were detached to reconnoitre the movements of a party of Boers who had been making a nuisance of themselves. The bushmen skilfully tracked these Boers to the junction of the Orange and Sea Cow rivers, and watched them making relaxed preparations to spend the night there, totally unaware that they had been followed. From their elevated vantage point Dallimore and his men quietly discussed the situation. Dallimore was inclined to attack. Others were less keen, arguing that they would be greatly outnumbered and the more prudent course would be to send a messenger back with an urgent request for reinforcements. Corporal Elliott agreed strongly with Dallimore. He argued that the Boers could move on before the reinforcements arrived, and the bushmen might therefore lose the crucial advantage of surprise. Besides, if the bushmen chose not to attack they 'would miss a good fight'. His advocacy was decisive.

There are conflicting accounts of the ensuing engagement, but it is clear that Corporal Elliott played a leading role in a notable exploit. The bushmen waited quietly in drizzling rain as the cold blackness of night descended. Eventually, when the Boers were all asleep, Harold stealthily advanced towards their camp. In the dark (together with, perhaps, one or two troopers) he succeeded in rounding up all the enemy's horses, and managed to lead or drive them away from the camp without disturbing their sleeping riders.

During the night the bushmen positioned themselves around the camp. At dawn they unleashed a sudden volley of shots. The startled Boers ran for their horses; unable to find them, they took cover and returned fire. There was a sharp fight lasting about half an hour. It ended when one of the blacks used by the Boers to assist with the care of their animals, who had been captured by the bushmen when he went looking for the missing horses, was sent back to the Boers with a message from Dallimore: they were surrounded, the captain asserted, and if they did not surrender he would bring his big gun into action against them. Dallimore actually had no such gun, but the bushmen had maintained such a heavy fire from concealed positions that the beleaguered Boer leader, convinced he was surrounded by a far superior force, complied. When he realised he had surrendered to a group numbering half his own he was overwhelmed with shame and fury. Dallimore and his fifteen bushmen, who emerged from the engagement without casualties, returned proudly to Henniker's column with their remarkable booty of 27 Boers, six blacks, and 54 horses.

As well as displaying great bravery in the execution of this bold tactical manoeuvre which had such productive results, Harold was probably influential in its conception. His absorption in military history had familiarised him with such exploits. He had perhaps even rehearsed a similar plan himself either in his imagination or during one of the war games he had played in the paddock behind Elsinore. Dallimore certainly had a sufficiently high regard for Harold to be very responsive to his suggestions.

For his contribution to the tactical coup Corporal Elliott was honoured with a special parade before Colonel Henniker and an appreciative telegram from Lord Kitchener. Moreover, on Dallimore's recommendation Harold was awarded the Distinguished Conduct Medal (DCM), the most prestigious award available to a British or colonial soldier of his rank other than the Victoria Cross. Harold was euphoric. After all his reading about military accomplishments and his dreams that he might some day achieve something special in battle himself, he felt profoundly gratified and ecstatically proud. In reflective moments he imagined the excited reactions of family and friends back home, and wondered how long it would be before they became aware of his distinction.

The incident was sufficiently noteworthy to be mentioned within a week in British and Australian newspapers, but the only individual named in the brief initial accounts of this 'daring feat' was Dallimore. It was not until 26 March, almost four weeks after the engagement, that the Melbourne dailies reported that two members of the Victorian Imperial Bushmen had been singled out for honours: Tivey had been awarded the Distinguished Service Order (DSO) for his leadership at Philipstown, and Harold had received the DCM for 'particularly daring' gallantry. This announcement thrilled the Elliotts at Ballarat, and there was also delight and satisfaction at Ormond, where MacFarland's suggestion of a congratulatory message was accepted with alacrity. 'Hearty congratulations from Master Tutors Students Ormond College', proclaimed their cable, which was sent the following day and received by Harold a week later. 'Corporal H.E. Elliott' became the subject of a paragraph in the 'Personal' column of the *Argus*, a section reserved for individuals of the highest renown: 'At Ormond College', it said, 'he was well liked, left most of the talking to others, but was always to be depended on when it came to action in the football field or elsewhere'.

Since Harold was ambitious for promotion and had clearly proved his worth as a soldier, it was not surprising that he had been considering whether to emulate the numerous members of Australian contingents who had attained commissions in British units. With the DCM to his credit, it was understandable that the Royal Berkshire Regiment was attracted to him as a prospective subaltern, especially in view of the high reputation the Victorian bushmen had won for themselves. The bushmen, however, were reluctant to lose someone of his calibre, especially with Tivey's C Squadron lacking its proper component of officers. Special arrangements were made to keep him. His commission in the 2nd Royal Berkshires was cancelled, and he remained with the bushmen as an attached subaltern.

The bushmen continued their arduously widespread patrolling. Still operating as part of the column headed by Henniker of the Coldstream Guards, they were now detached from the larger formation commanded by Plumer. They kept the Boers in their vicinity under relentless pressure. These Boer units frequently lost men and horses, and had to keep constantly on the move to evade their pursuers; because of this harassment they found it much harder to obtain the provisions they desperately needed. But it was tough work for the bushmen, too. Logistic complexities arising from their extensive movements were not always overcome. At times the column had to halt because it had almost run out of food for its weary men and horses. The men were often sick as well as hungry—more VIB lives were lost to disease than as a result of Boer bullets. They also had to contend with a climate that baked them by day, froze them at night, and inflicted sudden devastating storms. As Tivey remarked, 'people in Victoria have no idea of the difficulties the troops have to face in this country'.

There was also the ever-present risk of a dangerous skirmish. Elliott was involved in a clash near Steynsberg on 23 March, when the Victorians confronted a large band of Boers on the move. Caught in the open under concentrated enemy fire, the bushmen were lucky to escape; several men had their clothes cut by bullets. On 26 April, the day all five squadrons of the contingent were at last reunited, two bushmen were killed when a small D Squadron party was ambushed while patrolling. Early in May Henniker's column was ordered to pursue a band of Boers into rugged high country. Since then, as Tivey reported over a fortnight later,

> we have had no rest, started on the 5th with a night march through the mountains and have been chasing and fighting Boers every day through awful country, have been in touch with them all the time and have cleared them out of their strongholds. We were over mountains five and six thousand feet above sea level, and it was bitterly cold at night.

On 10 May C and D Squadrons were detached from the column for patrolling activity west of Doornbosch. The following day they encountered Boers in large numbers, and there was a sharp engagement before the enemy fell back. On 12 May Lieutenant Elliott was one of three officers accompanying 40 bushmen from C Squadron who came across a much bigger group of Boers at a farm. A fierce fight ensued. As well as superior numbers the Boers had the advantage of surprise and were ensconced in prepared positions, but the bushmen still succeeded in forcing them to retire. According to Tivey's account of the affray, the capture of an important hill by Lieutenant Elliott and a few men was a significant factor in the successful outcome. Elliott was one of seven Victorians singled out for special mention in column orders. Having buried a much-admired trooper under a cross constructed by the Coldstream Guards pioneers, the bushmen resumed their patrolling in very wet weather. After covering ten miles they were about to halt for the night when they were deluged by a heavy snowstorm. The men were 'nearly frozen', Tivey noted. Another officer described it as 'the most miserable night we have ever had on the veldt'.

By this time the Victorians and their horses badly needed a rest. After months of such strenuous work they felt worn out, and many of them were also suffering from an influenza virus sweeping through their ranks. The frustration felt by those bushmen including Elliott who had been stuck at Marandellas had been well and truly assuaged by their gruelling campaigning. They had covered over a thousand miles on horseback (and many more by train); they had endured extremes of climate as well as acute tension and peril; yet with persistence, courage, and verve they had made a valuable contribution to the British cause. 'I would like to say a word about the Victorians', wrote Edgar Wallace, the noted London *Daily Mail* correspondent. 'Victoria is a colony which has produced some splendid soldiers, but no better nor finer troops have ever been put into the field than those men who form part of Colonel

Henniker's column'. With their stint of service about to end, the Victorian Imperial Bushmen received messages of thanks from Henniker and Kitchener prior to their departure.

Some officers either stayed in South Africa or travelled to England, leaving only nine of them to accompany the unit home on the *Orient*. It left Cape Colony under Dallimore's command on 22 June. During the voyage Lieutenant Elliott acted as the unit's adjutant, which was no sinecure; the ship had a rough passage, and there was considerable sickness on board. Moreover, the men had been discharged and fully paid for their services before the journey began, a practice later discontinued because it tended to leave men who had already attracted a certain notoriety for wildness even less amenable to discipline. Elliott made his intentions clear when he threw the troublemakers' Crown and Anchor gambling apparatus overboard. 'You'll find yourself in the big bath one of these nights', they threatened, but he maintained discipline undeterred. Kenneth Mackay, commander of the New South Wales Imperial Bushmen (and a well-known politician and writer), who was also returning on the *Orient*, was most impressed:

> This young officer performed the duties of Adjutant for the Victorians on board the 'S.S. Orient' in a manner about which I cannot speak too highly. Under exceptionally difficult circumstances he showed an amount of tact which was most praiseworthy while his capacity for hard work is remarkable.

Despite the murky presence of mid-winter fog, it was a memorable day when the *Orient* landed at Port Melbourne on 12 July. The bushmen received a rousing welcome home as they marched through the city to the ceremony and lunch awaiting them at the Exhibition Building, where they were presented with medals and showered with praise. The Prime Minister, Edmund Barton, congratulated them for their efforts, reminding them that since their departure Australia had become a nation and the whole country was very proud of them. Another speaker read out a letter of appreciation from Colonel Henniker, who described the bushmen as 'a credit to Australia and the Empire'; he wished that 'from such contingents an Imperial regiment could be formed'. The assembled onlookers and well-wishers reacted to this message with considerable enthusiasm—such glowing praise from the commander of a legendary unit such as the Coldstream Guards was the ultimate accolade. 'It was', according to the *Age*'s account, 'by this time close on 4 p.m., so the amount of justice the men did to the luncheon can be readily conceived'.

At the end of the lunch the formalities were concluded, and the men were at last free to join the relatives who had been waiting for hours to give them a proper greeting. Harold, looking tanned and fit, was soon surrounded by the Elliotts, who flocked to make a fuss of their particular hero. Not only had he enlisted sixteen months earlier as a humble young trooper and returned as Lieutenant Elliott DCM; above all, as far as they were concerned, he was safe and sound.

The delighted response to Henniker's letter reflected the respect and admiration widely held in Australia for Britain and its institutions. But Harold had formed an unfavourable opinion of the British army after seeing it at close quarters. As he recalled two decades later,

> I remember well when I volunteered for the Boer war the jests that met us at every turn at the idea that we could compare ourselves with the British Regular Army, and it was cheerfully asserted that we would run at the first fire. To some extent we were impressed by these assertions, but in that war we compared ourselves side by side with the best troops that Britain could produce, and failed to discern any marked superiority in courage or discipline to ourselves.

In fact he was very critical of procedures in some British units, especially practices routinely adopted by the Coldstream Guards to instil discipline:

> The Guards are extraordinarily smart in answering an order, and they explained to me how the unfortunate recruit is trained in this respect. If a sergeant-major, walking about, sees a recruit cutting up tobacco to put in his pipe he calls him to do something, and if the man pauses to put the tobacco into his pipe before obeying the call, he is charged with 'hesitating to obtain an order' and is severely punished. He must drop everything at once and answer the call. This is not imagination on my part. As a prospective subaltern in the British Army, I paid close attention to all these customs, about

> which a very efficient sergeant-major gave me minute instructions. A favourite method of quieting an obstreperous man who is drunk and very abusive is to gag him with his own socks.

Being eager to learn, Harold liked hearing grizzled non-commissioned officers (NCOs) of the Coldstream Guards recount their experiences; he tried to get them yarning whenever he could. 'Many of them were old sergeants with up to twenty years service', he later recalled, 'and an extra tot of rum saved from our allowance would mostly lead to something of interest to us youngsters'.

Harold's perceptions were also influenced by encounters with former British soldiers now serving in his own regiment. The unfavourable impression created by the ex-Imperial sergeant-major he had clashed with at Marandellas was reinforced by other incidents. Some of them concerned a VIB sergeant who had previously been a gunner in the Royal Artillery; according to Harold, he was 'very insistent on his dignity'. One evening, after an exhausting day's trekking on the veldt, that sergeant summoned a young bugler—who was described by Harold as 'being the average cheeky Australian larrikin'—and ordered him to take his (the sergeant's) horse to a nearby well and water it. 'Go to hell', retorted the bugler. 'You water your own bloody horse'. The sergeant placed the bugler under arrest and made a big fuss about insubordination; the bugler was sentenced to one hour's imprisonment in the field. Offenders so sentenced were tied to a wagon wheel in spreadeagle fashion, but this notorious practice in the British army was abhorrent to Australians and the bugler's comrades refused orders to impose it on him. Elliott's adverse impressions of certain British soldiers and procedures were instrumental in his decision not to proceed with his commission in the 2nd Royal Berkshire Battalion.

Despite this aversion to joining a traditional British unit (which many Australians were doing), he was nevertheless keen to return to South Africa somehow or other. He liked soldiering, despite its dangers and hardships: it was something he found absorbing, and he had certainly shown he was proficient at it. Like all soldiers, he had wondered how he would react when under fire for the first time. To his relief he had passed this personal test satisfactorily, and had gone on to acquire a reputation for admirable coolness and courage in action. He impressed not only his superior officers such as Dallimore and Mackay but also troopers who served in the ranks with him: one of them described Elliott 30 years later as one of the finest men he had ever met. Although Elliott had left Australia with few illusions about the reality of armed conflict, reading about war was not the same as experiencing it firsthand. He was now familiar with not only the horrors of war, but also the basic role of the common soldier—in particular, that odd mixture of long periods of relative tedium punctuated by occasional bursts of terrifying danger. Far from being discouraged, however, Harold found military life exhilarating; with a high regard for soldierly prowess very widespread in Australia at the time, he also found it profoundly fulfilling. Accordingly, as long as the fighting in South Africa lasted, he wanted to be in it. There were rumours and predictions of an imminent end to the war, as there had been for some time, but the conflict still dragged on. The British were unable to quell the Boers' lingering resistance, and could not persuade them to agree to peace terms.

An opportunity to return to South Africa soon presented itself. Major J.F. Thomas, a senior officer in the first New South Wales bushmen's contingent, sought governmental approval for his proposal to organise another contingent to be made up of returned soldiers who wanted to go back to South Africa. Hundreds of men wished to do so. Some had been unable to find work since their return, some were restless or unable to readjust to civilian life, and some felt they would have better post-war prospects on the veldt than in Australia. The new Australian federal government had no plans at that stage for more contingents, and official recognition was not forthcoming. However, arrangements were made for the men recruited by Thomas to be given 'indulgence passages', which enabled them to travel free of charge to Cape Town (apart from the cost of their meals, 1/6 per day, which they had to pay). There they would join one of the irregular locally raised units crying out for experienced reinforcements, skilled horsemen in particular. The troopship *Britannic* was made available to transport them, but the announcement that the ship would be conveying New South Welshmen and Queenslanders on indulgence passages without calling at Melbourne led to an agitation by Victorian returned soldiers, who ultimately succeeded in having the *Britannic*'s itinerary altered to include a stopover at their capital city. When the *Britannic* visited Melbourne to collect 105 Victorians on 24 August, they came aboard under Lieutenant Harold Elliott's command.

Because Australian soldiers, bushmen especially, had established a notorious reputation for independence, indiscipline, and wildness, the captain of the *Britannic* was not at all pleased to learn he had to transport hundreds of Australian ex-soldiers back to South Africa in an unofficial capacity. His misgivings were reinforced when he finally arrived in Melbourne some 30 hours late after being delayed by bad weather. A British officer, who had been involved in the supervision of the Victorians waiting to board the ship, was relieved to see him. 'Thank God you've turned up, old man', said this officer, 'these are the worst lot I've ever had to deal with'.

Being in charge of these men was clearly a challenging task, but Elliott evidently handled it very capably. Even the pessimistic troopship captain conceded that the men soon 'settled down … and we had very little trouble with them during the rest of the time they were on board'. Some of the men harboured secret plans to pick up a civilian job away from the fighting, but they had a rude awakening when several staff officers came aboard the *Britannic* as soon as it reached Cape Town and insisted they all had to enlist in one of the irregular units or return immediately to Australia. They made their choices, and went their separate ways. Major Thomas subsequently became involved in the celebrated Bush Veldt Carbineers courts-martial, which resulted in Lieutenants Harry 'Breaker' Morant and Peter Handcock being sentenced to death by firing squad; a third accused Australian, Lieutenant George Witton, was also convicted, but was gaoled rather than shot. Witton had served in the VIB, and was Elliott's former quartermaster-sergeant; Elliott knew him 'very well'. Thomas acted as the defendants' lawyer, and became immortalised in the film *Breaker Morant* as the character portrayed by Jack Thompson.

Harold Elliott had no involvement in the controversial escapades of the Bush Veldt Carbineers. Having considered his options, he obtained a commission with the Cape Colony Cyclist Corps. This unit had been formed only nine months earlier, but had already done well in a number of engagements. Lieutenant Elliott was assigned to the northern region of Cape Colony at Prieska, where he was appointed Assistant Press Censor in mid-October. But this was not a congenial role for someone who yearned to involve himself in a combatant capacity, and he was soon looking for a position in a well-credentialled mounted unit. To boost his chances, he wrote home in search of further recommendations to supplement testimonials he had already obtained from Mackay—'I am sure he is absolutely conscientious and trustworthy'—and the VIB commander, who saluted 'your brilliant record' with the bushmen. There was a warm response from John Garbutt of Ballarat College, who described Elliott as 'a hard-working, loyal, trusty and true gentleman'. Another mentor during his years at Ballarat, Presbyterian minister Dr Cairns, attested to his 'diligence and integrity', 'excellent moral character', and reliability 'in any position of trust'. Harold also received a fine recommendation from MacFarland:

> He proved himself a man of sterling character and of blameless life. He was also a good industrious and intelligent student ... Lieutenant Elliott has received a good education, he is a man of quiet determined character, and I can confidently predict that he will do thoroughly any work which he undertakes.

Elliott decided to join the Border Scouts. This choice confirmed his willingness to place himself where there was strenuous work and intermittent danger. He would be operating in Cape Colony's North-Western District, an inhospitable region where martial law prevailed and there was 'not a railway or a made road or bridge through the whole of it'. The Border Scouts were hardy souls who had made an arduous, unglamorous, and very effective contribution to the anti-Boer cause. According to a British officer who served with them, they were talented as well as tough:

> the men could always tell whether distant dust was made by ostriches, springbok, locusts, or mounted men, and never made a mistake in their judgment. If a party of horsemen had passed over the road they could roughly estimate the number, and could tell how many horses were ridden and how many led. They travelled by night as easily as by day, always going straight across country and never on the track. Not a waggon of any sort accompanied the regiment, the blanket being under the saddle and an overcoat strapped in front. They carried no cooking-pots or food, as when on trek they only used meat. Spare ammunition was carried on horses.

Because they operated in areas so remote and so replete with enemy sympathisers, the British authorities felt unable to rely on getting money safely through to them, and stopped sending it. As a result the Border Scouts commander, Major Birkbeck, resorted to his own substitute currency. Since the jackal was something of an emblem to the unit (the men wore its skin on their hats), it was featured on the 'notes' issued by the Border Scouts paymaster that were made from cloth of various types, including commandeered blinds, sheets, and table-cloths.

After joining the Border Scouts in December 1901, Lieutenant Elliott was soon distinguishing himself again in hazardous circumstances. Six days into the new year he was in charge of a small group guarding an isolated post when a Boer force headed by Commandant Conroy raided it. The Boers were evidently hoping to capture hundreds of horses held at the post, but Harold marshalled his meagre garrison so skilfully that Conroy's Boers, despite their numerical superiority, were repulsed. It was another feather in his cap. 'I congratulate you and men with you it was well done', cabled Birkbeck. There was another telegram from none other than Lord Kitchener himself: 'Please tell Lieut Elliott that I am very pleased with his conduct and that of his men in driving off Conroy and saving horses'.

The Border Scouts and other units engaged in Cape Colony succeeded in keeping the guerrillas who were still active in the Cape confined to the far west and north-west, where they were least effective. Elsewhere the Boers' scope for manoeuvre was also declining and, though remaining defiant, they became more amenable to a negotiated end to hostilities. After a lengthy negotiating process the Boers agreed to sign peace terms in May 1902, and the war was over. Elliott remained with the Border Scouts until they were officially disbanded three months later.

Harold Elliott's flair for soldiering was clearly demonstrated in South Africa. It had been evident beforehand that his interest in military pursuits—whether reading about past commanders and battles, or practising drills in a peacetime context—was profound. He proved during the Boer War that when real bullets were flying his soldierly capacity matched his zeal. When he enlisted he was earnest and enthusiastic, but inexperienced and unknown. He returned after the war with a distinguished record, a burgeoning reputation in military circles, and justified confidence that he could command men capably in tough conditions and adverse situations.

CHAPTER FOUR

'Utmost Energy and Concentrated Perseverance': Solicitor and militiaman, husband and father

1903-AUGUST 1914

AFTER THREE YEARS spent away from formal study soldiering on the veldt, it would have been understandable if Harold Elliott found it difficult to readjust to university life. But there was no sign that this lengthy interruption hampered him in the slightest. If anything, he returned to his studies with an even more purposeful approach than before. Three years earlier he had decided to complete a full arts course before tackling any law subjects, only to enlist in the VIB a few weeks later. In 1903 he enrolled again in third-year arts, and recorded satisfactory passes in all his subjects at the November examinations.

He had not sat for the separate honours examinations in arts, but when he turned to law in 1904 he decided to strive for honours. The professor of law, Harrison Moore, was youthful-looking, slightly built, prim, and puritanical. He delivered precisely worded lectures in a Londoner's accent while obsessively twisting a pellet of wool between his fingers, 'pulling it to pieces as if separating the strands of an argument and rewinding it into a ball'. Although Moore felt his primary objective was to produce competent professional lawyers, he was intent on presenting the law in a broad historical and political context in order to avoid churning out blinkered practitioners whose main focus was on remuneration. His tuition won widespread acclaim. Harold Elliott responded to it superbly, tackling jurisprudence, law of property, law of contract, and constitutional history and law with outstanding results.

He attained honours in all four subjects—first-class honours and the exhibition in property and contract, a second and a shared exhibition in the other two.

> His was not the supremely brilliant talent that achieves success in sudden flight; there was no royal road to triumph prepared for him by nature; only by utilising the utmost energy and concentrated perseverance was he to win such prizes in the scholarship of law.

By the time he returned from South Africa Elliott was appreciably older and more self-reliant than the average college student, and it was not surprising that he spent part of his second university phase in private accommodation at 'Endersleigh', 201 Drummond Street, Carlton, rather than in Ormond. An impressive three-storey residence near Grattan Street, conveniently close to the university, Endersleigh was part of Holcombe Terrace, a stylish edifice in two-tone patterned brick and decorative iron lace. Alexander and Mary Campbell, both immigrants from Scotland, had recently acquired Endersleigh. Alexander Campbell farmed for many years in Tasmania before moving to Victoria, where he earned a living in various ways, including as a boarding-house proprietor (in Warrnambool) and as a storekeeper. Elliott came to know the Campbells and their four children very well.

His absorption in military pursuits continued unabated. On 1 March 1904, when the first Defence Act passed by the federal parliament created an Australian Militia, he joined one of the new militia units, the 5th Australian Infantry Regiment (AIR). Much of his spare time was devoted to regimental activities not far from Endersleigh at the Grattan Street drill hall, where young military enthusiasts savouring every anecdotal Boer War snippet they could scrounge were thrilled to find they had a lieutenant in their regiment who had been decorated for daring bravery in that conflict.

In 1905, the final year of his law course, Elliott returned to Ormond, where his younger brother George would also be residing while studying first-year medicine. Harold's glittering prizes at the end of 1904 had included an Ormond residential scholarship for the following year (worth £60), which enabled him to return to college without relying on his father for financial assistance of possibly distasteful dimensions for an independently inclined 26-year-old. An added attraction was the appointment of an inaugural law tutor at Ormond, H.C. Winneke.

George had an even more illustrious record at Ballarat College than Harold. As well as emulating him in being dux of the school, George had displayed outstanding talent as a footballer and runner, and was awarded a prestigious prize for being the most popular and admired student in the whole college. However, once George was at Ormond, neither Harold's example nor his exhortations succeeded in keeping George on the straight and narrow. George did not possess the resolute determination that his elder brother had in such abundance. Whereas Harold was a teetotaller, George was fond of a convivial ale. George's enjoyment of various distractions, which included playing in the popular Victorian Football League (VFL)—he managed to get a game in the Fitzroy team that went on to win the premiership that year—proved detrimental to his studies, and he failed to pass any of his subjects at the end of the year.

Harold, in stark contrast, completed his law course brilliantly. He had his distractions, too—his involvement with the 5th AIR in particular—but did not allow them to interfere with his main objective. In Ormond he shunned the tediously repetitive debates, still dominating Students' Club meetings year after year, about the desirability of having the *Bulletin* in the common room. His solitary participation in Students' Club affairs was his stint on the gymnasium committee, although he was also a member of a separate committee involved in the organisation of the university's Annual Sports Meeting in May. He entered two events himself, the shot-put and the hammer-throw; that he was victorious in both was testimony to his physical strength, and also indicates that he spent long hours sweating in the gym as well as supervising its use by others. But he remained supremely dedicated to his work. If high-spirited Ormond roisterers were indulging in such rowdy boisterousness that he was having trouble concentrating in his study, he was not averse to descending the stairs rapidly and threatening the offenders in no uncertain terms with drastic retribution if they did not pipe down. They invariably did. At the same time he generously allowed other students to use his notes, which were renowned for thoroughness and reliability (but not readability—his vigorous scrawl was not easy to decipher).

His involvement in the activities of the Law Students' Society included being a participant in an evening debate at a city cafe on the following topic:

> B applies to A to allow B to use, gratuitously, a wooden shed belonging to A, for the purpose of potting plants. A knows that the roof of the shed is in an unsafe and dangerous condition; B does not know it. A consents to B's using the shed. A does not think of the condition of the roof and does not tell B anything about it. Whilst properly using it for the above-mentioned purpose B is killed by the roof falling upon him. Has B's personal representative any cause of action against A?

In the debate Harold was given the task of arguing for the affirmative. Such occasions were pleasant social gatherings as well as useful scholarly exercises, but the key to success still lay primarily in one's ability to sustain the all-important solitary slog. It is true that a law degree could not be attained without intellectual prowess and a reasonably cool head at examination time (when the whole year's assessment was based on a few hours' answers). But even more crucial was the capacity to cope with the sheer grind. Students needed substantial persistence and determination to master the intricacies of tomes such as Pollock's *Law of Torts*, Snell's *Principles of Equity*, and *Personal Property* by Joshua Williams.

Elliott's results clearly demonstrated that he had all these attributes. Prospective honours students in final-year law were required to pass all their fourth-year subjects at the end of that year before presenting themselves at the Final Honour Examination in March of the following year. In November 1905 Elliott duly obtained passes in all his final-year subjects, then devoted much of the ensuing summer to revision while many of his friends and contemporaries were maximising their time at the beach. This gruelling conclusion to his tertiary studies involved further examinations in two subjects from third-year law as well as in three fourth-year ones. He had to outline and explain the doctrine of equitable estoppel; he had to evaluate the applicability in criminal cases of the maxim 'Qui facit per alium facit per se'; he had to elucidate 'the advantages and objections to inserting an attornment clause in a mortgage'; and much, much more. His results were very gratifying. He was awarded second-class honours, and shared (with George Crowther of Trinity) the coveted Supreme Court Prize for the top student in final-year law.

Aspiring solicitors with a law degree had to complete their articles before becoming eligible to practise. In view of his superb academic results Elliott was clearly a well-credentialled acquisition for any legal practitioner. After being engaged by the well-established establishment firm of Moule, Hamilton and Kiddle, he commenced his articles at their city office located at 55 Market Street. The senior partner, F.A. Moule, had already begun what would become a near half-century term on the council of Melbourne Grammar School, where he and his brothers had been among the earliest pupils. The youngest brother, W.H. Moule, had obtained a law degree, practised at the Bar, played Test cricket for Australia, and spent two terms in the Victorian parliament as MLA for Brighton before becoming a County Court judge in the year that Harold Elliott began his articles.

F.A. Moule's career had been less dashing. Having qualified as a lawyer himself via the more prosaic non-university route, he apparently preferred to employ solicitors who had done likewise. According to a lawyer who used to work at the firm, no law graduate became a partner there until F.A. Moule's nephew did in 1931. That did not mean he was averse to hiring young graduates with brilliant records—on the customarily exploitative terms for employees doing their articles. However, once the year's articles were up, the firm tended to dispense with these graduates. Retaining them as fully fledged lawyers would result in increased expenditure. This was something that 'sweet' F.A., as the tough martinet was known in some quarters, was not prepared to tolerate.

While completing his articles Harold resided at Endersleigh with the Campbells again. George boarded there, too, and made a better fist of first-year medicine in this different environment. Alexander and Mary Campbell had two sons, Neil and John, and two daughters, Kate and Belle. Neil was an accountant in Melbourne. John managed a pastoral station near Geraldton, Western Australia. Kate and Belle had contrasting personalities. Kate, six years older than Belle (and three years older than Harold), was a petite, gentle, sweet-natured woman with an air of unworldly diffidence; she helped her mother with the household chores at Endersleigh. Belle, whose full name was Isabella Rachel, had a more assertive and practical disposition. She was building a career as one of the band of competent women who formed the backbone of the successful Gilpin's retail chain stores.

Both sisters were attracted to Harold. In fact, he had been engaged once already. Dora Adamson, whose family lived near Lake Wendouree and knew the Elliotts well, had a vivacious, outgoing personality. When

Harold moved on from Ballarat to university he began making visits from Ormond to see Dora, now residing in Essendon, and a close friendship developed. The engagement was broken off by Elliott, for reasons that remain unclear; he apparently felt let down in some way. Once he committed himself to Kate Campbell, however (after some flirtatious dalliance with Belle as well as Kate), that relationship proved lasting. Belle accepted the situation loyally, and remained on good terms with both Kate and her future brother-in-law.

In August 1907, having completed his articles, Harold was formally admitted to practise as a lawyer. Moule, Hamilton and Kiddle apparently dispensed with his services when they became obliged to pay him more than a pittance. So, to further his legal career, Harold sought the assistance of Professor Moore. He received a glowing testimonial:

> I have pleasure in stating that Mr H.E. Elliott who was a student in the University classes in Law in 1904 and 1905 did excellent work throughout the course, and apart altogether from the distinguished position he won in his Examinations, established a high reputation for ability and strength of character.

For a time Harold was based at the Victorian country town of Stawell, where he practised as a solicitor with Arthur Wettenhall. The Wettenhalls were well known in and beyond the Grampians region for the quality of the merino sheep bred at their extensive properties; Arthur's younger brother Roly had resided at Ormond while Harold and George were there.

Harold then moved back to Melbourne. He bought a house, and entered into partnership with Glen Roberts, a 44-year-old solicitor who had been practising since 1892. Harold's impressive academic results and his conspicuous capacity and integrity made him a compelling proposition for a more seasoned solicitor on the lookout for a partner. The new firm of Roberts and Elliott was initially situated at the office address Roberts had been using for years in Collins Street near Elizabeth Street.

The house Harold acquired was in the north-eastern suburb of Northcote, which had become familiar territory. Kate had been living at 73 Darebin Street, Northcote since her family's move there from Endersleigh. Harold seems to have briefly resided there himself before acquiring 'Dalriada', a brick dwelling on a sizeable block situated a quarter of a mile east of the Campbells' house in the same street. He obtained loan finance for the purchase from his father (who held mortgages over a number of properties), and was as scrupulous about interest payments as if he had a formal contract with a bank.

Harold married Kate on 27 December 1909. It was a decidedly family affair. They were married at Dalriada under Presbyterian auspices with George and Belle the primary witnesses. The marriage certificate correctly recorded the bridegroom's age as 31, but Kate's was understated by a year and given as 33, perhaps to narrow the age difference (when Harold's parents married 42 years earlier their equivalent document was similarly inaccurate). There was, sadly, one notable absentee: Kate's elder brother Neil had died two months earlier after a four-year battle with tuberculosis.

George, who had returned to Ormond in 1907, was making slow progress towards his degree. He was too fond of sporting and social diversions to emulate his elder brother's dedicated approach to study. Now a well-known footballer, he was prominent in the University VFL team; a dashing defender, he captained University and represented Victoria at interstate level. To working-class football fanatics the University team was a curious phenomenon, represented by players of 'superior intelligence' who 'wore pyjamas and brushed their teeth'. University had an unfair advantage, they complained, because its medicos like George could teach their team-mates where to bump opponents most effectively. Harold was very interested in football, and proud of his brother's achievements; he just wished George could display more self-discipline around exam-time. Coincidentally, there was another VFL captain with the same surname: Fred Elliott, one of Carlton's finest ever players and the first footballer to play 200 League games, was famous throughout Victoria as 'Pompey' Elliott.

In 1911 Harold became a parent and lost one of his own in the space of a few months. In March Kate gave birth to a daughter; her parents honoured their younger sisters by naming her Violet Isabel. Harold was thrilled to become a father. He was an affectionate, involved parent from the moment he first glimpsed Violet: she 'caught hold of his fingers tight', gazed at him intently 'with sparkly bright little dark eyes', and he was instantly smitten. He enjoyed the frequent remarks others made about the strong facial resemblance between his little daughter and himself; he helped Kate weigh the baby each week to check she was growing satisfactorily; and when Kate sometimes felt daunted by the responsibilities of motherhood, Harold was supportive and tried hard to bolster her confidence. Thomas Elliott was a grandfather for only four months. Stooped and bent, he had been ailing with heart and blood pressure trouble. He died at Ballarat in July; Harold, Rod, and George carried his coffin at the funeral.

Next April Harold made a much more pleasurable return to Ballarat for his youngest sister Violet's wedding. He knew her husband, Dr John Avery, well: he was a Queenslander who had won an Ormond scholarship to study medicine, a course unavailable in his home state. Avery had met his future wife when he accompanied Harold and George to Elsinore during the shorter vacations of the academic year when it was not practical to return all the way to Queensland. He had supplemented his earnest proposal of marriage by taking Violet out in a boat on Lake Wendouree and threatening to sink it unless she said yes. They settled in Brisbane, accompanied eventually by her mother and elder sister Flory, who was unusually tall, frequently irascible, and did not marry. Harold had only one sibling, George, based permanently in Victoria after his sisters left the state. His other brother Rod had for some years been farming at Tocumwal in southern New South Wales. Rod was a jovial prankster who enjoyed the occasional visits to 'Toke' of his relatives (including Harold) as much as they liked his lively humour and practical jokes.

Kate had attended the Avery wedding in an advanced state of pregnancy, and in June 1912 gave birth to a son. He was named Neil Campbell in memory of the uncle he never knew. Once again Harold felt anguished about Kate's childbirth agony, but he was thrilled to have a son. Besotted with his children, he played merrily with them; they responded warmly to his heartiness, boyishness, and fondness for 'tishes' (kisses). At the dinner table Violet would sometimes sit on her father's knee; when Kate was wary at one stage about Violet eating meat he would playfully sneak her some of his while Kate was not looking.

All this time, while Harold Elliott was becoming a solicitor, husband, and father, he maintained his purposeful involvement in Australia's peacetime defence forces. It was a commitment that dominated his leisure hours. For almost a decade after graduating from university, he later claimed, he 'never had a holiday that was not spent in some military encampment or school of instruction'. There was no keener participant in militia activities, whether it was parade drill or tuition sessions, bush camps or training exercises. He was active in both the Naval and Military Club and the South African Soldiers' Association. Indeed, his closest friends outside his family tended to be fellow militia enthusiasts, notably James Stephen and Harry Duigan (both fellow lawyers), Bob Smith, Walter McNicoll, and Henry (Gordon) Bennett. Elliott continued to read voraciously about all aspects of soldiering past and present, and assimilated useful insights about command techniques from a wide range of sources:

> I used to read a great deal of poetry ... and Kipling has always been first favourite amongst my authors. I owe him a great deal in many ways. He is a great student of human nature and the light he throws upon it has often consciously or unconsciously aided me whilst endeavouring to learn how best to handle men.

His ability and dedication were very evident, especially in his characteristically thorough preparation for promotional examinations. After joining the 5th AIR as a second lieutenant in 1904, he became a lieutenant in 1905, a captain in 1909, and a major in 1911; for eight months he served as the regiment's adjutant. Confidential commanders' assessments authenticated the Victorian commandant's verdict that he was 'an excellent officer'. In 1907 Lieutenant Elliott was given the ultimate accolade of 'excellent' in three categories by the 5th AIR's colonel, who did not use that adjective anywhere in his assessments of the fourteen other subalterns in the regiment.

While he was gaining promotion he followed intently the evolving national debate about defence policy. Concern about Australia's defence preparedness was galvanised by Japan's arrestingly comprehensive defeat of Russia in 1905, and there were other unsettling international developments. Alarm spread throughout the British Empire after it was dramatically alleged in London that Germany was positioning itself to challenge British naval supremacy. Tensions also rose disturbingly during the Agadir Crisis and other scares. A 1909 editorial in the Melbourne *Age* told its readers they lived in 'a world that is going mad in preparation for a major war'. Agitation for comprehensive military training in Australia gathered more and more adherents, and a compulsory training scheme was introduced with Harold Elliott's wholehearted approval. One of the reasons that he devoted himself to militia activities with such passionate seriousness was because of his concern about Australia's vulnerability to Japan and Germany.

The advent of compulsory military training led to an overhaul of the militia structure as well as a large increase in its numerical strength. Major Harold Elliott, with other 5th AIR officers, joined a newly created battalion, the 60th Infantry, based in North Carlton. A year later, when another batch of cadets was drafted into the militia and further formations came into existence, he was promoted to command one of these new units, the 58th Infantry Battalion (Essendon Rifles). The nucleus of the 58th was a single Essendon-based company previously belonging to the 60th. Henceforth all eight companies of the 58th were to obtain their recruits from the Essendon area, including the nearby suburbs of Moonee Ponds, Ascot Vale, and Newmarket.

Right from the outset Lieutenant-Colonel Elliott forged the closest possible links between his battalion and the local community. He arranged for a formal ceremonial inauguration of the unit at Essendon on 19 July, and a special church parade the following day. His impetus led to the formation of a citizens' committee to support the battalion's activities, particularly in sport, military competitions, and fund-raising. Elliott used sport wherever possible to help the local community identify with the battalion. For the unit's colours he chose the red and black of the popular Essendon VFL team.

Colonel Elliott outlined his views on discipline for officers and NCOs of the 58th in a lively and informative treatise full of historical allusions. In particular, it was sprinkled with insights derived from his Boer War experiences. He adopted an anecdotal approach: 'I strongly hold that a single example or illustration teaches us more than a whole book of abstract theory'. Among the anecdotes recounted in Elliott's fluent, compelling style was a predicament that vexed Tivey in South Africa, when a VIB trooper became lost and some of his comrades refused orders to move on unless a search party was detached to look for him:

> A squadron of Australians hot, dusty and dry are pushing fast along a road in that 'scorched and scornful land', their waggons toiling along in the rear deep in dust with a few men told off as escort. One of these men—call him Trooper X—sees a buck at a little distance,

> he will he thinks slip off the waggon and secure a choice supper. Corporal Z in charge of the escort thinks it no harm, he lets him go, he will he imagines rejoin in a few minutes. At any rate he will get in to-night as he only has to follow the track. The man goes off—he is not a very good hunter—the buck sees him and makes off a good way, then starts to feed. The trooper follows. He thinks he will get behind a clump of bushes and stalk him. He cautiously approaches, reaches the bushes and finds the buck gone. He searches awhile and then gives it up. By this time he is a good way from the road and the waggons have gone, even the dust from them is not in sight. However he will by taking a short cut diagonally to the track soon catch up. He hurries on. He strikes a patch of prickly bush, it does not seem of any great extent so he resolves to go round it on the side further from the roads, he goes on and on, so does the bush ... Darkness comes on ... He sits down to rest for awhile and loses all sense of direction. He is lost and already feels the pangs of thirst and hunger. Let us return now to his comrades. Camp is reached. After waiting some time Corporal Z reports that Trooper X is missing. But it is dark, nothing can be done until morning. Morning dawns. The officers discuss the matter over their hurried meal. The Captain anxiously scans his instructions. He has been ordered to reach and hold a certain drift or ford by a certain time. He sees already by a glance at his map that he has not covered as much as he should have done in the time. He must push on or his mission will be fruitless.

Elliott's skilful presentation of these episodes—with flair and realism, using the present tense for added immediacy—was most effective in enabling the 58th officers and NCOs to imagine themselves confronted by similar problems in equivalent situations. He gave them his conclusions with characteristic directness. Corporal Z should never have acquiesced in the trooper's departure in the first place, and the missing trooper (who in fact survived his ordeal after being found by the search party in a distressed state) 'in the circumstances would have thoroughly deserved his fate' if he had been 'left to die and rot'. Moreover,

> Had that squadron been properly trained they would without doubt have left Bill X to the vultures and his bones would be

> bleaching in the scrub to this day. However cruel that may sound to you it is war, and you must educate yourself to face it ... it is war and it is discipline, and war and discipline are not humane ... it is not the slightest manner of use disguising it and sugar coating your discipline in time of peace, for the sugar will, I assure you, suddenly disappear and melt away in the field, and you will be left with the pill in all its naked bitterness to swallow ... The least hesitation or delay in obedience (more especially in modern times) for a few minutes may well mean the difference between the losing and the winning of a battle, and on you lies the onus of seeing that it does not occur. If your men and NCOs are properly trained such an incident could not occur. If Corporal Z had known his job Trooper Bill X would have been brought back to the waggon quick and lively, before he had gone 20 yards, and brought up before the Captain to be dealt with for falling out without permission.

Colonel Elliott cautioned his officers and NCOs to be very wary of the understandable urge to be popular with the men under them. While 'within bounds this desire is laudable enough', pursuing it indiscriminately could lead to a breakdown in discipline and, therefore, to disaster. Moreover, even the strictest discipline, provided it was administered impartially in a fair and just manner, could in fact increase the popularity of the commander concerned. He cited the retreat of the British army to Corunna in 1809, referring to Napier's multi-volume history of the Peninsula War and quoting lavishly from *The Recollections of Rifleman Harris*, a private in the brigade commanded by General Craufurd that comprised the rearguard during the retreat. Elliott used graphic excerpts from the Harris book to emphasise that Craufurd's adherence to the fiercest discipline in the most appalling conditions was instrumental in the brigade's exceptional feats of endurance. Craufurd's men, Elliott stressed, retained a profound affection, even worship, for their commander despite his strong-willed severity. Elliott was impressed by the way Craufurd combined strict impartial discipline with considerate attentiveness to his men, and also admired his willingness to use forceful methods to ensure they were appropriately looked after.

Elliott was trenchantly critical of Australian officers who had displayed less than wholehearted commitment to their training exercises. A certain company commander who did not fully comply with an order

> at a Bivouac we had some years ago ... because he considered that his men were tired ... was guilty in my opinion of a gross breach of discipline. If his men were so tired that they could not do duty properly, it was his bounden duty to go to his Colonel and tell him straight out that his men were too tired. If the Colonel disagreed and sent them out his duty was done and he was absolutely bound to see that [the order was completely obeyed]. The responsibility for that would be on the Colonel's shoulders ... As it was it made the whole thing a farce. Neither the subalterns, NCOs or men derived the slightest use from what they did. The officer concerned has not to this day the slightest idea that anyone knows of this, but I was the Adjutant of that Regiment and it is the Adjutant's duty to find out these things and I know that that officer though in many respects a good officer is not to be depended on as absolutely straightforward and honest.

On another occasion 'the half battalion I was in' received an order

> to occupy a certain hill. The Major in command took us a little way towards the foot of the hill till he got behind a hedge, halted, looked at it hard (it was very steep), looked at us and back towards the C.O. Then he led us into a grassy hollow under some shady trees and told us to have a sleep. 'Tis too damned hot, men, to trouble about the hill at all', said he. This is the sort of thing that ruins discipline. How can an officer expect his men to obey him when he sets an example like that?

He did not want to see that kind of attitude in the 58th:

> Always act on manoeuvres as if you were actually on service. That is what they are held for. The Government are paying you good money to act as if you were at war, and if you don't so act you are getting money on false pretences.

Despite his criticisms of some unspecified officers, Elliott was optimistic about the overall potential of Australian soldiers. In general they had plenty of initiative, which was not necessarily detrimental to discipline. According to Elliott, the correct definition of initiative was

> the independence based on intelligence which prompts an inferior to promote the ends of his leaders when the latter are no longer present. The enforcement of discipline does not mean or imply the destruction of initiative.

Furthermore, Australian soldiers were relatively bright:

> Their average intelligence is far higher than that of the average Tommy Atkins of the British Army, they are quick to appreciate the necessity for the strict obedience of orders under certain circumstances. For example on a night march in Africa in attempting a surprise on the enemy, we never had the least trouble in preventing men smoking or striking matches in the line of march. They saw readily enough that all our exertions would be in vain if one of us put the whole show away by striking a match.

But it was a different story altogether in the British units serving alongside them. Elliott had heard taunts flung at native-born Australians like himself that 'you'll never be the men your fathers were', but he was confident these sneers would prove mistaken: 'I honestly believe that with discipline there will be no troops in the world comparable with our own'.

The intensity of his commitment to military preparedness was also demonstrated in a stirring pep talk he delivered at an officers' training school shortly before he became commander of the Essendon Rifles. A director of this particular school, Elliott exhorted the trainees to apply themselves devotedly to their military work:

> That way, and that way alone, I would impress upon you, lies the safety of Australia—our children's heritage. Without that effort Australia's rising sun, the badge of its armies, may well be quenched in blood. The cheerful homesteads around us, through which we have wandered in our pleasant play, at war may well be laid desolate; their owners ruined; their cattle ruthlessly slaughtered, to bring us the sooner to our knees; our great cities laid in ashes,

> unless we cravenly yield them at the first summons; our wives, our mothers and our sisters rendered at the best homeless and desolate; at the worst, dishonoured or slain before our eyes. These things are the result of sloth and unpreparedness.

It was not just prospective army officers who were receptive to such a message in 1913; plenty of Australians who had nothing to do with soldiering agreed wholeheartedly with these sentiments.

He also urged the trainees to bear in mind that any neglect in their training might have harrowing consequences in a real fight:

> Will you be thinking of this good man and that good man lying dead, wounded or missing, and thinking: Did I do right or not in taking this or that action? Will I have to account for these men's lives, or not? If you have well and truly and zealously applied yourselves to the task of mastering the science and art of war, your conscience at least will be easy, however heavy your heart; but if you have neglected your opportunities and looked upon your connection with the Battalion as merely a sort of amusement, or as a means of attaining some sort of social distinction (poor as it is), then you will be as Judas was, for like him you will have betrayed a sacred trust.

With his forthright approach and passionate seriousness, Elliott was making a name for himself. Tallish and heavily built with the powerful chest and shoulders of a noted shot-putter, he was clean-shaven with a big reddish face, brown eyes, and dark hair (though Kate was beginning to notice grey shoots emerging). He was regarded in militia circles as a commander of impressive intellect and strong opinions, a hefty fire-eater ever-ready to be fiercely critical of anyone not doing what he thought they should be doing. Though quietly spoken normally, Elliott when steamed up had a roar that could be heard a long way away. And it was not just the rank and file at the receiving end—if his officers did not meet his exacting standards he did not spare them, either.

Yet that did not diminish the admiration many of his men had for his forceful personality and vigorous methods. There was a straightforward openness about him that they appreciated (except when on the receiving end of one of his withering outbursts). Utterly and artlessly sincere, he was not adept at concealing his feelings, especially concerning what he saw as 'matters of conscience': in fact, he regarded speaking frankly on such issues as fundamental to his self-respect. This was despite the shyness that still troubled him, if less acutely. He now managed on most occasions, and in most company, a direct, uncomplicated, and attractive geniality, without ever impressing as a smooth or accomplished mixer.

Admiration for Elliott in the militia was not, however, universal. Shortly before he transferred from the 60th Infantry to take up command of the Essendon Rifles he was involved in a bizarre dispute with a brash 25-year-old lieutenant, Tom White, who commanded D Company in the 60th. There had been antipathy between the pair for years—stemming, according to White, from an exchange during their days in the 5th AIR, when Elliott had taken a dim view of the way that White, then a junior subaltern, had disagreed with him in a discussion about machine-gun tactics. Be that as it may, Elliott considered that White had an insubordinate manner and could be occasionally cavalier about obeying orders he disagreed with. White felt Elliott was headstrong and unduly dictatorial.

The bitter dispute between them arose in April 1913 when White refused to comply with Elliott's request to postpone two D Company social gatherings, a ball and a smoke night, which White had planned to hold in June. With D Company about to become the nucleus of the newly created battalion he had been promoted to command, Elliott told White that he wanted to organise a major function of his own for D Company at that time. But White replied that the dates had been fixed, with deposits paid to secure the Essendon Town Hall as the venue for both the ball and the smoke night. Accordingly, he doubted whether the arrangements could be altered. Elliott's fervent desire to make a success of his new command burned deep within him, and he was furious to find that his plans to start off on the right foot were being thwarted by someone he disliked. He told White that permission was necessary to hold the functions. White replied that the battalion commander had given his blessing verbally. Elliott (who was second in command of the 60th) countered that written authorisation was required, and he would make sure White did not get it. The perplexed commander of the 60th, Lieutenant-Colonel F.A. Foxall, who had at times found Elliott a difficult subordinate, wished the problem would go away. He tried to engineer a compromise solution, without success.

The squabble soon degenerated into farce. On 8 May Elliott discovered that D Company had decided to have a smoke night the following evening instead of their two proposed functions in June. He reacted by turning up during business hours at the office where White worked and placing him under arrest for insubordination. (Men under Elliott's command were used to his unusual habit of declaring them to be under arrest for minor disciplinary breaches and then releasing them afterwards.) After finding out the identities of the organising committee who were responsible, along with White, for the decision to hold this substitute function, Elliott visited them in their respective places of employment and arrested them, too. One of them was a teller in a bank, where the sight of Elliott marching in to cross-examine him and then gravely place him under arrest was, to say the least, a diverting spectacle for waiting customers.

Foxall, who was, in White's opinion, intimidated by Elliott's insistence that proceeding with the smoke night represented a serious disciplinary offence, persuaded White on 9 May to call at Elliott's office with a compromise proposal. But Elliott would not have a bar of it. When he learned that the function had not yet been cancelled, he ordered White—in a bellow that startled the staff of Roberts and Elliott—to accompany him immediately to Foxall's office. As they walked down Collins Street together, White did not mince words in telling Elliott exactly what he thought of his domineering conduct. With Elliott by now 'almost apoplectic', Foxall decided regretfully that the smoke night would have to be cancelled, even though the caterers were already at the Town Hall getting the function room ready. Elliott made sure this decision was implemented by turning up at the Town Hall himself, impounding the food, and ordering the bewildered town clerk not to allow anyone inside. After the men arrived, unaware of the late cancellation, White presided over an informal alternative gathering in the street outside the hall.

The following day an account of this extraordinary affair was published in the Melbourne *Herald*. Elliott wrote to the newspaper threatening a libel suit, although he had dubious grounds (and ultimately did not sue). White was approached by solicitors acting for the *Herald*, and agreed to assist them by providing a detailed written statement. By then a military court of inquiry into the affair, requested by

White, had commenced under the jurisdiction of three 60th officers, Major W.R. McNicoll and Lieutenants H.T.C. Layh and R.H. Henderson. White received well-intentioned advice from several officers that it was in his best long-term interests to back down and express regret for the imbroglio, but he was no longer prepared to make conciliatory gestures. After the inquiry had taken testimony from witnesses, he stubbornly refused to accept that the written record of evidence was completely accurate. The alleged omissions were insignificant, but the inquiry had to go through the evidence all over again. Foxall was livid.

Although White was ultimately cleared of Elliott's charge of insubordination, his unappeased resentment prompted him to pursue redress. Initially he sought an additional inquiry into the circumstances of his arrest by Elliott. When this request was denied (on the compelling ground that the issue had already been dealt with), White then alleged that Foxall had inappropriately reprimanded him. Eventually, however, he decided to let the whole matter rest.

It had not reflected well on either of the protagonists. Elliott had certainly confirmed that he was an absolute stickler for discipline, but had made himself look ridiculous in the process. Since it was his deeply felt yearning to make a successful start as a battalion commander that had produced his over-reaction in the first place, it was ironical that his conduct could only diminish his reputation in a local community where it was so important to him to make a good initial impression. His performance at the Essendon Town Hall, where he startled onlookers by arriving suddenly and then charging around the supper room, fanatically packing away the food that the caterers had laid out on the tables, was hardly auspicious.

Still, first impressions are not always lasting ones. Before long it was evident to anyone who took an interest in the Essendon Rifles that its inaugural commander had abundant zeal and capacity. He was a hard taskmaster who frequently roared at his men (and sometimes at his officers), but his demanding methods instilled effectiveness. That he quickly managed to overcome any misgivings entertained by influential Essendon residents was demonstrated by the remarkable success of a military fete held in March 1914 at Queen's Park, Moonee Ponds. The fete was conceived in order to raise funds for the district's cadets and militiamen so they could acquire various facilities such as band instruments, gymnastic equipment, and camp requisites. The Victorian

Governor opened it, and among other notables present were the Premier, W.A. Watt, and the Essendon mayor, J.F. Henderson, who was actively involved in the organisation of the big occasion. Queen's Park had 'never looked better', large crowds turned up to have a look at the wide range of stalls and the military displays, and battalion funds were boosted by almost £400.

In mid-1914 Harold Elliott's family life was a source of solace as well as satisfaction and delight. A devoted parent, he observed the activities and development of his 'wee bairnies' with abiding fascination. He had a lot of fun playing with them: 'gallopy gallopy' ('rides' on his knee) and hide-and-seek were particular favourites. Although an affectionate and attentive father, he had a very busy life; while he was at work, or out on militia business either in the evening or at weekends, there were inevitably times when Kate found two demanding toddlers quite a handful. In these circumstances her sister Belle generously assisted Kate with the children and the housework. Equipped with a more practical disposition than Kate, she was soon playing a significant role in both the children's upbringing and the domestic routine at Dalriada. Violet dubbed her 'Baaby', to Neil she was 'Dear', and both names stuck.

Harold and Kate were a contrasting couple. He was tall and thickset; she was petite and slender. His rushed, vigorous scrawl was hard to decipher; hers was neat and clear. He tended to bolt his food, keen to complete his meal and get on with whatever else he had to do; she would urge him to slow down. She was not overly decisive; he had more than enough decisiveness for both of them. Tidiness was a priority for her, but never an attribute of his; she maintained a spotless house, and spruced him up for the office and the parade ground. For Harold, home represented a haven from the pressures of a competitive outside world; for Kate, it was the very essence of her existence. His volatile temperament prevented him from reacting placidly to disappointment or controversy; she tried to keep smiling and stay cheerful at all times. When he exploded one Saturday at the football—his sense of protectiveness while watching George, a fearless player, was probably at the heart of it—Kate was embarrassed; afterwards he was sheepish and apologetic, she was forgiving.

Being a man of his time, Elliott regarded the domestic front as principally a female domain, and tended to defer to women on household matters. The dominating assertiveness familiar to the Essendon

Rifles was much less evident at Dalriada. When it did occasionally surface, Kate (and sometimes Belle) was capable of meeting fire with fire. Domestic discord, however, was happily rare. Those who knew Harold and Kate or saw them together had no doubt they were a devoted couple. Kate, like others, admired Harold's unswerving adherence to values then widely esteemed—honour and duty, hard work and manliness, thrift and temperance. Harold called her 'Kit', 'Katie' or (in a fond tribute to the sweet-natured graciousness he adored) 'my sunshine lady'. He was her 'Dida'.

Kate accepted the priority her husband gave to military pursuits. (If she had not, of course, the marriage could hardly have prospered.) She understood that if Australia became involved in armed conflict he would feel impelled to participate. It was an eventuality she dreaded; she knew her man too well. At an impersonal level she acknowledged, like most Australians, that it was appropriate for Australia to support Britain in the almighty struggle that was, according to knowledgeable people in disconcerting numbers, sooner or later likely to be generated by the combustible elements in Europe. But the threat war would pose to her family circle made her feel vulnerable. Kate tried, though, not to dwell on her private fears. She supported Harold heartily, empathising with him as well as she could in his triumphs and his troubles—as he did for her—and restricted herself to gentle rebukes for his propensity to resort to the milder 'b' profanities (bloody, bastard, and bugger) in his forceful exhortations to the men of the Essendon Rifles.

The other big part of Harold's life, his legal work, was also going well. The firm of Roberts and Elliott was progressing satisfactorily. Its office was now situated at 84 William Street, near Collins Street, in the recently completed Queensland Building. This was an impressive structure of Barrabool stone (like Ormond College) built to house the state headquarters of the Queensland Insurance Company. Harold was pleased with the way his relationship with his partner had developed; their respective families were very friendly as well. Although Glen and Katie Roberts lived with their three sons in the decidedly middle-class world of Burke Road, Camberwell, six miles away from the less well-to-do environs of Northcote, the Roberts and the Elliotts often socialised together. Katie Roberts had an attractive and insightful personality, and her eldest son, 20-year-old Eric, had a special admiration for Harold.

Elliott's legal work, military commitments, and parental

responsibilities left him limited leisure time for other activities. He liked chess, still enjoyed riding and shooting, and remained interested in football and athletics, but his chief recreation was reading. Military titles featured prominently, of course, but did not dominate: along with Kipling, his favourite writers included Jane Austen and Jeannie Gunn (author of *We of the Never Never*), and he also acquired texts on Indian and Greek mythology. Elliott was not musical, and not one for late nights. A non-smoking teetotaller, he was very partial to his cup of tea (especially the way Kate brewed it). He and Kate liked gardens, and relaxing in pleasant outdoor settings. One of her cousins, Ina Stewart, often accompanied them on enjoyable outings (by tram or train) to places like Studley Park, or further afield to Healesville or the Dandenongs.

In mid-1914 campaigning was underway for an election for both houses of Australia's federal parliament when war clouds gathered ominously in Europe. Harold Elliott had welcomed Labor's contribution to Australia's enhanced defence preparedness, but he was a most unlikely ALP voter. Essentially a middle-class conservative, he read the *Argus* and agreed with its advocacy of free trade rather than the protectionist views propagated by its rival, the more progressive *Age*. With sectarianism regrettably pronounced in Australia, he was, like many other Protestants of Anglo-Scottish descent, inclined to be suspiciously hostile to Roman Catholics, especially if they were fond of Ireland. He supported the White Australia Policy, and accepted the conventional notions of the day about the superiority of the Anglo-Saxon race. (At one particular drill session the Essendon Rifles failed to meet his exacting standards when practising a ceremonial march. 'Do it again', he roared, 'that wouldn't satisfy a bloody Chinaman!') Like many other men who manage to rise from disadvantaged origins to a more elevated station in life through self-discipline and hard work, he tended to believe others could do the same if they wanted to badly enough. This perspective, which inevitably aligned him politically with Labor's opponents, understated the significance of Londonderry. Without detracting from the determination and commitment underpinning his success, it was the Londonderry proceeds that had enabled him to escape from rural poverty.

The 1914 federal election resulted in a convincing victory for the Labor Party, which returned to office with Australia already at war. As part of the British Empire, Australia had become involved when Britain declared war on Germany after its invasion of Belgium. Britain was aligned with France and Russia in this cataclysmic conflict, while Austria–Hungary supported Germany.

Reactions to Australia's participation varied. Publicly expressed hostility was minimal. There was probably a good deal of muted wariness, but it was overshadowed by the ardent enthusiasm displayed by those Australians who expressed their support in vehement pronouncements or exuberant refrains of 'Rule Britannia'. Although many of the enthusiasts probably grasped that the forces involved would be immense, there was a widespread belief that the war would be decided relatively quickly. Few Australians were aware that recent advances in military technology, which significantly advantaged the defensive side in an engagement, would lengthen rather than shorten the conflict. Although certain discerning observers concluded that this trend had been exemplified in the Boer War, for Australian martial enthusiasts in 1914 a far more significant impression arising from their country's most recent participation in armed conflict was that casualties had been relatively light. Australian casualties in South Africa were too small to constitute a forbidding deterrent in 1914; in Harold Elliott's Victorian unit more bushmen died of disease than because of enemy bullets.

The rush to enlist reflected a conviction that the cause was worthwhile as well as the widespread expectation that the war would soon be over. Most Australians combined nationalistic allegiance to their own country with a fervent attachment to Britain. They felt affectionately sentimental about the land of their forebears and proud of the pre-eminence of the British Empire, which they regarded as the standard-bearer of civilisation around the world. At the same time they felt uncomfortably vulnerable about Australia's security; they looked apprehensively to Britain, its navy in particular, to protect them. In that context any genuine threat to British power was a serious danger to Australia, and it was infinitely preferable to deal with the ominous situation overseas rather than on Australian soil. Another possible influence on the early impetus to enlist was the notion that this conflict represented a superb opportunity for a newly federated nation to make its mark internationally as a worthy member of the British Empire.

Individual Australians held this dual loyalty to Britain as well as to their own nation in varying proportions. For example, the strong imperial orientation defining the work of Brudenell White, Australia's pre-eminent military administrator in 1914, was altogether absent from the nationalistic outlook of the architect of the pre-war universal training scheme, J.G. Legge. Harold Elliott's perspective was much closer to Legge's than to White's. As Elliott grew up he was encouraged to feel proud of the relatives on both sides of the family who had served with distinction in Britain's armed forces, but his own experiences in the Boer War had left him anything but starry-eyed about the British army. His disenchantment was reinforced when he read *Scapegoats of the Empire*, a book written by his friend George Witton, who still felt bitterly resentful about the treatment he and his comrades in the Bush Veldt Carbineers had received from British military authorities.

However, despite this measure of disillusionment with British soldiery, the dictates of duty and desire pointed in the same direction for Harold in August 1914, as Kate knew they would. After a century relatively free of major wars, a massive conflagration had erupted in Europe with most of the world's great powers involved and Australia an eager participant. Much of Elliott's life had been devoted to preparing himself so he would be able to contribute effectively if and when such a conflict arose. He had benefited from his extensive military experience, both in the ranks and as an officer, without becoming over-seasoned like some of the other militia commanders, who were soon exposed by the rigorous demands of combat as being too old or unfit.

Unlike them, Elliott had just turned 36 and was in robust health. Since his university years his girth had spread markedly, but despite this increased weight he was still the very embodiment of a vibrant man of action. If anything, his strapping physique made him an even more imposing figure in uniform. His attributes as a commander included a capable and adaptable intellect; considerable experience; absolute dedication; formidable willpower; self-confidence and decisiveness; proven courage under fire; administrative competence; strength of character; a certain charisma; and familiarity with Australians of diverse backgrounds—rural and urban, poor and comfortable, working-class and professional. The looming war was going to be the biggest challenge of his life. He was itching to embrace it.

CHAPTER FIVE

'He Knows How to Make Soldiers':

Preparing the 7th Battalion

AUGUST 1914-APRIL 1915

AN EXPEDITIONARY CONTINGENT was expeditiously organised. It was called the Australian Imperial Force (AIF). Its infantry division consisted of three brigades: one from New South Wales, the second from Victoria, and a third from the other four states. Command of the Victorian brigade was given to J.W. McCay. Talented and industrious, ambitious and irascible, McCay was not yet 50 but already had an impressive array of achievements to his credit as a teacher, solicitor, militiaman, and politician. This was in spite of his uncanny flair for alienating people unnecessarily.

On 14 August Harold Elliott was appointed to command the 7th AIF Battalion, one of the four battalions in McCay's 2nd Brigade. Elliott, by far the youngest of the sixteen original AIF battalion commanders, had already been considering which officers he would like to have in any battalion led by him. He had even drawn up a provisional list. After being notified by McCay of his appointment, he quickly contacted the men at the top of his list. Among them was Walter McNicoll, headmaster of Geelong High School. 'Look here Mac', said Elliott, 'I have been appointed to a battalion command—will you come as my second?' 'Certainly', replied McNicoll.

Other militia officers approached by Elliott acquiesced as readily as McNicoll, but he was disappointed by the unavailability of some that he wanted. The territorial composition of the 7th Battalion influenced his selections. His unit had specific recruiting zones; some were familiar to him from his militia years (Essendon/Moonee Ponds and Parkville/North Carlton), but most were not. Concluding that comradeship and morale within his battalion (and, as a result, its proficiency) would be enhanced by maintaining pre-war associations between its officers and men as far as possible, he decided to incorporate these links into the unit's internal structure right from the outset. Accordingly, the eight companies of the battalion were each given their own geographical affiliation. Volunteers coming forward from Brunswick and Coburg were to form A Company; enlisters from Parkville and North Carlton would belong to B Company; men from the Goulburn Valley and north-eastern Victoria would join C Company; from Essendon and Moonee Ponds, D Company; from Footscray, Spotswood and Bacchus Marsh, E Company; from Castlemaine, Kyneton and Daylesford districts, F Company; from Bendigo, G Company; and from Echuca, Swan Hill, the Murray Valley and north-western Victoria, H Company.

This arrangement ensured that his objective would be met as far as the rank and file were concerned, but what about the officers? Pursuing the territorial ideal would inevitably involve the appointment of officers he hardly knew, and he was acutely aware that the selection of appropriate officers was crucial to the ultimate effectiveness of his battalion. Elliott tackled this problem with characteristic decisiveness. He sent telegrams to the militia commanders of the areas militarily unfamiliar to him, asking each of them to forward a list ranking in order of merit the officers and NCOs volunteering in his region. Within 24 hours he had received some replies, had asked some officers from rural Victoria to come to Melbourne, and had started interviewing them. He became so engrossed in this process that he forgot a scheduled meeting with McCay, who was predictably irate (Elliott could hardly pretend he would have displayed equanimity himself if a subordinate had been too busy to remember an appointment with him).

Slightly more than half the officers selected by Elliott for the 7th were well known to him. He was especially pleased that four he particularly liked were eager to serve under him again—31-year-old Williamstown engineer Jimmy Johnston, architect Geoff McCrae and the widely esteemed Henderson brothers, 22-year-old Rupert and 20-year-old Alan. Lawyer Charles Mason had been a lieutenant in the same bushmen's unit as Elliott during the Boer War as well as a captain in the

Essendon Rifles; schoolteacher Charles Denehy had been a lieutenant in both the pre-war 60th and 58th Battalions. Also from the 58th came W.L. 'Birdie' Heron, Jack Scanlan, Earl Chapman, Bert Heighway and handsome, strapping Claude Swift — each young, keen, unmarried second lieutenants who were leaving clerical jobs behind them. Other officers chosen by Elliott after years of close militia association with him included 28-year-old Alf Jackson, Longwood farmer Fred Tubb and 29-year-old bank clerk Bert Layh. It was a tribute to Elliott's ability that all these men, who were most familiar with his capacity, personality, and methods, were very willing to serve under him in the perilous challenges of real conflict. The three members of the board of inquiry investigating the regrettable clash between Elliott and T.W. White — McNicoll, Layh, and Rupert Henderson — all accepted positions in the 7th.

The officers appointed to the 7th who had not served with Harold Elliott in a militia unit would at least have heard of him before August 1914. However slight their acquaintance beforehand, they soon knew him very well indeed. To lead E Company, the men from the western suburbs, Elliott chose Captain E.A. McKenna and two Footscray residents, 23-year-old chemist Les Blick and Irish-born Shannon Grills, an assistant factory manager. A 31-year-old school teacher, Bob Weddell, was placed in charge of F Company. Allotted to G Company were dentist Herbert Hunter, a renowned Bendigo identity who had been an outstanding athlete and footballer, and two other Bendigo men, 24-year-old clerk Stan de Ravin and 26-year-old lawyer Eric Connelly. That golden city was also represented in the 7th Battalion by Chris Finlayson, who became its adjutant. Elliott gave command of H Company to the town clerk of Echuca, Captain Ivie Blezard, who had enlisted (like Elliott) as a trooper in the Boer War; with Blezard in H Company were Lieutenants Charles Davey of Kerang and Denehy (then of Rutherglen).

While Elliott was busy choosing his officers, the hundreds of volunteers presenting themselves at enlistment centres around Victoria ensured that there would be no shortage of men for those officers to lead. To be eligible for the AIF these volunteers had to be between 19 and 38 years of age, in good health, at least five feet six inches tall, and able to achieve a minimum chest expansion of 34 inches. On 17 August Fred Tubb, a shortish extrovert who had already been notified by Elliott that he was to be the 7th Battalion's transport officer, addressed about two dozen young men from Euroa. 'Tubby' (as he was widely known, though in physique he was the opposite) told them he had been authorised to recruit local volunteers for the AIF, and he wanted to give them some advice before they committed themselves. The war would be no picnic, he assured them; some would be returning disabled, some would not be returning at all. 'It might sound awful', he added, 'but I feel I should warn you because you're all so young'. 'What about you?' one of them countered. Tubb was frank: 'I want the chance to win a Victoria Cross'. Besides, he added, 'I've never been to England' and 'I've got no ties, I'm not worried'. A few of Tubb's listeners were deterred by his sobering advice. The remainder accompanied him to the pre-embarkation training camp at Broadmeadows.

Colonel Elliott interviewed one of these Euroa lads, labourer Clarrie Wignell, and quickly sensed that the strongly built 16-year-old before him had lied about his age. The conversation, according to Wignell, went something like this:

> 'How old are you?'
> 'Nineteen.'
> 'When were you born?'
> 'I don't remember.'
> 'You don't know? Surely you know.'
> 'Well, when you're a newborn baby you don't know that.'
> 'Don't act like a newborn baby now, we don't want newborn babies in the bloody battalion. Why can't you tell me when you were born?'

At this point Wignell blurted out that his family was not well off, and he had been doing tough work from an early age; he was used to roughing it, he was handy with a rifle, and he could match anyone at swinging an axe or a pick and shovel.

> 'Attention! Height?'
> 'Six foot and half an inch'.
> 'Weight?'
> 'Thirteen stone.'
> 'It's not for me to say you're a liar, you're just as much a man as I am.'

So Clarrie Wignell was in, but his Euroa mate Billy Morgan's interview with Elliott ended differently. 'Sorry, son', concluded Elliott. Morgan, bitterly disappointed, protested immediately: 'you took my cobber and he's nearly a year younger than me'. 'Well, he's a better liar than you are', responded the colonel.

On 19 August Elliott's unit, having reached about half its nominal strength, joined the other three fledgling battalions of the 2nd Brigade for an arduous march from Victoria Barracks to Broadmeadows. They were in motley clothes, their marching was primitive, and many of them found twelve miles of 'dusty, foot-wearying trudge' a gruelling challenge, but they were buoyed by the ovation they received from thousands of enthusiastic onlookers along the way.

The Broadmeadows training camp on first acquaintance was 'a green plain rather high and wind-swept, with rows of pine trees and an old homestead'. A privately owned property of some 150 acres located about half a mile from the main road to Sydney, it had been offered by its owner to the Defence authorities, and was in the process of being rapidly transformed. The local shire had been trying unsuccessfully for years to obtain a decent water supply in the area; the army managed to have over four miles of pipe laid and water flowing within five days. A telephone connection was hastily installed, post and telegraph facilities were established, and even the nearest railway station a mile away was swiftly upgraded.

Elliott lost no time in getting down to the business of producing a different kind of transformation. His aim was to mould the hundreds of individualistic civilians under his charge into the makings of a cohesive fighting unit in a few short weeks. Addressing the 7th Battalion officers and NCOs shortly after their arrival at Broadmeadows, he declared that the raw material at their disposal was equal in quality to the essence of Cromwell's famous Ironsides, 'whose proud boast it was after fifteen years of service that during that period no enemy had ever seen their backs'. It was their task, he declared, to make the 7th as outstanding as the Ironsides. The notion that Australians were not amenable to military discipline was nonsense, he insisted. On the contrary, provided the reason for discipline was given and understood, they would submit to it eagerly. He assured them he would be imposing the strictest discipline, which would not only maximise the battalion's proficiency but also, he believed, make the 7th Battalion second to none as a unit within the whole AIF.

He was as good as his word. His men began a rigorous training routine. They were up early for pre-breakfast physical exercise, often a jog-trot to the station and back. This was followed by a combination of drill, marches, shooting practice, manoeuvres, and lectures for the rest of the day and sometimes during the evening as well. Through it all their commander was a dominating presence and the toughest of taskmasters. Exacting and explosive, he exhorted them and exhausted them as he demonstrated by his every action that he regarded the proper preparation of the 7th Battalion for combat as an undertaking of the utmost importance. The battalion began to take shape and assume an identity of its own. It was allotted the colours brown and red (soon to be referred to as 'mud and blood').

Adverse weather accentuated the arduousness of the training regime. During long route marches torrential downpours drenched the battalion. Poor drainage and heavy pedestrian traffic turned the rich clay soil into a quagmire. Saturday 19 September 'was a terrible day out here', Geoff McCrae told his mother; 'we were all soaked through and were ploughing through the rain and mud from nine in the morning until 4.30 in the afternoon'. With drying facilities inadequate, before long throat complaints were almost universal. Elliott himself had to go home to Dalriada for a weekend to recuperate. It was all too depressingly reminiscent of Langwarrin in 1900, but at least he could use his experience of that unhappy precedent to avoid making similar mistakes; he was certainly prepared to act decisively on issues affecting the welfare of his men. He firmly believed that his months as a private and corporal with the bushmen, when he had a real taste of what it was like to be at the bottom of the military hierarchy, were immensely valuable to him as a commander. 'One learns exactly what the men have to put up with, and can learn to do things and the need for doing things for their welfare as one can learn in no other way'.

Those who joined the 7th Battalion had varying motives for enlistment. Some felt strongly that Australia was obliged to aid Britain, a sentiment shaped by educational influences, by social conditioning and in many instances by family links as well. Others who were in tedious jobs or unemployed were motivated more by a sense of adventure and the once-in-a-lifetime prospect of travel overseas. A proportion felt the need to impress or escape from particular women. Many made a spontaneous decision to be in it with their mates. Most were probably influenced by the prevailing wisdom—which Harold Elliott evidently accepted—that the war would not last long.

They came to the battalion from different backgrounds. When the captain of Melbourne Grammar enlisted, classes were suspended in his honour; the whole school swarmed down St Kilda Road to Victoria Barracks, and cheered as Billy Kent Hughes arrived in the first group of volunteers. After being accepted into the 7th Battalion, he soon impressed Elliott. Promoted to sergeant in E Company, Kent Hughes found himself dealing with mettlesome livewires from the industrial strongholds of Footscray and Williamstown, a world away from the rarefied, affluent ambience of Melbourne Grammar. Enthusiasm for the cause was no less evident in the western suburbs, where the ranks of 'the Bulldog Company' were filled 'with great exuberance'. Kent Hughes handled the challenge of his new environment well. His company made him an honorary member of the Waterside Workers' Federation.

While the 7th Battalion had its share of tough characters and hard cases, they were complemented by young men of uncommon idealism. Having promised his mother that he would say his prayers each night, 16-year-old Clarrie Wignell did so only after lights out with a blanket over his head, but the intimidating presence of worldly larrikins and ruffians did not deter 19-year-old Wangaratta postman Albert Coates from kneeling down in front of them to say his prayers before turning in on his first night at Broadmeadows. Very familiar faces to Elliott were Sergeant Jack West, a noted footballer who had played with George Elliott in the University team, and Ken Walker, whose sister Lyn was George's girlfriend. Walker's closest mates, Bill Elliott (no relation) and unassuming, absent-minded Ellis 'Teena' Stones, were among the numerous stalwarts of St Thomas's Harriers Club in Moonee Ponds who joined the 7th Battalion. Another, Jim Bowtell-Harris, was to become one of the battalion's best-known personalities, but his initial encounter with his battalion commander at Broadmeadows was anything but auspicious:

> 'What is your name?'
>
> 'Bowtell-Harris, sir'.
>
> 'Hyphened name, eh? No hyphens in this battalion—your name is Harris.'

Morning roll-call on 25 August revealed that the 7th Battalion had reached (and in fact exceeded) its allotted numerical strength. It did so before any other battalion in the 2nd Brigade, largely because Elliott waived the stipulation that volunteers without militia experience had to be rejected. This instruction had caused difficulties and delays, which in his view hampered the 7th more than the other 2nd Brigade battalions as its recruiting areas were more widespread than theirs, and included regions where militia units had never existed. He therefore resolved to overlook it when evaluating volunteers who were suitable in all other respects.

When McCay found out about Elliott's recruitment policy, however, he took a dim view of it. The brigadier directed Elliott to discharge everyone without the requisite experience; Elliott spiritedly defended his approach. Eventually they compromised. McCay would suspend judgment for three more weeks; if he could then identify the men who lacked the necessary experience, Elliott promised to discharge them. Meanwhile, as the men continued with their demanding training schedule, Elliott reminded them that the battalion was over strength. This was a powerful incentive: to be sent home unwanted in the atmosphere then prevailing was tantamount to disgrace. At the end of the three weeks Elliott paraded his battalion, and they marched past the brigadier. Afterwards McCay confessed, to his astonishment and Elliott's delight, that he could not point to a single man whose lack of previous service was detectable. 'What's the use of our compulsory training scheme?' remarked the brigadier, amazed that after only a few weeks he could not distinguish between volunteers with little or no pre-war training and men who had been trained for years. Again Elliott had a different view. It was that very scheme, he replied, that had produced the trained officers and NCOs who turned the men of the 7th into potential soldiers so quickly.

Civilians flocked to Broadmeadows on the designated visitors' days. During the first Sunday that the camp was opened to the public some 20,000 visitors made the journey from Melbourne; the two extra trains made available became eleven, but even they could not cope with the demand. A week later there were 34 special trains and, according to some estimates, no fewer than 60,000 visitors. Among them was Sergeant Kent Hughes's mother:

> we started for camp at 9.30 in a taxi and lunched with Col. Elliott ... about 30 officers and 4 ladies, we had actually flowers on the table but the tablecloths looked khaki colour. I sat next the Col. and liked him very much. We all had Irish stew.

When Kate Elliott's recently married cousin Ina Prictor accompanied her to Broadmeadows one Sunday with Violet and Neil, the colonel was, as usual, absorbed and uninhibited with his children. They playfully scattered grass in his hair; he placed Neil's tiny feet inside his boots.

These weeks of pre-embarkation training were punctuated by numerous farewell functions. Every Melbourne suburb, each country district, and many diverse institutions wanted to honour their particular quota of AIF representatives. Footscray council gave their volunteers a special send-off, but it did not quite go according to plan. 'The lads cheered and booed through the pompous speeches like kids at a Saturday matinee, and then fell upon the eats and liquor, swept aside plans for a concert, and proceeded to chat up the girls.' Elliott was not at that function, but did attend a special dinner at Ormond College, where MacFarland and a senior resident student, Keith Doig, paid tributes to the AIF's Ormond men; Elliott, on their behalf, spoke briefly in reply.

He was also present at a memorable function for the 160 men from Essendon and district soon to depart. Nearly all of them were in the 7th Battalion; many had also belonged to the Essendon Rifles before the war. The Essendon Town Hall supper room 'was beautifully decorated with flags, bunting and other patriotic emblems, and the tables were nicely decked out with the most tempting of eatables'. Each soldier was given a scarf, handkerchief, and pipe and tobacco (or, if not a smoker, a pocket book). The festivities included a 'patriotic concert', and there were a 'good many encores' as the 'immense audience' expressed its appreciation. The mayor made a speech, referring to Colonel Elliott in glowing terms, and asked the pianist to play 'For He's a Jolly Good Fellow'. The audience joined in enthusiastically.

Moved by this stirring tribute, Elliott spoke feelingly in reply. He offered his sincere thanks on behalf of the men and himself for the 'magnificent reception and hospitality'. To have been chosen as a battalion commander was a great honour, he emphasised, and he hoped he would prove worthy of it. Interrupted at this point by a burst of applause, he proceeded to mention that parents of some of the '1023 boys' under his command had told him they were glad he was their commander; he hoped when they came back those parents would still think so. Having asked the mothers who had entrusted young sons to his care to remember him in their prayers while the AIF was away, he assured them he would do his best to be a father to those lads until they returned. Many parents who were terribly anxious about their departing sons derived some reassurance from his heartfelt remarks, which they often recalled during the worrying months ahead.

Victorian AIF formations marched through central Melbourne on 25 September. It was 'the greatest parade that had ever been seen' in the city, enthused the *Argus*. In marked contrast to the march to Broadmeadows five weeks earlier, the impressive cohesion and discipline of the AIF units confirmed their readiness to embark. However, departure was delayed owing to concern about marauding German warships. For yet another week repetitious training continued and rumours flourished. At last, on 16 October, official word came that the 7th would be embarking in two days' time. Next morning, which was Caulfield Cup day, roll-call disclosed a number of absentees without leave. After their return they were ordered to parade before Colonel Elliott. What he said to them was to be remembered with much merriment:

> Never before have I seen such an array of horse-lovers. My interest in the animal has always been limited to using it for carrying me over distances I would otherwise have to walk. I have never been attracted to horse races, and much less to the duties a stable entails. I am glad to have discovered your attachment at so opportune a time, as it solves any difficulty associated with the care of the horses we are taking over with us. You can all expect to be called upon to act as horse batmen for the duration of the voyage.

On 18 October, after reveille at 5.00am, the 7th Battalion marched to Broadmeadows station, travelled by train to Port Melbourne, and was aboard the troopship it was to share with the 6th Battalion, the *Hororata*, by midday. Information about troopship movements was carefully censored, but sufficient knowledge of the battalions' departure had spread to attract a sizeable crowd to bid them farewell. As the *Hororata* slipped away from the wharf on that sunny afternoon, with bands playing and onlookers cheering, there were surging and conflicting emotions on board. After their monotonous training and the uncertainty and strain of their long-postponed departure, it was a relief to the men to be actually going. 'One and all were heartily tired of Broadmeadows and the surrounding country', wrote Kent Hughes, 'since every hill for miles around had been attacked and defended' repeatedly. Mixed with this sense of relief was a heightened awareness that they were leaving loved ones and familiar surroundings that they might never see again. A temporary halt at Williamstown enabled final messages to be sent ashore by boat. Elliott, busy with a multitude of tasks, scrawled a hurried parting note to Kate:

> Goodbye now my darling. Give a big kiss to each of my darling bairns. Don't forget to write often and often even when you don't hear from me because I will be lonely for news of my loved ones.

A week later the *Hororata* reached the convoy rendezvous of King George Sound near Albany at the south-western corner of Australia. The voyage had been favoured by pleasant weather and generally smooth seas, but with two battalions on board conditions were decidedly cramped. Elliott pronounced himself satisfied with the top-deck cabin he was sharing with McNicoll, but McCrae described the accommodation allotted to other 7th officers as 'veritable dog-boxes'; meanwhile, the rank and file slept in hammocks, and 'resembled sardines in a tin'. Exercise was limited to half-hour bursts of physical drill, undertaken daily by each company in turn, and an occasional boxing or fencing contest. Seasickness and inoculations were grudgingly endured. Gambling was sufficiently rife for Elliott to take preventative action. A more acceptable feature of the voyage was music: the battalion bands played for two hours each day, and there were three pianos, an organ, and a number of gramophones which were frequently in use. At least congestion was eased somewhat at Albany, where Major-General W.T. Bridges, the AIF commander, inspected the *Hororata*; seeing for himself how crowded it was, he arranged for a 6th Battalion company to be transferred to another ship. When Elliott heard about a report sweeping Melbourne that the *Hororata* had been sunk with no survivors, he sent Kate a reassuring telegram: 'All well don't believe any rumours Elliott'.

'Very fine sight', Elliott noted in his diary when describing his first impressions of the assembled convoy. It certainly was. The *Hororata*, which left King George Sound on 1 November, was one of 28 troopships conveying the AIF in three parallel columns a mile apart, with half a mile separating each ship from the one behind it; the *Hororata* was the eighth ship in the starboard column. On its right flank was the Japanese cruiser *Ibuki*, one of four naval watchdogs protecting the convoy from German raiders. Also on guard duty were a British armoured cruiser and Australia's own modern cruisers *Melbourne* and *Sydney*. Behind the AIF transports another ten troopships carried the New Zealand contingent. The whole convoy was over seven miles long. The splendid spectacle of these columns of ships, proceeding evenly across the vastness of the ocean in perfect formation, provided a continuous reminder for everyone involved that they were engaged in a momentous enterprise. As the AIF's last glimpse of Australia, the Albany coastline, disappeared from view, sentimental reflections gathered momentum aboard the *Hororata*. Harold Elliott was not immune, as he told Kate:

> The first day out of Albany I was very lonely for you and my dear bairns, so I got out your photo and fixed it in my cabin. It is a great comfort to me ... Every day I think of you and of our dear little pets ... If you should never see your old man any more dearie you will at least be able to remember this, that during all our wedded life your old man was happier and more content than ever before in his life and he never found a single fault in you nor regretted for a single atom of a minute that he loved you and wedded you.

On the morning of 9 November, as the convoy was passing the Cocos Islands, it became evident that a German naval presence had been detected. Most suspected—correctly—that it was the *Emden*, a cruiser renowned for audacious exploits in the Indian Ocean and the main threat to the convoy. The *Sydney* left its protective post guarding the troopships and steamed away out of sight, while the *Ibuki* dramatically powered forward to place itself between the convoy and the enemy cruiser. '[We] noticed the Jap boat on our right flank start off at tremendous speed with columns of black smoke just pouring from her four funnels', observed Elliott. The usual drills and lectures continued on the troopships, but most of those involved were wondering what was taking place beyond the horizon. Shortly after eleven o'clock came a stirring message from the *Sydney*, 'Emden beached and done for', which was swiftly circulated among the transports. There was universal jubilation that this menacing threat had been removed, and immense satisfaction within the AIF that an Australian ship had been responsible for the demise of a notorious enemy raider.

Elliott was pleased with the way his officers were getting on together. They were, as Geoff McCrae observed, 'a very busy and happy family', who entertained themselves with diverting banter at meal-times and in numerous other ways when duties permitted. McCrae, for example, was passing on the rudiments of engineering to Lieutenant Tubb during spare moments, and learning chess from the capable second-in-command of the 6th Battalion, Elliott's friend Major Bennett. The officers' camaraderie was particularly evident during the various ceremonies commemorating the crossing of the equator.

On 17 November the *Hororata* left Colombo, which Elliott described as 'very picturesque', and reached Aden eight days later. With the weather now hot and sultry, 'the chief occupation', according to Kent Hughes, 'seems to be to sit and perspire'. 'I have never perspired so much in all my life', wrote McCrae, 'each morning when I awake the bed and pillow looks as if a bucket of water has been poured over it'. The quest for congenial diversions in these oppressive circumstances led to an approach to Colonel Elliott for a lecture to the men on his Boer War experiences. This address, delivered on 27 November as the convoy made its way along the Red Sea towards Suez, was characteristically forthright. Elliott's scathing criticism of some British units he had encountered in South Africa—one particular regiment, he recalled, was known as 'the Scarlet Runners'—was distasteful to at least one English-born member of the 7th Battalion.

A significant decision affecting the AIF was announced the following day. It had been intended to transport the Australian and New Zealand forces to England, where they were to undergo further training before being sent to the Western Front, but these arrangements had been altered. Instead, the men learned, they would be disembarking in Egypt. As this decision was digested, its implications were discussed and analysed. Aboard the *Hororata*, Elliott told Kate, there were

> all sorts of speculations as to what it meant. The general conclusion come to was that the weather would be too cold for our men in England just now and we were to put the finishing touches on our

> training in Egypt and we would be in a central position from which we could be employed anywhere. It will seem strange to be amongst scenes where Julius Caesar and Anthony and Cleopatra and Nelson and all the old people fought and died.

The consensus on board the *Hororata* had, in fact, assessed the situation correctly. A Canadian contingent, as eager as its Australasian equivalents to make a wholehearted contribution to the British cause, had been sadly disillusioned by its miserable experience of inclement weather and inadequate facilities at Salisbury Plain. Conditions became so appalling that its 'training' degenerated into a struggle to stay alive. It was obvious to Australian representatives in London that Salisbury Plain would be disastrous for the AIF coming straight from the tropics. They told British authorities that Egypt would be much more suitable, and their urgent representations were heeded. Furthermore, since the convoy's departure from Australian waters Turkey had entered the war as an ally of Germany. With Egypt under British control although nominally Turkish territory, the likelihood that Turkey would challenge Britain's presence in Egypt now a state of war existed between them made it prudent for British strategists to station the Australasian forces there.

During the voyage Elliott wrote to Kate regularly. At times he missed her terribly—'I was most awful lonely for my wee sweet wife on those days'—and longed to take her in his arms again, gaze into her 'dear bright eyes and sunshine face' and kiss her 'dear lips and cheek and chin'. At such moments he found it comforting to have a photo of her to look at; now and again he gave it a kiss. In his letters he interspersed matter-of-fact accounts of shipboard developments with outpourings of intense affection:

> Now Kit old girlie that's just about all the news so what about a bit of lovemaking. Dear old girl will you please cuddle up nice and close ... with your dear old loving arms about me and tell me how much you love me—'cause you do love me you know something scandalous. Your dear old sweet face is smiling down on me as I write and the wee sweet bairnies too. It will be just about Xmas or New Year when you get this and I do with all my heart wish you a very merry Xmas and a bright and happy New Year ... God bless you for all your sweetness and love to me. All my association with

> you has helped me to be a better and truer man and I hope I shall deserve to have had you for a wife and to have had the happiness of being your husband. My little sweetheart, you are a wonderful little woman and you don't know it the least little bit. There is no one that ever I met that has your sweet unselfishness and grace.

Colonel Elliott and his men had a memorable day when the *Hororata* passed through the famous Suez Canal. The canal itself was an impressive feat of construction, and the men were intrigued by the soldiers from different nations guarding it, by the varied vegetation beside it, and by the people from unfamiliar cultures toiling to make their living near it. On 6 December the 7th Battalion was transported by train from Alexandria, the port of disembarkation, to Cairo, and then by tram to within a mile of their destination, Mena camp. 'Very interesting journey', remarked Elliott, delighted when McCay 'specially complimented' him on the battalion's discipline. 'Everything points to a considerable stay here', he concluded after arriving at Mena, situated about ten miles from Cairo near the famous pyramids and the Sphinx. His men spent their first night on the desert sand in awesome proximity to these extraordinary structures, so powerfully evocative of ancient civilisations and mysteries.

Elliott was eager to explore the AIF's new surroundings. On the day after his arrival he walked to the pyramids and climbed the biggest. He also inspected the Sphinx, various temples, and the work of an archaeological team from Harvard University. The following day he accompanied Bert Layh to Cairo, 'a wonderful city'; they saw 'magnificent dress-stuffs and jewellery', and palatial residences like 'Toorak mansions'. On 11 December, when the 7th Battalion's training recommenced in earnest with a short march into the desert, Elliott was fascinated when he came across rich limestone formations from an ancient sea bed.

But his appreciation of these discoveries was outweighed by his abhorrence of local characteristics and customs. He was appalled by the cavalier approach to personal hygiene displayed by the Egyptians he encountered. They were 'filthy in the extreme', they lived in 'hovels' with 'donkeys and camels and fowls', they had no qualms about urinating 'up against the walls everywhere', and you had to 'hold your nose for the stench'. Even a special experience like inspecting the pyramids was 'marred by the filthiness of the Arabs and the consequent stenches'.

Elliott was also scathing about what he saw as the Egyptians' dishonesty and rapacity. Tourists had been swindled in Cairo for decades, and from the time Australian soldiers arrived in Egypt they were persistently harassed by petty criminals and unscrupulous scoundrels. Egyptians in general quickly acquired a notorious reputation within the AIF for untrustworthiness. 'Take them all in all they are about the biggest thieves and cheats unhung', Elliott pronounced within a week of his arrival. Also, though no prude, he was disgusted by the brazenness of prostitution in Cairo. 'People's hair would stand on end in Melbourne', he assured Kate:

> Can you imagine women sunk so low as to allow dogs and it is said donkeys to connect with them for exhibition. Yet if you go in certain quarters of this city great bloated black hags run after you and ask you to see Donkey and girl etc and leer at you. Can you imagine the police of any civilised place permitting such things. A black fellow followed me half a mile the other night wanting to take me to women. I told him I had no use for them. Then he said you like to see small boy with de girl. I believe this is one of the common exhibitions at the *better* class places. I refused. He then became confidential. You not afraid Captain English soldier see you—I tek you nice quiet place—nobody see you—nice French girl. I had to wallop him with my stick to get rid of him.

Not all Egyptians were scoundrels and pesterers who flagrantly fleeced travellers, but Harold Elliott's perceptions were typical of the AIF generally. The pre-war focus on racial difference in Australia—the widely accepted White Australia Policy had been extensively debated in parliament and enshrined in legislation—accentuated the tendency of Australians to regard other races as inferior. In view of their own cultural heritage and the conduct of the Egyptians they encountered, it was not surprising that Elliott and his men reacted as they did. A small proportion, however, found the fleshpots of Cairo enticing, especially with recreational alternatives initially minimal. It was weeks before the 7th Battalion boxing stadium was constructed and Mena had its own cinema theatres. The stadium was erected by a 7th corporal, a builder in civilian life, and managed with entrepreneurial flair by Lieutenant Wally Conder. Launched as a 'Stupendous Scene of Stoush' with the enterprising Conder as chief spruiker and referee, its regular bouts provided popular entertainment and welcome revenue for battalion funds.

Elliott became indignant when hovering Egyptians trying to sell fruit or other merchandise disrupted a parade or exercise. He told them to go away; they ignored him or pretended not to understand, so he resorted to more persuasive measures. On 18 December he took the battalion out on a long march. His men ploughed steadily through the sand for four gruelling miles, with a trail of vendors struggling along behind in the dust, huge baskets on their heads, wondering when the battalion would stop so they could at last transact some business. When Elliott did eventually call a halt he arranged for one of his men who could speak Arabic to let them know that if they were not out of sight in half an hour all their goods would be confiscated. They left reluctantly. On other occasions when coercion was required he would suddenly activate his big black horse and, standing in the stirrups, would theatrically draw his sword, roar at the hawkers and gallop towards them—a display of intimidation that scattered the disrupters and amused his men. Before long it was noticeable that vendors left Elliott and his battalion alone, though they kept pestering other units. This contrast did not escape McCay, who, while repeatedly complimenting the 7th's discipline, reprimanded the 8th Battalion commander for allowing his men to buy fruit while the brigadier was addressing them.

McCay selected the 7th to represent the brigade at the ceremonial proclamation of Egypt as a British protectorate (a procedural measure to rectify Britain's uncertain legal status in Egypt), which occurred in Cairo on 20 December. Elliott regarded this as pleasing recognition for his battalion. He told his men it was an honour, but left them in no doubt he would have preferred some real action. The 7th left Mena before sunrise, and set off for Cairo—covering half the distance 'in pitch darkness'—to take up its allotted position lining a street. It was, concluded the colonel, 'a very creditable performance'.

Ten days later the 1st and 2nd Brigades assembled in a corner of Mena Camp within sight of the pyramids for a formal review by Australia's High Commissioner in London, Sir George Reid. His stirring speech impressed Elliott and many others who heard it:

> I have seen some fine things in my time from Australia, but you are the limit ... The youngest of these august Pyramids was built 2,000

> years before the birth of Christ. They have been the silent witnesses of many strange events. Can they ever have looked down upon a more unique spectacle than this splendid array of Australian soldiers massed in their defence?

The march past afterwards was 'a grand sight', according to Tubb, who felt the 7th, with Colonel Elliott at the forefront 'looking splendid', marched 'the best of the whole crowd'.

These formal occasions injected some variety into the battalion's gruelling training routine. At least after Broadmeadows they were more hardened to it, but ploughing through ankle-deep sand and a cloud of dust under a scorching sun for mile after mile encumbered by heavy equipment was tough toil. Sometimes they stayed out in the desert on overnight exercises when all they had to keep the bitter chill at bay was what they carried on their backs. 'Training was hard', recorded a 7th private:

> We would leave early in the morning out all day chasing bayonets over the sand return almost to camp in the evening. But not quite. [We] would take up an outpost position, dig trenches, take turns at standing to all night and off again into the Desert next day for a hard day's gruelling and finish up with a 400 or 500 yards charge yelling like Dervishes.

'There is little or no news to tell you', Elliott informed Kate, 'we go out and dig trenches in the blessed old desert and walk around in it and come home and go out and do it some more next day'. He encouraged his soldiers to sing while marching. 'What about that song "Marching, marching"?' he would call, trying to enliven a flagging company, and tired men would wearily respond:

> Marching, marching, marching,
> Always bloody well marching,
> When we're dead and in our graves
> We will bloody well march no more.

The close mates who were 'the three musketeers' from Essendon—Ken Walker, Teena Stones, and Bill Elliott—were doing it hard along with the rest of the 7th. Writing to Teena's mother, Bill claimed no other battalion was being trained as strenuously as theirs: 'Pompey has been working us like the very deuce every night and only giving us enough time for sleep of a day then out for more work'.

As that letter indicates, Colonel Elliott had acquired a nickname. During pre-war days in militia circles he had sometimes answered to 'Bob', but his new sobriquet, derived from the champion Carlton footballer Fred 'Pompey' Elliott, proved more enduring. He did not initially like it, especially when local newspaper-sellers were bribed to approach his tent early in the morning and chant 'Egyptian Times, very good news—death of Pompey the bastard'. But he gradually grew accustomed to the nickname, well aware that once it had become common parlance within his battalion—let alone beyond it—he had no choice in the matter.

His reputation as a leader was growing. A 25-year-old labourer in the 7th eulogised him in a letter home:

> My colonel is the whitest man I know. I would follow him anywhere even to certain death. He is my ideal soldier, the best loved man in the battalion. God bless him.

His men grumbled now and again about his rigorous methods, but it was obvious to them that his aim was to mould the 7th into a first-rate combat unit. He 'may be hard', wrote one, 'but he knows how to make soldiers'. (In some AIF formations there was resistance to the notion that superiors had to be ritualistically saluted, but Elliott claimed this was not a problem in units commanded by him because his men understood that saluting was simply a means to an end: without the habit of instinctive obedience they could not expect to become part of an effective fighting force, which was precisely why they had volunteered in the first place.) From their viewpoint the fact that he had won the DCM as a corporal was important; it signified that he had not only experienced real combat, but had also distinguished himself in it with conspicuous bravery. He clearly knew his stuff, and treated his responsibilities with the utmost seriousness. Whether or not his soldiers survived would partly depend on their superiors' capacity, and they were glad their colonel was someone they could trust to make competent decisions under pressure. Moreover, he was absolutely straight, and incapable of deviousness: you knew where you stood with Pompey. They also appreciated the way he took a personal interest in them as individuals, even though he had over a thousand men under his command. 'One of my boys a very fine young fellow Pte Lubke died the other day … from pneumonia', Elliott told Kate in a letter from Egypt, 'he was such a good fellow and as strong as a giant'.

Also instrumental in Elliott's growing reputation was his personality. Numerous commanders tried to be exacting disciplinarians during the Great War, and ended up being despised as callous, sadistic martinets. But there was nothing austere or aloof about Pompey. He was a larger-than-life character, full of exuberance and vitality, with idiosyncrasies that appealed to his men and boosted their anecdotal repertoire. In physique and demeanour he was the epitome of a fighting leader. His face often gave the impression that he was ready to wage war at a moment's notice, and he had a notorious habit of roaring indiscriminately at privates or company commanders if he felt they were performing inadequately. To be the target of one of his withering tirades was an unpleasant ordeal for even the hardiest souls. 'Some of the men appear to be terrified to death when they come before me' for misconduct, he confided; occasionally he could see their 'knees fairly knocking together with fright'.

If someone else was the victim, however, it could be amusing to be an onlooker. Shortly after the 7th Battalion's arrival at Mena he took his men to the pyramids for a short walk and gave them an hour's sightseeing. But when the time came to form up again there were two men from F Company missing (they were still exploring the inside of a pyramid). 'Captain Weddell', bellowed Elliott in front of the whole battalion, 'is there no discipline in your company?' On another occasion, when some 20 men from C Company absented themselves from parade to visit Cairo, the colonel was furious: 'Captain McKenna', he roared, 'where the bloody hell are all your men?' And signallers on battalion exercises in the desert came to dread their colonel's stentorian call from afar to 'get off that bloody line'.

Part of Pompey Elliott's distinctiveness was the mystique he created around his big black charger, Darkie. During inspections Darkie consistently seemed to demonstrate an astounding ability to detect even infinitesimal irregularities. He would draw the colonel's attention to unshavenness, unsteadiness or improper attire by stopping, throwing back his ears, and stretching out his neck. In fact it was Pompey, an accomplished horseman, who was directing his well-trained steed by subtly nudging Darkie's neck. He would then pretend that Darkie had spotted the irregularity. Many 7th men became convinced that the horse had extraordinary powers.

The most famous Pompey anecdote, and one of the most celebrated AIF episodes of the entire war, was the 'hat story'. Elliott's nationalistic outlook shaped his preference for the felt hat rather than a cap or British-style pith-helmet, which were then in use partly because felt hats were in short supply. At battalion parade one Wednesday morning he noticed that a particular private was resplendent in a newly acquired helmet, and galloped across to him. 'My God, you look like a field-marshal', he bellowed. 'Get rid of it'. He turned to survey the assembled companies, raised himself in the stirrups, and announced that he could see too many helmets; every man in the 7th, he ordered, had to be wearing a felt hat at parade the following morning. 'I don't care where you get them, but you must all have one', he declared, adding that those without would find themselves cleaning sanitary pans.

There are multiple versions of what happened next. According to an authoritative account from an eye-witness, Colonel Elliott concluded the parade, rode to his tent, handed his horse to his groom, and strode to the adjacent marquee housing the officers' mess to have lunch. At the end of the meal he put his right hand down under his chair to collect his hat.

> We all became aware of some violent reaction in Pompey; his hand moved in a vacuum—the hat was not where he believed he had put it. Jumping to the conclusion that this may have some connection with his last words to the battalion, he thought that some member of the mess was playing a joke upon him. Promptly he darted his hand under Major McNicoll's chair, but the [major] got there first, and, pulling his hat out, satisfied Pompey that that was not the hat he was looking for. Then Pompey thrust his hand under Padre Hearn's chair, but with the same result.

He loudly summoned his batman, Tom Stafford, who was directed to search his tent for the missing hat. Stafford reappeared and informed him that it was definitely not in the tent.

> Pompey's habitually ruddy complexion turned now to a blazing red. All members of the mess were ordered to stand at their places, and, having thus immobilised them, Pompey went from chair to chair inspecting each hat in turn. But Pompey's own hat was not among them. Pompey's next move was to order the Adjutant to fall-in the entire battalion in tent groups, each group in front of its tent. Every tent was to be searched and every hat examined … Pompey directed the search himself, wearing a cap.

An occupant of the first tent to be searched could not resist such a tempting opportunity. 'What is that 7th Battalion man doing on parade without a felt hat?' he demanded, imitating a sergeant-major's bark. Elliott wheeled around angrily. 'Who said that, Mr Heighway?' he snapped to the nearest officer. 'I'm sorry, sir, I've no idea', replied Heighway (who conceded afterwards he did indeed have a pretty good idea). 'Unless you quickly find out and parade him', retorted Pompey, 'you can regard yourself as under open arrest'. Heighway was not too concerned. Placing his officers under arrest from time to time was just one of Pompey's renowned idiosyncrasies; indeed it was an occupational hazard for any officer commanded by him.

Pompey whirled away furiously to resume his extensive search, but did not find the hat. Realising he would be breaching his own order if he failed to obtain a felt hat in time for parade next morning, he hurried into Cairo hoping to acquire one. To his relief he did manage to get hold of a possible replacement, although it was too small and the khaki dye applied to it reacted with sunlight to produce an odd pink hue. By obtaining it he felt he had foiled the hat-snatchers, but there was considerable suppressed mirth in the ranks when he appeared at parade wearing this peculiar ill-fitting substitute and struggled valiantly to retain his dignity.

What happened to the missing hat remains a mystery. Since the back of Pompey's seat at mess was near the edge of the marquee, it was certainly possible for someone outside to filch the hat by reaching in underneath his seat. Various identities were suspected. A 7th man on guard nearby admitted years later that he knew who took it, but refused to name the perpetrator. Some speculation apparently implicated Major Blezard, who had already told Elliott his order was unreasonable because there were simply not enough felt hats available; Blezard, a kind-hearted, popular officer, sometimes intervened when he felt his colonel's exuberance needed to be curbed. However, while amused by this episode, he repeatedly denied any personal involvement, and he was inside the marquee at the time anyway. The most likely culprit was Private Bill 'Sandy' Marshall.

Why did Pompey's exhaustive search fail to locate it? Careful burial in the desert sand was one suggested explanation; others claimed that it was quickly passed on to someone in the 6th Battalion. About a month later Kate Elliott in Melbourne received a hat purporting to be the missing one through the post; once again various identities were suspected of involvement in this exploit without anything conclusive being established. Partly because of these uncertainties, the story of Pompey's hat became embellished by rumour and hearsay. Numerous versions flourished. It became a famous piece of AIF folklore, a development not unrelated to the parallel emergence of Pompey as one of the most legendary characters in the whole force.

In due course Pompey came to appreciate the funny side of the hat story, but the incident that amused him most during the AIF's period in Egypt occurred when the 7th was marching from Cairo to Mena. The battalion happened to pass a group of hawkers and their tethered donkeys just as one of those animals, a male, was showing conspicuous interest in a nearby female of the species. The passing soldiers reacted to this spectacle with ribald laughter, which annoyed the owner of the amorously inclined donkey. He darted over to it and gave one of its ears a savage twist, whereupon the donkey's desire deflated quickly. Shortly afterwards the battalion's leading company, headed by its captain marching along in fine style with the senior sergeant just behind him, encountered a horse-drawn carriage containing two attractive women. One of them bowed and smiled to the captain, who gave an enthusiastic salute in return. Instantly a voice from the ranks was heard: 'Twist his ear, sergeant'. Pompey enjoyed telling that story for the rest of his life.

Lord Kitchener, Britain's Secretary of State for War, decided to combine the AIF and the New Zealand soldiers based in Egypt into a corps, to be called the Australian and New Zealand Army Corps (ANZAC). He appointed one of his personal favourites, General W.R. Birdwood, as its commander. Short, slight, and ambitious, Birdwood had acute limitations in tactics and organisation. He was more intent on mixing with men under his command, whether in or out of danger. This characteristic was to win him considerable popularity, even though his contrived affability was ridiculed as 'Birdie's bull'. Elliott's first impression of him was favourable enough: the 'little chap' was 'very pleasant spoken indeed, quite genial and nice in fact', he noted.

But shortly afterwards an incident during a tactical exercise led to a tense exchange between them. The 7th Battalion was ordered to take a particular hill, a manoeuvre observed by Birdwood and his senior staff officers including Brigadiers-General H.B. Walker and R.A. Carruthers. Elliott issued his orders in writing to his company commanders, who were about to move off when Carruthers intervened, asserting that an alternative method should be adopted. After the exercise was completed as Carruthers had directed, Walker, unaware of his intervention, told Elliott that the operation had been conducted unsatisfactorily and explained how it should have been performed. Elliott, predictably annoyed, produced his original orders, which showed that he had wanted to do it exactly as Walker had just outlined. 'I then turned to General Birdwood', Elliott later recalled, 'and said "Sir, how can I tell what to do if one of your staff takes my battalion out of my hands, makes mistakes with it and then leaves me to be blamed in consequence?"' Birdwood hesitated, according to Elliott, before replying that Carruthers should not have taken over the battalion, but the best solution to a tactical problem was a matter of opinion and Carruthers had for years led one of the best battalions in India. At the time Elliott felt that Birdwood 'didn't seem annoyed' by his forthright protest, but he later revised that assessment.

Early in February 1915 the Turks made their predicted attack against British forces guarding the Suez Canal. Elliott received an urgent summons late at night:

> I was just in the middle of a sound sleep when I was called by the Adjutant to say that the Brigadier wanted me so I hustled off down with Major McNicoll in my pyjamas and an overcoat. We got there all right and were told we were to march at 10.30 a.m. tomorrow morning to Cairo and there entrain for Ismailia on the Suez Canal where we will arrive about 10 p.m. Nothing but fighting kit is to be taken and as we hear that the Turks are advancing on the Canal it may mean fighting.

Only two AIF battalions were being dispatched; to be chosen as one of them was another gratifying honour for the 7th and its commander. When Elliott and his men arrived at Ismailia, they were told that they 'would be called into the firing line at daylight for sure as the Turks were coming on'. This promised to be the real thing at last.

Elliott ordered everyone to be ready for action at a moment's notice. This meant going to sleep with all clothes on, even boots. Up early next morning, even more animated and purposeful than usual, Pompey first visited the latrines, which consisted of holes in the sand. Unaware of his presence, the drowsy man alongside kept missing the target. 'Damn it, man', objected the colonel, 'what do you think these holes are for—to piss into or piss out of?' Pompey then went looking for the designated duty officer, who that day was Denehy, and found him sound asleep. Having abruptly ended his slumbers with a characteristic roar, Elliott saw the embarrassed lieutenant struggle into the trousers he was supposed to have slept in. 'By God Denehy', boomed Pompey, 'it'll be back to Australia for you, and without your bloody pants too'. He then caught sight of someone else who had not fully complied with his overnight directive. This unfortunate sergeant never forgot what followed:

> I got picked up for not having my boots on. Doubtless, the whole Battalion had theirs off too, but they were able to get them on while I held the undivided attention of the C.O. for a few minutes. You can understand what that meant. We all knew Pomp, and on that occasion his 'bark' was positively ferocious.

Having whipped himself and his men into a fever pitch of anticipation, Elliott was frustrated when it proved to be all in vain. On their first morning at Ismailia they received reports from British aircraft that the Turks in their vicinity had fallen back some ten miles. Skirmishes continued elsewhere along the canal, but the AIF battalions were not engaged. There were several false alarms for the 7th: at one stage half a company was set to occupy front-line trenches that the Turks were rumoured to be approaching, but then word came that the enemy was 30 miles away and retreating rapidly. Elliott's men had eight days of suspense; the men heard guns firing and saw distant shellfire through telescopes, but they did not fire a single shot themselves, and the closest they came to the Turks was having to escort some prisoners. It was all a great anti-climax. With the enemy firmly repulsed from the canal by other soldiers, Elliott and his battalion returned to Mena on 12 February.

Later that month the AIF's conduct in Egypt became a highly controversial issue when distorted versions of a dispatch sent to Australia by the official AIF correspondent, Charles Bean, began circulating within the force. Tall, wiry, and bespectacled, Bean was humble and humane, principled and nationalistic. A journalist from Sydney, he was unknown to Elliott and many others who formed an unfavourable initial impression of him as a result of this episode. The dispatch in question, written at the request of General Bridges, was designed to prepare Australians for the distasteful reality that a number of undesirables were being returned home because of their escapades in Cairo. Bean's sober assessment repeatedly stressed that only a tiny proportion of the AIF was involved in this misbehaviour, but this crucial point was obscured in the edited extracts that were cynically sensationalised.

Any suggestion that the AIF was harming Australia's reputation was repugnant to many of its members. Geoff McCrae was incensed: 'I would like to get my hands on that reporter' who has secured 'for us the abuse rather than the gratitude of our country', he fumed. Major John Gellibrand, a Tasmanian orchardist of considerable intelligence, insight, and humour who had been appointed to Bridges's staff by virtue of his training and experience in the British army, observed that there was 'no denying that we left Australia with a lot of men that were useless to God and man and that we are in the process of getting rid of them'. It was also true, Gellibrand felt, that the Australians were remarkably willing to risk venereal disease in Cairo: 'they don't care what it is as regards looks, colour, age, health, they are "afflamés pour les femmes" and in they go and later in to hospital'. However, he wished his friend Bean had not written the contentious article.

Elliott agreed. For some time his frustration with the misbehaviour of several 7ths had been eroding his pride in the battalion. 'It is just scandalous', he told Kate,

> the way a few men are going on getting us a very bad name with everybody. They get on the drink and go with women and get disease and cheat the nigger cabdrivers ... I am out of all patience with them. They go down to Cairo and stay there piggishly drunk

> for two or three days and we have to send men for them and they fight them and knock them about shamefully.

Accordingly, 'I am sending back to Australia this week three or four wasters I am sick and tired of punishing and who are no manner of use to us at all'. Nevertheless, 'with the exception of a few bad eggs', he wrote, 'the men have in the face of tremendous temptations placed before them behaved wonderfully well'.

> It was only a very very few out of the total number who played up and by writing home as [Bean] did a great many people will believe everyone was playing up here ... Some of the men were very angry and wanted to catch Mr Bean and tar and feather him. It was a great pity it was ever sent.

A particular grievance arising from Bean's dispatch prompted Elliott to involve himself directly in the controversy. Bean's article singled out men wearing the ribbon denoting service in South Africa as disproportionately prominent among AIF wrongdoers. Bitter protest meetings of aggrieved Boer War veterans ensued in Egypt and Melbourne. They had been 'grossly libelled and were naturally very angry about it', explained Elliott, who was prominent at the Mena gathering and an office-bearer in the South African Soldiers' Association (Victoria). 'I soothed them as best I could and told them I was taking steps to get redress'.

Elliott submitted an official request to McCay asking for a detailed statistical analysis to be made, in order to establish whether Bean's 'charges ... against soldiers with South African service' could be sustained. Referring this request to Bridges, McCay stated he could 'see no objection ... to exact data being obtained', but Gellibrand, who had served in the Boer War himself (although in the British army), advised Bridges to reject it. Statistics could not be conclusive, Gellibrand contended, because some men wore the South African ribbon without entitlement; besides, to collect the data—presumably for publication—would not be conducive to proper discipline. In due course McCay received an official reply from Gellibrand that the question of defending the character of soldiers in the Australian division was a matter for Bridges alone, and the 'suggestion that official steps should be taken to collect information for unofficial publication is not approved'. Bridges, having asked Bean to write the article in the first place, clearly wanted to nip the disaffection it had produced firmly in the bud. Former Boer War soldiers at Mena were organising a gathering which Bean had agreed to address, but it was cancelled after Bridges intervened. 'The General', Bean wrote, 'was absolutely opposed to the meeting'. Another of the measures Bridges took was to rebuke Elliott for his involvement. According to Elliott,

> I was summoned to attend before General Bridges with General McCay. The former soundly reprimanded me. I insisted, however, on standing my ground, and said that as we felt aggrieved we ought to have the matter investigated. In the end General Bridges came to see my point of view, and he promised to see if he could do what I asked. Nothing however so far as I ever heard was done for us.

Concerned his battalion's image had been tarnished by the reaction to Bean's dispatch, Elliott did what he could in private letters home to repair the damage. 'Katie you have no idea of this city', he emphasised, assuring her in three successive letters how proud he was of his soldiers.

> The men I have under me are, taking them all round, the finest lot of fellows you could raise anywhere in the world. I work them very hard indeed. Marching and drilling or digging trenches in the heat and dust which rises round you like a choking fog. You must stand up for my boys Katie.

Elliott also wrote to J.F. Henderson, the former mayor of Essendon:

> In point of fact, the behaviour of the Division here ... was, in my opinion, exemplary. Capt. Bean stated the cases of misconduct were confined to about one or two per cent. Judging from my own Battalion ... this is exaggerated, as I find, on working it out, that the percentage of cases of gross misconduct is under ½ per cent.

After outlining the extenuating circumstances in detail—'the vilest concoctions are sold to the troops as genuine liquor'—and providing an account of the battalion's trip to Ismailia, Elliott reaffirmed that the overall 'behaviour of the men ... has been exemplary and their work in the field has received the highest praise from the Brigadier'. He added some particular reassurance for Essendon people. Apart from a hospitalised corporal,

> all the Essendon boys are in splendid health and with hardly an exception have gained weight, and their parents and friends would be delighted with their robust appearance.

This letter was published in the *Essendon Gazette* on 29 April. By then many Essendon lads were far from robust.

On the last day of February the men of the 3rd AIF Brigade left Mena for Alexandria, where they were to embark for a secret destination. Elliott was informed that his battalion and the rest of the 2nd Brigade would soon follow. As at Broadmeadows, however, they had to endure a frustrating delay. They had to be ready to depart at short notice and were keen to go, but had to put up with more of the training grind as the weather deteriorated. As well as more heat and more flies, the approach of summer brought fierce sandstorms, reducing visibility and morale while plastering everyone and everything with grimy grit. 'To-day is as hot as Hell with a gale blowing in from the desert', McCrae told his sister; 'the air is as thick as peasoup with dust, everything is covered with it'. Within a fortnight he was finding the conditions even more trying:

> The training this week has been most strenuous more so than at any other time and such weather to carry it out, heat and blinding sand storms. My eyes were all silted up and my mouth so parched that I often lost the power of speech. I had to suck pebbles to make my tongue pliable.

Like other AIF units toiling in the desert since December, the 7th Battalion became infected with discernible staleness. 'We are all heartily sick of the sand and dust of this place', wrote Elliott, 'and the men are losing interest in their training'. Two days later they endured a dreadful sandstorm, their worst yet.

The remaining AIF units at Mena paraded on 29 March for an inspection by the newly appointed commander of the Mediterranean Expeditionary Force, Sir Ian Hamilton. He singled out the 7th Battalion for special praise. 'You have a very fine regiment', he told Elliott. 'I congratulate you'. For Elliott, who had not been feeling well, hearing his men complimented by a distinguished general for being 'wonderfully steady' was the best possible tonic: 'The Colonel was tremendously pleased', a 7th signaller noticed. Five days later, at last, came the order to move that Pompey and his men had been yearning to receive. They were delighted. 'Well we are on our wanderings once more', Elliott notified Kate. 'We have seen the last of Mena Camp, thank heaven for that, and before dawn we will have seen the last of Cairo, and three times thank heaven for that'. They would hardly have felt so buoyant if they had known what destiny had in store for them.

CHAPTER SIX

'Hardly Any Left of the Poor Old 7th Battalion': Initiation at Gallipoli

APRIL-MAY 1915

WHEN ELLIOTT AND his men received orders to leave Egypt they were not notified of their ultimate destination. They had still learned nothing definite about the whereabouts of the 3rd Brigade, which had left over a month earlier. The rumour mill, however, was in full swing. No-one in the 7th Battalion was surprised when confirmation came that it was to join the 3rd Brigade at the island of Lemnos prior to participating in a forced landing at the Dardanelles.

It would do so under reshuffled leaders. The internal structure of AIF battalions had been overhauled to conform to the system adopted in the British army. The eight companies of Elliott's battalion were transformed into four 'double companies' comprising four platoons each. Elliott preserved the territorial basis of the battalion by combining what were formerly A and B Companies in the new A Company, the previous C and D Companies in the new B Company, and so on. Further changes became necessary when McNicoll was transferred, having been chosen to replace the ailing commander of the 6th Battalion. Elliott chose Blezard to succeed McNicoll as the 7th's second-in-command. The company commanders became Mason, Rupert Henderson, Jackson, and McCrae. Elliott had a profound regard for McCrae, who had a charming, amiable, and upright personality; his only shortcoming as an officer, in his colonel's opinion, was his reluctance to engage in the vigorous chastising that came so naturally to Pompey.

In fact Elliott was very satisfied with the officers he had selected eight months earlier: 'All the officers have turned out very well indeed', he wrote. 'I would not change any of them in spite of the fact that I still rough them up occasionally'. At one stage his misgivings about Birdie Heron led to a stern reprimand for excessive drinking shortly after their arrival in Egypt, but Heron's conduct was no longer causing concern. And Elliott's threat to send Denehy home when momentarily displeased with him at Ismailia did not reflect the colonel's real appreciation of a capable, conscientious, and considerate officer. Elliott was delighted with the continued development of officers who had served under him in the militia, notably Johnston, Layh, and the Henderson brothers. He was also impressed with those less familiar to him before the war. Blick, the shortish lieutenant from Footscray, had been 'splendid'. So had Blezard. And they had all mixed in well—McKenna, for example, had become McCrae's closest friend. Elliott felt they were 'all such good pals that the loss of one will create a terrible blank for those that are left'.

This melancholy observation was triggered by Elliott's perception of the task the AIF had been given. His battalion would be participating in an enterprise fraught with difficulty—a forced landing from the sea at a fortified coastline manned by enemy soldiers who would be defending their homeland and expecting an imminent attack. British and French forces were to undertake concurrent landings elsewhere on the Gallipoli Peninsula. The objective was to overcome Turkish resistance on the peninsula, allowing the fleet unimpeded passage through the Dardanelles to Constantinople, with the ultimate aim of knocking Turkey out of the war. The invading forces would be assisted by British and French ships, which had attempted unsuccessfully to silence the forts guarding the Dardanelles, initially by sporadic bombardment and then by a full-scale onslaught on 18 March. These purely naval assaults only alerted the enemy; the likelihood of another attempt by a combined naval and military force gave the Turks—and the Germans providing them with crucial guidance—time to prepare. There was now little scope for surprise, an asset of vital importance in any attack and especially crucial in a forced landing of this kind. Before the 7th Battalion even left Egypt, one of Pompey Elliott's men, having a haircut in Cairo, was assured by his barber that the AIF would be going to the Dardanelles and would never succeed there.

The AIF was ill-served by the complacency and incompetent

planning of the British strategists who conceived the Gallipoli venture. It is true that they were constrained by their obligations to the principal theatre of conflict, the Western Front. The clashes there between massive armies had produced not the short war that had been widely predicted but a stalemate, as both sides dug themselves into trenches snaking across France and Belgium. Attempts to break the deadlock had resulted in appalling casualties for the attackers. But even allowing for their inability to devote maximum resources to the Dardanelles, Winston Churchill, Kitchener, and their War Cabinet colleagues were culpably inept in their deliberations about Gallipoli. Their judgment was faulty, their reasoning unsound and at times contradictory, and they arrogantly underestimated the Turks' fighting capacity. Less than a decade earlier an official appraisal of a notional British offensive at the Dardanelles had concluded that any such attack was doomed to fail; but this sober report was ignored as the Gallipoli concept generated a momentum all its own.

To make matters worse, the complex operation was prepared with extraordinary haste. After the gamble was authorised and General Hamilton was appointed to command it, he had to find his staff from officers not engaged at the Western Front, and he had to be on his way to the Dardanelles within 24 hours. He and his hastily assembled staff then had to formulate detailed plans for the assault and overcome a multitude of daunting tactical, logistical, and administrative problems, all in a few weeks. Inevitably, the organisation was inadequate. One English columnist wrote that Hamilton would have often made more extensive preparations for a recreational shooting trip than he was able to make for the Dardanelles. When Britain and its allies launched a comparable landing against the Germans during the Second World War they took over a year to plan it.

The AIF's pre-eminent organiser, Brudenell White, was startled by his superiors' overconfidence and complacency. General Walker, Birdwood's chief staff officer, was so appalled by the proposed landing that he wanted to make a strong protest—apparently to the Australian government directly—in order to have the whole operation cancelled. However, Birdwood and Bridges felt differently, and their optimism prevailed. Elliott certainly had no illusions. 'There is no disguising the fact that the enterprise contemplated may turn out to be exceedingly dangerous', he admitted on 22 April.

Elliott and other battalion commanders, dressed like sailors, had scrutinised possible landing sites during reconnaissance cruises aboard British battleships. On their initial inspection they were conveyed by the *Queen Elizabeth*, then the most powerful ship afloat. In a brief address General Hamilton informed the assembled commanders that they were about to attempt a feat that had not been accomplished since William the Conqueror invaded England in 1066; if they succeeded, their achievement would be even greater than Wolfe's victory at Quebec in 1759. 'It was a wonderfully interesting trip', enthused Elliott. 'During the observation we were shelled by the enemy', but fortunately the 'closest shot was a full 400 yards away'. Intelligence reports based on aerial reconnaissance revealed that the enemy was busily fortifying the peninsula. Developments at the Western Front had confirmed that determined defenders able to utilise artillery, barbed wire, and machine-guns could make things very difficult for an attacking force. Clearly, Elliott and his battalion had an awesome challenge ahead of them.

Like many of his men, Elliott found his thoughts turning to home and loved ones with growing intensity. 'I want to come back and see you and my darling bairnies oh so much', he assured Kate, yet his commitment to his command responsibilities was unwavering; besides, 'I would love to do something great in the war'. How were these aspirations to be reconciled?

> I want you to pray good and hard for me that on the day of trial I may shut out of my mind all thought of you and of my sweet ones and remember only my country and my duty. It will be hard for you to ask this my loved one but it is only by such sacrifices that our country can survive, and it would be better that you lose me and we win the war than that we should lose the war and you keep me. It is very very hard my love even to contemplate the thought of never seeing you again yet we both must pray that when the time comes I shall have no thought of self.

Elliott's characteristic openness was consolidated by the no-secrets pact he and Kate had agreed to maintain in their wartime communications. Kate sometimes felt that her correspondence lacked content, but Harold treasured every snippet: 'I read your letters over and over again for fear I miss a word of them'. News from home was precious, and it was wonderful 'when you are far away to think that someone loves you

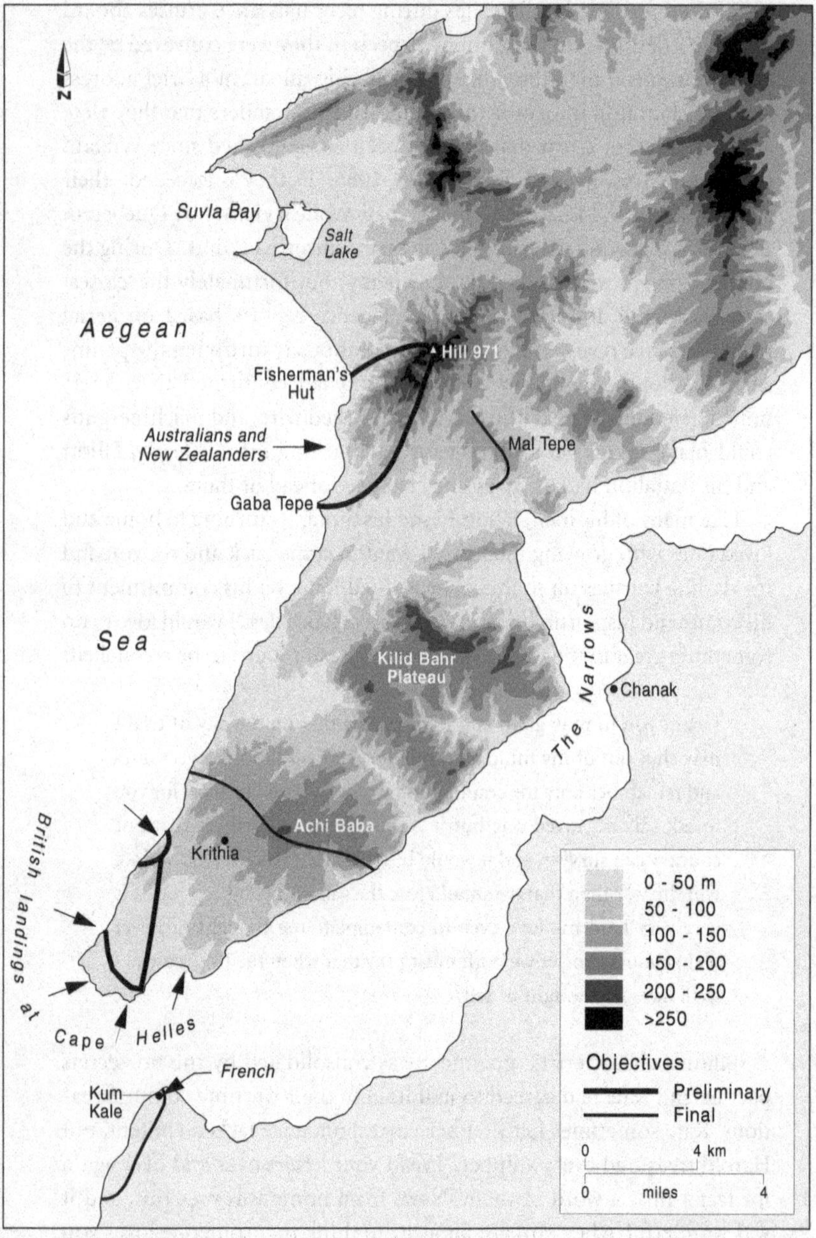

Gallipoli landings, 25 April 1915

so truly and well and is watching and waiting for news of you'.

However, with the Gallipoli venture about to be launched, unsettling news from home rocked him. A bombshell from Belle informed him that Kate was in hospital recovering from an operation; Belle had taken three months' leave from work to look after the children during Kate's recuperation. Understandably perturbed, he wrote home anxiously, wondering what the operation was for (apparently some problem affecting her teeth), but soon had to put it out of his mind. The landing, having been postponed for two days because of bad weather, was to take place at dawn on Sunday 25 April. Elliott left Lemnos on Saturday morning aboard the *Galeka*. With him was his battalion (less Mason's A Company, which was travelling on the *Clan Macgillivray*) and the 6th Battalion under McNicoll.

Sleep was elusive on that last night before their appointment with destiny. The stakes, as well as the perils, everyone sensed, were substantial; exhilaration vied with nervousness as the dominant emotion. There was one universal preoccupation: how would they acquit themselves in the great test that was rapidly approaching? For most, it was the experience of being under fire for the first time, and how they would react to it, that was monopolising their thoughts. At least Elliott knew what it was like to be a target for real ammunition, but he was well aware that leading an infantry battalion into action in an operation of this magnitude and complexity—there had been no bigger amphibious assault in the entire history of warfare—would be a challenge. His misgivings about the enterprise only strengthened his resolve to do everything in his power to make his battalion's contribution as successful as possible.

Surveying his men with a fatherly eye as they quietly prepared themselves, he felt proudly confident they would do well. However, like many others, he could not help wondering about casualties, and whether he would become one himself. Elliott's friend Major Bennett was similarly reflective as he mingled with the 6th Battalion on the *Galeka*:

> Moving among them, one could see a look of determination in every man's face. They were very silent. Many were the prayers offered that night. All were anxious as to how they would behave under fire on the morrow ... They knew that the reputation of Australia was in their hands ... They knew of the great difficulty of their task and they knew that the operation was extremely

> hazardous. They knew, too, that casualties would be heavy. It was a solemn voyage.

Most of them were thinking of home; some were imagining their family's reaction if the next day proved their last. Many Australian soldiers wrote to loved ones that night. A 7th Battalion officer, Alan Henderson, penned a letter to his parents:

> At last we make our final move and very soon we will have started to do what we came away for and have waited so long to do. While you are in church tomorrow thinking of us, we may be needing all your prayers ... but everything is ready and everyone quietly confident of success. It is going to be Australia's chance and she makes a tradition out of this that she must always look back on. God grant it will be a great one. The importance of this alone seems stupendous to Australia while the effect of success on the war itself will be even greater.

The landing was to be undertaken initially by the 3rd AIF Brigade, with the 2nd Brigade to follow. These units were to be later reinforced by the 1st and 4th AIF Brigades and a brigade of New Zealand infantry. The landing was to take place near a prominent promontory called Gaba Tepe, which jutted into the sea on the western side of the Gallipoli Peninsula. Gaba Tepe itself was strongly guarded by barbed wire and machine-guns, and an artillery battery was known to be located nearby, but there was no wire at the chosen landing site a mile to the north. The landing force was supposed to take control of the ridge rising from Gaba Tepe to the commanding height over four miles away known as Hill 971 (almost 1,000 feet above sea level), together with the extensive area of precipitous slopes and ravines situated between this ridge and the coast. The terrain was so extraordinarily rugged that it would have been a tall order in peacetime, but the attackers also had to contend with a tenacious enemy already alerted by the naval assaults to expect an imminent invasion; the Turks did not know, however, where the landing(s) would be attempted.

The task allotted to the battalions of the 2nd AIF Brigade was to establish themselves on the left of the 3rd Brigade, extending the area seized in a northerly direction and capturing the vital high ground at and around Hill 971. Elliott's 7th Battalion was to be responsible for the left flank. If everything went according to plan, this would extend from the approach to 971 back to the beach near a point known as Fisherman's Hut, over two miles away (the capture and retention of 971 itself was the 5th Battalion's assignment). The 2nd Brigade was to be conveyed from its transports to shore in a number of 'tows', which consisted of a small steam pinnace towing three connected rowing-boats containing between 40 and 50 soldiers each. When the battalions of the 2nd Brigade landed, they would be guided to a particular rendezvous by staff officers, who would choose the most suitable location in the prevailing circumstances.

In the early hours of 25 April 1915 the *Galeka* quietly made its way towards Gallipoli in total darkness. The moon set shortly before three o'clock, leaving only the stars to dilute ever so faintly the enveloping blackness. The three companies of Elliott's battalion (who were to depart from the *Galeka* first, followed by the men of the 6th) had already had a hot breakfast of stew and tea. They were lined up on deck, their equipment checked, ready to disembark. Sharp stabs of apprehension surged from tightly knotted stomachs. Visibility was minimal, but all eyes were fixed on the distant, just-discernible coastline. They could not see the tows ferrying the first wave of the landing force, but knew their 3rd Brigade comrades were silently approaching the beach. The strain was immense as they waited and waited, wondering when the landing force would be detected and how vigorously it would be opposed—factors which would, of course, crucially influence their own fortunes when their turn came.

At last, just before 4.30am, the yellow flare of a beacon suddenly penetrated the darkness, and the crackling sound of shooting—initially sporadic, then continuous—became clearly audible. For another quarter of an hour, as the night sky began to pale with the approach of dawn, the *Galeka* steamed towards the coast, reaching its designated position punctually at 4.45. But there was no sign of the tows supposed to be meeting the *Galeka* to convey its men to the shore. The captain of the *Galeka* reacted boldly, moving his ship 600 yards closer to the beach, but the tows that should have arrived after depositing their quota of the 3rd Brigade ashore still failed to appear.

An artillery battery at Gaba Tepe now took aim at the *Galeka*. Menacing projectiles roared towards Elliott and his men with a fearsome screech, burst with a sudden thunderclap and dispersed their lethal shrapnel ominously close. This salvo, a novel experience for nearly everyone aboard, prompted plenty of deep breaths and surreptitious wiping of clammy hands on thighs.

Colonel Elliott joined other senior officers at a hastily convened conference. The naval commander, who had ultimate responsibility for the ship and the men, said the shelling was too dangerous to wait any longer for the tows, and the men would have to row themselves ashore immediately in the *Galeka*'s own lifeboats. Elliott objected. He was well aware that even the most carefully made plans often come unstuck in the chaotic turmoil of battle; he knew that in such situations the ability to react resourcefully and devise feasible alternatives was one of the attributes of a competent commander. But this change to his battalion's role could have disastrous consequences. The disembarkation arrangements would be thrown into disarray because they had been based on the carrying capacity of the rowing-boats in the tows, and the *Galeka*'s lifeboats were much smaller. Furthermore, few of the men were used to rowing. They would be more vulnerable on their way to the beach without the protective machine-guns mounted in each of the steam pinnaces. And, crucially, it was the naval personnel in the pinnaces who were to guide them to the appropriate place on the beach. Because of inadequate precision in the planning of the operation, and excessively restricted circulation of vital information about it, all Elliott knew about his battalion's intended landing position was that it was towards the left of wherever the 3rd Brigade had managed to get ashore. Nevertheless, having made these objections, Elliott deferred to the naval commander. 'You are in charge', he acknowledged. 'If you give me a direct order I will obey it'. The naval commander reiterated that the *Galeka* was in real danger of being sunk by enemy shelling and the soldiers would have to disembark immediately.

Elliott ordered B Company to get into the lifeboats. Although the advent of dawn was gradually increasing visibility, it was still not clear precisely where the first wave had landed. He was acutely conscious that his instructions, through no fault of his own, were inadequate: 'All the direction I could give them as to the landing place was to keep to the left of the 3rd Brigade'. Into the first boat clambered B Company's commander, Major Jackson, and about 35 men. Three more boatloads soon followed. These four boats headed off close together, containing most of the initial D Company men from Essendon. Observing them intently, Elliott noticed Captain Layh perched awkwardly. 'Keep your bum down Bertie', he called out. The remainder of B Company accompanied Lieutenant Swift into the fifth boat. Elliott decided it was now time for him to go, and he climbed into the sixth boat with Lieutenant Grills and the first portion of C Company.

Being towed in by steam pinnace, as arranged in the operation plan, would have required the men to row only the last fraction of the distance from ship to shore after being released from the pinnace. Rowing all the way in, under fire, was a very different proposition: although the *Galeka*'s captain had brought his ship closer to the shore than any other transport, the beach was still some 1,200 yards away. But everyone was keyed up, and the oars were wielded to good effect. When the fifth and sixth *Galeka* boats were 400 yards from the beach, a pinnace materialised at last and towed them the rest of the way.

The closer they came to the shore, the louder the noise of gunfire grew. A shot from a Turkish rifle resembled the sharp crack of a cricket ball hit powerfully by a bat; machine-gun fire 'was an altogether more intense sound, like pneumatic riveters on a boiler plate'. Intermittently obliterating all other noise was the crescendo of shellfire. Shrapnel shells were rocketing from Gaba Tepe towards the defenceless boats with an unnerving shriek—like the roar of several trains hurtling through a tunnel together at top speed—before exploding with a loud bang and scattering their deadly contents, which spattered into the water or thudded into Australian flesh. British warships retaliated with a thunderous bombardment of powerful high-explosive shells. Although no-one in Elliott's boat was caught by shrapnel, the near-misses led to quickened pulses and churned stomachs. Elliott did what he could to steady the men with him, and puzzled about the irreconcilable difference between the looming cliffs in front of them and the less forbidding coastline they were supposed to be approaching.

As they neared the shore the men became anxious to get out of the boats as soon as possible. There was a discernible bank on the far side of the narrow beach; after feeling vulnerable and unable to retaliate for what seemed like ages, they were keen to get themselves ashore and utilise whatever cover the beach afforded. They were weighed down by waterlogged clothing and equipment, slippery stones gave them an awkward underwater footing, and some were disconcerted by the dead bodies and blood-red tinge in the water; but they were all desperate to escape the menacing fire aimed at them. (In other boats some were too eager: underestimating the water depth and encumbered by their heavy equipment, they drowned.) A few minutes' strenuous wading brought them ashore, and Elliott, Grills, and Swift shepherded their group towards some temporary cover. Elliott told them to wait there while he ascertained where they were to go next. It was now almost 5.30am.

Ahead of them was supposed to be an open plain which they were to cross before climbing a low hill. Instead they found themselves confronted by utterly different country—rugged ridges and ravines covered by obstructive, waist-high undergrowth. From the little stony cove where they had landed, the most prominent feature was an exceedingly steep hill some 300 feet high rising directly above them. Elliott realised that the AIF had been put ashore at the wrong place. (The traditional explanation of an unexpectedly strong current has been increasingly discredited. It is more probable that the mistake occurred simply because—as Elliott concluded at the time—naval personnel could not distinguish the coast clearly enough in the darkness.)

The orders for the landing had specified that after reaching the beach the battalions of the 2nd Brigade would be guided forward by one of two designated staff officers. Elliott went looking for them. He was told that neither had landed. McCay had not yet arrived either; Elliott was in fact the first senior officer of the 2nd Brigade ashore. He then asked for the whereabouts of the 3rd Brigade's Scottish-born commander, Colonel E.G. Sinclair-Maclagan, an experienced and capable leader. Told that Sinclair-Maclagan had established his headquarters near the top of the precipitous hill towering over the landing site, Elliott hurried away in that direction.

As his powerful frame scrambled up the incline, retracing the footsteps of the 3rd Brigade first wave who had charged straight up in the dark, he experienced the same difficulties with the terrain as they had. Besides having to contend with the slope itself—steep enough to be challenging for anyone—he found that the tangled, prickly scrub was sometimes too dense to penetrate and forced frequent changes of direction. The rough, gravelly soil made it hard to keep a foothold. Whenever he lost his balance and clutched around for support, a wrong choice could have painful consequences—barbed bushes ripped through clothing and scarred the skin underneath. Plenty of bullets were flying about, but at least the trench at the top of the hill was no longer occupied by the Turks who had been shooting down from there when the AIF began climbing up towards them.

During Elliott's ascent the wounded Australians passing him on their way back to the beach indicated the fierceness of the fighting up ahead, and the piteous cries he heard from dying soldiers were heart-rending. But the little that could be done for those poor souls was a task for others, and he had steeled himself not to allow such distractions to affect his main task—ensuring the correct decisions and actions were taken to enable the 7th Battalion to play its part as effectively as possible. Moreover, at this early stage any avoidable delays in sending AIF units where they were most needed could affect the outcome of the battle. So he pressed on determinedly until he found Sinclair-Maclagan. By the time he did, after a quarter of an hour's arduous climbing, his cheeks were red and he was puffing hard.

His conversation with the brigadier was brief. Sinclair-Maclagan, as the most senior commander ashore, was endeavouring to retain control of an operation that had gone so astray he had already decided, on his own initiative, to amend it drastically. He had in fact been pessimistic about it all along. During a reconnaissance cruise on 14 April he had observed that if the coast was 'strongly held with guns' it would be 'almost impregnable', and before leaving Lemnos he told General Bridges that 'if we find the Turks holding these ridges in any strength I honestly don't think you'll ever see the 3rd Brigade again'. Now, to Elliott, he quickly confirmed that the AIF had been put ashore about a mile north of the intended landing place; because of this, he added, the original plan could not be implemented. Having concluded that the most appropriate course in these circumstances would be for the 2nd Brigade to come in on the right of the 3rd Brigade rather than on its left as planned, he ordered Elliott to collect his men on the right of the AIF's position. Elliott returned to the beach as quickly as he could. Both the operation plan and Elliott's preparatory visualisation about how his role might unfold had been based upon the assumption that his battalion would have responsibility for the extreme left; yet within minutes of his arrival ashore he had been directed to place it on the far right.

Arriving back at the beach, he relocated the fifth and sixth *Galeka* boatloads under Swift and Grills. He panted up to them, told them to proceed to the southern end of the cove in accordance with

Sinclair-Maclagan's instructions, and began looking for other 7th platoons to send there also. Before long he had collected D Company and part of C Company, but was unable to find the rest of C Company, his machine-gun section or any of Jackson's B Company who had filled the first four *Galeka* boatloads. He discovered that A Company had landed from the *Clan Macgillivray* and been directed to a relatively protected forming-up area about 400 yards inland. Elliott then sent all the 7th men he had assembled on the beach to this spot, which became known as the Rendezvous. From there some of them were immediately ordered forward to the fighting taking place on the 400 Plateau, a prominent feature adjoining and overlooking the Rendezvous.

Elliott was busy reorganising the 7th men at the Rendezvous when McCay arrived. The brigadier told him that because the 5th Battalion had been delayed the 7th would have to take over its task of capturing the all-important Hill 971 almost three miles away. Elliott concluded that Sinclair-Maclagan's switch of the 7th to the south had been a temporary manoeuvre to shore up the right flank until other units became available, and its ultimate role was still on the left as originally planned. He accordingly ordered all 7th platoons left at the Rendezvous to follow the portion of his battalion that had already gone forward to the 400 Plateau, with a view to beginning an advance in a north-easterly direction towards 971. Still puzzled and increasingly concerned about the whereabouts of B Company, half of C Company and his machine-gun section, he positioned himself at the entry to the Rendezvous, where detachments of the 2nd Brigade were continually arriving, and acted as a general directing post while looking anxiously for the missing 7th cohorts. After a while he lifted his gaze to the slope leading up to the plateau where he had sent his battalion, and saw the last company disappearing from view; on the crest, supervising this movement, he recognised the stalwart figure of Captain Hunter. Elliott decided it was time to join them.

He was about to hasten forward when McCay reappeared. Following his brief conversation with Elliott, McCay had chanced upon Sinclair-Maclagan, who told McCay he wanted the whole of the 2nd Brigade inserted on the right of his brigade instead of on its left. McCay was understandably taken aback to discover that the operation, especially his brigade's part in it, had been so radically altered. Sinclair-Maclagan assured him it was essential, and there was no time to lose; McCay acquiesced grudgingly. It was in order to notify Elliott of this fundamental switch that McCay caught up with him at the Rendezvous. The brigadier said he now wanted the 7th to be inserted into a gap in the AIF front line between two 3rd Brigade battalions on the 400 Plateau. Adjusting quickly to this unexpected change, Elliott sent the necessary messages to his company commanders on the plateau. He subsequently received a message from one of them, Rupert Henderson: 'Have been ordered to advance 300 yards beyond the position you have assigned to me'. (McCay had given this order to Henderson, Elliott noted afterwards, 'without reference to me'.) Although Henderson sent further messages back to him, Elliott was having trouble maintaining contact with his other companies on the plateau; his second-in-command, Blezard, had been severely wounded in the chest, picked off by a sniper after waving his men into position.

Sensing that the situation up ahead was fluid and precarious, Elliott felt even more torn between his desire to be with the men he had sent forward and his growing concern about the others he had been unable to find. He still hoped to find traces of them as 2nd Brigade detachments kept arriving at the Rendezvous, and he was reluctant to leave his directing post; but when he received word from Henderson that a large force of Turks was advancing, he decided that he ought to climb up to the plateau and ascertain what was happening there. As before, he took no notice of the enemy projectiles flying around, until a sharp jolt to his right ankle followed by acute discomfort confirmed that this was one bullet he would be unable to ignore. It quickly became clear that he was significantly disabled and unable to carry on.

He felt annoyance and frustration more than anything. To be knocked out of the fighting at a critical time when his men needed his guidance (and without having seen a single Turk) was intensely galling; more excruciating, in fact, than the pain in his foot. He refused to be evacuated immediately. Not until he had arranged for ammunition to be brought forward and for messages confirming his disablement to be sent to McCay and Mason (who, with Blezard wounded and Jackson missing, was now in command of the battalion) did he reluctantly agree to be carried away on a stretcher. After his wound was patched up he was helped down to the beach. He had to lie there for hours.

The haste, complacency, and contempt for Turkish military prowess that had infected preparations for the landing were particularly evident in the arrangements made to care for the wounded. According to a senior AIF medical officer, Colonel Neville Howse VC, the extent of the neglect 'amounted to criminal negligence'. Some of his colleagues accused the responsible British authorities of 'murder'. For an operation of this scale the provision of medical facilities was scandalously deficient. There was only one hospital ship, the *Gascon*; there were nowhere near enough doctors and other medical staff; their supplies, from bandages and dressings to stretchers and surgical instruments, were woefully inadequate; and, when predictable problems ensued, attempts to rectify the shambles were hampered by culpably defective communication links with the top-level medical administrators.

There were inordinate delays. Despite desperate efforts by overwhelmed doctors and orderlies, thousands of wounded soldiers endured monstrously prolonged suffering. Small boats carrying dozens of stricken men—who were wet, hungry, and seasick as well as injured—approached the *Galeka* and several other transports which had been urgently utilised to take the wounded away from Gallipoli (though they had little or no medical staff or facilities on board), only to learn that each had no room for more. Some men with grievous wounds received no proper treatment for days. Many preventable deaths occurred and numerous avoidable amputations eventually had to be performed. Alan Henderson, the 20-year-old 7th Battalion lieutenant who wrote such a stirring letter on the eve of the landing, died at sea after being placed aboard one of these transports.

Morning became afternoon, and still Harold Elliott lay waiting on the stony beach as the battle raged above and around him. His foot was throbbing and he was uncomfortable in his wet clothes, which had been saturated when he waded ashore and further moistened by the sweat generated by his purposeful exertions during the battle. But he could tell he was in better shape than many others around him. His long wait on the exposed beach ended at last when he was carried aboard the *Gascon*, which departed for Lemnos at 9.00pm. From there he was transported to Alexandria, arriving on the morning of 29 April. The following day he was admitted to the Australian hospital near Cairo at the Heliopolis Palace Hotel.

Recovery was slow. The wound itself did not heal quickly. It took weeks longer for his foot to regain enough strength for him to get about. He also suffered a severe bout of bronchitis. Triggered, he was convinced, by the hours he had to wait lying in damp clothing after being shot, his illness threatened to develop into pneumonia, and for a while caused the hospital staff acute concern: it 'really troubled me more than the wound, I think'.

While regaining his strength he had plenty of time for reflection. In pre-war days he had advised would-be officers that if you do everything possible as a commander yet your unit sustains severe casualties, then 'your conscience at least will be easy, however heavy your heart'. As Elliott reviewed the landing, his heart was heavy indeed, but his conscience was clear. Many a commander could have been bewildered or rattled by the varied instructions Elliott received, but he had responded readily and decisively. His bravery and selflessness set a fine example to his men, increasing their regard for him. Clarrie Wignell, one of the Euroa lads recruited by Lieutenant Tubb, sent a letter home about the landing:

> The poor old Colonel got shot in the leg and had to leave, and when they attempted to carry him to the boat he said, 'No, there are plenty worse than I to go first'. The men love him.

Not all the AIF commanders distinguished themselves. Shortly after General Bridges landed with Brudenell White around 7.30am on 25 April, they were puzzled to find a 3rd Brigade colonel still on the beach with his head pressed into the bank. When they saw his terrified face they understood. Bridges later found McCay similarly unhinged by the stress and turmoil of the battle. According to White, McCay

> was completely lost and his grip on things seemed gone. He could not orient himself. Bridges came along with his yard and a half stride and wanted to know what the hell he was doing ... As Bridges grew more and more angry I saw McCay's face change. He began to get a grip on himself and before long he was in complete control.

Courage and capacity in battle can fluctuate. Some soldiers manage to be consistently outstanding, but the performance of others can differ significantly from one engagement to the next or—as with McCay at the landing—can even vary considerably during a battle.

Both Bridges, one rung above McCay in the military hierarchy, and Elliott, one rung below, had similar views about McCay: his intellect commanded respect, but his pedantic argumentativeness could be annoying. At the landing, at a stage when Elliott was closer to the action than McCay, he had suggested that it was time to consider an order to dig in; the brigadier responded that he was running the fight, not Elliott. McCay's abrasive manner made him unpopular with the rank and file, as did his tendency to assume the worst of them in battle. Soldiers who were keen and brave but not sure exactly where to go—because their platoon commander and senior NCO had been killed, or for other plausible reasons—took understandable umbrage when McCay swore at them, accused them of cowardliness and threatened them with his revolver. Elliott was unenthusiastic about McCay's performance at the landing:

> Brigadier McCay, although he deservedly gained considerable fame as a brave man, was far from being an ideal commander. He had little faith in anyone's ability save his own and constantly interfered with the arrangements properly belonging to his Battalion commanders ... which completely deprived them of any initiative and any responsibility.

Elliott's misgivings before the landing were vindicated by what occurred on 25 April. Because the terrain was so 'rugged, broken and trackless', he concluded afterwards, the area to be seized by the landing force was 'far too extensive'. He was appalled by the level of casualties his battalion seemed to have sustained, but felt 'very proud' of his 'magnificent' men who had done 'wonderfully well'. Elliott was keen to hear the experiences of every member of the 7th he encountered during the ensuing weeks. He had talked with some while waiting on the beach; he also had 80 wounded 7ths with him on the *Gascon*, while others from his battalion were admitted to hospital at Heliopolis. He was soon able to piece together a reasonably accurate picture of what had happened.

The 7th was not the only AIF battalion to lose its cohesion after landing at such an unexpected place and then complying with emphatic instructions to push forward rapidly. It was not surprising that companies, platoons, and smaller groups became detached and intermingled with other units. Both the missing half of C Company and the machine-gun section, Elliott learned, had climbed the steep hill overlooking the beach (as he did when looking for Sinclair-Maclagan) and involved themselves in the desperate fighting beyond. The officers leading those C Company men (who included McKenna and Conder) were severely wounded; the machine-gunners suffered such heavy casualties that 21-year-old Lance-Corporal Harold Barker found himself in charge (and rose to the occasion superbly). Elliott also heard disturbing reports of casualties in the fighting on 400 Plateau, which he had been about to scrutinise when he was wounded.

What he discovered about the missing men of B Company moved him profoundly. Whereas the fifth and sixth boats (the latter containing Elliott) had been collected by a pinnace and guided to the shore, the first four boatloads had rowed themselves all the way from the *Galeka* to the beach without any assistance. All they knew about where they were supposed to be going was that they had to aim to the left of wherever the 3rd Brigade had landed. They accordingly headed towards the northern-most flashes of fire they could discern ashore in the emerging dawn. Shrapnel was bursting over other boats away to the south, but their main concern was the volume of rifle and machine-gun fire aimed at them from the shore; they could see the bullets cutting into the water ahead of them. They realised they would be sitting ducks, but they did not hesitate.

Time seemed to stand still while they rowed steadily towards the danger zone. Jackson, Layh, and Heighway were in the leading boat; Ken Walker's fellow 'musketeers' from Essendon, Ellis 'Teena' Stones and Bill Elliott, were among the rowers, feeling acutely vulnerable, expecting a bullet in the back at any moment. But at no stage did they waver. Having rowed about three-quarters of a mile since leaving the *Galeka*, they encountered the gunfire in earnest about 50 yards from the beach. It was a hail of bullets. One by one the rowers were hit, and slumped down. Others immediately seized their oars. Another of the rowers from Essendon, Harold Elliott later wrote,

> [a] little red-headed laddie named McArthur, scarcely more than eighteen, was shot through the femoral artery and the blood spurted from his thigh as the water squirted into the boat ... A sergeant attempted to bind it up. 'It's no use, Sergeant', he cried, 'I'm done', yet he rowed on until he swooned from loss of blood, and a comrade took his place.

Teena Stones was hit by a bullet that rebounded from his oar and scythed its way through the bones and flesh in and around his left knee; he 'tried to keep rowing but it was no good'. Of the original rowers in the leading boat, only Bill Elliott was not hit. Heighway, at the tiller, was hit through the chest. The impact nearly knocked him into the water. Layh saw him slide into the bottom of the boat, where he began to twitch and kick disconcertingly before he stopped quivering and attempted to operate the tiller with his foot.

At last the boat scraped the shore, and those able to get out lost no time in doing so. In the process more were hit, including Layh (ironically, in view of his colonel's last words to him, in the left buttock). He managed, however, to scramble across the beach with other survivors, all of them desperate to reach the flimsy sanctuary afforded at this part of the coast by grass-tufted sand hummocks. They tried their utmost to return the enemy's fire, but the fusillade aimed at them seemed, if anything, to intensify. Alongside Layh (who had collected another wound in the calf) a man was hit three times. In agony, he begged Layh to finish him off; another Turkish bullet made his request redundant. To find out how many from the leading boat were still going, Layh called out to the men around him. Only six answered. Bill Elliott was among the silent. Layh thought he and the rest would soon be history, too, sensing that the Turks in the vicinity were about to come down from their strongpoint and rout his outnumbered remnant. In an attempt to deter these Turks, he ordered his men to make their bayonets visible above the sand hummocks to indicate they were about to charge.

To the great relief of Layh and his comrades, the torrent of enemy fire tormenting them suddenly ceased. They were soon joined by survivors from the other three B Company boatloads. Casualties in these boats had also been severe. About 140 men had left the *Galeka* in those first four boats, but only around 35 mustered on the beach with Jackson (who had been wounded three times), Layh and Scanlan. They had arrived directly opposite the 7th Battalion's original objective, almost a mile north of the cove where Colonel Elliott and the rest of the battalion had landed; the withering fire aimed at them had come, in fact, primarily from the direction of Fisherman's Hut. Jackson hurried away to get help for the wounded. Layh and the others eventually decided to make their way along the beach towards the main AIF position. Variable cover and menacing Turkish fire made this a difficult task; one machine-gun held them up for hours. By the time Layh arrived at the cove it was nightfall, and he had only eighteen of the initial 140 men still with him.

Harold Elliott was particularly stirred by the plight of his wounded men in front of Fisherman's Hut. The Turks had maintained a concentrated fire on the leading boat, even after it was clear that everyone in it was either dead or gravely wounded. As bullets ripped into the boat—Heighway 'could smell the burning paint'—it became so riddled with holes that it began to fill with water, compounding the fear and misery of the men trapped inside. Pinned down by the bodies of their comrades as well as by merciless enemy fire, they became aware that liquid of a gruesome crimson hue was swishing ominously around them. Teena Stones was desperate to staunch the blood pouring from his and others' wounds, but he had a dying mate lying across him and 'it was impossible to get him to move'.

They stayed there in this pitiful state for well over an hour before assistance from the hard-pressed medical units to the south materialised. Stretcher-bearers carried Stones ashore, checked the flow of blood from his wound by wedging his camera into the hole where the back of his knee used to be, and transferred him a mile along the beach to the cove where most of the AIF had landed. Like his colonel, he had to lie there for hours. Shrapnel burst intermittently above, inflicting a further wound on the man alongside him. When he was at last taken off the beach, his was one of the batches of unfortunates who were ferried from ship to ship before being placed on a crowded transport for an agonising journey to Alexandria. He then joined his colonel at the Heliopolis Palace Hotel, where amputation of his leg was only narrowly averted.

Like Teena Stones and Alex McArthur, many of the B Company men who suffered terribly in front of Fisherman's Hut were young Essendon lads who had served under Elliott's command before the war. Elliott was greatly affected by their ordeal. He often referred to it in subsequent years, sometimes with graphic, lyrical intensity:

> The water gained in the boat and flowed around them, its blue turning a ghastly red with the blood of the wounded and dying. Still the hellish hail of fire continued, it did not cease when the boat grounded but swept over them, still piercing the writhing bodies

> through and through ... Oh those leaden minutes of agony, how slowly, how dreadfully they passed by.

'I wonder', Elliott reflected, 'what people in Australia thought of that dreadful slaughter'.

On 28 April the Melbourne *Herald* published in its final edition a brief official announcement that the AIF had participated in a landing at Gallipoli. Despite fervent yearning in thousands of Australian homes for more detailed news, only the most meagre information filtered through for several days while more and more Australians were notified (prior to soldiers' names being publicly announced) that their relatives in the AIF had become casualties. The full gravity of the situation swept through Essendon on Saturday 1 May, when the clergymen—who had been given the sombre task of informing soldiers' next-of-kin that their loved ones had died at the Dardanelles—were busy dealing with the consequences of the fighting in front of Fisherman's Hut. With rumours circulating wildly, many Essendon families waited in dread to see if they would be approached by these messengers. Among them was the Stones household; Bill Elliott had been boarding with them for some years. Confirmation of his death came in a poignant cable from Teena: 'Wounded leg Bill gone Ellis'. Many families were similarly grief-stricken in Bendigo, Footscray, and other areas that had given their sons so willingly to the 7th Battalion. With all regions of Australia represented in the landing force, there was anxiety and gloom throughout the nation.

Kate was notified on 30 April by the Defence Department that her husband had been 'slightly wounded'. Elliott himself arranged for a cable to be sent to his partner Roberts: 'Walker and I wounded neither seriously advise wife Elliott'. His first letter home was to Kate on 3 May. 'I hope you are not worrying too much', he wrote, concerned about her health in the wake of her operation. He then turned to his news:

> Well now last Saturday morning before daylight we Australians started to land about halfway along the Gallipoli peninsula ... The formation was like Sandringham at home. A narrow strip of beach with high cliffs above rising in successive ridges to 400 feet or more. Such a scramble it was to get to the top and we were weighed down with three days rations and packs. We threw the packs off on the beach and left them. The enemy's guns a couple of miles south

shelled our boats as they approached the beach ... Of course, we suffered heavily.

Elliott was far from well when he wrote. The landing actually occurred on a Sunday. He admitted in his next letter he had no idea what he had written in its predecessor.

In Australia the heavy burden of AIF casualties was known several days before any detailed account of the landing was published. It was not until 8 May that a dramatic dispatch by an acclaimed English war correspondent describing the AIF's landing reached Australians, who reacted with exaltation and relief that their countrymen had displayed such courage and dash in undertaking their difficult task. As they read with pride that there had been 'no finer feat in this war than this sudden landing in the dark and storming the heights', emotions already churned up by the casualty lists were further stirred by the realisation that Australia had made a spectacular impression in an international setting.

Events at Gallipoli that same day were guaranteeing that many more homes throughout Victoria would be plunged into misery. The British landings at the southern tip of the peninsula had also resulted in severe casualties and limited progress for the invaders. Reluctant to concede that the foothold established at Helles represented the limit of the British advance there, General Hamilton felt that another thrust towards the village of Krithia was justified before the conflict in this sector stagnated, like the Western Front had, into static warfare from entrenched positions. Together with the New Zealand brigade, a brigade from the AIF Division was to be detached to assist with the assault: Bridges decided on McCay's 2nd Brigade. In Elliott's absence his battalion was under the temporary command of Lieutenant-Colonel Gartside, a senior 8th Battalion officer with Boer War experience.

Having been conveyed by trawler to Helles, Pompey's men had the distinct misfortune to come within the orbit of Major-General A.G. Hunter-Weston, a British divisional commander. It was the performance of commanders like Hunter-Weston that endowed British generals in this war with a notorious collective reputation for blinkered incompetence (monstrously unjust though it was, of course, to many of them). Hunter-Weston was bombastic and gruff, 'self-important and vain'. Inflexible and reckless, he had an obscenely cheery indifference to the casualties his men endured as a result of his ill-considered offensives. Obsessed with hygiene, he 'inspected the latrines whenever he visited a unit'. Having commanded a brigade in the early fighting at the Western Front, he had been withdrawn after reputedly going 'off his head'.

Hunter-Weston directed a series of abortive attacks towards Krithia beginning on 6 May. Each was hampered by British artillery shortages, confusion about the location of the Turkish positions being attacked and, above all, Hunter-Weston's ineptitude. Apart from three roughly parallel ravines and a gentle slope towards the Turkish positions, the terrain was relatively flat and open, providing minimal cover (altogether different from the sector the 2nd AIF Brigade had just left). Hamilton suggested that a night advance might be appropriate. Hunter-Weston, however, rejected his chief's sensible advice, and proceeded to launch a number of unimaginative, repetitive set-piece thrusts in quick succession. In each instance he ordered an advance a long way uphill in broad daylight towards Turkish machine-gunners and sharpshooters who had uninterrupted visibility. On each occasion the British, French, and New Zealand soldiers who had to attempt the impossible were given preposterously little time to prepare themselves for it. All these attacks failed comprehensively.

Unfazed by these developments, ebullient as ever, Hunter-Weston was eager to oblige when Hamilton indicated he was keen to persevere. The conspicuous failure of Hunter-Weston's approach had reinforced Hamilton's preference for a night advance, but Hunter-Weston was still opposed to this method. Hamilton was intelligent, cultured, and courageous, but his sensitive temperament did not possess the forceful driving power (which Pompey Elliott had in abundance) to impose his will on subordinates. Again he declined to overrule his divisional commander; once more there were fatal consequences. On 8 May, after another predictable attack had predictably failed—launched by Hunter-Weston in mid-morning, as usual, after the Turks had breakfasted and been alerted by a brief preliminary bombardment—Hunter-Weston ordered the devastated New Zealanders to repeat the exercise in the afternoon. Hamilton decided to cancel this renewed attempt and, in a desperate gamble, ordered instead an ambitious general assault involving other units in the vicinity as well as the New Zealanders.

Late in the afternoon of 8 May the men of the 2nd AIF Brigade, so far mercifully spared from Hunter-Weston's fiascos, were settling into new surroundings well behind the front, cooking their evening meal and preparing rudimentary shelters for the night. Out of the blue McCay received a message ordering his brigade to advance towards Krithia and beyond. There was, absurdly, only half an hour to attend to all the organisational arrangements and move up to the front line to begin the attack. After being hastily alerted by brigade headquarters, Gartside felt able to give the 7th companies (who were to comprise the right half of the leading waves, though they were then three-quarters of a mile behind the existing front) only two minutes to get ready. In effect, the brigade had been directed to advance along an exposed spur for three miles although they would encounter the same Turkish fire that had demolished a series of similar attacks before any of these advances had managed to progress a sixth of that distance. A 7th private, having just returned after delivering a message to a British unit up ahead, was amazed to learn that such a suicidal manoeuvre had been ordered. He wanted to guide the battalion forward along a protected route that he had discovered via one of the ravines, but there was no time to reconnoitre or to consider such alternatives.

As soon as they emerged into the open they were shelled by Turkish shrapnel. Rifle and machine-gun bullets buzzed around them with growing intensity. 'Come on, Australians', McCay repeatedly called, and others took up the cry:

> The fire of small arms increased but the heavily loaded brigade hurried straight on, heads down, as if into fierce rain, some men holding their shovels before their faces like umbrellas in a thunderstorm.

Inevitably they lost heavily, but the survivors kept going until their numbers were too thin to go further. They dug in where they were, 400 yards short of the Turkish trenches, still over a mile from the village of Krithia. It was a marvellous display of heroic courage. Onlookers likened it to the charge of the Light Brigade.

It was also a product of murderous and futile folly. Gartside and many others were killed, and the agonies of the wounded were heart-rending. Later that month, after the shattered remnants of the 2nd Brigade had rejoined the AIF, British units at Helles successfully advanced towards the Turkish trenches at night—the penny having dropped at last—with minimal casualties. These manoeuvres were a prelude to another attack on Krithia; this was better planned than its predecessors and began auspiciously before withering, owing to a crucial tactical error by Hunter-Weston, who, astonishingly, had recently been promoted to corps commander. In July he was evacuated from Gallipoli suffering from sunstroke. He 'should surely have been shot', concluded one of Pompey Elliott's men, 'as he was equal to at least a division of Turks against us'.

News of the 2nd Brigade's exceptional charge soon reached Elliott. He was delighted to learn that onlookers from other countries 'were astonished at the reckless daring of our men', but appalled by the magnitude of the casualties: 'They tell me there is hardly any left of the poor old 7th Battalion'. By 30 April, in fact, the 7th had suffered more casualties than any other AIF battalion. The Krithia losses completed a devastating initiation for Elliott's unit.

There were hardly any of the original officers left. Two had been retained offshore on other duties—Tubb, as battalion transport officer in charge of the horses, and McCrae, on a temporary secondment to an engineers' unit. Of the remaining 29, only two combatant officers were still going strong, Grills and Weddell. Both knew they had been very lucky. 'A man never realizes ... what a terrible thing war is until he has been through it', wrote Grills after Krithia. 'Anyone fortunate enough to get off with his life in this Bloody Struggle ... ought to thank God'. Jackson, Layh, and Heighway were away undergoing treatment for wounds received near Fisherman's Hut; Chapman, also hit during the fighting there, died, as Alan Henderson did, on the way to Alexandria. Killed during the battle further south on 25 April were McKenna (who bled to death after his leg was blown off), Blick, and Davey. The severely wounded included Blezard, Conder, Connelly, Denehy, Mason, and Swift. Scanlan had emerged unscathed from the ordeal in front of Fisherman's Hut, but received a bullet in the chest at Krithia and was sent home to Australia.

De Ravin had a lucky escape. Having offered his men a final cigarette before the landing, he had pocketed the emptied container, joking that bibles and packs of cards had saved soldiers' lives before and a cigarette case might prove just as handy; after he waded ashore that case actually proved his salvation, deflecting a bullet that struck him over the heart. But he was not so lucky at Krithia, where an enemy projectile smashed his big toe. Birdie Heron emerged from the landing with two head wounds from shrapnel, but rejoined the battalion in time to collect another in the charge at Krithia; this third one proved more serious, resulting in the loss of an eye. Jimmy Johnston, having missed the landing because of an infected throat, lived up to his colonel's high expectations by his conduct at Krithia, but was gravely wounded in the charge when several bullets hit him in the stomach. The adjutant, Captain Finlayson, whose wedding was a social highlight of the training period at Broadmeadows, sustained multiple fractures in his right leg, which eventually had to be amputated. Also hit at Krithia was Captain Hunter, the famous athlete–footballer who had assured the people of Bendigo on behalf of that city's original enlisters that 'there would be no beg pardons', and 'while all could not expect to return they were prepared to take a sporting chance'. Wounded in the foot, he was taken to the rear; he was lying on a stretcher having his wound dressed when a stray bullet happened to strike him, with fatal consequences.

That was not all. Elliott was dismayed to hear that Rupert Henderson had been killed at Krithia. 'It is dreadful for the Hendersons to have lost both their boys like this', he wrote, 'they were so splendid and brave all through'. McCrae, having 'passed through a most awful week of mental stress' aboard a 'luxurious' ship while his 'men and brother officers were short of rest, food and water and fighting for their very existence', felt 'awfully sorry for the Hendersons, it must be a terrible blow losing two sons like that'. The elder brother of Rupert and Alan, a teacher, was interrupted in the classroom one morning and handed a message. 'When Henderson read the telegram', one of his students later wrote, 'he turned white and rushed from the room'. The mother of these sons, an indefatigable volunteer for many years in a host of social service activities, had a nervous breakdown in 1915. The Bishop of Bathurst, headmaster of Trinity Grammar School during the Hendersons' years there, described Rupert in May 1915 as the finest individual he had ever had in his charge.

About a week after Pompey Elliott heard about Rupert Henderson's death, he also learned that Jimmy Johnston had succumbed to his wounds and that General Bridges had been fatally wounded. 'What will be the end I wonder', he mused. His feelings about the decimation of his battalion and the loss of officers he particularly admired were candidly expressed in a letter he sent to the Henderson family with his 'deepest sympathy'. Alan, he wrote, was in the firing line the whole time from the landing, encouraging the men to advance and holding them to it when their losses counselled retreat ... Rupert first learned of his death just before leaving the Gaba Tepe landing place for Cape Helles. He was informed of Allan's death by Lieut Johnston, who had not landed in the first instance here owing to illness but had gone to Alexandria with wounded and returned in time to take part in the great charge near Krithia, which has rendered the name of the Victorian Brigade and in particular the 6th and 7th Battalions famous throughout the Army here, in which both Rupert and he fell. I have felt the death of these two more than all the others and they are many, for the 7th Battalion at present is little more than a name. Both Johnston and Rupert came in a peculiar degree under my instruction in the 5th AIR and both had they been spared would have earned a great name. I asked both personally to join me in the 7th before they had decided to volunteer and I never had the slightest reason to doubt my judgment, but every day confirmed it more and more. No one could have been more loyal and trustworthy than they, and indeed all my officers, proved. But I feel peculiarly responsible for their deaths and though there is no doubt that they would have come in any case, I cannot forget the fact that it was by my invitation they came ... I enclose a scrap of paper which you may treasure. It is the last message I received from Rupert. I was wounded a few minutes afterwards.

CHAPTER SEVEN

'May I Never See Another War': Steele's Post and Lone Pine

JUNE–AUGUST 1915

POMPEY ELLIOTT REJOINED his battalion at Gallipoli early on 4 June. Shannon Grills was

> awakened by a tremendous cheer and on looking up found that Col. Elliott had returned. Talk about a commotion. The old boys were extremely pleased to see the Col. return and resume command of the 7th.

Grills led Elliott to a nearby hill where a detached company of the 7th was on garrison duty. The impromptu reaction there was just as fervent (and somewhat perplexing, presumably, for the Turks). 'Three hearty cheers rang out', noted Grills. The men were 'beaming with smiles of delight' as their colonel mingled among them, 'shaking hands and having a chat with those whom he recognised'. These spontaneous ovations were gratifying, but there were 'only about half a dozen of all the Essendon boys left, and only a little over a hundred of all the men I took from Broadmeadows'. At least some of the less severely wounded were, like Elliott himself, gradually returning. Pompey was delighted by the reappearance of any of his originals, officers especially. Geoff McCrae arrived on 11 June, Alf Jackson came back a week later, and Bert Layh followed shortly afterwards. Contingents of reinforcements materialised from time to time. Pompey welcomed each batch of recruits with

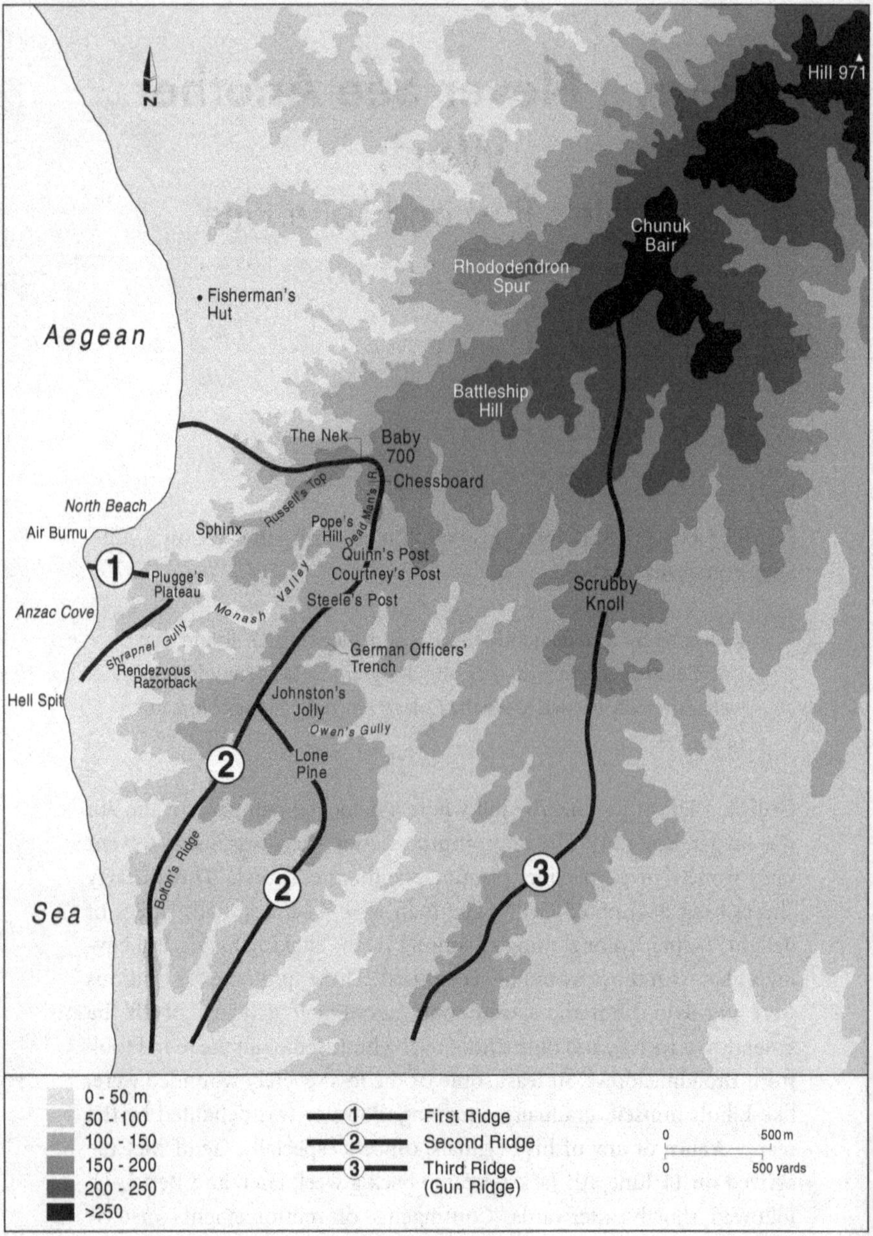

Anzac positions

a spirited address that left them in no doubt that they had a high standard to emulate.

While Elliott was away the acronym Anzac (derived from the Australian and New Zealand Army Corps) had commenced its enduring association with the Gallipoli campaign. The narrow, crescent-shaped beach, 1,000 yards long, where most of the landing force had come ashore, was officially named Anzac Cove on 29 April. Anzac was being used as a shorthand label for both this landing place and the whole combat area. In addition, the soldiers from Australia and New Zealand involved in the enterprise were beginning to be referred to as the Anzacs.

The area captured at the landing had been transformed since 25 April. Elliott was impressed:

> there is a wonderful change in this place since I was last here. The scrub has been mostly cut down for firewood etc and all the hillsides are like rabbit warrens where we live ... everywhere there are immense trenches for our protection. In many places these are 9 or 10 feet deep. Fortunately there has been very little rain and the subsoil is very porous, so that it is nice and dry.

Nevertheless it was obvious that the limited positions held by the invaders fell far short of their ambitious objectives. The Turks still controlled the ridge rising from Gaba Tepe to Hill 971, the third ridge encountered by the Anzacs as they progressed inland. The soaring height immediately above the beach (climbed by Elliott when looking for Sinclair-Maclagan), now known as Plugge's Plateau, comprised, together with its southern shoulder, the first ridge. Beyond Plugge's, across a deep valley called Shrapnel Gully, was the second ridge, which extended from the sea south of the main landing site in a north-easterly direction. Some Australians had penetrated beyond the second ridge on 25 April without being able to consolidate. The positions established along this ridge north of the 400 Plateau—the posts known as Steele's, Courtney's and Quinn's—represented the limit of the advance. Quinn's Post, where Turkish trenches in front were in some places only a few yards away, and the enemy could overlook the Anzacs from their left, left rear, and right, was the precarious apex of their whole position. Yet Quinn's was only three-quarters of a mile from the beach. The Anzacs, then, were confined to a small triangularly shaped area. The coast and the positions on the north flank roughly resembled the two shorter sides of a right-angled triangle, while the longest side extended south-west from Quinn's along the second ridge to the sea.

When Colonel Elliott rejoined the 7th Battalion it was in reserve south of Shrapnel Gully on the relatively protected western slope of a narrow spur known as the Razorback, which descended from the 400 Plateau towards the beach. The battalion had been 'resting' there, apart from occasional stints in support trenches, since returning from Krithia on 17 May. The rest was illusory because of the strenuous toil performed by soldiers at Anzac away from the front trenches. The transformation in the roads, trenches, and dug-outs that Elliott found so striking had been achieved by the exertion of men having a spell from the strain and danger of front-line duty. Besides this construction work, the lugging of food, water, and ammunition was a never-ending chore, and they were always liable to find themselves called upon for special tasks like dragging big guns up steep slopes into carefully chosen positions. The advent of systematic mining, to extend the Anzacs' trench network and to undermine Turkish positions, added another arduous activity to the growing list of 'rest' duties.

For practically everyone at Anzac, whether in or out of the trenches, it was a tough and dangerous existence. They had to put up with abundant hard work, insufficient sleep, tightly rationed water, and a generally monotonous diet. Their health began to deteriorate as flies became a major problem. Enticed by unburied bodies, uncovered latrines, and miscellaneous refuse, flies were soon present in vast repulsive swarms, dispersing dysentery and diarrhoea in epidemic proportions. 'It is very hot here and the flies are awful', wrote Pompey. There was also a plague of lice that spread universal discomfort. The biggest problem of all, the ever-present danger, was simply a fact of life for everyone at Anzac. Although the improved trenches and dug-outs had partially reduced their vulnerability, the Anzacs, unlike their counterparts in other wars and in other theatres in this war, were confined to such a small area that anyone in it was potentially under fire the whole time. Of course, some spots were more dangerous than others; but since everyone in the AIF was well within reach of a Turkish bullet or shell, each soldier had to adjust to the reality that at any moment he or the close mate beside him could suddenly be killed.

There was no respite from this continual threat. Pompey Elliott had been back with his battalion in its relatively protected position for only a few minutes when the Turks shelled it. 'We rushed for our dug-outs on the side of the hill', he told Kate, but two men were hit. The bombardment caught one at a latrine, and the other, a cook, at his work station. Both died. Even the treat of a refreshing swim was risky, because the Turks shelled the beach frequently.

Elliott now had to adjust, more thoroughly than before, to the way the war was being fought. Having heard about the phenomenon of prolonged trench warfare that had taken root at the Western Front, he quickly familiarised himself with conditions at Anzac, where the opposing combatants had become similarly bogged down and essentially static warfare prevailed. This situation had arisen because the war happened to occur during an era when the state of military technology bestowed significant advantages on defenders. The advent of the machine-gun and barbed wire, and the enhanced effectiveness of rifle fire (increased range, quicker firing, and smokeless powder), all contributed. In these circumstances even the most able generals struggled to devise effective methods of attack that did not produce hideously high casualties for the attackers. Some senior commanders were culpably slow to adapt to the new conditions; incompetent butchers like Hunter-Weston made a habit of ordering murderous advances. At Anzac the advantages possessed by defenders were very evident. The invaders had been unable to attain their objectives at the landing and subsequently; so, too, were the Turks completely unsuccessful in their attempt to drive their opponents into the sea on 19 May.

Bombs, unfamiliar to Australians before the landing, became a feature at Anzac. They were particularly effective in close-quarters fighting at places like Quinn's. After being startled by these lethal fizzing cricket balls, the Australians tried to counter them by manufacturing their own improvised 'jam-tin' bombs and forming specialist squads of bomb-throwers. But the Turks retained a considerable advantage by virtue of their superior quality and supply of this important weapon.

The most distinctive characteristic of the new style of warfare, however, was the terrifyingly destructive power of artillery. This was more evident at the Western Front than at Gallipoli, where both the Turks and their adversaries had to make do with shortages of heavy guns and ammunition. The Anzac batteries, moreover, had to operate in a cramped, hilly environment that did not suit them. Nevertheless, while the saturation bombardments routinely adopted in France were unknown at Gallipoli, shellfire in smaller doses at the peninsula proved potent and devastating.

A week after Elliott's return the 7th Battalion's post-Krithia recovery period came to an end. On 11 June the 2nd Brigade took over responsibility for trenches that the 1st Brigade had been holding near the centre of the inland perimeter at Anzac. Initially the 5th and 8th Battalions occupied the front line while the 6th and 7th, having suffered more severely in the early fighting, were in reserve. Elliott described his new dug-out so Kate could imagine him in it:

> You would laugh to see my home. Fancy a place just long enough for me to lie down in comfort, cut out in the side of the hill some eight feet in. My bed is a shelf of earth left some five feet from the top while the remainder is cut some two feet deeper. When the hill falls away near the front it is built up with sandbags so that you can imagine a square cut out of the side of the hill and roofed over with a few boughs and a water-proof sheet. I am quite safe from anything except a high explosive shell and from even that unless it happened to lob right in through the roof, and that has only happened to one man, one of all the lot here. Only his legs were found for burial.

For the time being it was that odd combination familiar to soldiers, long periods of inaction punctuated by bursts of heightened danger:

> At this moment except for one or two rifle shots at intervals of a minute or more you would hardly dream that a war was going on. It is a lovely day, and although nearly all the tall scrub on the hillsides has been cut down and burnt for fuel, the hillsides are still green and pretty. In a few minutes I suppose it will all start again, the crackling of the rifles, the rattle of the machine guns and the boom of the cannon, the long whistle of the shells which often arrives before the shell itself and allows you to take cover if only you knew where it was going to lob.

Intermittent Turkish shelling continued to be the main hazard. On 12 June Elliott happened to be talking to McCrae when shells landed 'quite close to us', killing two men and wounding four others. Later that month Elliott had a particularly close shave when a shell landed in his dug-out, missing him by inches. For a frightful moment he 'expected to be blown up' by this unwelcome visitor, but it failed to explode. The first man on the scene, the battalion quartermaster, said Pompey 'was halfway through the Lord's Prayer before he realised that it was not going off', a quip Elliott enjoyed recounting afterwards. He had other near misses, particularly while swimming, but continued with his regular dip. It was 'the most beautiful sea water', he told Kate, 'so clear that you can stand up to your neck in the water yet count your toes on the firm sandy bottom of the sea'. Other recreational pursuits were few, but he did manage to outmanoeuvre Grills in their first chess encounter since the day before the landing.

When the fighting at Anzac stabilised, the Turks controlled important positions near Quinn's known as the Chessboard and Dead Man's Ridge. From there they not only overlooked Quinn's and other Anzac positions from the left and left rear; they also had a superb view down Monash Valley, which was the continuation of Shrapnel Gully and the main artery between the beach and Quinn's. Their command of this vital route was an influential factor for the first month or so after the landing. During this period Turkish sharpshooters hit many Australians undertaking tasks that required their presence in Monash Valley. The activity continued nonetheless—being shot at along Monash Valley was accepted as an occupational hazard. By the end of June, however, the deadly skill of crack Anzac snipers, stalking their prey patiently from carefully concealed posts, had transformed the situation. After famous duels between opposing marksmen, the Australians and New Zealanders managed to curb their Turkish counterparts so effectively that venturing along Monash Valley became much less risky.

Among the finest AIF snipers were the 7th Battalion group Elliott installed in a specially designed post above their bivouac. Percy Carne from Bendigo had won numerous prizes for rifle-shooting. Sergeant Wally Fisher, a Frankston plumber and the eldest of nine brothers who all enlisted in the AIF, was a renowned marksman. Farmer Hal Young, the champion of the St Arnaud Rifle Club, had been a sergeant in the 8th Battalion before accepting the offer of a commission in the 7th at the end of May. Elliott was confident his group of snipers could cause the Turks a great deal of trouble:

> we have put a tunnel in and then a crosscut to the face of the hill and put two men with a steel plate loopholed in front of them. One watches with a telescope and the other fires on to the Turks' trenches up on what we call the Chessboard ... There is one spot in which we can fire right into a trench at 1100 yards and it must annoy the Turks considerably.

Elliott's confidence was quickly vindicated. His team of snipers was in position at dawn with all their specialised accoutrements—telescopes, binoculars, verniers, and telescopic and peep sights—and remained there, he wrote, 'until the last gleam had faded from the western sky, sweeping with their glasses backwards and forwards across and again across the Turkish lines'. Maintaining this painstaking vigil hour after hour in sweltering midsummer heat was not easy: 'we had to be in the sun all day', wrote Carne, and it was 'very hot in our position'. They soon discovered that a smartly dressed officer was making a regular morning visit to a particular Turkish post at the head of Monash Valley, where he would chat briefly with the men on duty, borrow a rifle, and fire a couple of ritualistic shots into the valley. The Australians, watching him so intently they could even see his gleaming teeth, decided to plan a surprise for his next visit. Carne and his team duly accounted for their long-distance quarry. Immediately afterwards they observed consternation at and around the Turkish post. They did not know it at the time, but they had deprived the Turks of a distinguished commander who was about to lead an important assault towards the Nek and Russell's Top (crucial positions on the Anzac left), an attack that went ahead without him but was unsuccessful—partly, Elliott later concluded, because of this inspiring commander's absence.

Early in July Elliott and his men relieved the 8th Battalion in the front-line trenches. The 7th's numbers had been gradually increased by reinforcements and returning originals, but illness was a major problem. Both Major Weddell and the battalion doctor, Eric Gutteridge, were evacuated sick on 3 July. The battalion was still barely half its nominal strength, and a good many of its members were inexperienced recruits. On 3 July Elliott moved into his new position on the second ridge at Steele's Post. From this perch high above Monash Valley there was a superb view of the expansive sea and, above it, consistently glorious sunsets. Pompey inspected the trenches three times daily, to check the condition of parapets, loopholes, and wire, to keep his men on their toes, and to appraise the latest activities of the Turks opposite.

In front of Steele's was an important enemy stronghold known as German Officers' Trench. The Turks had established a machine-gun there that was ideally placed to fire in enfilade—the most lethal angle of fire, especially for a machine-gun—northwards along the Anzac line, towards Quinn's in particular. Being only 50 yards east of Steele's, this machine-gun post had been an early priority in the Anzac mining initiatives. The Turks, unsettled by their opponents' tunnelling, endeavoured to countermine, but had less expertise and even less adequate equipment than the rudimentary implements available to the Anzacs. Tension underground was acute; AIF miners could often hear the digging of their counterparts opposite. When Australians heard Turks digging very close to a tunnel they were pushing forward from Steele's towards German Officers', it was decided to explode the mine on 25 June. The explosion entombed Turkish miners, unnerved their countrymen in the vicinity, and left a large crater 20 feet in diameter between the Australian tunnel and the Turks' trench at German Officers'. Elliott had just taken over at Steele's when another Australian tunnel near German Officers' was blown up in similar circumstances, damaging Turkish trenches and unsettling the occupants.

The Turks, evidently anxious about AIF intentions at German Officers', singled out Elliott and his men for a severe retaliatory bombardment the following day. Shells descended with a piercing shriek and exploded in massive eruptions. The earth trembled, and dust, sandbags, tools, chunks of timber, and fragments of mangled humanity rocketed skywards.

> Three men were killed, all of them old 7th men. Two of them had been wounded on the first day 25th April with me and only got back a fortnight ago. Six others were also wounded, none badly. I had rather a narrow escape myself. I was going along the fire trench to encourage the boys when a shell burst in the parapet ... Three men were partly buried under the debris and I was covered from head to foot in dust and debris but was quite all right and helped to yank the others out.

A day later the Turks again bombarded Steele's, and Elliott had another narrow escape:

> I went along the trench to see where a shell had burst and to find out if anyone was hurt … when a second shell came and burst in front of me covering me with dust and the smoke of the explosion. Two or three men dashed out of their dug-outs and rushed to pick up my pieces, and were much astonished to find that I wasn't twopence the worse … [Later,] seeing four men watching for the enemy I sent away the two men in the middle leaving only the two end ones. I had just gone a few steps away when a shell came and blew in the whole trench. It was nearly 8 feet deep and it was filled right to the top with dirt and sandbags. The two men I had left were still there and still looking through their periscopes but not particularly happy. I was afraid the Turks might try an attack and hopped up and started to fill up the sandbags again, but the men said they would do it and that my life was too valuable to risk like that … About six or seven others were buried in the debris including my crack shots Sergt Fisher and Sgt Carne.

Howitzer-induced burial was ghastly. Smothered victims were gripped by understandable panic and the terrifying dread that they would not be extricated before they suffocated or another shell arrived to obliterate both them and their rescuers. Afterwards, shattered nerves tended not to recover quickly. 'My mates and myself were suffering from shock today after last night's experience', wrote Percy Carne, who had just set off to hand in a letter to his mother when the shell arrived that buried four of the sniping team. 'It shook my nerves a bit as it would have blown me to pieces if I had not shifted to post the letter'.

Shortly after lunch on 8 July Elliott was at battalion headquarters when an engineer burst in and announced that 'Turks are in our tunnel'. Galvanised by this disturbing news, Elliott immediately directed Grills and another 7th officer, Cedric Permezel, to organise a party to drive the Turks out straightaway. After they rushed away to attend to this, Elliott reconsidered. He had no knowledge of the situation himself; he had never been inside these particular tunnels. (It was the engineers, rather than the infantry commander on the spot, who had specific responsibility for the tunnels; apart from a few sentries and working parties carrying out excavated earth under the engineers' direction, infantrymen were encouraged to stay away.) Reviewing his instinctive reaction, he felt he should find out more about the situation before sending men to deal with it. Accordingly, he hurried forward himself to investigate, collecting along the way two men, who happened to be newly arrived reinforcements, to accompany him into the tunnel.

This tunnel, he later recalled, was 'about 80 yards long' and dug in a 'zigzag' fashion in order

> to localise the effect of a charge should it be blown in at any time. It was so low that I could not stand up in it. It was so narrow that two men could not pass in it. It was pitch dark. To have carried a light would have meant making myself an aiming mark. Every step you made ... echoed along the gallery and at every turn you might expect to have a bayonet stuck in your ribs.

Into this forbidding gloom the trio proceeded, the colonel in front. They had cautiously progressed almost to the end of the tunnel when there was a sudden flash in front of Elliott's face and a cry behind him. A Turkish bullet fired at close range had miraculously missed him, passing under his left arm and striking one of his terrified companions; they both ran for their lives, convinced that their colonel (who had remained silent) had been killed. Elliott, his pistol raised, quietly pressed himself into the side wall, where he was less of a target to his adversary hovering around the next bend, and paused to see if the enemy would advance. A few minutes later the nearest Turk fired again. He missed. After waiting for 'what appeared an interminable time', Elliott heard movement behind him. Sensing that the party he had ordered Grills and Permezel to organise might be arriving, he crept back towards this noise. 'Is that you, Permezel?' he whispered. There was no reply.

It was indeed Captain Permezel, but he and Grills were startled by this question and suspicious of Turkish trickery in the darkness. The men who had left Elliott in the tunnel had insisted that a bullet had gone right through him and he must be dead. Permezel had bravely volunteered to lead a small group into the tunnel to retrieve the colonel's body, and was understandably wary about accepting that he was alive after all. Eventually Permezel asked this unknown inquirer to identify himself, with a nickname. The reply, 'Bob Elliott', settled all doubts; Permezel had a long association with Elliott in the militia and was very familiar with his pre-war nickname. Elliott then led Permezel and his men back to the furthest point he had reached. He then instructed

Permezel to organise a chain of men all the way back to the tunnel entrance so that filled sandbags could be passed along for a barricade, which the colonel would erect himself. Hearing voices, the Turk resumed firing, but kept hitting the side of the tunnel harmlessly. Permezel urged Elliott to allow him to build the barrier, but Elliott refused and rapidly erected a breastwork two sandbags thick. After completing it he withdrew from the tunnel.

The engineers, headed by Lieutenant R.J. Dyer, resumed control of the situation. They successfully devised an explosion that destroyed the portion of the tunnel occupied by the Turks and created a new crater, known as Dyer's, in front of the barricade Pompey had built. As arranged by Elliott, a squad of Australians headed by Ken Walker immediately rushed the new crater and fortified it.

There was another sequel to Elliott's duel in the tunnel. Brudenell White gently told him it was not really appropriate for a lieutenant-colonel to risk himself undertaking tasks of that nature. There was even a special AIF order decreeing that minor enterprises should be led by junior officers, not senior commanders. Afterwards Elliott maintained that he had acted properly:

> It must be remembered that veteran troops were rare at that time, and it was impossible to say who was the man to entrust to such a task. No one could say what was the thing to be done until you had seen the place.

The hazardousness of the assignment also influenced his decision:

> I believe that no officer should order his men to go where he is afraid to go himself ... Frankly I was afraid to go, but since I could on that very account not order anyone else to go, I went forward myself to investigate.

Whatever his superiors thought, this celebrated exploit reinforced his reputation within and beyond his battalion for remarkable, selfless bravery. It became an article of faith among the men he commanded that he would never send a man anywhere he was not prepared to go himself. Three months later Kate Elliott received a letter from the mother of a 7th Battalion corporal:

> My boy spoke of Colonel Elliott performing the bravest deed he had ever heard of, but that it would take too long to explain, also would not pass the Censor. His men think the world of him.

Late on 11 July senior AIF commanders learned that they had to assist a major offensive to be undertaken at Helles the following morning. Their role was to prevent Turkish units from being withdrawn from Anzac and transferred south. Several feints along the Anzac front were hastily organised. One involved Pompey Elliott and his men; he was ordered to arrange a bomb assault from Dyer's crater. (Earlier attempts to simulate attacks at Anzac had resulted in excessive casualties. Birdwood directed that in undertaking feints on this occasion the Anzacs should not leave their trenches, apart from one manoeuvre on the far right. But preparations were rushed, and this instruction was not passed on to Elliott.) Pompey assembled his officers, told them frankly that the enterprise would be dangerous, and asked for a volunteer to lead it. Lieutenant Norman Greig nominated himself; he was a Scotch College (Melbourne) teacher who had arrived with the third batch of 7th Battalion reinforcements just before the Krithia charge.

Accompanied by eleven other volunteers, Greig climbed out of Dyer's at 8.15am in broad daylight and charged towards the other crater. The attack, Elliott recorded, 'was completely successful at first'; startled Turks in the crater were quickly overwhelmed. But their comrades in nearby German Officers' then retaliated, showering Greig and his men with bombs. With two men killed and all the rest, including himself, wounded, Greig ordered his party to return via the broken-down tunnel. The gallant lieutenant was last seen 'standing at the tunnel-mouth, revolver in hand, his head bleeding, holding back the Turks while his men retired'. He refused to be captured, and was eventually killed by a bomb. Sacrificing himself to keep the Turks at bay, he enabled all his wounded men to scramble back to safety.

Long-range Turkish shellfire, which had continued to torment Elliott's men at Steele's, resumed with redoubled intensity. No other part of the Anzac front was shelled more heavily. Lieutenant Tubb, who had at last been allowed (after repeated requests) to leave his transport section and rejoin the battalion, arrived at Steele's early on 10 July, and was given 'a hearty welcome' by Elliott, Grills, and McCrae. He found his first glimpse of Anzac—this 'huge rabbit warren', he described it—

'most exciting and interesting', but three shells landing nearby were 'frightening'. Up early the following morning, he had a tense stint on guard at Dyer's crater, then endured another burst of enemy shellfire. 'One cracked just above my head giving me an awful fright', he wrote, 'I got smothered in dirt and rubble'. The Turks bombarded them again that afternoon:

> Shells are bursting about us still. They make my heart go pit a pat ... They've smashed our trenches about an awful lot, destroyed some of our dugouts ... By jove I can hardly write—I don't like the blooming howitzer shells.

The following day it was worse:

> We have experienced an awful time this morning, got shelled terribly ... trenches are smashed to pieces. Had a rotten time digging out some of the men. Feel knocked out ... I got bruised and half buried twice ... All my men are fatigued and suffering from shock ... The strain and shock is very tiring. All the old boys need recuperating badly.

'I hope I can stick this game out', he concluded doubtfully after only three days at Steele's. One of those 'old boys', sniper Percy Carne, was buried by a shell for the second time in a week. Afterwards his health broke down completely, and he was sent to England for a prolonged recuperation.

Elliott was devastated by the ordeal his men endured. For 'the past week our trenches have been a hell upon earth' and 'I have no heart to write, even to you', he told Kate.

> Men were blown to pieces by shell or crushed to death by the masses of earth blown down upon them, but Katie the boys are wonderful. They stick it out and the call for picks and shovels or stretcher bearers never fails to be answered though often another shell sends these willing workers into eternity. Poor Capt Permezel had his leg frightfully shattered. It is said he must lose it. Poor old Ken Walker was always the first to lead a party to the rescue of those buried in the trenches, not once but dozens of times. For a long

> time he was fortunate, I often saw him with his face set and pale but never shrinking. At last three or four nights ago a fragment of shell went right through his body. Our Doctor did not give any hope of his being saved at all but news of his death has not reached me, so I am beginning to hope against hope for it was a frightful wound and the poor boy bore it without a murmur ... Oh I do hope his life will be saved.

Then there was Sergeant Garner, one of his original 'Essendon boys':

> everybody is talking of him. He was dangerously wounded on the first day through the chest, but continued to fight until exhausted by loss of blood. He recovered and was just back a few days when he had both legs blown off by a shell the day before yesterday. He never uttered a groan nor lost consciousness. He told the bearers to stop as he was being carried past a fire and asked them to light his cigarette ... When he got to the Doctor he was as cheery as possible, nodded to his friends near and said 'Well Doctor, have I got even a fair sporting chance' ... I hope he does survive, poor chap.

He then described the outstanding valour of that 'fine young officer' Norman Greig.

> I am proud of them all Katie, but oh my heart is breaking to see them, my hair is nearly quite grey with the worry and grief of it all to see them dying so. We are like men under sentence of death, for every day takes its toll of us. We are worn out too ... It is only by the blessing of providence that I am alive ... for every day these wretched shells explode and cover me with dust and grime. So far I have avoided being buried, but any day may bring it or worse upon me. But God is good and maybe your prayers will prevail. I am in excellent bodily health but I am broken hearted at the loss of my brave boys ... May I never see another war.

Permezel, Walker, and Garner all died of the effects of their wounds.

Colonel Elliott's frank report stating that his men were worn out was supported by medical officers, and was instrumental in the decision to withdraw them on 19 July after sixteen harrowing days in the front line.

Although a senior artillery officer who had recently arrived from France insisted that Elliott's men had not experienced a genuine bombardment by Western Front standards, the combination of relentless strain and overwork (particularly the need to keep repairing repeatedly wrecked trenches) had left them severely overwrought. Many were suffering from the condition that was to become known as shell-shock. Elliott was immensely relieved when their ordeal ended:

> It is terrible to be in those trenches where we were ... and hear those big shells coming towards you, and you have just got to stay and wait for them to blow you all to pieces or pass you by if your luck is in.

The 7th Battalion was back in the same reserve position it had been occupying when he rejoined it on 4 June:

> For myself I am fairly comfortable, but the men have to work very hard at fatigue work, getting food up and mining under the enemy's trenches etc ... I am still well in health but very sad for my poor boys.

Despite these feelings he was soon cracking the whip with his usual zest. On the first morning after his men were relieved, the 7th Battalion was ordered to provide a working party of 50 men at 4.15am. Despite the best efforts of the NCOs involved (according to Tubb), the squad arrived for duty late. Elliott bellowed his disapproval. Later that day there was a repeat performance, which left Tubb, one of his greatest admirers, distinctly unimpressed:

> The C.O. roared on the Sgt Majors and me last night for not supplying 25 men for fatigue at a minute's notice ... The C.O. is unjust and unreasonable at times but he does it all for the best I suppose.

If ever it was appropriate not to enforce the highest disciplinary standards—and in pre-war days even such a stickler as Elliott had conceded there were circumstances when it would be permissible to relax them—it would be hard to imagine a more suitable time. He was painfully familiar with the ordeal they had just endured, and knew just as well as Tubb how unfair it was to saddle them with strenuous tasks when they were supposed to be resting. It was in fact Pompey's vigorous protest that they were 'getting absolutely exhausted by continuous fatigues' which resulted in some lightening of their workload. But he was determined to prevent any possibility of a slide in the impressive standards achieved by his battalion, and was perhaps also motivated by concern about the training the reinforcements had received.

There had been questions at Anzac at an early stage about the instruction AIF recruits were receiving from British regulars in Egypt. That the 7th's 'reinforcements apparently have not had much training' was clearly evident to Grills in May; the colonel (not then returned to Gallipoli) 'would go mad if he saw them at work'. Since then the tendency for AIF reinforcements to arrive at Anzac unable to use a rifle, and unfamiliar with basic drill movements, had been accentuated by Birdwood's policy of rushing them across from Egypt with minimal delay. The 'new men we are getting', Elliott observed in June, 'are hardly trained at all'.

With a bittersweet mixture of sadness and pride, Pompey identified with the 7th Battalion completely. 'I am very proud indeed of my lads in the 7th', he declared, reviewing its deeds and casualties for correspondents including J.G. Latham and lawyer J.C. Richardson:

> I don't think the record can be much surpassed by any Regiment in British History ... All my officers that I picked myself turned out splendidly, and I am delighted with them and the boys but almost broken hearted at their fate.

In this frame of mind he reacted angrily when he learned that disparaging remarks about the 7th had been made by an 8th Battalion officer, Captain E.T.J. Kerby, whose men were unimpressed when the 7th's front-line stint at Steele's was shortened. Pompey could be uninhibited himself about shortcomings he perceived in other units (though quick to give praise when he considered it merited). But any aspersions on his beloved 7th were intolerable, and he resolved to make an issue of them. Kerby was paraded before the 7th, and his comments were read aloud. The battalion 'was justly incensed', according to Tubb, who knew Kerby, having lunched with him in Egypt. Kerby had been 'making serious mistakes and talking too much', Tubb felt, but he was not enthusiastic about Pompey's vigorous pursuit of the matter. Three days later Kerby was evacuated sick.

On 21 July Elliott realised he was the only one of the twelve initial battalion commanders still at the helm of his unit. That same day also saw the departure of Grills, the only one of Elliott's original officers who had been with the battalion ever since the landing. Grills had been severely shaken when buried during an enemy bombardment on 13 July —'a horrible sensation'—and had been feeling increasingly ill, battling diarrhoea and sleeplessness, for a week. Pompey could have done without these unpleasant reminders of the rapid turnover of Anzac leaders. He was not the only veteran preoccupied with pessimistic reflections.

No-one was better placed to detect the AIF's moods than its official correspondent, Charles Bean. His earlier unfortunate image in the AIF (arising from the dispatch Bridges asked him to write about misconduct in Egypt) had been erased by his meritorious conduct since. From the morning of 25 April—when he came ashore under fire and paused on the beach to photograph the men landing with him rather than search for cover immediately—Bean's bravery and dedication to his work had made him a widely admired figure. Unlike other correspondents content with safe, distant, and often distorted reporting, Bean lived at Anzac with the soldiers, and was painstaking in his endeavours to ascertain the truth. Armed with the facts, he could then write faithfully about the AIF's experience, in contemporary reporting for the newspapers and also in the history of Australia's part in the war that he was later to write. He had already had miraculous escapes. Under torrential fire at Krithia he had accompanied the 2nd Brigade's remarkable advance and, disregarding his own safety, helped many of the wounded lying in the open; Elliott's friend McNicoll acknowledged that he would have died if Bean had not rescued him.

Outwardly Bean was gentle and unassuming, idealistic and unworldly, but his determination underneath was the mainspring of his courage and remarkable productivity. He visited a variety of units, inspected dangerous positions, and compiled copious notes; he scorned sleep, preferring instead to write up his articles, catch up with his diaries, or obtain a firsthand glimpse of the action whenever he discovered or sensed something doing. After reports of his contribution at Krithia spread throughout the AIF, he was welcomed, especially in the

2nd Brigade, whenever he called on information-gathering visits. He had already conducted detailed interviews with Elliott, Grills, and Layh about the landing.

With rumours circulating in July that a massive break-out from Anzac was in the offing, Bean detected from his unique vantage point a subtle change of mood among AIF veterans.

> They had pictured themselves fighting perhaps for a year or more, and had imagined the majority then returning, as they had done from South Africa, marching through the well-known streets and cheering crowds of their home city, and arriving back among their families with strange tales, interesting 'souvenirs', and thrilling experience. Now for the first time the perception came to many ... that for them the prospect was one of battle after battle, in which, in the long run, there must almost certainly be one of two endings. They felt themselves penned between two long blank walls reaching perpetually ahead of them, from which there was no turning and no escape.

Their pride and sense of duty ensured they would not shirk, but the grim unavoidable outcome, they concluded, was that sooner or later they would be either killed or severely wounded. That Pompey Elliott was thinking along these lines was revealed in the letter he wrote to Richardson after the 7th was withdrawn from Steele's:

> I had some rather narrow shaves myself but fortunately have survived so far. I am wondering daily how long this immunity is to last and quite expect to go out in the next advance but of course am hoping for the best.

That next advance was imminent. Preparations for a renewed offensive at Anzac had been maturing for months. The main aim was to secure Hill 971 and the adjacent heights that were the Anzacs' objectives on 25 April. It was intended to surprise the Turks by attacking this vital high ground from an unexpected direction. After proceeding northwards from Anzac at night, a number of formations would make a co-ordinated enveloping movement inland. Some of them, notably Brigadier-General Monash's 4th AIF Brigade, would have to advance across exceptionally difficult terrain (even harder to penetrate in darkness), but the architects of the offensive were hoping to take advantage of the Turks' confidence that an assault through that part of the peninsula was impossible. Assisting this main thrust—and hopefully compounding the enemy's confusion—would be a number of diversionary attacks, together with a new landing by five British brigades at Suvla Bay four miles to the north. Such ambitious operations required extensive preparations: dug-outs for eight additional battalions, for example, had to be constructed at Anzac. The necessity to keep the Turks in the dark led to the employment of many Australians, even those who most deserved a proper rest like Pompey Elliott's battalion, on unpalatable night-time labouring chores.

After months of indecisive, static conflict and abundant death, horror, disease, lice, and grime, Pompey Elliott, like the Anzacs generally, welcomed the opportunity to participate in a bold break-out designed to end the deadlock at Gallipoli. But he was not at all enthusiastic about his battalion's allotted role. The main diversionary attack at Anzac was to be an assault on the Turkish positions on the 400 Plateau. This important feature comprised two lobes split by a valley known as Owen's Gully. The larger and more southerly lobe had been called Lone(some) Pine—because of the solitary tree then visible upon it—while its northerly neighbour had acquired the picturesque name of Johnston's Jolly. On 6 August the battalions of the 1st Brigade were to commence the offensive with a charge towards the Turks' stronghold at Lone Pine. The 6th Battalion was then to capture German Officers' Trench.

Meanwhile the 7th Battalion, in association with the 12th, was to be prepared to follow with a possible attack at Johnston's Jolly. Storming Lone Pine would be difficult enough for the battalions of the 1st Brigade; at Johnston's Jolly the Turkish defences were even stronger, the distance between the opposing trenches was greater, and the Turks would by then be thoroughly aware that a major offensive was under way. Elliott concluded that his men would be attacking a large number of securely entrenched and expectant Turks supported by machine-guns with three tiers of fire. The 7th Battalion was severely depleted, even after assimilating six separate contingents of reinforcements. Johnston's Jolly would clearly be a tough nut to crack. Others shared Elliott's misgivings. Birdwood had overruled objections from his chief staff officer, Brudenell White, and the divisional commander, General Walker, who felt an attack on Johnston's Jolly was tactically unnecessary and beyond the capacity of the units chosen to do it. They did not manage to persuade Birdwood to abandon it, but their views influenced him to make this part of the offensive provisional.

Elliott, then, had to proceed with the organisation of an attack he deplored, while keeping to himself his fervent hope that it would be cancelled. His pessimistic mood infected his welcoming address to the latest batch of reinforcements on the eve of the offensive. After minimal training they had been rushed to Anzac Cove, where they arrived in darkness, disembarked before dawn, and climbed up to their new abode. Ushering many of them up was their acting sergeant, Bill Dunstan, a 20-year-old Ballarat clerk with militia experience. He had joined the AIF back in Victoria only two months earlier, and there had been similarly meagre training for most of his comrades in the 6th Reinforcements of the 7th Battalion.

Raw and taut, gazing wide-eyed around their new surroundings in the dim, early morning light, they assembled nervously to hear pearls of wisdom from their famous colonel. Their introduction to this bulky figure with his comprehensively cropped hair was, to say the least, disconcerting. It was not just that he was an unlikely looking commander, 'dressed like a fifth rate tramp' with 'boots unlaced' and 'no visible rank'; what he told them in a brief blunt address made it abundantly clear they had a very bleak future indeed. He made them 'feel like worms', one affirmed. Another was struck by his assertion that within a couple of days they would probably be either in hospital or dead. Tubb, very familiar with his colonel's idiosyncrasies, described it as 'a characteristic speech', but Elliott was even more forthright than usual because he was convinced that attacking Johnston's Jolly would be absolute folly.

Many 7th stalwarts agreed. Lieutenant Gil Dyett, having returned to Australia to enlist after being in South Africa at the outbreak of the war, arrived at Anzac in June with the fifth batch of 7th Battalion reinforcements. On 6 August, a few hours before the offensive was to begin, he happened to receive an appetising array of preserved fruit and other foodstuffs from a comrade in Egypt. For anyone who had been at Anzac a week (let alone months), these were luxurious delicacies. Dyett invited Lieutenants Noel Edwards and 'Curly' Symons to join him in consuming them. Edwards, Bendigo's first enlister in the AIF, had been consistently impressive. Capable and courageous, irrepressible and inspirational, he looked after his platoon assiduously, and his men thought the world of him. Symons, a 26-year-old commercial traveller, had served with Elliott in the militia and, like Edwards, had enlisted in the 7th Battalion shortly after war was declared. As they hopped into Dyett's pears, cherries, and figs, the Bendigo-born trio discussed their prospects of surviving the proposed attack. Each felt that this would be his last meal; they would 'never see dear old Bendigo again'.

At 5.30pm on 6 August the men of the 1st AIF Brigade launched the Anzac offensive with a dramatic charge at Lone Pine. After fierce hand-to-hand fighting they succeeded in establishing themselves in the enemy trenches. It was a stirring spectacle for the onlookers awaiting their turn in the offensive. 'That charge will live for ever in history', enthused Elliott, who felt the 1st Brigade did 'magnificently'. That the Turks would strive to recapture their lost trenches was not just expected, it was fervently desired—the main aim of this Lone Pine assault was to draw the Turkish reserves in the Anzac zone into the fight, so that they would be unable to protect the heights of Hill 971 and Chunuk Bair from the advancing 4th AIF Brigade and New Zealanders. An hour after the battle began, Elliott was ordered to return bombs allocated to his battalion's attack. Subsequently he was asked to provide a company to help thwart an imminent counter-attack at Lone Pine, and he immediately dispatched B Company under Tubb. While Tubb and his men were on their way, Elliott was then requested to provide a further detachment, to assist the 6th Battalion's attempt to capture German Officers' Trench later that night. In view of this pruning of his battalion it was becoming less and less likely, Elliott felt, that the Johnston's Jolly attack would eventuate.

But preparations for it had to continue, just in case. Noel Edwards was busy nearly all night. He was in charge of a party of 60 men whose task was to deal with the plentiful barbed wire between the opposing trenches at the Jolly. They tackled the problem in two ways. Edwards and some of these men ventured bravely out into the open and hauled in as much wire as possible with rakes and grappling irons. Their alternative method involved the attachment of a blanket (folded for double thickness) to two pieces of wood, creating something resembling a wide stretcher for the men to place on the wire as they advanced across it. At 3.15am on 7 August Elliott was notified that a sufficient number of these 'blanket screens' had been constructed and stacked ready for use.

Shortly afterwards the 6th Battalion tried again to capture German Officers' Trench—at the insistence of White and Walker after the failure of its first attempt three hours earlier—but this gallant effort was equally unsuccessful. Like Elliott, his friend Bennett, the commander of the 6th, had been unimpressed by the task allotted to his battalion in the offensive. It was, he considered, conceptually flawed and too onerous. After his misgivings were vindicated by the failure of the initial attack, Bennett had been appalled by his superiors' insistence on a repetition. When that second attempt miscarried, and he was then told to try a third time, he exploded. His furious reaction was instrumental in the abandonment of any further ventures at German Officers'.

Equally unsuccessful were the diversionary attacks by dismounted AIF light-horsemen at Quinn's, Dead Man's Ridge, and the Nek. All these operations involved futile uphill charges in daylight across the open towards Turkish strongholds. Whereas commanders at Quinn's and Dead Man's, like Bennett, acted decisively to minimise losses once the futility of attacking there was confirmed, the assault at the Nek was pursued in the succession of brave but pointless attempts later immortalised in the film *Gallipoli*. Elliott claimed afterwards that his battalion's proposed attack at Johnston's Jolly would have been just as disastrous. He was very relieved when it was cancelled. 'We were saved from meeting the fate of the 8th and 10th Light Horse, who were practically exterminated attempting a similarly hopeless task', because 'we were urgently needed' elsewhere.

On the morning of 8 August he and his men were sent to Lone Pine. A battle had been raging there for almost two days. Flagging AIF units were trying to stave off repeated Turkish counter-attacks. Directed to the right of the Pine, where the inferno was fiercest, the 7th Battalion companies filed through a narrow communication tunnel connecting the old AIF front line to the newly established forward posts. Their destination resembled an excavated maze. It was honeycombed with trenches and traverses, bomb-stops and barricades. Some were incomplete; some had clearly been constructed very hastily; some were reinforced with protective overhead cover. It was 'like an underground city', wrote Elliott, with streets 'cut through criss-crossing everywhere'. Awaiting his men in this labyrinth were scenes of indescribable horror, which even the most callous veterans found hard to stomach. Cluttering the narrow pathways were dead and dying men from both sides in appalling numbers, lying two and three deep in some places. It was impossible to avoid walking on them. Compounding the assault on the senses and sensitivities of Elliott and his men were the revolting stench and deafening noise. The exhausted AIF survivors were so drained that Elliott was able to gain from them hardly any of the useful local information customarily transmitted during a relief.

Assessing the situation rapidly, Elliott arranged for the extension and improvement of existing trenches, ordered the construction of new ones, and distributed his men among the various posts under his control. From two of these posts, Elliott realised during his inspection, there was a good view of a Turkish communication trench some 400 yards away. Wally Fisher and other renowned 7th Battalion snipers were soon causing consternation along it. Perhaps in retaliation, a sharp bombardment opened up from a faraway Turkish battery; Fisher and other snipers were hit. This was an unnerving experience for the newest reinforcements, whose few days on Gallipoli had been a nightmare beyond their most terrible imaginings. Elliott reassured them personally, but the first of a series of almost continuous bombing attacks began soon afterwards. The Turks were determined to regain their former Lone Pine positions. Not only were they committed to recapturing any ground yielded as a general principle; they knew, and Elliott's snipers had just confirmed, that in this particular instance the loss of their positions had left considerable Turkish territory exposed and vulnerable. Moreover, they were still unaware that the attack at Lone Pine was essentially a feint.

This series of Turkish attacks continued with little respite for some 20 hours. They were pressed with particular intensity while the 7th Battalion was settling in that afternoon, and also from 7.00pm that evening. The most violent attack of all began as dawn was breaking and lasted for most of the morning. Elliott and his men endured a ghastly ordeal. They were vastly outnumbered, in terms of both men and bombs. Elliott's company commanders repeatedly called for more bombs, and Elliott himself made urgent requests to brigade headquarters. But the quantity available to the 7th, compared to their opponents' supply, was relatively small. Ferocious fighting continued hour after hour. The rising casualty toll further clogged the congested trenches, making it increasingly difficult to get ammunition forward. When bombs did materialise, the absence of the 7th Battalion's squad of trained bombers meant that specialists were not available to use them with maximum proficiency. Summoned to Lone Pine at 6.00pm on 7 August, the 7th's bombers had almost all become casualties before the core of the battalion arrived.

Elliott was again justifiably proud of his battalion. By this stage the men he was commanding were minimally trained newcomers or, if they had been at Gallipoli long enough to become capable veterans, were in most cases severely weakened by a combination of dysentery, overwork, and a monotonous diet. They were tired from lack of sleep before they even arrived at Lone Pine. Baking daytime heat further sapped their energy. They were subjected to rifle and machine-gun fire of such intensity, Elliott noted, that at its peak 'every periscope raised above the line of trenches was instantly smashed and even the bayonets were shattered by the hail of bullets'. Hordes of Turks kept coming at them, deluging them with bombs, which they either tried to stifle with sandbags or picked up—risking an explosion in their hands—and threw back at the enemy. Brave men were going down everywhere. As the survivors kept shooting and stabbing, smothering or hurling back the lethal hissing grenades, they could not avoid treading on their valiant comrades. Elliott 'had never experienced such fighting'. The strain on those remaining was immense as the gruesome carnage continued. They were sustained by their pride in themselves, their mates, and their cause, and by rumours that the offensive was going well elsewhere apart from the setbacks at German Officers' Trench.

Their courageous resistance was also profoundly influenced by their commander. Bean's wide-ranging observation of a multitude of units during the war convinced him that the quality of any unit was substantially attributable to the calibre of that unit's leadership. The way the 7th Battalion hung on at Lone Pine against overwhelming odds confirmed that Elliott had instilled into it his own indomitable staunchness. In this battle, a byword for savagery in the AIF, his men fought with tremendous courage and tenacity. It was as if they were collectively demonstrating with Pompey-like vehemence that they would keep defying the enemy as long as any of them remained able to do so. Elliott was there in person, embodying that attitude himself. Larger than life as usual when battle was joined, he encouraged, rallied, and exhorted his men, twice drawing his own revolver when a Turkish breakthrough seemed imminent. A man fighting alongside him was hit by a bullet that 'smashed his head like an egg shell'; Pompey was 'splashed from head to foot with [his] blood and brains', and was 'not exactly a pleasant sight'.

How best to allocate his men was a perplexing challenge. With overcrowding in the front trenches aggravating the congestion problems and increasing casualties (among Dyett's A Company recruits in particular), Elliott arranged for these trenches to be occupied as lightly as possible, with reserves nearby under whatever cover could be utilised. He had to respond to the Turks' threats to various posts under his command while contending with steadily mounting losses of officers and men. Reshuffling the dwindling forces at his disposal was like a continuous juggling act of increasing complexity.

> I had ... to try and keep everybody cool and steady and send reinforcements where needed, only just sufficient and no more so as to spin them out as long as possible, and when men came to me to implore me for bombs which I hadn't got and for reinforcements I could not spare (or they could not hold out) to tell them to go back and fight with bayonet and rifle until they were dead, and they did it.

While all this was occurring he also displayed subtlety and insight in dealing with the new arrivals. Some of them, not surprisingly, found the stress of this terrible battle beyond them:

> I had about 170 raw recruits shoved in just before the fight, most of these fought like demons but a few broke down. I found one fellow wandering about without a rifle, all trembling. I took him to a place which had a dark tunnel in it, and told him to watch that and if he moved an inch I would blow his brains out. It really led to our own lines and there wasn't a Turk anywhere near it, but he didn't know. After about an hour he got alright, and I sent him back to the fight. Another came back trembling all over so that he couldn't hold his rifle. I told him if he couldn't fight to fill sandbags. He went at it like a madman—you never saw a man work like him—but it pulled him round. Later I saw him fighting as well as the rest.

It was the vulnerable section of trench on the southern side of Elliott's sector known as Number 1 Post that caused him most concern. Initially in charge there was Dyett, but he was severely wounded soon after the Turks launched their most violent attack just before dawn on 9 August. Elliott sent Lieutenant Jack West (friend and former football team-mate of his brother George) to take over. After a while a bullet struck West in the forehead. Elliott saw him carried away against his will 'with a frightful gash on his head', struggling with the stretcher-bearers and shouting deliriously at the top of his voice: 'Bombs wanted! Bombs wanted! Tell the Colonel we can't hold it unless he sends bombs and reinforcements, bombs and reinforcements!'

Elliott then directed half a dozen men under Hal Young to Number 1 Post. On arrival there, Young found a redoubtable private, Castlemaine labourer Tim Shadbolt, holding up the Turkish attackers single-handedly. Young's party sprang to Shadbolt's aid, but the Turks' advantage in bombs was crucial. Within an hour all had become casualties, Young with three separate wounds and Shadbolt with a severe facial injury that ultimately cost him an eye. To retrieve the situation Elliott sent along Lieutenant Hec Bastin, an NCO in the original 7th who had now, reflecting Elliott's high regard for him, succeeded Grills as adjutant. Bastin led a charge which drove the enemy out of Number 1 Post, but his arm was severely wounded in the process. Like West, he did not want to be sent to hospital, but Elliott insisted. The colonel was then informed that the Turks had captured this post.

Having been impressed by the 'cheerful reports' throughout the night from Symons, who 'had kept his men well in hand and in great heart though suffering heavy losses also', Elliott decided to send him to Number 1. After receiving Elliott's summons, Symons left his posts in the care of a couple of capable corporals until Tubb arrived to take over. Elliott explained the situation to Symons, provided him with a party of ten men to lead, and directed him to retake Number 1. 'Goodbye Symons', he concluded, aware that every officer he had sent there had been badly hurt, 'I don't expect to see you again, but we must not lose that post'. Symons shook hands, saluted, and led his men away. He was immediately bowled over by an exploding bomb, which would have maimed him if a comrade had not managed to curb its impact by flinging a couple of sandbags on it just in time. Symons picked himself up and continued on his way to Number 1, where he and his men regained control of the post.

While Symons was retrieving the situation at Number 1, a tremendous struggle was under way 70 yards to the north at the post he had left. Inspired by Tubb's intrepid leadership, the meagre remnant there (reduced to less than a dozen) was hanging on tenaciously, though vastly outnumbered. Tubb had directed two men, Corporals Webb and Wright, to deal with the enemy bombs, either by throwing them back or smothering them with discarded Turkish overcoats. The rest of Tubb's men were at the parapet, blazing away with their rifles at the onrushing Turks. Tubb was actually above the parapet, shooting with his revolver, and his daring example induced similar bravery from his men:

> 'Good boy!' he shouted, slapping the back of one of them who by kneeling on the parapet had shot a sheltering Turk. As the same man said later: 'With him up there you couldn't think of getting your head down'.

Catching enemy bombs and throwing them back was, of course, a highly hazardous business. Wright was killed when one exploded in his face. Webb continued with this dangerous method until a bomb blew up in his hands, severing them both. He walked out of the Pine, but died shortly afterwards. Bombs in quick succession knocked out most of the others.

The only men still able to assist Tubb, now bleeding from several wounds, were Bill Dunstan, the recently arrived Ballarat clerk, and 22-year-old Alex Burton, one of the Euroa originals. The sandbag barricade safeguarding their position was blown up by Turkish bombers advancing along the trench towards them. With revolver fire Tubb repulsed these attackers, while Burton and Dunstan rebuilt the breastwork. The Turks wrecked it again, and attacked once more. Undeterred, the Victorians drove them away and re-erected the barrier. This process was repeated a third time, before an exploding bomb killed Burton and severely wounded Dunstan. Dazed but dauntless, Tubb obtained a few men from a nearby post to continue the fight, but the Turks decided to persevere there no longer. Tubb's survival, he himself acknowledged, was 'miraculous'.

Similar feats of gallantry occurred at other posts where the fighting was also desperate. Noel Edwards particularly distinguished himself during that long night, inspiring inexperienced recruits in his platoon with his bravery and encouragement. Afterwards one of them claimed that he 'deserved a VC if ever a man did'. With his premonition of imminent death stronger than ever, Edwards took advantage of a temporary lull in the fighting to write a cheery letter to his parents describing the meal he had shared with Dyett and Symons. The Turks launched another attack shortly afterwards. Edwards fought with reckless zeal, shooting at least eight Turks before an enemy bullet found him.

Early in the morning of 9 August the divisional commander, General Walker, having come forward to appraise the situation personally, told Elliott it was essential to keep the attacking Turks at bay. If necessary, Walker added, he and his staff would occupy the trenches themselves. Elliott assured him the 7th would hold on. Savage fighting continued all morning. It was not until about midday that the enemy attacks began to peter out. 'Hang on boys', Pompey called encouragingly, 'we've got them'. The 7th Battalion was relieved shortly afterwards, and trudged wearily out of the Pine. Observing the exhausted survivors as they passed, General Walker congratulated Elliott on their magnificent effort and assured him it would not be forgotten.

Such praise was well deserved, but the battalion had again lost heavily. According to documents found on dead Turkish soldiers, Elliott told Kate,

> we had over 3,000 Turks against us in those attacks. I never had more than 600 and finished with only about 200, but we held the trenches. Consequently the 7th and your old man would be apt to get swelled heads for all the nice things said about them. A staff officer told me yesterday that that attack was considered the most desperate battle that has taken place anywhere on the Peninsula.

However, 'you could have my share of all the glory of the battle', he declared sadly, in exchange for just 'one of the poor boys who died or was mangled to death there'. Symons, as D Company commander, led 150 men and four officers into Lone Pine. Next morning there were nine left. The inexperienced reinforcements who had arrived a few days earlier fared particularly badly; few of these lambs emerged unwounded from the slaughter. A 5th Battalion man who answered a call for volunteer bomb-throwers was sent to Lone Pine:

> the first person I seen was Pompey Elliott ... You could say anything to him in the line, but not a word out ... I said to him 'Where's this

> great 7th Battalion?'... He said 'You'll find them lad, they're in there, you'll find them as you go in'. They were in there all right, there was nobody alive. They'd blown the end of the trench down and enfiladed them. Dead Australians, all 7th Battalion.

Of all the officers hit, only one did not manage to survive—Noel Edwards, whose premonition sadly came true. Tubb was thrilled that his colonel was 'very pleased' with him, but it was a long time before he was fit enough to return. Bastin and Young did not rejoin the 7th for a good while either. West and Fisher never did. Nor did Dyett. Deafened, concussed, and with numerous other wounds (the most serious, in his back, inflicted spinal damage), Dyett was carried down to the beach, where his multiple injuries and lifelessness resulted in a blanket being reverently placed over him prior to burial until someone noticed him move.

General Walker was as good as his word. Before long he arranged for Major Gellibrand to ask Elliott which of his men had most contributed to the successful defence. Pompey, like his men, was worn out. Deciding which men to include in this list was 'a difficult task where so many had died doing their duty'. Of those he nominated, Symons, Tubb, Burton, and Dunstan eventually received the ultimate award, the Victoria Cross. A year earlier, when Tubb warned the young Euroa volunteers he had gathered to think carefully before signing the enlistment papers, and one of them asked why he was going, he had admitted he wanted to have a crack at a VC. Tubb and one of those recruits who heard his cautionary advice at Euroa had ended up winning that coveted medal together, with Burton's death in the process a poignant vindication of Tubb's warning.

The bomb that knocked Bill Dunstan out left him blinded for months, and the metal embedded in his head gave him severe headaches for the rest of his life. Before he enlisted he was keen on a Ballarat girl whose parents were snooty about their daughter's romance with a bootmaker's son. 'You can marry my daughter if you come back with the VC', the mother loftily told Dunstan. He did. (When his award was announced, it was sensational news in Dunstan's home city; his future mother-in-law heard the newsboys trumpeting the headline story—'Ballarat Hero Wins VC', they yelled—but she declined to buy a paper herself. 'Wouldn't be anyone I know', she reputedly sniffed.) West, Edwards, and others also deserved recognition, but four VCs to one battalion in a single action was, Elliott believed (mistakenly), unprecedented in British military history. Wright and Webb, along with two other NCOs, were awarded the DCM.

The fate of Webb seemed to symbolise for Elliott the 'horrible nightmare' of Lone Pine. 'Fancy seeing a man you knew blinded and with both hands blown off trying to get up on his feet'. One of Pompey's original Essendon boys, Webb had been (as his colonel knew) orphaned as a youngster. It was most distressing to watch him stagger towards the doctor with his 'bleeding shattered stumps held out in front of him'. Trying to describe what it was really like at Lone Pine was no easy task, but Elliott gave his lawyer friend Richardson a graphic glimpse:

> The weather was hot and the flies pestilential. When anyone speaks to you of the glory of war, picture to yourself a narrow line of trenches two and sometimes three deep with bodies (and think too of your best friends, for that is what these boys become by long association with you) mangled and torn beyond description by the bombs, and bloated and blackened by decay and crawling with maggots. Live amongst this for days ... This is war and such is glory —whatever the novelists may say.

The 7th Battalion's contribution at Lone Pine was outstanding. But the success the AIF achieved there—not only winning the battle, but drawing all available Turkish reserves into the fight—was not matched elsewhere in the August offensive. Monash's 4th AIF Brigade was unable to accomplish the extremely difficult task it had been given. The New Zealanders did manage to ascend Chunuk Bair, but their tenuous perch on the summit was lost when the British battalions relieving them were driven off by determined Turks in vastly superior numbers. Contrasting pointedly with the Anzacs' dash and determination was the languid British ineptitude at Suvla. The brigades involved in the Suvla shambles had a more difficult assignment than most Australians appreciated, but many AIF soldiers concluded after this fiasco that Britain's military prowess was decidedly overrated.

After a brief rest the 7th Battalion had to return to the Lone Pine trenches it had vacated 48 hours earlier. 'The sights were absolutely indescribable', wrote Elliott.

> The dead still lay and putrefied where they had fallen, and the first thing I did was to dig huge pits in the bottoms of the trenches and simply stack them in as they were. The poor fellows engaged in this awful work had to be fortified with liberal doses of rum to keep them going. It was splendid how they worked too. The sight and smell often made them retch and vomit but they kept on, and now the trenches are habitable and getting nearly as strong as our original position.

Having attended to that hideous problem, Elliott and his men were now free to concentrate on the Turkish soldiers opposite who were still alive. They were showing no inclination to resume their counter-attacks at Lone Pine, where the position captured by the Australians was gradually strengthened as the 7th and 1st Battalions alternated in 48-hour shifts. In the process, Elliott told Kate, 'we discovered quite a number of interesting points of view from which we could shoot Turks', and it was 'very amusing to watch them scatter'. Pompey interrupted one of his routine inspections to have a long-range shot himself. A private alongside, eager to please, was observing through a periscope. 'Got him, sir!' he shouted approvingly. Pompey was not conned by this transparent flattery. 'Got him be damned', he retorted, 'the bullet's not halfway there'.

As before, Elliott was striving to maintain strict discipline when it might have seemed tempting to relax his exacting standards temporarily. It was not an easy path to follow, 'yet by doing it I am keeping up the spirit and pride of the 7th in themselves'. Despite his reluctance to vary his rigorous approach, he was confident that his standing among his men remained high. As he put it, 'I don't think they'd swap me for any other Colonel about'. However, his battalion did have to adjust to a different commander. Within hours of writing those words to Kate he was feeling 'much off colour'. He resisted the doctor's verdict that he should be evacuated, but began to feel worse and worse. His temperature climbed to 102 degrees. Eventually, like Weddell, Grills, and countless others, he became too sick to carry on, and left Anzac on 28 August.

CHAPTER EIGHT

'Great and Fearful Responsibility': Evacuation and elevation

SEPTEMBER 1915–JUNE 1916

ELLIOTT DID NOT return for months. Pleurisy was diagnosed, and he was sent to England. He had severe 'pains all over', the 'bed clothes were wringing wet with perspiration', and 'one night I thought it was the end of things for I couldn't breathe lying down but had to sit up in bed all night'. During the voyage his diet was limited to Bovril and condensed milk. He became 'dreadfully thin' and 'terribly weak'. By the time the ship arrived at Devonport on 12 September he was over the worst, but he was hospitalised and kept under close observation. A medical board gave him two months' sick leave, and advised him to continue his gradual convalescence in London.

He spent his first night in London at Berners Hotel. Situated close to Oxford Street, near Soho, Berners provided accommodation of a good standard and was imbued with a certain stylishness, without aspiring to the stateliness of its most elite equivalents. Elliott enjoyed his stay. From then on, whenever staying overnight in London, he made a beeline for Berners. On 23 September he was transferred to Digswell Place, the grand Welwyn residence of Lieutenant-Colonel Percy Buckley, the principal military adviser on the Australian High Commissioner's staff. Elliott was overwhelmed. 'Most beautiful place I have ever seen', he enthused; his hosts were 'too kind for words'. Other Digswell Place convalescents included 7th Battalion officers he had not seen since the landing, Stan de Ravin and Jack Whitelaw. There was plenty of spirited reminiscing, especially when Mason and Tubb came up from London for a visit. Being with congenial companions in tranquil surroundings was a good recipe for recovery, but 'I seem to have lost all power of endurance', Elliott told Kate, frustrated that his former strength and stamina remained elusive for weeks.

But he was well enough to travel to the north-east in October. Since arriving in Britain he had been endeavouring to get in touch with his and Kate's relatives. After making contact with his father's brother Robert and receiving an invitation to stay, Harold spent a 'very pleasant' fortnight based at 'Dene House', Gateshead (near Newcastle) with his uncle and aunt and their children: 'though I never saw them before a week ago, it is as if I had known them all my life'. They showed him an old stone house that had been his grandparents' home over 60 years earlier. He took the opportunity to fit in a bit of sightseeing, including visits to Edinburgh and Durham, before journeying to Boston, Lincolnshire, to spend an enjoyable few days with another cousin, Nellie Peaston, and her family. As in Newcastle he was urged to stay longer, but he had tracked down some of his mother's relatives in Wales and was keen to meet them, too.

So he made his way to Trevor, a small town near Llangollen, to meet two sisters whose great-grandfather was Thomas Janverin, the naval officer in Nelson's Trafalgar fleet who was also Harold's great-grandfather. These new-found second cousins, Emily and Laura Edwards, had married a pair of brothers whose family had a successful tile-manufacturing business. Wary of manipulative imposters, they appraised this solidly built stranger in unfamiliar uniform with probing questions. Once they were convinced he was genuine, he was again deluged with kindness.

As Elliott discovered, the naval tradition had continued in this branch of Janverin descendants. The father of the sisters who met Harold at Trevor, J.F. Tottenham, had also been a captain in the British navy. His son, an admiral, was serving under Jellicoe in the North Sea. Emily and Laura showed Harold some genealogical treasures, including one letter dated 1690. There was also fascinating 1799 correspondence from their mutual great-grandfather, who had written with vivid frankness about his experiences with Lord Nelson's fleet and his chief's notorious relationship with Lady Emma Hamilton.

Elliott stayed with Emily Edwards, her husband, and daughter Pattie at their residence, Bryn Oerog, a comfortable two-storey house set in spacious grounds. Each evening a gong sounded at 6.45pm to remind everyone it was time to dress for dinner. The view from his bedroom window looked across an extensive garden to sheep and cattle grazing languidly; beyond, barges slowly meandered along a winding canal. Lone Pine seemed a long way away. Visiting all these relatives had proved very worthwhile, but it was 'a terrible rush round and I have felt tired at nights'. Although their bounteousness had ensured that the weight lost during his illness had well and truly reappeared, he had not yet regained his customary vitality. He was 'greatly constipated and suffering from piles'.

While grateful for the warm hospitality bestowed upon him, he suspected it was partly attributable to his rank.

> I have the feeling that if I had not been a 'Colonel' my welcome, except for my aunt (who is a darling) and my uncle who is a fine old chap, in all probability would not have been so hearty. But then one has no right to look a gift horse in the mouth.

Although he 'had a very pleasant time' in Britain, 'it wasn't home a bit'; he felt homesick for his own family, who 'know that I am a very ordinary sort of person but who love me all the same'. Many Australian soldiers did regard England as 'home', and felt thrilled about being there; Pompey Elliott was not one of them. The Suvla fiasco had been a disillusioning eye-opener for some Anzacs who had hitherto subscribed to an unwavering faith in all things English. To Elliott, it merely confirmed that there was no justification for having England and the English—especially its soldiers—on some lofty, exalted pedestal.

Pompey's disparagement of British units had already alienated one of his NCOs. Shortly after the horror of Lone Pine, English-born Ted Pinder overheard Pompey savagely denounce the British effort at Suvla. To Pinder, such sweeping vilification was monstrously unjust, and confirmed that Elliott had a fundamentally jaundiced perspective. It was not just that Elliott had been scathingly (and, to Pinder, offensively) critical of certain British formations during his Boer War address on the *Hororata* a year earlier. Pinder felt that anti-English prejudice was also evident in an incident in July 1915 involving Albert Tonks (who hailed from Birmingham) just after the harrowing stint at Steele's Post.

Tonks, trying like many 7ths to furnish himself with makeshift protection from the searing midsummer heat, had pulled his groundsheet over a small hole and utilised his bayonet to peg a corner of it. Pompey spotted this unorthodox use of a bayonet, and pounced. 'After roaring away in his usual fashion', Pinder recalled, Pompey concluded his diatribe with these words: 'Fine this man ten shillings, Sergeant-Major, and double it because he's a Pommy'. Pinder's account of this incident, though uncorroborated and written nearly half a century afterwards, has the ring of truth. Elliott was certainly prone to such outbursts, and Pinder dated it precisely at a time when Pompey was on the warpath so aggressively that even an admirer like Tubb was describing his behaviour as 'unjust and unreasonable'.

It was while Elliott was travelling around Britain meeting relatives that the award of the four Lone Pine VCs to the 7th Battalion became publicly known. Tubb and Symons, both then in England, were inundated with congratulations, and there were numerous jubilant messages for Pompey too. He was, of course, 'delighted that the boys got their VCs', and initially made light of the fact that he had been overlooked for an award himself, a surprising omission to many Australians aware of his contribution.

> When I think of some of those who have got honours lately and that I have been passed over I may feel envious, but when I think of what my boys have done and that it was I who trained them for it I am consoled ... I have had such a lot of letters from the boys, many of them crippled for life and not one complaining, but all glorying in having been one of the 7th. This to me is far above any personal award, for I got to feel for the Regiment and the men in it as I feel for you and my wee bairnies.

Pleasing reports in Kate's letters of his glowing reputation among returned 7ths—even though he had been a demanding disciplinarian—reinforced his confidence that 'their respect is genuine, and that is what I value more than any slab of the Alphabet that I can be given'.

'Your old man is not much of a hero', Pompey reflected. He was 'often pretty scared', but managed with determination and willpower to conceal his apprehension; his men thought he was fearless. His main concern was not fear of pain so much as the prospect of finding himself in a situation where he had to be responsible for an unavoidable order that would probably result in nearly all obeying it becoming casualties. At Lone Pine, when 'death seemed very near to us all', numerous 7ths said they could not hold their positions without more men and bombs:

> I told them to go back to their posts and die there, and they went, and were carried by me all torn and wounded a few minutes later. It was as if I actually placed those bodies, living and warm, like bricks to stem the torrent. But though I made them hold, still the decision did not rest with me. I had the order from the General to go there and hold the place to the last man, and we did it.

The possibility that he might have to be responsible for such an order himself filled him with dread.

It was impossible not to think about casualties. Still preoccupied with anguished thoughts about the first fortnight's toll, fine officers like Jimmy Johnston and the Hendersons in particular, Elliott was also dwelling on the more recent losses, notably Ken Walker:

> I suppose poor Lyn is very sad about Ken. I have been intending to write to her ever since, but feel somehow that I cannot. I think it would break me up completely if I met them. He was such a fine boy and they loved him so much, and he was fond of them too. And when I think of all these things I cannot write.

Homesickness did not help. There were times, he told Kate, when he reminisced wistfully about lolling on the family couch, his head in her lap, while she smiled fondly down at him and caressed his hair. Returning home would be marvellous, and would certainly have been possible 'had I chosen to make the most of my sickness as some are doing'. But that would be tantamount to shirking. Unthinkable, even though 'I want to kiss you all over'. Kate was putting on a brave face. She did all she could to be supportive. Her letters were an 'inspiration' to her husband. They did not dwell on her unceasing anxiety about him, which had impeded her recovery from her operation. She was glad Belle was still living with her and helping with the children; Harold was effusively grateful for his sister-in-law's contribution.

Elliott returned to Gallipoli on 7 December. With the 7th then in reserve, Geoff McCrae met him at the beach and accompanied him up to the battalion's bivouac. Not far away was the 22nd AIF Battalion. In that unit were two men Elliott was keen to catch up with, Corporal Jack Campbell (his brother-in-law) and Major Bob Smith. He found both fit and well. Smith, a tall, solidly built 34-year-old who worked in his family's wool-scouring business, had become a close friend while serving with Elliott in the militia. In August 1914 Smith was one of the first Elliott approached to become an officer in the 7th, but he declined because his wife was about to give birth. Campbell, a 37-year-old farmer and Kate's only surviving brother, was station manager of a property near Geraldton, Western Australia, when war was declared. He resigned that position to go to the war, but enlisted in Melbourne so he could spend time with his mother and sisters before leaving Australia. He had a cheery, affectionate, and responsive nature; Violet and Neil were particularly fond of their 'Uncle Jack'.

Conditions at Anzac had been transformed during Elliott's months away. Instead of oppressive heat and fierce fighting, the weather had become decidedly wintry, and each side was content to remain largely on the defensive. The long-suffering Anzacs now had to endure fierce blizzards and numbing iciness (though snow was a pleasing novelty for many of them). There were numerous cases of frostbite and exposure. Some men froze to death. At Suvla, where torrents of putrid water cascaded wildly along the trenches, there were even drownings.

This deteriorating weather reinforced the misgivings about the Gallipoli enterprise aired by some British strategists since the failure of the August offensive. The Turks would soon have at their disposal more heavy artillery than before, they contended, and it would be preferable to avoid the ordeal of winter at Gallipoli—when the weather would be an even more formidable enemy than Turkish soldiers—and deploy the British and allied forces more usefully elsewhere. This view had increasing adherents, despite the likelihood (accepted by both advocates and opponents of evacuation) that casualties in any withdrawal would be heavy. After prolonged consideration, the British government decided early in December to proceed with an evacuation.

Preliminary measures had been authorised by the handful of Gallipoli commanders aware that evacuation was being considered. With secrecy crucial, they pretended that these changes had been necessitated by the onset of winter conditions. Rumours began to circulate about a withdrawal, but not many soldiers believed them. When Pompey Elliott heard that Lord Kitchener had visited the Anzacs, including the 7th Battalion, his reaction was one of regret that he was unable to be present; he had no idea that Kitchener had come to assess the proposed withdrawal for himself. Even four days after Birdwood learned that the government had directed the evacuation to proceed, Elliott was still unaware. 'We have been told that we won't have much chance to write for some time after this', he told Kate only a week before the scheduled departure. 'I don't quite know what is in the wind'. Brigadier-General Monash, notified that afternoon, likened the impact of this 'stupendous and paralysing' news to 'a thunderbolt from a clear blue sky'.

Most Australians were stunned to learn that the whole force was to leave. Withdrawal essentially meant failure. Like everyone at Anzac, Pompey hated to admit that all the courage displayed, all the hardships endured and, in particular, all the lives lost had ultimately been in vain. The prospect of leaving dead mates behind was especially painful. Equally sobering was the probability of significant casualties during their departure. Since the evacuation would be a gradual withdrawal, obviously the last men to leave would be at most risk. Nevertheless officers in every unit were inundated with fervent pleas from men desperate to be in the rearguard. The principle governing selection was supposed to be suitability rather than insistent volunteering, but it was rumoured that Pompey had nominated himself, and perhaps his battalion as well, for a leading role. This is plausible. He developed something of a reputation for offering men under his command for difficult tasks. Both Elliott and his battalion did end up with important rearguard responsibilities.

Anzac and Suvla (but not, initially, Helles) were to be evacuated. From Anzac there were more than 40,000 men to be withdrawn. Some had already left. Under the scheme directed by Brudenell White there was to be a series of gradual daily withdrawals until about half the overall number had gone. The remainder, just over 20,000, would then be taken off over two successive nights. During this final phase, the climax of the operation, Elliott would become the rearguard commander of the right Anzac flank, while the 7th, as the 2nd Brigade's last remaining battalion, would be safeguarding to the very end an important sector near Lone Pine.

Secrecy was paramount. Elliott, characteristically treating his responsibilities with the utmost seriousness, impressed upon his men the crucial importance of keeping the Turks in the dark. He even ordered that anyone heard talking about the evacuation would be court-martialled. So when an inebriated private (who had managed to get hold of a jar of rum and sampled the contents) began trumpeting his delight that they were leaving, Pompey was immediately animated, and called for someone to silence him urgently. Nearby happened to be one of the 7th's originals, Harold Schuldt, a humane and popular corporal. He tried to obey his colonel's directive, but struggled to curb the rowdy drunkard. It was only after he resorted to a desperate, inexpert uppercut that he achieved the desired result (and dislocated a finger that was still misshapen half a century later).

Evacuation preparations were in full swing when an interesting device was brought to Elliott's notice. Its inventor, 20-year-old architectural modeller Bill Scurry, had only been at Gallipoli a few weeks, but was well known to Pompey, having served under him as a lieutenant in the Essendon Rifles. Assisted by his mate 'Bunty' Lawrence, who had attended the same school and church as Scurry and enlisted with him in the 7th Battalion's 8th Reinforcements, Scurry had designed a simple but ingenious apparatus for a self-firing rifle. Water in one container was allowed to drip gradually into another underneath, with the lower one attached to a rifle trigger; eventually the lower receptacle became sufficiently heavy with water to make the rifle fire. With every endeavour being directed to the organisation of a withdrawal unbeknown to the Turks, the potential usefulness of such a device was obvious—especially to Pompey, who had already told his officers and NCOs that if any mechanism could be devised to help deceive the Turks it might well prove invaluable. He was instrumental in arranging for the invention to be tested at Anzac headquarters. It worked, and the heads were impressed. Scurry and Lawrence were detached from other duties to manufacture a collection of these special rifles.

Tension mounted as the climax approached. The weather and the Turks had both been helpfully benign, but either could easily sabotage the carefully planned operation. After sunset on the scheduled penultimate day, 18 December, 10,200 soldiers departed (including a contingent of 206 7th Battalion men under Major Layh), leaving 10,000 to be evacuated on the final night. Because they were to leave at different stages, they were classified in three separate parties known as 'A', 'B', and 'C'. The 230 'A' party men in the 7th Battalion, like their counterparts in other units, were to begin leaving the trenches at dusk. Major McCrae was to follow with his 'B' party contingent, commencing at 9.35pm. At this stage Pompey Elliott would be moving to brigade headquarters (the brigadier having departed with the 'B' parties) to take over command on the right Anzac flank, which involved supervising the final withdrawal of 'C' parties from five different battalions as well as a small contingent from brigade headquarters. It would be a testing, nerve-racking assignment. Being as familiar with military history as anyone at Anzac, Elliott appreciated the danger with the utmost clarity. But he welcomed the challenge, and regarded his appointment as an honour. Not the least attractive feature was the implicit recognition of his potential for promotion.

He was intensely frustrated when an injury prevented him from playing his part fully. On 18 December he slipped and fell, wrenching his left ankle so severely that there was some concern he might have broken it. He tried to carry on, arranging for a makeshift crutch to be made so he could 'stick it out and stay with the boys to the end', but the following morning the brigadier insisted that he had to leave straightaway if he was unfit. At midday Pompey unwillingly left Gallipoli for the last time. 'It was very disappointing ... after I had made all the arrangements and everything was working beautifully'.

Nowhere in his wartime correspondence to Kate or anyone else, not even in the privacy of his diary, did he describe precisely what he was doing when he hurt his ankle. Long after his death 7th Battalion veterans provided corroborative accounts of what happened. In pre-war days Pompey had noted approvingly that both General Craufurd of Corunna fame (a particular hero of his) and the renowned Boer leader General de Wet had occasionally resorted to brutal summary punishment in order to maintain discipline. It was apparently in emulating them that Pompey injured himself. Coming across someone from the 8th Battalion who was, according to Elliott, committing some misdemeanour, Pompey delivered an impromptu reprimand. 'Go to buggery, I'm not in your 7th', was the quick retort. Enraged, Pompey sprang forward to deal forcibly with this insubordination. His impudent quarry darted away. Pompey set off in hot pursuit, but lost his footing and tumbled heavily down a steep bank.

So Pompey was absent on the momentous last night. Again the weather was propitious, the sea calm, and the enemy unsuspecting. As scheduled, the 'A' and 'B' contingents left the trenches in turn, and made their way along pre-arranged routes to the beach. Mettlesome 'C' parties, anxious but determined, remained thinly scattered along the trenches for several hours, knowing that their prospects of survival would be minimal if the Turks suddenly detected the withdrawal and attacked in strength. At around 2.00am the last 106 of the 7th Battalion began moving out. A dozen stalwarts under Major Jackson stayed on to cover their departure. This extraordinarily tense three-quarters of an hour seemed much longer. Eventually Jackson directed two of them, Scurry and Lawrence, to activate the self-firing rifles in their sector. This done, the gallant band then nervously descended to the beach.

It was a memorable walk. Strips of hessian covered their fixed bayonets to prevent any glittering in the moonlight. Like their comrades before them, they had layers of torn-up blanket under their boots to muffle the sound of tell-tale tramping. As they proceeded through murky tunnels, along vacated trenches, and past eerily empty dug-outs, the impulse to disobey orders and run was almost irresistible. They made it safely to the pier, where one of the last boats was waiting for them, and were soon on their way.

The whole operation, directed brilliantly by Brudenell White, was an astounding success. The withdrawal of the whole force with only two minor casualties was regarded as miraculous. There was tremendous jubilation in the AIF. But Pompey Elliott had mixed feelings. Although delighted that the evacuation had been such a triumph, he was back at Heliopolis hospital 'in the same old ward as last May' with another throbbing foot and an acute sense of frustration. Being unable to participate fully in something so conspicuously special was bad enough; that he had been prevented by a somewhat embarrassing incident made him feel worse. He was, like many Anzacs, amazed that success had been so complete. 'I still cannot understand how, unless their eyes were blinded, we could have eluded their vigilance, for in many places the trenches were only a few yards apart'.

Again he took weeks to recover. He had regular massage treatment in hospital, but 'whenever I attempt to walk the ankle seems to give way'. Not for the first time he was, he admitted, a 'very impatient' patient. Rejoining the 7th Battalion on 9 January, he was 'still lame' over a fortnight later. His ankle was uncooperatively slow to heal, but he managed to get about with it tightly strapped, using a horse whenever possible.

Elliott was reunited with his battalion at the AIF's new Egyptian base, Tel-el-Kebir. The 7th was being replenished by the influx of reinforcements and the return of sick or wounded veterans. As soldiers, however, many of these recruits were raw, and had to be licked into shape. So hundreds more Australians became familiar with Pompey's vigorous training methods. Like their comrades before them, they experienced the full repertoire—the intimidating demeanour, the bellicose roar, and the big black horse with a remarkable eye for parade misdemeanours—and duly accumulated their own collection of Pompey stories. As usual when he was on the warpath, onlookers not on the receiving end tended to find his tempestuous tirades amusing. Some, though, felt uncomfortable: roaring at his officers was inappropriate, they felt, in front of the rank and file.

Convinced that the 7th Battalion had been the most outstanding unit at Gallipoli, Colonel Elliott gave the assembled reinforcements a stirring account of its achievements, exhorting them to live up to this fine record. Wrongdoers could expect no leniency. When Pompey did not recognise an offender brought before him, he would usually ask if the culprit was an old 7th. If so, he received a stiff penalty because he 'should have known better'; if a new recruit, he would get the same punishment to ensure he knew better in future.

On one occasion the battalion was awaiting the order to fall in when an AIF general happened to pass by, and none of the nearest men saluted. Spotting this neglect, a 7th officer raced over and arbitrarily chose one of them to charge as an example. It was 'Bunty' Lawrence. Ordered to appear before the colonel, Lawrence found him 'seated in the mouth of a bell tent, looking as savage as a Jersey bull'. Pompey came straight to the point. 'Private Lawrence, charged with not saluting—how do you plead?' 'Not guilty, sir', replied Lawrence. The officer laying the charge outlined what had happened. Pompey turned back to Lawrence.

> 'Why didn't you salute?'
>
> 'Didn't see him, sir'.
>
> 'What fine do you consider necessary to make you remember to salute an officer when you see one?'
>
> 'No fine at all, sir'.
>
> 'Let me tell you a story. When I was at the Boer War I was only a lieutenant, and I went past a sentry and the sentry presented arms to me. I said "There's no need to present arms to me sentry, you

> only present arms to a major or above", and the sentry said "I knew that sir, but I was only practising". Now that's what you ought to do. You ought to salute your sergeant. And if you're not sure, salute anything that looks like an officer.'

As the colonel paused for a moment, Lawrence could not restrain himself: 'I often have to do that, sir', he interjected. Pompey was so enraged by this cheekiness that the tent seemed at imminent risk of collapse. 'Fined seven days' pay!' he bellowed.

Despite this intimidating purposefulness, Elliott was feeling 'sad and weary'. He was tired of all the browbeating and castigating he felt he had to do in order to maintain the battalion's efficiency, and bitter about promotions and awards in other units he thought undeserved: 'I get very much annoyed at times at the unfairness of it all'. In successive letters to Kate he relived Lone Pine in graphically grim detail: 'the trenches were full of dead men and blood and brains—I wonder will I ever be able to forget it all'.

> While I feel pretty well generally, I am not quite myself in that the least opposition excites me to great anger. I do my best to control it, but a man gave me a bit of cheek the other day and I nearly had a fit I think. I suppose it is a result of the strain and worry.

Receiving letters from Kate and Belle with news and photographs of the children did wonders for his morale, and a letter from England also helped. Its author, Major Weddell, described what had happened when Symons was presented with his VC. Ushered in to have a brief private chat with the King, Symons was asked about his regiment. The 7th Battalion had won four VCs already, Symons replied; it had suffered more casualties and done more fighting than any other at Anzac. Encouraged by the King's responsiveness, Symons went on to say that he could not understand why the colonel of a battalion with such a fine record, having been through so much of it and been wounded himself, had not even been mentioned in dispatches. The King summoned his secretary, asked him to note the name 'Colonel Elliott', and promised Symons he would inquire into this apparent oversight. Fancy Symons 'talking to the King like that', Elliott observed, 'it was good of him'.

Shortly afterwards Elliott learned he would be leaving the 7th

Battalion. On 15 February he was instructed to take command of the 1st AIF Brigade. Pompey arranged to have a stirring farewell message communicated to each member of the 7th. He would depart with 'the utmost regret', it began. Recalling the battalion's earliest days at Broadmeadows and its accomplishments since then,

> I can give you no greater praise than to assure you that you have fulfilled in every respect the expectations I then formed of you. You have cheerfully submitted to the severest discipline imposed on any regiment in the Australian army, recognising that it was imposed from no capricious desire for punishment, which is distasteful to me, but with the deliberate intention of making you the best regiment in the army.

While it would be 'boastful to assert that we have become the best regiment in the Australian army', the 'facts speak for themselves'. The 7th had sustained more casualties than any other battalion, he claimed, and its achievements and awards for gallantry were second to none.

> You have never yet failed to accomplish any task set you ... To each and all of you I tender my sincere thanks for the cheerful readiness with which you have always carried out my commands and wishes in the camp, in the trenches or on the field. I desire no better compliment, praise or reward. H.E. Elliott.

A comprehensive post-Gallipoli overhaul of the AIF had led to Elliott's promotion. Thousands of sick and wounded veterans were emerging from hospitals, and recruiting campaigns in Australia had produced abundant reinforcements. With the New Zealand force also enlarged, an Australasian army of two corps was created. The AIF, having previously contributed two infantry divisions and part of a third, would now provide five in this new Anzac army. Moreover, to conform with changes then occurring in the British army, a large number of new artillery and subsidiary units were simultaneously created. The architect of this massive reorganisation was Brudenell White.

Part of the process proved distressing. In order to spread the hard-won AIF experience around the expanded force, the sixteen battalions involved at Gallipoli from the outset were divided in two; half of each unit became the nucleus of a fresh battalion. After the split in Elliott's former unit, for example, half remained with the 7th and the other half was transferred to form the experienced core of the newly created 59th Battalion. Many veterans found this rupture painful. Elliott administered it sensitively. Long afterwards, one veteran recalled Pompey telling him that though he had been one of those earmarked for the 59th he could stay with his mates in the 7th if he wished. Elliott also acknowledged the widespread dismay in his farewell message:

> Though it will be hard for those named for transfer—as it is for me—to sever their connection with the 7th, I appeal to them to put their sentiments aside and firmly resolve to make the old 7th proud ... that the 59th Regiment sprang from this battalion. Let each regiment give a cheer when it meets the other in the field or on the march, and feel proud to know and recognise each other wherever they meet.

With new units being created, soldiers throughout the AIF were evaluating their options. One 7th stalwart who was considering a transfer to the Camel Corps asked a mate, an ex-jockey serving as Pompey's groom, to find out what his boss thought. A message from Pompey came back via the groom: a horse had only two ways of kicking, but a camel had seven. The inquirer decided to forget about a transfer.

Elliott was initially ill at ease as a brigadier, missing familiar faces and feeling daunted by his new role. 'It is a great and fearful responsibility', he wrote. Because the 1st Brigade men were all from New South Wales

> I don't know a single soul amongst them all ... I don't know who are the good ones and who cannot be trusted, and I am away from all my pals, and all these 4000 lives may depend on me—if I don't make up my mind what to do quickly enough, or if I make it up wrongly.

Pompey inherited the capable brigade staff assembled by his predecessor, Colonel Nevill Smyth VC. He appreciated their capacity and helpfulness, but was disappointed that they were all English:

> This always more or less riles me because it always hints at inferiority in Australians—that they are not good enough for these jobs. But still they are all nice boys, and there is nothing too great a trouble for them to do for me.

British officers had behaved before the landing as if 'they had no sort of use for us at all', but now, after the AIF had distinguished itself at Gallipoli, Egypt was 'just swarming with British officers eager for jobs with the Australians'.

The vacancy Elliott filled at 1st Brigade was created by Smyth's promotion. On 29 February Elliott learned that Smyth's elevation would no longer be going ahead. Smyth would be reverting to brigadier, and had asked for his previous command. In the circumstances Elliott accepted that Smyth was entitled to it. When Birdwood and White suggested the 14th Brigade as an alternative for Elliott, he replied that he would prefer the 15th if possible, since it was a Victorian brigade. This request was granted.

He was delighted. Besides being a Victorian unit, the 15th Brigade included the 59th Battalion, the offshoot of the 7th.

> I have Major Layh and all the other 7th boys who were sent over to the 59th Battn under my command again. I have the 57th, 58th, 59th and 60th Battalions, all Victorian and all old 2nd Brigade men. We will have to work very hard to knock things into shape, but I love the work with my own men.

With the 57th, 58th, and 60th similarly connected to their respective 'parent' battalions, the 5th, 6th, and 8th, Elliott's familiarity with those 2nd Brigade units would also be helpful in his new command. He began enthusiastically exploring ways to emulate in the 15th Brigade the territorial affiliation with Victorian districts that was, he felt, a success in the 7th Battalion.

His delight was short-lived. He took a dim view of the battalion commanders earmarked for his new brigade. Elliott's confidence in his ability to make discerning assessments when appointing subordinates had been reinforced by his pride and sense of vindication in the performance of the 7th Battalion officers he had chosen so carefully in

August 1914. He was satisfied with one of his battalion commanders, Cam Stewart, the former 5th Battalion adjutant now in charge of its offshoot, the 57th. But he was decidedly unimpressed with the other three. Command of the 58th had been given to solicitor C.R. Davies, previously second-in-command of the 28th Battalion. At the helm of the 59th was E. A. Harris, who had a farm in north-west Victoria near the selection where Elliott grew up, and had left Australia, like Davies, as part of the Second AIF Division. Appointed to the 60th was J.W.B. Field of the 8th Battalion, an experienced officer out of action since his severe head wound at Krithia. None of them, Elliott felt, was likely to provide the type of vigorous leadership and insistence on discipline that he desired in a battalion commander. He would be far more comfortable with competent officers he knew and had essentially trained himself, such as Bob Smith or Bert Layh—subordinates familiar with his methods and temperamental quirks.

Elliott's start with the 15th Brigade confirmed these impressions. At the 1st Brigade a cohesive staff ran things like clockwork, and he felt there was not much for him to do. Starting a brigade practically from scratch was altogether different. A machine-gun company was formed; a school of instruction established for officers and NCOs; a vigorous training program instituted for the rank and file. During this busy time Elliott became adamant about not wanting Davies, Harris, and Field. He decided to try to replace them with Smith, Layh, and the 40-year-old deputy commander of the 29th Battalion, Harry Duigan, another experienced officer who had served with Elliott in the militia. Pompey also concluded that he would prefer to do without several other officers he had been given: 'If only General White will support me ... I will feel happier with men I can fully trust and rely upon to keep discipline'.

His efforts to achieve his objectives included a visit to Bob Smith and applications to White and the Second Division commander, General Legge, seeking approval for Smith's transfer. His letter to White suggested that Smith could be exchanged for Harris:

> Please do what you can to help these arrangements to take immediate effect. The 59th Battalion under Layh and 57th under Stewart are progressing favourably, while the 60th and 58th are at a standstill owing to no officers coming forward to serve under them.

Approval from Brudenell White, however, was not forthcoming. The enlargement of the AIF was already complex enough without the additional complication of an urgent War Office request—in response to the massive German attack launched at Verdun on 21 February—to send Australian divisions to the Western Front as quickly as possible. Because the First and Second AIF Divisions had been earmarked for imminent transfer to France (rather than the Fifth, containing Elliott's brigade), White's main priority was to get them right. It was inevitable, White admitted, that in such an immense reorganisation some newly promoted officers would be slow to impress; if they were in units staying longer in Egypt, there was more scope to give them an extended trial.

Snatching a few moments during a hectically busy period for him, White dictated a letter to Elliott outlining his position. 'I would not for anything damp your enthusiasm, and ... I have the greatest sympathy for your territorial scheme', he began diplomatically,

> but instead of going at it "neck and crop", would it not have been wiser to *work towards* the territorial idea than to have attempted to get it at *one jump*? It seems to me that the result of your effort has been to disunite you from three of your battalion commanders, and this is not a happy start. One has always to bear in mind too that these fellows' reputations are in your hands and are of course just as precious to them as your own is to you. I am going into the whole thing to see what can be done and the General [ie, Birdwood] wishes to help you, but your precipitancy has not made it easy for us. I am sorry that it is not possible to give you carte blanche in the way you suggest ... to get men from other infantry battalions; as you know the 1st and 2nd Divisions are about to move, and their efficiency for the time being takes priority over yours ... you say that you will not countenance any blocking of transfers where it is clearly to the advancement of the applicant to obtain the appointment in question. May I suggest to you that the advancement of the applicant is a minor thing to the efficiency of the whole? All this sounds a little more of a rebuke than I actually intend, but I hope shortly to get a chance of talking it over with you as a friend. Do not rush into it too hard; such a reorganisation as we are attempting is unnatural enough, and nature dislikes sudden eruptions.

Elliott received a similar response from Legge. 'I sympathise very much with your desires, but am sorry to say they are not practicable under present circumstances', wrote the Second Division commander. He had 'already let a number of officers go', and 'making further changes' when they were about to depart was 'out of the question'.

Pompey regarded the denial of his request as an implicit reflection on his judgment, and he was appalled by the consequences for his brigade. White's letter, intended as a soothing mollifier, was like a red rag to a bull. Pompey was still livid when he compiled a spirited reply. It was not at all correct to suggest that

> I have allowed my preference for the territorial idea to cloud my judgment of men. Stewart of the 57th does not in the least belong to the territorial idea, but he is far and away the best man for the job he has, is doing it very excellently and I shall strongly recommend his confirmation in the position ... Rather than have an inefficient battalion commander although belonging to the territorial area, I would abandon the whole thing.

Elliott had asked a number of Western Australians about Davies, and 'the verdict was all the time unfavourable'. Moreover, Elliott doubted that a single commander in the brigade where Davies was best known would take him even as a second in command: 'Does this go for nothing?' As for Harris,

> I have been unable to find anyone whose opinion I value at all who thinks the least of Harris as a commander of men. Am I wrong in believing that you thoroughly agree? Major Coulter, 8th Battalion, who was left behind to instruct the 21st Battalion when they relieved the 8th Battalion at Steele's Post (and he is no very rigid disciplinarian himself) was so disgusted by the slackness and lack of discipline shown by the 21st Battalion when under Harris that he actually paraded him (Harris) before Brig-Gen Smyth, and Harris was soundly reprimanded ... Similarly with regard to Field. I have seen him at Mena carrying on outposts. It was a sight for the Gods. Even his old friend Colonel Bolton reported against him as a possible second in command. Field admitted as much to me the other day.

There was much more about Field, and a great deal about promotion policy:

> With regard to the question of transfers of officers injuring the efficiency of the whole, I contend that it will have the very opposite effect. Of what interest is it to a man to be earnest, zealous and untiring in his work if it will merely result in his battalion commander refusing to part with him. No doubt ... you yourself would be a brilliant adjutant and the salvation of a man like Field. The Division is the worse off because of your promotion, but is the efficiency of the whole not served by advancing you to your present position? Is this same argument not to be applicable to everyone then, or is it only to apply to the Staff? I tell you your argument is totally wrong if it involves this. Everyone who is worthy of it should be pushed on irrespective of the inconvenience it may cause the man who loses by the advancement.

The more he wrote, the more intemperate he became:

> The territorial idea was adopted not as an end in itself, but as a means of inspiring enthusiasm in men who feel just a little sore in being cast out of the fold of the old battalions. If I seemed to you to have pushed the idea hastily you were wrong; nothing, as you will now perhaps admit, has been recommended without the gravest consideration. The reputation of the men upon whom I have reported adversely may be sacred—to me, the lives of the men who may depend on them [are] more sacred still, and in two cases, viz Field and Harris, I fear greatly for those entrusted to them. But ... this matter lies with you for decision, and on your head be the blame if you find for any reason that you cannot follow my recommendations ... As I asked before, do you desire an efficient brigade or will any old thing do? ... I conscientiously believe my judgment of these men is just, and my recommendations are made in the sole interest of the efficiency of the force. Upon investigation you may conclude that my judgment is wrong ... then do your plain duty and relegate me to the 7th Battalion, to the Base, or to Australia as your conscientious judgment may determine is the right place for me. Reputation or no reputation, I ask no one to bear what I will not readily stand myself.

Birdwood was infuriated by this extraordinary letter—so angry (Elliott later learned) that he was inclined to accept the implicit invitation to send its author back to Australia. It was only after White demurred that Birdwood relented. Birdwood's reliance on White's capacity and judgment was already evident, and White knew Elliott much better than Birdwood did. The courage and awkward affability that Birdwood showed in his frequent visits to forward positions, combined with his shrewdness in self-promotion, had won him superficial popularity (although many Australian soldiers found 'Birdie's bull' increasingly irritating). But for a general of his eminence and reputation he had pronounced limitations. His grasp of administration, organisation, and tactics was ordinary; on his return from these sociable trips forward, he was unable to provide a reliable tactical appreciation of the position he had just visited. In fact, Birdwood was only able to make these outings and maintain his voluminous correspondence with highly placed politicians, soldiers, administrators, and other influential individuals because White, more self-effacing and less ambitious, was doing the bulk of the real work.

Whereas Elliott retained an overall respect for White's capacity (while vigorously disagreeing with some of White's decisions that affected him personally), he detected Birdwood's essential shallowness with commendable insight relatively quickly. It was preposterous, Pompey insisted, to suggest that 'I should hesitate to differ from him and tell him so. He ... has not handled Australians as long as I have, and has not studied them as I have done'. Pompey correctly suspected that Birdwood's primary motive in scheming to remain with the AIF was self-interest. He would not have been surprised to learn that Birdwood was equally assiduous in striving to prolong his (dependent) association with White.

That Birdwood regarded Elliott's conduct as inexplicably bizarre was underlined in one of his letters to George Pearce, who remained Australia's minister for Defence throughout the war. Birdwood told Pearce he would have to review his previous recommendation supporting Elliott's promotion:

> I am sorry to say he does not seem to have become at all well, and I am very doubtful as to whether it will be possible to confirm him, though I trust he may improve. He suddenly seems to have become a bull in a china shop, and has already put up the backs of three of

> his commanding officers. I have every sympathy with the territorial feeling as likely to produce esprit de corps, and for that reason it was that I put him to the 15th Victorian Brigade. He, however, apparently wishes to ride the territorial system to death, and because he happened to find officers commanding battalions who were not Victorians, he at once seemed to make a set against them, and reported upon them as useless.

Birdwood was repeating (presumably in ignorance?) the distortion of Elliott's motives that his forceful letter had sought to correct. Pompey had objected to the three battalion commanders because he felt they were incompetent rather than because they were not Victorians—two of them *were* Victorians! Also affecting Birdwood's perception of Elliott's performance early in 1916 were the reports that he and White were receiving from Elliott's immediate superior in his latest post, Brigadier-General G.G.H. Irving, who was filling in as interim commander of the Fifth AIF Division until McCay returned to Egypt to take up that appointment. Irving was an experienced administrator, but had never commanded soldiers in battle. Elliott 'drove Irving ... nearly wild', Birdwood told Pearce. From Elliott's viewpoint, however, Irving had been obnoxiously overbearing, 'giving himself considerable airs over me', and issuing directives and reprimands in 'things that I reckon he had nothing to do with in my Brigade'.

In Pompey's blistering letter he had invited White to check his specific allegation against Harris (that the 21st Battalion had been undisciplined at Steele's Post) with Smyth. It is unclear whether Birdwood or White ever followed this up, but Harris did approach Smyth about it. The upshot was that Smyth wrote to both Harris and Elliott denying the allegation. Elliott, not for the last time in controversy, had harmed his case by making damning assertions—based not on his own firsthand knowledge, but someone else's uncorroborated account—which proved to be inaccurate.

The controversy was revived when the Prince of Wales reviewed the 15th Brigade on 22 March. To Elliott, the 'pink-cheeked', 'very shy' 21-year-old prince looked about 16; they shook hands, and chatted briefly about boxing and football. Also in attendance was Brudenell White. He and Elliott had a spirited private discussion. According to Elliott's diary account, White conceded

> that he knew that one at least of the battalion commanders was no good, old Field, but said he must have a trial. May the Lord have mercy on the battalion.

White concluded, Elliott told Kate,

> by saying I would have to take them or leave myself ... I am sick and tired of the whole thing. They know that these men when they get into action are likely to ... mess things up and get their men uselessly slaughtered, but they say we must take them. Then of course if the 15th Brigade makes a failure I'll have to take the blame. It is a lovely prospect isn't it.

It was during this controversy that George Wieck joined Elliott as his senior staff officer. A 34-year-old Queenslander, Major Wieck was a full-time soldier of capacity and experience (including eventful Boer War service as an 18-year-old); Elliott was soon raving about his 'splendid Brigade Major'. Wieck, not overawed by Elliott's larger-than-life personality, was prepared to express opinions unpalatable to his chief. But on this issue he was sympathetic, concluding that AIF Headquarters knew or sensed that the three commanders in question were inadequate, but wanted proven incapacity before resolving to get rid of them. Elliott reluctantly accepted the situation:

> I had a talk with Field and Davies and Harris and told them my recommendations were not being followed and that I proposed to obey my orders ... and try and make a brigade out of this show, and pointed out that the lives of 1000 men hang upon each of them.

That same day McCay assumed command of the Fifth Division. Elliott was unenthusiastic: McCay was 'not a bit popular ... with either officers or men' because of his abrasiveness and reputation as a glory-hunter eager to risk infantry in rash enterprises. Pompey felt that this sweeping denunciation was excessive; although critical of McCay's grandstanding and bigheaded tendencies, he respected McCay as a soldier. McCay's arrival released Irving to take over command of the 14th Brigade. The remaining brigade in McCay's division, the 8th, had been formed in Australia under 49-year-old Edwin Tivey, the urbane stockbroker who was Elliott's squadron leader during the Boer War. But it was McCay's other brigadier who dominated Birdwood's initial briefing:

> I have told McCay of the difficulties I have had, and that I rely upon him to keep an eye on Elliott, and I hope make a good Brigadier of him, but that if he finds that impossible he will have to be replaced.

McCay summoned Elliott for a chat within hours of his arrival: 'had to endure more talking to re battalion commanders', Pompey noted wearily in his diary.

In this frustrated, aggrieved mood, Pompey's jaundiced attitude to the individuals imposed on him was very evident. J.D. Schroder was ordered to report with his section to the 15th Brigade. Arriving at 3.00am, he and his tired men did not attend the customary pre-breakfast session of physical jerks that morning.

> I was awakened from a very deep sleep by a roar which resembled that of a bull at large thirsting for gore. Standing in the doorway of the bell tent was a huge figure, riding breeches on, no leggings, boots unlaced, a flannel shirt with one brace over the shoulder and one dangling down the side. Not wishing to be outdone in the roaring line, I did a little myself, the result being that within five minutes I was sojourning in the guard-tent and my section was at physical jerks. Needless to say who our early morning visitor was. I was released later in the day by Major Wieck, and I realised that the tales of Pompey's exploits and discipline at Gallipoli had not been overrated.

Schroder was glad he did not incur Elliott's wrath regularly, as a certain 58th officer did. 'Call yourself a soldier,' Pompey would rant at this unfortunate, 'you're not even a wart on a soldier's arse!'

In another incident Elliott happened to be 'walking among his ragged veterans from Gallipoli, looking more like a butcher's offsider' than a brigadier, when several 'immaculately dressed reinforcement officers' approached, just arrived from Australia. Pompey was unimpressed. 'Don't want them' was his abrupt reaction. 'But, sir', a staff officer persisted, 'they are sent from Corps HQ.' Pompey was insistent: 'Send them back! Send them to Cairo! Send them to Hell!' Thrusting a thumb towards his rugged old hands nearby, he said 'I'll make my officers from those fellows'.

While all this was happening he had an unexpected visitor, General Walker. After congratulating Elliott on his promotion to brigadier, Walker volunteered that he had come especially because he felt he should apologise as a matter of honour for the outrageous ill-treatment Elliott had endured. Uppermost in his mind was his fervent promise to Elliott that the 7th Battalion's magnificent Lone Pine contribution would not be forgotten. He wanted to assure Elliott that he had kept his promise, submitting Elliott's name at or near the top of his award recommendations. By the time these awards were published, Walker continued, he was lying wounded in a London hospital, but he was so astounded by Elliott's omission that he insisted on getting up to make a personal protest to General Hamilton. Taken aback by Walker's sudden advent, Hamilton replied that Elliott's name had been deleted from the list before it reached him.

Elliott thanked Walker for taking the trouble to recount all this, and reassured him that the 7th Battalion's four VCs and numerous other awards were ample fulfilment of his promise. A professional soldier might believe a lack of recognition could affect his post-war career, Elliott pointed out, but this state of affairs did not apply to a solicitor like himself, so Walker need not worry about it any further. 'But it is an honour', Walker persisted. Pompey agreed that it certainly would have pleased his family.

Late in March Elliott went to Cairo to be initiated as a mason. In the AIF masons were prolific; he knew many himself. 'Nearly every officer of the original 7th was one', observed McCrae, 'and I found it an "open sesame" on the Peninsula'. Whatever Elliott made of the peculiar rituals of freemasonry, he was comfortable with its fundamental aims and ideals. He would have endorsed McCrae's private assessment that anyone able 'to keep all the precepts of Masonry ... would be a perfect man, unselfish, liberal and charitable'. The requirement of committed faith in a supreme being was no obstacle. After Elliott's elevation to brigadier, responsible for 4,000 men 'whose lives rest on my judgment', he began to 'feel sometimes I am the instrument of the Lord and doing his work in my own way to end this dreadful war'. The sectarian overtones of freemasonry were not uncongenial either. With sectarianism perniciously prevalent in Australia (though less so in the AIF), he had, like thousands of Australian Protestants, been infected with latent anti-Catholic prejudice.

After the First and Second AIF Divisions left for France, the divisions of the Second Anzac Corps had to safeguard the Suez Canal in their place. With most of the local trains transporting the departing divisions, Elliott learned late in March that his 15th was one of the unfortunate brigades required to make the move from Tel-el-Kebir on foot. Marching across the desert for some 35 miles with a meagre water ration would inevitably be a severe test. McCay queried the necessity for the march with the corps commander, Alexander Godley, a leader of mediocre ability and obnoxious personality. To Godley, it was an order from the Commander-in-Chief in Egypt, and that was that. McCay persevered, presenting his objection personally at British headquarters, but was told that rail transport was unavailable and the march had to be done. The Fifth Division's trek to its destination, Ferry Post, was broken into three stages, to be tackled a day at a time.

Irving and his 14th Brigade men set off first. They endured a terrible ordeal. Baked by intense heat, their water bottles soon empty and their feet blistering painfully in new boots, they sank into the heavy, burning sand up to their knees. A cloud of dust and flies added to their misery. The brigade disintegrated into a rabble. Men fell out all over the place. Many, delirious with thirst and exhaustion, were barely alive. Medical and other units were rushed to the rescue, and encountered scenes of dreadful suffering. There were reputedly a number of deaths.

Elliott's 15th Brigade followed two days behind. To minimise the ordeal he chose a different route after personally inspecting the various options and consulting officers familiar with them. He also adopted a different march timetable, arranging for short halts at regular intervals (and being sensibly flexible about them), together with a long break in the middle of the day when the heat was at its worst. A carefully selected rearguard attended to stragglers. During the march itself the driving force of his tempestuous leadership was more evident than ever, enriching the ever-growing fund of Pompey anecdotes. Probably his biggest challenge was to ensure that men overwhelmed with raging thirst did not drink the tempting but disease-ridden liquid in the adjacent sweetwater canal. Energised by his memory of the disastrous consequences of indiscriminate thirst-quenching during the Boer War and aware that he had to compensate for his battalion commanders' shortcomings in the enforcement of discipline, he roamed far and wide on his famous black horse, ranting and roaring. When one man

> gave me cheek and refused to fall in ... I drew my pistol and pointed it at his head and swore I would blow his brains out on the spot if he didn't obey orders. The pistol wasn't loaded, but I frowned at him and he concluded he'd better march.

Another man forgot the ban on smoking and unthinkingly lit a cigarette. Pompey pounced on this infringement immediately. 'Who lit that?' he bellowed. Having identified the offender, he added ominously 'I should shoot you'. 'If you shoot him, *I'll* shoot *you*', came a voice from the ranks, just as menacing. Its owner was arrested. Asked by Pompey afterwards for an explanation, he replied that he would respond like that to anyone intimidating his brother (the smoker). Pompey arranged for this private to be sent forthwith to a school for NCOs, reasoning that anyone who could stand up to him in full flight was a man of mettle with leadership potential.

Newly arrived units of engineers placed under his command for the march were totally ill-prepared for this gruelling experience. They became rebelliously uncooperative. With their own officers unable to control them, at one stage they responded to Elliott's exhortations with hoots, jeers, and insolent suggestions that he should get off his horse and carry a bloody pack himself. Pompey responded by riding right in among his most strident detractors, daring them to repeat this to his face. No-one did. He replaced the engineers' officers, and there was no further insubordination.

About 140 of the 3,348 men under Elliott's command fell out during the three days. But the rearguard played its part well (only four had to go to hospital), and the brigade marched into Ferry Post as a cohesive formation. It was, in the circumstances, an impressive achievement. McCay, apprehensive after the disastrous precedent of Irving's brigade, bestowed lavish praise on Elliott and his men.

But the drama was not yet over. Elliott and his thirsty men had been told that water would be ready for them when they arrived. But they found no water available at Ferry Post. Elliott complained to McCay. It was coming, McCay repeated. When it had still failed to materialise hours later, Pompey issued a vigorous protest. It was outrageous to deprive men of water in the desert, he thundered, and their understandable fury could escalate into mutiny. He threatened to march them back across the Suez Canal to Ismailia in order to get them a drink. After further late-night inquiries he was assured that the precious liquid would be available at 5.30 the following morning.

Up at five o'clock, Pompey found 'men were actually licking the taps to moisten their lips, and many of them had been sleepless all night from the torments of thirst'. Half an hour later no water had transpired. Pompey galloped away in search of the local chief engineer in charge of the pumps. This man deflected Elliott's wrath by explaining that the Egyptians did not provide him with enough water for the soldiers in camp, and he was under strict orders anyway not to start the pumps before eight o'clock because the noise interrupted the slumbers of General Godley and his Corps staff.

Remounting his horse, Pompey raced off to Corps headquarters. There he eventually 'unearthed a young pink-faced British staff officer clad in blue silk pyjamas, who came out yawning and looking very cross at being thus unceremoniously disturbed from his slumbers'. Pompey's message was blunt. After tersely outlining the position, he told the staff officer that if the water was not turned on in five minutes he would be marching his men to Godley's headquarters to tell the Corps commander precisely how they felt about the situation. If there was any problem about obtaining the cooperation of the Egyptian civil authorities, he would be delighted to provide a firing squad to deal with them. Immediately galvanised, the staff officer issued the necessary directives, telephoned the chief engineer to instruct him to start the pumps, and the water was flowing within Pompey's stipulated deadline. Afterwards Elliott was unapologetic but philosophical when McCay warned him that a repetition of such conduct was bound to get him into trouble.

Another Fifth Division brigadier was in real trouble. McCay concluded that Irving's defective arrangements had been primarily responsible for the 14th Brigade's disastrous failure. Irving was sacked, and sent home to Australia. Birdwood's correspondence suggests that as far he was concerned the biggest blot on Irving's performance was not the ordeal endured by 14th Brigade footsloggers during the march, but the fact that their distressing experience prompted them to give Irving a spiritedly hostile demonstration shortly afterwards at a time when the Prince of Wales happened also to be present. Elliott was no admirer of

Irving and gathered that his leadership during the march had been undistinguished, but still felt sympathetic: 'We should never have been ordered to do the march at all in weather like that without water carts, and yet he was blamed for its failure'.

A week after the desert march Elliott received a letter from a stranger. Rose Taylor was wondering whether her 'very dear brother' Fred Wright, killed at Lone Pine, was the Corporal Wright of the 7th Battalion mentioned (according to the newspapers) in one of General Hamilton's despatches. She also asked 'if you could let me know any particulars of his death'. Her only other brother had been 'missing' at Gallipoli since May:

> it is hard to bear, but it would be harder still to have had them stay at home when King and duty called them. I do not say that we do not suffer because we do. My mother is … a widow 61 years of age, and it is a severe blow to her, but oh I am as proud of my mother as of my boys, she is as brave and true as they were.

A clergyman brought news of Fred's death. Her mother wavered momentarily, crying 'My son, my son', then

> drawing her hands over her eyes which were blinded with tears said your mother will be as brave as you were my son, just as though she was speaking to him, and quoted that beautiful passage of scripture that … fits our fallen men so well, greater love hath no man than this that he gaveth his life for his friends. I felt so small and mean at the side of her, and realised that she was a mother worthy of the soldier sons she had lost. I do not know why I have told you all this unless it is to let you know that while our boys are playing the game the women they leave behind will all do the same.

That scripture passage was more apt than she knew. As Pompey outlined in his reply, Fred Wright was in Tubb's heroic group at one of the most vulnerable Lone Pine posts, protecting his comrades by smothering Turkish bombs or catching them and throwing them back, until one exploded at the wrong time and killed him. Writing again to thank Pompey for his reply, Rose Taylor said she had 'spoken to so many of your old Boys', and the way they talk about their commander would make him 'a very proud man indeed'. There was more. 'My mother wishes me to add that an old woman's prayers follow you wherever you may go.'

In May Elliott received another moving letter from Australia, this time from Katie Roberts, the wife of his legal partner. She had read some of Elliott's letters to various Melbourne friends and had been in contact with Kate Elliott. Sensing General Elliott was severely run down, Katie Roberts decided to send him 'a little bit of a lecture' (as she described it) about taking more care of himself. 'We all at this end appreciate the absolutely magnificent work that you have done and are doing', she wrote, but to deny essential respite to a 'military genius' who was 'invaluable to our Empire' would be folly. 'If you have headaches and are always tired might that not be a proof to you' that it was time for a spell, she urged. 'For the sake of our Empire ... for the sake of your dear little wife ... and for the sake of your beautiful children—Give to yourself the justice you would insist on being given to other people'. Admitting that such a pep talk was 'extremely bold of me', she went on to assure him that his 'kind and thoughtful' letter to the bereaved parents of Cedric Permezel was 'genuine balm to those bruised hearts'.

> We can gather from what you say something of what you have had to endure, and we get a glimpse of what the awful sacrifice of so many bright young lives has meant to you. I do wish it was possible to let you know how much real deep and genuine affection goes out to you from so many hearts at this end. It would be a help to you, if such a brave true soul ever needs human help.

Elliott was touched. 'It was a very nice letter', he acknowledged.

In fact, his health and morale had improved considerably since the gloomy February phase that Katie Roberts was counteracting. This improved mood had much to do with the progress he felt the 15th Brigade had made under his exacting leadership. It was a tough slog, especially on outpost duty in the desert where hot windstorms left everything covered in sand. 'I have had to work hard ... but I have got my own Brigade pretty nearly as good as the old 7th used to be', he reported proudly in May. His tendency to identify himself wholeheartedly with his unit was no less apparent as a brigadier. Ever mindful of comparisons with counterpart units, Elliott was pleased when he concluded that the 15th Brigade was outperforming the other brigades in the Fifth Division, Tivey's 8th and the 14th under its new commander, 42-year-old railway administrator Harold Pope. Of course, he was especially delighted when his brigade's merit was confirmed by his superiors. He was now feeling more appreciated by them. McCay, Godley, and the Commander-in-Chief of the British forces in Egypt inspected the brigade on 11 May and were most complimentary.

Elliott was feeling much happier about the calibre of the 15th Brigade's officers. 'I am gradually, just as I have always endeavoured to do, building up round me a very fine lot of young officers', he told Kate; he was 'getting rid of the useless ones' wherever possible. Andrew Morrow, whose prominent Ballarat family Elliott knew well, was 'doing very excellent work' in the 59th Battalion. Majors A.J.S. Hutchinson and Tom Elliott (no relation), both talented Duntroon graduates of outstanding promise, had been specially recruited by Pompey from the Light Horse. Doing well in the 60th were two lieutenants who had arrived in Egypt with a reinforcements batch in January, 27-year-old Maffra farmer Tom Kerr and 21-year-old university student Dave Doyle.

He would have liked more ex-7th officers in the 15th, but was delighted that three originals were among them. With the 57th was Charles Denehy, the schoolteacher with a literary bent and impressive twirling moustache, who had been severely wounded at the landing. Rejoining the 7th in September, he was in charge of one of the last parties at the evacuation. Pompey's satisfaction with Bert Layh's transfer to the 59th at the helm of its ex-7th component had been vindicated by his competent, vigorous leadership since. And Pompey was especially pleased that Geoff McCrae had accepted his request to join the 60th. Wounded twice at Gallipoli, McCrae contracted paratyphoid fever after the evacuation and was almost invalided to Australia. After a protracted recovery he joined the 60th as second-in-command in mid-May. 'He is a great favourite with everybody, officers and men', Elliott enthused.

Pompey's growing contentment was reflected in his appearance. 'People tell me I look ever so much better', he reassured Kate, 'quite as young looking' as before the Gallipoli landing. 'The only difference I myself can detect is that my hair is much greyer than when I left you'. His buoyant frame of mind was unshaken by a recurrence of his ankle trouble and a painful new injury, a cracked collarbone sustained after his horse tripped and fell at full gallop. For a while he was limping around with an arm in a sling, but remained on duty. He had even become grudgingly reconciled to the presence of the three unwanted battalion commanders, although he repeatedly railed in private about how much more he could have achieved with the brigade if he had competent commanders instead of those 'old fossils' (Field was 51 and Davies 45, but Harris was 36 and two years younger than Elliott!).

In mid-May, during a week of extreme heat, Field became severely ill and was sent to hospital. 'I am sorry for him', noted the brigadier, 'yet if he only will not come back it would be the greatest possible blessing to the Battn and the Brigade'. His wish was granted: Field was invalided back to Australia. To replace him as commander of the 60th Battalion, Elliott applied for Duigan to be transferred from Tivey's brigade. In the meantime McCrae took over as acting commander. Under his leadership the 60th, Elliott noticed, quickly improved.

Elliott was hardly likely to invite Field to contact his family back in Melbourne, but he did encourage a number of his returning men to do so. Some visited Kate, as did relatives of men who had served under her husband. One of these callers was the mother of Les Blick, the 7th lieutenant killed at the landing; she gave Kate a photo of her son. Elliott was pleased. 'He was a splendid boy Katie, everyone in the regiment officers and men seemed to love him'. The first anniversary of Anzac Day shortly afterwards was commemorated with ceremonies in Australia (and Egypt, France, and England) and long lists of In Memoriam notices, which became a sad feature of newspapers during the war years and afterwards. Among them were tributes to Lieutenant Leslie Colin Blick containing touching allusions to 'little Leslie', the son he never knew.

Fond references to his offspring continued to be a regular refrain in Elliott's frequent letters to his family. He repeatedly urged Kate and Belle to tell him all about their activities—'I am so sorry to be missing all their little children's ways'—and he cherished the photographs of them he received from time to time. 'I am eagerly looking forward to more snapshots', he told Kate in May. 'They are just about keeping me alive'. He was tickled pink to learn that three-year-old Neil had startled Kate by approaching a uniformed stranger on a Melbourne tram for an impromptu conversation because, Neil later explained, of the small 'wed-and-bown' coloured shoulder patch identifying this soldier as a 7th Battalion man. Others sensed Elliott's intense attachment to his children. Brigadier-General Tivey, now his equal after being his squadron commander in South Africa, had (perhaps because of this) a somewhat uneasy relationship with Pompey during the Great War, but when they were together Tivey knew he could generate a convivial atmosphere by talking about Elliott's children.

Early in June it became evident that the move to France that Elliott and his men had been anticipating for weeks was at last going to happen. During their last few days in Egypt Pompey's satisfaction with the development of his brigade was repeatedly reinforced. After an inspection of the various Fifth Division transport units, McCay told Elliott that 'the turn-out of the 15th Brigade was the best in the Division'. McCay's senior staff officer, Lieutenant-Colonel C.M. Wagstaff, had already described the 15th Brigade's progress, considering it had only existed for three months, as 'marvellous'. Then, just before their departure, another of the brigadier's unwanted 'old fossils', Colonel Davies, became seriously ill. The brigade had to leave without him. Elliott's response was similar to his reaction to Field's illness: 'I hope the old chap doesn't come back for the sake of his regiment, but apart from that I wish him no harm'. Davies, like Field, never returned to the 15th Brigade. All these developments were positive portents for Pompey, reaffirming his confidence that his brigade—and its commander—were ready to play their part in the struggle against the formidable German army in the principal theatre of conflict, the Western Front.

CHAPTER NINE

'The Slaughter Was Dreadful': The battle of Fromelles

JUNE–JULY 1916

THE JOURNEY FROM Egypt to the Western Front was a memorable experience. Leaving the heat and endless desert sands behind them, the Australians enjoyed a tranquil Mediterranean voyage followed by an enchanting trip through southern France at its midsummer finest. As their trains transported them northwards, the Anzacs were enraptured by the beauty of the countryside and the warmth of the welcome they received along the way (not least from attractive French girls, who were presented with spontaneous gifts of bully-beef and other tokens of endearment). For the Australians this glimpse of France represented real civilisation, a stirring glimpse of the world they had come so far to protect from the depredations of German Kultur. Brigadier-General Elliott was impressed: 'The weather at present is perfect and the country is something glorious, so wonderfully fertile, and the people are very kind and nice'.

On 27 June Elliott arrived at his allotted brigade headquarters in the locality of Steenbecque. Situated about 20 miles west of Armentières, Steenbecque was 'a lovely little village some distance behind the firing line though near enough to hear the guns'. He was billeted in the house of a local doctor named Brunet. Docteur Brunet and his elder son Jean were away with the French forces, but Madame Brunet and the rest of her family—stepdaughters Maximiliene and Marie Therese, and son Pierre—had remained at Steenbecque. At first Elliott found the Brunets shy and withdrawn. The language barrier was a problem, but he and Madame Brunet did their best,

> I with my broken French and she with her broken English. You would die laughing to hear us, but we can manage to get hold of every word of each other's meaning ... sometimes we get stuck, and we have to get out the family dictionary to find out what the other is talking about.

Elliott helped to break the ice by showing the Brunets some recent photos of his own children. Madame Brunet became 'quite excited over them, and wanted to know their names and all about them'. The thaw continued, with Maximiliene playing the piano and singing for Elliott and his officers. Before long the brigadier and the Brunets were getting along famously.

Their friendship spoke volumes for their assessment of him. The Brunet women were wary about having strange men staying in their house; the behaviour of some British soldiers at Steenbecque had been, Pompey gathered, undistinguished. Elliott's scrupulous moral propriety ensured he would not be a candidate for what some of his men called horizontal refreshment, but he knew of course that many in his brigade had amorous inclinations and would find women willing to accommodate them. The inevitability of mutual dalliance was one thing, but intimidating coercion was quite another:

> when we were placing the men in the different houses I was always very careful to tell them that if the men ever annoyed them in the least to come and tell me at once and I would punish them very severely, and one lady nearly cried and said thank you very very much indeed ... Her husband is away at the war and she seemed sad to have to take the men into her house, and quite brightened up after I spoke to her.

Being billeted with local inhabitants well within earshot of the guns was just one of the adjustments the Australians had to make. The tremendous power of the guns themselves was another. Elliott's battalion had endured harrowing shellfire at Steele's Post, but the terrain and restricted ammunition supplies limited the impact of artillery at Anzac. It was a different story at the Western Front. 'There was a terrific bombardment about dusk last night', Elliott noted in his first Steenbecque letter, 'it seemed to make the house tremble'.

On 4 July, when he and Wieck were driven forward in a motor car (a novelty in itself after Gallipoli) for their first glimpse of the quiet sector three miles south of Armentières that the 15th Brigade would soon be taking over, other differences quickly became apparent. Fortification methods were altogether different. Because deep digging in these flat, marshy fields of northern France produced shallow, waterlogged ditches instead of the solid trenches and tunnels familiar to Anzac veterans, walls of earth and sandbags had been erected to form a parapet and parados, with a raised wooden track (made of 'duckboards') in between for soldiers to walk along. They were not really trenches at all, but passages between elevated barricades. The thickness of the front rampart was being considerably extended, but the vulnerability of these barricades to shellfire was disturbingly obvious. However, the construction of small tramways to transport food and stores, the ready availability of water (piped forward), the provision of steel helmets and gas masks, and the supply of vital necessities such as sandbags, timber, flares, and maps together with bombs and ammunition in quantities that were the stuff of dreams at Gallipoli, did reflect a certain sophistication, reinforcing the Australians' perception that they were now at the main arena.

In mid-1916 Britain had 55 infantry (and five cavalry) divisions in France. Among these 55 were eight Dominion divisions, half of them Australian. With allied formations (predominantly French), they opposed the mighty German army along a meandering scar snaking across Europe from northern Switzerland to the North Sea. The shape of that line had hardly changed in 20 months, despite all the attempted advances and all the hideous carnage since October 1914.

When Elliott and his brigade arrived at the Western Front there were two major offensives affecting the strategic situation. The French were preoccupied by the relentless pressure still being exerted by the Germans at Verdun (about 170 miles south-east of Steenbecque) four months after they had launched the massive assault there that had prompted senior British strategists to press for some, at least, of the AIF divisions to be transferred to France as soon as possible. The British countered with an immense thrust at the Somme. Progress was slow and casualties colossal—57,470 British soldiers were killed or wounded on the first day of the offensive—but the disappointing results were

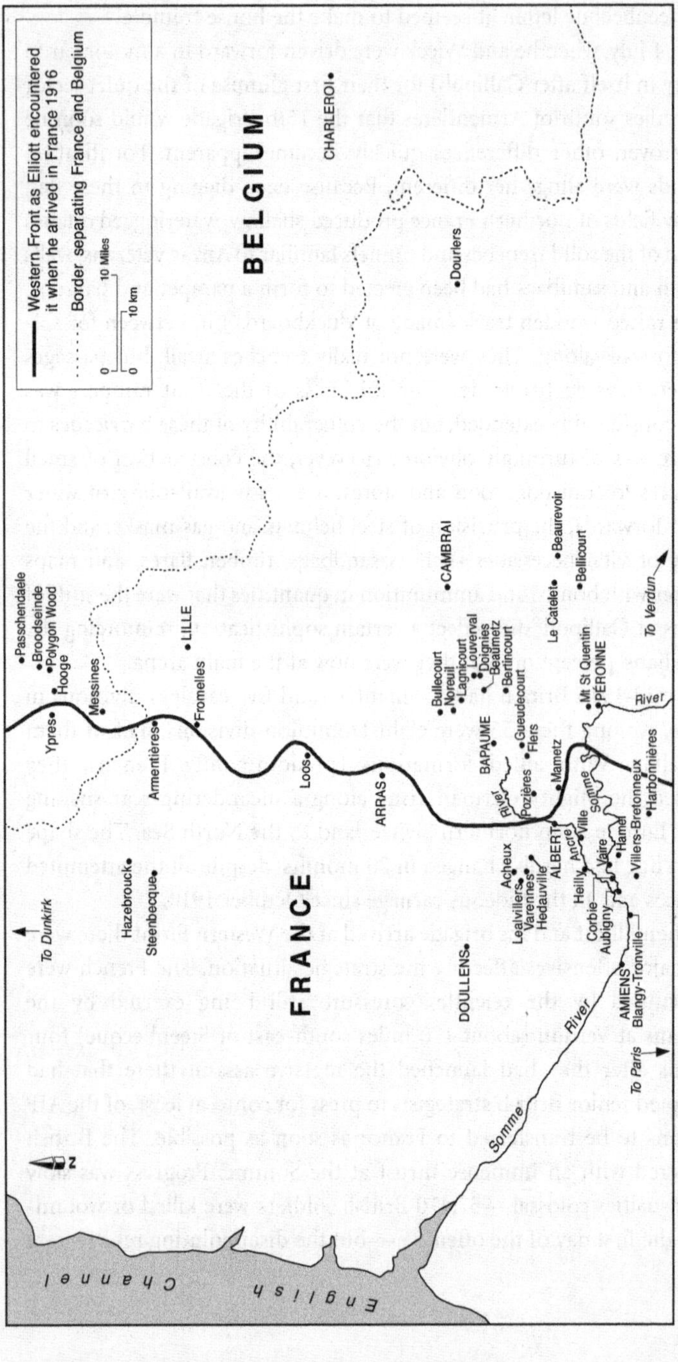
Western Front as Elliott encountered it when he arrived in France 1916
Border separating France and Belgium
0 10 Miles
0 10 km
BELGIUM
FRANCE
English Channel
N
To Dunkirk
To Paris
To Verdun
CHARLEROI
Dourlers
Passchendaele
Broodseinde
Polygon Wood
Hooge
Ypres
Messines
Armentières
Fromelles
LILLE
Hazebrouck
Steenbecque
Loos
ARRAS
DOULLENS
CAMBRAI
Beaurevoir
Bellicourt
Le Catelet
Bullecourt
Noreuil
Lagnicourt
Louverval
Doignies
Beaumetz
Bertincourt
Gueudecourt
Flers
BAPAUME
Mametz
Pozières
Mt St Quentin
PÉRONNE
Harbonnières
Villers-Bretonneux
Hamel
Vaire
Ville
Acheux
Lealvillers
Varennes
Hedauville
ALBERT
Heilly
Corbie
Aubigny
AMIENS
Blangy-Tronville
Ancre
River
Somme
Somme River

The Western Front: places of significance to Elliott

masked by distorted reports full of optimism.

A week after the launch of the Somme offensive the Fifth AIF Division was ordered forward to make its front-line début. The men of the 15th Brigade had been put through a supervised initiation to real gas; this demonstration of the effectiveness of their gas masks was a prudent confidence-booster. On 8 July Elliott farewelled the Brunets, and his brigade began a testing route march towards the front.

Elliott was satisfied it was ready. He was delighted with his staff. Wieck was a 'splendid' brigade major. The staff captain, 20-year-old R.G. Legge, a nephew of the commander of the Second AIF Division, had distinguished himself at both Duntroon and Gallipoli. Legge was 'a good little chap for work', wrote Pompey, but 'over fond of the girls when he gets a chance'. Not that the brigadier was complaining: Wieck and Legge were 'a wonderful help', and 'seem to think of everything'. Geoff McCrae, having led the 60th superbly since Field's departure, was confirmed as that battalion's commander. Command of the 58th, vacant after Davies's illness, had gone to Elliott's former deputy in the 7th, Alf Jackson. Pompey still had misgivings about his other 'old fossil', Harris of the 59th, but was convinced the brigade was in fine shape. Though not complacent—he knew that he and his men had much to learn about this new environment—he felt confident the 15th was well prepared after its months of instruction and arduous training for its first taste of trench warfare.

Other well-placed observers agreed. Birdwood, predictably impressed with Tivey's polished style and agreeable manner—such a contrast to Pompey's uncompromising forthrightness—visited the Fifth Division shortly after its arrival, and wrote to Pearce afterwards:

> Tivey has arrived with his Brigade, and I must say he always strikes me most favourably. I mentioned this to McCay, saying that I presumed that he regarded Tivey as his best Brigadier, and rather to my astonishment he told me that he could not say he considered this to be the case at present.

Birdwood's astonishment stemmed not just from McCay's revelation that Tivey was not his best brigadier. It was surely McCay's opinion that Elliott was entitled to that particular accolade that really startled Birdwood. The fact that Birdwood hid this from Pearce suggests he was still aggrieved about Pompey's strident objection to the 'old fossil' battalion commanders four months earlier.

At 6.00am on 12 July General Elliott formally took charge of the 15th Brigade's portion of the front. After all his years of earnest endeavour to equip himself to be a first-rate soldier, he was now in command of more than a mile of the British line in the biggest war there had ever been. It could have been a proud moment, but he was far too busy to indulge in such reflections. The 15th Brigade had been allotted the western third of the Fifth Division's front, which faced southward towards the village of Fromelles in German-occupied territory. In this sector the width of no-man's-land between the respective forward trenches varied considerably, but it was at its widest opposite Elliott's brigade, extending to more than 400 yards in places. It was a customary initiation in a quiet part of the line; only twice since the stabilisation of the Western Front had there been fierce fighting near Fromelles. Elliott and his men began familiarising themselves with their new surroundings, accumulating and assimilating knowledge about the techniques and procedures of trench warfare European-style, as well as the special requirements of their particular sector. They had scarcely begun when Elliott had some stunning news to digest.

On 13 July McCay was notified that the Fifth Division would be participating in an imminent full-scale assault on the German lines. The origins of this extraordinary decision were essentially twofold—the failure of the Somme offensive to live up to expectations, and the delusions of a British corps commander, Lieutenant-General Sir Richard Haking. Information had reached the Commander-in-Chief, General Sir Douglas Haig, that the Germans were transferring men to the Somme in order to reinforce their hard-pressed defenders there. British strategists were impressed by the idea of a demonstration or subsidiary show of strength at some suitable spot elsewhere. If the Germans could be induced to wonder whether a major new offensive might follow, they would have second thoughts about moving units to the Somme.

Haking, like Hunter-Weston of Krithia infamy, was one of the pernicious incompetents who managed astonishing ascents in the British army during the Great War. A product of the exclusive Staff College (where he cemented his crucial friendship with Haig), Haking had expounded his unqualified faith in the merits of an ultra-offensive approach in several books on military tactics before 1914. According to

Haking, even if a defending force was stronger than the unit attacking it, the attackers 'will win as sure as there is a sun in the heavens'. The absurdity of such nonsense in an era dominated by heavy artillery, machine-guns, and barbed wire was starkly exposed by wartime experience. Remarkably, Haking's philosophy did not change, although he was himself implicated in a number of comprehensive reverses.

Even more remarkably, he kept getting promoted. Beginning the war as a brigadier, he was given a division in 1914, and was further elevated to the command of XI Corps by September 1915, when he was involved with Haig in the catastrophic debacle of Loos. Afterwards, the mutual support of Haig and Haking not only enabled them to avoid blame for this fiasco; it was instrumental in Haig's promotion to Commander-in-Chief in December.

A close observer of Haking during this period was the senior staff officer of the 46th British Division, Lieutenant-Colonel P.W. Game. He was to become a household name in Australia as Governor of New South Wales when he dismissed Premier Jack Lang in 1932 after protracted, selfless consideration (in contrast to Sir John Kerr's premature ambush in 1975). It remains a striking insight into Haking's character that someone of Game's integrity and reliability should depict him in December 1915 as 'a vindictive bully'. There was more: two months later, Game described Haking as 'really impossible, untruthful and a bully and not to be trusted'.

The crucial factor in the complex sequence of events leading up to the decision to launch an attack at Fromelles in July 1916, the solitary constant among the fog of high-placed indecisiveness, was Haking's vigorous advocacy. The 'planning' before the battle was a shambles. Most of the main players were distracted by their focus on the momentous Somme action to the south. There was uncertainty about whether there should be just an artillery demonstration, or a combined onslaught involving infantry and artillery (and, if so, which units should undertake it), or no operation at all. But Haking, who had been advocating an assault in the Fromelles area for weeks, brushed aside the waverers and the sceptics. So keen was he to make the attack as substantial as he could get away with that he proposed to push on to the Aubers Ridge, the higher ground behind the German lines that provided excellent observation of British positions. (Haking 'was always very keen to take the Aubers Ridge', a British brigade major then in XI Corps recalled drily, 'and always told us if we behaved ourselves we should be allowed to attack it'.) But Haig refused to countenance the idea of transforming a limited feint into a grandiose attempt to capture the Aubers Ridge.

Haking should have been deterred by his familiarity with alarming precedents. In May 1915 he was involved in an ambitious attempt to seize that very ridge. The assault completely failed, and there were 11,619 British casualties. A subsequent bid to capture the Aubers Ridge, launched to assist the battle of Loos, resulted in another emphatic failure. And most recently of all—only a few weeks earlier, while Pompey Elliott was settling in at Steenbecque—Haking himself directed a venture closely resembling the operation proposed for the 15th AIF Brigade.

This took place at a salient in the German line two miles away known as the Boar's Head. The aim was to deliver a feint attack in order to deter the enemy from transferring reserves from this normally quiet sector to the Somme. Two Sussex battalions of the 39th Division carried out the attack. A participant later wrote that with 40 divisions concentrated on the Somme it was 'absurd' to expect the Germans to be duped by an incursion of merely two battalions: 'the conception of the attack was so futile that nothing but failure could have resulted'. The date of the operation was altered several times, the shooting of the gunners allotted the task of destroying the enemy's concrete gun-emplacements was 'shockingly bad', and the Germans had a good view of the rushed British preparations, so the attack came as no surprise to them. 'Come on Sussex', they called contemptuously as they confronted the attackers with a 'prompt, severe and accurate' bombardment and withering machine-gun fire. Some Sussex infantrymen managed to penetrate the German lines temporarily, but were overwhelmed by the fire concentrated upon them. The attack had to be abandoned.

British casualties (1,153 killed, wounded, and missing) were very heavy considering the numbers engaged. Haking nevertheless concluded that 'as a raid' the operation was 'highly successful' and 'greatly improved the fighting value' of the 39th Division. Failure at Boar's Head was hardly the divisional commander's fault, but he was sacked while the real culprit remained. There was another British corps commander who tried, unjustifiably, to attribute responsibility for a 1915 reverse to one of his divisional commanders, and initiated steps to sack him; this corps commander narrowly escaped dismissal himself. Haking's conduct a year later was similarly reprehensible, but there was no condemnation or day of reckoning for him.

Pompey Elliott knew nothing of this Boar's Head engagement as he threw himself into the hectic preparations for the Fromelles fight. There were a thousand and one things to think about. Under the plan the Fifth AIF Division was to join the 61st Division of Haking's XI Corps in a combined attack towards a salient in the German line as it curved around a prominent strongpoint known as the Sugarloaf, an elevated concrete bastion bristling with machine-guns. The 15th Brigade, being stationed on the western third of the Fifth Division's front, would be in the centre of the attack, with Pope's 14th AIF Brigade on its left and the 184th British Brigade on its right. Even apart from the ominous Boar's Head parallels, it was a decidedly ambitious undertaking. Both infantry divisions were very inexperienced. The fact that the formidable Sugarloaf was situated opposite the divisional boundary separating the Fifth AIF from the British 61st meant that sound co-ordination between these divisions was an even higher priority than it would otherwise have been.

Most significant of all was the haste of the preparations. The minimal time allowed prevented this work from being done exclusively at night, a grave handicap when the Germans enjoyed such superb observation. From their Aubers Ridge vantage point they could study the increased daytime activity and see the supplies being rushed forward, and they drew the obvious conclusion. Moreover, the effort involved in toiling round the clock to bring up thousands of bombs and large quantities of different types of ammunition, as well as all the essential rations, wire, picks, shovels, tins of water, engineers' stores, ladders (for parapet scaling), and various other necessities, ensured that the men would be anything but fresh when the attack was launched. Godley, who would be lending the Fifth AIF Division to Haking for the operation, had no qualms about any of this. Neither he nor his (all-British) staff raised any queries. Objecting to proposed undertakings that were unjustifiably risky or demanding for the men under his command was evidently not in his repertoire.

As for McCay, he was delighted that his formation, the last of the four AIF divisions in France to arrive, would be the first to be used in a major operation. Elliott felt that McCay allowed his satisfaction with this development to override his perception of the difficulties:

> if I had been in McCay's position [I] would have protested about having to attack such a position ... Not that it would have done much good, I suppose, because the move was ordered from [above], but McCay was terribly anxious that it shouldn't be stopped and made no mention of the difficulties facing us.

He wanted to lead 'the first Australians to have a big fight in France, and so get a big splash'.

The artillery's role would be crucial. The fundamental problem British strategists had been grappling with ever since the Western Front became deadlocked was how to get their own men across no-man's-land and installed in enemy positions and beyond. In mid-1916 a viable solution was still eluding them, although appropriate artillery protection was clearly part of the answer. Adapting to novel conditions of war was not easy, admittedly, but whatever tolerance might have been due to the military planners has been swamped ever since by revulsion at the dreadful loss of life that ensued because senior British commanders were such slow learners, unable to absorb the lessons of failed offensives such as Neuve Chapelle, Aubers Ridge, and Loos. Progress was being made, but it was very gradual. An innovation—sending the infantry forward close behind a protective mobile screen of shellfire (the 'creeping barrage')—was beginning to attract adherents.

Essentially, however, artillery techniques had changed little since the start of the war. Gunners still went through their customary process of conducting a kind of practice shooting session at designated targets. This 'registration' was observed by an artillery officer sent forward for the purpose, who had to assess whether his battery's shells were hitting the particular trench or strongpoint allotted to it. When he was satisfied that the target was located, the appropriate ranges, elevations, and strengths of charge used by each gun were recorded, and the guns became silent until they resumed firing, with these readings reset, when the bombardment began in earnest.

There were several flaws in this process. Fog, mist or other unsuitable weather conditions could prevent the forward observation officer from discerning where the shells were actually landing. Even if he believed they were on target he was sometimes mistaken. Weather changes between prior registration and the bombardment proper could subvert accuracy. Besides, the guns themselves were not, at this stage of artillery evolution, precision instruments. Dozens of shells fired from a particular gun, even if settings and weather conditions remained unchanged, would not land in the same spot. Accurate shooting was also impaired by the varying quality of the shells.

It was no easy task, then, even for seasoned gunners, to provide the infantrymen with the support they desperately needed, and the artillery arrangements for Haking's Fromelles attack made the attackers' already onerous task more difficult still. For a start, the gunners of most of the batteries allotted to the operation had even less experience than their infantry comrades. Among the formations lent for the engagement to supplement the guns of the attacking divisions were the batteries of the Fourth AIF Division. Back in Egypt the artillery brigades of both the Fourth and Fifth Divisions had been gutted in March to enable the First and Second Divisions to hasten to France in an appropriate state of readiness. Recruitment, organisation, and training in the denuded batteries had to start afresh, and the effects of their disrupted development were still evident in July.

The significance of this inexperience—the gunners of the British 61st Division were also new to France—was heightened by the frantic haste of the preparations. Registration was rushed, inevitably, with adverse consequences for the gunners' accuracy, precisely when the infantry was relying on them to quell recognised strongpoints such as the Sugarloaf. At the time, recalled the staff captain of the British brigade attacking on the far right, the artillery program seemed 'ludicrously inadequate' for the task of dealing effectively with objectives like concrete machine-gun emplacements. 'Hopelessly insufficient artillery both in numbers and training', concurred an officer on the 61st Division staff.

Pompey Elliott's concerns about the operation were reinforced by the artillery's inexperience and also by his consultation with the British brigadier whose men would be attacking alongside the 15th Brigade. Brigadier-General C.H.P. Carter was an experienced 52-year-old career soldier of pronounced limitations. It was presumably no coincidence that he had not been given a field command in this war until May 1916. According to a senior officer in his brigade, Carter 'demonstrated daily his ignorance of the requirements of war'. Gruff, awkward, and uninspiring, he had a peculiar obsession with signs. Elliott was disturbed to learn that Carter was intending to send his men out through openings in the front-line breastwork known as sally-ports (a directive to this effect had emanated from Haking).

The disastrous experience of the 6th AIF Battalion at German Officers' Trench a year earlier had left many Australian leaders disenchanted with this method. It was all too easy, Elliott told Carter, for a sally-port to become clogged. As soon as a few men were hit near the opening, the narrow passage to it would become completely blocked, and confusion and failure would inevitably result. Carter replied that he was prepared to give sally-ports a try, and if Elliott's advice proved correct he would simply send the men over the parapet instead, as Elliott recommended. But that was no consolation to Pompey, who felt that attempting such a change of plan in the middle of a battle was asking for trouble. It would certainly not be as straightforward as Carter seemed to think.

With Pompey's pessimism about the operation growing, he learned that a staff officer from Haig's headquarters (GHQ) had travelled up from the Somme to see how the preparations were progressing. He persuaded this visitor, Major H.C.L. Howard, to accompany him forward. Elliott and Wieck gave Howard a guided tour of the front line, and took him to a spot in no-man's-land affording a useful view of the Sugarloaf and the ground the 15th Brigade had to traverse. Pompey explained his intention to position some of his brigade's machine-guns in the gap between his right and the British left opposite the Sugarloaf. If the British emerging from their sally-ports did not manage to keep up with his men alongside, and the 15th Brigade's right flank became exposed, at least these machine-guns would be positioned to provide covering fire. Howard vigorously approved. Elliott showed Howard the orders he had prepared, and asked his companion if there were any improvements he could suggest. Howard could not offer any.

On their way back to brigade headquarters Pompey told Wieck to keep going, and drew Howard aside for a private word. He produced a pamphlet he had been given containing the accumulated wisdom of two years of trench warfare, quoted its recommendation that no attack should be made where the width of no-man's-land exceeded 200 yards, and reminded Howard that his own brigade had to cover at least twice that distance before reaching the German front line. Acknowledging that he had only been at the Western Front a few days, Pompey gave Howard his frank assessment: the attack had no hope of success. What then, he added, 'man to man and strictly between ourselves', was Howard's assessment?

Howard was visibly moved. He replied with equal frankness that he expected it would be 'a bloody holocaust'. Pompey then urged him to go straight back to Haig and say so. Howard promised that he would.

Elliott never saw Howard again, but it seems that Howard's (in effect, Pompey's) representations to Haig influenced GHQ to appraise Haking's proposed attack more rigorously. Haig indicated that he did not want the attack to proceed unless there was definitely enough artillery and ammunition to enable the enemy trenches to be captured and consolidated. Further conferences ensued. The army commander between Haig and Haking in the military hierarchy, General Monro, was ambivalent. But Haking was adamant, insisting that the resources at his disposal were clearly sufficient and he was absolutely confident of success. Moreover, the infantry were 'worked up to it' and so 'ready and anxious to do it' that any backtracking would be bad for morale. In fact, as Pompey Elliott knew, Haking was spouting absurd nonsense. When heavy rain and mist prevented the attack from taking place on 17 July as scheduled, there was intense relief among those who were to carry it out. Preparations had been so rushed that the men of both infantry divisions were practically exhausted.

'I confess I have very great doubts as to whether the attack can be a success', Elliott admitted before learning of the postponement. He was still concerned that his men had too much ground to cover in crossing no-man's-land. Besides, they were 'pretty well worn out'; the whole affair had been far too 'hastily improvised'. Postponement was a relief, but daunting difficulties remained. Guns had been 'rushed into position' with insufficient time allowed for registration, Pompey noted. There were 'not nearly enough communication trenches to prevent congestion', and 'if they are blocked up there will be hopeless confusion'.

General Monro's qualms about the operation prompted him to make a last-minute attempt to have it cancelled altogether. But Haking's blustering optimism prevailed. The weather cleared, and the attack was fixed for 19 July. Disaster loomed with a terrible inevitability.

It was to be a strictly limited operation. Two battalions only from each brigade were to advance; no further units were to be committed without Haking's authorisation. Elliott's initial intention was to use the 57th and 58th, the battalions of his brigade most familiar with front-line conditions and the ground to be covered in the assault. After the postponement, however, he changed his mind. The men were exhausted after the hectic preparations, and part of the 58th had been caught by a severe burst of enemy shellfire:

> My poor boys are getting pretty badly knocked about … Poor fellows, some of them were dreadful sights after the bombardment … I saw one huge hole made by a shell … 15 feet deep and about the same square. So you may judge what a man is like when one of these hits him. About 20 we could not find at all.

There were, Elliott discovered, other problems in the 58th. The trenches it vacated were left 'in a filthy state', confirming that disappointing 'slackness' had developed in that battalion. Alf Jackson, Elliott's old friend and colleague, had taken over command of the 58th twelve days earlier. Jackson had been wounded in three places when leading the Essendon boys at the Gallipoli landing; later, in Pompey's absence, he had been acting commander of the 7th Battalion. Despite this record and their long association, Pompey had declined to recommend Jackson to succeed him as commander of the 7th because he felt that Jackson's leadership had deteriorated. The reason became starkly apparent when Pompey became aware the day before Jackson was due to lead the 58th into action that he could dice with death no longer. The prospect of having to place his life at grave risk once more had reduced him to a 'nervous wreck', unable to face the ordeal without resorting to copious consumption of rum. Elliott had Jackson replaced straightaway. Hastily transferred from the 57th to lead the 58th was another of Pompey's ex-7th originals, Major Denehy.

The 57th and 58th, then, were replaced as the 15th Brigade's assaulting battalions by the 59th (led by E.A. Harris, with Layh as second-in-command) and the 60th (commanded by McCrae, with Tom Elliott as his deputy). In fact, Tom Elliott was not then with the 60th. Pompey, convinced that the 21-year-old major had uniquely outstanding potential and could become an Australian Kitchener, wanted to keep him out of such a perilous and probably pointless engagement, and seconded him to brigade headquarters as Wieck's assistant. With the 60th about to enter the front trenches for the first time, McCrae implored the brigadier to return him. McCrae had concluded (like many others) that his deputy was 'a real military Genius' who would, he assured Pompey, be invaluable with all the organisational arrangements. 'Elliott himself was anxious to go', wrote Pompey, 'so at last with great reluctance I let him go'.

Sentimental thoughts of home and family dominated the hearts and minds of many 15th Brigade soldiers during the last hours before the attack. Pompey was no exception:

> I am writing this in the morning and about 6 o'clock this evening we will start a battle. Nothing like what is going on down on the Somme, but in other wars it would be a very considerable battle indeed. I have taken every precaution that I can think of to help my boys along, and am now awaiting the signal which will launch so many of my poor boys to their death. They are all eagerly awaiting the signal, and we hope to so pound the enemy's trenches that we won't have much loss at all ... I am going up to watch the assault from our front line. I cannot stay away back here. If mischance comes I can only say God bless and keep you my own dear little true wife and helpmate and [may] our little sweet pets comfort you always ... My will is in the safe at the office.

Geoff McCrae wrote a lyrical letter to his family:

> Today I lead my Battalion in an assault on the German lines and I pray God I may come through alright and bring honour to our name. If not, I will at least have laid down my life for you and my country which is the greatest privilege one can ask for. Farewell, dear people, the hour approacheth.

Tom Elliott penned a brief note to his 'darling sister':

> Just a line to let you know all well ... Some operations are pending so must cut this short ... Don't worry about me, I'll be alright.

Each of the attacking battalions was to advance in four waves. After their departure the front line was to be occupied by part of the designated 'third battalion' in each brigade, the companies concerned having moved forward for this purpose from the support position known as the '300 yards line'. These companies were also to assist the assaulting battalions by providing digging and carrying parties as required.

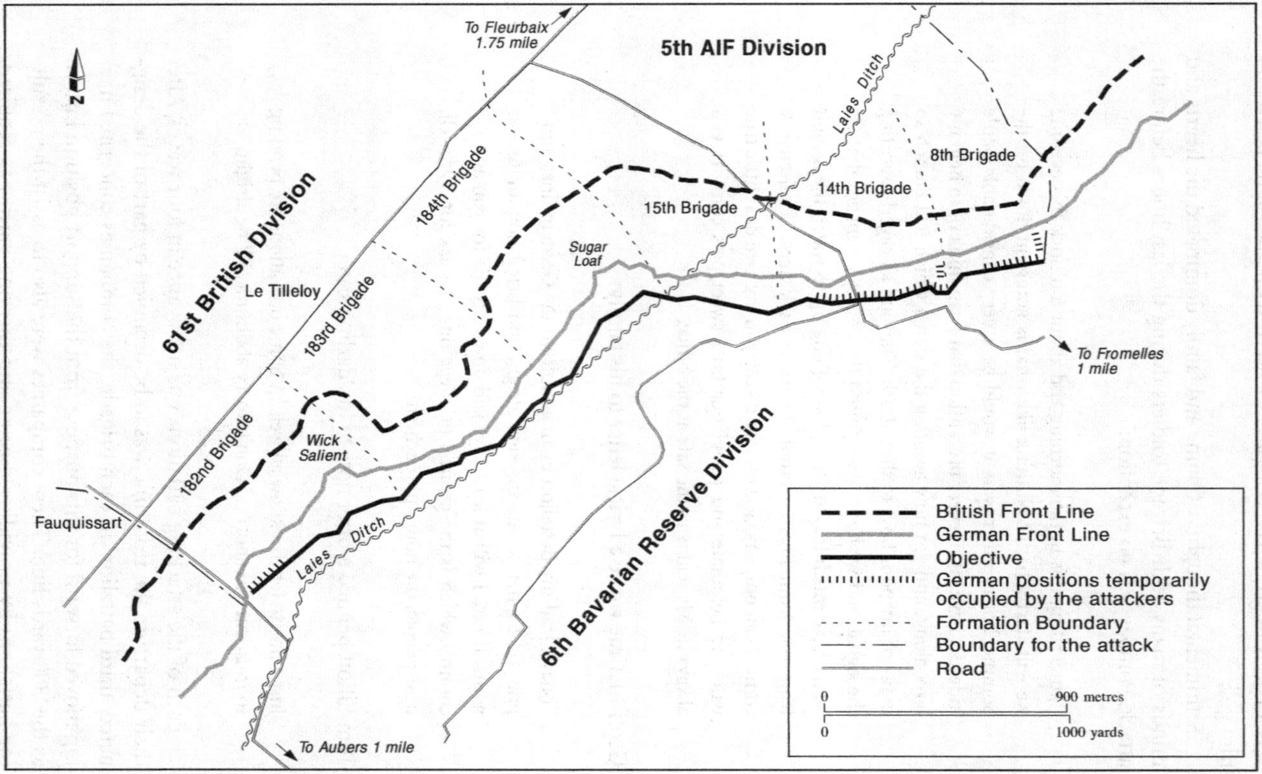
To Fleurbaix
1.75 mile
5th AIF Division
N
Laies Ditch
8th Brigade
14th Brigade
15th Brigade
184th Brigade
61st British Division
Sugar
Loaf
Le Tilleloy
183rd Brigade
To Fromelles
1 mile
Wick
Salient
182nd Brigade
6th Bavarian Reserve Division
Fauquissart
Laies Ditch
To Aubers 1 mile
British Front Line
German Front Line
Objective
German positions temporarily
occupied by the attackers
Formation Boundary
Boundary for the attack
Road
0
900 metres
0
1000 yards

The battle of Fromelles

The battle of Fromelles

Formations and Commanders

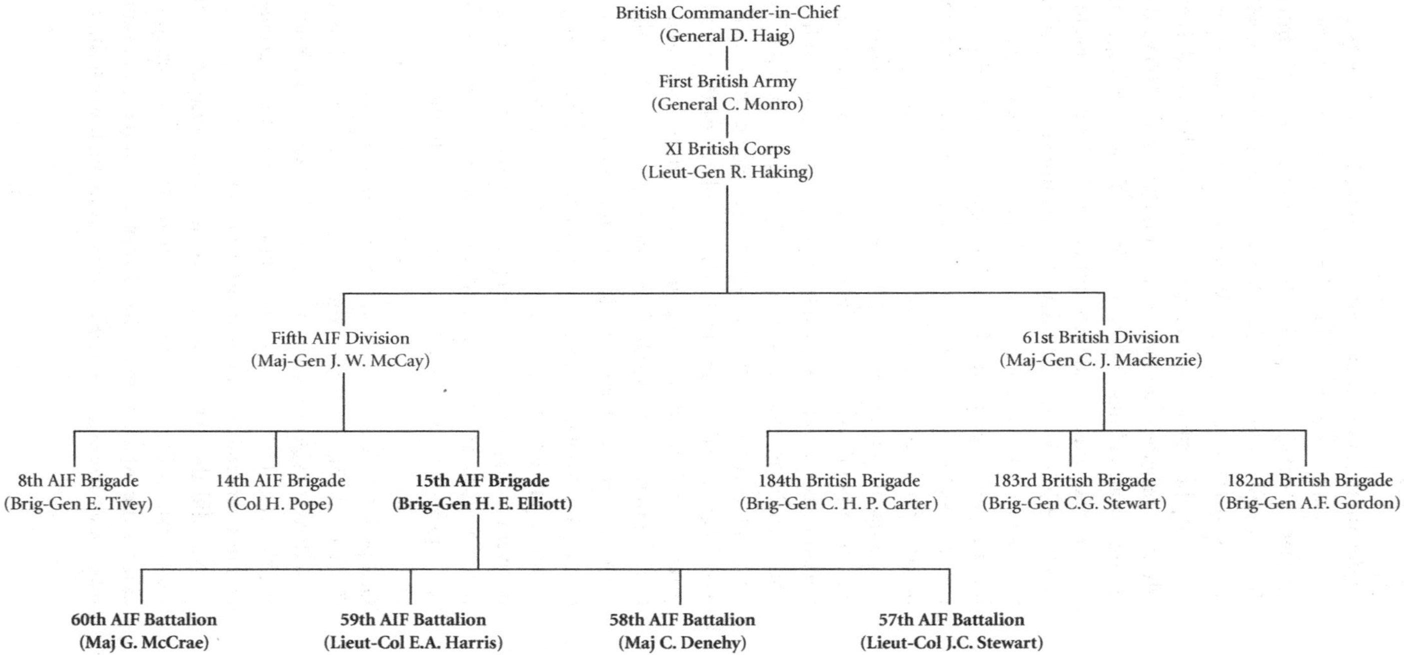

British Commander-in-Chief
(General D. Haig)
First British Army
(General C. Monro)
XI British Corps
(Lieut-Gen R. Haking)
Fifth AIF Division
(Maj-Gen J. W. McCay)
61st British Division
(Maj-Gen C. J. Mackenzie)
8th AIF Brigade
(Brig-Gen E. Tivey)
14th AIF Brigade
(Col H. Pope)
15th AIF Brigade
(Brig-Gen H. E. Elliott)
184th British Brigade
(Brig-Gen C. H. P. Carter)
183rd British Brigade
(Brig-Gen C.G. Stewart)
182nd British Brigade
(Brig-Gen A.F. Gordon)
60th AIF Battalion
(Maj G. McCrae)
59th AIF Battalion
(Lieut-Col E.A. Harris)
58th AIF Battalion
(Maj C. Denehy)
57th AIF Battalion
(Lieut-Col J.C. Stewart)

Under these arrangements the remaining battalion was to remain in reserve some distance behind the 300 yards line, with brigade headquarters situated even further back (almost two miles from the front line). Pompey nominated the 58th as his 'third battalion', with the 57th in reserve. He decided to leave Wieck to coordinate messages during the battle at the rearward headquarters, while he based himself at an advanced brigade headquarters at Trou Post on the 300 yards line (with communication links back to Wieck and forward to Legge in the front line) so he could more directly influence the course of events.

On 19 July, a fine clear day, the preliminary bombardment of the German trenches began at eleven o'clock and continued with growing intensity for seven hours. By mid-afternoon, when all guns were blazing, the sights and sounds were awesome. Exploding monsters of destruction descended in quick succession, catapulting geysers of earth skywards, hurling metal fragments far and wide. The Germans retaliated with a bombardment of their own, catching some men of the 60th Battalion as they moved forward to join the 59th in the front line, but both battalions were in position, ready to go, by 3.30pm. Nerves were taut, and there were over two hours to wait while these terrifying enemy missiles crashed down and rocked the trembling earth beneath them, but it was heartening to catch a glimpse through the haze and dust of the German trenches 400 yards ahead being battered with similar severity.

Also boosting their morale was the presence of their brigadier, braving the front-line danger alongside them with a willingness shared by few equivalent commanders. At such a time, with his men about to go over the top, any leader worth his salt would obviously encourage his men and keep whatever misgivings he had about the operation to himself. But Pompey was genuinely impressed with the way the Australian and British guns were pounding the German trenches; it was by Gallipoli standards a substantial bombardment. 'Boys, you won't find a German in those trenches when you get there', he enthused amid the thunderous explosions. He and his men, however, were not aware that the German fortifications and dug-outs were much deeper, stronger, and less penetrable than their British equivalents.

Nor did they know that the tremendous noise of the British and Australian shellfire was more impressive than its accuracy. Haking had assured the attackers beforehand that they would be advancing in the wake of an irresistible artillery bombardment; it would have

> cut all the wire, destroyed all the enemy's machine gun emplacements, knocked down most of his parapets, killed a large proportion of the enemy, and thoroughly frightened the remainder.

In fact, observers reported during the bombardment, the artillery was not satisfactorily dealing with the Sugarloaf. Even after arrangements were made in mid-afternoon for heavy guns to give this all-important bastion extra attention, there was still concern that inadequate damage had been inflicted. Officers in the 60th Battalion, looking across no-man's-land to the enemy fortifications they would soon be attacking, could see plenty of German wire uncut and at least three machine-gun emplacements undamaged. Afterwards a senior artillery commander complained that he had been severely handicapped, not only by the hasty preparations that had prevented him from familiarising himself sufficiently with the battlefield and registering his batteries properly, but also by such basic oversights as the near-total absence of support staff and, incredibly, the lack of a decent map to make sense of the messages he received during the battle.

Having returned to the 300 yards line, Pompey watched and listened intently as the attack unfolded. Because the front trenches were furthest apart in the 15th Brigade sector, the 59th and 60th began climbing over the parapet into no-man's-land at 5.45pm, a quarter of an hour before the shellfire supporting them ceased. As his men moved forward, right on time, the sound of German rifle-fire could soon be heard despite the continuing bombardment, closely followed by the ominous rattle of a machine-gun fired from the Sugarloaf. All the same, the operation proceeded like clockwork as far as he could tell. Observation from his vantage point was limited, but his brigade advanced as ordered in four successive waves five minutes apart. After a while, although the German artillery maintained its severe retaliatory cannonade, the enemy small-arms fire subsided. 'Attack appears to be successful', he reported to Wieck.

A few minutes later, however, Major Layh, who had accompanied the 59th advance, reappeared. Colonel Harris had sent him back to report that the battalion (forming the far right of the AIF attack) had been held up halfway across no-man's-land and could penetrate no further. Pompey, influenced by early signs of success on the 15th Brigade's left, sent Layh back to Harris with a message urging him to try again. Then, concerned that he had received no word from the 60th although telephones had gone out with the fourth wave, he directed his newly appointed intelligence officer, Lieutenant Dave Doyle, to get in touch with Geoff McCrae. Venturing out into no-man's-land, Doyle was soon a target for 'very heavy' machine-gun fire. 'How I got through I don't know, being absolutely in the open', Doyle wrote afterwards. Unable to get across towards McCrae, he eventually managed to get in touch with the 59th, and returned with a message from Layh that any further advance was impossible.

In the continued absence of definite news about the 60th, Elliott presumed that McCrae and his men had established themselves in the enemy trenches without managing to get information back by messenger or telephone. He obtained McCay's authorisation to supplement the attack with the two companies of the 58th not already engaged in various digging and carrying duties, and to bring the 57th forward to replace the 58th in the front trench and 300 yards line. German shells were pounding not only the 15th Brigade's front line but also the communication trenches behind, and no-man's-land as well. Telephone wires were repeatedly smashed (though the line connecting Pompey to Wieck was maintained throughout), and the route forward was now so damaged that the 57th and 58th Battalions had to dash desperately across the open to reach the pre-attack front line. Out in no-man's-land, where the 59th had been held up, Colonel Harris was severely shaken when one of these powerful projectiles exploded nearby; he escaped physical injury, but was incapacitated with shell shock. Notified of this development, Pompey immediately directed Layh to take command of the 59th.

Meanwhile Elliott was beginning to receive disturbing reports of heavy casualties. The breakdown of the 59th's attack had been caused, exactly as he feared beforehand, by the problems the British alongside had experienced in getting forward from their sally-ports. A vital part of their task was to establish themselves in the German strongpoint at the Sugarloaf salient; any failure there would have alarming implications for the whole attack. It was difficult to ascertain how the 184th British Brigade had fared—here too the haze, dust, and dearth of information from the attackers left baffled local commanders shrouded by the notorious 'fog of war'—but the early signs were not encouraging.

Confirmation that the 184th had not attained its most crucial objective materialised when General Carter informed Wieck that there would be a renewed bombardment of the Sugarloaf prior to a fresh attack. Shortly afterwards Wieck received a further message from Carter: 'Am attacking at 9pm. Can your right battalion co-operate?' After Wieck quickly conveyed this request to advanced brigade headquarters at Trou Post, Elliott decided, logically enough, that his allotted reinforcement, the half-battalion of the 58th that had just arrived in the front line, should advance to help this renewed British attempt to seize the vital salient. He and Wieck attended to the necessary arrangements.

> The[se] two companies of the 58th were commanded by Major Hutchinson, a young graduate of Duntroon, son of a Tasmanian clergyman, and a boy of the finest type that his country produces. Before the actual order to advance, the men—as was often the case with Australians, especially when first in action—could be felt straining like greyhounds on the leash, and were not easily restrained from anticipating the word of command.

When it was given, in the fading twilight as night closed in, 'they went forward with splendid dash opposite the Sugarloaf, carrying with them a number of survivors of the 59th'. However, to Pompey's amazement and dismay, there was no sign of any advance alongside from the 184th British Brigade that his half-battalion had gone forward to support.

There followed a puzzling series of directives. Haking could not make up his mind what he wanted. At 9.25pm McCay passed on to Elliott Haking's belated notification that the 61st Division was 'not attacking tonight', and authorised Pompey to 'withdraw 59th and its reinforcements' (that is, the half-battalion of the 58th under Hutchinson) if the attack that had just been launched was 'not likely to succeed'. Earlier, when Pompey asked McCay for further reinforcements (influenced by his assessment that casualties in the 15th Brigade seemed severe), McCay had refused this request. At 10.30pm, however, McCay not only affirmed that the 61st Division was going to make another attempt on the Sugarloaf after all; he was prepared, he informed Elliott, to authorise the 15th Brigade to throw the 57th Battalion into the fray—precisely the additional reinforcements Pompey had earlier sought in vain—if it would help the brigade attain its original objective. Pompey responded warily to these contradictory messages. The 60th was 'believed to be still' in the German trenches and the 59th had not yet reached them, he reported at 11.16pm. As for committing the 57th and making another attack, he could not 'guarantee success' because the enemy machine-gun fire was 'very hot', but he was 'willing to try'.

Shortly afterwards Pompey was handed a chilling message from Denehy, one of the most devastating he ever received. Pompey immediately passed on its disastrous tidings to Wieck:

> Following message from Maj Denehy indicates that the attack of this Bde has completely failed, such men of the 60th as actually reached the enemy's trench being killed or captured, the two coys of 58th mown down when close [to] enemy's trench and very few came back. Message begins: Men of all battalions are coming back from no-man's-land and fully expect that they will gradually drift back to the line. Many men are wounded, many are not. Very many officers are casualties, including Majors McCrae, Elliott and Hutchinson, all of whom are reported dead, and seems impossible to reorganise ... Report seems to be unanimous ... that not a single man of the 15th Brigade is now arrived in enemy's trench, as enemy's flares are coming from the whole of the front allotted to this Bde. I am now organising the defence of our original trenches.

Pompey asked Wieck to 'notify Division and ask for instructions'. McCay, accepting that the 15th Brigade was 'of no further use for attack', directed Pompey to abandon the assault altogether and concentrate on re-establishing his brigade in its original front line.

The fighting was over for Pompey and his men, but the suffering was not. It was a night of agony. Australians have rarely—perhaps never—known a more tragic 24 hours than the battle of Fromelles. Those lethal Sugarloaf machine-guns, unsubdued by the artillery, had inflicted calamitous casualties on the 15th Brigade. W.H. 'Jimmy' Downing, a 57th Battalion private, later recorded his impressions:

> Stammering scores of German machine-guns spluttered violently, drowning the noise of the cannonade. The air was thick with bullets, swishing in a flat criss-crossed lattice of death ... Hundreds were mown down in the flicker of an eyelid, like great rows of teeth knocked from a comb ... Men were cut in two by streams of bullets [that] swept like whirling knives ... It was the Charge of the Light Brigade once more, but more terrible, more hopeless—

> magnificent, but not war—a valley of death filled by somebody's blunder.

The 60th Battalion was practically annihilated. This fine unit had gone into action over 900-strong, its talented leaders and well-trained rank and file eager to perform well in its first engagement. Next morning, when the shattered battalion assembled after being withdrawn, only 61 men and a few officers answered the roll-call (a small number of other unwounded men gradually turned up later). Lieutenant Tom Kerr, still in shock after losing so many friends and collecting wounds himself in the ribs and shoulder, was staggered to find himself acting battalion commander. Ascending the parapet to advance with the third wave, he had expected to glimpse the previous lines pressing forward ahead of him, but there was no movement at all. He could see plenty of Australians, but they were all lying still. When, shortly afterwards, Doyle tried in vain to get across and find McCrae (as directed by Pompey), the battalion commander and hundreds of his men had already perished in the knee-high shaggy grass of no-man's-land.

The 59th, the other assault battalion, had suffered almost as badly, and the fate of the nine o'clock attack under Major Hutchinson ensured that casualties in the 58th were also considerable. The official figures, when ultimately finalised, confirmed the magnitude of the disaster:

	Officers	Other ranks	Total
57th Battalion	2	33	35
58th Battalion	11	237	248
59th Battalion	20	675	695
60th Battalion	16	741	757
attached formations	3	66	69
			1804

Worse still, there was an unusually high proportion of fatalities. The toll of AIF soldiers killed in action tended to be about a quarter of the number of wounded, but at Fromelles the proportion of the 15th Brigade's casualties who were killed was much greater.

There were appalling casualties in all three AIF brigades engaged at Fromelles. Unlike Pompey's 15th, which had more no-man's-land to cross and was closest to the Sugarloaf machine-guns, the 8th and 14th Brigades had succeeded in capturing 1,000 yards of the enemy's front system, but were puzzled by the shallow ditches they encountered as they pushed on in search of the rear German trenches Haking had instructed them to seize. It was typical of Haking's direction of the battle that these supposed trenches proved to be non-existent. After fierce fighting during that long night of 19–20 July, their exposed positions eventually proved untenable in the face of German counter-attacks from several directions simultaneously. They were forced to fall back, like the 15th Brigade, to their original pre-attack front line. Only on the far right did a British battalion manage to seize and briefly retain part of the enemy line, before being overwhelmed by German shellfire and counter-attacking bomb-throwers.

During the engagement 1,547 British soldiers were killed or wounded. Losses in the Australian Fifth Division amounted to no fewer than 178 officers and 5,355 men—all this in less than 24 hours. Of all the forces engaged in this conflict there were few divisions, if any, that recorded a higher toll in one day throughout the war (and hardly any battalions sustained more casualties more rapidly than the 60th did at Fromelles). Remarkably, in one night, the AIF's participation at Fromelles had resulted in a staggering toll—equivalent to the *entire* Australian casualties of the Boer War, the Korean War, and the Vietnam War *put together*. Casualties in the German division that repulsed the assault amounted to about a quarter of those experienced by the attackers. Within that division, in a regiment situated opposite the 15th Brigade, was a 27-year-old dispatch runner who managed to avoid injury during the battle. If he had been less fortunate at Fromelles, the twentieth century might have proceeded quite differently. His name was Adolf Hitler.

There was no more distressing sight for Australians in the whole war than the scene in the AIF front line after the battle of Fromelles. Devastated trenches were packed with dead and dying men. Shocked observers groping for words to describe the carnage resorted to the analogy of a butcher's shop. Corporal Hugh Knyvett of the 59th was one:

> The sight of our trenches that next morning is burned into my brain. Here and there a man could stand upright, but in most places if you did not wish to be exposed to a sniper's bullet you had to

> progress on hands and knees. If you had gathered the stock of a thousand butcher-shops, cut it into small pieces and strewn it about, it would give you a faint conception of the shambles those trenches were.

According to Downing, 'the sandbags were splashed with red, and red were the firesteps, the duckboards, the bays'. It was the '[m]ost awful scene of slaughter imaginable', wrote Doyle.

Stretcher-bearers toiled devotedly, some with improvised stretchers, but the casualties were overwhelming. With communication trenches inaccessible—damaged by enemy shellfire and jammed with further casualties—it 'was an hour's hard work for four men to carry one to safety'. At 7.00am on 20 July the 15th Brigade's front trenches were full of men still awaiting medical attention after having been wounded the previous afternoon and early evening. Many had to remain there much longer. Some did not survive the wait. There was another heart-rending spectacle for anyone looking out towards no-man's-land, where Australians 'could be seen everywhere raising their limbs in pain or turning hopelessly, hour after hour, from one side to the other'. The slightest movement attracted merciless fire from the Germans, but undeterred volunteers risked their lives in attempts to rescue stricken comrades.

Meanwhile Layh, Denehy, and Legge were striving to reorganise the defence of the 15th Brigade's sector. Shaken participants in a failed attack tended to be concerned about an immediate enemy counterthrust, especially after a reverse as severe as this one: with the trenches wrecked and occupied thinly by able-bodied defenders, there was every reason for the survivors to feel vulnerable. To Denehy, it seemed that he and Layh had 'a tremendous length' of line to safeguard considering the paucity of men available to defend it and the intensity of the shellfire exploding along it. Midway through that long and terrible night Legge advised Pompey that 'the front line at present could not be held against a counter'; but after hasty fortification repairs, and further reorganisation by Layh and Denehy, the staff captain was able to report that the situation was much more satisfactory.

At one stage Pompey decided to inspect the state of affairs in the front line himself. Schroder accompanied him:

> Pompey got tired of sitting in advanced brigade headquarters, and took me up the line with him. What had been ordinary sandbagged trenches were now heaps of debris, and it was impossible to walk far without falling over dead men. Although the Hun had a barrage down and there must have been dozens of machine guns operating from the Sugarloaf, Pompey never thought of ducking, but went from battalion to company headquarters and so on right along the line. A word for a wounded man here, a pat of approbation to a bleary-eyed digger there, he missed nobody. He never spoke a word all the way back to advanced brigade [headquarters] but went straight inside, put his head in his hands, and sobbed his heart out.

Later Pompey was unable to conceal his distress from his men. Neil Freeman, then a 58th Battalion lieutenant, declared more than two decades after the battle that

> I ... will always have before my eyes the picture of Pompey ... the morning after Fromelles, tears streaming down his face, shaking hands with the pitiful remnant of his brigade.

Also then present was another officer, Captain Bill Trainor of the 57th. Pompey's agony was palpable; his eyes were filled with tears as he came over to Trainor. 'Good God Bill, what's happened to my brigade?' he lamented. A 58th Battalion survivor was struck by Pompey's compassion and the intensity of his anguish as he tearfully urged to the shocked, weary men trudging past him that the disaster was not his fault.

Throughout the night hundreds of maimed men managed to struggle back to the Australian front line, some with limbs detached, some hobbling, some on all fours. While forward with Schroder, Pompey came across a 59th officer with a shattered leg crawling along desperately, and suggested he should get help from the stretcher-bearers. 'There are thousands behind me who can't even crawl', Lieutenant Stewart Smith replied. 'Let the bearers get them first'.

The pitiful plight of helpless comrades inspired deeds of exceptional gallantry. Some rescuers made many hazardous trips into no-man's-land. Pompey later recorded that two of his 'lads ... went out under fire six times bringing in wounded comrades, until one was at length killed and the other badly wounded'. The Germans made few

Above Harold's parents, Helen and Thomas Elliott

Below The Elliotts' farmhouse at Charlton photographed in the 1980s; this was the second home Harold lived in (not the basic hut that was its predecessor)

Above 'Elsinore', Ballarat

Below Law student on the verandah at 'Elsinore'

Above Ormond College football team 1899, with Harold Elliott at centre of back row

Below Lawyer

Above Officers of 1st Battalion, 5th Australian Imperial Regiment: seated in the front row are Harold Elliott third from right, Thomas White far right and F.A. Foxall third from left *AWM H18374*

Below Kate, Neil (partly inside his father's boots) and Violet visit the colonel at Broadmeadows, September 1914

Above A brief spell during the 7th Battalion's arduous desert training in Egypt before the landing at Gallipoli: from left, Captain McKenna, Lieutenant-Colonel Elliott, Major McNicoll and Captain R. Henderson *AWM H15590*

Below 7th Battalion men keen to make the most of a visit to Cairo *AWM J5576*

Above Landing, 25 April 1915: Harold Barker (7th Battalion) photographs comrades descending rope ladders as they leave their transport, the *Galeka AWM J5589*

Below Landing, 25 April 1915: Charles Bean's photograph shows small boats conveying 7th Battalion men from the *Galeka* (far right) to the shore; aboard the ship in the centre, the *Novian*, were General McCay and a small part of the 7th Battalion *AWM G894*

Above Landing, 25 April 1915: As the boats near the shore some of the occupants have already been hit

Right Australian dug-outs behind Steele's Post on the slope up to the second ridge; Elliott's 7th Battalion endured a harrowing stint at Steele's in July 1915 *AWM G942*

Above Left With Major Wieck at Steenbecque; Elliott described his 'splendid' brigade major as being 'always cool, always busy'

Above Right Geoff McCrae, who served under Elliott as an officer in the 7th Battalion and the 15th Brigade; Pompey admired him profoundly

Below General Birdwood (with raised arm) in discussion with Brudenell White
AWM E94

concessions, although at times they did allow Australians to carry casualties in unhindered, especially while efforts were made to secure formal ratification of an impromptu truce arranged with the enemy by two Australians of the 8th Brigade. McCay, however, disallowed it in accordance with Haig's specific order forbidding such agreements; Haking and Monro endorsed McCay's decision. Under military law, in fact, McCay was entitled to authorise a local suspension of arms without his superiors' ratification.

Rescuing continued despite the collapse of the truce. Brave 57th men were particularly active, readily helping the other stricken battalions in Elliott's brigade. Conspicuous in this selfless work was 30-year-old Captain Norman Marshall, son of a well-known Presbyterian minister and Ormond College identity. A Gallipoli veteran, Marshall was building a glowing reputation as an intrepid leader after beginning the war as a private. 'One of my mates is out there and I want to go and get him—will you come?' Marshall asked Sergeant-Major Bill Knuckey, who agreed to help. It was a dangerous assignment, but they managed it successfully. Working closely with Knuckey was Sergeant Simon Fraser:

> we must have brought in over 250 men by our company alone. It was no light work getting in with a heavy weight on your back—especially if he had a broken leg or arm and no stretcher bearer was handy. You had to lie down and get him on your back, then rise and duck for your life with the chance of getting a bullet in you before you were safe.

Also among Marshall's assistants were Captain Harry Cameron and Bob Salmon, a 24-year-old lieutenant and former Ballarat College student Pompey had known in pre-war days. One morning Fraser was observing over the parapet at daybreak:

> I saw two figures in their shirts and no hats, running about halfway between our lines and the Germans: they were our captains Cameron and Marshall hunting for more wounded.

Not all the prominent rescuers were in the 57th. Dan Toohey of the 59th, a 7th Battalion original earmarked for return to Australia after several unsuccessful operations on a painful Gallipoli wound, had returned to his unit instead as a stowaway. Pompey, delighted to have him back, quipped that he should be court-martialled for deserting hospital without permission. Toohey made an outstanding contribution at Fromelles. During the battle he indefatigably ensured that ammunition kept coming forward, and afterwards—again under heavy fire—with three others rescued 25 men from no-man's-land. Pompey estimated that around 300 men of his brigade were brought in, with about 30 rescuers becoming casualties in the process.

Charles Bean was down at the Somme, where the other three AIF divisions were about to be thrown into the British offensive at Pozières. He was aware that an attack at Fromelles was under consideration, and had discussed the proposal with Brudenell White: 'I hate these unprepared little shows', White told Bean on 17 July. On the night of 19 July Birdwood assured Bean that no assault would eventuate for at least 24 hours. Next morning Bean was startled to learn that the attack had taken place. He immediately hastened north to Fromelles, borrowing White's car for the purpose. Arriving early in the afternoon, he visited each brigade in turn:

> Poor old Tivey looked quite over done—with eyes like boiled gooseberries ... Elliott was dead asleep when I called—but McCay came in and woke him up. When Elliott came out I felt almost as if I were in the presence of a man who had just lost his wife. He looked down and could hardly speak—he was clearly terribly depressed and overwrought.

British authorities tried to mask the magnitude of the catastrophe in their official communiqué:

> Yesterday evening, south of Armentieres, we carried out some important raids on a front of two miles in which Australian troops took part. About 140 German prisoners were captured.

Bean was flabbergasted. 'What is the use of deliberate lying like that?' he fumed. 'The Germans know it was an attack—they have numbers of our wounded as prisoners'. The cable he hastily drafted about the battle for Australian newspapers referred to the engagement as an 'attack' rather than mere raids, and described AIF casualties as 'severe'.

According to another contemporary report by an Australian,

> Our men … are disgusted to find the operation described in brief paragraphs in the London papers as an Anglo-Australian raid. They think that fierce fighting for eight hours under terrific gun fire might be considered a battle.

Contributing to Bean's anger was his conclusion that the Fromelles operation had been utterly futile. As White had told him on the 17th,

> We may deceive the enemy for two days; and after that, he knows perfectly well that it is not a big attack, and that we are not in earnest there. We don't get anything that does us any good—the trenches are hard to keep, and … two divisions [are ruined in the process].

It was, as Pompey Elliott had predicted as well as White, a monumental folly. If the feint had been limited to an artillery demonstration without infantry involvement, the Germans might well have wondered whether this bombardment was the prelude to a major offensive. But once only two infantry divisions attacked on a narrow front it was clear this was not a major offensive, so the Germans could, if they wished, transfer units from the Fromelles sector to the Somme with impunity. Besides, they obtained from a casualty or a prisoner a copy of Haking's order, which *told* them it was a feint. And anyway, even if the attack had somehow succeeded in capturing all the ground as planned—despite the non-existence of the German rear trenches specified by Haking—it would have resulted only in an untenable bulge pushed into the German line that would have been subject to flanking fire and even closer observation from the Aubers Ridge.

Haking's conclusion was predictably different. 'From my experience in this attack I am quite convinced that with two good Divisions' and the same amount of guns and ammunition 'we can carry and hold the line whenever it is desired', he claimed. Haking contended that 'the artillery work turned out even better than I expected', the wire was 'properly cut', and 'the assaulting Battalions had a clear run into the enemy's trenches'. This assessment remains astounding: Pompey's men were mown down in their hundreds by the Sugarloaf machine-guns that should have been dealt with by the artillery. The Australians, according to Haking, 'were not sufficiently trained to consolidate the ground gained', and the 61st British Division 'was not sufficiently imbued with the offensive spirit'. 'With two trained Divisions', he added absurdly and insultingly, 'the position would have been a gift after the artillery bombardment'. In fact, as Bean affirmed, 'it may be doubted if any infantry in the world could have crossed No-Man's-Land where the 15th Brigade failed', and many British survivors of Fromelles resented what one of them described as Haking's 'abominable libel … on a gallant division which was massacred through no fault of its own'.

Most bizarre of all, Haking concluded that the attack had 'done both Divisions a great deal of good'. Considering that the Fifth Division had lost 5,533 men in one night, that comment surely qualified Haking to be certified rather than retained at the front. Yet, incredibly, his friend Haig tried a fortnight later to promote him further, to the level of army commander. This proposal was so preposterous that it provoked a reduction in GHQ's powers over promotion. Although any further rise for Haking was stymied, Haig's support and protection ensured that he could not be removed; Haking the Butcher, as he became fondly known, remained in command of XI Corps until the end of the war. He evidently learned little from the various disasters he presided over: even late in 1918 he was still orchestrating futile, costly Fromelles-like attacks.

The battle of Fromelles was a repetition of Haking's Boar's Head fiasco on a larger scale. Parallels were plentiful. Preparations were rushed, inadequate and visible to the enemy. There were several postponements. The shooting of the gunners who were supposed to be dealing with vital German strongpoints was sadly astray. Both ventures were ill-conceived, inflicting heavy casualties on the attackers while failing to achieve the ostensible objective of deceiving the enemy. And afterwards the corps commander who had directed both doomed enterprises with chilling incompetence managed to describe them as beneficial to the units slaughtered while undertaking them. On the afternoon following Fromelles Haking sent the Australians a farewell message of fatuous bluster, full of hollow claims about the operation he had catastrophically botched. 'I wish you all still a more complete victory in your next attack', he concluded, 'and I hope I shall be somewhere near when it takes place'. That closing sentiment was hardly reciprocated. After Fromelles it was obviously in the AIF's best interests to operate as far away from Haking the Butcher as possible.

That same day, after his chat with Bean, Pompey Elliott dashed off a sorrowful letter to Kate.

> The battle is over. My brave boys have done all that man could do ... the British Generals ... say we accomplished our object, which was to keep the Germans from moving their reserves from in front of us down to the Somme, but we paid a fearful price ... Poor Geoff McCrae is missing and reported killed while most gallantly leading his battalion ... Bert Layh is safe. He had a beastly experience. He dashed out — a huge shell burst and blew him into a deep 10 feet hole full of mud and water and half drowned or smothered him, and it was only with the utmost difficulty that he got out. He suffered greatly from the cold for the water here is ice cold. Still he will be all right ... I think over 2000 of my own Brigade alone are killed, wounded or missing, and very very many of these will be killed, as the Germans fired at them as they lay all night and all today ... many many must perish slowly and miserably of starvation and want of attention in that no-man's-land. God help us all, it is cruel indeed. I had several narrow escapes yesterday from shells, being covered up with debris several times, but am still perfectly well though very very sad. The casualties will be worse I fear than even the landing at Gallipoli. I have indeed hardly any officers at all left, and must start to rebuild the Brigade all over again. I must stop now dear, for I am very weary and there is still much to do to help the boys.

Three days later he was in a bitter mood when he wrote to Emily Edwards.

> God knows why this enterprise was ordered, apparently as a feint to distract the enemy's attention from the Somme area. However ... the Division was hurled against the German trenches without anything like adequate preparation, and although we broke the German line and captured nearly two hundred prisoners the slaughter was dreadful and at length we were ordered to retire ... I am glad to say that my poor boys behaved magnificently. We attacked in four waves and there was not the least hesitation in any one of

> them although they saw the preceding waves going down before the machine guns like corn before the reaper ... One of the best of my Commanding Officers was killed and practically all my best officers, the Anzac men who helped to build up my Brigade in Egypt, are dead. I presume there was some plan at the back of the attack but it is difficult to know what it was. One can only say — It was an Order. I trust those who gave the order may be made to realize their responsibility.

On 21 July he wrote to Geoff McCrae's father. George McCrae's adoration of his youngest son, Elliott knew, was unusually intense. This made the task of writing about Geoff's fate all the more difficult, but Pompey did not flinch. 'Dear Mr McCrae', he began, 'It is with the utmost regret that I must announce to you the death of your son Geoffrey'. Aware the news would have already reached the family by cable, Elliott went on to outline the details George would be longing to know. It was a frank letter. His view from the outset, he wrote, was that the attack 'was doomed to failure, for we had no sufficient reserves and the artillery bombardment was far from being sufficient'. The ensuing slaughter was like the charge at the Nek

> on a tenfold scale. They were met by a storm of shrapnel shells and a hail of ... bullets. Geoff led the fourth wave of his Battalion in person and although he saw the preceding waves going down before the storm he never hesitated an instant when the moment came, and every man of his followed him instantly ... Geoff's regiment was practically annihilated.

Two days later Elliott wrote again to let George know Geoff's body had been retrieved:

> Dear Mr McCrae, I have just returned from attending poor Geoff's funeral ... His body was recovered in the face of much difficulty and danger after three attempts owing to the enemy opening fire on the bearer party on each occasion. The chief credit for recovering it belongs to Capt Norman Marshall 57th Battalion ... and some of Geoff's own men who volunteered to form the bearer party.

Geoff was 'a true soldier and gentleman ... in every way', Pompey concluded, signing off with 'the very sincerest sympathy on behalf of myself and my Brigade'.

As well as writing to bereaved relatives Elliott drafted numerous recommendations for gallantry awards. He did not allow the cynicism he felt about the administration of the awards after his own Lone Pine injustice to affect his conscientious nominations. It was 'not merit alone' that decided these awards 'as I know to my cost', he declared, 'but at least no unworthy names will be submitted by me whatever happens'. His tribute to Norman Marshall's work was surprisingly rejected, but Kerr, Toohey, Cameron and Salmon each received a Military Cross. Simon Fraser was mentioned in dispatches. Private Reg Poulter, who (Elliott wrote) 'courageously volunteered and successfully carried an important message' from practically under the German parapet all the way back to the 15th Brigade's front line 'under a withering machine gun and artillery fire'—and made no fewer than eight trips across no-man's-land to deliver messages or rescue wounded—was awarded both a Military Medal and a Russian Medal of St George.

Elliott also did what he could to obtain recognition for some officers who died in the fight. Geoff McCrae was mentioned in dispatches after Pompey submitted that his 'courage and devotion to duty cannot be spoken of too highly', and he had 'received no reward' despite being repeatedly recommended at Gallipoli. For Major Hutchinson Elliott recommended the award of a posthumous VC. He led the two 58th companies in the nine o'clock attack 'with great dash and resolution and actually reached a position near the German wire', well ahead of the point reached by the earlier attack on this part of the battlefield. 'Here he ordered his men to take cover while he made a personal reconnaissance of the wire to discover an opening'. He persevered alone, despite continuous enfilade machine-gun fire, until he was killed. No VC for Hutchinson was forthcoming. Pompey was not surprised: in the citation some reference to the failure of the 184th British Brigade to make its concurrent advance would have been unavoidable, thereby recording 'a shameful betrayal of gallant men' who 'were hopelessly and helplessly massacred'.

The brigadier was especially sad about the death of the man he had predicted would become an Australian Kitchener, Major Tom Elliott. His arrangements for the 60th Battalion's attack—after Pompey reluctantly acceded to McCrae's request to allow him to participate in it —were 'remarkably thorough and complete'.

> He accompanied the 2nd wave of the attack, and was killed while encouraging the men to move forward. His early death thus unfortunately terminated what promised to be an exceptionally brilliant career, and it can safely be said with the utmost regret that this officer's death is the greatest individual loss the Brigade has suffered since its formation.

What happened on 19 July dominated Pompey's thoughts for weeks. 'I can honestly say that ... I neglected nothing that I can think of to aid my boys', and the failure of the attack was 'no fault of mine'.

> General McCay said he was very pleased with the 15th Brigade work and with me and my staff for all the arrangements we made for the battle. Not a single thing I am proud to say went wrong with our arrangements ... I would have been broken hearted if I had neglected anything that would have helped my boys. For instance in the 14th Brigade they sent up a whole lot of hand grenades to the front line, and when their poor boys opened the boxes they found no fuses in them. I had thought of this, and had a dump where all the grenades were examined a mile behind the front line, and all the ones without fuses were taken out, and I had an officer who understood the whole thing and some men under him putting the fuses and detonators in before they were taken near the firing line.

Moreover, after the battle the British 61st Division staff expressed particular gratitude for the invaluable assistance provided by the 15th Brigade machine-guns Pompey had positioned on his right flank opposite the Sugarloaf. Still, he knew there was no room for smugness:

> There's such a lot to be thought of every time. Of course every fight we are in helps me by giving me experience and one is less likely to forget essential things, but I have a dreadful lot to learn. Two at least of the Generals of the British Division next to us who did so badly have been sacked, and one of ours too.

The British generals dispensed with were Carter and the commander of the 183rd Brigade on his right, which had also made hardly any headway across no-man's-land. Elliott concluded that the dismissal of Carter, at least, was related to the fiasco of the revived British bid to capture the Sugarloaf. Carter had approached the 15th Brigade and asked it to 'co-operate' with his brigade's 9.00pm attempt, but neglected to let Wieck and Elliott know that this attack, along with other renewed thrusts along the 61st Division's front, had been subsequently cancelled (by Haking, who was evidently unaware that Australians were to be involved). Carter and his staff may not have expected the 15th Brigade's support to encompass a full-scale frontal assault; it is conceivable that by 'co-operate' they envisaged assistance such as covering fire from machine-guns carefully positioned for the purpose. But whatever aid they had in mind, they should certainly have informed the 15th Brigade that it was no longer needed. As a result of this culpable oversight, the 58th Battalion companies under Hutchinson went forward on their own in an advance that was, Bean later wrote, 'one of the bravest and most hopeless assaults ever undertaken by the Australian Imperial Force'. Stationing liaison officers at the headquarters of adjoining units to ensure smooth co-ordination—or, in other words, to avoid appalling mishaps like this one—was not then, regrettably, the usual practice it later became.

In a number of post-war accounts of the battle, including Bean's *Official History*, it has been suggested that leaders of other units, notably the Fifth AIF Division, were also partly responsible because they could have informed the 15th Brigade that Carter's brigade would not be attacking. However, these interpretations presume that McCay and Wagstaff at Fifth Division knew that the 58th Battalion companies had been assigned to *advance concurrently with Carter's brigade*; it is by no means clear that they did. Responsibility for this fiasco belongs overwhelmingly with Carter and his staff. They asked for the assistance in the first place; they should have ensured that the 15th Brigade was informed that they no longer required it.

The Australian general sent home was Pope. At one stage after the battle McCay had been unable to wake him, and concluded that he was in an alcohol-induced stupor. Pope insisted he was simply in a deep slumber, a natural reaction after acute stress and sleep deprivation, and regarded his dismissal as a monstrous injustice. Pompey was sympathetic:

> I am sorry for him. He did well in the fight, but next day it is said he was so cut up that he took some drink and he was in such a state with his nerves that he was incapable of commanding his men if there had been a côunter attack, and so he was sent home.

It was a terrible ordeal for all the commanders. Tivey, like Elliott, was reduced to tears by the sight of his shattered brigade.

Afterwards Pompey was tormented again and again as he reflected on the calamitous losses resulting from such a pointless enterprise.

> I am very sad for poor Geoff McCrae and young Andy Morrow. Do you remember Hugh Morrow who used to visit me in Drummond Street. Andrew was his young brother. He was such a wee chap when I first knew him ... He was always so bright and cheery. He led his men on magnificently until near the German trench a piece of shell struck him in the face and crushed it in fearfully. His men carried him out and I was hopeful he would live though he would have been badly disfigured and he was [a] very handsome lad — but he died next day from shock. I am afraid it will go very hard with his poor old mother. He was her youngest boy and the apple of her eye.

Wally Vaile and Jack Bowden, Morrow's friends and fellow 59th lieutenants, also died.

> They were great pals and ... all went out in the charge together. Bowden was killed outright ... Vaile was shot through both ankles, and his arm was all smashed up. Morrow died in the Ambulance and Vaile got as far as Calais, it was the exposure and loss of blood that killed Morrow and him. Yet when they were carried in both were so brave and bright, not a word of pain or complaint, and Vaile never seemed to think of himself but only of Jack Bowden. He wanted him brought in, but in his bravery Jack Bowden had pushed far out to the enemy's trenches, and in spite of many gallant efforts the boys could not get his body in.

But it was not just the loss of Geoff McCrae and Tom Elliott — 'both magnificent young officers', he assured another correspondent — and

Andy Morrow and his mates that caused Pompey such anguish, although their loss alone was devastating enough. Over 1,800 officers and men in his brigade had obeyed orders, done their best, and become casualties in a catastrophe that he had predicted and tried to prevent. That his arrangements for the battle were creditable, in contrast to those of other commanders involved, was no consolation. The ghastliness of Fromelles seared his soul, reinforcing his conviction that too many British commanders and units were unreliable. Many of his men concluded likewise. The battle of Fromelles remains perhaps the most tragic 24 hours ever experienced by Australians. It was certainly the worst day Pompey Elliott had ever known.

CHAPTER TEN

'I Really Cannot Imagine How They Live Through It': Winter at the Somme

AUGUST 1916–MARCH 1917

ELLIOTT'S BRIGADE WAS unfit for any major offensive assignment for months. The 59th and 60th Battalions were so depleted that for a while they were combined for administrative purposes as if they were a single unit. For almost three months the 15th Brigade remained in the Fromelles sector, which reverted to its customary state of relative inactivity after the futility of attacking there had been confirmed by Haking's disastrous venture. Elliott applied himself to the task of rebuilding his brigade all over again.

Officers were needed desperately. Always on the lookout for officer material, Pompey was more assiduous than ever in his efforts to attract suitable candidates. Some he obtained from the 4th Light Horse (a squadron of this Victorian unit had accompanied the AIF infantry to France as divisional cavalry). Other officer vacancies were filled by 15th Brigade NCOs who had been brave rescuers at Fromelles, including Dan Toohey, Bill Knuckey, Hugh Knyvett and Simon Fraser. Awareness of Knuckey's willingness to accompany Norman Marshall on dangerous rescuing enterprises was crucial, Knuckey himself was convinced, in the willingness of his platoon to follow him as an officer. Rank-and-file respect for newly appointed officers was far from automatic; Knuckey's experience vindicated Pompey's promotion choices.

The AIF's aggressive harassment—intermittent artillery bombardments, sporadic mortar assaults, occasional infantry raids—

disturbed the relative quietness of the Fromelles sector following the battle. These raids, rapid incursions to unsettle the German formation opposite, maintained pressure on the enemy, but the price in casualties was sometimes excessive. The 15th Brigade's first raid, exactly a month after the Fromelles battle, was undertaken by the 57th Battalion and directed by Norman Marshall. At least sixteen Germans were killed, an enemy machine-gun was captured and another destroyed, documents and other materials were seized, and the defending unit identified. But the 56 raiders sustained 19 casualties, including two fine officers who were both killed. The 'good ones are always getting it', Elliott reflected sadly. It was 'harder and harder to replace them'. Consecutive letters to Kate featured this melancholy theme. 'If only some of them, the Hendersons, McCrae and one or two more could have come through it all right', he wrote, 'it is terrible to have the good ones go one after another'.

In mid-September there was another raid, this time by the 58th. Its organisation by Captain Harold Ferres was impressive, and the raiders secured identifications and inflicted considerable damage, but their casualties (five killed, five wounded) again saddened the brigadier:

> I begrudge them very much. The results seem so inadequate for the loss of these fine boys, but on the other hand a shell landed in a patch of 10 boys who had come to get their breakfast at the cook's fire and eight of them ... were wounded all at once, one seriously.

Distressing losses seemed unavoidable whatever his men were doing.

Another incident that particularly upset Elliott concerned his keen young protégé Bill Scurry, who had devised the ingenious drip-rifle used at the Gallipoli evacuation. Scurry had been awarded the DCM for his ingenuity on Elliott's recommendation. Afterwards, having been promoted to brigadier, Pompey thought of Scurry when he had to find someone to create from scratch the light mortar unit that had become part of an infantry brigade's structure. Scurry had no idea what a trench mortar looked like, but the brigadier's offer was compelling. 'Pick three officers and 60 other ranks, any you like in the brigade', urged Pompey. Scurry accepted. Now a captain (he was a humble lance-corporal when he and 'Bunty' Lawrence created the drip-rifle), Scurry applied himself with such zeal and proficiency that only a few weeks later the 15th Light Trench Mortar Battery performed creditably at the battle of Fromelles.

Light mortars operated in the 15th Brigade more effectively, Pompey was convinced, than they did elsewhere. Mortar batteries in some other brigades had an uneasy relationship with the infantry, who did not like the retaliatory enemy shellfire the mortars tended to provoke. In contrast, he and Scurry instilled a spirit of mutual co-operation; infantrymen in the 15th Brigade eagerly nominated troublesome enemy posts for Scurry's mortars to deal with. Elliott was delighted with Scurry's 'splendid work ... he has a real genius for soldiering'.

On 3 September, however, an unusual German shell, brought to Scurry for examination, exploded while he was scrutinising it. His multiple wounds included the (eventual) loss of a finger, a severe chest injury, and almost total blindness in one eye. Pompey was dismayed. Informed of the hospital's verdict that Scurry was unfit for further service, Pompey urged the doctors to reconsider. Scurry was 'the best and most enthusiastic officer in my brigade without exception', he declared. 'I would sooner have him with one eye than a dozen others with both eyes'. But medical authorities confirmed that Scurry should return to Australia.

Elliott was experiencing near misses himself. One night he and Dave Doyle tried to locate a suspected spy allegedly signalling to the Germans from behind the Australian lines. Weary after searching unsuccessfully, the brigadier wrote, they had paused for a breather 'when a bullet zipped just over my head and struck him in the side, and he fell forward on me'. Doyle's wound was 'pretty serious'. He was evacuated to England. The frequency of such incidents 'makes one become a fatalist':

> This morning ... a poor boy was struck in the face and blinded by a piece of shell just as I passed him ... it is just heartbreaking to see these fine boys maimed and broken like that every day.

Elliott fantasised about having 'a holiday in the country where everything is quiet and Katie and I are walking along holding each other's hands and telling each other all the news'.

> I am very sad these days sometimes, thinking of poor old Geoff McCrae and all the other boys. I wish we could get away from this spot. It will be always associated in my mind with their loss, like Lone Pine will be with the losses there ... I am tired of all this—every day I must plan ... how to kill men.

After yearning to get away from Egypt only a few months earlier, it now seemed 'years and years since I was there'.

Compensations were few. Not even an overdue decoration could cheer him up. In mid-September he learned that he had been awarded the Russian Order of St Anne:

> I don't know much about it ... I suppose it is a scheme to palm off some old thing upon me, and keep the best for someone else ... But I suppose it is better than being passed over completely as in Gallipoli.

After making enquiries, however, he conceded that it seemed 'not a bad Order to have at all'.

At least he was feeling better about his battalion commanders. Colonel Harris, disabled by shellshock in no-man's-land on 19 July, had confessed to Elliott that after such an unnerving experience he doubted whether he could face another battle. Pompey tactfully thanked him for his contribution and wished him well in the future, but privately reacted to his departure from the brigade with heartfelt relief. At last all three of the 'old fossil' colonels had gone. Cam Stewart at the helm of the 57th retained the exacting brigadier's confidence. Charles Denehy had performed very capably at Fromelles in challenging circumstances, having been plucked from the 57th to command the 58th just hours before the battle. Elliott was delighted that the transfer of his friend Harry Duigan from Tivey's brigade had been approved. With Duigan in charge of the 60th and Bert Layh leading the 59th, Pompey was certain his brigade would have its best quartet of battalion commanders since its inception.

On 29 September he left France for a badly needed holiday. While it was a beneficial spell from the trenches, he was too busy to have the complete rest he needed. Beginning in London at Berners Hotel, he accepted an invitation to spend a couple of pleasant days at Digswell Place with the Buckleys. He then visited AIF training camps at Salisbury Plain, paying particular attention to the 'depot battalion' that was the designated reinforcement source for his brigade. From there he travelled by train to Christchurch on the south coast to see one of his new-found British relatives, Alicia Carter, a cousin on his mother's side (widow of an admiral and sister of Emily Edwards). Mrs Carter was still coming to terms with the recent loss of her eldest son at the battle of Jutland. Returning to London, Elliott visited

> various hospitals where I knew my boys were, and saw a number of them. I am sorry that few of them were making any satisfactory progress towards recovery. It will be a long time before most of them are fit, if they are ever fit at all.

Aware he had been 'looking a bit dilapidated' of late, Elliott acquired a new uniform in London. Even Pompey admirers felt this was overdue; 'we were all a bit ashamed' of his shabby attire, Captain Kerr of the 60th admitted in August. Stylish dress was never a Pompey priority. Utterly unpretentious, he tended to be contemptuous of soldiers who were conspicuously spick-and-span, staff officers from higher formations in particular. Moreover, he begrudged expenditure on clothes when he was trying hard to save: the cost of his new outfit 'was just something awful'. Anyway, even if he had felt motivated to take more care about his appearance, his bulk and temperament were daunting obstacles. Whatever he was wearing soon became crumpled, looking as if he had slept in it.

Nevertheless, ever the disciplinarian, he insisted that men under his command had to be properly dressed. Diverting incidents ensued. Because Pompey preferred a belt rather than braces to keep his trousers up, he would often leave his braces hanging down; sometimes he forgot to hoist them back over his shoulders when this became appropriate. At formal parades he would be haranguing some unfortunate private about a button infringement, unaware how incongruous this reprimand was when his own braces were dangling sloppily from his midriff. Pompey's arrest in London for impersonating an officer also generated widespread amusement. Military policemen refused to believe that such a scruffily dressed man could really be a brigadier. There were red faces all round when this misunderstanding was eventually resolved.

Before returning to his brigade Elliott was reunited, for the first time in two years, with his sister Violet and brother George. Violet had been in London for months, waiting impatiently to see her husband, now an AIF medical officer, but Jack Avery had only recently been granted leave. It had been a frustrating situation. As Harold acknowledged when periodically canvassing whether Kate might come to London, Violet Avery's experience was not an encouraging precedent. Pompey was on his way back to the front when he caught up with George at Wimereux (near Boulogne). In 1915 George had married Lyn Walker after at last qualifying as a doctor (having started his course a decade earlier). He subsequently enlisted, like Jack Avery, in the medical corps. Harold was particularly fond of his youngest brother, and they had much to discuss, not least the recent marriage of their brother Rod.

Elliott and his brigade were transferred to the Somme shortly after his return. Haig had persisted with the Somme offensive despite mostly unsatisfactory results and an immense casualty toll, Australians very much included. Fierce fighting around Pozières and Mouquet Farm had resulted in no fewer than 22,826 AIF casualties in less than seven weeks. The ends hardly justified the means or the losses, but Haig was determined to persevere, even during winter.

The impact of summer showers on the Fromelles trenches had convinced Elliott that winter at the Western Front would be grim, but the reality was worse than even he had expected. The brigadier and his men were about to endure an unimaginable ordeal in the worst conditions experienced by the AIF during the entire war. British forces, relentlessly attacking since July, had pushed the Germans up to eight miles back, but the territory gained had been churned by innumerable shells into a surreal wasteland of death and destruction. As the Fifth AIF Division made its way towards the Somme battlefield, the onset of winter rains was turning the bleak shell-cratered landscape into a gluey morass. With all transport now confined to a few major roads, the increased pressure left them impenetrably congested.

While the 8th and 14th Brigades were sent straight into front-line trenches north of Flers, the 15th Brigade began with a stint in reserve three miles behind at Montauban, one of the pulverised villages that had become a boggy pigsty. 'The ground was very wet and muddy and there was practically no shelter', Wieck noted. Elliott was furious that the previous British occupants had left the area 'in a perfectly filthy condition'. Learning that 150 tents were obtainable from a supply depot some nine miles away, Elliott and Wieck immediately arranged for them to be collected, but clogged roads made this impossible. In these new surroundings, unlike the Fromelles sector, 'the roar of the guns is continuous by night and by day', Elliott reported. On 24 October he decided to have a look up ahead:

> Everything is desolation. The shell holes overlap and no semblance of buildings remain, just heaps of rubbish. I was quite knocked up by the walk and heavy going. Communication trenches are practically impassable with mud.

With his men scheduled to relieve the 14th Brigade in the front line, Elliott went forward again three days later to discuss changeover arrangements. It proved an even more trying excursion. Battling a severe cold, Pompey decided to take Darkie this time:

> I rode up yesterday and it took over 6 hours to go 3 miles up and three back. My poor old horse was quite knocked up floundering through shell holes up to the knees in mud and water. Once he fell with me and I thought I'd never get him up again for the mud was like glue and he simply couldn't lift himself at all.

On the 29th, amid persistent rain, Elliott inspected the front-line trenches his brigade had taken over:

> They were wretched in the extreme. Full of sloppy water and mud, in places over your boots. No sanitary arrangements ... Large numbers of dead, even in the trenches, with only a layer of dirt thrown over them ... Enemy shelled our headquarters considerably.

Next day there was more torrential rain. Conditions deteriorated even further.

As Corporal Downing recorded, the men were exhausted after slipping, sliding, and wrenching themselves forward through 'mire to the thighs at best, to the middle at worst'. When they tried to extricate themselves from the most tenacious mud the noise 'was like the tearing of sheets of cloth'. Some men and mules could not be extricated at all. A front-line stint in these putrid, dugout-less ditches, Downing wrote, was sheer torment:

> Hands and faces protruded from the slimy, toppling walls of trenches. Knees, shoulders and buttocks poked from the foul morass ... Our clothes, our very underclothing, were ponderous with ... mud ... There was no hot food, and no prospect of it ... We

> were soaked from head to feet (the feet that were never dry all that winter) with sweat and icy mud. We did not sleep, but waited in a torpor as the minutes crawled past ... We were mud to the eyes; our chilled fingers bled. Everything we touched was slimy.

Downing exemplified the plummet in AIF morale during this unusually severe 1916–17 winter:

> We just go into the line again and again until we get knocked. We'll never get out of this. Just in and out, in and out, and somebody stonkered every time. Australia has forgotten us, and so has God. I wouldn't wish my worst enemy to have to put up with this.

Elliott was full of compassion for his 'poor boys' having 'a terrible time' in these 'dreadful' trenches, with 'practically no sleep or rest' for three days at a time. Despite his heavy cold, he did what he could to hearten them, leaving his headquarters (an old German underground dug-out) to plough through the muck in regular front-line visits before breakfast:

> When I went round the trenches of course I got sopping wet just like the boys, but we had a fire in the end of the dug-out and I promptly went to bed until my clothes were dry again and did not put them on again until quite dry.

For miles around there was utter desolation—'mud, mud, mud everywhere', wrote Elliott. It was 'one vast bog', affirmed Wieck.

Attacking in these conditions was inconceivable, grotesque. Not only would attackers scarcely be able to drag themselves across the quagmire; it was impossible to get provisions, ammunition, and other prerequisites forward to them. But Haig decided to keep pressuring the Germans, and the Fifth Division was ordered to undertake an attack north of Flers that had been initially scheduled for 25 October before being repeatedly postponed because of the weather. The task had been allotted to the 14th Brigade with the 57th Battalion assisting; Elliott was warned that his whole brigade might become involved. To Pompey, any notion of attacking in such conditions was 'madness', and could only be contemplated by individuals unaware of the real situation.

He decided to rectify this himself. Having reconnoitred the position with Lieutenant-Colonel Wagstaff, McCay's senior staff officer, Elliott protested forcefully to McCay that the operation was impossible. Wagstaff concurred. McCay thereupon telephoned Brudenell White at First Anzac Corps and passed on what Elliott and Wagstaff had said; he added that because of their assessment he was not going to authorise the attack unless specifically ordered to do so by Birdwood, who would accordingly be responsible for the consequences.

The upshot was further postponement and reconsideration. On 3 November the Fifth Division was relieved, and Elliott briefed the 7th AIF Brigade commander, Brigadier-General J. Paton, who was new to the sector. A few days later Elliott learned that Paton's brigade had suffered a severe repulse in attempting a similar advance. There were 819 casualties in the 7th Brigade, including Paton himself. Attacking in such conditions—the worst the AIF ever endured—was preposterous, Bean concluded. Some 7th Brigade men were so exhausted by the effort of getting forward to the front line that they were weeping from sheer fatigue with the attack about to start. Elliott felt understandably vindicated. 'I am glad I saved our poor boys from the attempt', he wrote; 'fancy attempting a charge' with 'mud up to your knees'.

By then he was preoccupied with an altogether different concern. The increased need for AIF reinforcements after devastating recent casualties had prompted Australia's Prime Minister, W.M. Hughes, to raise the issue of conscription. Following a bitter campaign, a referendum on the question had been held on 28 October. Elliott was appalled to learn that a majority of Australians had voted against conscription. 'Isn't that a scandal', he raged. 'I feel that our country has disgraced us'. He had been emphasising the need for reinforcements ever since mid-1915. To Elliott, if Australians would not volunteer in sufficient numbers to do their duty in this almighty struggle, compulsion was obviously necessary. Astounded by the people's verdict, he responded by unleashing instinctive prejudices:

> I cannot understand it. I suppose it was the Catholics that were against England as usual, together with all the cold footers and wasters ... I hope we will never hear anything again about the loyalty of the Irish. They are a lovely lot.

Hughes had presumed that the AIF would vote overwhelmingly for conscription. He had arranged for the soldiers' voting to be conducted early enough for him to be able to trumpet this anticipated large majority before polling day in Australia. The AIF did record an overall majority in favour of conscription, but the narrow margin was far short of the emphatic endorsement Hughes was expecting. Instead of advertising the soldiers' vote far and wide before 28 October, he refused to release the figures for five months.

Voting in the 15th Brigade took place on 19 October. 'I am afraid lots and lots of the boys here have voted against', lamented Elliott. Although profoundly disappointed, it was symptomatic of his compassionate identification with his men—such a significant factor in his success as a commander—that he reacted sympathetically to their motives for opposing conscription. He could understand why 'men who have to stand in the front line and bear it all—frost and snow, rain and hail, bullets, bayonets, shells and bombs night and day' were reluctant to compel relatives and friends to endure such 'dreadful suffering' against their will. Not even in private letters did he castigate those in his brigade who had voted 'No', though he was repeatedly scathing about anti-conscriptionist campaigners.

That Germany had to be defeated, for Australia's sake as much as any nation's, had been Elliott's firm conviction 'from the very instant war was declared'. It was 'very, very certain' that if Germany won the war, Australia itself would be in peril: 'The Germans themselves make no secret of the fact that if they can get it they will take it'. If so, everyone in Australia would then experience 'all the horrors we see about us'. According to Elliott, peace terms should not even be considered as long as the German army remained outside Germany. He endorsed the conscriptionist claim that even a conflict involving millions could be so finely balanced that the provision of more Australians could make a difference, although his own recent experiences at Fromelles and Flers suggested that if Australia did provide more men they would probably be massacred in futile enterprises. Concern that unwilling conscripts might diminish the quality of the AIF's performance influenced some Australian soldiers to vote 'No', but Elliott was confident he could extract a satisfactory standard of efficiency from unpromising raw material.

His frustration that Australians remote from the conflict were prepared to vote against the views of on-the-spot military experts like himself was understandable, but perhaps this very detachment enabled them to make a longer-term judgment in a way that he, in the centre of the action, could not. Australia's future had already been gravely compromised by the loss of so many of its brightest and best, such as Geoff McCrae. If it really was necessary to send more soldiers to the Western Front slaughter-house, it was arguably not in Australia's genuine long-term interests to be the nation providing them.

For a while at the Somme the 15th Brigade happened to be in pleasing proximity to the 7th Battalion. Reunited former comrades exchanged hearty greetings and swapped tales of Pozières and Fromelles. Pompey himself was inundated with well-wishers. Many reiterated a sentiment he had often heard from 7th veterans since his departure: they would like to transfer to the 15th Brigade. Charles Mason, Jack Scanlan, and Shannon Grills, former 7th officers incapacitated at Gallipoli, had all joined the 15th Brigade after recovering in Australia. Elliott heard fervent similar aspirations expressed when he visited the 7th on 26 October. It was a jovial interlude with spirited handshakes and reminiscing. But at one point, with his successor Lieutenant-Colonel Carl Jess present, Pompey said 'Well, boys, if any of you are not satisfied you know where to come—we're just camped across the road'.

That pointed remark reflected Elliott's differences with Jess concerning George Ball. Pompey had recommended Jess as his successor. Jess had not served in the 7th before commanding it; he began the war as Monash's staff captain before becoming brigade major of the 2nd Brigade. Ball, a tall, Russian-born immigrant who had been in Australia only three years when the war began, was one of the 7th Battalion's finest front-line soldiers. He was 'absolutely fearless', Pompey enthused, 'always doing some reckless job'. Wounded at the landing, Ball was awarded the DCM on Elliott's recommendation for remarkable gallantry at Lone Pine. Ball's undoubted leadership potential was undermined, Pompey felt, by his imperfect grasp of English. Reluctantly, Pompey decided not to make him an officer because his inability to understand or write precise messages might let him (and those fighting alongside him) down in a tight corner. Ball's fondness for liquor was another concern. Whereas Pompey had been tolerant—'he was such a splendid chap that I always shut my eyes hard'—Jess punished him repeatedly for drunkenness.

In the trenches, however, Ball was outstanding. At Pozières he was 'magnificent', and in a subsequent raid he single-handedly dealt with half a dozen Germans. Although recommended for a VC, he was only given a bar to his DCM. Disappointed, he hit the grog again and was arrested. Elliott intervened—'I went over and asked Jess couldn't he let him off in view of his services'—to no avail. Jess had been stung, Elliott surmised, when Ball blurted out that Pompey used to visit the front line regularly, but Jess was rarely seen there; this was a widely held view, as Pompey knew. Elliott then asked Ball if he would like to transfer to the 15th Brigade. Ball applied immediately, but Jess refused to acquiesce. Returning to the front line soon after, Ball was struck by a shell fragment and killed.

Elliott and his brigade returned to front-line duty in the Gueudecourt sector (not far from Flers) on 20 November, taking over from the most elite British formation, the Guards. During the changeover Elliott and the guardsmen discussed their experiences. He had a reminiscent chat with the able chief staff officer of the Guards Division, Lieutenant-Colonel C.P. Heywood, who had, as a Coldstream Guards subaltern, served in close proximity to Elliott in the Boer War while the Victorian Bushmen were attached to Henniker's column. Elliott was interested to learn that the Guards had spent months near Fromelles; then part of XI Corps, they had resisted Haking's desire to launch a series of attacks with a view to capturing the Aubers Ridge.

Prompted by Elliott's account of the AIF's grim Fromelles experience, Major-General G.P.T. Feilding, the Guards Division commander, remarked that the Guards were supposed to attack there, but decided not to because the operation would have been a disastrous failure. 'What happened?' asked Elliott. 'Nothing', replied Feilding, explaining that the Guards' reputation was 'beyond reproach'. The Australians had now established an equivalent reputation, Feilding added, endorsing the way McCay had challenged the proposed attack at Flers. Feilding advised Elliott that whenever he was given a task that he was convinced after careful reconnaissance was impossible, he should do what a Guards commander would do: refuse to carry out the order without instructions from a superior specifically overriding his recorded protest. Only a few days earlier, in fact, an order by Heywood directing one of the Guards brigades to capture two enemy trenches contained an escape clause specifying that if conditions were unfavourable the brigadier concerned was 'at liberty to postpone the operation'. The attack did not take place. Elliott's discussions with the guardsmen reinforced his determination to protest if directed to undertake any more operations like Fromelles or Flers.

The Guards were inadvertently implicated when Elliott incurred Birdwood's wrath shortly afterwards. Birdwood happened to ask a 58th casualty if he had seen any Germans, and was told he had seen dozens but was not allowed to shoot at them. Birdwood angrily demanded an explanation from Elliott. The brigadier denied all knowledge of any such order (and sensed Birdwood disbelieved him). On making enquiries, Elliott discovered that front-line guardsmen had told his men during the changeover that they were not to fire at the enemy unless the Germans fired at them.

Elliott followed this up with Brigadier-General C.E. Corkran, commander of the Guards brigade his men had relieved. Corkran confirmed that the Guards had established a tacit understanding with the Germans opposite, and provided a compelling justification for it. The British front trenches were situated on the forward slope of a hill under direct enemy observation, and communication trenches to the front line were impassable or non-existent; yet the terrible ordeal endured by front-line soldiers could be partially alleviated only if food, dry clothing, and equipment could be conveyed to them. With firm dry ground much closer behind the German front than it was behind the British, it seemed obvious to Corkran that the British would benefit much more than their adversaries from a non-provocative arrangement. Elliott agreed.

> I reported this conversation to General Birdwood and asked him to see General Corkran, and pointed out that a policy that was considered good enough for the Guardsmen who had always been held up to us as the mirror and pattern of efficiency and discipline was hardly to be condemned in us ... He did not seem pleased at the way I put it.

Birdwood ended the understanding. Front-line suffering increased, and by more on the British side, Elliott was convinced, than on the enemy's.

On 22 November, having decided to see for himself the state of the trenches his men had just taken over, Elliott left his headquarters early in the afternoon intending to spend the night in the front line. Accompanying him was Lieutenant Hugh Knyvett, who had impressed him with the quality of his scouting work after being commissioned from the ranks following Fromelles. On their way they encountered a sharp enemy bombardment, which necessitated a deviation from their intended route. The forward position comprised an erratic broken 'line' of thinly occupied shell holes, not easy to find in the dark. 'We got almost inextricably tangled amidst the slush and shell holes', Elliott wrote, 'and after wandering for hours found ourselves at last in the 8th Brigade lines to the right about 800 yards off the position we intended to reach'.

How they were to proceed from there was not straightforward. Knyvett was confident he knew the best way, but Elliott was not so sure. Getting around in the shell-scarred slime, Pompey explained later, could be

> terribly puzzling in the dark owing to the dozens of trenches which get in your way. Often you cannot cross them when you reach them, and you go along to find a crossing, and before you know where you are they have bent round, and when you do cross them it is so dark and you cannot see anything that will enable you to pick up your original line of march.

It was not uncommon, in this sector particularly, for soldiers of both sides to turn up mistakenly in enemy-held territory.

Elliott opted to stay put while Knyvett checked that his preferred direction was correct. Knyvett set off. An hour later he had not returned. The brigadier had an uncomfortable wait. It was a bitterly cold night, and he was wet through. Eventually Elliott decided he could wait no longer. He made his way slowly back, arriving 'very wet and muddy at 2am next morning'. His misgivings about Knyvett's route proved correct. Knyvett had almost walked into a German sentry, who fired at him as he scurried away into a shell hole. One of the bombs the Germans threw after him rolled against his leg and exploded, inflicting multiple wounds. The bombers then searched for him unsuccessfully. With his legs useless, Knyvett crawled painfully back across part of no-man's-land before being rescued. It was just as well that Elliott had been prudent.

Meanwhile Elliott was grappling with another affliction tormenting his long-suffering trench-dwellers:

> It is dreadfully cold and frosty … The frost dries the ground wonderfully, but the men in the front trenches suffer shockingly from trench feet when their feet get frozen and gangrene sets in. It is so far back to the ambulance and it takes so long to get them from the front line that they are too far gone when they reach the ambulance to have their feet saved.

Various preventative measures were adopted. Rubber gum boots were issued, and officers and NCOs were directed to ensure that feet were regularly massaged with whale oil. Efforts were redoubled to get duckboards forward and to provide the men regularly with dry clothing and warm sustenance.

Elliott, desperate to alleviate the hardships, was at his wits' end.

> I have tried to work out ways of sending hot food up to the line … I have so much on my mind … It is dreadful that these poor boys have to suffer like this. Fancy a six foot trench half full of muddy slush in which you have to live for three days at a time.

'I lie awake all night at times trying to find a way to help them', he admitted. He passed on to McCay his own ideas, together with suggestions by his men that he had adopted. Some were instituted beyond the 15th Brigade. One of his officers came up with a thermos-like conveyance to keep provisions hot on their way forward. This contrivance, Elliott reported proudly, 'has been taken on throughout the whole British Army'.

But it was distressing to feel so powerless despite his strenuous efforts:

> The weather continues to be the absolute limit. Today pouring rain and snow. Many of the poor boys are very sick. I really cannot imagine how they live through it all. The ground is so sodden with rain and so shaken with shell fire that it is hardly possible to dig a trench at all. When it is dug the sides crumble in almost at once from the rain … The men stay there three days at a time. During this time it is practically impossible to get any sleep as there is nowhere to lie. The men get a little sleep propped against the side of the trench, but then the frost comes and freezes the sludge and their poor feet get frozen and unless you get them back quickly their

> feet get gangrene and their toes drop off. We have to leave them there three days as otherwise the awful toil of marching up every day through the mud would simply knock up every man we have, and the men themselves prefer to do the three days at one go than face the awful walk. It is a horrible walk, too. Fritz notices almost at once where a track is worn in the mud and shells it all night, and most of the tracks have an avenue of mangled corpses all along the border of them.

The Fifth AIF Division 'has the worst sector along the whole British front', Bean concluded.

On 14 December Elliott was on his way to the front line with Major Greenway of the brigade engineers when 'suddenly without any warning a huge shell ... exploded with a deafening roar' just behind him. Elliott was flung violently forward as Greenway, just ahead, spun round anxiously. Greenway grasped the brigadier in his arms as they were showered by spattering mud and enveloped by a pall of smoke. 'Are you hurt sir, are you hurt?' Greenway shouted. Fortunately for them both, the gluey mud had prevented the shell from dispersing properly, and Elliott was unscathed. But that night when he went to bed he realised he had not escaped altogether.

> Although I felt as sleepy as usual I could not go off at all. If I dozed the least little bit I would suddenly give a nervous jump and wake right up again ... This made sleep impossible.

After three nights of this he consulted Keith Doig, the recently arrived 60th Battalion doctor. Doig had been a colleague of George's during his medicine course, at Ormond College, and on the football field. The Ormond farewell dinner in September 1914 that both Elliott and Doig (as senior resident) had addressed seemed half a lifetime ago. Doig prescribed a sleeping draught for the brigadier. That evening, having taken it, Pompey was 'into a lovely sleep' by 7.00pm, but at 12.45am a German shell arrived

> about 20 yards from my door and nearly shook the place down. I tried to get off again and had rotten luck. I dozed off about a dozen times and had frightful nightmares each time. I fell off bridges and

> got blown up by shells, and went into a big house or hotel to find Katie and found dozens of bedrooms all round the place and did not know which was hers, and got into a terrible state because I had to go away as I thought without having seen her. This dream was brought on by Katie's letter I had just read saying how disappointed she would have been had she come to England and waited for months like Violet, and then had had to go away home without seeing me. I was nearly scared to death to go to sleep again after that, and was glad morning came at last.

After a good sleep the following night, however, he was soon feeling much better.

With 1916 drawing to a close, he was about to spend Christmas apart from Kate and the children for the third year in a row. He was convinced it would not be the last. Having heard rumours that Russia was contemplating surrender, and feeling concerned about the implications of Germany's triumph in Roumania, he was pessimistic about the strategic outlook:

> I have always thought that it would be all over by Xmas 1917, but I begin to fear I will never see home again ... It seems to me that never before have we been in such awful danger of being defeated, and you know what that would mean—the end of the British Empire. Certainly Australia would go to the Germans.

He was particularly concerned about the Germans acquiring their own tanks. This British innovation had been unveiled on 15 September. Next day, before he had seen a tank himself, Elliott was enthusing that this 'new thing' was 'the most promising implement of war we have yet invented'. It was, he explained, like 'an enormous slug moving so slowly over anything at all—trees, wire, trenches, even steep embankments'. The prospect of the Germans developing their own filled him with dread:

> I confess that the thought of these lumbering monsters coming down upon us is awful to contemplate. There is such a feeling of helplessness in regard to them. Infantry have no chance with them at all. If you get in their way they simply come and tread on you or shoot you to bits.

At the end of another harrowing year, with victory seemingly further away than ever despite all the losses and all the hardships, Elliott was in a sombre mood. 'I do miss poor Geoff McCrae very much', he wrote on the last day of 1916. 'He had a particularly bright happy disposition'. Cedric Permezel, Jimmy Johnston and the Henderson brothers all had special qualities too:

> They were one and all animated with a wonderful personal loyalty to myself. And now all are gone. I shall not look upon their like again—that is certain ... If I myself should fall in France I should like to be buried near poor Geoff.

He described the appearance and position of Geoff's grave in detail for the distraught McCrae family, who reacted to their bereavement by seeking all sorts of information about Geoff—the location of the cemetery, and how to get there; the farmhouse he stayed in on his last night alive, and how to find it; the identity of his batman, and how to contact him; the personal effects Geoff left behind, and how to retrieve them. Elliott replied to these and other requests patiently and at length, and did what he could to soothe their aching anguish:

> I can assure you that Geoff fulfilled the highest expectations you ever formed of him, and he will do honor to those soldier ancestors of his where he has joined them.

Elliott was also missing his family. He wrote to Kate every few days, as she did to him. Throughout these stressful years apart they gave each other unstinting harmonious support. Friction was minimal. He was annoyed when he found his first letter home after the Gallipoli landing reproduced in the *Argus*—'Beach Like Sandringham' ran the headline—but his disapproval evaporated when he learned that a journalist who had overlapped with him at Ormond had persuaded Kate to release it for publication. Late in 1916 Kate heard from Ina Prictor that a certain officer had been critical of McCay in a letter to a solicitor friend. Presuming the unnamed correspondent was her husband, she proceeded to take him to task. However, Elliott denied writing any such letter, pointing out that he had altogether different views about McCay. Kate apologised profusely.

Such misunderstandings, however, were rare. Elliott was always sympathetic to concerns expressed in her letters—vexatious house-hunting, ill-health in the family, the redback spider in the cubby-house. He kept her regularly informed about soldiers she knew, her brother Jack in particular. Sensing her tendency to scrimp selflessly in his absence, he repeatedly urged her to put some weight on her slender frame. And he treasured her letters:

> I had started on foot at 9pm and got here after 12. The mud and slush most of the way was quite up to the knees and I had fallen over into many shell holes, so you can imagine the state I was in, but I found a heap of letters awaiting me including two from you … Muddy and tired out as I was I read them all before I went to sleep, and was quite cheered and comforted by all your kindness and love.

Kate was intensely proud and supportive of her husband. His frankness to her about his experiences and feelings consolidated her loving empathy. She needed little encouragement to wax eloquent to friends about 'Daddy' and his doings, identifying totally with his aspirations and associations. Kate willingly invited to her house those wounded officers who accepted Pompey's encouragement to contact her, attended the Governor-General's presentation of the VC to Bill Dunstan, and (though not at all an attention-seeker and hardly a natural administrator) accepted a prominent role in the 15th Brigade 'depot' —an association formed to organise the dispatch of supplementary rations and to streamline requests for information about particular soldiers from anxious relatives and friends. Not wanting to add to her husband's burdens, she did her best to keep her worries from him—the biggest, of course, being concern for his own safety. Whatever she really thought, she assured him she was confident that her prayers for his safe return would be heeded.

Although proud of her husband's reputation, Kate regretted that some of the Pompey stories his men liked telling attributed (mildly) coarse language to him. After the Gallipoli evacuation she told him so. 'There is no use denying it', he replied,

> I did swear sometimes and it did good Katie … it made them pay attention to what I said. I don't like it Katie a bit more than you do, but I do everything calculated to make my boys do what I want.

Now he was a brigadier, he assured her, he would no longer have to swear. Before long he had to modify this assurance. His battalion commanders were to blame, he told Kate, and he had lectured them accordingly:

> I made them all laugh by telling them my wife said she had heard all sorts of stories about me including one that I had developed a habit of swearing at the men, that you had said you didn't believe it and hoped if it were true I would stop it at once. That I had thereupon written to assure you that having been promoted to command a Brigade I now had four Battalion Commanders to do all swearing necessary and I would be able to be good. That after the march from Tel-el-Kebir unfortunately I had to write again, and confess that instead as in the 7th swearing for 1 only I found I had to swear for 4, ie for the whole Brigade. This very much amused them, but I assured them I was not a bit amused at the prospect and they would have to do their job and relieve me from the necessity for swearing at their men.

Kate was not placated, and he had to revisit this issue after Fromelles:

> You need not worry dear about the swearing. I don't have to do it now at all. I leave it to Bert Layh and the others. Some of them are quite good at it too.

In fact, 'I would pass for a Sunday School teacher anywhere at present'.

As before, whenever Kate aired misgivings about the content of her letters, he was reassuring. 'You would not think your letter was uninteresting if you saw me reading it over and over about six times so as to be sure I haven't missed anything'. But if ever she (or Belle) felt like that, he reiterated, just a description of whatever the children were up to would enthral him. His thirst for news about them was insatiable. Belle frequently sent photos of them; he kept asking for more. Receiving a letter from his five-year-old daughter in her own handwriting for the first time ('Dear Dida, I love you, Violet') was a special milestone that he noted in his diary amid all the military developments.

Elliott did what he could from afar to remain an involved parent. He deeply regretted being unable to see his children grow up, but was aware that his remoteness did not preclude him from shaping their development. In one sense, he felt, it might even help. Because the children had placed him on a higher pedestal than they would have done at home—'while I am so far away they cannot see all the holes and faults in me'—they were perhaps more receptive to his influence, he conjectured, than they might otherwise have been.

However, the remarkable letters he wrote to his children underlined how unfortunate it was for them that he was not around during these formative years. He had a marvellous talent for communicating with children. Surely no commander in any combatant nation in this war regularly described military developments like this:

> Since I wrote to you before we got a lot of big waggons like traction engines and put guns in them and ran them 'bumpety bump' up against the old Kaiser's wall and knocked a great big hole in it and caught thousands and thousands of the Kaiser's naughty soldier men and we killed a lot of them and more we put in jail so they couldn't be naughty any more, but then it started to rain and rain and snow and hail and the ground got all boggy and the waggons got stuck in the mud and the old Kaiser has such heaps and heaps of soldiers that he sent up a lot more and thinned them out where the wall wasn't broken and started to build another big wall to stop us going any further ... it is very very cold here and the Jack Frost here is not a nice Jack Frost who just pinches your fingers so you can run to a fire to warm them but a great big bitey Jack Frost and he pinches the toes and fingers of some of Dida's poor soldiers so terribly that he pinches them right off. Isn't that terrible ... And the naughty old Kaiser burnt down every little house all round here and Dida's soldiers have to sleep out in the mud or dig holes in the ground like rabbits to sleep in. And all the trees are blown to pieces by the big guns and there is no wood to make fires and Dida's soldiers have to make fires of coal and the waggons are all stuck in the mud so Dida's soldiers have to carry it through all the mud and everything they eat and wear has to be carried too. And Dida's soldiers get so dreadfully tired they can hardly work or walk at all. Isn't that old Kaiser a naughty old man to cause all this trouble. Now goodbye dear little laddie. Give dear old mum a kiss and tell her Dida's coming home soon and that you will grow up soon and you won't let any old Kaiser come near her ...

As those parting words suggest, Elliott gave his young son clear signals that it was a man's duty to protect the womenfolk in the family. He was a devoted father with a rare talent for relating to children at their level, but he was a man of his time concerning the different expectations he had of his son and daughter. It was not that he gave less encouragement to Violet than Neil—he was encouraging her to strive to be top of the class before she even started school!—but it tended to be in different spheres. Prompted by his admiration of Tom Elliott and other 'splendid boys from Duntroon' who had served under him, Pompey was already contemplating sending his four-year-old son there so Neil could 'learn to be a soldier properly', as distinct from picking it up on a spare-time basis as he had. He was clearly hoping that Neil would develop sturdy soldierly attributes, both physical (a strong chin was desirable) and temperamental. On one occasion, with Belle occupied on the phone, part of the fire escaped onto the linoleum; Pompey was gratified to learn that Neil displayed initiative, sweeping it up promptly all by himself. And in a pep talk about dealing with bullies, he wrote that if 'any naughty boy' was ever rough or said 'cheeky things' to either Violet or Neil, it would be appropriate for Neil to 'punch him real hard' to stop him behaving 'like an old Kaiser Bill'. 'Don't you be frightened if he is a big boy', he added, 'if you punch him good and hard he will start to squeal for mercy'. On the other hand, the specific activities that Elliott encouraged Violet to continue with were her piano-playing and knitting, saying grace before meals, and helping Kate roll the butter.

It was hardly surprising that Violet and Neil, in their own way, became absorbed in the war. Instead of the customary bedtime story from a book, they often clamoured for a 'story about Dida', which usually had a military flavour. Neil's imaginary play often featured shells and 'Kaiser Bill' characters; he liked singing 'Onward Christian Soldiers' and, as the man of the house, sometimes pretended to be practising his shooting prowess in order to be ready to protect his mother, sister, aunt, and grandmother. But in his prayers he asked God to stop the war. Violet wanted to become a nurse so she could help look after Dida's wounded soldiers, and talked about having some special flowers with her when at last she met her father again. 'It is very nice of you to promise to bring me flowers when you come to meet me', he replied fervently, 'but you will be the only flower I want … best little fairy lady in all the world.'

Just before Christmas McCay was replaced. With his Gallipoli wound still troublesome, he was finding it increasingly difficult to carry on as Fifth Division commander in the appalling conditions, and his reputation among the men was permanently tarnished by his connection with the Krithia charge, the desert march, and the Fromelles disaster. Elliott believed that the sweeping criticism of McCay was excessive, and felt impelled to stick up for him. To Pompey, McCay's biggest weakness had been his willingness to attack unquestioningly whenever he was told, but the way he associated himself with Pompey's Flers protest indicated that he was reconsidering his former approach (a change Elliott believed he himself had engendered). McCay was 'undoubtedly one of our ablest generals', and there was 'no one I personally would sooner serve under', wrote Pompey. 'Whatever his faults he does know his job and he is a wonderfully brave man, as brave as anyone I've ever seen'.

Sensing that McCay would be despondent about relinquishing the last field command he was likely to hold (he was transferred to head the AIF depots in England), Elliott wrote him a considerate letter: 'I told him if he ever goes to war again and wants a soldier he can ask for me and I'll go with him'. The gesture hit the spot, as McCay's reply confirmed:

> It is not often in a man's life that he receives so generous a letter, and one that makes him very proud, but yours I will keep and value always for the splendid friendship and undeserved appreciation it expresses ... It is a rather bitter pill to see the shelf so near, but I must just take things as they come.

McCay's successor as Elliott's immediate superior at Fifth Division was 52-year-old Major-General J.J. Talbot Hobbs. A London-born architect who had migrated to Western Australia in 1887, Hobbs had commanded the First Division's artillery since the outbreak of war. Short and wiry in physique, and sometimes nervously hesitant in speech, Hobbs was capable, determined, and meticulous; he was a disciplinarian without evincing McCay's austere manner. Elliott's initial impressions were not favourable:

> He has put a red flag on the front of his motor car so the men can't say that they didn't know he was in the car, and whenever they see

> the red flag car pass they've got to salute it. He is splashing round making a terrible fuss.

Having heard that C.R. Davies, the former 'old fossil' commander of the 58th Battalion, had returned from Australia and was looking for an appointment, Elliott became concerned that the reputed friendship of Hobbs and Davies, both West Australians, might result in Davies being posted back to the 15th Brigade: 'If they try to force him on to me again there will be a deuce of a fuss', he threatened.

The advent of Charles Mason, who had served with Elliott in South Africa as well as at Gallipoli, enabled him to kill two birds with one stone. His recommendation led to the appointment of Mason as head of the Fifth Division training school with the temporary rank of lieutenant-colonel. Not only was Mason well-suited to that post; once he was in it, transferring him to fill any vacancy that might arise at the level of battalion commander in the 15th Brigade would be, as Pompey realised, relatively straightforward. Mason's availability would help Elliott thwart any plans to saddle him with officers he did not want, such as Davies. And there might well be vacancies to be filled—Duigan was away sick, and an injury to Layh was threatening to sideline him for weeks. To fill in for Layh at the 59th, the brigadier chose Grills; Pompey had considerable regard for Scanlan, who had also recently joined the 15th Brigade, but he was away on staff-work training. Pompey's satisfaction with Cam Stewart's sound leadership of the 57th had continued; he was acting brigadier whenever Pompey was on leave. Denehy of the 58th was also, Elliott felt, 'doing most excellent work'.

But the 60th was a worry. In Duigan's absence the acting commander during the most trying phase of the winter was Major F.V. Trickey, an officer Pompey had tried to get rid of back in Egypt. Overwhelmed by the appalling conditions, Trickey submitted that he and his staff had done 'everything humanly possible', but Pompey was scathing about his leadership: 'a more utterly useless officer in the face of the least difficulty I have never yet met'. Trickey was banished and, pending Duigan's return, Pompey resorted to installing his staff captain, Legge. Well aware of Norman Marshall's potential, Elliott arranged for him to attend a special training course for prospective battalion commanders.

In mid-January, fortified by a fortnight away from the trenches and a CMG in the New Year's decorations, Elliott returned with his brigade to Gueudecourt. The sector they had left a few weeks earlier was looking very different, the brigadier told Kate:

> It has snowed here for two days and last night there was a hard frost, and all the world around is like a huge wedding cake with icing sugar on it. The frost has made a hard crust on the snow and it crackles under your feet as you walk. It is very pretty but very cold.

In this environment digging work was more onerous and, at times, impossible (though trench walls thankfully no longer kept subsiding). Night patrols were more visible against the white background, and traffic routes showed up more clearly in aerial photographs, presenting artillery on both sides with obvious targets.

However, despite these drawbacks—and the intense cold—the new conditions were a tremendous relief. The exhausting mud had gone. Mobility returned. Supplies could reach the front-line soldiers more easily and more often. And the recipients found themselves able to move about more freely, a development that boosted their morale as well as reducing the incidence of trench feet. Elliott's resolve to do his utmost for his men was unremitting; he believed that they were looked after as well as possible. Bean, whose dedicated roving around the AIF had given him a good idea of what was feasible, was amazed to find that Pompey had installed kitchens close enough to provide his front-line soldiers with three hot meals each day.

But illness, exacerbated by the extreme cold, remained a major problem despite Elliott's endeavours. In the 60th Keith Doig evacuated Duigan and Kerr on the same day; Duigan, seriously ill, was delirious and had a very high temperature. Twice, seven weeks apart, Wieck described the situation at brigade headquarters as an 'epidemic'. At one stage half the headquarters personnel were sick in bed. Legge, for example, had a fortnight's sick leave in January, but four days after his return had to go away again.

Pompey himself had to cope with persistent ill-health. Early in December he was diagnosed with bronchitis, and was ordered to bed. He took over a week to recover, only to relapse a few days later. 'I get nearly better, then (as today) I get very wet and cold visiting the trenches and get right back to where I was again', he explained. 'I go to bed just after dinner at night because I cannot keep warm anywhere else'. He struggled on with inflamed throat and choky cough until 26 January, when he was laid low with influenza on top of the chronic bronchitis. Doig, increasingly concerned, kept him bedridden, but he was determined to remain on duty. By now it was so glacial that when Doig went looking for firewood his hands were too cold to hold the axe:

> Shell holes of water are frozen right to the bottom. Ink is frozen. The mud is frozen and of course we are frozen.

'Even in bed one's feet feel like ice', Elliott affirmed; the doctors 'say I will get pneumonia or pleurisy if I stop here much longer, so I've given in to them at last'. He agreed to have a prolonged break at the end of his brigade's period in the line. Until then he was supposed to stay in bed.

Bob Salmon, Doyle's successor as brigade intelligence officer, did not succumb to the headquarters epidemic. He had become Pompey's usual companion on his regular rounds of the forward positions, usually around dawn, whenever the brigade was on front-line duty (and the brigadier was not confined to bed). Pompey liked to amuse himself by testing whether the icy veneer above the shell holes would support his considerable weight. On 23 January he went forward early with Salmon:

> On way back tested the shell holes for thickness of ice—found one that would bear us both. The ice was nearly 3 inches thick, the upper two-thirds crystallised, the lower one-third as clear as glass. Also saw some very beautiful frost effects on a wire netting screen in front of a battery.

His companion was not as enthusiastic about these diversions. According to Salmon, Pompey used to bounce about on the ice, full of boisterous exuberance and joie de vivre, and say

> 'Here we are full of life, and we might be blown to bits any moment and we don't care a damn'. He would only laugh when I suggested he should not speak like that in the plural.

Salmon had a keen eye for potential amusement himself. Pompey, Salmon knew, was so fed up with what seemed to him a stream of impractical directives emanating from Corps headquarters far to the rear that he had threatened to send any Corps staff officer he came across to the front line for 24 hours. Accordingly, when Salmon learned that a major from Corps headquarters (unidentified by Salmon, but probably Major S.S. Butler) wanted to visit the 15th Brigade, he was eager to help. With Pompey sick 'in bed in his miserable surface dug-out doing his best to keep warm and dry', Salmon was looking forward to some entertaining 'fireworks'. He was not disappointed:

> On reaching the dug-out I pulled the waterproof sheet aside and said 'Major ——from Corps headquarters to see you, sir'. Pompey nearly leaped from his sleeping bag and, before any courtesies could be exchanged, roared 'Do you know what I am going to do with you?' 'No', was the answer. 'I am going to take you to the line and keep you there for 24 hours'. The major protested, but Pompey insisted as he was trying to climb into his issue pants. In the end the major convinced Pompey that it was a matter of extreme urgency that he be back at Corps headquarters as soon as possible. On being then asked the purpose of his visit, the major replied that he had brought some cakes from the Chief of Staff. A gruff goodbye was exchanged, and the visitors departed. The only remark that I could catch as they passed along the duckboards was 'Extraordinary!'

An official party of civilians visited the 15th Brigade on 11 February. Pompey, still unwell, asked Salmon to look after them. Salmon guided them forward until they were 400 yards from the front line. According to Elliott, Salmon then

> told them they would have to stoop down very low and crawl because ... the Bosche ... would shell them if he saw them. So down they got on hands and knees and painfully crawled the last quarter of a mile over the frozen mud and ice in the bottom of the trench, while he walked along comfortably in rear of them nearly busting his sides at the look of them.

Chuckling about this episode afterwards, Pompey and his talented intelligence officer (who had started at Ballarat College as a seven-year-old shortly after Elliott left) reckoned they might have fewer unwelcome visitors in future.

On 1 February the 15th Brigade assisted an adjacent assault by a 4th Brigade battalion, which was initially successful before being repulsed by a German counter-attack. Elliott had advised Brudenell White beforehand that this operation should be tackled differently. Having frequently urged during the winter that local tactical objectives could be attained with much fewer casualties if his brigade's light mortars had a more prominent role, Pompey was particularly frustrated when these mortars were not used on this occasion. He was convinced they could have exacted a severe toll on the German counter-attackers. An amended version of the operation was carried out a few days later. Again the assault was initially successful and once more the Germans counter-attacked, but this time the 15th Brigade was asked to help. Anticipating this request, Pompey had his mortars already in position, and their contribution was a crucial factor, he and Wieck believed, in the failure of the German counter-attack.

There was in addition an important raid by the 57th Battalion to organise. Hobbs, also involved in the preparations, was proving to be a worrier: after a conference he attended had exhaustively canvassed the artillery's role, he phoned Elliott, anxiously wanting to change an aspect 'we had already fully discussed ... and agreed'. The operation was a distinct success. In a swift and devastating vindication of Elliott's faith in his brigade's light mortars, the raiders inflicted severe casualties on the enemy while sustaining few themselves. Furthermore, information derived from the prisoners and materials captured was in the possession of Army headquarters only half an hour after the start of the raid, a record-breaking feat. Birdwood sent a warm congratulatory telegram, and Hobbs reacted with such ecstatic delight that Pompey's concerns about their relationship dissolved in an instant. However, 'the effect of being up all night and the excitement sent my temperature away to glory'; Doig insisted on his immediate departure. Hobbs 'gave me a very nice lunch', organised a car to Boulogne, and 'said I must not on any account hurry back'.

In London he reported to an AIF medical board, consulted a dentist, and luxuriated in his first bath for a month. He then went to Harrow to see Duigan and his wife. It was Duigan's seventh week in bed battling pneumonia, bronchitis, rheumatism, and kidney trouble, and he was 'just skin and bone'. To Jessie Duigan's relief, Elliott accepted that her husband should not return to France, and arranged a position for him in England. Invited to stay with the Buckleys again, Elliott spent a couple of days at Digswell Place before travelling to Wales for a relaxing week at Bryn Oerog, where he consolidated his friendship with Emily Edwards; they corresponded frequently after his return to France.

Towards the end of his stay his brother George joined him. George was worn out after devoted endeavours as the 56th Battalion's doctor to alleviate the winter sufferings of that unit, efforts glowingly commended (as Harold knew) by George's superiors. They discussed the recent birth of George's first child, Jacquelyn, enjoyed each other's company in the picturesque Bryn Oerog surroundings, and returned to London together. Pompey then went to Buckingham Palace, where he shook hands with the King and was presented with his CMG. On 12 March, refreshed by his break, he returned to France, where interesting developments were under way and an unusual opportunity awaited him.

CHAPTER ELEVEN

'Simply Paralysing the Old Boche':

Pursuit to the Hindenburg Line

MARCH 1917

DURING THE MID-WINTER misery Elliott had been pessimistic about the strategic situation, expecting the Germans to launch an awesome onslaught within a few months. Instead, while he was recuperating in England, the Germans retreated. This was a stunning development; but, as Elliott cautioned correctly, the enemy would be 'falling back … only to take up a stronger position to the rear'. Senior German strategists had concluded that their most effective path to victory lay in a policy of full-scale submarine warfare to restrict England's food supplies. While this naval strategy was taking effect they decided that Germany should remain on the defensive militarily. They therefore pulled back their forces at the Western Front to the heavily fortified Hindenburg Line (as it came to be known), which had been under construction for some time. This manoeuvre involved a retirement that varied in depth, and was as much as 30 miles in some sectors; in front of the AIF the new line was twelve miles away. After such a miserable winter, it was an uplifting contrast to be advancing in pursuit of a retreating enemy. Bapaume had been a primary objective, and an increasingly remote one, during the costly assaults of 1916; Australians occupied the town on 17 March, encountering minimal resistance, and glimpsed Germans scampering away in the distance across unravaged green countryside. It was an exhilarating turn of events.

Later that day Elliott was delighted to learn that he had been chosen to command a composite formation charged with the task of pressing forward to harass the German retirement. He was given two infantry battalions, a light horse squadron, and detachments of artillery, machine-gunners, engineers, and ambulance. His formation would be one of two advanced columns pushing forward ahead of the AIF; the other, led by Brigadier-General Gellibrand, would be operating on Elliott's left. It was a role well suited to Pompey's vigorous leadership and tactical grasp, and the prospect of exercising a semi-independent command in these transformed conditions of open warfare was enticing.

But he would be operating on a tight rein. Haig had instructed that the pursuit had to be cautious. With the Germans retiring voluntarily, Haig was wary of a counter-thrust; moreover, the pursuers would eventually encounter resolute defenders in strength, and he regarded the imminent Arras assault as a much higher offensive priority. He authorised the advanced columns to take advantage of opportunities to harass the retreating enemy as they arose, but made it clear that more substantial attacks were unlikely to be justifiable. Within these guidelines General Sir Hubert Gough's Fifth Army, which contained the Australians on its far right, was directed to push forward expeditiously to the Hindenburg Line; this would enable it to provide optimum assistance when the Arras offensive was launched further north by the Third Army. Gough opted to use an advanced column from each division of his army then in the front line. In the AIF sector Brudenell White concluded that the most appropriate way to give effect to the intentions of Haig and Gough would be to impose strict limits on the daily progress of the Australian columns; Hobbs agreed. Elliott became acutely frustrated by these constraints.

Construction of the Hindenburg Line was not yet complete, and the Germans tried to delay the pursuit with sporadic resistance from various villages and cannily placed strongpoints along the way. The pursuers also encountered systematic German destruction. Many found this repugnant, including Elliott:

> If you saw the way they have treated this country you'd never speak to a German again. They've even bashed the poor kiddies toys to pieces and burned them and chopped down all the fruit trees and put poison or nightsoil into the water.

The infantry battalions Elliott commenced the pursuit with on 18 March were the 59th and 60th. His column soon found itself under fire. Its light horse patrols, cantering about ahead to provoke hostile attention so the German dispositions could be pinpointed, were fired at from Frémicourt, the first village along the main road north-east from Bapaume. Three 59th companies converged on Frémicourt, and with the aid of the light horse quickly established themselves in the village, capturing several Germans in the process. A homestead half a mile to the south known as Delsaux Farm was the next significant obstacle. Strong protective wire restricted the manoeuvrability of the light horse, but the infantry proceeded to envelop the defenders, who were eventually forced to withdraw. They left behind an order disclosing the German rearguard plans in this and adjoining sectors. The pursuers then pushed on to the next village, Beugny.

Elliott had long been convinced that envelopment was a most effective offensive tactic:

> Such a movement paralyses the action of men who, if attacked frontally, would put up a desperate resistance. They see these columns near and far passing them by without attention, they see their hope of retreat or reinforcement cut off, they realize that resistance will mean in all probability certain death by the bayonet, and their morale collapses.

He ensured his men were thoroughly drilled in envelopment, and reminded his battalion commanders that

> the enemy in fighting a rearguard action would probably adopt the recognised plan of holding strong points with intervals between them. I pointed out that if we attacked these strong points we would be playing the enemy's game for him ... they should on the contrary endeavour to penetrate between the points, and the enemy's garrisons would then be compelled to retreat to avoid being surrounded.

The men were in fine fettle, but after static months in the trenches it was not easy to adjust to open warfare. At Frémicourt, instead of methodically outflanking the rearguard elements they encountered, too many men in the 59th gravitated towards these defenders. They were drawn to the skirmish as if by a magnet, wrote Wieck, who shared Pompey's faith in envelopment but realised that good soldiers tend to be attracted to a fight. There was another legacy of prolonged trench warfare. Initially 'our men were very nervous about moving in the open', Wieck observed; 'even one distant rifle shot would send a whole platoon to ground'.

After the uneven performance at Frémicourt, Elliott was delighted by the sweeping success at Delsaux Farm a few hours later. It was, he wrote,

> a very difficult position to take. The enemy had a beautiful field of fire down an even grassy slope and were in a fine well-dug trench with deep dugouts. Any attempt at a frontal attack would have led to useless slaughter and it took a long while to ascertain the flanks of the position and penetrate through the line.

A young British staff officer seconded from GHQ to 15th Brigade headquarters went forward to have a look. He returned unimpressed. 'The advance guard are just sitting on their tails smoking', he reported in disgust. He was astonished to learn shortly afterwards that both the farm and the Germans' withdrawal plans had been captured. Pompey explained the procedure to him, especially the importance of a patient, gradual manoeuvre.

Elliott had good reason to be satisfied with the first day's work. Considerable progress had been made, and his senior officers had performed superbly. During his year with Wieck Pompey had repeatedly praised his 'splendid' brigade major, who was 'always cool, always busy'; on the first day of the pursuit Wieck was outstanding. Roving tirelessly, he found the transport and guns in desperate need of an alternative route forward, and organised it for them; embarked on an extensive solo reconnaissance of the column's unprotected right flank, and found two villages completely unoccupied; rode across to the British alongside, and asked them to fill the gap; and, on his return to the AIF sector (after covering over 50 miles on horseback during the day), had a narrow escape when a Lewis-gunner mistook him for a German. Bob Salmon did well, too. As Pompey's liaison officer with the light horse squadron, Salmon was at the forefront of the action; he was one of the first to enter Frémicourt, and kept his chief informed with accurate, up-to-date reports. Legge and others on Elliott's capable staff also distinguished themselves.

On 19 March the 60th Battalion took over from the 59th as the foremost infantry. In order to avoid a repetition of Frémicourt, Pompey arranged for the 60th to advance in two columns, to be led by Dave Doyle and Tom Kerr. On the left Doyle's men succeeded in extricating the Germans from Beugny after manoeuvring around it. A platoon headed by Eric Walker (Ken's brother, who had transferred from the 4th Light Horse) was harassing this retirement effectively when it was attacked by a separate German formation of cavalry and infantry. For a while there was 'a lot of excitement and nearly hand to hand fighting', Walker noted, but eventually the Germans withdrew. Over on the right Kerr's men were confronted by German detachments defending Lebucquière, Vélu, and Vélu Wood with the assistance of well-sited machine-gun posts. The task of dislodging them was made even more difficult by the failure of the British to move up alongside, despite Wieck's personally conveyed request. This enabled the Germans on the right flank, particularly those occupying the village of Bertincourt, to hinder the pursuit with sporadic enfilade fire. Elliott strengthened his right with reinforcements, which included a 59th company; a replacement battery for his delayed artillery materialised and made its presence felt.

In due course his men gained control of Lebucquière, Vélu, and Vélu Wood, and then shivered through a rugged night. Although the change to open warfare was exquisitely welcome, the weather was still a major hindrance; the pursuers had to contend with severe cold and occasional frost and snow. On the evening of 19 March Walker's platoon 'dug in after a fashion and sat all night in pouring rain, cold and tired'.

Elliott was increasingly concerned about the situation on his right flank. Dictating a message to Hobbs, he resorted to the formula recommended by Feilding of the Guards to emphasise his concern about 'being continually exposed to enfilade fire' from the right: 'I shall advance according to my instructions but must disclaim responsibility for disaster due to counter attack from that direction'. This sentence was deleted, however, when the message was sent, presumably because he decided to deal with the situation himself. He directed a 59th platoon to capture Bertincourt in combination with the light horse, even though that village was situated slightly outside his specific zone of operations; when Bertincourt was secure he would resume the advance. He informed Hobbs, who approved these arrangements and immediately informed the 20th British Division alongside. Acquiescence from Hobbs was hardly surprising: the instructions Elliott received from Fifth Division had specified that he had to organise his own protection on the right flank.

At 10.25am on 20 March Layh advised that Bertincourt was 'clear'. Elliott's force was now free to concentrate on the capture of Morchies on the left and Beaumetz on the centre–right. Both battalions were weary, but the 59th advanced on a wide front and was installed in Morchies by midday. The 60th found Beaumetz a tougher nut to crack, but the enveloping approach insistently advocated by Pompey once again proved successful, and the defenders were eventually forced to withdraw. The pursuit was now approaching the main German rearguard position in front of the Hindenburg Line, and Elliott was instructed to halt.

His headquarters was inundated with congratulations after this impressive three-day advance, but there was an altogether different reaction from the corps commander. Birdwood was livid about developments at Bertincourt. The Australians who occupied Bertincourt were relieved by British cavalry, who left a nine-man patrol to safeguard the village and were quickly driven out of it. When Pompey discovered this, he ordered a 59th platoon to reoccupy it. Again he promptly reported his action to Hobbs, who routinely informed the 20th British Division alongside. Pompey was understandably frustrated by the inability or unwillingness of the British on his right to provide the measure of assistance that would have prevented the Germans from hampering his column's activities from that direction. It was 'once bitten, twice shy' as far as he was concerned. He insisted that the garrison in Bertincourt had to be strong enough to deal with any further Germans who might materialise, and he refused to hand responsibility for the village back to another flimsy patrol of British cavalry. 'The platoon in Bertincourt will remain there until the 20th Division infantry reaches that village', he declared uncompromisingly in a message to Hobbs early on 21 March. Arrangements were then made at corps level for the 20th Division to occupy Bertincourt as an infantry outpost. Elliott kept his platoon there until this occurred. A company from the 20th Division turned up belatedly on 23 March.

Birdwood was inclined to overreact to anything unorthodox that might jeopardise his standing in the eyes of influential British traditionalists. It was no coincidence that he was cranky about an incident involving both the cavalry and a neighbouring infantry division that happened to belong (because of the formation boundaries) not just to another corps but to another army. It was probably during a visit by Birdwood, White, and Hobbs to advanced guard headquarters on 22 March that Pompey became aware of the corps commander's spleen. Apparently Pompey tried to explain, but Birdwood would not listen.

Elliott became even more aggrieved when White said he would have to modify his 'Napoleonic ideas'. Two decades later White described Pompey as 'really an amusing figure' during the advanced guard operations, when 'he was picturing himself as J.E.B. Stuart' (a famous commander in the American Civil War) and imagining 'the whole German army was retiring before him'. In view of Elliott's historical consciousness, he was no doubt aware of parallels with military encounters of the past; more relevantly, his decisions relating to Bertincourt had compelling justification. Hobbs and Wieck both had misgivings about Pompey's idiosyncratic tendencies, but shared his concern about the situation on the right. 'Always a weak spot', Wieck noted when describing the sizeable gap, which he estimated at one stage to be no less than five miles wide. 'Our exposed right flank', Hobbs advised Birdwood, 'is and has been a constant source of anxiety to us during the advance'. Moreover, Hobbs's endorsement of the way Elliott dealt with the situation was consistent with Birdwood's own instructions that the advanced columns had to be responsible for guarding their own flanks. Pompey was convinced that his concern about the right flank was appropriate and his response in the circumstances was justified. He felt that White should have understood the tactical realities, and resented the remark about his 'Napoleonic ideas' as an outrageous slur. It rankled for years.

The tighter leash that restrained Pompey after Birdwood and White disapproved of developments at Bertincourt left him feeling more frustratingly fettered than ever. 'You will not advance beyond the line Velu Wood–Beaumetz–Morchies until further instructions are given', he was ordered on 21 March. 'Except for urgent tactical reasons operations of your force must be confined within the divisional boundaries'. Elliott's column had to mark time to allow neighbouring formations to catch up:

> I was under absolute orders not to advance a foot, and I had to watch the Bosche digging trenches like fury night and day where he had none at all in front of me, and I could do nothing but fret and fume and swear.

On the left flank the advance of Gellibrand's column had initially been rapid, but his rash attempt to capture Noreuil on 20 March resulted in a severe reverse that left Gellibrand also in Birdwood's bad books. Pompey had to swing his left flank back as a result.

The main priority on the Australian front was now Lagnicourt, a village south-east of Noreuil just outside Elliott's designated boundary. This attack was allotted to the 7th AIF Brigade, which relieved Gellibrand's formation; Elliott's column, after its impressive advance, was well placed to assist. Meanwhile the exhausted 59th and 60th Battalions were relieved. To Elliott's chagrin, they were replaced in his advanced guard not by the units he predictably wanted, the 57th and 58th of his own brigade, but the 29th and 30th Battalions from Tivey's 8th Brigade.

Early on 23 March the Germans attacked Beaumetz with a detachment of storm-troops. Elliott, in the advanced guard headquarters at Frémicourt, was informed at about 5.30am that the 29th Battalion had been driven out of the village his men had captured three days earlier. He ordered the 59th forward to deal with the situation. In fact, the men on the spot achieved this themselves by counter-attacking spiritedly before the reinforcements arrived, and at 6.30am Elliott was able to reassure Hobbs that these endeavours were progressing satisfactorily.

But Pompey was not satisfied. Proud of what his advanced guard had achieved and bitter about his superiors' attitude concerning the Bertincourt controversy, he sensed that the 57th and 58th would have resisted more effectively than the 8th Brigade battalions he had been given. He was incensed that this German attack had been even temporarily successful. According to Wieck, Pompey was apoplectic, reacting as if it was a personal insult that the enemy would have the temerity, the effrontery, to take such liberties with men under his command. Corroboration of Pompey's frame of mind came from one of his most fervent admirers, Scanlan, who visited advanced guard headquarters that morning. 'Counter-attack me, would they? I'll teach them', Pompey thundered in Scanlan's presence. From an adjoining room Wieck could hear Pompey cursing and pacing about furiously: 'I'll teach the bastards to attack me!' he raged. He was still fuming when Wieck joined him.

'I'm going to give the bastards a lesson', he told Wieck, announcing that he was going to arrange an immediate advance towards the next two villages, Doignies and Louverval. Wieck was taken aback. This notion flouted the explicit directive from Hobbs forbidding Elliott from progressing beyond Beaumetz and Morchies. Wieck reminded Pompey of this order, even fetching it to show him. But Pompey was fed up with these chafing restrictions. 'I don't care if I hang for it' he proclaimed, in a defiant flourish characteristic of a commander who from time to time threatened to shoot wrongdoers under his command but never did. He told Wieck to summon several unit commanders in the advance guard. When they arrived he outlined what he had in mind, and instructed Wieck to compile the appropriate orders. Wieck asked Pompey if he should tell Fifth Division headquarters about this operation. Pompey said no.

After drawing up the orders, Wieck returned to his room for some solitary reflection about his predicament. Standing up to Pompey in full flight was not for the faint-hearted, but the Hobbs directive was unambiguous, and Elliott's operation not only contravened it but seemed to him a risky undertaking as well. Wieck decided to draft a message to Fifth Division. He took it in to Pompey, and indicated that if Pompey would not authorise its dispatch he would do so himself. It was now Pompey's turn for a few moments' quiet contemplation. Wieck, standing stiffly at attention, waited for an answer. Eventually it came. 'Send it', said Pompey.

The message, dispatched at 7.30am, reported that Beaumetz was 'practically recovered' and that Elliott was 'preparing counterattack to drive enemy right back probably including Doignies'. According to Wieck's subsequent account, there was a swift response. A message from Hobbs stated that the operation should be halted until he himself arrived to discuss it. Before long both Hobbs and Wagstaff turned up, and asked anxiously if there was still time to stop the men going forward; Wieck replied that they were on their way. Hobbs then went into Elliott's room and the attack was 'countermanded'.

The surviving records, however, show that the reply from Fifth Division to Elliott's 7.30am message was not sent until 8.50am: 'Divisional commander does not agree to your pushing on to Doignies at present'. Pompey quickly responded that he had 'held up movement' as ordered, but the 'opportunity of recovering any prisoners captured by the enemy will be lost should my original intention not be followed out immediately'. This rejoinder prompted an elaboration from Fifth Division, which was sent to Elliott at 11.30am:

> It is not considered advisable to attack Doignies at present. If however you can satisfactorily organise an attack and capture Doignies and Louverval to-night the attempt can be made on the lines suggested yesterday by the Army Corps Commdr. Discuss with Colonel Wagstaff on his arrival and wire your decision.

Meanwhile other messages were circulating as the picture in Beaumetz became clearer. Around midday Pompey notified Fifth Division that the situation there was 'very satisfactory': German casualties were considerable, and the performance of 'all our troops engaged' was 'distinctly good'. 'Splendid work', came the reply, 'Divisional Commander very pleased'.

In the diary Hobbs kept throughout the war he often described rebukes he had to deliver to subordinates, and regularly recorded his daily movements, meetings, and conferences. On both 22 and 24 March, for example, he mentioned visits to Elliott. Yet his entry for 23 March contains no reference to any visit to Elliott, and no hint that he was displeased with his tempestuous brigadier. Furthermore, there is no mention of any such visit by Hobbs in either the official 15th Brigade diary compiled by Wieck, the Fifth Division diary or Elliott's private diary for that day; the Fifth Division diary states that one of Wagstaff's assistants, Major D.M. King (the GSO II), visited Elliott. And though Pompey often wrote passionately about setbacks and grievances in his diary, the entry for 23 March was a low-key reference to what he saw as a missed opportunity:

> Fine day but very cold. At 4am enemy attacked at Beaumetz after a bombardment but was driven off. Afterwards I planned an attack on him but this was forbidden by HQ 5th Div. I think we could have easily got Louverval and Doignies.

So, far from Hobbs hastening forward to reprimand Elliott and cancel this decidedly imprudent attack—the impression arising from

Wieck's recollections, and the version promulgated by Bean in the *Official History* and elsewhere—Hobbs was in fact pleased with the morning's developments, and apparently did not visit Elliott at all. In addition, King (or perhaps Wagstaff) did so primarily to find out whether Elliott wanted to carry out the attack in question (which even Birdwood had recommended!) later that same day. Moreover, as Bean acknowledged, an implicit flexibility about the advanced guard's daily limits had developed between Elliott and Hobbs; on the very next day, for example, Pompey was authorised to launch operations beyond Beaumetz. It was not until around 6.00pm on 23 March—and primarily because of information secured by one of Pompey's machine-gunners, Lieutenant Harry Trevan—that Hobbs decided to withdraw the option he had earlier offered Pompey of an operation that evening:

> In view of probable attack by enemy on Beaumetz cancel suggestion in my G.S. 249 for night attack on Doignies and Louverval. All further enterprises involving the attack on villages will not be undertaken without reference. Acknowledge.

'Acknowledged', Pompey acquiesced immediately. Trevan, who distinguished himself more than once in the Beaumetz fighting, had shot a troublesome enemy sniper and then found on his body a diary note suggesting that the Germans would probably attack Beaumetz again.

Was Pompey's urge to drive the Germans back on the morning of 23 March as rash and reprehensible as Bean concluded? Elliott did concede after the war that he wanted 'to teach the enemy a lesson', and the sight of Pompey all steamed up at his headquarters during a crisis did prompt more than one observer to presume that his brainpower had become a casualty, missing in action. Despite the storm and tempest, however, Elliott's intellect could still function effectively: 'what looks like rashness may well be nothing but careful calculation', he contended. He consistently maintained after 23 March that 'an extraordinarily favourable' opportunity to capture Doignies, Louverval, and Lagnicourt with bold envelopment methods had been wasted. If his column had been authorised to advance immediately towards these villages, Pompey argued, defensive enemy fire from them would have been hampered by the Germans falling back from Beaumetz. Moreover, the fact that detachments of storm-troops had to be called on to attack at Beaumetz confirmed that the rearguard Germans in front of him had such little appetite for further fighting that they practically

> would have bolted if you stamped your foot at them ... Corps and Division seemed so blessed 'windy' about my position at this time that they would give me no discretion, and the wonderful tactical advantage which we had gained by getting behind the enemy's line ... was simply frittered away.

The counter-argument that this next group of villages were tougher obstacles—being part of the main enemy rearguard positions in front of the Hindenburg Line, this argument ran, the Germans would be more resolute in defending them—cut no ice with Pompey. His envelopment methods had done the trick so far, and he saw no reason why they would not overcome resistance in the villages ahead. Furthermore, the Germans' desire to retake Beaumetz only confirmed that his advanced guard was significantly disrupting the enemy's withdrawal. There was every reason to push on at once, Elliott concluded. It was immediately after a failed advance that soldiers at the Western Front tended to feel most vulnerable; in general, the sooner a counter-attack could be launched, the greater the chance of success. Doignies, Louverval and Lagnicourt would have to be taken eventually, and a swift, daring envelopment could achieve the desired result at a much lower price in casualties than any subsequent adoption of more conventional set-piece methods.

This assessment was, Pompey felt, vindicated by the subsequent operations to seize these villages directed by other AIF commanders. When the 14th Brigade captured Doignies and Louverval on 2 April, George Elliott was greatly impressed by the bravery of the attackers; but the AIF casualties in that one night were more than Pompey's advanced guard sustained in its entire eleven days of operations. 'I told my brother at the time that both places could have been taken with one tenth of the casualties and he was rather indignant', wrote Pompey, but 'he did not understand tactics'. Gough's biographer, a senior commander himself, concluded that the Fifth Army's pursuit to the Hindenburg Line was hindered because of a lack of 'highly trained advance guards, quick to see a fleeting opportunity, ready to take a calculated risk'. Pompey Elliott's column was clearly an exception, and it was no coincidence that Gough was lavish in his praise of its achievements.

Whether Elliott's proposed attack early on 23 March was advisable or not, his reluctance to tell Hobbs about it until persuaded to do so by Wieck was hardly justifiable, as Pompey apparently admitted to Wieck afterwards. What happened that morning at Elliott's headquarters underlined Wieck's significance. The effectiveness of any commander was influenced by his senior staff officer. A complementary blend of attributes between the two was vital, and the relationship between Elliott and Wieck was no exception. While Pompey readily acknowledged the calibre of his brigade major and recognised the importance of Wieck's contribution, there were other commanders who owed a much greater debt to their chief staff officers. The most conspicuous example in the AIF was Birdwood himself.

That the Germans were concerned about the progress of Elliott's advanced guard towards the incomplete Hindenburg Line—a reasonable inference after they attacked Beaumetz on 23 March—was confirmed beyond doubt when elite, specially trained storm-troops were brought from faraway Valenciennes to make another attempt at Beaumetz early the following morning. The defenders they encountered were the battalions Pompey had repeatedly sought, the 57th and 58th, who had relieved Tivey's units during the night. This time the attackers were repulsed without penetrating into the village at all.

Afterwards Elliott was authorised to direct an advance to a nearby enemy strongpoint. It was, he later recalled,

> a very pretty little attack by the 59th Battalion ... to prevent the enemy from massing here for his counter attacks on Beaumetz. It was a real little parade stunt. Brilliant sunshine, green meadows, with overhead artillery and m[achine] g[un] fire—the men moving in artillery formation under shell fire, breaking into lines of scouts and skirmishers as they came under musketry fire. They advanced by rushes, the sections supporting by covering fire. This was the only time during the war except the Krithia attack where, as far as I know, the attack was carried out strictly as we practised it at Broadmeadows and Mena Camp. The enemy could not stand it and fled helter skelter.

Later that day, 24 March, a 57th party drove the Germans out of an isolated farmhouse on the main Bapaume–Cambrai road north of Beaumetz. With the advent of a vigorous Canadian cavalry brigade easing concern about enemy activity on the right flank, the next important encounter for Pompey's advanced guard was the Lagnicourt operation on 26 March. This engagement landed Pompey in further controversy.

His column was to help the 7th AIF Brigade capture Lagnicourt by executing a complementary advance south-east of the village. An encounter during a relief two months earlier had left Pompey decidedly unimpressed with the 7th Brigade's commander, Brigadier-General E.A. Wisdom. Nevertheless he was keen to provide the maximum possible assistance to Wisdom's brigade. Bean, who knew more about the AIF than anyone, paid Elliott this glowing compliment in his account of Lagnicourt:

> No commander in the AIF was more eager than Elliott to assist to the utmost any force acting on his flank, and on this, as on other occasions, he was anxious to do even more than was asked or expected.

On 21 March, as soon as Pompey was notified that one of his battalions would be participating, he directed the 60th Battalion to begin preparing for the operation. He ensured that its officers went forward to familiarise themselves with the ground, and organised arrangements for 'exceptionally thorough co-operation' with the 26th Battalion, the 7th Brigade unit that would be advancing alongside the 60th. This thorough planning was stymied when the operation was postponed. It was not until about an hour before the rescheduled start that the 26th's commander realised that the 58th would be undertaking the role in the attack previously allotted to the 60th. How this misunderstanding arose was 'difficult to trace', Bean concluded, but 7th Brigade headquarters was surely to blame. With the 7th and 15th Brigades responsible for the detailed arrangements, Wieck's operation order issued the previous afternoon specified that the 58th would be participating instead of the 60th, and a copy of this order was earmarked for the 7th Brigade. Moreover, a battalion commander in Wisdom's brigade described the standard of communication during the operation from 7th Brigade headquarters to his own as 'execrable'.

The upshot was that co-ordination was hampered, but the 58th companies advanced independently towards their objective. They had limited artillery support, and had to contend with at least three times as many German machine-guns as the 7th Brigade units encountered in making the main attack. The 7th Brigade men entered Lagnicourt, but their fragile hold in the face of an enemy counter-attack prompted Wisdom to make an urgent appeal to Elliott for assistance. Pompey reacted decisively. Having already handed control of the 58th to Wisdom, he ordered the 59th forward into the fight and arranged for another battalion to be ready to follow suit if needed. As so often occurred, however, those on the spot managed to deal with the situation before reinforcements arrived. The Germans fell back, leaving Lagnicourt in Australian hands. Afterwards Wisdom complained about the substandard support he received from the 15th Brigade.

This allegation predictably riled Pompey. He apparently heard about it when General Gough visited his headquarters the morning after the battle. Wisdom had claimed that his men would have secured more prisoners at Lagnicourt if the 15th Brigade had responded more promptly to his appeal for assistance. Wieck was able to scotch this notion straightaway by producing a pile of messages that had passed between Pompey's headquarters and Wisdom's brigade. Not only had Pompey positioned more units of his brigade to participate in the battle than he had been asked (because, he later claimed, he predicted the counter-attack that eventuated); he had also sent a 15th Brigade liaison officer to the 26th Battalion—a prudent measure not reciprocated by Wisdom—and had arranged for a direct telephone connection between the 26th and his 58th. This link was severed when it was disconnected at the Second Division end, a dereliction not without precedent.

Pompey contended that his reaction to Wisdom's plea had been prompt and appropriate, and if there was mediocre co-ordination, as Wisdom alleged, the 15th Brigade was certainly not to blame. Gough agreed, and concluded that the 15th Brigade had done even more than it had been asked. So did Bean. In fact the threat from the German counter-attack had already been overcome even before Wisdom heard about it, let alone by the time his request for aid eventually reached Elliott. Pompey's experiences during the advanced guard operations entitled him to conclude not only that Wieck was not weak but that Wisdom lacked wisdom.

During Gough's visit Elliott learned that he and his men were about to be withdrawn for a well-earned rest, but before they were relieved they were involved in several more engagements. On the afternoon of 27 March the 58th Battalion took control of the Lagnicourt–Doignies road, capturing in the process a machine-gun crew and, at another strongpoint, a further machine-gun, a trench mortar and portable searchlights. The Germans defending this strongpoint tried to confuse the oncoming Australians by shouting 'Retire, retire' at them. 'Retire be buggered' was the immediate response, followed by the bayonet, and the defenders fled. The Germans then retaliated with a sharp bombardment and counter-attack. Many of the 57th Battalion garrison at the tactically important farm on the Bapaume–Cambrai road were hit, and the survivors were driven back. Captain Keith McDonald learned of this development as he was returning with his 59th company to Beugny (having been sent forward as part of Pompey's response to Wisdom's plea). He decided on his own initiative to direct his tired men to that farm. They reoccupied and secured it. Stewart was aggrieved about this unauthorised involvement in an engagement under his direction. To mollify Stewart, Pompey said that he would reprimand McDonald, but he was in fact delighted with the impromptu intervention and recommended McDonald for the MC.

Elliott's intense pride in the achievements of his men during the pursuit was evident in the letter he dashed off on 28 March:

> My word Katie my boys have been making a name for themselves. They far outreached the British and even the Australians, and for three whole days we were absolutely forbidden to advance one step further to allow the others to catch up on each side of us. Every day there was some new exploit that brought congratulations to one Battalion or the other ... Even the Army Commander ... actually came along yesterday to see us, and several days before he sent his staff capt ... to take note of my methods of attack which were simply paralysing the old Boche ... the boys have done marvellously brave things for me ... Stewart, Layh and Denehy have been simply splendid ... So far I haven't done a single thing wrong and taking all in all everyone is astonished at the smallness of the loss with which we have accomplished so much. So far not a single officer has been killed, though one was rather badly wounded and

> three or four others slightly wounded. I suppose about 60 men have been killed and about 300 wounded for over a week's fighting, and the German losses have at times been simply dreadful.

A day later, after they were withdrawn, he was in a buoyant mood when he wrote to Kate again:

> We finished up last night. I would dearly have loved to have pushed on and captured two other little villages from the enemy. I had all the plans ready but the men, poor boys, were so tired out and had done so splendidly that when the Divisional General offered to take us out I raised no objection ... The old Bosche cannot fight very well in the open, and my boys have found it out and are eager for the job. It is lovely to see them fight. They go out as if they were going to a parade, never a check or halt, and then ... the old Bosches jump out and run for their lives when we get a few hundred yards from them and our guns open up on them and smash them as they scoot for cover. It is just the fun of the world.

An end to the war was still distant, he assured George McCrae, but the Australian soldiers, if adequately reinforced,

> will come back with a Reputation that will never fade or grow dim. I never saw men in such heart as our men are now. Their speed and dash in attack is equalled by no troops at present in the field, and in stubbornness of defence and endurance of shell fire they equal anything I have ever seen or read about. It seems to me that in their present form they are literally unconquerable.

CHAPTER TWELVE

'Too Weary and Worn for Words':

Bullecourt and a well-earned rest

APRIL–AUGUST 1917

ON 7 APRIL Elliott and Wieck attended an important briefing at Fifth Division headquarters. The long-planned Arras offensive was imminent, and would include an assault by the Fourth AIF Division on the Hindenburg Line itself near Bullecourt. 'I fear we will be checked for quite a while by the Hindenburg Line', Elliott informed Kate. 'The wire there is from 400 to 600 yards thick'. A powerful preparatory bombardment was supposed to deal with the wire, but a change of plan led to a disaster of Fromelles-like dimensions. Frustrated that it was taking days for the artillery to clear a path for the infantry, Gough, the army commander who had impressed Elliott during their brief recent contact (but not the AIF leaders familiar with his impulsive tendencies at Pozières in 1916), seized with alacrity the dubious notion that tanks could deal with the wire. In fact, the tanks failed miserably. Most broke down, and the few that did turn up were not much help. One fired mistakenly on the Australians it was supposed to be assisting. Two brigades of the Fourth Division managed the extraordinary feat of fighting their way into the Hindenburg Line without artillery support, but they eventually had to retire. Casualties were catastrophic. This dreadful fiasco at Bullecourt reinforced Australian misgivings about British tactical competence. A profound contempt of tanks throughout the AIF was another legacy.

In mid-April the Fifth Division marched to the rear for a proper rest. The 15th Brigade's destination was Mametz, about ten miles back.

Anzac Day anniversary commemorations were a highlight. A holiday was declared, and the brigade assembled for a sports meeting in the afternoon. Pompey had a prominent role, presiding and acting as chief judge. It was 'the best time we've had for seven months', Doig declared. In the evening there were a number of celebratory dinners, including 'quite a swanking feed' which Pompey enjoyed at Fifth Division. The benefits of tranquil surroundings and warmer weather were soon evident. 'It is so peaceful', enthused Elliott, 'and the boys seem so happy and well and bright'. The 'weather is not warm — it's hot', Doig observed, yet just '3 weeks ago it was snowing hard'. It was 'by far the best rest ... since we left home', Elliott reported.

That same day the Second AIF Division began another desperate battle at Bullecourt. There was less impulsive haste this time, and artillery was used to deal with the wire instead of tanks. But the planning was again defective, and casualties were again distressingly numerous in the AIF brigades engaged — Gellibrand's 6th, which did well, and the 5th, commanded by Elliott's old friend Bob Smith, which did not. Repeated attempts were made to extend the breach in the Hindenburg Line that the Australians had achieved at such terrible cost, but the Germans were just as intent on dislodging them. Fighting of rarely surpassed ferocity raged for days. This second battle of Bullecourt was supposed to involve, within the AIF, only the Second Division, but the First Division was drawn in and it was eventually deemed necessary to interrupt the Fifth Division's rest as well.

At 8.16pm on 7 May a message arrived directing the 15th Brigade to return to the front. The following day, while his men were making their way back to the battle zone, Elliott ventured up to have a look at the AIF salient east of Bullecourt to be taken over by his brigade. Artillery activity was almost constant, Elliott discovered:

> [A] shell came right into the Communication Trench and seemed to burst in my face in that I actually felt the heat of the explosion. It half buried me into the dust and mud it threw up ... yet neither myself or either of the two guides were damaged in the slightest beyond the fright we got.

The devastating German shellfire on the AIF salient and its approaches also included gas projectiles. Several 59th officers, including Bert Layh, were unable to accompany their battalion forward because of the effects of gas inhalation. The 58th Battalion took over the left of the AIF position, where the fighting was particularly savage, with the 57th on its right, the 59th behind in support and the 60th further back in reserve. Pompey's men had not been in position long when the Germans attacked and gained ground on the left, but the 58th swiftly drove them back.

The ordeal endured by Pompey's men as they moved forward near Bullecourt was graphically described by Downing:

> Scraps of shattered bodies obtruded from the obscene earth. The country became more and more abominable, more and more desolate. Steel helmets, rusted rifles, parts of equipments, broken iron stakes, lengths of barbed wire were mingled in the tormented soil ... Doubling through a ravine, full of shattered limbers and guns, torn equipment, disembowelled mules and dead men, full of the noise and the stink of bursting shells, full of flying lumps of red-hot steel, burring and whizzing and whining — sweating as we wound through a battered trench, cringing and recoiling as the shells burst almost in our faces, we came to a place where a white-faced officer with a streak of blood on his brow sat under a bank of earth, directing the incoming men ... Stretcher-bearers worked like demons, sweating and panting as they stumbled over the rough ground with their limp and moaning burdens. Batteries of field-guns flashed and slammed behind us. The sky was lit in the east with the flare and flicker of the German artillery. It was a place where every sight, every sound, meant death — the screams of someone dying in agony, the monstrous clash and rumble of the guns, flinging hundreds of tons of shells each minute on our line, the swish of bullets, the pop of gas-shells. There was nothing that was not ugly, distorted and horrible — nothing but the heroism of flesh contending with steel, and the flares in their diabolical beauty, filling with light that place of terror, so that German machine-gunners, strapped to their guns and straining their eyes as they sought a target in the night, might fill the hillsides with another kind of death.

On 11 May Elliott learned that the British on his left would be making another attempt to install themselves in Bullecourt. His brigade was directed to assist with a complementary advance alongside. The German positions earmarked for his brigade, Elliott wrote, included strongpoints

> bristling with machine guns in concrete emplacements and fenced with wire entanglements. As they were within 50 yards of our barricade the artillery could not fire on them without grave danger to us as the shots could not be observed closely owing to the configuration of the ground behind, and if we withdrew our men from the barricade during the bombardment it was certain that the Germans (who are pretty wide awake in this respect) would re-occupy them and part of our line with them. These strong points in addition to being a formidable obstacle to our advance were a protection to a deep sunken road about 10 to 15 feet deep running from the German positions to their rear works. This road formed their main artery of communication with the village, and it was certain that if we could storm the strong points and occupy the sunken road effectively the Germans' grip on the village would be greatly weakened.

The solution, Pompey concluded, lay in a weapon he had frequently extolled — the Stokes mortar. His plan involved a hurricane bombardment from his light mortar battery, followed by a three-pronged infantry assault. First of all, a concrete machine-gun emplacement facing the Australians had to be rushed and conquered; beyond that first objective, a sizeable German-held portion of the Hindenburg Line had to be captured, together with numerous adjacent dug-outs near a tactically important crossroads; thirdly, that intersection had to be converted into an Australian strongpoint, a manoeuvre involving the subjugation of further enemy strongholds positioned west of it. Hobbs gave Elliott's plan the green light. To carry it out, Elliott selected, logically enough, Denehy's 58th, the AIF battalion closest to these strongpoints (supplemented by two companies of the 60th). That afternoon Elliott rode across to discuss arrangements with his British counterpart who would be directing the simultaneous operation on the left, Brigadier-General H.R. Cumming. 'I noticed he was rather old and indecisive', Pompey noted, and 'had no plan to use his trench mortars'.

Elliott left the detailed planning to Denehy, the schoolteacher with the twirling moustache and fondness for music and literature who had served under him throughout the war and in the pre-war militia. Denehy's capacity and reliability were founded on painstaking diligence rather than dynamism and dash. Earnest and loyal, he was the epitome of the caring battalion commander devoted to his men. Denehy 'worships his Battalion, and it really is very very fine', observed Pompey, 'but I believe he thinks of it all day and dreams of it at night.' This was a case of the pot calling the kettle black if ever there was one; but Pompey, far from being critical, was most appreciative, knowing Denehy would do his utmost to implement the brigadier's instructions. As a 58th officer put it, 'if Pompey told Denehy to order the 58th to go into no-man's-land and stand on their heads, Denehy would do it'.

At 2.30pm on 11 May Denehy summoned the senior 58th officers to his headquarters. 'You've got the tough one, Mickey', he said apologetically to Lieutenant R.V. Moon, the unassuming 24-year-old bank clerk whose A Company platoon, comprising 28 men and two Lewis guns, had the task of storming the concrete machine-gun nest facing the Australians. Moon was one of the 4th Light Horse NCOs who had transferred to the 15th Brigade to fill officer vacancies after Fromelles. B Company's role was to take control of the German trench and nearby dug-outs. Leading B Company was Captain Norman Pelton, a 35-year-old schoolteacher whose kind-heartedness was evident in the condolence letter he had recently written to the mother of a young St Arnaud private, full of 'admiration for your brave and gallant soldier boy'. Denehy gave the third task in the operation (securing the crossroads and beyond) to C Company. Its commander, Jimmy Topp, an amiable, effervescent lieutenant, had just returned to the 58th after doing particularly well at officers' school.

At midnight Denehy called another meeting to confirm final arrangements:

> I shall never forget the conference I held at my headquarters prior to the attack, all the Company Commanders were cheery and optimistic, and I could not help feeling a glow of satisfaction when I saw and spoke with the men I trusted as leaders.

The officers listened intently as Denehy went over their respective tasks again. When he had finished Topp spoke up: 'Well it's my birthday tomorrow, sir'. 'A good omen', remarked the colonel. The others jovially congratulated the birthday boy (who was turning 37). They all shook hands, wished each other well, and headed away to their starting points.

Their prospects of success plummeted before the operation even began. During the tense lead-up to zero hour the Germans unleashed a 'terrific bombardment on our line'. It was, Pompey considered, 'the worst I've ever been under'. Hobbs, watching from the rear, described it as 'the heaviest I think I have yet heard'. According to Downing, 'over the whole of the forward area every living thing seemed blotted out by the intensity of the barrage'. Two Lewis-gun crews were buried and, Elliott lamented, the vital Stokes mortar battery was also hit:

> One section of Stokes Mortars with crew and ammunition vanished into space and no trace of guns or crew (except a fragment of a base plate of one gun) has ever been seen since. A second section with its gun, crews and ammunition was completely buried as they stood under the debris thrown up by a huge shell ... This left only one section of Stokes guns in action under Capt Freeman, a young Warrnambool officer ... At the very second fixed for him Freeman opened fire, but he had ... to engage 3 targets instead of one ... and consequently lost time in traversing. Nevertheless in 5 minutes his crews hurled 115 projectiles into the enemy's works ... Then the infantry stormed across.

Moon and his platoon dashed forward towards the first objective, Moon leading the way, flinging bombs vigorously. They encountered fierce resistance. Moon and other attackers were soon hit, but he kept rallying his men despite a severe facial wound. Inspired by his leadership, his platoon took control of the strongpoint. Moon then led his men to the fight for the second objective, where they found B Company struggling, unable to prevail against numerous German reinforcements emerging from an extensive dug-out system nearby. Some of Moon's platoon wavered, but Moon himself was undaunted, even after a second wound left him dazed and deafened. 'Come on boys', he kept calling, urging them to stick with him. 'We would have followed him anywhere, he was that game', one wrote afterwards. With the outcome at the second objective very much in the balance, Moon's leadership proved decisive. He organised the positioning of a Lewis gun so it could partly enfilade the Germans in the trench. They became disconcerted and fell back. Moon pursued them, initially on his own. Some Germans took refuge (which they intended to be temporary) inside their dug-out entrances. These retreating defenders greatly outnumbered their pursuers but Moon, along with some quick-thinking comrades, detected a fleeting opportunity and pounced, rushing to the dug-out entrances and firing inside. The occupants were trapped.

So far so good for the attackers, but sustained German fire from the west indicated that the British advance alongside had been less successful, rendering the third AIF objective practically impossible in daylight. Moon had been hit again, but because of the uncertain situation on the left he refused to leave. With sweat and blood cascading down his face, he sat down for a brief rest. 'My word it was a hard fight', he said, 'I've got three cracks and not one good enough for a Blighty' (that is, of sufficient severity to require evacuation to England). He then had an impromptu conference with two other 58th lieutenants, who agreed that the Australian dispositions should be altered. This reorganisation was in progress when Moon was again wounded — his jaw was broken, and twelve teeth were shattered. Even then he lingered to satisfy himself that the adjustments to AIF positions were proceeding appropriately, before consenting to be assisted to the rear. Later, after nightfall, the Australians took control of the vital crossroads unattainable in daylight, bringing this difficult three-pronged operation to a successful conclusion.

Elliott and Denehy were delighted. Their men had overcome tremendous shellfire and determined defenders to seize 300 yards of the formidable Hindenburg Line and associated strongpoints, in the process capturing five machine-guns, three flame-throwers, two bomb-throwing machines, and no fewer than 186 prisoners (most of them trapped by Moon and fifteen or so comrades) while accounting for many other Germans as well. Pompey especially enjoyed hearing about the response of a certain German officer. Ensconced in one of the big dug-outs with his unit, he kept ordering his men out to deal with the attack before making a belated appearance himself:

> when at last the spick and span [commander came] to the surface he found all his own machine guns already mounted on the parapet by Lieut Trevan, a young Kerang (Victoria) machine gun officer, each pumping bullets at 500 a minute after the fleeing remnants of his force. I am told his face lengthened about a foot.

The operation was 'one of the best little stunts we have put up so far', Elliott claimed proudly, 'and too much cannot be said for the pluck and energy of Col. Denehy's boys'. Their 'experience must have been quite as bad or worse than Lone Pine, and they stood it magnificently'. Doig, well forward during the battle, was inspired by what he saw and 'proud to be an Australian'. Inevitably, in such ferocious combat, a heavy price was paid. There were 245 casualties in the 58th Battalion, and it was not the only unit to suffer. Bill Knuckey, Simon Fraser, and Reg Poulter, all exceptional at Fromelles, were equally gallant at Bullecourt but less fortunate — Knuckey was severely wounded, and the other two were killed. In the 58th Norman Pelton, the compassionate captain, became the subject of condolence letters himself after being struck by a shell; Jimmy Topp was shot after guiding his company to its objective, and did not survive his birthday. They 'were both killed ... leading their men most gallantly', Elliott wrote, but it was 'Mickey' Moon who monopolised the superlatives. Pompey had doubted if Moon had the makings of an officer, but he was sceptical no longer: 'carrying on with his jaw broken and 3 other wounds as well' was exceptional gallantry, and 'I am going to send his name in for the VC'. Moon became the only member of the 15th Brigade to be awarded that coveted decoration.

The 15th Brigade, having achieved its objectives so successfully, was replaced in the line by the 173rd British Brigade. Its commander was the youngest general in the British army, 28-year-old Bernard Freyberg, DSO, VC. Freyberg was impressed by Elliott, and especially liked the informal way he and his colonels worked out arrangements together. Moreover, according to Freyberg, the Australians' methodical collection of their wounded, despite having to 'run the gauntlet through the enemy artillery fire', was 'a wonderful sight, that got completely under one's guard and made us all very proud to be fighting alongside such men'.

Elliott became aggrieved with both the British brigades he encountered at Bullecourt. Among the weapons his men collared on 12 May were machine-guns of a new type never previously captured, but a unit in Freyberg's brigade claimed to have captured them in a report which was fabricated. It was only after the 15th Brigade protested and furnished receipts that the correct attribution was made. Pompey's grievance with the 91st Brigade, which had attacked on his left on 12 May, also concerned a false report. This one claimed that the 91st's advance had driven the prisoners captured by Moon and his comrades into the 58th's arms. Pompey reacted strongly: 'I stoutly contradicted this — and the matter dropped'. In fact, the inability of part of the British 91st to get forward had led directly to the dismissal of its commander, General Cumming. Pompey, unimpressed with Cumming, would not have been surprised (although Cumming may well have been harshly treated).

In June, Elliott was given ten days' leave. After crossing to London, he called at Wandsworth Hospital, and visited his brigade's training battalion at Salisbury Plain. He then headed to Bryn Oerog with Bert Layh. Both needed a good rest. Elliott was 'feeling really tired out', and he was concerned about Layh, who was recovering slowly after being gassed at Bullecourt:

> I ... brought old Bert Layh along here to get better. He has to be very careful yet as his heart goes up to about 120 beats a minute with any strenuous exertion such as walking up a hill or walking quickly. Hence he won't be able to see the beauties of the country about, but it is lovely all the same here — so quiet and peaceful.

On their second morning at Bryn Oerog Elliott slept in till nearly ten o'clock, a most unusual occurrence for him. 'I did feel such a fool being so late for breakfast, but I suppose it only shows how much I needed a rest'.

His brigade was enjoying a proper rest at last. He returned to find his men well back at Rubempré, savouring their most sustained break from front-line duty since arriving in France. They were revelling in the sunshine. Warmer weather 'did much to help the men to shake off the evil effects of the winter spent in the mud', Wieck concluded. Elliott, too, welcomed the advent of

> real Australian summer scorching days ... The country still looks green and lovely, and the little woods invite you to go and lie under the shade all day with a book.

Elliott still had misgivings about Hobbs. 'I never feel any confidence in him', he told Kate. Hobbs was earnest and well-meaning, and congratulated him effusively when the 15th Brigade did well, but he doubted whether the divisional commander had the strength of character to support him in a tight corner: 'I know if the least thing went wrong I could expect no defence from him no matter how blameless I might be'. With his short, frail stature and nervy manner, some observers felt Hobbs did not look or sound like a general; he lacked 'the power of command', Bean concluded in mid-1917. And Hobbs's misconceived appraisal of an advanced-guard exercise on 2 July convinced Elliott he was deficient in tactical acumen as well. Pompey reiterated his preference for McCay, who, 'with all his faults', was 'a brilliantly clever man and a fine soldier'.

In July 1917 Elliott learned that Wieck was being transferred to Monash's staff at Third Division. Hobbs nominated as Wieck's successor Captain G.A. Street. A law student at the outbreak of war, Street was an original Anzac in the 1st Battalion and had been staff captain at the 14th Brigade for the past year. Handsome, charming, and a cricket devotee, he was a stylish product of a well-to-do background and Sydney Grammar School. In Pompey's opinion, however, Street was demonstrably unsuitable. He understandably wanted someone competent and reliable as his brigade major and right-hand man, and he was familiar enough with the 14th Brigade officers (his brother being among them) to be convinced that Street was not appropriate. Elliott felt that Street's advancement owed more to social leverage than to ability.

For some time Pompey's firm preference, should a successor to Wieck become needed, had been, typically, a military enthusiast he had largely trained himself, Jack Scanlan (formerly of the Essendon Rifles and 7th Battalion). The backgrounds of Scanlan and Street were altogether different: Scanlan, a coachbuilder's son, had attended Christian Brothers College, St Kilda, and became a clerk in the Customs Department. Pompey concluded that devious influences were at work to further Street's preferment, and sensed that a British regular on Hobbs's staff was primarily responsible. With both Street and Scanlan recommended for staff training in England, it was no accident, Pompey felt, that Street was sent to the prestigious Staff College at Cambridge, whereas Scanlan was diverted to Salisbury Plain and thus sidelined. Elliott conceded readily that Street was likeable and well-intentioned, but described him as 'not in the same class' as Scanlan in terms of ability. Pompey was infuriated to have someone he considered 'a social butterfly' foisted on him:

> He was a wealthy man, who was able to shout car trips for some of the senior officers in Paris ... His thoughts were always with his best girl in London, and he could not sleep in anything rougher than silk pyjamas at ten guineas a suit.

From Pompey's perspective it was a repetition of the trouble over his initial battalion commanders back in Egypt. As in March 1916, he protested vehemently that the lives of his men would be unjustifiably endangered by an unsuitable appointment. But he could not persuade Hobbs, who seems to have demonstrated precisely the staunch resolution in defence of an embattled individual that Elliott had believed to be absent from his make-up. Pompey, of course, saw this differently. Hobbs was 'as phoney as an eel', he told Belle; 'you can pin him to nothing at all':

> I am fed right up to the back teeth with soldiering ... It would just about sicken you the way influence is worked to get good jobs for fellows who are not worth twopence ... I do wish McCay had not gone. He at least was a man and a soldier, and did not work by underhand means.

Pompey found the whole business abhorrent and draining, but felt impelled to persist. He managed to extract a concession from White that Street would be transferred if this proved necessary:

> But this was only in consequence of my asking to be sacked rather than be compelled to take him on, and there is not much pleasure in the position for me. The youngster is a very decent boy, and it is very hard on him after being appointed to be sacked. It is harder on my boys though if ever one be sacrificed through his want of knowledge ... The worry of it though is just awful and I am thoroughly sick and tired of the whole thing and so weary and worried that I feel ... as if I'd carried a load of about 10 tons up the biggest and steepest hill in the world and had just thrown it down too weary and worn for words and no desire and no ambition but to be clear of it all and get back to my dear old darling loving wife and never go out of her sight again.

On 25 July, the day Wieck left, Street started awkwardly. He 'proved an utter failure' at drafting orders, Pompey wrote, and showed 'an entire ignorance' of the relevant field service regulations.

Other developments were more gratifying. The tactics that Elliott's column had used in March became the basis for instruction in advanced guard principles at the prestigious Senior Officers' School, Aldershot. The quality of his leadership during those pursuit operations was also recognised, he learned in July, by the award of the DSO. Though disinclined to get carried away by such decorations, 'I was, I must confess, rather keen on getting that DSO because I felt I had been done out of it unfairly in Gallipoli'. Still, the slaughter and destruction continued unabated, and he had been away '3 years and no end in sight yet':

> I look perfectly fit and well, but I seem to have very little stamina left in me. After a period of work at all strenuous, particularly if I am worried a lot as I am now, I feel myself as weak as a child somehow as if I had not one ounce of push or go left in me, and I am dreading another winter like last one ... It's a weary world, Katie love, and I can see little light.

Elliott kept encouraging Kate to allow herself an occasional treat, but she was as frugal as ever. Writing home in August, he thanked her profusely once again 'for the way you are reducing that old Debt' (to his father's estate, administered by the Ballarat Trustees company), and wondered whether his accumulated 'deferred pay' (the proportion of his AIF income retained by the government until the end of the war) might enable him to pay the debt off altogether. Now and again he wondered about the legal practice he had left behind. He sometimes felt pessimistic about whether he would find former clients still using his firm after he had been away four years or more. This was not really a reflection on his partner, Glen Roberts, and the others in the firm who would be doing their best; rather, it was a recognition that the personal touch was important, and in his absence some clients might switch to other solicitors more familiar to them than Roberts was. Elliott had continued to correspond with Glen and Katie Roberts. Their son Eric, a pilot in the Australian Flying Corps, had written to him from Egypt. Eric, who idolised Elliott, had wanted to be in the 7th Battalion, but its commander preferred to avoid having to send such a close family friend into a perilous situation. 'I couldn't take Eric', Elliott told Glen; 'it would be like taking my own son'.

Eric's cousin Len Stillman, however, was in the 15th Brigade. Enlisting in mid-1915 after qualifying as a lawyer, Stillman had embarked as a 31st Battalion NCO and was wounded at Fromelles. Afterwards, possibly acting on a suggestion from Katie Roberts (Stillman's aunt), Elliott arranged for him to be transferred from Tivey's brigade to the 60th Battalion and commissioned. He 'seems a nice boy' though 'rather thin and pale' was the brigadier's first impression of this new 23-year-old officer. Stillman proceeded to distinguish himself at a school of instruction and in stints as the 60th's acting intelligence officer and as Assistant Provost Marshal at Fifth Division. 'I ... wish that all my young officers were as promising as your nephew', Elliott told Katie Roberts in March 1917. A few weeks later Stillman was at 60th Battalion headquarters with his colonel when Pompey entered. 'How are you Stillman?' the brigadier began. Stillman saluted, replied politely, and they shook hands. He was dumbfounded by what followed. According to Stillman's subsequent account, Pompey then turned to the colonel:

> "What do you think of this boy of yours (that was I), Colonel? He wrote to his Aunt, who is a friend of mine, and told her he had seen me recently and that I had spoken very nicely to him, and that usually meant trouble. Ha, ha!"

Stillman was mortified with embarrassment:

> Of course I nearly swooned. Now as it happens I did write something of the sort to Aunt Katie in a jocular sort of way and she apparently either wrote to the Brigadier direct or told his wife ... The Brigadier is not a man to be trifled with (that's why he is such a great soldier).

Katie Roberts might know H.E. Elliott, her husband's partner, Stillman wrote, but Brigadier-General Pompey Elliott was a very different character: 'I assure you they are as distinct as Dr Jekkyl [sic] and Mr Hyde'. Pompey had made a similar impression on other officers in his brigade. Captain John Aram, a 31-year-old St Kilda accountant, informed his mother in mid-1917 that he had just had an interview with 'my friend the Brigadier tonight and he was very sweet, so I can look for a good slathering in the near future'. Writing again twelve days later, Aram confirmed that Pompey had recently 'been very nice to me, whether or not it is the calm before the storm I cannot say'.

Like Stillman, Elliott's brother George was building a fine reputation in the AIF. He had been recommended for the MC after his outstanding contribution at Bullecourt. But the popularity of 'Doc' Elliott in the 56th Battalion stemmed from his fun-loving camaraderie as well as his bravery and medical work. Unlike his teetotal brother, George was very keen on a convivial ale or three. After several rounds of drinks at the Fifth Division's military tournament on 12 July, he happened to spot Brigadier-General Elliott deep in serious conversation with eminent commanders. To the amusement of onlookers, George strolled up behind them, thumped his brother vigorously on the back and greeted him heartily: 'Hullo Pompey, how are you?'

> The surprised general wheeled round with a look of thunder on his face, which softened somewhat when he recognised who was responsible for the informal greeting. He tried, however, to cool the 'doc's' ardour by a sign which drew attention to the quality of the little gathering.

George would not be deterred: 'I don't care a damn who you're talking to with all those ribbons on your chest, you should be glad to see your little brother.' Indeed he was. Pompey was very fond of George, and was pleased to catch up again when George visited on 30 August. Flourishing a cute photo of daughter Jacquelyn, George asked for a loan because he needed spending money for the leave he had just been granted. Pompey acquiesced readily, stifling his disappointment about relinquishing nearly half the next £50 he was about to send home to expedite the Ballarat Trustees repayment.

Pompey had not seen Jack Campbell, on the other hand, for months. He had been mildly intrigued by this lack of contact with his amiable brother-in-law until an explanation materialised from Belle and Kate. Their mother, as Jack's next-of-kin, had been officially notified of his hospitalisation with venereal disease. Gonorrhoea resulted in his absence for over three months. Although he was on the best of terms with Pompey, it is hardly surprising that Jack shied away from discussing this turn of events with a brigadier-in-law of forceful personality who, though no wowser, adhered scrupulously to a strict moral code. Elliott, however, was not judgmental about Jack's predicament, and kept hoping to see or hear from him. Of Pompey's other family connections in the AIF, Eric Walker had been ruled medically unfit and sent home to Australia, and Jack Avery had been promoted to the command of a hospital at Salisbury Plain.

The 60th Battalion had a new commander. Norman Marshall would have revelled in the 15th Brigade's pursuit operations, but he was in England attending a special school at Aldershot (and getting married). Elliott's confidence in him was vindicated when he excelled in his course, and the brigadier had no hesitation in endorsing his promotion to command the 60th:

> Fancy Katie, joining as a private and now Lieut. Col. with a Military Cross as well and pretty sure of a DSO too before long. And his men just think the world of him too. This is in the 57th. I hope the boys in the 60th will like him as well. I feel sure they will too in a very little time.

He was right. Marshall was a natural leader. Energetic and fearless, dashing and inspiring, he became one of the most popular commanders in the AIF. No task was too daunting for this perennially cheerful daredevil — he was always willing to 'give it a fly'. A champion boxer in pre-war days who also enjoyed football and convivial camaraderie, Marshall ensured that the 60th officers had a lively time out of the line. According to Dave Doyle,

> after dinner in the officers' mess there would very frequently be an impromptu boxing tournament, the Colonel arranging the bouts, acting as timekeeper, referee and occasionally barging in and engaging both contestants himself.

Marshall would also organise nocturnal horse-back excursions to selected estaminets. Doyle again:

> So off we'd go and a good time would be enjoyed by all. Often on return in the small hours of the morning if the moon was bright the

> Colonel would lead us cross-country — over fences and ditches straight for home. No matter how thick the night had been, everybody would be on parade first thing next morning and no excuses would be accepted.

These exploits did not impress Pompey. Marshall 'lets his officers go in rather too much for drinking and acting the goat to please me altogether', frowned the brigadier. Moreover, in the battalion Marshall had just left, Stewart's 57th, Captain Aram, a teetotaller, felt that excessive drinking by the officers was routine.

But such foibles did not disturb the fundamental confidence Elliott had in his colonels. Marshall was an outstanding leader, and he also rated Cam Stewart highly. Experienced, reliable, and cool in a crisis, Stewart was definitely brigadier material, Pompey felt. As for Denehy, he sometimes demonstrated a lack of the quick-thinking decisiveness that came naturally to Marshall and also to Layh, but made up for this in other ways. Denehy was 'coming on excellently', Elliott wrote in mid-1917, and thoroughly deserved his DSO for Bullecourt. Elliott regretted Layh's continued absence, but he was pleased that the new commander of the 59th was Mason. He had engineered Mason's appointment to head the Fifth Division school in case one of his colonels became incapacitated, and events worked out precisely as he had envisaged. One of his battalion commanders did have to be evacuated, and on hand, ready to step in as the logical replacement, was Mason, the experienced 39-year-old lawyer who had served with Elliott as an officer in South Africa and the militia as well as in the 7th Battalion. Pompey was delighted to have another colonel he knew and trusted. Once again, he felt his judgment in appointing subordinates was vindicated. Mason was doing 'very well' at the 59th, he reported in July; 'I am wonderfully fortunate in my Battalion Commanders'.

Apart from preferring Scanlan to Street as brigade major, Elliott was also highly satisfied with his own staff. Legge was back as staff captain. Pompey had disciplined him earlier in 1917 for being too 'fond of his bed'. Legge loathed freezing dawn starts, when he had to cut short his sleep and swing into action straightaway; Elliott, who customarily retired early, was unsympathetic. When Legge 'was very sulky and slow' early one frosty March morning, Pompey, fed up, banished him to Fifth Division with a note explaining his dismissal. Elliott sensed it was 'a very nasty shock' for Legge, 'but it will I think do him the world of good'. It did. Legge was talented and had served him admirably, Pompey acknowledged, and it was good to have him back. He

> learned a lot of Wieck's ways of doing things ... and I think I taught him a lesson when I sacked him that time. He is a lot different now and is doing good work for me. I should have very much greater confidence in him than I could possibly have in Street.

Elliott was delighted with his brigade as a whole. He felt it was in excellent shape. During its lengthy break away from the front line the emphasis had initially been on rest and recuperation after Bullecourt, but increasingly from June onwards the main focus became preparing for its next assignment. Elliott's men practised shooting, route marching, crossing pontoon bridges, and various attacking manoeuvres. They did these exercises sometimes as a brigade, sometimes at night, and sometimes competitively as separate battalions, companies, and platoons. This rigorous training program was not just carried out under the brigadier's exacting supervision; it was approvingly scrutinised by more senior commanders including Hobbs and Birdwood, and impressed such august observers as Haig and the King. More than ever Elliott was convinced that the 15th Brigade had nothing to fear from comparisons with equivalent formations. 'The boys are just looking splendid', he enthused, 'and I am certain they will do splendidly next time we get into action'.

As that day grew nearer, Elliott had renewed doubts about his own fate. After Kate wrote that young Neil had said he wanted to give his father a 'truly and really kiss' instead of yet another substitute smooch on a letter, that touching complaint triggered a melancholy response:

> Dear wee chap I wonder if ever I'll see him again. I sometimes think my luck cannot last much longer. I have had so many narrow escapes.

He signed a brief codicil amending his pre-war will:

> In the event of my death I desire that my son Neil Campbell Elliott on attaining the age of 21 years shall be entitled to any medals and

> orders now or hereafter belonging to me. In all other respects I confirm my said will.

'I've been so long away and I am so tired and worn out', he wrote wearily. However, there was no way his resolve and commitment would slacken in the slightest. As he steeled himself for what might be one last effort, his devotion to duty, regardless of the personal cost, remained absolute:

> There will be a great and terrible battle soon I think, Katie ... and I expect we will be in it. If we do get a chance at the Bosche I intend to make the most of it — if possible break through their lines somehow. It would be worth any sacrifice to get them on the run really and truly going back ... If anything should happen to me you will know that at last I am in peace away from the troubles and worries that so afflict me, and that I have done my utmost to do any job they have ever given me to do.

CHAPTER THIRTEEN

'I Would Have Gladly Welcomed a Shell to End Me': The battle of Polygon Wood

SEPTEMBER-NOVEMBER 1917

IT WAS HAIG'S keenness to launch an offensive in the north that resulted in the challenging task Elliott and his brigade were given in September 1917. Haig had long fancied the notion of a drive north-east from Ypres across the fields of Flanders to the Belgian coast. A successful onslaught there would not only begin the process of liberating Belgium from German occupation, the objective that had ultimately prompted Britain to enter the war. It would also dislodge the Germans from both the tactically important Belgian ports and the advantageous higher ground east of Ypres. But how likely was this ambitious Flanders venture to be successful? Haig's detractors in British strategic circles were sceptical; previous offensives under his direction afforded little basis for optimism. But with the French and Russian armies in very ordinary shape in mid-1917, Haig felt that the onus was on Britain to do something. Eventually he was reluctantly authorised to proceed.

Pessimism was understandable after three years of stagnation. But there were lessons to be learnt at the Western Front, and some commanders were learning them. With the refinement of artillery techniques, the innovation of Stokes mortars and Lewis guns, and the adoption of the creeping barrage (a mobile curtain of shellfire moving forward at a pre-arranged pace just ahead of the advancing infantry it was protecting), a carefully planned attack on a limited portion of enemy trench now had a good chance of success. There had previously been a critical gap between the end of a set-piece preliminary bombardment and the arrival of an attacking force at its objective, but this window of opportunity for defenders was gradually closed by the increasing sophistication of the creeping barrage. Such innovations had impressed Elliott, and convinced him that with careful preparation fewer lives need be lost in making successful attacks. 'Our Artillery and trench mortars are so perfect now', he wrote in February 1917, 'it is only very occasionally that one should have to charge in the old bull at a gate fashion'.

But these improvements did not pave the way for a decisive breakthrough. The ultimate war-winning stroke that Haig in particular hankered after remained as elusive as ever. Even a well-prepared and initially successful advance tended to run into trouble as attackers pushed forward beyond the range of their supporting artillery. The defenders could usually rush reinforcements (particularly by rail) to the threatened area more quickly than the over-extended attackers could get their guns forward.

The answer, some perceptive commanders began to realise, was to aim at a series of achievable step-by-step advances instead of an unrealistic big breakthrough. Under this 'bite and hold' approach the idea was to choose a feasible chunk of enemy-held territory; unleash an irresistible protective barrage; get the infantry forward close behind it; mop up any lingering resistance; consolidate the captured ground in order to ward off any hostile response; and then stay put for a few days while the guns were brought forward and thorough preparations were made for the next phase in the offensive.

In June 1917 General Monash's Third AIF Division participated in a successful advance by General Plumer's Second Army at Messines, five miles south of Ypres, that came to be hailed as a bite and hold classic. Before this battle, with his division about to participate in a major operation for the first time, Monash had nervously acknowledged that the cards seemed stacked against attackers at the Western Front, but success at Messines converted him into a bite and hold enthusiast: 'I am the greatest possible believer in the theory of the limited objective', he declared.

Was the Flanders campaign to be based on bite and hold techniques, or was it to be another bid for the big breakthrough? Haig was ambivalent, but made his preference clear by his choice of commander to direct it. Instead of Plumer, who was familiar with the area and had just supervised the Messines triumph, Haig put Gough in charge, influenced by his reputation for decisive dash and vigorous pursuit. After conspicuous preparations and a bombardment lasting more than a fortnight, the offensive began fairly well on 31 July, but ran into severe difficulties in August. Enemy resistance was effective, and the attackers' problems were magnified by the impact of rain on a clay battlefield where the water level was high and the drainage ruined by shellfire. Haig responded by switching to an unambiguously bite and hold approach, relegating Gough to a subsidiary role and reinstating Plumer as commander. With the well-rested Australian divisions about to become involved in the offensive (which became known as the Third Battle of Ypres), this was a pleasing development in AIF circles. After Bullecourt the prospect of attacking under Gough was distinctly unpalatable.

About Plumer, on the other hand, there was no such concern. If there was one principle becoming ever-clearer at the Western Front, it was that careful preparation was essential if attackers were to have some chance of success, and no army commander heeded this lesson more effectively than Plumer. Methodical and painstaking, he and his first-rate chief-of-staff Major-General 'Tim' Harington managed to instil in the units fighting under them a well-founded confidence that they had attended to every possible organisational detail before committing men to confront the enemy. The talented Plumer–Harington partnership had already impressed Monash and other AIF leaders.

Elliott was soon singing the pair's praises as well. With preparations for the next phase of 'Third Ypres' in full swing under their capable direction, Plumer scrutinised a simulated 15th Brigade attack on 8 September. 'He is a funny little red faced man, very white hair and moustache', Elliott reported, 'but is a good General'. And of all the British staff officers Pompey encountered during the war, Harington was 'the only one ... who ever impressed me that he had a proper conception of his job'; this Pompey defined as the adoption of appropriate measures 'to save the infantry casualties'.

That simulated attack on 8 September featured new methods introduced in response to the system of defence now being adopted by the Germans. In the continuing evolution of Western Front tactics the Germans had instituted a system of defence in depth, eschewing rigid lines of trenches in favour of a more fluid structure based on hundreds of mutually supporting concrete machine-gun nests. These blockhouses, shrewdly located and practically impervious to shellfire, became known to their assailants as pillboxes. A pillbox could be vacated when necessary much more quickly than a deep underground dug-out, and could also be used as an effective springboard for counter-attack. This was a crucial attribute: the German policy was now to occupy the front lightly in scattered posts, allow any advance towards them to penetrate so the attackers could become over-extended and vulnerable, and then hit back hard with a swift and sudden counter-thrust. The British had also come to favour defence in depth, but the main focus in the AIF's training in the lead-up to Third Ypres was new offensive tactics, in particular how to deal with pillboxes and German counter-attacks. Platoons were now encouraged to see themselves as self-contained units, equipped with their own specialist sections (bombers, Lewis-gunners, scouts, snipers, moppers-up) to overcome pillboxes and other enemy strongpoints on their way forward, without being so held up in the process that they lost the protection of the creeping barrage.

During the long spell enjoyed by most of the Australians there were briefings and drills galore to familiarise them with these new methods. At the 15th Brigade Elliott supervised this training with characteristic robustness. During one exercise Lieutenant Charles Noad, a 15th Brigade newcomer who had just completed an officers' course after being wounded at Pozières, became a target for the unmistakeable Pompey bellow:

> '*Who's* in charge *here*?'
>
> 'I am, sir' (from Noad).
>
> 'What are *those* men *doing there*? A bloody *lance-corporal* wouldn't have them doing *that*!'

Also influential was Wagstaff's successor as Hobbs's chief-of-staff, Lieutenant-Colonel J.H. Peck, who had demonstrated admirable bravery, skill, and humour in a variety of AIF appointments since 1914. Peck was able to pass on useful insights gleaned from the battle of Messines, where the AIF encountered the German defence in depth and implemented the new attack methods successfully. Pompey's confidence that his men would be able to execute them proficiently was vindicated by their performance in the brigade exercise on 8 September, when Plumer 'said he was pleased with my boys'. The following day the 15th Brigade was advised to get ready for an imminent move to Belgium.

So Elliott had to steel himself, together with thousands of veterans under his command, for a return to the slaughterhouse. They knew the horror awaiting them. They knew that their senses and sensibilities would be violated by deafening noise, hideous stench, appalling sights. They knew that the damage their nerves had sustained in previous exposure, unhealed even after such a prolonged rest, had left them less equipped than ever to cope with such an ordeal. Pompey in particular, whose temperamental endowment was hardly phlegmatic, had to muster tremendous willpower to maintain, in circumstances of paralysing stress, the distinguished leadership he had so far displayed.

Elliott arrived at Steenworde with his brigade on 17 September, aware the AIF was about to spearhead the step-by-step resumption of the Third Ypres offensive. The First and Second Divisions were to launch it on 20 September, with the Fourth and Fifth Divisions to undertake the second phase a few days later. '[From] what I can see it's going to be "some" fight that we're going into', Elliott told Belle:

> if my luck is out I know you'll do your best to help [Katie] and the wee people over the stiles till they are able to look after you ... The guns are booming like the waves on the shore again—drumming to call us to battle and for many of us beating our funeral marches at the same time. If I could leave [Katie] and the wee people a little more money I would go willingly since men must die that we may be quit of the old Kaiser and his soldiers, and it may as well be me as the next man ... my poor boys have to face it all time after time, and it is up to the officers (even the highest) not to shrink from what their men have to face. But whether we shrink or whether we don't, we must each and all go into it with what courage we can muster.

The first battle was an uplifting success. On 20 September the Australians advanced close behind an awesome barrage, their determination and confidence redoubled because two AIF divisions were attacking side by side for the first time. All objectives were taken, German morale was shaken, and the sadness over individual losses was countered by the elation in the AIF at such a comprehensive victory. Elliott was delighted:

> Our boys particularly the old 7th have made a glorious advance and captured a whole lot of Bosches and driven [them] back a long way ... That will be another feather in our boys' caps for the British troops have been blocked along this line for about a month. I hope we will do as well when our turn comes, which will be very soon now.

It was not until later that he learned that Major Fred Tubb VC had been hit. Wounded by a sniper after gallantly leading his men towards a group of nine pillboxes (all eventually captured by his company), Tubb was being carried back on a stretcher when he was struck by a shell. He was rushed to a dressing station, but did not survive.

On 20 September the Australians had attacked on a 2,000-yard front and successfully advanced, in three stages, about a mile along the main ridge east of Ypres. The next step, once the guns were brought forward, involved a further advance of about three-quarters of a mile on a similar front. If this operation went according to plan, a third battle was envisaged: a drive to the crest of the ridge following its northward curve towards Broodseinde. In the second step two AIF divisions were once again to move forward side by side in the centre of the attack, while the British X Corps conforming on the right secured that flank and Gough's Fifth Army carried out a similar task on the left.

Dominating the Australian sector of the advance was Polygon Wood. This formidable stumbling block comprised a tangle of shattered trees, obstructive undergrowth, shell craters, trenches, and pillboxes together with a creek, a riding track, and a prominent mound providing sweeping observation for the Germans. The western side of Polygon Wood had been the Australians' final objective on 20 September. Their task in the second battle was to sweep through it and establish themselves beyond it. The Fifth AIF Division, being fresher than the Fourth, was given the harder task on the right. Two brigades from each division were to attack. Hobbs chose Elliott's 15th and Brigadier-General C.J. Hobkirk's 14th as the Fifth Division's assaulting brigades, with the 15th in the more onerous position on the right of the divisional front, the 14th on its left and Tivey's 8th behind in reserve. Pompey's men, therefore, had been given the most demanding task of all the brigades involved in the battle.

The attack was to be undertaken in two distinct parts. First, an advance of half a mile would be made to the far (eastern) edge of Polygon Wood (the red line). After consolidation and reorganisation, the advance was to resume with a further drive east of about 350 yards by fresh units to the final objective (the blue line). Elliott allocated the first phase to the 60th Battalion, with the 57th and 59th to undertake the later advance to the blue line. The 58th would occupy the front line before the battle, and remain there as a garrison and brigade reserve after it started.

Elliott's decision on the 58th's role was perhaps influenced by the absence of its commander as well as the fact that it had suffered more than any other 15th Brigade battalion in its last engagement (Bullecourt). Denehy, increasingly troubled by the stress of command, was granted a fortnight's leave in September. Returning shortly before the battle, he was placed in charge of the Fifth Division nucleus (the portion of each unit now customarily kept out of a major action to facilitate the restoration of morale and esprit de corps should heavy casualties be incurred). The 58th went into action under Major Neil Freeman, a 27-year-old solicitor and renowned footballer from Geelong, which had strong links to the 58th. Freeman lacked experience as a battalion commander, but Pompey was convinced he was a leader of abundant promise. He so distinguished himself at the Aldershot course for prospective colonels that he had been offered (but rejected) a position there as an instructor.

Two 58th companies filed smoothly into the 15th Brigade's portion of the shell-cratered front in the south-west corner of Polygon Wood late on 23 September. The following night they watched a relief of the British troops on their right degenerate into confusion. What they saw did not inspire confidence in the 98th British Brigade, which was to make a complementary advance and secure their flank in the battle. Nor did the unwillingness of the 58th's newly arrived front-line neighbours, the 1st Middlesex Regiment, to occupy the disturbing gap between them and the Australians; this task was, under the stipulated formation boundaries, unquestionably the 98th Brigade's responsibility. The commander of the furthest right 58th company, Lieutenant Hugh Boyd, did his utmost to persuade the British to extend leftwards, but it was not until a squad under Sergeant Jack Colclough, a 33-year-old farmer, spent all night digging across towards the Middlesex that the gap was partly closed.

Meanwhile Pompey Elliott was being frustrated by several disruptions to the 15th Brigade's preparations. Shortly before the battle Legge departed, having been promoted to brigade major in the 14th Brigade; he was replaced by Roy Gollan, a 25-year-old Geelong journalist. Elliott's familiarity with his new staff captain was limited to the months Gollan had spent in the 58th Battalion in 1916. In this major operation, then, Pompey's principal assistants would be a brigade major he lacked confidence in and a staff captain he hardly knew. Moreover, although he was well accustomed to improvising by now, the headquarters assigned to his brigade—a sizeable dug-out in a vast mine crater at Hooge (three miles east of Ypres)—was, he felt, demonstrably unsuitable. On his arrival there he found the dug-out very wet and already occupied by the headquarters of other units. He had to 'reduce Brigade Staff to an absolute minimum, and even then it was absolutely impossible for them to gain any proper rest or to have proper organisation or to arrange for the record of events'.

Elliott was also perturbed by the late arrival of the operation order from Fifth Division. There was not enough time for the contents to be properly absorbed, passed on, and implemented. With his brigade scheduled to attack at dawn on 26 September, he organised a conference with his battalion commanders at Hooge crater on the evening of the 24th, primarily to discuss issues arising from the divisional order—which did not materialise until 10.30pm, after the conference had concluded.

One directive in the order particularly annoyed the brigadier. In his brigade's extensive training for its next assignment it had practised attacking on a three-company frontage. According to Pompey, this method was adopted with Hobbs's imprimatur, was practised 'with great success', and was eminently suited to his brigade's task at Polygon Wood (advancing through woods had been a feature of the 15th Brigade's training routine as long ago as June). When the Fifth Division operation order arrived, however, it prescribed a two-company frontage for the attack (and, because the advance to the blue line was to be undertaken by two battalions, each of them would have to adopt a one-company frontage). Elliott sought permission to use the method his men had practised, but Hobbs insisted that any such variation was out of the question. His order had been approved by White and could not be altered, he insisted with dubious justification. By then, however, the 15th Brigade's preparations were being dislocated by the most serious disruption of all.

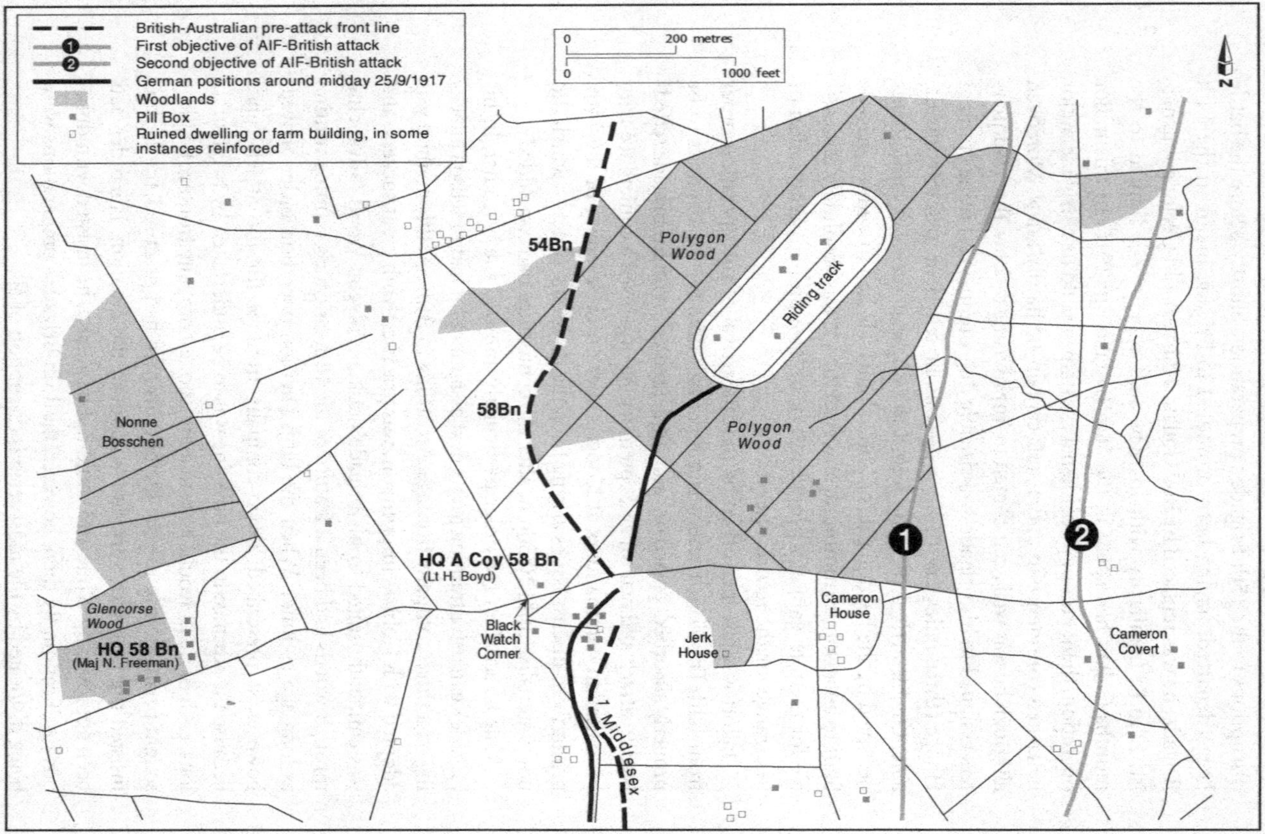
British-Australian pre-attack front line
First objective of AIF-British attack
Second objective of AIF-British attack
German positions around midday 25/9/1917
Woodlands
Pill Box
Ruined dwelling or farm building, in some instances reinforced
0
200 metres
0
1000 feet
N
54Bn
58Bn
Polygon Wood
Riding track
Polygon Wood
Nonne Bosschen
Glencorse Wood
HQ 58 Bn
(Maj N. Freeman)
HQ A Coy 58 Bn
(Lt H. Boyd)
Black Watch Corner
1 Middlesex
Jerk House
Cameron House
Cameron Covert
1
2

The battle of Polygon Wood

The battle of Polygon Wood

Formations and Commanders

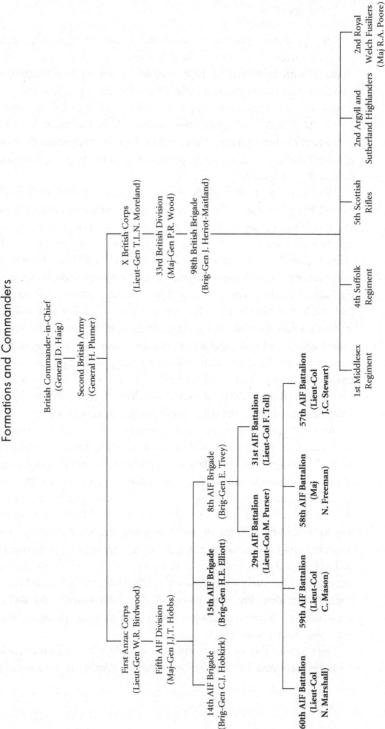

- British Commander-in-Chief (General D. Haig)
  - Second British Army (General H. Plumer)
    - First Anzac Corps (Lieut-Gen W.R. Birdwood)
      - Fifth AIF Division (Maj-Gen J.J.T. Hobbs)
        - 14th AIF Brigade (Brig-Gen C.J. Hobkirk)
        - **15th AIF Brigade (Brig-Gen H.E. Elliott)**
          - **60th AIF Battalion (Lieut-Col N. Marshall)**
          - **59th AIF Battalion (Lieut-Col C. Mason)**
          - **58th AIF Battalion (Maj N. Freeman)**
          - **57th AIF Battalion (Lieut-Col J.C. Stewart)**
        - 8th AIF Brigade (Brig-Gen E. Tivey)
          - **29th AIF Battalion (Lieut-Col M. Purser)**
          - **31st AIF Battalion (Lieut-Col F. Toll)**
    - X British Corps (Lieut-Gen T.L.N. Moreland)
      - 33rd British Division (Maj-Gen P.R. Wood)
        - 98th British Brigade (Brig-Gen J. Heriot-Maitland)
          - 1st Middlesex Regiment
          - 4th Suffolk Regiment
          - 5th Scottish Rifles
          - 2nd Argyll and Sutherland Highlanders
          - 2nd Royal Welch Fusiliers (Maj R.A. Poore)

The Germans, stunned by their defeat on 20 September and correctly sensing that another British attack was imminent, tried to thwart it with an assault of their own. At 5.15am on 25 September a ferocious bombardment suddenly descended on the 58th and 1st Middlesex, and immediately began to inflict sizeable casualties. Never before (as British intelligence later concluded) had German artillery concentration been greater. Never before had the 58th endured such intense shellfire. Germans in large numbers were spotted advancing behind this onslaught.

Lieutenant Boyd reacted decisively. Leaving his headquarters (a formidable pillbox near the crossroads at the south-western edge of Polygon Wood known as Black Watch Corner), Boyd fired the SOS signal, moved forward to the front line with his support platoons, and took control there. Major Freeman sent Boyd two further platoons from battalion reserve. The Middlesex, overwhelmed by this tremendous assault, fell back in disarray. The Germans made strenuous efforts to drive the 58th back in similar fashion, but did not succeed. A Prussian officer, leading his men from the front, materialised near the gap that Sergeant Colclough's squad had attempted to occupy. Colclough, arriving seemingly from nowhere, bayonetted him, hit the ground again to evade enemy machine-gunners, and then shot the next two closest Germans. His resourcefulness deterred other attackers in the vicinity. They wavered, turned back, and sought cover in nearby shell holes.

Pompey's men held on with superb tenacity. The alarming German penetration on the right enabled enemy machine-gunners to assail the 58th with oblique and enfilade fire. Boyd responded by swinging some of his men around to face the flank incursion, but they also had to contend with menacing machine-gun fire from low-flying German planes. When Boyd realised the Germans had reached the Middlesex support line he sought from Freeman, and was given, the two remaining platoons in battalion reserve. To reach the front line, these reinforcements had to go through an avalanche of German shells. Inevitably some men were hit, but the survivors persevered spiritedly and joined their beleaguered comrades. Boyd was proud of the 58th's morale and skilful resistance in a very tight corner, but he felt that the situation 'was becoming hourly more precarious'.

The shellfire was exceptionally intense, extensive, and prolonged. Pillboxes captured by the AIF five days earlier were particularly targeted. The Germans knew their precise location, and correctly presumed Australian commanders were occupying them. An evident priority was the redoubtable pillbox near the eastern edge of Glencorse Wood, 600 yards behind the support line, which was chosen by Freeman as his headquarters. Although its structure survived numerous direct hits, the concussion was so severe that pigeons inside it (used to carry messages) did not survive; outside, there were numerous casualties as runners and others in the immediate vicinity were hit. Similarly, Elliott's headquarters at Hooge crater, two miles behind the front, was a 'very unhealthy' place that was 'shelled all the time' (Stewart later wrote).

Even further back the shellfire was also extraordinary. Hobbs was on his way to Elliott's headquarters early that morning for a final discussion about the next day's attack, but the barrage he encountered while proceeding east along the Menin Road to Hooge convinced him it would be suicidal to venture any further:

> I stopped numerous convoys, cars and men from going to almost certain death. Dumps were going up in all directions. Motor lorries and cars burning along the Rd, broken down wagons, dead men and horses. I tried to get on but after going on for about 500 yds found the Road completely blocked. I hesitated and then decided to go back. 3 minutes after a lorry full of ammunition just ahead of where I stopped blew up with a tremendous explosion—a very narrow escape indeed.

It was obvious that this German onslaught would succeed in sabotaging the AIF's Polygon Wood operation unless the disturbing situation on the right could be swiftly retrieved. Just before nine o'clock a message reached Elliott from Freeman requesting a company of reinforcements. Pompey immediately arranged for a 60th company to be sent forward. That battalion was supposed to be spearheading the attack in 20 hours' time, but the brigadier had little alternative. There would clearly be no AIF attack at all unless this incursion was repulsed. He instructed Freeman to get in touch with the Middlesex and organise a combined thrust to eject the Germans and regain the front line; Freeman was to let him know when this counter-attack was to begin so he could co-ordinate a barrage to support it. Freeman did his utmost, but could find no Middlesex officer able to make the arrangements.

Hobbs could not get to Hooge, but Marshall, Stewart, and Mason managed to present themselves there for a ten o'clock conference at Elliott's headquarters. The brigadier had summoned them for a briefing on the divisional order, particularly to clarify the unpalatable change in attack formation insisted on by Hobbs. There seems to be no record of Pompey's mood at this stage, but it was presumably explosive. That his men had to discard a method repeatedly practised by them and suitable for their task was infuriating; discovering this change so late that he had to put his battalion commanders' lives in great peril to tell them about it was intolerable. Visiting Hooge crater then was decidedly dangerous, as Mason testified:

> The appearance of the place baffles description; the approaches were being heavily shelled and bombed, the dump was wrecked and ammunition and bombs were littered all round, and several motor lorries were wrecked and one blazed fiercely.

While Elliott was with his colonels they also discussed the situation on the right, and the possibility that further reinforcements might be required.

Their conference had just concluded when a message arrived from Brigadier-General J.D. Heriot-Maitland, commander of the 98th Brigade. This message stated that the 1st Middlesex would be counter-attacking at two o'clock to re-establish themselves in their front line. Heriot-Maitland had not formally taken over command of the sector when the Germans launched their assault, and remained unaware for some time that his brigade was being attacked. While considering his response he was told not to concern himself with the need to have fresh men for the following day's operation; recapturing the front line had to be his main and immediate priority. This instruction came from Major-General P.R. Wood, who was commanding the 33rd British Division for a few months in the temporary absence of the unimpressive temperance zealot who led it for two years, Major-General R.J. Pinney.

Elliott had already sent a second 60th company into the fight, and now decided to send its last available company as well (the other being engaged, like two of the 57th, on carrying duties). About this time a concerned 58th officer, having made his way to Hooge crater to suggest that Freeman could do with a company of reinforcements, received instant reassurance when he approached the brigadier. 'A company', replied Pompey, 'my boy, you shall have the whole of the 60th'. Elliott directed Marshall to accompany the last 60th company forward and take charge there when he arrived. Pompey then sent another message to Freeman, instructing him to support the 2.00pm British counter-attack with the 60th Battalion reinforcements he had been given. The brigadier also outlined the barrage organised for this advance, and advised that Marshall was moving forward to take over.

For Boyd and his weary 58th stalwarts hanging on resolutely, the news that Marshall was coming to their aid was heartening indeed. As Bean acknowledged, in a 'tight corner the mere knowledge that Norman Marshall was in charge would give confidence to all Australians who were aware of the fact'. Boyd had already been buoyed during this most harrowing day of his life by an encouraging message from Marshall.

But relentless German shellfire continued to make it very difficult for reinforcements and carrying parties to get forward. A lieutenant supervising a 57th party lugging ammunition to a dump at Glencorse Wood was killed close to Pompey's headquarters, and a number of his men were hit. The 60th company engaged in similar toil suffered so severely that Marshall had to send another lieutenant to reorganise it. For the other 60th companies, advancing to reinforce the 58th, the barrage deluging Glencorse Wood was a nightmare. As they gallantly proceeded in single file, a few yards apart, along the track that was the only way forward in the treacherous, shell-cratered wilderness, it seemed inconceivable that they could escape the thunderous missiles crashing all around them. The commander of B Company and over 20 of his men were hit, and A Company soon lost over 60, including two officers. These casualties seemed miraculously light, so devastating was the shellfire.

Boyd, in accordance with Elliott's instructions (conveyed via Freeman), arranged for some of the 60th reinforcements to advance in support of the scheduled 2.00pm counter-attack by the 98th Brigade. However, there was no sign of the Middlesex. Two companies of Argyll and Sutherland Highlanders managed to establish a partial line in the 98th Brigade's sector, but it was still well behind the previous front and 350 yards behind Boyd's position. Boyd's anxiety about the vulnerability of the exposed 60th men was accentuated by his glimpse of Germans massing ominously ahead near the pillbox-reinforced strongpoints known as Jerk House and Cameron House. Eventually, around five o'clock, Boyd decided to withdraw this 60th fragment.

Shortly afterwards, having been delayed by a communication mix-up, Marshall and his intelligence officer, Lieutenant Stillman, arrived at Freeman's headquarters. They quickly appraised the situation. Stillman felt 'things were becoming very serious on the right'. Marshall sent Elliott a frank assessment:

> Am at 58th Battalion headquarters. Position appears bad. Enemy reported by [Boyd] at 5pm to be again massing near Jerk House and Cameron House. Brigade on our right have not retaken their front line and can get nothing definite from them. Our right is still intact but line is now badly knocked about and would have very bad time if attacked in flank. Enemy aeroplanes flying very low and machine-gunning freely. Have formed the opinion that enemy intend counter-attacking at dusk. Enemy barrage very heavy on our support and reserve lines and it is almost impossible to get reserves [forward] until dusk ... Consider you should insist on the British Brigade on our right retaking their front line at once and link up with us otherwise relief tonight must suffer very severely. Intend sending two companies into line at dusk or as soon as possible thereafter. Still suffering heavy casualties.

Marshall then proceeded further forward to confer with Boyd, who was delighted to see him. For twelve hours the 31-year-old Bendigo dentist had carried the harrowing front-line responsibility for a critical situation that was being followed with concern by all his direct superiors in the military hierarchy right up to the Commander-in-Chief himself. (Major-General Harington was to write in his biography of Plumer eighteen years later that it was a 'very disconcerting' time, 'which I remember well'). Boyd had risen to the challenge superbly, but was glad to hand over at last to someone more credentialled. Marshall 'at once grasped the situation tho he had not seen the front on any portion of this sector', Boyd later noted admiringly, and directed the only 60th company not yet called into action to bolster the right flank straightaway. Its commander, 35-year-old Wilfred Beaver, had overlapped with Harold Elliott at Ormond College during a distinguished scholastic career before becoming a magistrate in Papua, where he collected material for a book later published with the title *Unexplored New Guinea*. The way Beaver led his company straight to the thinly held position it was to reinforce 'was worthy of great praise', Marshall considered, but just as Beaver arrived he was fatally wounded.

Back at Hooge crater Elliott received a message from the 98th Brigade shortly after Marshall's front-line report arrived. Marshall had highlighted the plight on the right, urging Elliott to exert maximum pressure on the 98th Brigade to rectify the situation. Pompey had been sceptical of earlier British claims that the 98th had recaptured its front line, a recovery not verified by Freeman. The vague message from Heriot-Maitland that arrived within minutes of Marshall's appraisal merely confirmed Pompey's impression that the British had no idea about the state of affairs on their front or even where their units were. With minimal help to be expected from that quarter, and with Freeman describing the situation in similarly pessimistic and precarious terms as Marshall, Elliott reacted with characteristic decisiveness: he committed another of his battalions to the fray, Cam Stewart's 57th.

Among the 57th's men wondering what the next day's battle might bring was its vivid chronicler 'Jimmy' Downing. 'Despair, hope, despondency and resolution fought for the possession of each soul', he observed, as shells 'roared and moaned incessantly' and 'ragged iron whirled and burred'. Moving forward earlier than expected in response to Pompey's urgent summons, Downing and his comrades sensed the shellfire intensifying. Then they reached Glencorse:

> There was a crash close by, a red flame, flying sparks. Another—and two men in the flash, toppling stiffly sideways ... one with a fore-arm partly raised, the other lifted a little from the ground, with legs and arms spread-eagled wide—all seen in an instant—then a second of darkness, then shells, big shells, flashing and crashing all around ... we stumbled past the reeking bodies as nearly at a run as our exhaustion permitted—heads down as though it were a hurricane of rain, not ripping steel. By the red and flickering light of the shell-bursts men were seen running and staggering, bent low. They dropped into what had been a trench, ... enduring with tautened faces, lying close to the ground, crouching as they burrowed for dear life with their entrenching tools, while the storm of steel wreaked its fury on tortured earth and tortured flesh. There were on all sides the groans and the wailing of mangled men ... The

> smell of burnt explosive was thick and pungent. Bodies, living and dead, were buried, tossed up, and the torn fragments buried again.

Before the 57th Battalion began its approach to the front, Charles Noad, nervously preparing to go into action for the first time as an officer, was heartened by the philosophical fatalism of his experienced captain, Herb Dickinson. 'Go for your life', Dickinson advised Noad, 'if your name's on it you'll get it and you can't do much about it'. Noad's platoon was practically decimated in Glencorse Wood. One of his worst moments occurred when the column led by Dickinson halted and Noad heard men calling for the captain. As Noad feared, one of the shells bombarding the wood had Dickinson's name on it. After further casualties Noad found himself in charge of Dickinson's shaken company. As well as Dickinson, two other company commanders were killed while the 57th proceeded through that dreadful place, Captain Aram and Lieutenant Gerald Joynt (whose brother was to win the VC with the 8th Battalion).

Elliott had directed Stewart to 're-establish any part of our right flank which is abandoned, and form a flank to connect up with the British'. Stewart coolly scrutinised the situation with his adjutant and Lieutenant Roy Doutreband, his intelligence officer. Their personal reconnaissance confirmed that the 98th Brigade, despite its claims to the contrary, had no men in its sector (though some had joined the Australians on the 15th Brigade's right) forward of the Argyll and Sutherland Highlanders, who were positioned well behind the AIF front. Stewart distributed his men for maximum flexibility. One company filled the gap on the right between these Highlanders and the existing 15th Brigade front (in accordance with Elliott's instructions). The other three companies were positioned in reserve nearby, ready for use as and where needed.

It was now inconceivable to Elliott, as he told Hobbs in no uncertain terms, that his brigade could attack Polygon Wood the following morning. The 98th Brigade's promise to regain its front line, virtually a prerequisite for the planned operation to succeed, had not been kept. In view of its performance so far, the likelihood that it would be able to fulfil its obligations if the attack went ahead as scheduled had to be slim. The consequences for Elliott's men, vulnerable to flanking fire as they advanced, would be calamitous. Besides, his own brigade had already suffered acutely. The 58th had been severely mauled, and the 57th and

60th, two of the designated assault battalions in the operation, were in no shape for such a role. Moreover, the relentless German shellfire, as well as making it impossible for units to approach Polygon Wood without sustaining heavy casualties, had disrupted the attack preparations in other ways. Practically all the supply dumps accumulated for the operation had been destroyed. The important tape-laying to pinpoint assembly positions might well be detected by the Germans who had penetrated on the right. Tapes already positioned to mark forward approaches had been shot away. Nearly all the specially trained 58th guides had become casualties.

Elliott pointed all this out vigorously to Hobbs, who responded that the operation had to proceed nevertheless. This decision had been made, not without considerable anxiety, at a higher level; there would be significant modifications arising from Pompey's forceful representations. Accepting that the 57th, 58th, and 60th were too shattered and shaken to participate as assault battalions, Hobbs directed that the advance to the red line would now be carried out by the 59th, and two battalions from Tivey's brigade in divisional reserve would undertake the second phase. As for the all-important issue of the 98th Brigade's capacity to get forward on the right, Hobbs assured Pompey that redoubled pressure was being applied to Heriot-Maitland by his superiors to ensure that this occurred, and at least the British commanders were now conceding that their earlier reports that their men had regained their front line were mistaken. As well, special counter-battery action would be taken to subdue the enemy artillery that had tormented Pompey's men.

It was with 'the utmost anxiety' that Elliott rapidly overhauled the arrangements for the attack. The extra units he had been given would be operating in most unfamiliar territory: 'not a single officer, NCO or man of the two 8th Brigade Battalions had ever been as far as Brigade HQ, and it was necessary for us to provide guides for them even to that place'. Pompey immediately notified Marshall—'Division insists carrying out plan'—asking him to inform Freeman and Stewart of this decision, and to take responsibility for the front-line organisation of the attack (guiding the assault units to appropriate starting positions in particular) while Stewart took charge of the defence.

Elliott's other battalion commander, Mason, was on his way forward with the 59th when he learned to his surprise that his men would be undertaking the advance to the red line instead of the second-phase task they had practised. But this last-minute switch affecting the 59th was the least of Elliott's worries. Confident that Mason's men were familiar enough with the whole operation to adjust to their changed role satisfactorily, he was far more concerned about Tivey's battalions and the problem of getting supplies forward to replace the destroyed dumps. Frantically busy, Pompey did not waste words when Mason called at his headquarters. He quickly confirmed that the operation was on, and the 59th was to do the first part instead of half the second.

> 'So do you know what to do?'
> 'Yes', replied Mason.
> 'Well then, go and do it'.

Just after midnight the commanders of the 8th Brigade battalions assigned to the second phase, Lieutenant-Colonels Muir Purser (29th) and Fred Toll (31st), arrived at Hooge. Elliott gave them a hurried briefing in the limited time available.

During that tense, busy night Pompey's men did him proud. Freeman's weary 58th survivors were relieved in the front line by the 60th. Marshall, establishing his headquarters at Black Watch Corner, directed the preparations in the forward area. In allocating the vital tape-laying tasks, he shrewdly adhered to arrangements anticipated until the last-minute changes. His own intelligence officer, Stillman, set the tapes for the red line battalion, even though the 60th Battalion had been replaced in the attack; likewise, Doutreband did for the 31st Battalion what he had been expecting to do for the 57th, and Lieutenant J.W. Francis did the honours for the left blue line battalion even though his own 59th was attacking in the first phase. Guides from the 58th Battalion led the assault battalions forward from Hooge crater to Black Watch Corner. Sentries from the 57th and 58th were posted en route to prevent anyone missing his way in the dark. A 58th company formed a protective screen in front of the assembly positions. Two 57th companies (one without any officers after Glencorse Wood) and a 58th party made a sterling contribution carrying rations, water, Stokes mortars, grenades, and other ammunition to Black Watch Corner.

All these preparations benefited from the Germans' understandable belief that they had succeeded in preventing the scheduled AIF operation. This conclusion prompted them to ease their shelling of AIF positions during the night (although Doutreband's ten-man tape-laying party was caught by a sharp bombardment, and only one beside himself was not hit). Even so, it was an impressive display of brigade cohesion. Mason was full of praise for the assistance his men received as they proceeded smoothly forward and Stillman efficiently led them to their assembly positions. 'Everything went without a hitch', Mason enthused. There was the odd hitch affecting the movement of the 8th Brigade battalions, but they were correctly assembled in time. 'The last man was accurately placed in his position exactly 20 minutes before zero', Pompey declared proudly, 'in spite of difficulties which at first appeared insurmountable'.

The men under his command had done superbly, but he was powerless to alleviate his greatest concern of all—the situation on the right. Heriot-Maitland had arranged for two battalions to move forward during the night and recapture the front-line sector yielded by the Middlesex. The battalions assigned to this task were the 98th Brigade's reserve battalion, the 4th Suffolk Regiment, and a unit borrowed from the 19th British Brigade, the 5th Scottish Rifles. During that long and worrying day Birdwood and Hobbs had repeatedly urged Major-General Wood of the 33rd British Division to retrieve the situation on his front, reiterating their concerns in a visit to his headquarters. Responding to this pressure—instigated, of course, by Pompey's incisive reports—Wood approved Heriot-Maitland's arrangements and told him (at 7.30pm that night) that the reinforcement units should advance 'as soon as possible as the Australians were hard pressed on their right'.

The Scottish and Suffolk battalions had a challenging task. They had to move forward very much in the dark. Not only was it well past nightfall; the area they were entering was unfamiliar to them, and the location of the British and Germans within it was unknown. All the same, their rescue effort was lamentably mismanaged. Guides from 98th Brigade headquarters led them forward. The Scottish men followed their guide for over an hour before realising he was obviously lost—he had led them back to their start-point. Accordingly, there was no sign of them when the 4th Suffolk arrived at the joint pre-attack assembly point. The Suffolk commander proposed to move on without them, but Heriot-Maitland instructed him to wait. Two hours later he was still waiting. Just when he learned that Heriot-Maitland had changed his mind and directed the Suffolks to proceed on their own, a Scottish company belatedly arrived. There were further delays, occasioned by a thick mist hampering visibility, a sharp German bombardment, and uncertainty about the whereabouts of some Scottish companies. At one stage the Suffolks were poised to advance, but their commander told them to take cover because of enemy shellfire. In the end neither battalion managed to get into position to follow the British barrage forward, and they ended up 800 yards short of their objective.

Elliott was unaware of this sequence of events until shortly before the attack was to be launched, when a runner arrived at Hooge crater and handed over a message from Keith McDonald, Pompey's liaison officer at 98th Brigade headquarters. It was the 'intention' of the British 'to push forward quickly at zero and to get into touch with the barrage as soon as possible after zero', McDonald reported, but three companies of the 98th's left attacking battalion (the unit advancing next to Pompey's brigade) had 'lost their way'; hopefully 'at least one company ... will try to get as close to the original front line as possible' by the time the Australians began advancing. After the assurances about the strenuous endeavours the 98th would be making, Pompey understandably concluded that its effort had been demonstrably inadequate. Suspecting the worst, he had already instructed Stewart to 'be prepared to protect right flank of our attacking waves should British Battalions not make good their old line during the night'. But he recognised that the 59th, 29th, and 31st would just have to do their best without proper support on the right.

The support they received from the artillery, on the other hand, was outstanding. According to Bean, the barrage descending

> at 5.50 on September 26th, just as the Polygon plateau became visible, was the most perfect that ever protected Australian troops. It seemed to break out, as almost every report emphasises, with a single crash. The ground was dry, and the shell-bursts raised a wall of dust and smoke which appeared almost to be solid. So dense was the cloud that individual bursts, except the white puffs of shrapnel above its near edge, could not be distinguished. Roaring, deafening, it rolled ahead of the troops 'like a Gippsland bushfire'.

However, as the 29th and 31st Battalions moved forward with the 59th behind this superb barrage, a problem arising from their late inclusion soon emerged. The 59th, manoeuvring in precise accord with Elliott's intentions and its previous training—a thin screen in front, and the following waves at appropriate distances behind—was disorganised by the determination of some 8th Brigade men to get forward as quickly as possible in order to avoid being hit by the inevitable retaliatory bombardment. The 59th's orderly progress, then, was soon disrupted by the unexpected tendency of the 29th and 31st to push through it. Mason's men also had to contend with resolute resistance from German defenders in a number of pillboxes.

At one of these pillboxes there was a critical encounter involving one of Pompey's 7th Battalion originals. John Turnour, a theological student at Bendigo, had just turned 21 when the war began. He enlisted straightaway and became a private in Herbert Hunter's Bendigo company, along with Noel Edwards and numerous other now-fallen comrades. Throughout the war he had remained in, and very attached to, that same company, transferring with a number of its members to the 59th, while collecting numerous wounds along the way. Now a lieutenant, he was looking forward to the honour of commanding this company for the first time at Polygon Wood when Elliott, aware of his record and propensity for getting hit, nominated him for a role in the nucleus. But Turnour protested to Mason, and Pompey reluctantly allowed him to participate in the operation.

With the attack held up by machine-gunners in a large pillbox, Turnour organised his men into various shell holes forming an approximate arc facing the pillbox, and told them to be ready to rush it. He then placed himself directly opposite the front of the pillbox (and the forward loophole the machine-gunners were firing through), stood up, waved his men forward, and charged. Although repeatedly hit, his determination and forward momentum carried him on until he fell, riddled with bullets, in front of the pillbox. By monopolising the defenders' attention with such selfless gallantry, he enabled his men to rush the pillbox successfully. The bombers did their deadly work, and within seconds all resistance from the score of Germans in the pillbox ceased. Pompey later claimed that its capture, by creating a gap in the structure of mutually supporting pillboxes, paved the way for the encirclement and capture of others, and thereby contributed substantially to the 59th's progress.

The Germans resisted sternly. Of the six officers who accompanied the two leading 59th companies forward, Turnour was one of five to be hit. Nevertheless Mason was able to report at 6.45am that his men were consolidating at their objective. Pompey, waiting and wondering back at Hooge, was delighted. Mason's other news—no sign of the British on the right—was much less encouraging, if hardly a surprise.

This British failure soon became a major problem to Elliott when he realised that because of it the 8th Brigade battalions he had been given were refusing to push forward to their objectives on the blue line. Toll of the 31st was unequivocal. 'Troops on right have not advanced. Am not advancing further', he declared in a message that reached Elliott at 8.26am. Half an hour later a runner panted in to Hooge crater with a note from Mason confirming Toll's refusal. Elliott referred the situation to Hobbs, who insisted that Toll had to push on as planned, while a flank barrage would provide the protection not forthcoming from the 98th Brigade. Pompey immediately informed Toll. A later joint message from the 31st and 29th stated that they had sustained few casualties in reaching the red line, and were 'losing heavily from machine gun fire' while remaining there, but they would be staying where they were rather than pressing on to the blue line because of the unprotected right flank. 'Whatever justification Col. Toll may have had for failing to push forward', Pompey concluded, 'Col. Purser of the 29th had none'.

Elliott urged both units to get moving, an exhortation he reinforced when word came that the 14th Brigade on the left had reached their final objective (an accomplishment hindered by Purser's reluctance to advance). '14th Brigade have secured their part of the blue line', Pompey affirmed. 'Push on at once and report progress'. Two hours later he had still heard nothing from the 29th or 31st to indicate that they had moved at all. Thoroughly frustrated, and having more confidence in his own brigade's officers (a view which the morning's events, from his perspective, seemed to have vindicated), Pompey directed Mason to tell Toll and Purser that they either had to get the 31st and 29th to advance or he (Mason) would have to supersede them, by order of the brigadier, and take charge of their battalions himself.

The situation on the right flank, as far as Pompey was concerned, 'continued for some time to remain very obscure'. Retaliatory German shellfire after the launch of the attack had been ferocious. Downing was there:

> The barrage continued without intermission for twenty-four hours, and what the men endured could never be described, for the effect of shell fire is horrifying out of all proportion to the number it mangles and kills. Each inch of ground was tossed and churned ... a thousand times ... the mangling, ripping thunderbolts crashed rapidly as a roll of kettle-drums.

The 57th company directed to advance behind the assault battalions and protect the right flank had been unable to do so because of this shellfire. But Stewart and Marshall arranged for the 60th further forward to assume this responsibility instead. Although little information about developments on the right was filtering back to Elliott, it was clear enough that the German penetration there was proving a substantial hindrance.

The meagre news that Pompey did have was hardly reassuring. Stewart reported that the 'whole area is still being intensely shelled and any movement is most difficult'. There were fewer than 100 men left in the 58th, and his reserve had been reduced to one small company (Noad's). The various companies and platoons he had assigned to the fierce combat on the flank were all now 'lost to me'. Numerous runners and officers 'sent forward have disappeared'.

Meanwhile the situation was being reshaped by an initiative from the 33rd Division. Major-General Wood, evidently also impatient with the 98th Brigade's lack of progress, decided to detach a fresh battalion, the 2nd Royal Welch Fusiliers, from his divisional reserve and send it forward—through ground gained by the Australians rather than his division's fenestrated front—to make an advance south-eastwards from the 15th Brigade's right flank. This attempt was scheduled for midday.

The 2nd Royal Welch Fusiliers became one of the best-known battalions in the entire British army by virtue of the post-war literary accomplishments of some of its soldiers. A regular battalion with a proud history, the Welch had been involved in almost every significant British military engagement since 1689. The battalion was in France within a week of the outbreak of war in August 1914, and suffered severely at the Somme in 1916. Among its officers were Robert Graves and Siegfried Sassoon, who were to become acclaimed as two of the finest memoirists of the Great War; both wrote vividly and at times controversially about their service with the Welch. In very different style was

Old Soldiers Never Die by Frank Richards, a fine account from a rank-and-file perspective by a Welsh ex-miner who served with the battalion in India and Burma before 1914 and continuously at the Western Front.

But the most outstanding memoir of all, especially from a historical viewpoint, was Captain James Dunn's *The War the Infantry Knew*. Dunn, just like Pompey, followed years of university study with enlistment as a trooper in the Boer War and was awarded the DCM for gallantry in South Africa. In the Great War Dunn was regimental medical officer of the Welch (equivalent to George Elliott's position in the 56th AIF Battalion) from November 1915 until May 1918, but was, as Graves affirmed, 'far more than a doctor'. Tactically astute as well as exceptionally courageous, Dunn was not only frequently to be found in the firing line; he would often go out on patrol with the Welch and, Graves wrote, 'became the right-hand man of three or four colonels in succession'. Richards was another Dunn admirer:

> he was the bravest and coolest man under fire that I ever saw in France ... I always thought he was more cut out for a general than a doctor and that he certainly would have made a better one than most of those who were.

The Welch came up via a long detour through AIF-captured territory. With their colonel away on leave, the acting commander was Major R.A. Poore, a 47-year-old stutterer whose DSO in the Boer War testified to his bravery. Having arrived shortly before midday at Black Watch Corner with the outstanding young pianist (and friend of Sassoon's) who was temporarily his assistant adjutant, Poore discussed the situation with the Australians and then supervised the deployment of his platoons. The widely admired Welch adjutant was soon fatally wounded, two company commanders were hit, and the Germans managed to land one of their heaviest shells in a deep trench then occupied by Poore, the pianist, and another Welch officer they were conferring with, killing all three. The command vacuum was spontaneously filled by Dunn himself (a development unmentioned by the modest medico in his book). The Welch advanced valiantly, but encountered a hail of intense machine-gun fire that prevented them from reaching their objective—a cluster of pillboxes beyond Cameron House (and some 1400 yards east of Black Watch Corner) known as Cameron Covert.

They managed to establish themselves at Jerk House but not Cameron House, which was 'desperately defended', Elliott pointed out, and 'a formidable obstacle to the advance':

> It was on a slight eminence giving excellent fire command in all directions and although at times our men and the Royal Welsh Fusiliers were on three sides of it, it could neither be approached or silenced owing to the fact that the "Pill Boxes" in Cameron Covert effectively protected its flanks and rear.

Frank Richards, stationed for most of the afternoon near Black Watch Corner, was well and truly back in what he called 'the blood tub':

> The ground rocked and heaved with the bursting shells. The enemy were doing their best to obliterate the strong point that they had lost ... a dud shell landed clean in the trench, killing the man behind me, and burying itself in the side of the trench by me ... It was ... the first time I had been in action with the Australians and I found them very brave men. There was also an excellent spirit of comradeship between officers and men.

Richards knew he was fortunate to have survived such a fierce and prolonged bombardment:

> Not one of us had hardly moved a yard for some hours, but we had been lucky in our part of the trench, having only two casualties. In two other parts of the strong point every man had been killed or wounded.

Not far away Dunn was trying to compile a brief report for Heriot-Maitland, but the 'writing was interrupted several times by the quantity of soil that was thrown about us'.

Information from a prisoner indicating that an enemy attack was imminent seemed confirmed when hundreds of advancing Germans came into view beyond Cameron Covert. Seeking a stronger defensive position in response, the acting commander of the most advanced Welch company authorised his men to fall back to Jerk House. Many withdrew further. Onlooking Australians, angered by this excessive voluntary retirement, remonstrated vehemently with the back-pedallers; some even halted retiring Welch parties by threatening to shoot them. A 59th lieutenant who did so was later thanked by two apologetic British captains who were embarrassed about this unforced withdrawal. (One of them might have been Dunn; Richards saw him stop some Welch who were falling back.) In fact, this German attack foundered before it really began, thanks to timely artillery intervention.

But General Wood, the British divisional commander, was increasingly frustrated by the lack of progress on his front and its impact on the whole operation. Striving once again to invigorate the 98th Brigade, Wood directed Heriot-Maitland to 'make every endeavour to advance to the blue line'; it was 'of utmost importance that right flank of Australians should be covered by you'. But Plumer had already given up on the 33rd Division. The Commander-in-Chief approved his proposal that a fresh division should be transferred to his army 'in order to complete the work which the 33rd Division had not been able to carry out'.

Progress was much more satisfactory on the left of the 15th Brigade front. Stan Neale, an ex-7th Battalion veteran now a captain in the 59th, was particularly prominent, rallying the retiring Welch and ensuring that his battalion reached the correct objective (some Australians had halted prematurely, believing they were on the red line). Shortly afterwards a spontaneous manoeuvre by 59th men dealing with counter-attacking Germans brought them forward almost to the final objective, an advance which made the 29th's task of consolidation on the blue line relatively straightforward.

Pompey, then, was free to concentrate on expediting progress on the right. It was time, he decided, to use Marshall in a more offensive capacity. The 60th colonel had been busy supporting the 59th and 31st Battalions: he had been supervising the provision of reinforcements and supplies, the care of the wounded, and the safeguarding as much as possible of the right flank as the advance progressed. Liberating Marshall from these responsibilities at dusk on 26 September, Elliott directed him to organise an attack towards the main stumbling block on the right, Cameron House. With units considerably scattered and intermixed, Marshall initiated reorganisation and patrolling. About midnight he and Stillman inspected an advanced position held by Australians in the British sector. From there Marshall decided to reconnoitre further forward with Stillman and a small party. After venturing over 100 yards, they discerned a pillbox up ahead. Marshall proposed a raid. His companions agreed to give it a fly. They succeeded—the pillbox and those of its occupants who survived the skirmish were captured. Marshall arranged for the Australian line to be brought forward to this strongpoint, then led his party on further.

For some time Marshall remained unaware that the pillbox he had just acquired and failed to recognise in the dark was the very heart of Cameron House. He informed Elliott merely that he had captured a pillbox and a few prisoners, adding that he was still probably hundreds of yards short of Cameron House. Of Marshall's subsequent adventures as he proceeded towards Cameron Covert, Pompey knew nothing. A separate patrol was sent out to clarify the situation on the right; its report that Cameron House was in Australian hands left Pompey puzzled. When the sketchy information reaching Hooge crater (as Street noted) 'continued to be somewhat contradictory', Pompey decided at dawn on 27 September to resolve the uncertainty by going forward to see for himself. Peck, alarmed by the risks involved, tried to dissuade him, but Pompey was insistent.

Grimly purposeful, he was accompanied on this front-line visit (as in similar circumstances at Fromelles) by Schroder. On their way forward they came across an unwounded 15th Brigade officer in what Pompey concluded were suspicious circumstances. 'Your men are up there fighting for their lives—what are you doing?' he challenged accusingly, threatening to shoot this officer for dereliction of duty, before allowing himself to be persuaded by Schroder that such on-the-spot punishment might be a trifle hasty. They pressed on, passing Stewart's headquarters pillbox (and presumably startling the occupants) about seven o'clock. Fortunately the German shellfire had died down and things were relatively quiet by the time Elliott reached the front line and began an extensive inspection. Schroder remembered it well:

> with mud and slush up to our knees, Pomp took short cuts and missed nothing. The boys who looked abjectly miserable when we arrived at the various pillboxes and shell holes managed to raise a grin when the old man spoke to them.

Elliott's appearance so far forward amazed the Welch. 'It was the only time during the whole of the war that I saw a brigadier with the first line of attacking troops', marvelled Richards. Dunn was stunned. Having lamented earlier in his book that it was 'rare for anyone who combines authority and nous to be on the spot', he described a brief conversation 'the Australian Brigadier … called "Pompey" by his men' had with two Welch officers: 'He told them that there were few, if any, Germans in front of our position, he had "been to look"'. That a general would undertake such intrepid personal reconnaissance was a revelation to Dunn, who was also impressed to find the AIF colonel in charge of medical arrangements well forward: 'Was one of ours ever within the shelled zone when there was the greatest need for him to know how things were being done, and what might be needed?'

Pompey's comprehensive front-line inspection was crucial to the outcome of the battle. The morale-boosting, invigorating effects of his visit were considerable, but the tactical initiatives arising from it were even more significant. His first impressions were dominated by the chaos of the battlefield. 'I never saw such a scene of confusion, men of all regiments mixed up all over the place, dead of all regiments lay aside the enemy everywhere'. But he quickly discerned that a sweeping success was within reach, and some well-placed pressure could achieve it.

> I arranged with Marshall to consolidate Cameron House and the wood called Cameron Covert … Urged on the Welsh officers who still survived to reorganise their men. Ordered Mason to push forward to the junction of Cameron Covert and Polygon Wood and consolidate along the eastern edge of the Polygon Wood which runs northwards from there. I found Col. Toll of the 31st and Col. Purser of the 29th Bn in a dugout. The former I sent to reorganise his Bn which was much disorganised in Polygon Wood and to lead them forward to the blue line. Col. Purser I sent to establish a HQs with his Battn in their area and to make a report on the situation there. I then returned to [my] HQs and made a full report to Division. Shortly afterwards received the gratifying intelligence that Toll had made good the blue line and Marshall strongly established in Cameron Covert. In the afternoon we further got word that the British had now pushed right in and got the remainder of the blue line. This was in consequence of my report on the situation.

Essentially, Marshall and his men (assisted by the 15th Brigade's Stokes mortars) had pushed forward on the morning of 27 September in the British sector in and around Cameron Covert until they were *beyond* the final objective. This assisted the 31st Battalion to advance on Marshall's left in order to link up on the blue line with the 29th; it also facilitated an afternoon advance by the Welch and other British units to plug the gap on Marshall's right. The Germans unleashed a furious retaliatory bombardment—'the heaviest I have ever known', wrote a 58th lieutenant—but it eventually eased, and the 15th Brigade was withdrawn that night. Marshall handed over a frontage of 250 yards in the 98th Brigade's area.

It was an outstanding achievement by Elliott and his men. All objectives were attained, and the victory was won in circumstances of the gravest adversity. Despite the units engaged becoming unusually intermixed, the 15th Brigade had demonstrated admirable cohesion. Among the participants in Marshall's exploits at and beyond Cameron House were lieutenants from the 57th and 58th as well as his own officers. At one stage Noad was in charge of a party comprising men of the 57th, 59th, 60th, 31st, and Welch Battalions. And Mason's glowing praise for the officers from other units, who enabled the 59th to move into position so smoothly before the attack, was matched by his commendation of the assistance he was given during the battle by the 58th's leaders, notably Majors Freeman and de Ravin (another original 7th officer to join Pompey's brigade). The victory was also a personal triumph for Elliott. Under his leadership, Bean concluded,

> the 15th Brigade and the troops reinforcing it snatched complete success from an almost desperate situation on the right ... His staunchness and vehemence, and power of instilling those qualities into his troops, had turned his brigade into a magnificently effective instrument; and the driving force of this stout-hearted leader in his inferno at Hooge throughout the two critical days was in a large measure responsible for this victory.

Elliott's leadership was all the more outstanding in the circumstances, because he had to cope with devastating news unrelated to his command while the battle was raging. During the advance by the 14th Brigade on his left, as he learned at around 3.00pm on 26

September, his brother George had been mortally wounded. George was in Chateau Wood, only a few hundred yards from Hooge crater, waiting to go forward with the 56th Battalion when

> a fragment of a shell struck him on the back of the head crushing his skull and he died a few hours later without regaining consciousness at all. They brought the news to me when I was tied to my office directing the fight and I could not go to him though they said he was dying. I hope never to have such an experience again. The effort to concentrate my thoughts on the task of defeating the enemy as the messages came through revealing each move and the changing phases of the battle to me seemed as time went on to turn me into stone and half the time I was like a man sleepwalking, yet I do not think I made a single error that I would not have made at [training] manoeuvres under similar circumstances.

George's death was bad enough, but during the battle Pompey also received appalling news from home. A letter arrived from his friend Charles Lowe, a barrister who had been a university contemporary and was to become one of Victoria's longest-serving and most respected judges. This letter informed Elliott that his legal partner since 1909, Glen Roberts, had involved their firm in dubious speculations and amassed huge losses in his absence, with the result that Elliott had become, he learned, liable for debts amounting to thousands of pounds. This was a disastrous turn of events, all the more devastating because Elliott was committed to an upright code of honour and morality, and struggled to suppress a sense of personal financial insecurity (although he had less need than most to worry, thanks to his father's estate). Moreover, his absolute adherence to financial probity was reinforced by his perception that spotless integrity was essential to his future as a solicitor. Now more than ever he had to summon all his willpower to maintain his focus on the unfolding battle. The unpalatable task of telling him the facts had evidently not been rushed; Lieutenant Len Stillman had known of his uncle's financial disgrace for at least a month.

After the exhausted remnants of his brigade were replaced in the line, Elliott had one last task to supervise before he could begin to unwind:

> I had made arrangements for the removal of my brother's body, and at noon or shortly after we buried him with military honours in the little military cemetery to the west of Dickebusch. And so our battle came to an end. I was so utterly weary of body and soul at this time that neither shells, bombs or gas had the slightest terrors for me. In fact I was more like a man in a trance whose power of sensation had for the time being [been] removed. After a sleep I felt better.

During the next few days his headquarters was inundated with congratulations for his brigade's outstanding feat. Birdwood and Hobbs both called to offer theirs personally. Plumer went so far as to thank Elliott for saving the British army from disaster. Prouder of his men than ever, Pompey described the 58th as his 'Stonewall Battalion', and assured its survivors that their stand on 25 September would become a military history classic. Reviewing the battle with his officers and men, he emphasised the importance of compiling detailed accounts of the fighting in order to produce an incontrovertible record of what the brigade had accomplished.

Not surprisingly, his men were more intent on resting and counting their blessings to have survived. Keith Doig, writing to his fiancée on the day his friend George Elliott was buried, admitted he 'had never been nearer death':

> crouched in a shell hole with the big shells dropping all around me, I felt quite resigned and just wondered where the shell would hit me ... I was blown off my feet three or four times, I was covered with earth thrown up by the shells, I was hit with small fragments, yet marvellous to say I came out unscathed.

'The Somme was bad, Bullecourt was worse, but this place beats all', Doig concluded. Brigade casualties (around 1200, with another 720 in the 8th Brigade units) proved to be 'heavy', Street noted, 'but not greatly so when the fierce nature of the fighting is taken into consideration'.

One particular casualty was preoccupying Pompey when he began his first letter to his family five days after the battle. 'I am very sad still', he told Kate:

> Poor old Geordie, I saw him dead so white and rigid and still and his loved ones left behind him. And we have buried him so far from home amongst strangers to him. I am so glad I was able to bring his body back from the shell torn zone to a little cemetery where the grass was smooth and green and we fired the volley over his head and laid him in the grave with the Union Jack flying over him and our great guns still roaring in the distance. Poor Lyn and poor little darling Jacquelyn. You must tell our bairnies to love them both well. Tell the little people that the horrid old Germans came on in thousands to kill Dida and his soldiers because we broke their wall down and tried to catch them all, and ... near Dida the Germans hit poor old Uncle Geordie with a shell and he died and has gone away to Heaven and we will not see him any more until we die too and go to Heaven and dear little Jacquelyn will never see her very own Dida at all ... then Dida's own soldiers got up and they chased those nasty old Germans back for a long way through the bush that is called woods here and they caught and killed such a lot of them and those that weren't killed ... have been sent away to jail again.

The stirring account of the battle that followed underlined his pride in his brigade. 'We have had a wonderful battle and a wonderful victory', he wrote. 'My boys have simply covered themselves with glory'. He was frank about his reaction when his forceful recommendation to postpone the operation was rejected, and he then had to reorganise the attack with most of the ammunition stockpiled for it unavailable, the newly allocated 8th Brigade battalions unfamiliar with the ground, the enemy barrage still unimaginably severe, and the neighbouring British unable to deal with the enemy incursion on their front. 'I felt appalled at the task', he admitted, but his officers and men had responded superbly:

> Many many have fallen but we have in the fight stamped our fame on a higher pinnacle than ever ... It is wonderful the loyalty and bravery that is shown—their absolute confidence in me is touching—I can order them to take on the most hopeless looking jobs, and they throw their hearts and souls not to speak of their lives and bodies into the job without thought.

Then there was the Roberts business. 'Oh Katie', he added, 'as if my other troubles were not enough'. He described how he had been grappling with the complexities of the battle when a letter arrived with shattering news of his partner's debts.

> I am sorry for poor Mrs Roberts. God help her. Try not to worry darling. It is a bitter blow to me as I fear the money coming from my father's estate at mother's death, which I was hoping would provide for the children should anything happen to me, will be taken from me for the creditors. I can conceive no more mean trick than this played on a man in my position. I think I could have the villain put in jail but it would only cause a scandal and probably ruin the business without releasing me from debt in the slightest.

He explained that he had arranged for Lowe and J.W. Begg, a lawyer from Moule's (where Elliott had done his articles a decade earlier), to extricate him from the mess on the least disadvantageous terms they could manage.

Elliott did not conceal from Kate that the combined impact of these two blows while he was already under immense strain was almost unbearable:

> I cannot tell you what I went through that night ... After I knew Geordie had died I would have gladly welcomed a shell to end me. I walked twice from end to end of our zone and along the front line in front of the enemy's machine guns and never a shot came near me. It may be your prayers that protected me.

Also shaping this reaction was a 'feeling now amongst some of us that we have so many friends true and tried on yonder shore awaiting us that we should be more at home there than here', as he told George McCrae (whose son he had very much in mind when writing this). Pompey 'felt almost guilty of disloyalty to them in being still alive and not accompanying them to the unknown'.

He wrote again to Kate the following day.

> I got today from the Ambulance people poor Geordie's watch, cigarette case and a few things he carried on his body, also the

> shoulder straps with the stars from his coat which I had cut off as a last memento for poor Lyn ... I feel still very sad and depressed. It is terrible to think of him dead, poor boy, one can hardly believe it. If I had not seen him dead and helped bury him I doubt if I could have realised it ... It is very bitter too to think of what Mr Roberts has done to us ... I think this is just about all for the present. I am too heartsore to write much.

Although he did not feel like writing amid all this torment, he was sufficiently perturbed by something Kate mentioned to scrawl a hasty separate note to Neil:

> My dear little laddie, Mum has been telling me that you were so sorry for being naughty that you wished you were a little girl like [Violet]. But if you ever changed to a little girl Dida and Mum would not have any little boy at all. And Mum and Dida would be dreadfully sad if they had no dear wee mischiefy thing like our laddie. Dear little chap, Mum and Dida love you so much that they don't mind very much when you are naughty. Of course Mum has to [scold] you because if she didn't you wouldn't know what was naughty and wrong to do ... Dida was sad when he heard that the little lad wanted to be changed to a girl. He loves his little laddie so much that he was sorry the poor little chap was not happy. So don't you worry a bit old chap. You just try your best to be good and if you forget sometimes and Mum has to spank you, just be a soldier and try not to cry very much and you will know that Mum and Dida love you just the same even when they spank you. Spanking isn't so bad if you feel quite sure that dear old Mum loves you just the same. Dear little laddie, I wish I was with you now to take you up on my knee and comfort you and tell you Mum and Dida will always love you. You must be very good and loving now to dear Lyn and dear little Jacquelyn because dear Uncle Geordie their Dida was killed by the beastly old Kaiser's soldiers ... You must love and help dear old Mum and Belle and Nana very much too and cheer them such a lot. If you love them a lot that will cheer them.

The third battle in the AIF's step-by-step operations east of Ypres, the advance to Broodseinde Ridge on 4 October, was another decisive victory. The bite and hold approach was clearly proving successful, but Haig's keenness to pursue it even after the weather deteriorated led to the ill-advised assaults that made Passchendaele notorious. The turnaround was attributable to 'the vile weather and the awful mud and the over optimistic opinions of our Higher Command who thought the Bosche were on the run', explained Pompey, relieved that his brigade was uninvolved in such dreadful enterprises. He was appalled to hear of attacks so ill-conceived that heavy losses ensued 'simply because the men got stuck in the mud and the Germans picked them off at their leisure'.

In the aftermath of Polygon Wood Pompey's determination to produce a comprehensive document recording his brigade's performance did not slacken. Under his stimulus 42 officers in his brigade provided their own personal narratives of the battle. Armed with these accounts, Elliott then compiled his own report and award recommendations, devoting considerable time and effort to the task. His report, a chronological account of developments from his brigade's perspective together with an analysis of the lessons to be learned, filled, when typed, 24 single-spaced foolscap pages. He compiled his award recommendations with customary care to ensure once again that within his brigade, irrespective of the custom in other formations, these honours were genuinely earned. There was no formula. Of the 26 officers, 35 NCOs, and 35 privates commended, there were 11 officers from the 59th yet three from the 58th, 22 NCOs and privates from the 60th but only 13 from the 59th. These detailed recommendations occupied another 20 pages. The final result was a remarkable document.

Pompey's continuing dissatisfaction with Street was evident in the report. The complications arising from the tendency of the 29th and 31st men to push through the 59th, Pompey contended, 'might have been avoided had the 15th Brigade staff sufficiently impressed on the COs 29th and 31st Battalions the necessity of keeping at all costs behind the 1st Objective troops'. His report also claimed that an oversight by Street contributed to the unwillingness of Toll and Purser to advance beyond the red line. On 10 October, when he finished the report 'with great relief', he rebuked Street for 'not keeping a proper record of messages'. 'I do miss Major Wieck', he lamented to Kate:

> The new boy is a very lovable chap but I have to think of every mortal thing and suggest every single thing he does. In his spare

> time instead of like Wieck always thinking of next day's or next week's work—unless he is actually doing a job of work I have set him—he goes playing bridge with the rest of my staff causing them to waste their time also. It is most unsatisfactory to me. I cannot sack him and it is no use rowing with him all the time. He is only a boy after all, but I feel it very much.

That letter also mentioned yet another narrow escape for its correspondent. With the 15th Brigade about to return to the front trenches, Elliott went up to Broodseinde Ridge with Denehy and his intelligence officer, Lieutenant Bruce Anderson, to have a look at the area they would be taking over. The Germans 'started firing little whizz-bang shells at us', Elliott reported, and 'poor Anderson got a badly smashed foot from a shell fragment'. The brigade proceeded forward on 13 October for a particularly unpleasant four-day stint. In vigorous bursts of shellfire the Germans unleashed their new mustard gas. Even back at brigade headquarters Elliott twice had to keep his mask on for hours. Casualties in his brigade were substantial. 'Very pleased to be out of the place with a whole skin', Pompey noted after he and his men were withdrawn.

A few days later the 15th Brigade's awards for Polygon Wood were announced. There were 66 in all:

> Mason, Norman Marshall and Neil Freeman each got DSOs. Cam Stewart got a bar to his DSO, and quite a heap of my boys got Military Crosses and DCMs and Military Medals. I am delighted.

Of the other recipients, Boyd, Noad, and Neale won the MC, Sergeant Colclough of the 58th (who reacted so decisively to the German attack early on 25 September) and a private who stopped the Welch retiring on the 26th were each awarded the DCM, and Downing was one of 41 NCOs and privates honoured with the Military Medal. Pompey received nothing himself, but assured Kate he was unruffled—the DSO he had been belatedly granted was the one he wanted most, and he sensed he would probably score the CB in the imminent New Year list. Although satisfied overall, he was disappointed that some recommended by him had missed out, including Stillman, who 'did splendid work, little if at all inferior to those who got Military Crosses', and told the lieutenant so himself. 'That pleased me almost as much as getting the decoration itself would',

Stillman enthused, 'because he doesn't send the recommendations on unless he thinks they are worth it'.

Elliott needed a rest and was about to go on leave, but decided to get in touch with Jack Campbell before departing for England. He had seen his brother-in-law briefly, the first time they had run into each other for months, just before the Polygon Wood battle. This encounter had prompted another of Jack's consistently cheery letters to Kate:

> I saw Harold yesterday. If you saw him you would be very concerned about his physical condition. I am afraid he will have to give up soldiering and do a bit of navvying. I have often heard of people being as round as an apple but he is rounder than any apple. If old Fritz could see him he would never say that there was a shortage of tucker in England or France … he looks absolutely in the pink.

Pompey was looking forward to catching up with Jack again, but it was not to be. Visiting his unit late in October, the brigadier was shocked to discover that Jack had been killed three weeks earlier. A grim-faced stranger, Lieutenant Frank Wright, broke the news. When their machine-gun company went into action, Wright explained, Jack was normally kept back with the transport, but because of casualties and the need to rest surviving officers he had participated in the 6th Brigade's attack east of Broodseinde on 9 October. Wright himself, after enduring a harrowing front-line stint, had to remain there longer than planned because there was no available replacement—until Jack arrived to relieve him. On 9 October Jack accompanied the infantry advance and played his part effectively from a forward position before a German bullet found him. The sense that Jack had in effect sacrificed himself for a brother lieutenant left Wright particularly devastated. So, too, was Pompey; he had not been informed earlier because Jack was circumspect about having a famous brigadier-in-law. 'General Elliott … seemed quite unprepared for my sad news', wrote Wright. 'I'm afraid it was a big shock to him as it has been to us'.

So Pompey had yet more melancholy tidings to send home. 'It is with a sad heart that I write to you again my poor darling wife', he began, before passing on the details provided by Wright.

> The bullet went in just under his left eye and he fell back dead instantaneously. That was one blessing, at least, poor old chap. They had to bury his body where he fell as the country is now so awful that it nearly kills the men bringing down the wounded, and so the poor dead must be buried in the fields where they fall. I will try later on to find exactly where the grave is. It is at present practically impossible to go anywhere near it by day ... if you show the least sign of life anywhere along that ridge by day you get hundreds of shells fired at you. I've been up and I know. The poor boy with me had his foot all smashed up but your old man got off. It is certainly wonderful how nothing touches me ... Give my love to poor Nana and tell her that I and the laddie will try to make up for poor Jack's loss.

However, by the time this letter arrived, 'poor Nana', Elliott's mother-in-law, who was still residing with her daughters (Kate and Belle) and grandchildren, was in a bad way. The news of her only surviving son's death had already arrived. Coming on top of George's death and other recent shocks, it triggered a disabling stroke from which she never fully recovered.

Having in quick succession directed a difficult battle, buried his brother, discovered he was probably financially ruined, and now learned unexpectedly of his brother-in-law's death, Elliott was more in need of a rest than ever. He also had to contend with a nasty facial rash caused by German mustard gas. 'It becomes itchy in spots and the skin comes off and watery fluid oozes out, making unsightly sores.' He was, then, looking forward to a recuperative break in England. After an early start on the last day of October, he was in a car on his way to Boulogne at 5.00am. From there he journeyed to London without incident, reported at the Horseferry Road AIF Headquarters, and booked himself in at Berners Hotel. It was a long day and he was relishing the prospect of a big sleep in a comfortable bed, but he had a very disturbed night. His skin complaint and the bombs being dropped on London from German planes did not help, but he was troubled most of all by an unsettling message which suddenly arrived from that other world he had just left. Influential feathers had clearly been ruffled by his Polygon Wood report. Brudenell White had ordered him to disclose how many copies of it existed, and to ensure that none were removed from the Western Front.

Only the day before, Birdwood and Hobbs had visited Elliott without mentioning his report, but neither had at that stage seen it. Although Pompey had completed it almost three weeks earlier, before arranging for it to be typed he had shown it to Captain F.W. Robinson, the Fifth Division's intelligence officer, who had been stationed at Hooge crater to interrogate newly captured prisoners. An exceptionally talented scholar and linguist (he had written a PhD thesis on Roman history in German), Robinson had enlisted as an idealistic non-combatant in the AIF Medical Corps, but was transferred to intelligence after his obvious suitability for work in that sphere was recognised. When asking him to vet the document, Elliott invited Robinson, a moralist of unimpeachable integrity, to check its contents with information available to him from other sources. Robinson did so, and assured Elliott that it was fine. Pompey then had it typed—a sizeable task in view of its length. Hobbs did not receive it until 31 October; Elliott left France early that morning. With remarkable rapidity his report was read, discussed, and adjudged so reprehensible as to warrant suppression so rigorous as to be almost unique in the experience of the AIF. Just after his arrival in London, Elliott was abruptly notified that the clampdown was already being implemented.

After his restless first night at Berners, Elliott returned to Horseferry Road the following morning and arranged for a reply telegram detailing the distribution of the report copies. Long afterwards he described what happened when he returned to his brigade after his leave:

> On my return I received a peremptory order from General White that all copies of the report in my possession were to be destroyed and every note and message upon which it was based were to be likewise destroyed, and my written certificate was required that this order had been obeyed.

According to Pompey, Birdwood also arranged for an officer to visit the AIF War Records Section in London to ensure that the report was removed from its unit war diaries.

Stunned by this heavy-handed suppression, Elliott privately sought an explanation from someone on the Corps staff. He was told that his report had infuriated White and Birdwood. Firstly, it starkly illuminated the problems caused by the delayed issue of Fifth Division's operation order, a tardiness primarily attributable to the fact that White's overriding corps order materialised so late in the piece. As well, according to Elliott's informant, Birdwood was incensed by the way the document highlighted the inaccurate British claims that their men had regained their front line and the contrasting reports submitted at the time by Pompey, which had established the truth.

When the suppression of Elliott's report was exposed after the war, Birdwood (unbeknown to Pompey) privately ensured that Bean, then writing his magisterial multi-volume history of the AIF, was aware of his version of the controversy:

> You probably know this was destroyed because Elliott, not content with abusing the British troops on his flank, also entered into the most severe criticisms of Hobbs and his staff and further on Tivey and the whole of the 8th Brigade! Hobbs came to me almost with tears in his eyes on the subject, saying that if such a thing was published it would be quite impossible for the 8th and 15th to continue to work together in harmony, while should the criticisms on himself and the 5th Divisional Staff be seen and believed in Australia he would never be able to hold up his head again.

According to Hobbs, Elliott's report was 'a severe criticism' of his divisional headquarters 'and others who were connected with the operation, rather than a narrative'. When Hobbs showed it to Birdwood, the corps commander 'gave orders that all copies were to be withdrawn and destroyed, and instructed me to get an explanation from Gen. Elliott'. Birdwood wanted to summon Elliott back immediately to present it in person, but Hobbs dissuaded him, aware that Pompey desperately needed a good rest.

Hobbs did not have to read far to find criticism of his staff. 'The delay in defining the Inter Brigade Boundary was a source of considerable embarrassment', Pompey asserted in the report's second paragraph, before moving on to the late arrival of operation orders from Fifth Division:

> I would most emphatically urge that Divisional Operation Orders be issued to Brigade before the Battalions have been moved up into the shelled areas and thus become more or less out of touch with

> Brigade Headquarters ... I feel sure that continued neglect to issue these orders earlier will sooner or later result in a disaster similar to that which overtook the 98th Brigade in these operations.

It was not just that their belated advent disrupted preparations; Hobbs's refusal to allow Pompey's men to use the attack formation they had practised had prompted the brigadier to conclude that his battalion commanders would have to make a perilous visit to his headquarters in order to clarify this aspect.

> I would respectfully suggest that the very utmost latitude should be allowed to Brigade and even Battalion Commanders to modify their formations (quite without restriction from higher authority) in accordance with the terrain of which they have made a personal reconnaissance ... provided the general principles of distribution and consolidation in depth be adhered to.

'The man on the spot is the best judge', Elliott affirmed.

As for Tivey's battalions, Pompey did not conceal the frustration he felt about their tendency to disrupt the 59th on its way to the red line, together with the unwillingness of Toll and Purser to get on to the blue line. Yet to describe his references to the 29th and 31st Battalions as 'the most severe criticisms of ... Tivey and the whole of the 8th Brigade', as Birdwood did to Bean, was an exaggeration more flagrant than anything in Elliott's report. In fact, Pompey was just as critical of his own staff in connection with both these concerns.

The disappointing performance of the British on the right could hardly have been covered up in the 15th Brigade's report, even if the most ardent attempt at concealment had been made. Pompey, by nature no muzzler, was justifiably proud of what his brigade had achieved in the circumstances, and knew that the true magnitude of its accomplishment could only be grasped if the full extent of the 98th Brigade's failure was understood. Yet he described the fate of the 1st Middlesex temperately (and less critically than a number of his officers). When the Germans attacked early on 25 September, he wrote, the Middlesex lines were 'pierced in many places', some 'isolated ... small parties ... surrendered', 'the survivors ... fell back ... and ultimately became totally disorganised, and the great majority ... straggled to the rear'. When

Freeman tried (as Pompey ordered) to organise a combined counter-attack, he was 'unable to find anyone in authority in the Middlesex Battalion'. Later, when a 60th Battalion company advanced as part of a joint counter-attack arranged at brigade level, the 'Middlesex attack did not develop', and that company was eventually directed to halt 'as there was still no sign of the Middlesex'.

However, the palpable edge in Elliott's references to the 98th Brigade reflected his assessment of the inadequate direction and staff work displayed by that formation's leaders. He was blunt about their contribution to the alarming uncertainty around dusk on 25 September. 'No reliable information whatever could be got from the 98th Brigade as to the situation on their front or even as to the situation of their troops', he declared, citing the vague message from Heriot-Maitland that prompted him to send Stewart and the 57th forward after Marshall's men. The 98th Brigade also figured prominently in the frank references he made to his anxiety about proceeding with the AIF's Polygon Wood attack. Owing to the 98th's 'state of confusion' he 'felt certain' it would not be able to play its part, and this 'extremely probable event' would imperil the whole operation. Vindication did nothing to mollify his scathing censure of its performance:

> The 98th Brigade made absolutely no attempt to advance during the night ... but abandoning any intention of doing so they had substituted, in lieu thereof, a pious hope of overtaking the barrage at zero.

Pompey was also intent on demonstrating the falsity of the conclusion by 98th headquarters personnel that their men had regained their portion of the front line during 25 September, a misjudgment circulated to other formations, including the 15th Brigade, and even published in Haig's dispatches. In demolishing this claim Pompey referred to it as a 'delusion' (twice), 'quite unfounded' and 'emphatically not the case'. His report did not add (though a pointed observation along these lines would have been understandable) that the added confusion arising from this false impression hampered the efforts his men were making to do the bulk of the 98th Brigade's task as well as their own.

It has been repeatedly suggested—even recently by well-credentialled historians—that the criticisms of the 98th Brigade's performance by Elliott and his men could be discounted because they were made in ignorance of the phenomenal barrage that descended on the Middlesex early on 25 September. Such suggestions are unfounded. Boyd's 58th company, the 57th and 60th men going through Glencorse Wood, and others in Pompey's brigade were all acutely familiar with the intensity of shellfire that the German gunners congregated for the pre-emptive enemy assault could generate. Pompey, for his part, was less critical of the Middlesex than of the 98th's leaders and the failure by other units in that brigade the following night.

The purpose of an operation report was to record significant events involving the unit concerned, and to list whatever lessons had been learned for future engagements. Among the 'Preliminary Instructions' issued by Fifth Division just before Polygon Wood was a reminder that after the battle each formation engaged had to provide a written account of its role in it, including observations relating to the 'reasons for the success or failure' of the operation. Pompey's report was not only exceptionally detailed and informative; it was also unusually candid. Normally such reports were blandly worded, more intent on obscuring undesirable aspects of an operation than revealing them; but not this one. Pompey asserted, for example, that resorting to the 2nd Royal Welch Fusiliers, 'a borrowed Battalion' from divisional reserve brought forward through AIF-captured ground, was 'on its face a confession of the failure of the 98th Brigade troops to get on'. It was indeed, although that sort of aspersion on a neighbouring formation was not customarily cast.

It is true, then, that Pompey's report was frank and forceful, but it was also factual and fruitful. His conclusions were measured, compelling, and based on evidence assembled in the report—cited messages in particular. There were no unsubstantiated assertions. Moreover, criticisms were balanced by praise; where credit was due it was given. While the belated arrival of operation orders from Fifth Division caused 'the greatest difficulty and delay', the preliminary instructions issued by that headquarters 'proved highly valuable in assisting' the 15th Brigade's preparations. Similarly, while Pompey vividly described his vigorous efforts to persuade Toll and Purser that their men should push on as arranged to the blue line, 'they were entitled to every credit that the training and discipline of their Battalions eventually secured success'. And while the British on the right repeatedly 'failed to advance as promised', the way the Royal Welch Fusiliers 'advanced in perfect line and very steadily until they reached their objective' under 'heavy shell and machine gun fire' on the afternoon of 27 September was 'greatly admired by our men'. Elliott's concluding 'Summary of Lessons to be Learnt from This Action' was a list of constructive conclusions covering the familiar (Stokes mortars being 'invaluable' in defence or attack) and the fundamental (the perennial problem of communication). Other worthwhile recommendations were scattered through his report.

Was such extraordinary suppression justified? In view of Elliott's anguish after devastating personal blows, it was predictable that his review of yet another 15th Brigade operation hampered by neighbouring British deficiencies—following Fromelles, Bullecourt, and the pursuit to the Hindenburg Line—would be forthright. Yet Pompey could claim, and did so afterwards, that the report he submitted did precisely what it was supposed to do (record of events plus lessons learned), and did this better than most. In the *Official History* Bean acknowledged that Elliott's report was 'ably compiled and very detailed', and his chapter on Polygon Wood diverged minimally from it. (An early draft described it, correctly, as 'easily the most valuable document' of all the records pertaining to the battle.) Burying the suppression controversy in a footnote, Bean referred to Elliott's 'strong criticism of his superiors' —significantly, the historian did not say it was false—and in effect dismissed Birdwood's distortion alleging that Pompey had disparaged the whole 8th Brigade by not even mentioning it. However, Bean added that Pompey's 'downright statements concerning the division on his right ... though he believed them to be true, were definitely untrue and grossly unfair', and he concluded that Birdwood's suppression was appropriate.

This conclusion is dubious. Although Bean did not elaborate, his assessment was presumably based primarily on the testy sentence in Pompey's report that the 98th Brigade 'made absolutely no attempt to advance during the night' of 25-26 September and 'substituted' instead the 'pious hope of overtaking the barrage at zero'. (Asked in 1982 about his reminiscences of Polygon Wood, Charles Noad, who revered Pompey, not only recalled the suppression of his brigadier's report; remarkably, he was able to recite that particular sentence almost word for word, even though the document containing it had been ruthlessly suppressed within hours of being typed and, in the intervening 65 years, had, it seems, never been published anywhere!) In fact, Pompey's scathing conclusion concerning the 98th Brigade's inadequate overnight performance was understandable in view of the 4.10am message he received from Keith McDonald, which was duly cited in his report and in his view substantiated his forthright condemnation on the information available to him. But even if Pompey was mistaken, was his exasperated criticism so reprehensible that it justified the banning of his whole report?

Another option, surely, was to tell the brigadier this sentence was unacceptable, and his report could not be received unless it, and whatever other passages Birdwood took exception to, were deleted or amended. At no stage was his superiors' reaction presented to Elliott in those terms. The suppression was outright as far as Pompey was concerned: there was nothing conditional about it. Readers of the *Official History* might have concluded otherwise, however, after Bean was persuaded by White to alter his brief account of the controversy. Before White's intervention Bean's assessment was that 'Birdwood ordered the report to be destroyed, but (fortunately for this history) a copy survived'. After reading this sentence, White urged Bean to change it:

> I do not think Birdwood ordered the destruction of Elliott's report. My recollection is that he declined to accept its receipt and retention as a record. It might be well to alter your wording in the foot note referring to this report—it rather gives the impression that you thought the refusal to accept it a mistake.

Evidently Bean was easily persuaded—'Correct this', he wrote alongside that paragraph in White's letter—even though Birdwood's earlier letter to him on the subject confirmed that the report 'was suppressed and indeed destroyed'. The published version in the *Official History* stated that 'Birdwood, with justice, refused to accept the report and to include it in the official records, but a copy survived'.

Bean refrained from mentioning that (according to Elliott) Birdwood not only ordered the destruction of all copies of the brigadier's report, but every note and message documenting it. His reticence enabled him to avoid some awkward questions. For the commander of the AIF to ban a document because it contains falsehoods, yet insist on the simultaneous destruction of the very evidence that would prove the veracity or otherwise of statements in it, merely invites the conclusion that the alleged untruths were, in fact, embarrassingly accurate. It is also odd, to say the least, for the AIF historian to be implicitly condoning the destruction of AIF historical material, especially a document he himself described as 'easily the most valuable' record of a notable AIF victory. Besides, the documentation consisted primarily of communications between the 15th Brigade and other formations, and there was not much point ordering the destruction of the message records at 15th Brigade headquarters unless copies held by various other formations were also pursued. No such action was evidently instigated. There is more than a whiff here of a hasty, unwarranted decision by Birdwood and White. As for Bean's verdict, the AIF was tremendously fortunate to have someone of his diligence and integrity as its chronicler, but it is clear that his admiration for White influenced his judgments on numerous issues that he had to deal with as war correspondent and historian. The suppression of Elliott's Polygon Wood report was a glaring example.

CHAPTER FOURTEEN

'Terribly Depressed and Pessimistic':

Another gloomy winter

NOVEMBER 1917–MARCH 1918

ELLIOTT DID NOT return to France until December. After spending much of his first week in England resting in bed at Welwyn, he felt well enough to visit his brigade's training battalion. He was pleased by what he saw at Salisbury. Having removed his old friend Alf Jackson from command of the 58th Battalion just before Fromelles, Elliott had heard disturbing reports about indiscipline in the training battalion under Jackson's lax leadership. He was instrumental in the replacement of Jackson by Bert Layh, who was now able to direct the training of the 15th Brigade's reinforcements, though he was not yet fit to return to France. Layh 'has already made a vast difference', Pompey found. Much less pleasing was the impact of this trip on his health. He had concluded that his gas blisters were just about healed, but 'the cold wind of Salisbury Plain … inflamed the tender spots on my face' and 'cut the tender skin like a knife'. His blisters were stinging so painfully that he hardly slept at all that night although very tired after his visit. Longer rest was prescribed, and he returned to Welwyn for three weeks. From there he told Kate about his transformed and 'rather startling' appearance:

> you would laugh to see me—they won't let me shave because the razor was spreading the infection and every little nick was becoming festered and horrid, so I'm a real bushranger now with a black beard with a patch of grey on the chin. It seems so queer for

> me to have white whiskers, but it is wonderful how old we are getting.

He was seven months away from turning forty. What he had been through recently, he reflected, would have turned anyone grey; he was sure his resistance to infection had been sapped. It was 'owing to being so run down' that 'I cannot throw off this trouble as easily as I should', he wrote. 'When I came over I had no color at all and rings under my eyes and not a kick in me'.

Elliott was stunned soon after his return to the 15th Brigade when Birdwood offered him six months' leave to Australia. British soldiers could return periodically to their loved ones, but there was officially no home leave in the AIF, not even for original Anzacs like Elliott. Birdwood, however, was quietly arranging for selected AIF veterans to be allowed home, sometimes as 'submarine guards' on transports or under some similar pretext.

No-one in the AIF had given more committed service than Elliott. Considering what he had just been through and the state of his health, few commanders were more deserving candidates for home leave. At the same time it would not have escaped Birdwood that the offer was a means of sidelining, temporarily at least, a volatile brigadier who had made a habit of involving himself in controversy and producing some of Birdwood's more difficult moments. Birdwood and White had already taken advantage of the ill-health of another nationalistic AIF general they considered difficult, Legge, forcing his return to Australia. Pompey was hardly Birdwood's ideal commander, but Birdwood respected the brigadier's fighting and leadership qualities, and plugged away with his awkwardly genial pleasantries. They had managed to get on tolerably well most of the time, even though Elliott lacked 'full confidence in him':

> he always gives me the impression that he likes everyone to adopt his views and gets annoyed if you don't, and I have never adopted his views where I thought they were wrong without a fight.

Birdwood 'sticks to us I think more for his own sake than for ours', Elliott concluded perceptively.

It was an exceptionally tempting offer. After more than three years away, Elliott was missing home and family more than ever. There was no end to the war in sight, or no victorious conclusion that he could see. If he were still at the Western Front in another year's time he and Kate would have spent nearly half their married life apart. And there was no AIF father sadder about missing so much of his children's formative years. 'Tell me all about the wee people', he was still imploring Kate and Belle, 'tell me everything about their hair and cheeks and chins and everything, I can never hear enough of them'. However, his profound sense of duty, and the determination and dedication that sustained his commitment to the war, were still intact. They had been jolted, severely jolted in fact, but not ruptured. He also felt intensely loyal to the men under his command. There would be difficult times ahead, he felt certain, and he had to be sure they would be properly looked after without him. His immediate response to Birdwood was to ask two questions. Would he get the 15th Brigade back after his leave, and would Stewart be in charge while he was away? Birdwood replied that he could guarantee neither, an answer that practically convinced Elliott to reject the offer, enticing though it was.

Afterwards he discussed the matter with Hobbs. Although Pompey would still have preferred McCay as his divisional commander (unlike Tivey and other Fifth Division officers), he and Hobbs had gradually developed greater mutual understanding and respect. Elliott told Hobbs frankly that he felt he could not take the leave unless he was considered no longer fit to command—had Hobbs noticed any decline in the 15th Brigade's efficiency? Not at all, Hobbs replied hastily, assuring him that the offer had been prompted by his ill-health. Elliott then said he felt all right again. In that case, Hobbs suggested, a decision could perhaps be postponed; they could wait and see how he was feeling in a month's time, and make a final decision then. They left it at that, but Pompey had made up his mind: 'I decided that I could not desert the boys at such a time'.

However, he was really far from all right.

> I told the boys on Sunday that I could not leave them—even to go home on leave—knowing what was in front of them this Spring. Yet sometimes I feel that I have reached the limit of my strength and that I cannot stand the strain much longer ... I am always tired and sometimes my head aches ... and my nerves seem all raw and aching.

There were other symptoms as well. For weeks he remained 'terribly depressed and pessimistic', he told Belle. Writing to his lawyer friend Richardson, he admitted to being 'very depressed and anxious at times' after his 'particularly trying' experiences. This was hardly surprising, of course—he had much to feel gloomy about.

> Here it's the last day of this sad old year 1917. I think it has held more of sadness and disappointment than any other year of my life. I am particularly in the Blues today. It is bitterly cold and there is nearly a couple of feet of snow on the ground. There have been no home letters for more than a month. Australia has turned down Conscription again, and England is so short of men that she needed everyone we could give her. Having no news I don't know what position my business is in with Roberts, and it is very worrying ... I see no hope of war finishing for long and long yet unless we give in. This failure of Conscription seems to me the first stage of giving up, and all our sacrifices will be in vain. It is all a hopeless muddle as far as I can see.

He felt appalled and alienated by the fate of the second conscription referendum in Australia. Having harshly criticised Prime Minister Hughes for his inaction on this controversial issue following his re-election in May 1917, Elliott was scathing about the anti-conscriptionist campaigners whose efforts were again rewarded after Hughes plunged the nation into further discord by calling another plebiscite on compulsion. Convinced that the outcome of the war was in the balance and reinforcements were desperately needed, Elliott called Archbishop Mannix a 'lunatic' for claiming that additional Australian soldiers would make no difference, and described his admirers as 'stark raving mad' for believing him. The referendum result was 'heartbreaking' and 'shameful'; it was 'pretty hard to keep on being proud of one's country'. This was a striking admission from such an ardent nationalist. Australia 'has deserted us', he concluded in a letter to J.F. Henderson (the ex-Essendon mayor) that found its way into the *Argus*. It was deplorable, Pompey felt, that Australia remained unique among its closest allies (New Zealand, England, and Canada) in adopting neither conscription nor the ultimate disciplinary deterrent for deserters, the death penalty.

Pompey's strongly held views were reinforced by the increasing likelihood of a massive German assault early in 1918. For months he had been predicting that the breakdown of Russian military capacity would have ominous implications for the AIF and its cause, because dozens more German divisions would become available for deployment in France. The Germans were planning a tremendous offensive on the Western Front in order to achieve a decisive breakthrough there before the Americans (who had entered the war against Germany in April 1917) could make a meaningful contribution. As a result, there was 'an awful time' ahead for the AIF, Pompey felt: 'just as I said would happen, all the guns and men from the Russian front are being piled up against us', and 'we are in for a terrific fight pretty soon'. It was hard to be optimistic when France was already 'bled white', the British army was 'by no means what it was', Australia had rejected conscription, and the Americans seemed to be taking ages to get organised.

Although the home leave proposal was prompted by Pompey's recent tribulations, when Birdwood made the offer he was not even aware of the brigadier's biggest worry. Elliott had resolved to keep to himself his grave concern about the state of his legal practice. Though blameless himself, he felt personally tainted by his partner's disgrace, and concluded that his chances of resuming as a reputable solicitor after the war would be maximised if knowledge of this repugnant scandal was minimised. It was a wretched state of affairs. Information reaching him from those now acting on his behalf was meagre. He had little idea about how retrievable the position was, or how much in debt he was. His powerlessness to do much about the situation gnawed at him. If he was killed, he wondered, might his entire estate be diverted from Kate and the children to repay Roberts's debts? It was impossible, no matter how hard he tried, not to worry. Unable to discuss his terrible anxiety with anyone, he could unburden himself only in letters to Kate and Belle (Roberts 'must have been mad'; 'I cannot understand it, and wonder sometimes if he has taken to drink or drugs'). No wonder he felt 'very lonely', and told Kate he longed to rest his weary head on her 'dear soft arms and breast'. Being deprived of mail for over a month by a disruptive strike at home was the last straw:

> goodness knows what I am liable for ... [W]ith this worry on my mind and often keeping me wakeful, I cannot think things out as they should be and my poor boys may suffer from this. I would

> almost rather know at once that I have been stripped of the last penny than have the thing hanging over me like this.

His concern gradually eased after intervention from an unlikely quarter. He had always appreciated the attractive personality of his partner's wife, Katie Roberts, a woman of charm and empathy who tended to write him detailed letters about his children straight after she had seen them. Even while full of fury and anxiety about what her husband had done, Elliott was considerate about the implications for her. His admiration was reinforced by her reaction to her husband's infamy. She wrote frankly and sensitively to both the brigadier and Kate Elliott, apologising for her husband's gambling 'folly—I can't call it anything else and I can't make any excuse for him'—and confessing that he had been rescued from similar trouble over a decade earlier only after his mother provided thousands of pounds. Now that another emergency had arisen, Katie Roberts did not confine herself to sympathy and well-chosen words. Emulating her mother-in-law, she contributed a considerable sum from her own funds—a 'loan' of £800, to keep the creditors at bay (this was all she could raise, and came primarily from an inheritance). There was no grandstanding about this admirable contribution—neither Kate nor General Elliott first heard about it from the donor herself. It was 'very kind of her', Pompey noted, 'she is unlikely to get any of it back again ... and there was no obligation on her to do it at all'. Her donation alleviated the crisis, enabling the practice to continue as a going concern with Glen Roberts on a small wage and every effort being made to reduce the liabilities he had accumulated. Pompey remained keen to discontinue his association with Roberts, provided the advisers handling his affairs in his absence were satisfied that it was in his interests to do so. It was 'a great relief' when he learned the partnership was to be dissolved, even though it was still unclear whether he would be personally liable for a proportion of the outstanding debts.

Elliott was also concerned at the end of 1917 about how his family was coping. 'I wish I knew how you all were', he wrote on Christmas Eve, 'I hope you are not worrying too much about all that has taken place'. The mail delays did not help, but he was moved by Kate's touching condolence after George's death was announced. 'Such a loving sweet letter it is', he wrote back. 'I don't know whatever in the world I have ever done to deserve such a wife as you'. The flow of empathy and support from

Kate did not slacken, but it became obvious that family morale was flagging on Elliott's own home front. It was not only soldiers in the AIF who were thoroughly war-weary; for Australians at home, the war prognosis seemed depressingly bleak. Since 1915 they had been governed in an atmosphere of almost perpetual crisis. The bitter divisiveness of the conscription campaigns and immense industrial unrest had exacerbated the tension—almost everyone had a relative or someone precious in the trenches. Too many had already received devastating news from afar, and were struggling to cope with anguished grief as a constant companion. The mother of Rupert and Alan Henderson, for example, was still unwell after her breakdown years earlier when both sons died in the first fortnight at Gallipoli.

Optimism was scarcely evident anywhere in Australia at the end of 1917, and Elliott's family was no exception. As he surmised, his relatives were having a 'very sad time' indeed. George, Harold felt, had always been his mother's favourite child; Helen was predictably devastated by his death. Harold's mother-in-law, Mary Campbell ('Nana'), was no less affected by the loss of Jack, her only surviving son; the stroke she suffered was precipitated by the shock of this sudden bereavement. Even Belle, the practical, down-to-earth pillar of strength in the household, wobbled under the strain. Lyn was struggling to come to terms with widowhood and the prospect of bringing up Jacquelyn on her own. Her concern about her financial circumstances led to a bitter argument with Flory, her notoriously cantankerous sister-in-law, about their respective entitlements to the Londonderry inheritance. Harold was perturbed about all this, but was moved more than anything (having just rejected Birdwood's offer of home leave) by five-year-old Neil's reaction to the loss of the uncles he adored. It 'just made my heart ache to go home and love the dear little desolate laddie when I heard of him asking me not to be killed or die or get sick'. He sent his anxious son a heartfelt response without delay.

Such letters helped Elliott retain a prominent place in his son's affections, although he and Neil had been apart for more than half Neil's life. When acquaintances spontaneously commented on the physical similarity between Violet and her father, Neil would assertively interject '*I'm* like my Daddy too'—clearly a desirable attribute as far as he was concerned. The brigadier maintained a regular individual correspondence with Neil and Violet as well as Kate and Belle; including the occasional letters he exchanged with 'Nana', he was corresponding separately with five members of the one household despite being very busy most of the time. He found letter-writing easier when his brigade was in the line rather than out—more newsworthy things tended to happen, he felt—and when responding to a letter he had just received. Writing quickly in his direct, fluent style, he was forever doing his utmost to boost the children's self-esteem, particularly Neil's:

> Mum has been telling me how hard you have been working at school and how good you have been to [Violet]. And I was so glad you told Dear you didn't want Mum's face changed. I wouldn't either, dear laddie. It's just the best face in all the world and I wouldn't change my little laddie either. He's just the best boy in all the world for Dida.

Neil remained very sad about his uncles. Even months after their deaths, Elliott told Milly Edwards, Neil was still maintaining 'he couldn't say his prayers "properly" unless he prayed for them as well'.

Elliott was thrilled by Violet's development:

> My word, you did astonish your old Dida this time. I never knew my little pet could write such a big fat grown up letter as that. It delighted me but I was a little bit sad too because I realized that my little pet girlie ... is growing up to be a big girlie who will soon write better letters than her Dida ... I am sorry ... to have missed all the lovely fun we could have had together.

Violet's neat letters, and the rebuke that he was told she had given Belle for untidy handwriting, prompted him to make an effort to be neater in his own correspondence to her. This was a big adjustment, considering he had been throughout his adult life a hasty, barely legible scrawler and an impatient form-filler who would repeatedly have to cross out mistakes that exemplified the adage 'more haste, less speed'. He commended Violet's helpfulness around the house (washing the dishes, polishing the cutlery, pouring tea for visitors), praised her patient fortitude when she had the measles, and was elated to hear she was top of her class:

> Now wasn't that just the loveliest bit of news in all the world to give your weary old Dida. If you gave your Dida all the money in the

world and all the medals and decorations and pretty things as well, he wouldn't have been nearly so pleased as with that bit of news.

Elliott was also pleased that the 1917–18 winter was proving less severe than he had feared. 'The weather here is not bad at all just now —a wonderful difference to last year', he noted with relief in February. But it was not exactly warm. One January morning it was so glacial that he could hardly write, and there was more snow about than the locals had seen for years. He was appreciative as ever of the marvels of nature: 'in the sun the snow crystals sparkle until the branches look as if they were all set with diamonds'.

The impact of winter was less severe not just because the climate was milder. Lessons had been learned after the AIF's soul-destroying experience of 1916-17. Instead of prolonged front-line duty knee-deep in abominable slime, the emphasis from mid-November 1917 onwards was on as much rest and recreation for the Australians as possible. The AIF divisions, now grouped together in the newly created Australian Corps, were rotated in the front line. It was no picnic there, but at least it was quiet most of the time, and each division had a lengthy spell away from it. Elliott and his brigade spent the second half of December and all of January clustered in villages so far back they could hardly hear the guns. It was 'a lovely place for a rest', wrote Pompey. With training curtailed by the profusion of snow, there was plenty of time to enjoy football matches, athletics, and more improvised amusements such as tobogganing. Other entertainments provided for the men included well-patronised cinemas, concerts, and canteens. The incidence of trench foot, a scourge in 1916-17, dramatically declined now that preventative measures were better understood.

The 15th Brigade began a three-week stint in the front line near Messines on 21 February. 'Things are pretty quiet generally', Elliott observed. Apart from sporadic shellfire and occasional raids, there was a sense of calm before the storm. The long-anticipated big German offensive was imminent. The Germans seemed to be biding their time until their preparations were complete; the Australians wondered where the massive blow would fall, and what would happen when it did. With GHQ keener than ever in this situation to keep track of the movements of German divisions, the 15th Brigade carried out a number of raids in March. As ever, Elliott was ambivalent: 'I always begrudge good men lost on these raids, though they have to be attempted at times to get information that is not otherwise forthcoming'. To his relief, these enterprises were successful and 15th Brigade casualties were minimal. On 3 March his raiders

> got in and out of the enemy's line without difficulty, killed a few Bosches and brought back two wounded prisoners. They were miserable specimens, and shrieked and yelled so loudly for mercy when they were caught that the boys said they drowned the noise of the barrage.

While keeping an eye on these raids Elliott also had to contend with the departure of several senior commanders from his brigade. Mason found the winter very difficult. 'The cold wet weather has affected his old wound and causes him great pain at times', Elliott observed. Mason eventually accepted another instructional appointment: he became commander of the Australian Corps School. Neil Freeman had also left the 15th Brigade, having been promoted to lead one of the battalions in Tivey's brigade, the 31st, which had participated at Polygon Wood under Elliott's command. 'He has got on splendidly', Pompey enthused. 'I did not want to lose him by any means, but when the chance came to him I would not try to stop him' (a practice not always followed, he believed, by other commanders in equivalent circumstances). Before long Hobbs told Elliott that Freeman had made the 31st Battalion 'twice as good as it was before he came'. Promotion also led to Cam Stewart's departure: he was chosen to command the 14th Brigade. 'I am very sorry to lose him', Elliott told Kate, but 'I am delighted at the promotion which he thoroughly deserves for the splendid work he has done'.

Stewart, Mason, and Freeman were all fine leaders, but Elliott was pleased that familiar faces of proven capacity replaced them. He was delighted to have Jack Scanlan taking over the 59th. Mason had done well, but Elliott regarded Scanlan as one of the most talented of his original 7th Battalion officers. Another, Bert Layh, was now judged fit enough to return to active duty, and succeeded Stewart in command of the 57th. Layh was 'not quite the same as before he got the gas', Pompey noted, but as a battalion commander he would not be undertaking hard physical toil and 'the Doctors say ... he will be quite all right out here'. Elliott was convinced that Layh could emulate Stewart and become a brigadier before long. Compensating for the departure of Freeman was the advent of Major Charles Watson, a 35-year-old architect who had served with Elliott a decade earlier in the militia. Watson had enlisted in the AIF at the outbreak of war. Elliott had invited him to join the 7th Battalion, but he had been retained in various important positions in Australia. Eventually released for overseas service, Watson joined the 58th Battalion in January 1918 and within a month was its acting commander. Eyebrows were raised in the 58th over the swift advancement of an officer who had spent so much of the war in Australia, but Pompey rated Watson so highly that he considered recommending the newcomer for the command vacancy at the 57th created by Stewart's promotion. It was primarily Watson's lack of Western Front experience that influenced the brigadier to prefer Layh. Denehy had returned to the 58th in November after a mustard gas ordeal even more severe than Elliott's; by March he was looking weary again, and Pompey arranged for him to have a month's leave. The impressive leadership Watson demonstrated while deputising for Denehy during this more extended period left Pompey convinced he had the makings of a fine battalion commander. Elliott's other colonel, Norman Marshall, had just returned from leave. He was positively 'blooming', Pompey observed, 'looking just the very picture of health'.

Elliott was confident that his brigade would not be found wanting in the approaching confrontation. In its most recent major engagement (Polygon Wood) his men had responded superbly to an awesome enemy attack. He had leaders he knew and trusted. And his own morale was recovering. His extended absence, those weeks he had been given to rest and recuperate, had been beneficial. The strategic situation was also significant. With the climax of the whole war seemingly imminent, there could be no greater incentive for Pompey. Instead of dwelling on his daunting recent troubles, racked by anxiety and depression, his frame of mind changed as he geared himself up to meet the looming challenge. He felt sure that his men would give a good account of themselves. For three years, ever since the Gallipoli landing, the AIF had done a lot of attacking. Those attacks had been usually ill-conceived, rarely worthwhile, and almost invariably costly in casualties. But the boot would be on the other foot this time. The fundamental priority for Pompey's men now—stopping the Germans from rampaging across Europe—was precisely the objective that had prompted so many to enlist in the first place. Most of them, Pompey sensed, were looking forward to the challenge. Experienced stalwarts, those young men with old faces, were quietly hoping they would not be among the unfortunates who happened to be on front-line duty when the onslaught began—the opening barrage was bound to be awesome—but they did want to be in front of oncoming enemy infantrymen at some stage. Like Elliott, they were confident they would prove more than a match for the attackers.

Pompey was not so sure about the British. His doubts had been reinforced by his experience at Polygon Wood and what he had been told about the more recent battle of Cambrai (where the British, having attacked successfully, were surprised and driven back rapidly by an unexpected German counter-attack). Cambrai had looked very promising at one stage, he told Kate, but the accumulated losses since 1914 had diminished the calibre of the British army: 'a lot of the British Troops now are unreliable and run away at times'. He decided to circulate a frank brigade memorandum on the subject. If the Germans attacked on the 15th Brigade's front 'I have not the slightest doubt' about the outcome, he declared. But what he had been told about Cambrai showed that the British could not all 'be relied upon to be alert'. The Guards were magnificent in that battle, but in another division 'the outposts were all asleep' and some 'demoralised' men 'retired without orders'. In other words, 'the discipline, training and courage of every unit in the British Army is not so perfect as it should be'. In the 15th Brigade, however,

> we have absolutely nothing to fear except through carelessness, inefficiency or misconduct. It is the absolute duty of every officer and NCO to ensure the utmost efficiency of his men in musketry by continually practising loading exercises and seeing that the arms are kept in good order by constant inspection, and that the very utmost vigilance and care is exercised by the patrols and sentries out in front of our line and by every man at stand to ... if for one moment this care is relaxed, disaster may descend upon us at any moment like an avalanche.

It was not expected that the Germans would unleash their main attack in the sector occupied by the Australian Corps. An assault further south was much more likely, but there were no guarantees: 'we must be prepared here for any eventuality', Pompey declared. There were briefings galore about the likely German tactics, appropriate defensive arrangements, and the latest intelligence from captured prisoners concerning where and when the onslaught might be launched. Pompey, vigilant as ever, supervised his brigade's work meticulously, instilling urgency, ensuring efficiency, and making it clear to everyone under his command that what lay ahead was a mighty fight that could decide the whole war, and the 15th Brigade had to be ready to play its part with the utmost commitment and proficiency. All his old verve returned as the long-awaited climax neared. He even concluded one letter to Milly Edwards with a Shakespearian flourish, quoting from memory with impressive accuracy as he predicted that the looming clash 'will be an occasion when Henry V's words at Agincourt might well be applicable':

> 'We few, we happy few, we band of brothers
> For he to day that sheds his blood with me
> Shall be my brother— …
> And gentlemen in England now abed
> Shall think themselves accursed they were not here
> And hold their manhoods cheap while any speak
> That fought with us upon St Crispin's day.'

CHAPTER FIFTEEN

'Never So Proud of Being an Australian':

Resisting the German onslaught

MARCH–APRIL 1918

IN MID-MARCH 1918 German shellfire intensified in the Australian sector. In particular, a big long-range gun repeatedly harassed the 15th Brigade, then in reserve. On 18 March, after days of this unwelcome attention, Elliott asked the Fifth Division to organise subduing counter-battery fire. The same gun kept persevering on the 19th, and the following day, Elliott noted, it was 'active all day and night'. On 21 March it was 'very persistent and annoying all day', inflicting casualties in the 57th and 59th Battalions, and landing several shells near his headquarters. Nearby a 'huge one landed in the road, blew a hole some 12 feet across … and shook the whole place'. To many Australians, this increased enemy activity signified the commencement of the long-anticipated German drive for victory, and later that day came confirmation. The Germans had launched their offensive south of the Australians, in a region familiar to them—among the villages initially attacked was Bullecourt.

This development was widely welcomed in the AIF. It certainly was in the 15th Brigade, Elliott felt:

> There is a feeling in the air that we are all glad he is coming, and that we will hit him up to some tune before he wins through.

Other Australians were delighted, including the official AIF correspondent Charles Bean:

> My heart and spirits jumped up 100 degrees. So the German was attacking after all—he was really going to do it. The bombardment was on a front of over 50 miles! ... I cannot say how relieved I felt ... One hoped almost beyond hope that they would ... [try to] end the war by an offensive this year. And they are doing it. One does not for a moment believe that they will succeed. The attack always loses more men than the defence; they will get 5, 10, perhaps 15 miles. They may very likely take Bapaume. But at the end of it their army will be brought up against an unbroken wall ... It is not an easy time for the actual battalions in the line ... But one cannot help rejoicing.

Delight soon turned to concern, then alarm. The Germans succeeded in driving the British well back. Day after day came news of ominous advances, particularly in the Somme region. On 21 March the attackers captured no fewer than 21,000 prisoners, and penetrated in one day as far as the entire 1916 British Somme offensive had managed in over four months. Bapaume fell, then Flers, Guedecourt, Montauban, and Albert. Much of the British Fifth Army under General Gough was retiring in disarray. Even Amiens, more than 40 miles west of the pre-assault front line, seemed threatened, and there was still no sign of the unbroken wall that Bean had confidently expected. A special order from Haig, the Commander-in-Chief, described the situation as 'a crisis'. Elliott's relatives were among countless civilians gripped by the 'crushing tension' expressed by Vera Brittain: 'into our minds had crept for the first time the secret, incredible fear that we might lose the War'. Gough was 'rested', replaced, and eventually relieved of his command altogether.

The Australians followed these developments with increasing concern. There was no indication that the sector they were holding would be subjected to a genuine German attack, and they waited impatiently to be transferred to where the action was. For top-level British strategists it was a critical situation, fluid as well as disturbing. Under considerable pressure they had to work out where the AIF could best be utilised. On 23 March Elliott and his brigade were directed to be ready to move at short notice: 'we are in for exciting times', predicted Pompey. Decades later a 60th private recalled a parade just before his battalion's departure, when Hobbs addressed the men and sounded emotional. 'What will happen, I wonder', Hobbs wrote in the privacy of his diary as he began moving south. 'What shall we be doing a week or a month hence'? Elliott was similarly reflective about 'the awful situation that I have long feared'.

On 25 March the 15th Brigade marched nine miles to Méteren. The men did well, even though it was their first march of such magnitude for some time and they were shelled on the way by a long-range gun that inflicted eighteen casualties. The morale of 'these splendid boys of mine' remained admirable, Elliott reported. From Méteren they were to be transported south (along with the Third and Fourth AIF Divisions, which were also on the move). The railway they would be using had been intermittently bombarded, anti-aircraft Lewis guns were mounted on the trains, and the situation they were travelling into was so desperate and uncertain it was possible they might have to detrain along the way and go straight into action. Elliott summoned all the senior officers in his brigade to a conference, where he insisted that the strictest discipline had to be maintained during the journey—ammunition was to be readily available at all times, and bayonets sharpened. On 27 March, when the first of the trains transporting his men departed, Pompey was aboard. As usual, the men were conveyed in crowded cattle trucks. It was a pensive journey, according to Downing:

> the carriages rattled and bumped as we smoked and wondered towards what dreadful things we were being whirled away ... So we drowsed and were wakened by the jolting of the truck, or by the discomfort of the hard corners of the heaps of rifles and equipment on which we were huddled, forty men in a space of fifteen feet by nine; and our dreams were of heavy things.

Elliott arrived at Doullens that afternoon without incident, unaware that a momentous meeting in that town the previous day had overhauled the top-level direction of the anti-German forces. Haig, who had consistently opposed the installation of a supreme commander above himself and his French counterpart, had decided in this alarming crisis to acquiesce in the appointment of General Foch, a combative Frenchman renowned as an uncompromising fighter, as Western Front generalissimo.

Pompey's journey south proved uneventful, but a later train transporting the 58th Battalion was not so lucky. Around 8.00pm a long-range shell suddenly hit it. There was 'an immense explosion', immediate calls for stretcher-bearers, but 'no panic', according to a nearby 58th sergeant who escaped injury. Sixteen were killed (including the quartermaster and his staff, most 'blown beyond recognition'), nine others were wounded, and eight horses also died. The shattered portion of the train was uncoupled, a burial party stayed behind to carry out its grim work, and the rest of the battalion continued on to Doullens.

Elliott's instructions were to position his brigade in and around the adjacent villages of Lealvillers and Acheux ten miles south-east of Doullens. Three 57th companies marched directly to Acheux, and were in position by dawn on 28 March. With brigade headquarters in a Lealvillers residence close to a British battery, Elliott slept only minimally; the house shook every time a gun fired. Up and about early on the 28th, Pompey personally inspected the 57th's outpost line to ensure that 'we should not be caught napping' if the British in front did not hold. Away to the left the 4th AIF Brigade had already encountered the Germans. Nine miles south of Lealvillers, Monash's Third Division had arrived to plug an alarming gap on the Somme; this had arisen from a culpable misinterpretation made by a rattled corps commander in Gough's army, who had reacted to a direction provisionally outlining the procedure in the event of withdrawal as if it was actually an order to retire. Elliott managed to obtain worthwhile information from them, thanks to the enterprising efforts on his behalf of Dave Doyle, who had recently resumed as his intelligence officer. Pompey was full of praise for Doyle's 'excellent work'. Doyle reciprocated: the brigadier was 'evolving order out of chaotic conditions', he observed.

As each of these AIF formations advanced towards the oncoming Germans, they were outnumbered by distraught civilians and demoralised British soldiers going the other way. Thousands of despairing women, children, and old men were struggling along with sundry possessions they had hastily gathered after finding with bewildering suddenness that their homes were threatened by the rapid German advance. Moving in the same direction were many dispirited British soldiers, who assured passing AIF inquirers that the Germans were not far away and advancing in overwhelming numbers. The Australians pressed on resolutely to confront the foe, unflustered and undeterred by the dismay all around them. They were proud, defiant, and confident—their splendid morale boosted, if anything, by the surrounding defeatism that underlined the importance of their task.

In fact, their advent transformed the mood of some of the distressed villagers who recognised these reinforcements as Australians. Worried women with crying children clinging to their skirts became immediately exultant, and decided to return to homes they had hastily abandoned. Some, weeping with joy and relief, cried 'Vive l'Australie!' These stirring scenes, as the AIF was rapturously welcomed back to the Somme, are among the finest episodes in Australia's entire history. The gruff reassurance that one of these rescuers gave a frightened Frenchwoman—'Fini retreat madame, beaucoup Australiens ici'—remains a national treasure. There were numerous moments similarly special. 'Pas necessaire maintenant, vous les tiendrez', enthused a venerable Frenchman. A nearby Australian asked someone for a translation. Upon being told ('Don't need to leave now, you'll hold them'), his laconic response spoke volumes: 'We'll have to see the old bloke isn't disappointed'. The outstanding morale of the Australians, despite the daunting circumstances, was repeatedly noted by observers, including Pompey Elliott: 'the boys ... marched here last night as full of jokes and looking as happy as if they had got leave to Australia'.

A week earlier the British front line had been 28 miles from Lealvillers, which was due west of the pre-offensive boundary separating the Third and Fifth British Armies. The German assault had fallen heavily on both armies; the Third had resisted more effectively than Gough's Fifth. When the blow fell on 21 March, the northern-most corps of Fifth Army had been V Corps, and the fragments of this formation that Elliott encountered in and around Lealvillers confirmed the damning impressions of its performance he had been hearing:

> Found a great many stragglers from British regiments, chiefly 5th Corps, who are drinking and looting out of control. I at once had all of the estaminets closed and picketed ... all accounts agree that the majority of the British battalions gave way to panic and could not be made to stand at all. The rot seems now to have largely stopped, but everything is in a dreadful state of confusion. The 5th Corps are particularly disorganised.

That corps was indeed in poor shape (its commander was sacked, for the second time, shortly afterwards). Other British formations had endured a harrowing time since 21 March; tens of thousands of defenders were understandably shaken and exhausted. However, the unavoidable conclusion is that the quality of British resistance was decidedly variable. Some units displayed the utmost grit and valour, but there were also discreditable episodes of disintegration and hasty, premature back-pedalling—even, in some instances, involving commanders and staffs as senior as corps level. Such incidents had an accelerating snowball effect: neighbouring formations tended to conclude that they had to conform or be outflanked and isolated.

Late on 28 March, with the situation still very fluid, the 15th Brigade received the first of a series of conflicting movement orders. Its instructions, eventually clarified, were to move further south-east towards Albert, and to concentrate in and around the adjacent villages of Varennes and Hedauville. Varennes already possessed historical significance as the place where Louis XVI and Marie Antoinette had been intercepted after attempting to escape from the revolutionaries in 1791. Hedauville was about to acquire a little notoriety of its own, in AIF annals at least.

Having marched through a cold and rainy night, Pompey's men were tired and wet when they reached their new positions. The brigadier organised a new outpost line, and directed the 59th and 60th Battalions to base themselves at Varennes while the rest of the brigade, including his own headquarters, occupied Hedauville. Hobbs had assured Elliott that Hedauville would be vacated when his brigade arrived; shortly after midnight Third Army had instructed V Corps to ensure that its men were out of Hedauville by 8.00am so the 15th Brigade could occupy it. However, to Pompey's surprise, he found the village 'crammed full of officers and men' of the 12th British Division (V Corps)—or, as he later put it, 'packed to the utmost of its capacity with fugitives from the British Army and, in addition, a small nucleus of officers'. The occupants included three field companies of engineers together with, it seems, some infantrymen of the 36th and 37th Brigades and a number of stragglers. At about 9.30am Pompey called at the Hedauville chateau. It was 'literally packed with officers, all of whom were still in bed', he observed:

> [The] staff officer who appeared to be in command ... was still in a very undressed state, stated that he had no orders whatever about leaving, and until he did so he could not move. He stated that there

> were 'plenty of other buildings' in the village for me to take as headquarters without turning them out. I said I had no desire whatever to turn them out, but pointed out that my orders ... were to occupy the village of Hedauville with two battalions, and unless his [men] moved there would not be any accommodation for my men.

As Pompey explained to this officer, Lieutenant Smith of the 37th British Brigade, his main priority was not to install himself in the chateau but to obtain appropriate accommodation for his men. They were waiting in sodden fields under persistent drizzle after marching all night, and had been warned to expect only one hour's notice of a possible further move to the very front line. In other words, it was a matter of Lieutenant Smith moving not just his officers from the chateau, but all his men right out of the village. 'Not wishing to appear the least unreasonable', Pompey pointed out afterwards,

> I told him ... I would try to get a building for headquarters and leave the men outside until midday whilst he was getting orders ... I found a ruined schoolhouse with all the windows shattered by shellfire, and with the yard defiled by human excrement. In one corner two British soldiers were dressing a pig they had killed. I remained here, wet through, until about midday.

Meanwhile Doyle rushed away to find out as much as he could. His purposeful roving proved productive. The most likely location of 12th Division headquarters (according to Lieutenant Smith) was Senlis, so Doyle went there first, only to find that the division had retired to a village five miles further back. He was told it had lost touch with its corps (which perhaps explained why the directive to vacate Hedauville had not reached Lieutenant Smith's detachment). In the course of Doyle's inquiries he came across a British machine-gun officer, who volunteered a scathing assessment of the 12th Division that was 'literally unprintable'. His unit had been attached to men of that division who 'ran away' without informing him, this officer explained, with the result that some of his men and guns were captured. Moving on to Varennes, Doyle found that his questions about the 12th Division fragment at Hedauville produced another contemptuous response. That detachment had 'been nothing but a nuisance', remarked a British officer previously associated with it. Back at Hedauville by midday, Doyle told Elliott what he had learned. Pompey responded decisively.

> I then sent for the acting staff captain, and asked him had he received any orders yet. He replied that he had not. I asked why he had not telephoned or gone to Varennes to find out. He replied that he had no telephone. I told him that I had a telephone he could use, and then, being irritated by his listless manner and want of interest, and by the fact that my men were being drenched to wait his convenience, I told him that I had formed a most unfavourable opinion from what I had heard of his division, and that his own want of energy and initiative were strong confirmation of what I had heard, and that unless he got orders and moved his men out of the village immediately, I would assume command and march them out of the village, if necessary, under arrest.

This assertiveness had the desired effect, just as similarly forceful action from Pompey had accomplished on previous occasions when the welfare of his men was at stake (most notably, in the aftermath of the notorious desert march in March 1916). Before long, Smith and his men had vacated the village.

A few hours later, as Elliott and his brigade were at last settling into their new billets, the situation changed dramatically once more. Out of the blue, while Hobbs was visiting Elliott at Hedauville, an order arrived directing the 15th Brigade to proceed immediately south to Corbie, a town near the junction of the Somme and Ancre rivers. This was a crucial sector. The German plan was to break through and separate the French and British forces, before wheeling northwards to drive the isolated British back to the coast; Amiens, a vital transport and communications centre situated on the Somme, was a primary goal. Corbie and the tactically important town of Villers-Bretonneux were ten miles east of Amiens. 'The covering of Amiens is of first importance', declared Haig.

One of the highest priorities then animating Pompey's British superiors was to prevent the Germans from traversing the bridges across the Somme near Corbie. This important responsibility had been entrusted to the 9th AIF Brigade (under Brigadier-General Charles Rosenthal) of Monash's Third Division, but GHQ decided that

Rosenthal's brigade was needed further south to bolster the vulnerable British defence of Villers-Bretonneux; Elliott's brigade was to replace Rosenthal's. While doing so it would be detached from Fifth Division and operate under Monash's command; a car would be provided to take Pompey directly to Monash's headquarters. This bombshell arrived from GHQ while Elliott and Hobbs were conferring. Elliott hastily summoned his unit commanders to brief them. The fact that AIF formations had to be broken up like this was, Hobbs felt, 'pretty sickening' confirmation of the magnitude of the crisis.

Elliott had been instructed that the 15th Brigade's stipulated route to Corbie would be determined at British Corps level, but notification was slow to materialise. Departure was accordingly delayed, but his men were on their way by 9.30pm. Corbie was ten miles south as the crow flies, but their designated route was much longer, and the previous night's marching had left them tired and drenched. By the time they reached Corbie, Pompey calculated, they would have covered about 20 miles, and those on outpost duty would have done another three to five as well. Nevertheless, they marched to Bonnay (a village two miles north of Corbie) in splendid style, 'close up and in good heart all the time', according to the brigadier, who met the brigade on its arrival. Not a man fell out the whole way, and the 58th Battalion was even singing as it entered the village. The brigade accomplished this fine exploit 'without turning a hair', Bean concurred admiringly.

In fact, the reality was somewhat different. As a 59th footslogger recorded, he and his comrades were struggling along, 'thinking we were never going to get there, everyone in a state of exhaustion, many having fallen out by the way, able to go no further'. It was not 'a matter of stoutness of heart, but a question of physical endurance'. When 'what was supposed to be the main body' was eventually directed to halt so the stragglers could catch up, everyone 'simply fell down with their packs still on, in a few seconds all snoring'. Downing wrote that the weight of their gear was 'an exquisite torture':

> We went through towns and villages, over cobble-stones, cart-tracks and high-roads ... shambling along, keeping the step, but with stumbling feet and hanging heads. The desire for sleep was a dull pain; rest seemed the sweetest thing in the world, but we bit our tongues and kept going. We drowsed as we marched, literally

> walking in our sleep, and in the five-minute halts at the end of every hour we dropped to the ground and slept. Some mechanically kept walking; we called to them to make them stop.

A 57th signaller remembered it similarly:

> I was just about dead to the world and marched in my sleep most of the time. At every halt I just flopped down and had to be waked when it was time to move on again.

Pompey's men persevered, however, and reached their destination. It was, in the circumstances, an exceptional feat. Pompey knew how special it was:

> I ... have seen them triumph in battles, and have greeted them beaten, but never disgraced, returning from a stricken field — they were proud moments; but I have never been prouder than when, on one occasion in France, we marched, at night, 26 miles ... When I arrived at General Sir John Monash's headquarters ... his staff officer said 'They will never get here'. But at the appointed hour ... the whole brigade marched in intact, in close and beautiful order, no man or horse missing from his place nor as much as a round of ammunition or a haversack missing, and without the loss of more than 100 yards in the length of the column. That was a great achievement.

Getting there was indeed an outstanding feat, but there was important work to do as soon as they arrived. The 15th Brigade's primary task was to protect the Third Army's right flank by guarding the Somme crossings near Corbie, and Pompey directed the 59th and 60th Battalions to secure them at once. The remainder of the brigade, including Elliott's own headquarters, stopped at Bonnay. Next morning Pompey was up bright and early to inspect the 59th and 60th positions:

> Found things very bad indeed. Officers and men had got in exhausted, in the main were sound asleep instead of looking to the defences.

It was perfectly understandable that they were tired out. However, in view of the desperate circumstances, he felt that he had no option but to crack the whip in his inimitable style:

> I proceeded to the Corbie bridge head and found that the 60th Bn had not yet taken it over. I went to the Bn HQs and found everyone resting, mainly asleep. I told them what I thought and that I proposed to put them under trial by court martial for negligence ... Thence to 59th Bn HQ and strafed quite a lot, thence home.

After lunch Pompey visited one of Monash's brigadiers to discuss the situation, before returning to the 59th and 60th. Again he found much to criticise. 'Strafed a number of officers for faulty dispositions', he noted (though an officer from Monash's division who visited one of the 15th Brigade posts was impressed with the spirited morale of the occupants). By the end of this long day Pompey was feeling as ragged as his weary men. 'It rained heavily all the afternoon and I got wet through — very tired'.

During this purposeful round of supervision there was a diverting incident. Pompey, in full flight as the exacting disciplinarian, was unable to see the funny side; but his companions, including Doyle and Bob Salmon, certainly did. At the first post they visited in the afternoon inspection Pompey was surprised to come across an isolated group, who sprang up and presented arms.

> 'What in the devil are you doing?'
> 'Outposts, sir'.
> 'What are your instructions?'
> 'To look out for you, sir'.

Long afterwards, Salmon could still recall the sequel vividly:

> Pompey was furious, inquired who was the company commander, and sailed off for his billet. On arrival at the company headquarters we first met the cook and his offsider. The cook was dressed in a long frock coat, lavender trousers, high-coloured flowing tie, fancy waistcoat and bell topper, and his offsider was dressed as a female

> in the brightest garb, really more feminine looking in parts than the most buxom wench. Both were inebriated, and when they recognised Pompey they sprang to attention in a sort of way and saluted. It was a most ludicrous sight, but Pompey almost bellowed with anger.

Salmon refrained from identifying the company commander and outlining what happened to him, but Pompey did arrange for two 59th officers to be replaced.

Having first ensured that Layh and Watson were absolutely clear about his requirements, Elliott decided to bring their 57th and 58th Battalions forward to relieve the exhausted 59th and 60th. Being in reserve had enabled the fresher incoming units to recover more quickly from the gruelling night marching. After the relief he summoned all the 59th and 60th officers to the church at Bonnay for a lecture covering the brigade's new responsibilities. Quoting liberally from Field Service Regulations—the manual he regarded as his military bible—he urged every officer to know the chapters concerning outpost and picquet duties off by heart, stressed the importance of ensuring that all the men were familiar with the billeting rules, outlined the finer points of defence along a river, and predicted where the Germans might attempt to cross. After the lecture Monash called at Elliott's headquarters to discuss the overall situation; he was keen to ensure that everyone, even working party personnel, was appropriately equipped to handle any sudden emergency. Senior officers of 15th Brigade and Third Division (including Wieck, now on Monash's staff) conferred about a new trench line, to be created by the 59th and 60th Battalions, to protect the outskirts of Corbie and neighbouring La Neuville should the British fall back further. The 59th and 60th men, responding to Pompey's vigorous stimulus, laboured to such good effect in constructing this line that Monash's admiring chief engineer volunteered that he had never seen men work so well. With Australians now safeguarding the critical Third Army front from Corbie to Albert, the situation north of the Somme was much more secure.

Pompey, however, remained gravely concerned about the vulnerability of the front south of the river. Holding the line there was the 14th British Division, which had not recovered from its misfortune in being in front of the main German thrust on 21 March. Even allowing for the immense power of that intimidating onslaught, the 14th Division's resistance had been, to say the least, disappointingly inadequate. A comprehensive British evaluation of that dramatic day concluded that 'the biggest collapse of a division' had occurred in the 14th, which

> did not fight well on 21 March. Its forward positions fell quickly; many men surrendered, and some hasty flights to the rear were observed.

The divisional commander was sacked on 22 March; within a week his successor (according to Haig's diary) 'went off his head with the strain'. Having been driven well back again on the 23rd, the 14th Division was relegated to a subsidiary role assisting the French, and then withdrawn altogether on 26 March. During the night of 3-4 April, under its third commander in twelve days, the 14th Division moved into its new position south of the Somme near Elliott's brigade. Pompey's concern about that sector was intensified by information provided by a pair of intrepid 60th Battalion lieutenants, 'Boyce' Pizzey (who had known Elliott before the war as a nearby resident in Darebin Road, Northcote) and W.R. Gannon, who had reconnoitred the British positions there. The front trench itself was solid enough, they told the brigadier, but there was no support or reserve line; 'very slack', concluded Pompey. With his own weary men toiling diligently to fortify the Corbie defences, the contrast, he felt, was glaring.

A higher priority for some British soldiers, it seemed to Pompey, was looting. With the French civilians vacating their homes and estaminets swiftly—many departed so suddenly that the Australians came upon numerous half-eaten meals left on tables—soldiers so inclined could avail themselves of a variety of provisions. There was plenty of wine to be had, fine champagne in particular. At one stage, with water in relatively short supply, some of Pompey's men were using champagne for washing and shaving. In such circumstances the notion that they would forego a more orthodox application for the beverage was unrealistic. Pompey's inclination to implement strong preventative measures was reinforced by his encounter with the intoxicated cooks on the day after his brigade arrived. Having issued strict orders and installed guards at all the main liquor repositories, he was soon satisfied that he had managed to curb excessive consumption within his brigade; but he became increasingly frustrated that his efforts were being undermined by lax British indifference. He was prepared to concede that a certain amount of petty larceny was inevitable. Systematic looting, however, was another matter altogether. The state of affairs in Corbie deteriorated to the point where there seemed to Pompey to be more British officers and men intent on 'looking for what they could loot than were fighting the enemy'. With the officers out of control, it was impossible to discipline their men. Other AIF generals, including Monash, Hobbs, and Rosenthal, became independently convinced that there was far more looting by British soldiers than by Australians.

When a British captain was apprehended in Corbie with a mess cart full of looted champagne, Elliott decided that enough was enough. After handing the culprit over to the military police, Pompey resolved on his own initiative to issue a notice declaring that the next officer caught looting would be summarily and publicly hanged in the Corbie market square, and his body would be left swinging there as a deterrent. He ensured that this remarkable notice was displayed prominently in Corbie. Underneath, in a postscript, Pompey admitted that the drastic penalty he was threatening was probably illegal, but he was prepared to do whatever was necessary to maintain order; if he ever had to execute his threat, he proposed to rely subsequently on a royal pardon. His vigorous intervention was influenced by his familiarity with historic campaigns, he told Milly Edwards afterwards:

> I have read so much military history that I knew what to expect and how to deal with it. Wellington and Moore's campaigns in Spain and Portugal were a good preparation for what I saw, and the Duke hanged and shot without remorse as the only way of keeping and restoring order.

Pompey particularly had in mind the uncompromising vigour of one of his heroes, General Craufurd, 'in flogging, hanging or shooting men who plundered or straggled from the rearguard' during the 1808-09 retreat to Corunna. In fact, Elliott, in a striking precedent five years earlier, had given officers and NCOs of his militia battalion a vivid account of how Craufurd had even threatened to hang a certain officer in order to achieve an objective he regarded as urgent.

Pompey made a big splash with his Corbie ultimatum. Looting ceased immediately. 'None seemed inclined to make of themselves a test case under the circumstances', he observed drily, 'and I never had the slightest trouble afterwards'. This was yet another colourful Pompey anecdote to add to an already long list, and the story soon became famous even beyond the AIF. 'That yarn has spread through the whole blessed British Army', he mused later that month, 'and promises to be still more widely known than the yarn of the hat' (which was now three years old, but 'I see it in all sorts of papers still').

The Germans launched another imposing assault towards Amiens on 4 April. They achieved a breakthrough on the 14th Division's front, a development that came as no surprise to Pompey:

> as I expected from the manner in which they were holding the line, they gave way very badly ... great numbers flung down their arms and ran away. The cavalry ... were consequently forced to give ground, and the situation looked disastrous.

The Germans established themselves in Hamel, and advanced ominously beyond. Dispirited British soldiers fell back in large numbers, together with a much smaller number of Australians from Rosenthal's brigade, who had been impelled to conform with the British retirement. On the scene south of Corbie near Villers-Bretonneux, the crucial town overlooking Amiens, was Charles Bean. He became convinced that Villers-Bretonneux, the key to Amiens, would soon be in German hands. In 'great gloom', Bean called at Elliott's headquarters to let him know, 'so that if Villers-Bretonneux were taken he would not be caught in the flank'. Pompey had already taken decisive action of his own. Having warned his battalions at an early stage to ensure that they were in a 'state of absolute readiness' to respond as directed in the emergency, he sent a message authorising methods of the utmost vigour to his senior custodian of the bridge across the Somme at Vaire (about a mile east of Corbie), Captain Ferres of the 58th, who was having difficulty rallying the 14th Division back-pedallers because their officers kept insisting they had been ordered to withdraw. Elliott ordered Ferres 'to stop all stragglers and compel them to fight'. Armed with this empowering directive, Ferres instituted wholehearted measures. Splendidly assisted by detached British cavalry parties eager to help, he collected about 500 British infantrymen and positioned them in a makeshift defensive line.

Elliott, having conferred with Monash, sent the 59th and 60th Battalions (previously in reserve) forward to join Ferres's British remnants. Companies of the 59th arrived first; the 60th came in later on their right. They found British cavalry units defending a sizeable portion of the front 'and doing it magnificently too', Elliott noted. The Germans kept coming, but were unable to penetrate further. According to Pompey,

> on the front the 59th had to hold there were 3 German Divisions opposed in depth, but the reception their leading files got turned the stomach of all who should have followed from the fight. One of my machine guns which I placed slightly forward of the line and protected by a swamp fired across the front and piled 200 German corpses in a ghastly rampart of slain before the survivors of the column concluded that they had urgent business elsewhere.

In fact, Elliott claimed proudly, his brigade actually gained ground there despite being so outnumbered. To the south Rosenthal's 9th AIF Brigade also retrieved the situation brilliantly, securing Villers-Bretonneux in dashing style just in time, while Elliott's men and the cavalry took control of the vital height north-east of the town known as Hill 104. The AIF's impact in the crisis was striking; as Pompey observed, 'the marvellous part of it is the smallness of our casualties'.

'The Australians and cavalry have fought magnificently', reported Sir Henry Rawlinson, the army commander who had replaced Gough, but the '14th Division did badly'. Bean agreed. Bearing in mind his disinclination to emphasise discreditable deeds or unworthy conduct in his published writing, the way he highlighted the contrasting contributions of the British infantry and cavalry in his considered appraisal of this engagement long afterwards in the Australian *Official History* was telling:

> The flight of the 14th Division's infantry came as a shock to the reinforcing troops, but Ferres was full of admiration for the cavalry: 'no men', he reported, 'could have done more than these cavalry men did'.

When Bean's able but devious English counterpart, J.E. Edmonds, artfully concealed this contrast in a typically misleading version for the British official history, Bean took Edmonds to task:

> the reader would not guess that there was a marked difference between the quality of the Cavalry and of the 14th Division. The events in the 14th Division's sector as described would be unrecognisable to anyone who saw them—the reader would conclude that the 14th Division carried out a well-conducted retirement. Actually the retirement was rather like a rout, and in most parts impossible to control.

Bean, unlike Edmonds, was there at the time and an eye-witness. In reply, Edmonds conceded that the 14th Division had low esprit de corps and by April 1918 'could not be depended on', adding that the general sacked on 22 March (after commanding the division for over three years) was 'never at any time of any use'.

On 4 April there were a number of rearrangements resulting from the German attack. The 15th Brigade was directed to remain in the front line it had just secured (another formation would take over responsibility for the crossings). The discredited 14th British Division was withdrawn, and replaced by the 3rd Cavalry Division. Because Pompey's men were now in the area of Fourth Army, it was no longer appropriate for them to remain with Monash's division (which remained north of the Somme as part of Third Army). They were to rejoin the Fifth AIF Division, which was about to begin moving south; until it arrived, the 15th Brigade would be transferred temporarily to the cavalry. Elliott was delighted. After having to contend with the shortcomings of weakened and deficient British infantry, it was splendid to be aligned (if only briefly) with the legendary cavalry. Monash also heartily approved of the changes:

> The Fifth Australian Division will, I hope, arrive overnight, and come in on my right flank, and this will be a great comfort and relief to me. These Tommy Divisions are the absolute limit, and not worth the money it costs to put them into uniform ...—bad troops, bad staffs, bad commanders.

The 15th Brigade, on the other hand, had been superb, Monash told Hobbs:

> Nothing could have been more splendid than the prompt action and excellent initiative of the Brigadier and all his staff and Commanders. The Brigade helped me over a very difficult period, and its very presence protecting the line of the river on my Right flank greatly heartened all my troops who were engaged in resisting a considerable pressure from the enemy ... I greatly admired Elliott's quickness of grasp and his resourcefulness in dealing with every situation as it arose; and also the promptitude with which he established most useful liaison with the troops, and the situation, south of the Somme.

In fact, the 15th Brigade's contribution south of the Somme resulted in praise even more gratifying to Pompey. It came from a commander of the prestigious cavalry, who acknowledged that the 59th and 60th Battalions 'arrived just in time to restore the situation'. The cavalrymen, their general assured Pompey, 'were very proud to have the opportunity of fighting alongside your splendid fellows', and hoped to do so again.

On 5 April the Germans made another attempt to break through towards Amiens. The main thrust was further north, but the 15th Brigade's sector was heavily shelled; the 57th, back in reserve near Corbie, suffered over 50 casualties. After the bombardment Pompey's men repulsed all enemy attempts to advance against them. The day's highlight for the 15th Brigade was an exploit by Corporal Doug Sayers, a 29-year-old Geelong engineer, and three privates who had been instructed by Ferres to protect the astutely sited machine-gun that had been so effective when the Germans attacked on 4 April. In the afternoon this 58th quartet was spotted by a patrol of 30 Germans, who set up a machine-gun they had with them and made other obvious preparations to attack the four-man post. Leaving two of his men where they were, Sayers and the remaining one manoeuvred deftly around to the Germans' flank, whereupon all four suddenly opened fire. Seven Germans were hit, and their officer ordered the others to withdraw. Sayers then directed his men to charge and, dashing forward, shot the German officer himself. The rest fled. They 'skedaddled for their lives, shedding arms and accoutrements as they ran', wrote Pompey, 'they never stopped till they got out of sight, and our fellows [were] laughing so they could hardly shoot, but they killed six and captured two' along with 'a beautiful automatic pistol of the latest type and fine pairs of Zeiss field glasses and some very important orders and maps'. The delighted brigadier recommended the three privates for the Military Medal (which they each received) and Sayers for the VC (he was awarded the DCM instead).

Pompey was not only enthusing about Sayers. The Corbie residence he had inherited as his headquarters (after the reshuffle of defending formations on 4 April) was, he wrote, 'a most glorious house, the finest I have ever been in', with 'exquisite' furniture, carpets that would 'make your mouth water' and exceptional collections of photographs, weapons, birds, flora, and fauna. In letters to Milly Edwards and his family back in Melbourne, he waxed eloquent in page after page of enraptured description, displaying the naturalist instincts his mother had detected and encouraged from an early age. In the billiard room, for example, 'ranged round the walls from floor to ceiling in cabinets of beautifully polished walnut was the most wonderful collection of gorgeous butterflies I have ever seen'. Outside, in the outstanding conservatory, he was delighted to find 'a lovely little Cootamundra wattle' in full bloom; he sent a small bunch to both Rawlinson and Birdwood 'as an omen of victory'. The magnificence of the art and furniture prompted Pompey to write to the French government recommending its removal so it would no longer be exposed to the probability of destruction by enemy shellfire; the authorities were most responsive to his suggestion. He also arranged for inquiries to be made about the butterflies, and found they belonged to the museum of Paris. They had been loaned to the owner of this opulent residence because he was classifying them with a view to writing a treatise on the subject. Assured by a grateful museum official that they were 'absolutely priceless', Pompey initiated steps to ensure that they, too, were protected. He was certainly doing it in style at Corbie. As well as 'the loveliest house in all the world to live in', he had two cars for the brigade to use, and the extra mobility for reconnaissance proved very handy. It was 'Boyce' Pizzey who initially acquired one of these vehicles. According to Pizzey, he was driving it along a Corbie street when he came across Pompey on horseback; Pompey was not slow to suggest that in view of their respective ranks an exchange of conveyances was probably appropriate.

Elliott ensured that his brigade maintained an aggressive outlook.

Intent on pushing forward wherever possible, he was even envisaging that his men could 'make Hamel untenable' for the Germans. At a conference with his battalion commanders on 6 April, he instituted a policy of reconnaissance by day and step-by-step advancement by night, with the forward posts being extended under cover of darkness. A small patrol under Ferres penetrated as far as Bouzencourt north of Hamel, and the 15th Brigade subsequently secured this village. To enable the reserve battalion, the 57th, to be less exposed to enemy shellfire, Elliott decided to move it back across the Somme to more secure billets; he directed his brigade major to arrange it and to let all the battalions know. In an aberration, however, Street's order to the other three front-line battalions was worded as if each of them was to withdraw across the Somme as well. Fortunately they queried it, and the error was corrected. Pompey was livid: 'trying to retreat in broad daylight over narrow pontoon bridges almost in full view of the enemy' would have produced 'a tremendous disaster, if not a massacre of the Brigade', as well as creating 'a break in our line nearly 3 miles long'. Pompey felt that his longstanding misgivings about Street's capacity had been vindicated. Hobbs agreed that, after a mistake of such magnitude, he would have to be replaced.

On 9 April the 15th Brigade was withdrawn for a break, and relieved by the 8th Brigade. Its commander was still Edwin Tivey, the prosperous 51-year-old stockbroker who had been Elliott's squadron leader in the Boer War. Pompey, increasingly contemptuous of what he saw as Tivey's pretentiousness, ingratiating manner to superiors, and laughable exaggerations of both 8th Brigade 'captures' and trifling personal 'wounds', took with him both the cars he had acquired (despite Tivey's pointed hints that they should remain where they were), and chuckled when the French authorities turned up to shift the ornate furniture and other treasures to safe storage soon after Tivey took over the Corbie residence. 'So where I had lived for a week surrounded by the luxury of millionaires with two motor cars, old Tivey came down to bare boards and horseback'. With the 15th Brigade now back in reserve, Elliott was able to write home for the first time since his men arrived at the Somme. On 8 April he had sent Milly Edwards a message to cable to Kate: 'Self and all commanders safe and well eighth April boys doing magnificent work winning golden opinions all love Elliott'. Apart from that cable he had been too busy to correspond with his family for over a fortnight, so he had much to tell:

> The AIF have hitherto accomplished nothing to be compared in importance with the work they have in hand just now ... we turned the tide that threatened to sweep over everything to Paris and the sea ... Australia [should] be proud of our boys.

Pompey certainly was.

> I was never so proud of being an Australian as I am today in spite of the failure of conscription. The gallant bearing and joyous spirit of the men at the prospect of a fight thrills you through and through—you simply cannot despair or be downhearted, whatever the odds against you, when you feel their spirits rising the more the danger seems to threaten. It is glorious indeed to be with them.

He was particularly pleased with the 58th Battalion. As well as pursuing a VC for Sayers, Pompey had recommended both Watson, who had been superb as acting battalion commander, and Ferres for the DSO:

> there is a wonderful fighting spirit in that battalion now. It is all due to old Denehy and his fatherly ways and the immense pride he takes in his boys. He is away on leave, he looked very tired [before he left] but he will curl his moustache more fiercely and proudly than ever when he returns and I tell him what the boys have done in his absence.

Elliott's letters to Kate vividly narrated his adventures. He outlined his vigorous anti-looting measures, raved about the wonderful treasures at his Corbie headquarters, and described how he dealt with the lieutenant who was unwilling to get his men out of Hedauville:

> He told me that his Division had moved and until he got orders from them as to where he was to go he could not move. I asked him where his Division was. He did not know. I asked had he sent [anyone] out to find where it was—No. I then saw that the blighter had no intention to move, that they were very comfortable there and didn't want to move and would take mighty fine care they didn't get orders. So I told him right there and then a few things I had found out about his Division and its

> fighting and running powers, and wound up by informing him that unless he and his officers and men were clear of the village by two o'clock I would send in an escort of my own men and march them out by force as prisoners. He got a nasty shock and was out of the village within the time fixed. He then had the [hide] to complain to his Division of the way I had treated him. In reply I let off some more steam and asked that a Court of Inquiry should be appointed to inquire into the conduct of the British officers and men in the village who had looted the whole place including the chateau. That startled them a bit, and the matter was dropped like a hot spud. I expected a snub from Birdwood, my usual portion from him, but nothing but a dead silence was the result. The fact is that I am at present so armed with written congratulations from the Lord knows who in the way of British generals that everyone concerned is mighty civil, and old Tivey looks down his nose at me as sour about it all as an old maid of 60. It is rather amusing you know, because I know the success of my brigade is not due to myself at all but the splendid officers and men I have got, and the only credit due to me is for discovering and pushing out the wretched duds that were pushed on to me in the beginning whom everyone now admits to be duds, but when I said so first I was near being crucified for it.

In Elliott's correspondence with Milly Edwards, his supportive cousin who had a son and other relatives in the British forces, he was particularly frank about the variable quality of the British units he had encountered. 'My own opinion', he told Milly on 12 April,

> is that a number of the British officers should be cashiered for gross neglect of duty and incompetence. A number of them have been under me of late and their apparent indifference is astounding. I actually overheard one say Well if the Bosche does get Amiens it won't matter to us, it's not 'our country'. The looting of the unfortunate French people's property, particularly wines, was a scandal ... The regular cavalry fought magnificently, and really saved the situation from irretrievable ruin. Their services should never be forgotten.

Pompey was also unstinting in his praise for the British machine-gunners who

> fought most magnificently whilst others fled, and hung on for two days to help us turn the tide though nearly absolutely exhausted. My boys were so delighted with them that to give them a chance of rest they supplied the guards on the guns during the periods of rest, and carried ammunition and supplied them with hot food and drink from their own pots and cookers.

(These machine-gunners were 'very grateful' for this 'great consideration', their commander assured Elliott; considering 'the experiences of the 24 hours previous to the arrival of your men', he added pointedly, 'it was a real pleasure to fight alongside men whom one could rely upon'.) It was undeniable, Pompey insisted, that some British infantry had behaved deplorably:

> No one as you know has been more ready to glorify the gallantry of the British troops—where I have found it true—than I. I would raise a monument a mile high to the cavalry and machine gunners who clung with us to wood and stream and hillock in desperate effort to stem and turn the tide ... There are hundreds of thousands in the British Army worthy of the utmost honour. There are hundreds certainly (perhaps thousands) who should be summarily and publicly shot or hanged for shameless misconduct.

On 9 April the Germans launched a big attack in Flanders. Once again they accomplished a substantial breakthrough; this was assisted by the defective dispositions of General 'Butcher' Haking, who became implicated once again in a disastrous reverse near Fromelles. A rapid advance ensued of alarming dimensions. Hazebrouck, a transport and communications centre as important in Flanders as Amiens was further south, was gravely threatened. Even the Channel ports seemed vulnerable. Haig issued to everyone under his command a forceful appeal that did not hide the gravity of the situation:

> Every position must be held to the last man: there must be no retirement. With our backs to the wall, and believing in the justice

> of our cause each one of us must fight on to the end. The safety of our Homes and the Freedom of mankind alike depend upon the conduct of each one of us at this critical moment.

This German advance in Flanders convinced the British to relinquish the ground gained in the costly Ypres offensive of 1917; what had been won in four months of terrible fighting was evacuated in three days. (In stark confirmation of Haig's folly in persevering at Passchendaele in appalling conditions, senior British commanders had privately acknowledged even before the Germans attacked in March 1918 that the bulge east of Ypres would become untenable if an enemy offensive eventuated.) With Amiens likely to be the objective of a renewed German assault, the developments in Flanders intensified Pompey's concern:

> The situation is bad indeed. It breaks one's heart to know that Polygon Wood and Broodseinde and all are gone again that so many of our boys died to gain, and Messines and Paschendale.

Growing concern about alarmist reports in this atmosphere of crisis led to a GHQ pronouncement and a characteristically forceful response from Elliott. Allegations were circulating that Germans posing as British officers were responsible for ordering premature retirements and spreading dire rumours (although such incidents, when investigated, tended to be attributable to mistaken or panic-stricken British soldiers). GHQ instructed that individuals suspected of disseminating such orders or rumours were to be immediately taken to the nearest commanding officer. On 15 April someone at 15th Brigade headquarters, hearing someone else assert that the Germans were marching on Hazebrouck, passed on this information to a signaller, who then told a batman that the enemy was in Hazebrouck but he was uncertain whether this was official. When Pompey became aware of this rumour-mongering at his own headquarters, he decided to issue a forthright edict on the subject: any individual caught in the act had to be 'treated as an enemy agent, placed under close arrest and tried by Court Martial'. This action was consistent with GHQ policy, but Pompey went further in a controversial additional directive:

> Should the Battalion be in action, and no satisfactory explanation is forthcoming from the man concerned, he will be summarily shot by order of the Battalion Commander concerned, and a record of the action taken forwarded, in writing, to these headquarters.

In Pompey's opinion the situation justified the sternest measures. 'Oh for a new Cromwell', he wrote.

The 15th Brigade remained where it was, in divisional reserve in front of Amiens. Its tempestuous commander, uplifted by the magnificent response of his men in the crisis, was more indomitable and inspiring than ever. Delivering rousing exhortations and dashing off stirring letters, he sent Milly Edwards a fervent morale-booster:

> I cannot tell you where we are, but think of what the Bosche most aimed for and plant my brigade right across the path. It is a great honour I feel to be placed there … we will hold him yet. You must tell every one to keep their spirits up—this is no time for softness and yielding … the boys are longing for him to come on … the more we see of him as a soldier, the more contemptuous of him do we become—his strategy and his tactics appear alike to have been copied from the locusts that devastate our fields at home on occasion … the whole military ability of the Teutonic race has advanced no plan beyond … the instinct of an infant grasshopper. In spots he must gain by such means a transient success, but will he win the war—never, if our hearts are stout and our brains cool and our arms ready to take advantage of opportunity … I must just stick it out like my boys—our backs to the wall but our faces and our breasts undaunted at all—facing the foe … Never fear the ultimate result.

CHAPTER SIXTEEN

'The Most Brilliant Feat of Arms in the War':

The battle of Villers-Bretonneux

APRIL 1918

DENEHY'S RETURN TO the 15th Brigade on 20 April led to a reshuffle of Elliott's battalion commanders. Watson had led the 58th superbly while Denehy was on leave, and Pompey was also pleased with his most recently promoted colonel, Scanlan. Unexpectedly, the battalion commander Elliott had become 'least pleased with' was his most renowned colonel, Norman Marshall. Pompey sensed that Marshall had been somewhat distracted by the presence in London of his wife and the imminent birth of their first child. Marshall 'is not the man he was', declared the brigadier; besides, compared to Watson in particular, Marshall 'does not know open warfare so well'. Other well-placed observers noticed no decline in the quality of his leadership. Marshall was 'the life and soul of this battalion', wrote the 60th's doctor, Keith Doig; it would be hard 'to find another CO in the AIF who had half the influence over his men'.

On 20 April Elliott learned that Watson had been nominated for transfer because of a sudden shortage of leaders in Cam Stewart's 14th Brigade. Elliott decided to have a chat to Stewart about Marshall. Pompey suggested that Stewart might like to have Marshall, the old friend who had served under him in the 5th Battalion at Gallipoli as well as the 57th in France; if so, and if Marshall were willing to transfer, Pompey told Stewart he would not object. Elliott's proposal arose from a combination of motives. Stewart was undeniably in difficulties; this generous offer would help a close colleague and further the overall AIF cause. At the same time, Pompey's perception of a slight decline in Marshall's outstanding leadership, coupled with the emergence of Watson as a fine commander, made the prospect of acquiescing in Marshall's departure less unthinkable than it would otherwise have been. Stewart, not surprisingly, was most interested in acquiring Marshall.

Elliott convened a conference of his battalion commanders on 21 April. He told them that Stewart had asked for Marshall, and they had to consider the ramifications for the 15th Brigade if Marshall's transfer was eventually approved. Pompey added that he was considering switching Layh from the 57th to replace Marshall at the 60th, promoting Watson to the substantive command of the 58th, and transferring Denehy from the 58th to the 57th (while Scanlan remained at the 59th). The brigadier emphasised the strong esprit de corps within the 15th Brigade—greater than in any other AIF brigade, he declared—and asserted that this co-operative spirit would be reinforced by these changes as well as helping to make them a success. Marshall expressed his regret at the prospect of leaving the brigade, but said he would be doing the right thing in the interests of the AIF as a whole if he transferred to the 14th Brigade to help out his 'old CO'. Layh, who had already commanded the 59th as well as the 57th, said he did not feel bonded to any particular battalion; if the brigadier wanted to shift him to the 60th he had no objection. The colonel who found the proposed changes most unpalatable was Denehy. Having been with the 58th since the eve of Fromelles, he felt affectionately attached to that battalion and proud of its record. He admitted that he would be sad to leave the 58th; however, like Marshall, he said if such a change would benefit the AIF he would be willing to transfer.

This provisional reshuffle was curiously sweeping. Elliott could have achieved a less disruptive rearrangement by simply shifting Watson to the 60th as Marshall's successor and leaving his other three colonels where they were. He seems to have been keen to keep Watson where he had been so impressive (at the 58th as Denehy's stand-in), but that does not explain why Layh had to be shifted as well. The brigade diary's record of the 21 April conference quotes Elliott as referring to the need for 'greater efficiency' without elaborating. More informative is a letter he sent to Denehy's wife later in 1918, praising her husband for making the 58th an outstanding battalion and leaving it 'at the hour of need' in order to fix up 'the 57th which had then fallen behind'. A decade later Elliott wrote that Denehy was 'in many respects my best and most reliable Battalion Commander'. Although Layh had the brigadier's full confidence, even admiration, it seems that Elliott had discerned some deterioration in the 57th's proficiency that made it more amenable to Denehy's painstaking, relatively nurturing style than to Layh's more vigorous (Pompey-like) methods.

On 20 April the 15th Brigade was involved in a reorganisation of the defending units situated in and around Villers-Bretonneux. Earlier in April the Australians had been holding the most vital stretch of British front extending some fifteen miles from Albert all the way to the Luce river south of Villers-Bretonneux. After the reorganisation the AIF's segment was reduced. The reassembled Australian Corps now held the British line from Albert to Hill 104 north-east of Villers-Bretonneux. Of the three AIF divisions occupying this part of the front, the Fifth (having now rejoined the Australian Corps) remained on the right of the Australian Corps sector, closest to Amiens. As part of the readjustment, however, its portion of front was moved northwards to enable it to occupy both sides of the Somme. According to Bean, Haig instigated this realignment, and having one formation responsible for co-ordinating the defence of an important geographical feature was consistent with 'sound military principle' (although, when the British had been retreating in disarray the previous month, Haig himself had contravened this axiom by fixing the Somme as the designated boundary between the Third and Fifth Armies). Rawlinson, implementing Haig's directive within Fourth Army, opted to allocate one main duty to each corps. Defence of the Somme would be the responsibility of the Australians, and the task of safeguarding Villers-Bretonneux would be entrusted to the British III Corps.

But would III Corps be up to it? That formation had endured a harrowing time during the German advance. Its leader, Lieutenant-General R.H.K. Butler, was inexperienced as a commander, having spent most of the war on Haig's staff; the Commander-in-Chief's estimate of Butler's capacity seemed higher than anyone else's. Butler's intimidating frown and remarkably bushy eyebrows were more prominent than ever when the Germans attacked his corps, then part of Gough's Fifth Army, on 21 March. He was, admittedly, in an unenviable situation. His corps was holding an over-extended stretch of front, it was being assailed by attackers in overwhelming numbers, and it contained the notoriously substandard 14th Division, which was to incur Pompey Elliott's wrath for its inadequate resistance north-east of Villers-Bretonneux on 4 April. Even so, Butler's leadership in the crisis was undistinguished.

With the 14th Division now banished, Butler's corps had acquired the 8th British Division, which took over the front in and east of Villers-Bretonneux under the reorganisation. This division had a better reputation than the 14th, having resisted on the whole more resolutely during the British retreat, but its losses had been severe and most of its newly arrived reinforcements were young and inexperienced. The commander of the 8th Division, Major-General W.C.G. Heneker, was widely disliked. An autocratic disciplinarian, Heneker 'was always breathing fire and slaughter from a long way behind the front' (according to the staff captain of a brigade in his division). His bullying instincts were liable to crumble when a valiant subordinate stood up to him, and he was not known for inspiring leadership in a tight corner.

Rawlinson's decision to make III Corps responsible for safeguarding Villers-Bretonneux was puzzling. He had himself recognised, when summoned to replace Gough, that his paramount goal was 'to keep the Bosche out of Amiens', and that 'one could not take over command at a more critical juncture'. Indeed, he had even staked his own reputation on retaining Villers-Bretonneux, so clearly was it pivotal to the fate of Amiens. As he knew, the AIF (with Elliott's brigade prominent) had been primarily responsible for halting the Germans' dangerous thrust towards Amiens early in April. It was increasingly apparent as that month proceeded that the Germans would have another crack at Amiens. By 20 April Rawlinson was certain it was imminent. 'I have done all I possibly can to prepare a really warm reception for the Boche', he asserted.

But is this claim sustainable? With Rawlinson acknowledging that he had no higher priority than the security of Villers-Bretonneux, it was hardly prudent—inviting trouble, in fact—to so arrange the formations under his command that the AIF was no longer involved in its defence. Rawlinson himself admitted that the divisions in Butler's corps, hastily reinforced to cover their losses since 21 March, were 'short of officers and have had little or no chance of training their new drafts'. On the other hand, he added (almost as if to convince himself), 'the men are not a bad lot and look as if they would fight well'; Heneker's division, Rawlinson claimed, had 'recuperated very quickly', and was 'now up to strength again with very good men'. Before long he was describing those reinforcements very differently.

Since 10 April Elliott and much of his brigade had been based four miles west of Villers-Bretonneux at Blangy-Tronville, a village situated alongside the Somme as it snaked south-westwards from Corbie towards Amiens. The main task of the 15th Brigade while in reserve was to press on with the fortification of defensive works between the existing front and Amiens. In particular, Pompey's men had to transform the Aubigny Line, a series of rifle pits a hundred yards or so apart when the 15th Brigade took it over, into a substantial obstacle extending two miles southwards from the Somme near the village of Aubigny to the wood behind Villers-Bretonneux known as the Bois l'Abbé. A recurrence of Elliott's severe bronchial symptoms confined him to bed for several days during April, preventing him from supervising this work closely; but Gollan (who was acting brigade major pending the appointment of a successor to Street) co-ordinated its organisation in association with staff officers from Fifth Division and various unit commanders on the spot.

Although Pompey and his men were ostensibly in reserve, the ever-zealous brigadier, convinced that another German thrust towards Villers-Bretonneux was imminent, had (with Hobbs's approval) positioned one of his battalions, Scanlan's 59th, in the Bois l'Abbé at the southern end of the Aubigny Line. Pompey instructed Scanlan to have the 59th ready to counter-attack immediately, in case the Germans managed to capture Villers-Bretonneux. He also urged all officers in the brigade to scrutinise a contoured model of the sector constructed at his request.

On 20 April various units of Heneker's 8th Division arrived to take over the portion of the front that had been vacated by the Fifth AIF Division in accordance with the reorganisation imposed by higher British commanders. Scanlan was surprised to find that the incoming Durham Light Infantry proposed to replace his battalion in the Bois l'Abbé with a solitary platoon. He informed Pompey, who was appalled. If the Bois l'Abbé occupants were driven out, the defenders in the Aubigny Line, which then included half of Elliott's brigade, would be enfiladed and gravely imperilled; the security of the Bois l'Abbé was 'absolutely vital to the preservation of our position', declared the brigadier. Instituting a policy of defence in depth was all very well, but having the bulk of the Durhams back in Blangy-Tronville would be no good if the Germans made forward movement from there difficult by unleashing yet another bombardment of gas shells (there had already been several in this area that very month).

It was bad enough that such a crucial position was being occupied by units that Pompey suspected were inferior and unreliable; doing so with faulty dispositions that endangered his own men was intolerable. He objected forcefully to Hobbs, who was sympathetic. Hobbs then queried the British arrangements with III Corps, only to be informed that Butler was aware of the dispositions and approved of them. Perhaps this was an occasion when Pompey's legendary forthrightness might have been more effective than Hobbs's accommodating tact. Elliott even suggested to Hobbs that the 59th could be sent back to support the Durhams, but Hobbs 'said it was impossible that we should move into the 3rd Corps area to do their job for them'.

Pompey's concern intensified. He persuaded Hobbs that a long trench should be excavated westwards from the Aubigny Line on the Fifth Division's right flank, ostensibly for 'communication' but in fact to protect the 15th Brigade men positioned there if the neighbouring British were driven out of the Bois l'Abbé. Two battalions were in the Aubigny Line, the 58th in the northern half and the 57th closest to the British (the 59th and 60th were back at Blangy-Tronville with brigade headquarters). Meanwhile a succession of newly captured Germans confirmed that another attack on Villers-Bretonneux was imminent.

On 23 April Pompey felt well enough to inspect the fortification work along the Aubigny Line. He was not impressed. The positioning of wire and machine-gun posts was defective. In some places there was a risk of machine-gunners inadvertently shooting their comrades; parts of the wire were kinked, thereby reducing the intended fields of fire; some machine-gun nests were not only incorrectly sited but inadequately concealed; and, along the perimeter of Aubigny itself, there was confusion about whether a certain wall or a trench some distance behind it was to constitute the main barrier. These defects, Pompey concluded, were the result of a flawed process. The officer with the overriding authority in such matters should not automatically be the chief engineer at divisional headquarters, who might well be deficient in tactical expertise; rather, he should be someone tactically proficient—in most instances, the infantry commander on the spot. Pompey was far from well, he was expecting a substantial and possibly crucial German attack any minute, and he was very busy trying to ensure every possible precaution was being taken to thwart it; but he managed to find time to dash off a frank statement outlining his concerns.

There were 'a number of points which caused me considerable dissatisfaction', Pompey declared in the forceful report he submitted to Hobbs. In places where the tactical wiring should have been 'absolutely straight'—because 'a gun cannot fire around a corner'—the Aubigny Line was 'radically defective', he contended. 'Already a considerable amount of work and material has I think been wasted', and it was 'very disheartening to the infantry soldier to see even a small part of his work scrapped and go for nothing'. The policy of relying on the divisional chief engineer, who might or might not have the necessary tactical knowledge, 'does seem to me to be courting disaster':

> The responsibility for the construction of the line and the provision for its security, both during construction and when completed, ought, I respectfully submit, to be thrown upon the infantry commander holding the line ... who presumably has got to fight in it.

Within hours, it was looking as if the men of Pompey Elliott's brigade who were holding the Aubigny Line might have to fight in it. Early on 24 April, just after 4.00am, Elliott received a message from the 57th Battalion stating that the Germans were shelling the Aubigny Line and bombarding Villers-Bretonneux. Elliott, not one to hesitate in such circumstances, immediately informed all his battalions that the anticipated German attack was probably under way, and dispatched liaison officers to the 8th and 14th AIF Brigades and to the reserve brigade (the 24th) of Heneker's division.

Swiftly discerning the probable German plan and devising an appropriate response, Pompey was soon issuing a stream of counter-attack orders. The 59th and 60th Battalions were to move through the 57th and advance on the north side of Villers-Bretonneux. The 59th was to skirt the northern edge of the Bois l'Abbé, and the 60th was to go forward further north near Hill 104. They were to join up north-east of the town and, swinging round towards the south-west, strive to re-establish a stronghold east of the town while cutting off the enemy attackers inside it in the process. Pompey told the 57th and 58th to be ready to support the 59th and 60th respectively in the execution of this bold plan. The 57th, he envisaged, could move round the south of Villers-Bretonneux and complete the envelopment of the town by his brigade. He directed the 59th and 60th to send out patrols for preparatory reconnaissance, and decided to establish an advanced brigade report centre and command post in a cowshed near the northern end of the Aubigny Line.

These dramatic developments happened to occur while the reshuffle of battalion commanders in the 15th Brigade was under way. Denehy, for example, was in the process of taking over at the 57th. In the circumstances it was sensibly decided to postpone these changes, and the colonels reverted to their accustomed commands. Denehy returned to the 58th. With Watson therefore deprived of a battalion command, Elliott decided to use him in a special intelligence role as information co-ordinator (in effect, as Pompey's eyes and ears) at the advanced brigade cowshed.

Elliott's arrangements for this 15th Brigade advance were essentially provisional. It was not yet clear whether the British had been driven back, and there was accordingly no certainty as yet that a counter-attack would be necessary. Pompey, however, had no doubt that it would be. His reaction had been 'entirely anticipatory ... in expectation of the British retiring', he later admitted. 'Unfortunately our previous experiences of them had left us fully prepared for this sort of thing'. Furthermore, as far as Pompey was concerned, General Butler's endorsement of the placement of a solitary Durham platoon in the Bois l'Abbé 'forbade us to hope that any intelligent military action could reasonably be expected from any of them from the Corps commander down'.

The messages gradually filtering through to 15th Brigade headquarters convinced Pompey that his assessment was spot on. At 7.40am a runner sent by the liaison officer he had stationed with the British panted in with a note indicating that the Germans seemed to have penetrated the front line east of Villers-Bretonneux. There was a sobering report from the 57th: a British artillery officer, hurrying forward to extricate his guns before it was too late, said that Heneker's men had retired halfway through the town. Then, from the liaison officer Pompey had sent to Stewart's 14th Brigade (the front-line Australians closest to Villers-Bretonneux), came the most disturbing news of all. This brigade, alongside Heneker's division, was yielding not an inch to the Germans, but men of its 56th Battalion located at Hill 104 could see enemy soldiers advancing north from Villers-Bretonneux. The unavoidable conclusion was that the Germans had taken control of the town and were proceeding to fan out behind the pre-attack British–Australian front line. These informative reports from the liaison officers Elliott had judiciously stationed contrasted with the limited news being provided by Heneker's division.

Pompey, predictably galvanised by these developments, decided to contact Hobbs on the telephone. In view of the alarming turn of events and the obvious need to restore the situation as soon as possible, Elliott urged Hobbs to give him the discretion to carry out the counter-attack he had organised and his men were all set to launch. 'He replied "Yes"' was all Pompey wrote when recounting the divisional commander's response. But Hobbs said more than that. His acquiescence was, in fact, heavily qualified. Pompey was only authorised to operate in the 8th Division's area if he received an 'urgent request' from the British to do so, and he had to keep Hobbs informed of whatever action he was taking. Meanwhile he could move his brigade forward to link up with the 56th Battalion, which was preparing a hot reception for the Germans north of Villers-Bretonneux along the road to Fouilloy.

But this restricted and provisional approval was good enough for Pompey. Interpreting it as basically a green light, he at once issued an order directing the 59th and 60th Battalions to proceed with the operation he had already initiated:

> Get in touch with troops on either flank. 57th Battalion will move as soon as possible echeloned to right rear of 59th and ultimately attack if required along railway to right of Villers Bretonneux clearing it by an enveloping movement. Scouts in front as soon as past Aubigny Line. All British troops to be rallied and reformed as our troops march through them by selected officers and on any hesitation to be shot. Battalions to maintain touch. 58th Battalion to prepare to move at once, reporting when ready. Objective is to restore our front line in prolongation of 14th Brigade. All units report when ready to move.

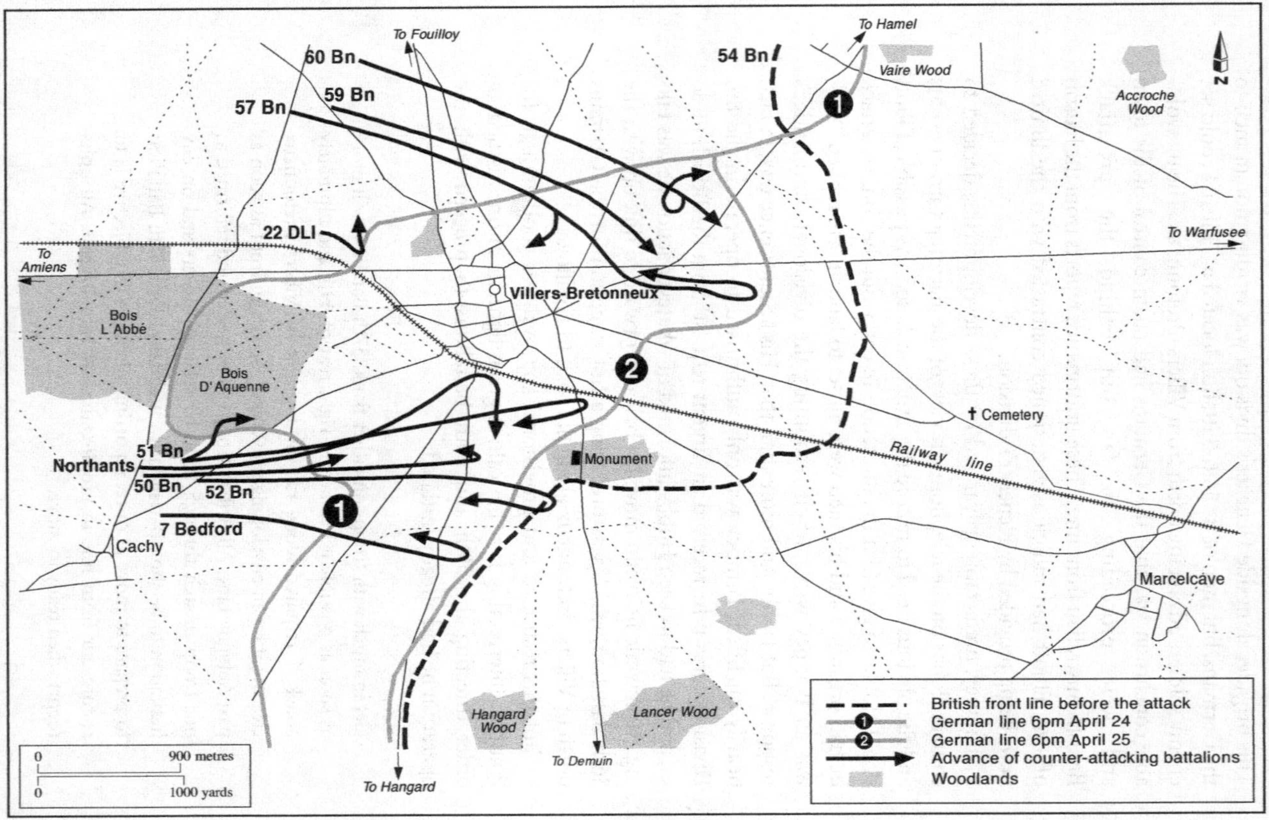
To Fouilloy
To Hamel
60 Bn
54 Bn
Vaire Wood
N
Accroche Wood
59 Bn
57 Bn
22 DLI
To Amiens
To Warfusee
Villers-Bretonneux
Bois L'Abbé
Bois D'Aquenne
Cemetery
51 Bn
Northants
50 Bn
52 Bn
Monument
Railway line
7 Bedford
Cachy
Marcelcave
Hangard Wood
Lancer Wood
To Demuin
To Hangard
0
900 metres
0
1000 yards
British front line before the attack
German line 6pm April 24
German line 6pm April 25
Advance of counter-attacking battalions
Woodlands

The battle of Villers-Bretonneux

The battle of Villers-Bretonneux

Formations and Commanders

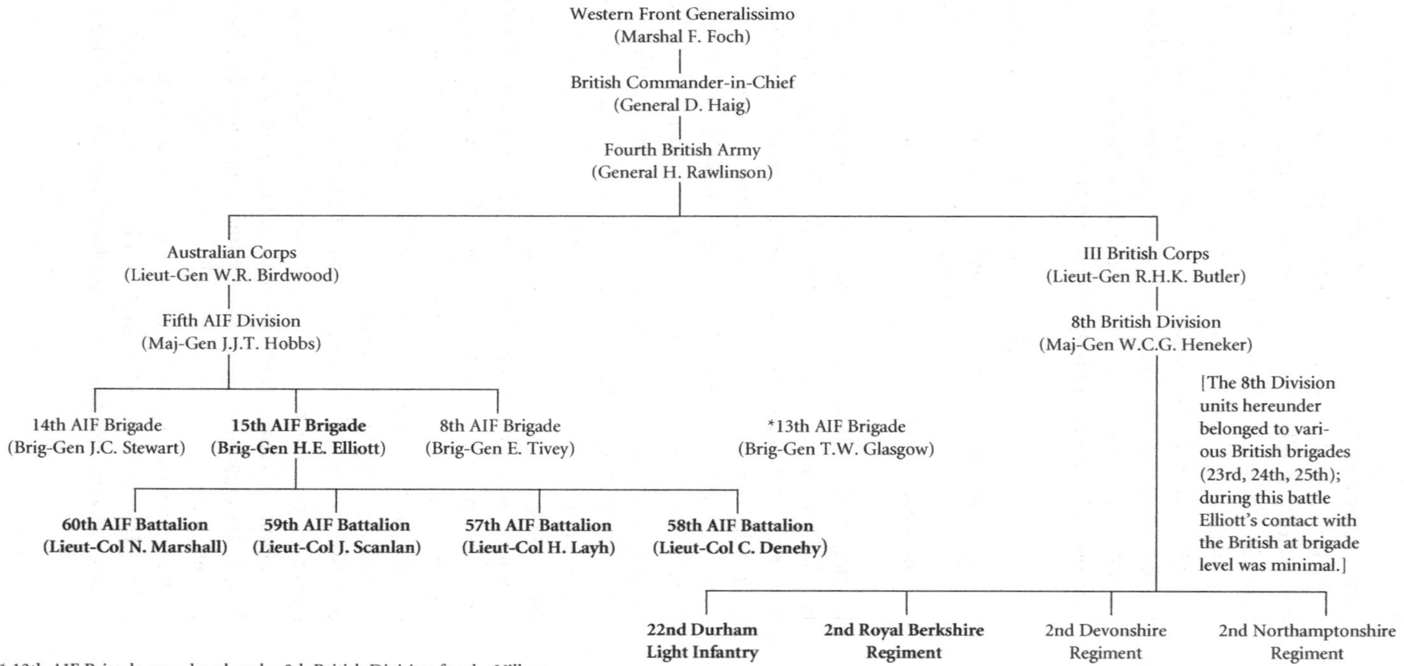

* 13th AIF Brigade was placed under 8th British Division for the Villers-Bretonneux counter-attack

Assisting the counter-attack would be the supplementary units allotted to the 15th Brigade, a troop of the 13th Light Horse and a battery of the Royal Horse Artillery. Rather than giving these units specific tasks, Elliott left the precise form of assistance up to their commanders after ensuring that the operation was carefully explained to both of them.

Hobbs, increasingly concerned about the 8th Division, rang Heneker to ensure he was aware of the latest developments and to find out what he was doing in response. According to the archival record of their conversation, Hobbs did not beat about the bush:

> Your troops have retired and our flank is in the air. Enemy is advancing from Villers Bretonneux towards Fouilloy … 15th Bde is coming in on the right of 14th Bde. Can we shell Villers Bretonneux? Are you going to make a counter attack?

Judging by the briefing that Hobbs gave Birdwood half an hour later, Heneker was not very forthcoming. 'We cannot get any information from 8th Div', reported Hobbs. That formation's headquarters had 'lost touch with their people', and 'we do not know whether they intend to counter attack'. At ten o'clock, when Hobbs had heard nothing further from Heneker, he was notified by Captain A.C. White, the liaison officer he had stationed at Heneker's headquarters, that the 8th Division was preparing to attack. Hobbs immediately phoned Elliott to inform him that the 8th Division was endeavouring to rectify the situation without outside help.

Both Australian commanders were convinced that Heneker's men would be unable to do so by themselves. But for the time being, Hobbs instructed, the 15th Brigade would have to stay put. Reiterating his directive that Elliott was not to move the brigade out of its area unless the British asked for assistance, Hobbs told him to keep it as intact as possible until such a request materialised, then to use his discretion, 'but be very careful how far you commit yourself and let me know immediately'. Pompey's compliance was reluctant but immediate. 'Stand fast as British are endeavouring to restore line themselves, but be ready for instant action', he ordered his battalion commanders.

Pompey then had to endure a prolonged and immensely frustrating delay. He had to cool his heels while Heneker ordered a series of counter-attacks involving various battalions in his division. None materialised. The 8th Division's only progress was a spontaneous advance of 150 yards by a small group in the wake of a tank, one of a number sent into action (with varying success) to counter the armoured vehicles the Germans had used earlier that morning. Hours were being frittered away, Elliott sensed, while the Germans were strengthening positions in Villers-Bretonneux that his brigade would surely have to recapture eventually: 'it was sticking out as plain as a pikestaff that we should have to counter attack sooner or later'. He at least ensured that his brigade derived some benefit from the delay by directing each of its battalions to send as many officers as possible forward to familiarise themselves with the ground, in case his proposed advance did eventuate.

Meanwhile Pompey's conviction that no successful counter-attack could be expected from the 8th Division was reinforced by reports reaching him from Watson, who was making splendid use of the light-horsemen allocated to the 15th Brigade and providing the brigadier with a stream of informative messages. 'My Light Horse patrol reports that English troops on right of 14th Brigade very low as regards morale and officers windy, fell back from last position without firing a shot', Watson reported early in the afternoon. Moreover, a corporal from the 2nd Royal Berkshires, the unit involved in the first of Heneker's abortive counter-attacks, turned up with 25 stragglers at Watson's report centre, and said (Watson told Pompey) that their major had told them 'to fall back to next ridge'. They 'had not suffered any casualties but shells had fallen close to them'.

Other officers under Elliott's command also formed unflattering impressions of the standard of British resistance. In the 59th Battalion John Christian, a 27-year-old lieutenant who hailed, like his brigadier, from the Melbourne suburb of Northcote, had led the preparatory reconnaissance that Pompey had ordered early in the morning. During the day Christian came across numerous British soldiers retiring; most were without arms or equipment and, as he observed, 'of course were useless' for defence purposes. Further back, the conduct of certain British artillery units was bitterly resented. Christian's commander, Scanlan, came across British gunners all set to open fire in poor visibility after they had withdrawn their guns a long way. The unsettled battery commander took no notice when Scanlan and Marshall warned him that he would be shooting into the 14th AIF Brigade and British infantrymen, and the Australians were only able to deter him by resorting to violent threats. And one of Scanlan's men saw Pompey remonstrating with British artillerymen about to skedaddle across the Somme: the brigadier was 'dashing about on his horse, brandishing a revolver, threatening to shoot the gunners if they pulled out'. The 'flabbergasted' gunners decided to stay (and were soon doing their bit).

In fact, the British had endured an undeniably harrowing ordeal. The Germans had launched their attack, as a staff officer in Heneker's division recalled, with 'a truly terrific bombardment that brought us bounding from our beds'; it was 'the heaviest of my experience', and 'the result was appalling'. Unnerved by this tremendous shellfire, the 8th Division men—many of them young, inexperienced, newly arrived reinforcements—then had to cope with a startling apparition. German tanks were emerging from the dense mist and smoke, and advancing remorselessly towards them. A British front-line officer later described how his company was 'raked' by unusually 'sudden, accurate and deadly' machine-gun fire. When it momentarily ceased he 'put his head up and saw an enormous and terrifying iron pill-box ... bearing straight down on him'. These tanks, creating havoc and some panic, spearheaded the Germans' rapid capture of Villers-Bretonneux. So swift was their progress that for the commander of the 2nd Devonshire Regiment, positioned south-west of Villers-Bretonneux well back from the front line (his battalion was supposed to carry out Heneker's second abortive counter-attack), the first inkling of the enemy advance was, Bean wrote, 'the appearance of the nose of one monster over the parapet of his headquarters'.

While Elliott was kept on the sidelines and his frustration and fury mounted, he was on the receiving end of an implicit rebuke. At 12.35pm Hobbs sent him a peremptory instruction, directing him to delete from his earlier order the sentence authorising his officers to shoot any of the British soldiers they encountered who hesitated when called on to rally. The order Hobbs was amending had been issued hours earlier; a copy had reached Fifth Division at 10.50am. If Hobbs found that sentence objectionable, why did he take so long to overrule it? The answer, Pompey suspected, was that Hobbs had himself been directed to act. He was probably right. The curt message was dispatched to Pompey from Fifth Division immediately after Peck, Hobbs's senior staff officer, had reported developments in a telephone discussion with Brudenell White, the power behind the throne at the Australian Corps. Moreover, in a subsequent conversation, Elliott sensed that Hobbs (whose recent experiences had left him decidedly unimpressed with the British) may not really have disapproved of the order.

Pompey always maintained that in the prevailing circumstances his action was warranted. At that 'extremely critical time' it was essential to stop the British 'fugitives', and his controversial order—which remained in force for some time after Elliott passed on his superiors' cancellation of it to his battalion commanders, because some of them were 'too busy to send it on further'—was implemented 'with excellent results'. It was 'not necessary to resort to extremes at all'. Like his notorious anti-looting execution threat a few weeks earlier, Pompey was confident 'no one would be at all likely to become a candidate for a Test Case to try the legality of the order'. Sure enough, when the 'panicky British ... were quietly but firmly informed' of it, they were 'by association with our men ... at once restored to discipline and sanity'.

Elliott also claimed that it was important to send a two-fold message to his own brigade. Some of his men, 'exasperated' by instances of British 'cowardice', 'were getting into a dangerous temper', and the order 'was directed therefore as much towards soothing this natural feeling of irritation of my men against the British as an actual direction to my officers to take action'. Furthermore, with historical episodes confirming that even the best soldiers sometimes get rattled and need steadying direction, it was also a prudent step 'to prevent the panic extending to our own troops'. Therefore, 'knowing my military history, I was prepared, even with my own troops—there were none finer in the world—to act as I did' in order to prevent any 'possibility of a general rout'. Bean was unconvinced. He described Elliott's action as

> a gross error of judgment and quite unnecessary; for, order or no order, his company and platoon leaders would, in the last resort, have tried to steady the defenders, whether their own men or the British, by threats of shooting.

As the hours ticked by on 24 April, and morning became afternoon, Elliott and his brigade waited impatiently to be called into action. Unbeknown to them there was plenty of activity behind the scenes, even if the endeavours that the 8th Division claimed to be making seemed distinctly unproductive. The news that Heneker's division had been driven out of Villers-Bretonneux caused consternation among his superiors, and produced a series of demands for a counter-attack without delay. Even Foch, at the very top of the military hierarchy, told Rawlinson in no uncertain terms that its immediate recapture was an urgent priority. Haig reacted to the unpalatable news by proceeding to Rawlinson's headquarters himself.

Rawlinson had already taken action of his own, prior to Foch's message and Haig's visit, ordering the 13th AIF Brigade (then billetted north of the Somme as part of his Fourth Army reserve) to march south at once 'to assist in the recapture of Villers-Bretonneux, which was imperative for the security of Amiens'. Meanwhile Rawlinson was hastily revising his optimistic pre-attack appraisal of Heneker's recruits a few hours after they had lost the crucial position he had staked his reputation on retaining. These 'reinforcements ... are composed of young boys who were under fire for the first time', he explained, and 'I fear that the heavy bombardment ... must have shaken these children a good deal' (an interesting assessment from the commander probably most responsible for those 'children' being there in the first place).

The commander between Rawlinson and Heneker, Lieutenant-General R.H.K. Butler, was becoming as frustrated with Heneker as Hobbs and Elliott were already. Having heard that Pompey's brigade was poised to counter-attack, Butler advised Heneker to 'await arrival of this Brigade and synchronise his attack with it'. But when Heneker claimed that this was impossible because his latest projected counter-attack was under way, Butler yielded. He then contacted Hobbs, and urged him to keep in close touch with Heneker. Even though Heneker kept insisting that his own units would be able to clear up the situation, Butler urged Hobbs 'to act as far as possible in close co-operation' with the obstinate 8th Division commander. Although Hobbs felt that his proffered assistance had been 'practically ignored' by Heneker, he obligingly contacted the British general again and reaffirmed that the Fifth Division was 'prepared to assist and co-operate in any way'. But the unsatisfactory status quo continued to prevail. The Germans had control of Villers-Bretonneux, and were no doubt strengthening their positions in and around the town as rapidly as they could. Heneker and his 8th Division were unable to remove them, yet kept rejecting offers and suggestions of assistance.

At this stage there was apparently a significant intervention by Rawlinson. A key figure in this development was Lieutenant-Colonel Edward Beddington, a capable staff officer (Brudenell White later claimed he had 'never known a better') now based at Rawlinson's Fourth Army headquarters after influential service on the staffs of Heneker and Gough. According to Beddington, Rawlinson told Butler (in Beddington's presence) to organise a combined counter-attack incorporating the Australians, and then sent Beddington to Butler's headquarters to ensure that the operation was carried out as prescribed by him. Beddington is unreliable on detail: 'my recollection ... is not too clear', he admitted in the version of events he gave the British official historian well after the war. In that account he estimated that Rawlinson's decisive conversation with Butler occurred at 2.00pm, and the version in his even less reliable 1964 memoirs timed it at 9.00am. It seems, in fact, to have taken place at about 11.30am. Moreover, Beddington claimed that from the outset he and Rawlinson felt that the operation they were authorising should be carried out at night, yet Rawlinson was ordering Butler at 11.30am to make this happen 'as soon as possible' (and seems to have assured Foch it would occur at 2.00pm).

Nevertheless, Rawlinson did insist that Villers-Bretonneux had to be recaptured—'We *must* get it back whatever happens', he declared in a letter that afternoon—and his timely intervention did evidently steel Butler to deal more firmly with Heneker. When the corps commander duly passed on Rawlinson's instructions, Heneker reacted oddly, as if quailing under pressure (a tendency characteristic of Heneker when his fragile assertiveness was challenged, according to some observers). Firstly, he rang Hobbs, asking the Australian commander he had treated shabbily for hours to come to his headquarters, because of some mysterious adverse development he could not explain on the phone (Hobbs sent a staff officer). He then rang Butler's headquarters in a state of evident desperation, and (according to the archival record) lodged a plaintive protest: 'Impossible to arrange counter-attack as we don't know where we are and where enemy is'. Butler's staff had to reassure the rattled divisional commander, who had wasted invaluable time arriving at that despondent conclusion and was contemplating a withdrawal of his own headquarters.

After protracted deliberations and discussions involving Butler, Hobbs, Heneker, a number of brigadiers (including Elliott), and numerous staff officers, a plan gradually crystallised during the afternoon. The 13th AIF Brigade, having been summoned from Fourth Army reserve that morning by Rawlinson, would attack south of Villers-Bretonneux; Elliott's brigade would execute an equivalent advance to the north, and join up with the 13th Brigade east of the town; and Heneker's division would assist in a subsidiary capacity, mopping up the Germans caught inside these two pincers. It was essentially the envelopment manoeuvre Pompey had been vigorously advocating and itching to launch since before dawn.

The 13th Brigade, having been placed under Heneker's command, was by now arriving west of Villers-Bretonneux after an eight-mile march from billets north of the Somme. Its commander, Brigadier-General William Glasgow, was a capable Queenslander whose previous commands had been in the Light Horse. Rugged and reticent, Glasgow lacked Elliott's emotional volatility and tactical flair, but was just as tough and resolute. He and some of his staff had earlier hastened to Heneker's headquarters, where the available information was vague and the atmosphere discouragingly bleak. Glasgow decided to find out what he could about the situation from those engaged further forward. After doing so, he called at Blangy-Tronville and spoke briefly to Elliott before returning to 8th Division headquarters, where he reviewed the latest developments with Heneker and attended a conference that discussed the forthcoming operation. At this conference Glasgow was unimpressed by what he considered the effete contributions of his counterpart brigadiers in the 8th Division (R.C. Haig of the 24th Brigade, then in reserve, was soon to be sacked, but Clifford Coffin of the 25th Brigade adjoining Stewart's 14th AIF Brigade had been awarded the VC in 1917, and G.W.St.G. Grogan was to win that decoration leading the 23rd Brigade a month later). During these discussions Glasgow insisted on several changes to the operation plan, postponing the start by two hours and altering the direction of his brigade's advance.

Was Elliott present during these discussions at 8th Division headquarters? His own records and recollections of the day's events make no mention of his attendance; it was only after Elliott's death that Bean realised that the reminiscences of the few surviving participants disagreed on this question. Glasgow and two of his staff officers did not recall Pompey being at Heneker's headquarters with them, and the communications records suggest that the main, and possibly exclusive, source of information for Elliott about the unfolding arrangements for the operation was Hobbs. This is logical. Contrary to a number of accounts—including the British official history—Elliott's brigade, unlike Glasgow's, was not placed under Heneker until very late in the piece. At 7.15pm Hobbs sought Brudenell White's advice about who should be controlling the operation; White suggested this was a matter for Butler to determine. It was only when this question was referred to III Corps shortly afterwards that Butler decided to place all units engaged in the counter-attack (a third brigade, the British 54th, was making a complementary advance to the south of Glasgow's brigade) under 8th Division for the operation; Elliott was not informed until after eight o'clock.

However, Glasgow's intelligence officer felt that Pompey did attend Heneker's headquarters at some stage, and the Fifth Division liaison officer stationed there, Captain A.C. White, was unequivocal. According to White, the morale of Heneker and his staff was low, and communication with the reserve 24th Brigade was non-existent; 'their ability to launch a counter-attack themselves was very slight'. When they learned that the AIF brigades would be doing it for them 'their delight was unbounded'. Elliott as well as Glasgow was at Heneker's headquarters, White assured Bean. The burly brigadiers 'seemed to dwarf the 8th Div staff', and Pompey had made a memorably cantankerous retort as they left. When Heneker, winding up the conference, said he wanted progress reports 'at least every hour', Pompey's response as he strode out the door was blunt: 'You'll be bloody lucky to hear from me before morning'. Such a remark is consistent with Pompey's frame of mind after Heneker had sidelined his brigade for most of the day. As late as 1936 Bean was still trying to clarify if and when Elliott was present at Heneker's headquarters, and apparently never managed to do so.

Whether or not Elliott was at Heneker's headquarters with Glasgow, it is clear that the Australian brigadiers had a subsequent conference of their own. Glasgow arrived at Blangy-Tronville at around 8.00pm (having been authorised to establish his brigade headquarters there with Elliott's), and they quickly compared plans. Making co-ordinated arrangements in such a hurry was not easy, especially as their brigades would be attempting to join up east of Villers-Bretonneux after advancing around different sides of it in the dark. As they evaluated the latest version of the operation blueprint, Glasgow spotted a potential snag concerning the interaction of the 57th Battalion with his own brigade, and suggested an alteration. Elliott readily agreed. He incorporated the change in the final briefing he gave his battalion commanders after summoning them to Blangy-Tronville—using his salvaged French cars to collect and return them afterwards—to ensure that they understood what their men had to do, despite the multiple amendments to the plan since he had initiated it some fifteen hours earlier.

Three battalions would be attacking in the 15th Brigade's complex night manoeuvre. The 59th and the 60th would advance around the northern side of Villers-Bretonneux towards Hill 104, as in Elliott's original plan—the 59th on the right, closest to the town, with the 60th on its left—until reaching the first objective, the road to Hamelet. There, the line was to swing round towards the south, pivoting on its right, and proceed to the road connecting Villers-Bretonneux with Hamel. According to the plan, the 60th would then be in touch with the right flank of Stewart's 14th Brigade, while the 59th on the right would have reached the main east-west Roman road beyond Villers-Bretonneux.

The 57th's role had changed most during the day. Concern that the 13th Brigade might not be able to reach the Roman road had prompted Hobbs to ask Elliott just after 5.00pm if his brigade could extend its final objective south of that major thoroughfare. Pompey acquiesced, directing the 57th to secure this extra ground, and making arrangements for that battalion to advance around the southern side like Glasgow's brigade—until Glasgow suggested, and Elliott accepted, that sending it around the north side might be preferable. At the last minute, then, Pompey directed Layh's battalion to advance behind the 59th. Two of its companies were to cross the Roman road and establish themselves between the 59th on that road and the 13th Brigade 500 yards south of it. The other two 57th companies would be tucked in behind, facing Villers-Bretonneux—protecting the brigade's rear in a role Pompey likened to 'a "shepherding" job as it is called in Australian football', and awaiting the nod to deal with the Germans inside the town.

Elliott arranged for the 59th and 60th to have Stokes mortars and extra machine-guns, and obtained 32 guides (one for each platoon in those battalions) from Stewart's brigade. He also ensured that the attackers were given a drink of hot tea and (as one of them recorded appreciatively) 'plenty of hot stew, as much as we could stuff into us'.

Pompey had given his men all the help he could in the circumstances. It was now up to them.

The operation was certainly a daunting challenge. Pompey's men had been on the alert since dawn. It had been a long, frustrating day. As one of their officers later wrote, they were

> eager, they had some knowledge of the ground, they felt that the crisis would not pass without offensive action for them … they … knew the fighting instincts of their commander, and they could not understand the delay.

Prolonged 'deadly suspense like this' was a severe strain, observed David Whinfield, a veteran 60th stretcher-bearer:

> Since 10 last night we have been rigged up all ready to march off to support and now it is to counterattack for some ground lost by the Tommies this morning. We were moving off at 10 last night, 4 am, 9 am, 1 pm, 5 and now 7. It is a terrible time. How will men hang on at this awful cruelty? Nerves are being shredded. Men's future strength is being heavily drawn from. My nerve is weak. It is too much for mortals.

(Despite his dread of the looming engagement, Whinfield managed to steel himself to participate so effectively that he was awarded the Military Medal.)

The manoeuvre now before Elliott's men was unusually complex. They would be carrying it out in the dark, against an enemy full of confidence after its comprehensive success that morning and its consolidation during the day. In addition, the artillery support for the counter-attackers would be minimal. Because the location of German positions was unclear and many British guns had moved back during the day to unaccustomed sites, neither a preliminary bombardment nor a creeping barrage was likely to be effective. With the element of surprise all-important, the artillery's contribution would be confined to brief bursts against a few specific targets after the counter-attack commenced. This hastily planned proposal to send two independent spearheads deep into German-held territory in the dark, with meagre artillery assistance and instructions to join up with each other, was certainly audacious. Compounding the audacity was the fact that one of the brigades involved was unfamiliar with the ground and had just marched eight miles to get to the rear of the battle zone.

It was an exceptionally risky enterprise, as many anxious insiders realised. Among them was Charles Bean, on the scene as usual when a significant AIF operation was in the offing. He had a soft spot for the 13th Brigade, which had incurred some 500 casualties at Dernancourt only three weeks earlier. That night he felt very pessimistic, as his diary attests:

> One cannot help thinking of our magnificent 13th Bde going over —as they may be doing now. I don't believe they have a chance … I scarcely think it will come off, surely … Went to bed thoroughly depressed … feeling certain that this hurried attack would fail hopelessly.

Others shared his concern. Downing felt that the operation had not even 'the remotest chance of success'. To a concurring 59th veteran, it seemed 'an almost impossible proposition'.

A worrying night was in store for every senior commander involved. Pompey Elliott was no exception. To ease the tension as he waited for news, he compiled a rambling response to an article he had spotted in a recent issue of the *British–Australasian* (a London weekly catering mainly for Australians in the United Kingdom) opposing the conferring of titles in British dominions. Elliott took a different view, attributing the widespread hostility to such titles in Australia to 'that same unworthy jealousy of success which is so unfortunate a blot alike upon ancient and modern democracy'—in other words, as he might have put it if writing in a later era, to the tall poppy syndrome. Titles justifiably awarded (and Elliott conceded that they were not always bestowed appropriately) constituted a useful incentive to perform worthwhile endeavours beneficial to the nation; the 'foolish clamor' for their abolition, he asserted, should be ignored. A potent factor in this hostility, he continued, was 'the boasted equality of man' that was 'a delusion and a snare':

> Men never have been and never can be 'equal'—in this world at least. Nowhere is this so fully exemplified as on the Battlefield … No one is quicker or more acute than our men to note the relative value of their officers. No one is abler to spot the 'dud', the

> incompetent and the cowardly, the cad and the cur, and act accordingly.

Some days later, when Elliott sent this treatise to the *British–Australasian*, he explained in a covering note how it came to be written, apologising if it seemed 'somewhat incoherent' in parts. It might seem a strange thing to do at such a time, he added, 'but when one has given an order' which 'means the certain death ... of many a dear friend'—'no matter what care or thought has been given to the preparations', and irrespective of 'whether victory or defeat crowns one's efforts'—the 'concentration ... required to write the essay dulls one's nerves a little to what is going on'. Elliott was not the only AIF general to occupy himself with correspondence at times of acute stress. It was 'the very best way of relieving the tension', Monash wrote that same month.

What was actually happening on the battlefield while Pompey was trying to distract himself from worry? His brigade had not started well. After the final clarifying conference at Blangy-Tronville, it was necessary for his battalion commanders to return to their units and brief their company commanders before the advance could begin. With zero hour at 10.00pm and the start line (the Cachy-Fouilloy road) two miles from their bivouac, time was tight for the assault battalions. The 59th and 60th were soon on their way, however, with the aid of guides positioned along the route as sentries. A snag then arose concerning C Company of the 59th, which was commanded by Captain Fred Bursey MC, who had started the war as a private in the 7th Battalion. One of the sentries advised Bursey not to venture across a certain area because the Germans had landed gas shells there. While detouring his men around this area, Bursey lost direction—it was well and truly dark by now—with the result that ten o'clock came and went without C Company putting in an appearance at the rendezvous. Because the allotted place of Bursey's missing company in the advance was on the far left of the 59th, closest to the 60th, the leading battalions were still not in contact when the attack should have started. Aggravating this inauspicious state of affairs was a German barrage on the road that was the assembly point.

The advent of Norman Marshall proved decisive. Marshall was on his way to the advanced headquarters Pompey had fixed in a quarry behind Hill 104; but, sensing that progress might be hindered by the particularly dark night, he decided to check on how things were going at the start line. The misty murkiness was intensified by the dust and haze of bursting shells and dense cloud cover; later, when the almost full moon was occasionally discernible through gaps in the clouds, visibility fleetingly improved. Marshall reacted to the confusion he encountered at the assembly point by taking control of the whole line. Directing that no-one was to advance without his approval, he quickly assessed the situation, assisted in particular by his trusted reconnaissance experts, Pizzey and Gannon, and the intelligence officer of his former battalion, Lieutenant Doutreband. Repeated efforts to find Bursey's company proving unsuccessful, measures to cover its absence were already being implemented; Marshall agreed that the reserve company of the 59th should replace it. At Marshall's instigation Pizzey, Gannon, and Doutreband had carefully calculated the compass bearings for the changes of direction during the advance; this and other information had to be passed on to officers in the replacement company. The brigade eventually moved off nearly two hours late.

It was a complicated manoeuvre, especially in the dark, but Pompey's men hurried forward to make up for lost time. They were 'tugging and straining at the leash', Scanlan noted. Keeping direction in the misty blackness was relatively straightforward, particularly for the 59th companies on the right, thanks to blazing buildings in Villers-Bretonneux which had been set alight by ancillary shellfire. Silent and resolute, Pompey Elliott's soldiers proceeded up the slope, taut with anticipation, excitement, and dread. Who would be the unlucky ones this time? Their splendid morale and determination were reinforced by the realisation that it was the third anniversary of the original Anzac Day, and they had an opportunity to commemorate it with a special exploit. The sporadic shellfire and obstructive wire they encountered on their way forward did not deter them. They pressed on until they reached the first objective, where there was a brief pause while the leaders checked positioning and direction. Bursey's missing company, having followed the advance after arriving at the rendezvous as the rest of the 59th was leaving it, now took up the forward position initially allocated to it.

Its scouts, pushed forward as a screen during this short pause, reported enemy soldiers close ahead. So did their counterparts in the adjoining 59th company commanded by another young veteran transferred from the 7th Battalion after Gallipoli, Captain Eric Young, a

23-year-old St Kilda bookkeeper; he had been wounded during the advance but kept going. Young responded to the reports that Germans were close at hand by strengthening the line with some cohesive adjustments and an extension of the right (towards Villers-Bretonneux). This movement was evidently detected; visibility had been increased by the buildings ablaze in the town. German flares went up; one landed near moving Australians and kept burning. They stopped still as one—a tribute to their training and discipline—but a machine-gun just ahead opened up erratically. In response Young gave, 'in a calm, easy voice' (according to a nearby sergeant), the order to charge.

With all the pent-up nervous energy that had accumulated during this long, suspense-filled day unleashed at last, Pompey's men sprang forward with a wild, terrifying yell. 'That ended any further attempt at checking direction', observed Scanlan, who described the raw spontaneous roar by his men as 'sufficient to make the enemy's blood run cold'. The whole line responded, the intimidating cry being taken up by the 57th men along with the 59th and by the 60th to the north. They all surged forward with an exhilarating, irresistible momentum. There was a desperate hail of machine-gun and rifle fire from the Germans, but the roar alarmed them, and their shooting was generally inaccurate. Most of them were caught by surprise and overwhelmed. Many were dispatched by the bayonet. According to Elliott, his men had perfected 'the throat jab', a thrust 'under the chin and upwards into the spinal chord' which was

> most deadly and difficult to parry ... Struck thus a man dies easily, quickly and painlessly, often without a cry or movement. Our men practise it assiduously ... and in a melee it makes them invincible.

The devastating 15th Brigade charge swiftly overcame all resistance in its path. Piercing various wired obstacles and exuberantly pursuing German runaways, Pompey's men penetrated deep into enemy-held territory.

While all this was happening Pompey was back at his headquarters waiting, wondering and writing his epistle to the *British–Australasian*. After his brigade left the first objective, he affirmed afterwards,

> the fight became a soldiers' fight purely and simply, and neither myself nor the Battalion Commanders could exercise any control

> upon it. The success was due to the energy and determination of junior commanders and the courage of the troops. I could only guess what was going on, but as there was no news of our men being driven back I was able to assume that all was going well.

Just after 3.00am, with incoming reports confirming satisfactory progress, Elliott asked Hobbs for permission to use his reserve battalion. Hobbs approved. Pompey contacted Denehy immediately, and gave him flexible instructions:

> Our attack is reported to have been very successful ... You will move at once into reserve line of front system ... You will be prepared (1) to reinforce front line if heavily counterattacked or (2) to further exploit success if conditions favourable by pushing along high ground towards Warfusee-Abancourt ... It must be left to your discretion as to how far you consider it safe to advance as both flanks may be somewhat exposed.

Indeed they were. On the left the tendency of the advancing companies to be drawn towards the fighting produced a gap between the 60th and the adjacent 14th Brigade, but awareness of this opening was only beginning to filter through to Elliott's headquarters. His main focus, as far as his brigade's flanks were concerned, was understandably the situation on the right, where the 57th was to link up with the 13th Brigade south of the Roman road.

How were Glasgow's men faring? Their progress had been severely hampered by enemy machine-guns among the trees to the left of their starting position. This wooded area was supposed to have been cleared that afternoon by Heneker's division, but assurances given to 13th Brigade leaders that this had been done were soon shown to be false when fire from machine-gunners ensconced there accounted for numerous 51st Battalion men. This impediment, which was threatening to stop the brigade's advance on the left, was only removed when Lieutenant C.W.K. Sadlier of the 51st led a party directly into the trees to deal with them; this dashing and successful initiative, described by Bean as 'extraordinarily bold', earned for its leader the Victoria Cross. Glasgow's men encountered further obstacles on their way forward—more machine-gun posts, wire, other strongpoints—and casualties were significantly higher than in the 15th Brigade. But they persevered, and some of them advanced close to their final objective before the surviving leaders decided that the most prudent option was to fall back and consolidate a position south of the centre of Villers-Bretonneux.

Accordingly, there was no sign of the 13th Brigade when the officers with the leading 15th Brigade groups were trying to work out where they should bring their exhilarating advance to a halt. Their decision to consolidate along the road to Hamel was also influenced by a measure of confusion about their ultimate objective. Bean and some other historians have been inclined to assign the blame for this uncertainty, in part at least, to Elliott, because the goal he had set for his men in his earlier orders did not coincide with the objective later fixed by Butler (and confirmed by Hobbs). Pompey, however, insisted that his final verbal instructions to his battalion commanders resolved this inconsistency: 'I never departed from the objectives given me by the Higher Command', he claimed. Anyway, in the circumstances, as Bean acknowledged, consolidating at the Hamel road was prudent and advisable.

While Elliott's men, then, settled for positions short of their goal, and the 13th Brigade ended up considerably further back from its objective, each formation had done enough to ensure the overall success of the operation. By dawn on the anniversary of Anzac Day it was clear that this daring counter-attack had proved a triumph, confounding the profound misgivings of even informed insiders like Bean. As awareness spread of the extent of the achievement, oppressive anxiety dissolved into rapturous relief. There had been 'a feeling of tenseness' and 'apprehension' at Heneker's headquarters, noted the AIF liaison officer Captain White, but 'when the wonderful result was known early next morning, jubilation was intense'.

Pompey was not one to rest on his laurels, especially when there were loose ends to tie up, and the situation in Villers-Bretonneux itself was unresolved. Responsibility for mopping up German resistance there had been allocated to two battalions of Heneker's division. The Durhams, assigned to Elliott for the operation, were to enter the town from the north, while the 2nd Northamptonshire Regiment did likewise from the south under Glasgow's temporary command. Pompey's brief association with the Durhams reinforced his condemnation of Heneker's division. Earlier, when trying to organise the mopping-up arrangements,

Pompey had found the Durhams commander elusive and, when eventually located, full of pessimism and indecisiveness.

Accordingly, he arranged that if the task allotted to the Durhams proved—as he anticipated—beyond them, part of the 57th would do it at daybreak. A report he received from Layh at 3.30am foreshadowed the implementation of this contingency plan: Germans were still resisting in Villers-Bretonneux, there was no sign of the Durhams, and Layh was confident that the 57th would be able to handle whatever mopping-up remained to be done inside the town at daylight. When Heneker rang Elliott at 4.15am and inquired about the progress of the Durhams, Pompey replied brusquely that he had no news whatsoever; judging by their commander's earlier frame of mind, Pompey added, they had probably not moved at all. Heneker said he would assign another unit to the mopping-up duties.

At daybreak on 25 April the 57th men provisionally earmarked for the mopping-up role commenced a left-wheel manoeuvre. Their two-fold aim was to clear north-eastern Villers-Bretonneux as they swept through it, and to establish themselves south of the Roman road with a view to linking up with the 13th Brigade. They performed their task superbly—almost too well, in fact. Methodically surrounding building after building, they captured so many enemy prisoners that they were unable to supervise the return of these Germans to the rear without jeopardising their capacity to form the new line east of the town. Fortunately they came across some British infantry who were able to take over as prisoner escorts. A company of the Durhams belatedly materialised, and the 2nd Royal Berkshire Regiment, the replacement mopping-up unit sent forward at Heneker's instigation, also helped. Although Glasgow was impatient to get his brigade closer to its original objective, his men could not do so in daylight; but that night, under cover of darkness, they moved into the gap—guided forward by, among others, Lieutenant Noad (who had distinguished himself at Polygon Wood)—and linked up successfully with Noad's battalion, the 57th.

The problem on the 15th Brigade's right was now fixed, but the gap on the left remained. During the night of 24-25 April Lieutenant 'Dick' Simpson, commander of the 60th's left company, tried repeatedly to locate the 54th Battalion on the 14th Brigade's right, but was unsuccessful. When Pizzey told Marshall about the gap on the left, Marshall came immediately to inspect it for himself. With daybreak imminent,

Marshall proposed that Simpson's company should send out yet another patrol; this time he would arrange for a separate party under Gannon to set off from the 54th to meet it. But Gannon's men and the patrol under Simpson encountered German posts, and were unable to connect with each other in the murk.

Simpson was a 25-year-old telegraph clerk and sporting enthusiast of high ideals from Ballarat. He had amazed veteran 60th officers when he managed to return to the battalion despite having minimal movement in his right arm after it was almost severed at Fromelles, and he was outstanding in this engagement. When he came across an enemy post, the Germans there surrendered; but before he could enter it a nearby machine-gun opened up. The whole patrol was hit except for Simpson and his sergeant, who dived for cover. This gun prevented a safe return in daylight, and his prisoners changed their minds about surrendering. But Simpson rose to the occasion superbly. He overcame all the Germans, dragged his wounded into the trench, and looked after them all day while controlling the post and sniping effectively. After dark on 25 April Simpson involved himself in the further endeavours made to bridge the gap. Connection was successfully established just before daybreak, but with an undesirably pronounced re-entrant in the Australian line.

While Elliott was considering how to deal with this situation he was distracted by a startling directive from his British superiors. On the morning of 26 April, with the 15th Brigade back in the Australian Corps but Glasgow's brigade still assigned to Heneker, Pompey became aware of III Corps pressure on both the Australian brigades to extend their advance, without delay, to what had been the British front line on 23 April. Heneker's headquarters, with evidently unquestioning compliance, instructed the 13th Brigade accordingly. Glasgow 'has received orders from 8th Division to carry out the advance at once', Elliott informed Hobbs.

Such a venture in broad daylight across unprotected terrain in the face of alerted, well-sited German machine-gunners would be very risky. Pompey described it as 'a hairbrained suggestion'. Hobbs, influenced by Elliott's forceful objection, persuaded Heneker and Butler to let Elliott and Glasgow decide what was feasible. The brigadiers were to send out patrols, and if this reconnaissance confirmed that a daylight advance was impossible, they could wait until dark. In mid-afternoon, however, the British scotched the whole idea (at least partly, Pompey assumed, because of his vigorous protest).

Elliott, now free to concentrate on fixing the unsatisfactory re-entrant on the 60th Battalion's northern front, approved Marshall's plan for a minor operation early on 27 April. A preparatory Stokes mortar bombardment was to deal with the closest German posts, but Pizzey and Gannon felt that this assistance did not compensate for relinquishing the all-important ingredient of surprise, which had proved so potent in the main counter-attack. The mortars did the trick as far as these targeted Germans were concerned, but (as Pizzey and Gannon feared) the attackers were quickly spotted by enemy machine-gunners further away, who responded with the hottest fire Pizzey had ever experienced. The 60th platoons hit the ground at once, and reverted to gradual progress by alternate rushes forward. With Pizzey, Simpson, and Gannon distinguishing themselves again as leaders, the 60th men methodically worked their way forward and secured their objective, capturing twelve machine-guns and some prisoners. At seven o'clock the enemy unleashed an accurate retaliatory bombardment and began assembling for a counter-attack. But the captured machine-guns were used to good effect, and with timely artillery support the 60th succeeded in thwarting this thrust before it even started.

The German barrage had been severe, however. In this minor engagement the battalion lost ten officers and 80 men, more casualties than in the main counter-attack itself. Among the killed, to widespread regret, was Lieutenant Simpson. Including these 90 on 27 April, the 15th Brigade sustained 455 casualties in the whole battle. The 13th Brigade tally was 1,009. With Fromelles and Bullecourt in mind as comparisons, Villers-Bretonneux was, Bean concluded, an occasion when 'Australian casualties, if fairly severe, brought a result out of all proportion to their severity'.

On 29 April the 15th Brigade was relieved, and withdrew to the Aubigny Line. The brigadier needed respite as much as his men. A few days earlier he had inadvertently ridden into a gas-shelled area: 'though I spurred up old Darky and galloped out of it at once, it did get into my throat a little'. It was only

> the very least tiny whiff, but my throat has been very bad since. I think it is getting better now and my heart and lungs seem all right, but I can hardly speak or swallow without considerable pain and I cough and cough like whooping cough until I am very sick and

> vomit up a lot of white frothy phlegm. The Doctor thinks I will be all right in about a week from now. It is beastly stuff. I hope I won't die of gas suffocation—at times I have been absolutely gasping for breath when a fit of coughing stopped—but I feel otherwise as good as gold.

At one stage during the fighting he had such 'a very bad fit of coughing' he felt he 'would suffocate for a moment', but his inflamed throat did seem to be benefiting from the compresses he was applying to his neck.

The congratulations and commendations pouring in to 15th Brigade headquarters did not help Elliott's throat, but they certainly underlined the magnitude of the feat he and his men had accomplished. In his first letter home following the battle, after an initial lament for the 15th Brigade's casualties, his pride in its superb achievement was evident:

> we have given the Bosche an awful hiding ... some of the British got tired or scared or something and ran away, and my boys had to take back the line from the Bosche and did it wonderfully. Regular "Bouquets" of praises have just been showered on us ... So far it has only got as far as the Commander in Chief. I suppose Gen. Foch and the President and the King may be will have a say in it yet. Some people say it is the absolute best thing done yet in the war ... our boys certainly did well. Some wonderfully brave things were done.

Birdwood, who called to express his appreciation in person, was one of the well-wishers proclaiming the feat as the finest accomplishment of the whole war:

> General Birdwood really tried to be nice to me yesterday when he came around about the splendid way my boys had behaved, but he rather looked as if I had made him swallow a bit of green apple. I wore my old Australian jacket and looked as disreputable as I could too. It's a joke on these spick and span soldiers to show them that Australians have a few brains sometimes.

Conspicuously absent from the congratulatory messages and visitors pouring into Blangy-Tronville was any expression of gratitude, even a telegram, from Heneker. But a compliment that Pompey relished came from a German prisoner. He claimed that his chiefs had tumbled to the clever British ruse of disguising the real number of Australian divisions, which had to be at least 20—for a start, he declared, there had to be five different 15th Brigades!

Hobbs was delighted, but along with his praise for the 15th Brigade came a rebuke for the report Elliott had submitted before the battle about defects in the Aubigny Line. Aggrieved officers at Fifth Division, the chief engineer in particular, were indignant about Pompey's frank strictures, Hobbs told his tempestuous brigadier. In the circumstances he felt he had no alternative but to pursue, on behalf of his staff, a retraction and an apology. As Elliott informed Milly Edwards, Hobbs

> came to see me yesterday and very decently begged me when I had a grievance never to put it on paper but to send for him and tell him verbally and he'd fix it up himself—but this he said, referring to the report he had with him, would cause civil war from its caustic criticism [of] superiors.

The really galling problem for them, Pompey added, was that his objections were 'perfectly correct': 'therein as in my Polygon Wood report lies the chief sting'. Hobbs affirmed in his diary that it was not so much the criticisms themselves that he took exception to, but the 'want of tact' that Pompey had displayed in making them. Elliott confirmed this when recalling their conversation years afterwards:

> He came to me and said they were all up in arms about it. I said 'Is my report correct or is it not'. His reply was something like this. 'That's the devil of it they can't disprove it, they are afraid that when they get back to Australia those reports will be brought up against them and do them a great harm which I am sure you would not want. So next time when things go wrong don't write in as you do and rub it in, but come and tell me verbally about it and I'll put it right'.

Although Pompey felt that the complaints by Hobbs's staff were 'puerile', he proceeded to compile, as Hobbs requested, a humble pie correction. He managed to combine deferential contrition ('I desire to most emphatically repudiate any intention whatever of criticising any member of your Staff', it began) with adherence to his fundamental point that the system was flawed: even if 'by good fortune one may chance to find a genius' as chief engineer, that 'cannot in my opinion alter the radical unsoundness of the policy'.

It was not just the writing of that retraction that made 30 April an uncongenial day for Elliott. A cluster of long-range enemy shells landed uncomfortably close to his new headquarters. The opportunity of a welcome rest in reserve was no guarantee of being out of harm's way. At the time he was writing to Milly Edwards:

> The night before last we were pretty heavily shelled ... I am having dug-outs built nearby at all speed, working night and day, as a refuge—so you see we are not foolishly brave ... I have just had a letter from my wife. She says ...

But Elliott's description of the latest family news was suddenly interrupted:

> That wretched gun has just put a shell right onto our lawn. I wasn't expecting it and it gave me a start—there's another, but it's gone right over by the bridge ... There's another shell now—a dud ... Another shell—pretty close up—confound it. I don't enjoy being shelled the least bit when I am two flights of stairs up and the bottom may go under me at any moment. Hence if you find this letter somewhat incoherent you will please allow for it as I must finish it ... Oh I'm in all sorts of trouble with people for speaking my mind too freely.

At this point Elliott gave Milly an account of the controversy about the 'quite indefensible' Aubigny Line:

> [The chief engineer's] feelings have been quite hurt by my remarks and I am to be put in my proper place. I am used to that by now and these reproofs roll off my feathers like water off a duck.

'Shelling stopped, no damage', his letter ended.

Before concluding it, however, Pompey admitted to making 'caustic remarks' about another matter 'which will probably lead me into more trouble'. He was incensed to discover that one or more of the other commanders involved in the Villers-Bretonneux counter-attack were apparently claiming to have originated it. What made Pompey see red was a congratulatory GHQ pronouncement (based on a formal message from Fourth Army), which stated that the counter-attack 'was admirably planned by III Corps', and its execution by the 13th and 15th Brigades (and other units) was 'deserving of the highest praise'. Haig did evidently believe Butler deserved credit for the planning. He had called at the headquarters of his protégé on 24 April after visiting Rawlinson, and (his diary records) 'felt very pleased at the quiet methodical way' Butler was 'arranging for a counter-attack to retake the village'.

From Pompey's perspective, however, this was a flagrant personal injustice. Yet again, he seethed, British commanders of higher rank had done him in the eye. He had been ready and willing to unleash his brigade as soon as the Germans launched their attack (which, he was certain, Heneker's division would be unable to resist), but had been prevented from doing so. After pacing about his headquarters like a caged lion for hour after hour, totally frustrated, he was at last given the nod to strike, the manoeuvre being essentially the one he had been itching to carry out all that time. Now that his men (with the 13th Brigade's assistance) had pulled it off, the British commanders who had prevented him from doing it in the first place—because their own units, so they said, would be able to do it unaided, a claim he felt all along was fatuous—now had the gall to claim the credit for conceiving the whole idea.

Pompey was livid. Hardly one to conceal his ire when riled about anything, he was certainly in no mood to take this lying down. He 'had to fight everybody to get permission to do it', he assured Kate, 'and when it was done they were all breaking their necks to get or share the credit'. Elliott showed the relevant orders and messages to Bean and his colleague, the recently appointed assistant AIF correspondent Fred Cutlack, to ensure that their dispatches 'do me justice'. Pompey was in a 'very aggrieved' frame of mind, Bean noted.

Elliott also mentioned his grievance in a letter to George McCrae:

> It was entirely to preliminary training that our very substantial victory was due. Now some people are calling it the most brilliant feat of arms in the war—we are supposed to have utterly ruined 3 Divisions, from each of which we had a large number of captives

> and killed more—and are endeavouring by all means in their power to claim the credit of it. Some who opposed my request in the beginning are now unblushingly trying to usurp the entire credit.

The three German divisions most involved in the assault on Villers-Bretonneux and its recapture by the Australians all sustained substantial casualties. One had just been transferred from the Russian front. The others (including a highly rated Guards division) had already lost heavily when opposed to the 15th Brigade earlier in April in the Hamel sector.

There were indeed, as Elliott surmised, a number of commanders claiming to have devised the operation. Butler did not distance himself from his superiors' praise. Even Heneker was jockeying for position in the credit queue. Having frittered away precious hours by insisting throughout the morning that his division would clear up the situation without help, only to conclude in despair that he could not organise a counter-attack because he did not know where his men or the Germans were, Heneker brazenly attempted to make a virtue of incapability, claiming it was his idea to carry out the operation 'under cover of darkness with a full moon'.

In fact, by pressing for an early evening start (until Glasgow insisted it had to be much later) Heneker—and Butler as well—were ensuring that the operation would be undertaken, initially at least, in daylight. And the prompt 8th Division endorsement of the rash III Corps proposal to push the Australian brigades forward in daylight on 26 April further impugns Heneker's dubious claim to be a judicious advocate of night enterprises. Illuminating the unreliability of Heneker's 'Narrative of Operations' is the astounding claim in it that his division had 'successfully accomplished' its preparatory task of clearing the wooded area on the 13th Brigade's left, with the result that 'the counter-attack was not interfered with from this wood at all'. In fact, the Germans who were positioned there practically brought the left of the advance to a halt—it was only able to proceed after the exceptional VC-winning exploit by Lieutenant Sadlier and his party—and Heneker himself asked Butler early on 26 April for tanks to deal with the Germans who were still there.

Pompey was not aware, however, that the commanders he regarded as usurpers were not confined to the British army. Hobbs, having heard about this GHQ pronouncement during a visit to 15th Brigade headquarters where Pompey was huffing and puffing about it, proceeded to record his own reflections in the privacy of his diary:

> Our people have had very trying experience with British people under whose control they have temporarily been. III Corps in an order issued claim credit for the admirable planning of the night operation on the 24/25th. I really planned it, but I felt I should never get the credit of it. My experience of higher British command this last 4 weeks has not been very inspiring and has at times been very trying indeed to me and my staff, and the conduct of some of the troops through the ignorance, neglect and I am almost tempted to say—but I won't, I'll say nervousness of their officers—has had a very depressing effect on me and I expect many of my officers and men.

After the war Hobbs reiterated his view that he was entitled to be recognised as the commander who planned the famous counter-attack.

As for Pompey, he maintained his rage on this issue for the rest of his life. Was he justified? Unravelling the complicated sequence of events on 24 April 1918 is a challenging exercise. It is clear that Elliott had formulated his plan by dawn, and copies of his orders implementing it reached Hobbs at Fifth Division during the morning. After Rawlinson directed Butler shortly before midday to organise a combined operation involving the Australians, Butler had (as his report stated) 'numerous telephonic conversations' with Hobbs and Heneker. During those discussions, Hobbs recalled long afterwards, Butler 'asked for my proposals in connection with the counter attack, which I gave him, and which with slight alteration were carried out ... that night'. Hobbs pressed his solution with a vigour born of exasperation:

> I was much upset at the time, and I need scarcely say Elliott equally so, with the refusal to accept our assistance early in the day, which I still believe would have been effective and have saved or, at all events, minimised the heavy losses suffered by the 13th Australian Infantry Brigade in the counter attack.

By contending that he 'really planned it', Hobbs was conceivably referring to his success in persuading Butler (and, through him, Heneker) that an envelopment manoeuvre, as instigated by Pompey, was the best approach.

But this notion—that Elliott's pre-dawn idea was translated to Butler that afternoon via Hobbs as conduit and advocate—is contradicted by Beddington's reminiscences. The recollections Beddington provided for the British official history (supplied after Rawlinson's death), and those in his little-known subsequent autobiography, emphasised the crucial intervention of the army commander he was serving (and promoted the significance of his own role in the process). According to Beddington, Rawlinson told Butler precisely how the counter-attack was to be carried out. He sent Beddington to Butler and then Heneker to ensure compliance with minimal variations, a task Beddington successfully accomplished. Result—a stunning triumph produced by the deceased army commander and his admirable, ultra-efficient staff officer.

However, Beddington's versions are marred by inaccuracies and exaggerations. It is true that III Corps records suggest that Rawlinson probably specified to Butler that the operation was to involve the Fifth AIF Division, the 13th Brigade, and Heneker's division, but how precisely he directed Butler beyond that is not clear. Among the indications that planning was not cut and dried at that stage are the tenor of the subsequent conversations involving Butler, Hobbs, and Heneker, and also Rawlinson's assessment that the operation 'was admirably planned by III Corps'. Although it was certainly feasible that the envelopment idea could have independently occurred to more than one commander, Elliott, as Bean acknowledged,

> in the week before the 8th Division came into the line, had more or less established it as the ready made scheme for recapturing Villers-Bretonneux, urging it, either personally or through General Hobbs, on most of his superiors.

Accordingly, his claim to have been its principal architect is compelling.

It was no wonder that the other commanders were eager to associate themselves with such a triumph. By recapturing Villers-Bretonneux in brilliant style, the counter-attackers not only confounded the widespread anxiety and pessimism about this perilous operation; they also succeeded in denying the enemy a tactically vital objective that was never threatened again—the dangerous thrust towards Amiens was stymied for good. The outstanding feat was acclaimed by numerous commanders all the way up to Generalissimo Foch, who raved about the 'altogether astonishing valiance' of the Australian brigades.

'In my opinion', wrote General Monash a week after the battle, 'this counter-attack, at night, without artillery support, is the finest thing yet done in the war, by Australians or any other troops'. Brigadier-General Grogan, a participant at Villers-Bretonneux himself, agreed. Long afterwards he described this 'successful counter-attack by night across unknown and difficult ground, at a few hours notice' as 'perhaps the greatest individual feat of the war'. To Grogan's staff captain, P.A. Ledward, it was certainly 'the most wonderful performance' he was familiar with in his entire war experience. Another English officer, Neville Lytton, whose vivid and varied war experiences included both hazardous front-line service and senior GHQ responsibilities, was well-placed to provide an informed assessment of the operation's significance:

> the importance of Villers-Bretonneux cannot be over-estimated. ... The Australians ... made a counter-attack at night which was completely successful ... one of the most astounding manoeuvres of the war. ... the battlefield discipline of the Australians must be absolutely perfect, no matter what their billet discipline may be ... Even if the Australians had achieved nothing else during this war but the recapture of Villers-Bretonneux, they would have won the right to be considered among the greatest fighting races of the world.

This marvellous achievement at Villers-Bretonneux was the culmination of the AIF's substantial contribution to the arrest of the German onslaught in March and April 1918. The Australians were of critical importance, and not just at the Somme. Earlier in April the First AIF Division was in the process of being transported south to join the other Australian divisions then securing the entire British front in the Somme region when it was hastily redirected north to Hazebrouck to counter alarming German penetration in that sector. One of its first units to arrive just in time was the 7th Battalion, which was rushed into the breach and instructed to hold a precarious portion of front no less than four miles long. In this desperate situation the staunch resistance of the battalion formerly commanded by Pompey Elliott was instrumental in a transformation during the next few days. The front was stabilised, and the Germans were halted before they reached Hazebrouck.

In these dramatic weeks, the climax of the entire war, Australians were influencing the destiny of the world as never before and rarely, if ever, since. The adjutant of the 2nd Northamptonshires at Villers-Bretonneux (who later became a major-general and a military historian) saluted 'the personal ascendancy of the Australian soldier on the battlefield which made him the best infantryman of the war and perhaps of all time'. Another British officer involved in the battle, Captain Ledward, was similarly eulogistic:

> it is my considered opinion that the Australians ... were better in a battle than any other troops on either side ... it seems to me indisputable that a greater number of them were personally indomitable ... I am glad they were on our side, and I believe that the journalists in spite of all they wrote about them didn't tell the half of their really heroic corporate qualities.

Will Dyson, the famous Australian cartoonist who was with Charles Bean at Villers-Bretonneux after joining the AIF as a war artist, included this tribute to his countrymen in a letter to his brother (the well-known writer Edward Dyson) shortly after the stunning counter-attack:

> the boys are more eager, cheerful, bucked up and full of fight than ever before. Weather is good, food is good and they are at the height of their reputation. What they have done is in so striking a contrast to what the others did not do .... God alone knows what terrible things are coming to them, but whatever they are they will meet them as they have met everything in the past. These bad men, these ruffians, who will make the life of Australian magistrates busy when they return with outrages upon all known municipal bye-laws and other restrictions upon the free life—they are of the stuff of heroes and the most important thing on earth at this blessed moment.

At this momentous time no AIF commander was more prominent or more controversial than Pompey Elliott.

CHAPTER SEVENTEEN

'A Profound Sense of Injustice':

The supersession grievance

MAY 1918

VILLERS-BRETONNEUX WAS the icing on the cake for Elliott's reputation. Now more renowned than ever as a fighting general and a real character, his outstanding leadership was widely recognised in the AIF, and the tempestuousness that had produced an abundance of diverting anecdotes was appreciated even more widely. No Australian commander was better known outside his own formation. Cutlack, Bean's assistant AIF correspondent, began his account of Villers-Bretonneux for the Australian newspapers with a vivid portrait of the famous brigadier:

> There is one man on the western front who ... loves to be in the thick of it. He is of big, burly build, with immense head and jaw; his large forehead is exaggerated by baldness at the temples, and a tuft of iron grey hair stands up in the middle of his head above the forehead—stands up permanently on end with sheer energy ... His every utterance—if it be but to ask the day of the week—he gives out with a lift of his chin like a challenge. The stoutest chairs creak under his weight. When he clasps his hands the sound is as of the foresail of a great ship as it luffs up into the wind. His heart is as big as the heart of an ox and as fresh as a schoolboy's. He has led his unit ... into every fight he could find. He thrives on the war. He dreams Homeric battles, it is said, every night of his life ... He fought the

> night attack on Villers-Bretonneux with several yards of flannelette shirting wrapped around his neck, for the gas-shelling had given him a sore throat. Wherewith he looked more like the great Lord Hawke than ever. His men have the greatest affection for him. They would probably like him just as much if he enjoyed a battle less. But the valiant bigness of the man takes their fancy, and they know they would never fail in a fight for lack of stoutness in him, their leader. Whenever his unit comes into action against the Germans it goes for them, as if in some resentment—caught from the spirit of its commander—that Germans should dare to stand in its way.

Morale in the 15th Brigade had never been higher. A mood of confidence and satisfaction was evident when Elliott lunched with his colonels at Blangy-Tronville on 29 April. As they reviewed the battle the brigadier asked his guests to submit the usual reports and recommendations for awards, and to arrange for other senior officers and the leader of every platoon to compile a narrative of the part each of them played in the operation. Elliott had already given Hobbs a brief interim account of the battle; he had in mind a more substantial document distilled from these individual statements, like his controversial Polygon Wood report. This get-together was more than a convivial review of a famous victory; it was also a farewell to Marshall, who was leaving the brigade the following day as part of the reshuffle postponed by the German attack on 24 April.

No impediment intervened this time. The 15th Brigade spent the whole of May in reserve after its celebrated April exertions. Not that Pompey's men were doing it easy—a rigorous fortification program kept them busy—but the brigade was able to adjust to the rearrangement of its battalion commanders without having to participate in dramatic front-line developments. Elliott even interrupted his supervision of this work by taking (with Hobbs's permission) an uncharacteristic day off, setting out one 'lovely spring' Saturday with some of his staff for a 'joy-ride'. Among those he visited in other AIF formations were his old friend McNicoll, Captain Symons (one of the 7th Battalion's Lone Pine VCs), and Monash and Wieck at Third Division headquarters. It was 'a most enjoyable time', but soon after his return Elliott was brought rudely back to earth. Long-range German shelling of Blangy-Tronville 'put me into the shrubbery, which largely spoiled its appearance'.

A few days later, news spread of significant changes affecting the whole AIF. Birdwood was to be promoted to lead the British Fifth Army. In anticipation of this elevation, Bean and others had for some time been considering the question of who should succeed Birdwood as corps commander and GOC AIF (administrative chief of the Australian force). The two leading contenders were Monash and Brudenell White. Haig, impressed by Monash's fine record in leading the Third Division, was inclined to anoint him for the corps; White's greatest advocate was Bean, who maintained a starry-eyed reverence for him and never warmed to Monash. Birdwood, aware that his association with the AIF in general and White in particular had done wonders for his career, recommended officially to the Australian government that he should remain GOC AIF, even though there was no guarantee that his army would contain any Australian unit. Monash, Birdwood advocated, should get the Australian Corps, and White should become chief-of-staff at Fifth Army with promotion to major-general—thereby continuing as Birdwood's right-hand man—because the 'experience to be gained should be of great value'. Beddington, who knew both Birdwood and White well, was not the only observer to surmise where the real value of such an appointment lay from Birdwood's viewpoint.

Bean was appalled by Birdwood's proposals. Impelled by his idealistic worship of White, Bean persuaded the well-connected journalist Keith Murdoch and other friends including Will Dyson to join him in opposition to these changes: 'we have lost our Trumper', Bean told Murdoch. Although White disapproved of this campaign and dissociated himself from it, Bean and his collaborators persisted; but the changes recommended by Birdwood were implemented, and remained in place for the rest of the war. There were also to be three new divisional commanders in the AIF. In addition to the vacancy created by Monash's promotion, the policy of maximising Australian appointments in the force had resulted in the departure of two British generals who had been commanding Australian divisions (Walker and Smyth).

It was on 21 May, with cables still flying back and forth between Birdwood and Australian cabinet ministers about the proposed changes, that Pompey Elliott became aware that important appointments were in the offing. His first inkling, apparently confined to the rumour that Smyth was to be transferred and replaced by Brigadier-General Gellibrand, was enough to perturb him. Gellibrand, Elliott's counterpart as leader of the other AIF advance guard north-east of Bapaume in March 1917, was a staff officer at Gallipoli and, before that, had served in the British army in England, South Africa, and Ceylon. Elliott had been in contact with Gellibrand from time to time during the war, but did not know him well. He was appalled that a British officer had been chosen when there was a well-credentialled Australian like himself available, and incensed that he had been superseded in the process (Gellibrand had not previously been senior to him). In high dudgeon he immediately wrote to White—'rather hastily', he admitted in his diary—to protest about 'the indignity of such an appointment'. He demanded to know why he had been overlooked, and even raised the possibility of appealing to the Australian minister for Defence.

White's spirited reply reached Elliott the following evening. 'Your letter has greatly pained me', it began. White proposed to discuss the matter fully in a visit to Elliott as soon as possible, but wanted to respond in part immediately. For a start, Pompey's diatribe clearly exemplified why he had been overlooked:

> your whole letter, even as a private epistle, is so intemperate that any tribunal judging it wd condemn you for a lack of balance and quiet judgment—even if it happened to contain the germs of genius which are supposed to be the counterpoise of eccentricity.

White dismissed Elliott's claim to have been superseded—appointments beyond the battalion unit were by selection only—and startled him with a revelation about Gellibrand:

> the British officer to whom evidently you refer is an *Austn* born there and now living there. Then as to yourself why all this great assertion? Do you think anyone doubts your courage? No one in the AIF, I assure you. Or yr ability? It is well known; but—you mar it by not keeping your judgment under complete control—your letter is absolute evidence. Finally you actually threaten me with political influence. You have obviously written hurriedly and I am therefore not going to regard yr letter as written. But let me say this: if the decision rested with me I should send you off to Australia without the least hesitation if calmly and deliberately you repeated yr assertion to seek political aid—and if you managed to raise a

> dozen 'politico-military' enquiries I wd fight you to a standstill on them!

In protesting about Gellibrand's nationality Pompey had left himself wide open. Gellibrand did have an extensive background in the British army, but was born in Tasmania and had returned there to live in 1912. (However, when it suited White in other contexts he acknowledged that Gellibrand was essentially British.) Elliott admitted that White's letter 'a good deal upset me, my nerves no longer being what they should be'. Only a few nights earlier his equilibrium had been further jolted by the burst of a big enemy shell alongside his headquarters chateau. He woke suddenly to a deluge of glass fragments and a reek of phosphorous, while his office downstairs was wrecked. Lieutenant Schroder was wounded, and Bob Salmon, also on duty, had a very lucky escape.

White visited Elliott on 23 May. They had a heated discussion. 'He said Birdwood would not promote me', Elliott told Kate afterwards. The brigadier then itemised his outstanding record.

> He admitted all that and said they had no General braver or more capable in the AIF, but I suffered from lack of control of judgment. Pressed to say what he meant, he could only say that I break out like a volcano if things don't go just as I want them.

White cited a number of examples—Elliott's protest about the battalion commanders initially allotted to the 15th Brigade; the forceful action he took to obtain water for his men after the notorious desert march; the controversies he initiated after concluding that neighbouring British formations had let his brigade down at Fromelles, Polygon Wood and elsewhere; his forceful anti-looting measures; and

> the row I had with a young staff officer who kept all my Brigade out in the rain until it suited him to get up about 10am in the morning after we had marched all night ... Now would you believe it possible that they are now dragging all this up to show I am not fit for a higher job. It is amazing and incredible. I should have thought that taking this in conjunction with my fighting powers, which he admits are not approachable, it would have proved that I was the very man for the job.

White's main priority was to persuade Elliott not to proceed with any protest. In his written reply to Elliott's diatribe, White indicated that he had not yet shown it to Birdwood in order to give the brigadier an opportunity to withdraw it, but he would oppose with the utmost vigour any attempt by Elliott to take the matter further. Now, in person, White maintained the pressure, clearly appalled by the notion that Elliott might appeal to Senator Pearce. Initially White denied that any such right of appeal existed. Elliott insisted that it did, and as a lawyer he ought to know. White then made it clear that if Elliott proceeded with this course of action he would be deprived of his command. According to subsequent accounts Elliott provided of this conversation, both publicly and privately, White said that he and Birdwood would regard any such appeal as an intolerable reflection on themselves, tantamount to an expression of no confidence. Whether a right of appeal existed or not, Elliott would find himself on his way home to Australia. White also gave the impression, Elliott subsequently claimed, that he would be first in line for any subsequent divisional vacancy.

This astute blend of intimidation and inducement did the trick. Pursuing his grievance to the limit promised to be a daunting course, especially for a commander with Elliott's profound sense of commitment to his men. He had been greatly moved by a letter he had recently received from Norman Marshall's mother, who described the relief pervading a Melbourne gathering of members and friends of the 15th Brigade when the announcement was made (by Colonel Duigan) that General Elliott had been offered home leave, but had opted to stay with his men: 'we all breathed more freely', she wrote. The brigadier withdrew his letter of protest, and decided not to proceed with the appeal.

Elliott's conviction that he was the victim of a monstrous injustice never wavered. Far from it. The discovery that Glasgow and Rosenthal had also been preferred to him for promotion redoubled his chagrin. Elliott had been promoted to brigadier-general at the same time as Gellibrand and Glasgow, but was a colonel well before both. Also influencing his reaction was his awareness that the increase in pay accompanying promotion to major-general would have been especially welcome, now that Glen Roberts had wrecked his legal practice. In those dark days when he was struggling to come to terms with what Roberts had done, he had consoled Kate and himself with the financial implications of a promotion which his record had entitled him to regard as within reach.

Elliott was not foolish enough to imagine that he would find it easy, but he had earned the opportunity by proving himself a fine brigadier, and he felt ready for the challenge. He was proud of the achievements of the men he led, justifiably proud—his own leadership, as informed observers such as Bean and Cutlack recognised, had been integral to the 15th Brigade's distinguished record.

Missing out on a division was an extremely bitter pill to swallow. He felt, as he put it, 'embittered by a profound sense of injustice'. After White had left at the end of their heated discussion, Pompey remained outside for half an hour, pensive and alone, before he rejoined his staff. One of them remembered what he said when he came in:

> My boy, if you want to get on in the army, go on leave to Paris, learn dancing, take lessons in deportment, learn to bow and scrape.

Other disappointed aspirants nurtured his sense of grievance. McNicoll and Tivey had been senior to all three of the promoted generals, and both protested about their rejection in tense interviews with White. Monash had supported McNicoll's claims beforehand. After Gellibrand succeeded Monash as commander of Third Division, a corrosive rift developed between McNicoll and Gellibrand of such magnitude that McNicoll asked to be relieved of his command and to be sent home to Australia. McNicoll asked Elliott if they could write together to the Defence minister; Pompey replied that they could communicate separately with Senator Pearce, but if they sent him a joint letter they risked being court-martialled for mutiny. At one stage Elliott had a conversation with Tivey about the appointments. Tivey claimed that when he protested to White about being overlooked, White had given him the impression that he would get the next divisional vacancy. Pompey concluded that he and Tivey had been conned by a 'paltry act of deception'. He was livid. 'It roused in me a deep and abiding sense of injury'.

Having to explain to aggrieved brigadiers why they had been passed over was yet another instance of White doing Birdwood's job. Elliott had been quick to discern Birdwood's shallowness, but when he criticised decisions and policies of the Australian Corps he did not blame Birdwood alone; he also accused White of shortcomings. White was an organiser of exceptional capacity and considerable charm. His planning of the Gallipoli evacuation was brilliant; but in France, compared to his flair for logistics and administration, it seemed at times that operational tactics were not his strongest suit.

It was during the dreadful 1916-17 winter, when inappropriate attacks were being ordered in appalling conditions, that Elliott had persuaded McCay to oppose the Flers operation scheduled for the 15th Brigade (which was subsequently undertaken by another AIF formation with disastrous consequences). At that time Pompey had also recommended to White that such enterprises should not be ordered without personal forward reconnaissance by the senior commander ordering them or a staff officer on his behalf; White had replied that such a policy could jeopardise the whole forward impulse. In this instance it was Elliott who was displaying the sound judgment that White accused him of lacking. (White seemed to demonstrate after the war a greater tolerance of commanders refusing to attack than he had shown during it.) Moreover, although one of White's most attractive characteristics was his self-effacing abhorrence of overt ambitiousness, his charm tended to fray under sustained strain and he had a steely resolve. He had earlier helped Birdwood remove General Legge from the AIF on specious grounds; Legge, like Elliott, was opinionated, forthright, and nationalistically Australian.

Although Elliott withdrew both his letter of protest and his intention to appeal to Senator Pearce, he remained determined to ensure that his grievance was put on record. He decided to compile a comprehensive account of the controversies that he believed had led to his supersession. It was a remarkable document:

> The complaint against me as laid down by General White is that I suffer from lack of control of my judgment and that this causes friction which would or might have disastrous consequences if I were raised in rank. In the event of my death I desire to place upon record, in justice to myself and my family, an account of every such incident.

Pompey then proceeded to review, in reverse chronological order, 21 controversial episodes, defending his conduct pungently in each instance:

(1) his report on the Aubigny Line;
(2) his instruction to shoot retiring British soldiers at Villers-Bretonneux who refused to rally when called on to do so;
(3) his frustration with Birdwood's refusal to endorse vigorous anti-looting measures against the British;
(4) his threat to execute looters at Corbie;
(5) his clash with the British staff captain who was slow to vacate Hedauville;
(6) his Polygon Wood report and its suppression by Birdwood;
(7) his vigorous opposition to the appointment of Street as his brigade major;
(8) his protests concerning false British claims of captured machine-guns and prisoners at Bullecourt;
(9) the occupation of Bertincourt;
(10) his criticism of Fourth Division operations involving his brigade in February 1917;
(11) his disparagement of attacking methods generally during the 1916-17 winter;
(12) his clash with Birdwood after some of his men followed a sensible non-provocation policy initiated by the Guards unit they had relieved;
(13) his protest against a proposed 15th Brigade attack which was later undertaken unsuccessfully by the 7th Brigade in November 1916;
(14) his criticisms of the Fromelles operation;
(15) the vigorous action he took to obtain water for his men after the desert march;
(16) his pointed remarks about the folly of ordering the desert march in the first place;
(17) his opposition to the transfer of certain officers he had appointed to the 15th Brigade;
(18) his vehement opposition to three of the four battalion commanders initially allotted to his brigade;
(19) the mild reprimand he received for risking himself in the tunnel encounter in July 1915, instead of sending a subordinate;
(20) his spirited protest in response to Bean's dispatch about undesirable behaviour in Cairo;
(21) his clash with Birdwood after a training exercise in Egypt.

In the overwhelming majority of these controversies Pompey's forceful defence was convincing.

Elliott's apologia also condemned Birdwood in the strongest terms for a circular he had issued in the wake of the Villers-Bretonneux triumph. This document, which infuriated Pompey, deprecated the growing tendency within the AIF to disparage the British. The Australians, according to Birdwood, had made such a name for themselves that running down their 'kith and kin' was 'not necessary for the full acknowledgment of the great work' they were doing. Pompey was incensed to discern an 'insinuation that when they speak as they do they are not telling the truth'; in fact, 'to my own certain knowledge the truth is being understated if anything'.

> It is the vilest libel upon us that was ever published to suggest that to add unworthily to our own fame we deprecated the efforts of our British comrades. I will go further and say that in some cases it would be impossible to libel the conduct of some British units.

Elliott cited the scathing reply by a British cavalry general to a request for barbed wire from a commander 'whose troops had behaved disgracefully'. (Pompey provided no identifying details, but this was surely General Harman of the Third Cavalry Division addressing a 14th Division officer on or about 4 April 1918.) The cavalryman's response, Elliott wrote, was to ask if

> it was proposed to put the wire in front or behind them, as judging by their performance that day he thought it was advisable to have something put behind them to keep them in their place. I do not think so cutting a remark or a juster one has been made by any Australian.

Pompey also described a recent incident involving an AIF front-line unit. This unit had submitted to the staff captain of a British formation (to which it was temporarily attached) an urgent request one afternoon for extra bombs. When no bombs had materialised by ten o'clock the following morning, the commander of that AIF unit went looking for the staff captain, and found him playing bridge. The Australian threatened to take his men out of the line if the bombs did not reach his men within half an hour; the staff captain put down his cards, made the necessary arrangements (the bombs arrived in time), and the Australian departed. 'By jove', the staff captain observed as he returned to the bridge table, 'stout fellers these Australians, but *so*cially—im*poss*ible!'

As usual, Pompey was careful to emphasise that his criticisms of some British formations did not apply to all of them. A 'very large number of the units in the British Army are doing magnificent work, quite equal to our own efforts', Elliott wrote in a covering statement to accompany Birdwood's circular when it was distributed in his brigade. However, he added,

> great numbers of men and officers have had to be employed who were obviously unsuitable for the task, except after long training, which it has not been possible to give them. While exercising the utmost firmness towards units and individuals on the battlefield we should, nevertheless, restrain our criticisms when out of the line and endeavour to set them an example in this as in other things, and help them whenever possible by advice and assistance.

Pompey showed this statement to Birdwood: 'though it seemed to my eye that he squirmed inwardly at its terms, he could make no comment' because it 'was all too true'.

Elliott was particularly riled by Birdwood's circular because he felt that the corps commander had done little or nothing to counteract 'shameless lies' propagated for years about alleged Australian indiscipline. Whenever his men had to find billets in a village they had not been in before, they tended to find the civilians there 'panic stricken' because of lurid tales disseminated by the British about Australians' 'savage brutality'. In fact, Elliott claimed,

> the inhabitants when they became better acquainted with our men preferred them to all others, not alone because they had more money to spend and spent it freely, but because of their far greater courtesy and gentleness towards the women, their love of children and love of helping in the farm work in which they were eager to assist.

As a result, his men had 'never left a French district without the people parting from us with the utmost good will and delighted to welcome us whenever we returned'. He himself maintained a warm correspondence with the first family he stayed with in France, the Brunets of Steenbecque.

It was not only because this persistent denigration was unwarranted that Pompey found it so repugnant. Also influential was a transformation of his own:

> Though myself possessing what may be called a good education, I am free to confess that the opinions and ideas which I had previously formed of the French People and their Institutions underwent the greatest possible change during my residence among them. The longer our stay in France continued, the more I found to admire.

His conversion was far from unique, he sensed:

> To a people so insular and isolated as we Australians undoubtedly were prior to the War, our experiences in this respect in France were undoubtedly an education and a very great pleasure. To our astonishment we found that though differing in language and race we were more closely allied in our mental development and real feelings with the French than with the English themselves.

Elliott bitterly resented Birdwood's double standard. With the British consistently terrifying French civilians by typecasting his men as barbarians, there had been no significant intervention by Birdwood. Moreover, looting was in fact more prevalent among British units than in the 15th Brigade, and Birdwood had prevented Elliott from dealing vigorously with British looters. Yet as soon as the boot was on the other foot and Australians began to cast scathing aspersions on the British after the inadequate performance of a number of their units, Birdwood, Pompey contended, had been mighty quick to pounce.

Even after providing a detailed account of 21 controversial episodes and exposing what he saw as Birdwood's double standards, Pompey's trenchant apologia was still not finished. He wanted to show that the decision not to promote him in May 1918 was the culmination of a pattern of hostile treatment by a corps commander resentful of his forthrightness and nationalistic outlook. He therefore included a lengthy account of how he had been mysteriously culled from the honours list for Lone Pine and oddly overlooked on other occasions as well. Only then did he bring this remarkable document to a conclusion.

Elliott had certainly fulfilled his aim of setting down his version of events for posterity in case anything happened to him during the war. But the contents of his apologia were dynamite, and he had to work out what to do with such an explosive document in the meantime. He decided to entrust it on a confidential basis to the head of the London-based Australian War Records Section, Captain J.L. Treloar. A shy, unprepossessing 23-year-old clerk, Treloar possessed dedication, zeal, and organisational talent in rare measure; he had served with the AIF at Gallipoli, and later for a time as Brudenell White's clerical assistant. Elliott and Treloar were developing a mutual respect and regard that was to endure. Treloar's trustworthiness was not in doubt. Earlier on, as Elliott knew, the only surviving copy of his suppressed Polygon Wood report had been taken to London and handed to Treloar (not by Pompey himself, but possibly by someone on his staff). Treloar was in an awkward position, but the document was clearly a significant war record, and he decided to retain it on a top-secret basis. It 'was smuggled to me and held by me with some trepidation', he later admitted.

While Elliott was compiling his lengthy apologia he also had to respond to a complaint emanating from the British staff captain he had evicted from Hedauville. Birdwood had directed Hobbs to obtain a statement from Elliott about the incident. Pompey's report covered the background to it in detail, and convincingly demolished the complaint (he incorporated this statement into his apologia as his version of that controversy, the fifth on his list of 21). 'I have as much reason to be proud of my English origin as anyone', he declared in the statement, citing the contribution of his relatives past and present to Britain's army and navy, and 'I gladly testify to the most gallant conduct' of the British cavalrymen assisting his brigade in April 1918. He also made a point of stressing that he did not want to 'place undeserving reproach upon anyone'. However,

> I feel strongly that the shielding of incompetent officers and unworthy conduct of individuals, particularly Staff Officers, ... adds to the difficulties we are in ... I shall be glad to give evidence in any Court of Inquiry that may be held.

Later in May, Elliott learned that Birdwood was leaving the Australian Corps to command Fifth Army, with Brudenell White accompanying him as chief-of-staff. 'I was never so delighted with anything in my life', Elliott enthused; 'we are well quit of them'. Pompey had never had much regard for Birdwood's ability. As for White, he

> is undoubtedly a very able man but he is now completely under General Birdwood's thumb, as he sees his future being made by sticking close to him and this is natural under the circumstances. But I cannot help thinking that it has more than once led to the betrayal of Australia's interests.

Pompey was very pleased that the new commander of the Australian Corps would be Monash. 'I have a great admiration for him', he wrote. 'I think I'll get on all right under him, couldn't do worse anyhow than under Birdwood'. Elliott's only regret was that Birdwood 'still retains the position of GOC AIF, but that arrangement I am sure cannot last long'. This understandable assessment encouraged him to nurture the hope that he might be promoted to divisional command after all. He had to have a strong chance, he felt, if some alternative to the Birdwood–White regime—Monash, presumably—was in charge of promotion, and Birdwood's continuation as GOC AIF hardly seemed compatible with departure from the Australian Corps.

However, Pompey's aspirations were dashed. Not only did Birdwood remain GOC AIF; he made it clear that there would be no promotion for Elliott. This became apparent when Hobbs turned up at 15th Brigade headquarters, and with a grim face asked Elliott outside for a private word. The generals formed a striking contrast in physique as they strolled into the garden together. Elliott wondered what was coming; his diminutive companion came straight to the point. Hobbs announced that he had been directed to reprimand Elliott in the strongest terms for the Hedauville incident, adding that Birdwood had indicated that the brigadier would receive no further promotion in the AIF because of the way he treated British officers. Elliott, stunned, reeled away in amazement. Hobbs gave him a consoling pat on the back: 'I had to tell you that, but by God you were right', he declared fervently.

For the rest of his life Elliott referred to this deeply felt grievance about being deprived of an AIF division as his 'supersession'. Whenever a promotion within an AIF battalion would result in an officer being overtaken by someone of lower rank, the necessity for that supersession had to be ratified after investigation by a higher commander, and the officer supplanted had to be notified. From the level of battalion command upwards, however, each appointment was determined by the personal selection of the GOC AIF, a method that enabled White to contend that the issue of supersession did not arise. Elliott dismissed this as sophistry.

He was not the only AIF general to become agitated about being superseded. In mid-1915 McCay felt so aggrieved by Legge's appointment to succeed Bridges that he submitted a formal protest, declaring that only his sense of duty prevented him from relinquishing his command 'rather than submit to the injustice done to me and the reflection on me that is implied by my supersession by an officer 6 years my junior as Colonel'. He even requested 'that this protest may be forwarded to the Australian Government' (in effect, exercising the right of appeal that White had denied Elliott). Nine months later, when Lieutenant-Colonel C.H. Brand missed out on a brigade command in the expanded AIF, he submitted what Birdwood described as 'a representation regarding his supersession'. And, most revealing of all, when the May 1918 appointments were submitted to the government for approval, the Defence minister was formally advised that the new divisional commanders 'will supersede' a number of officers (including Elliott). While it was understandable that White would dismiss claims of supersession as simply beside the point because of the nature of the selection process, it was predictable—especially straight after the Villers-Bretonneux triumph—that Elliott would feel not only superseded but intensely aggrieved about it.

Birdwood's correspondence indicated that Elliott was not even in the running for a division. The astonishing stream of chatty, ingratiating letters that Birdwood sent to an array of influential correspondents was crucial to his own reputation (and only possible because White was doing so much of his real work). Among the matters covered in Birdwood's letters to one of his regular correspondents, Senator Pearce, was his perception of how individual AIF commanders were going, and which of them were in line for promotion. He had shortlisted Gellibrand as a potential candidate for a division as early as March 1917, and anointed Rosenthal, an artilleryman without infantry experience, for promotion to divisional command even before he made his mid-1917 début as an infantry commander with the 9th Brigade.

Elliott was conspicuous in these letters by his absence. From March 1916 Birdwood did not mention him at all, either as a prospective divisional commander or when bringing Pearce up to date on the AIF's activities. At both Polygon Wood and Villers-Bretonneux, for example, where Pompey and his brigade had been outstanding, Birdwood referred to the 15th Brigade approvingly but avoided any reference to Elliott. In contrast, Birdwood's letter to Pearce about Villers-Bretonneux described Glasgow as 'a most excellent brigade commander ... of much determination and fine character', and pointedly associated Rosenthal with an 'excellent piece of work' by the 9th Brigade in a later engagement of much less significance. Birdwood's silence about Elliott was surely no accident—he clearly wanted to avoid giving Pearce any inkling that Pompey's superb record entitled him to be a contender for a division.

No further vacancy arose until the end of the war, but if one had it would have gone to Brand, with Wisdom probably next in line. Elliott's record was far superior to Brand's, and Pompey would have regarded any proposition that Wisdom might be preferred to him as preposterous after his first-hand experience of undistinguished leadership from the 7th Brigade commander in March 1917. However, Elliott was not even on the short list (nor was Tivey, despite White's assurances to each of them).

Was this treatment justified? It is true that the decision boiled down to personal selection by an individual authorised to choose (even if Birdwood, as his correspondence with Pearce confirms, lobbied unashamedly to keep that power to himself). From this perspective, one might conclude, Birdwood was simply entitled to make whichever decisions he thought best, and that was that. After all, that was how the system worked; Pompey had been making equivalent selection decisions affecting officers under his command throughout the war. But was it really appropriate to rule Elliott out? After the war Birdwood reiterated the case for the affirmative. Elliott was 'so entirely wanting in judgment and self-control that I should never have had a moment's happiness had he had an independent command like that of a Division', because he would be liable to involve his men in something 'without authority or reason'. However, the corps commander who would have been dealing with Elliott's alleged unreliability was Monash, not Birdwood. Elliott's admiration for Monash was as profound as was his distaste for Birdwood. It seems that Monash did not agree with Birdwood about Elliott, but he had little say in the appointments.

The 21 controversial incidents, as reviewed in Pompey's trenchant apologia, do not substantiate Birdwood's assessment. Only one of those episodes, the occupation of Bertincourt in March 1917, could be categorised as a possible instance of Elliott committing his men 'without authority or reason'. However, not only did he have compelling justification for the action he took in that instance, but he also ensured that neighbouring formations were informed, and Hobbs endorsed what he did (which was hardly surprising—it was consistent with an instruction from Birdwood himself that Pompey's advanced guard had to secure its own flanks).

White, it is true, described Elliott's offending characteristics more broadly, stressing his propensity to cause friction as a result of lapses in judgment and self-control. This broader perspective on Elliott's perceived shortcomings brings several other incidents from his list of 21 into the reckoning. Naturally, Pompey vigorously defended his conduct in each instance, but it is noteworthy that his immediate superior tended to agree with him even if Birdwood and White did not. Bertincourt was far from unique. For example, the 15th Brigade belonged temporarily to Monash's Third Division at the time when Pompey threatened summary execution for the next officer caught looting in Corbie. After disapproving rumblings began to circulate in higher British circles about this notorious notice, Monash 'fully upheld' Pompey's approach: 'the situation around Corbie was very critical indeed, and a strong hand was necessary to retain control'. Similarly, Hobbs was uncomfortable about having to reprimand Elliott for the Hedauville incident, concluding that Pompey's forcefulness was understandable on that occasion; he may also have been ambivalent about, rather than wholeheartedly critical of, the brigadier's instruction at Villers-Bretonneux to shoot British back-pedallers who refused to rally.

Not all the controversies Pompey had been involved in were featured in his apologia. It did not refer to his spontaneous resolve to order a counter-attack towards Doignies and Louverval on 23 March 1917, a decision that Bean evidently regarded as the biggest black mark against Elliott in the whole war. However, Bean's account of this incident is mistaken in several respects. Furthermore, when Pompey compiled his apologia he was responding to what White said were the reasons for his rejection. White did not refer to this spontaneous counter-attack, because (as Bean recognised) he was unaware of it. If White had mentioned it, Pompey would no doubt have included in his apologia a spirited defence of the decision itself, as he did on several other occasions.

But it was his initial unwillingness to tell Hobbs about it—until Wieck persuaded him to do so—that was indefensible. Still, all this amounted to in the end was a short-lived inclination that was nipped in the bud by Wieck, the superb brigade major Pompey valued so highly. If every commander guilty of an imprudent initiative that his staff persuaded him not to proceed with was thereby disqualified from promotion, few would have been eligible. When Harington, the chief-of-staff Elliott rated more highly than any other, was serving a very senior leader who made a habit of dashing off blistering missives in a furious frame of mind, he refused to send them. This happened repeatedly, whereas Pompey did not repeat his mistake—after March 1917, even when he issued an order as obviously controversial as his Villers-Bretonneux directive to shoot British back-pedallers, a copy was sent to Hobbs. As Elliott realised, a good blend of attributes in the commander–chief staff officer partnership was crucial. One of Gough's biggest problems, for example, was that his chief-of-staff for much of the war was a demonstrably unsuitable partner for him.

Elliott's biggest problem, in the context of his 1918 aspirations to promotion, was the perception that he was prone to go it alone, to act independently without heeding superiors' instructions or the exigencies of the overall tactical situation. This assessment by the Birdwood–White regime was accepted by Bean, but is it valid? In this connection it is illuminating to review the two big battles where his brigade was outstanding and his own superb leadership significantly influenced the outcome—Polygon Wood and Villers-Bretonneux. At Polygon Wood he had every reason to recommend postponement of the 15th Brigade's operation. The pre-emptive German attack had achieved a deep penetration on his right, inflicted sizeable casualties in three of his battalions, destroyed much of the accumulated ammunition, and played havoc with other AIF preparations. But when he was overruled, he proceeded to carry out the operation as ordered, and achieved a brilliant victory in circumstances of the gravest adversity.

The situation at Villers-Bretonneux would have tested the most patient, team-spirited commander. It occurred at a crucial time, even in the context of the whole war, and Villers-Bretonneux was obviously a critical position. Elliott was convinced the Germans would attack, convinced the British would be driven back, convinced his men would have to retrieve the situation, and convinced he had the plan that would enable them to do it. He was proved correct in every respect. It was obviously vital to launch the counter-attack as soon as possible, not only to give the Germans minimal time to consolidate, but also to utilise the lingering mist that had aided the enemy's attack. Early in the morning Elliott put the wheels provisionally in motion for the operation that he—and Hobbs—forever afterwards maintained would have done the trick and, bearing in mind the 13th Brigade's casualties, at a lower cost than was eventually incurred. But when Hobbs told him his brigade had to stand fast and wait, he obeyed orders. He was immensely frustrated, but he did what he was told. The injustice of the damaging perception that Pompey was not a team player was underlined by Bean himself in his account of Lagnicourt (March 1917):

> No commander in the AIF was more eager than Elliott to assist to the utmost any force acting on his flank, and on this, as on other occasions, he was anxious to do even more than was asked or expected.

This keenness to assist neighbouring formations was one of Pompey's many attributes as a commander. Even Brudenell White conceded 'he was a born soldier'. Tactically Elliott was astute, adaptable and, at times, innovative. Robustness, the ability to handle the immense stress involved in leading thousands of men when jolting shocks were inevitable and danger and death ubiquitous, was regarded by at least one well-credentialled study as the most important characteristic for any senior commander to possess. Elliott demonstrated, at Polygon Wood especially but also at Lone Pine and elsewhere, that he had this vital attribute. Also important was a good grasp of administration and supply, in order to instil confidence in the men under his command that they were being looked after as well as possible. Elliott showed up well in this respect, too: during the dreadful 1916-17 winter Bean was staggered to find that Pompey had positioned kitchens far enough forward to provide three hot meals each day for men in the front line.

Boldness, bravery, arranging good communications, instituting effective training methods, and utilising constructive conferences with subordinates were other recognised criteria for a top-ranking commander which Pompey clearly met. Elliott had always been a dedicated student of armed conflict, and in this war, by insisting that reports had to be submitted after an important engagement by every leader in his brigade—even down to platoon commanders—he accumulated a more informative picture than any of his AIF counterparts of what had actually happened in battles such as Polygon Wood and Villers-Bretonneux. As a result, he was better equipped to discern the lessons to be learned.

Elliott had also repeatedly demonstrated a capacity for the kind of flexible delegating that would have been increasingly required of him as a divisional commander. One such instance, at Villers-Bretonneux, concerned the additional units he was given, a Light Horse troop and a battery of the Royal Horse Artillery. Elliott did not assign a specific role to either; instead, he made sure that each commander understood the overall plan, and allowed them both to decide how they could best assist its implementation. This policy proved most successful. 'Nothing could exceed the zeal and ability of these two officers', Pompey enthused; both 'appreciated to the very highest degree the trust' given to them, and 'I have never been better served by anyone'.

The admiration was mutual. For the battery commander, Major A.W. van Straubenzee of the Chestnut Troop, it was a revelation to see the rapid response of Pompey's men to his orders, their keenness to get at the enemy, and their 'marked ability to use their rifles and machine guns'. Afterwards, in an honour bestowed by this famous unit only once before in its long history, van Straubenzee invited Elliott and his officers to become honorary members of the Chestnut Troop mess 'as a permanent record of the regard and admiration we had for them'. That rare distinction surely scotches the notion that Pompey was consistently, even compulsively, anti-British.

It was also at Villers-Bretonneux that Elliott made a special point of thanking the commander of the Royal Berks for his unit's welcome assistance with the mopping-up, which was supposed to have been provided by the Durhams. While Pompey predictably castigated the Durhams, he did praise the Berks appreciatively, just as he had lauded other British units such as the Chestnut Troop and the cavalry that his brigade fought alongside earlier in April. He was blunt and tempestuous, certainly, but he gave praise as well as criticism where it was warranted.

Another factor inevitably affected Elliott's willingness to dish out harsh criticism at times. He was all too aware that his men had been let down considerably by neighbouring British formations whenever they were involved in important engagements at the Western Front. Examples included Fromelles, Bullecourt, Polygon Wood, Vaire (4 April 1918), Villers-Bretonneux, and the pursuit to the Hindenburg Line (Bertincourt). Interestingly, both Monash and Hobbs were just as scathing as Elliott about some British units during March and April 1918, but expressed their criticism more discreetly. Unlike Pompey, they made sure Birdwood did not see or hear it.

As a combat formation, the 15th Brigade attracted rave reviews. Most memorable, perhaps, was Bean's tribute to this 'magnificent instrument, fit, like Cromwell's Ironsides, for the hardest military tasks'. On the compelling basis that the fundamental task of a commander was to persuade and inspire his men to fight well, Elliott was an outstandingly successful general. A feature of his leadership was his willingness, appreciated by his men, to share risks and dangers with them. He could never be accused, as Monash frequently was, of being unwilling to go forward himself to make an enlightening personal inspection. A few observers have suggested that, if anything, Pompey perhaps overdid this personal reconnaissance; but the evidence that his superiors regarded this tendency as excessive is minimal (and, if they did, Rosenthal was at least as 'guilty'). Pompey's style was the antithesis of remote, cushy chateau-dwelling; always deadly earnest, he was up-front in more ways than one. When Rawlinson issued an edict in April 1918 that there was to be no retirement from the British positions then held, Pompey's response was characteristic:

> I have accordingly given orders that when their last reserves are thrown in, every Battalion Commander and every member of his staff shall be armed with rifles and take their place in the firing line. The personnel of my Headquarters here are also organised in echelon to serve as final reinforcements, and finally, by my orders, myself and Staff Officers, when no other reinforcements are forthcoming from Division, proceed to the firing line to fight (as I hope) to the end.

It was a feature of Elliott's leadership that he was forever on the lookout for promising officer material, and always doing his utmost to ensure that appropriate individuals were sent to the various training schools. The school he established in his own brigade reflected his unflagging commitment to maximising the effectiveness of whatever formation he was commanding. Not only did Hobbs conclude that the 15th Brigade school was far superior to its equivalents elsewhere in the Fifth Division; it was, he enthused, 'one of the most perfect and successful schools I have ever visited'. At one stage, Elliott told Milly Edwards, the father of one of his men gave him a new watch after he had recommended the son for a promotion course. In reply Pompey thanked the donor for the gift, but urged him

> to get right away from the idea that his boy or he had ever been under the very slightest obligation to me ... It is because my boys know that they deserve their promotions to the full when they get them that they do not feel under any obligation to me, ... and they know that no matter how much I have helped them in the past, no matter who their friends may be or how friendly I may be to them, they will be smitten good and hard if they let me catch them out in the least degree.

'You've got men's lives in your hands', Pompey would remind his officers, 'if you can't do your job you're out!' Throughout the war, from the very first weeks at Broadmeadows, he was ruthless in dispensing with officers he felt were not up to scratch. Sometimes Birdwood and White overruled him, most notably when he objected to three of the 15th Brigade's initial battalion commanders and the appointment of Street as his brigade major (Pompey claimed with good reason to have been vindicated on all four objections).

Some of his men claimed that Elliott was not impartial. When assessing candidates for commissions he was inclined, they sometimes felt, to prefer aspirants with a good education. From the brigadier's viewpoint, however, this attitude was not a matter of favouring an old school tie, as some observers assumed, but a result of bitter experience. All too often during the war he found that men he had singled out because they were brave and had demonstrable leadership qualities tended, if their educational background was limited, to struggle in certain other requirements (fluent written expression and absorption of technical information, among others).

A classic case was Private Milton Brockfield of the 59th Battalion, a labourer from a Victorian coastal town. As Pompey was aware, Brockfield 'repeatedly displayed brilliant courage in the field', particularly at Polygon Wood, where he vigorously rallied a large number of retiring Welch Fusiliers; impressed, the brigadier recommended him for the DCM and an officers' training course. But the instructor's report was damning: Brockfield 'has a great opinion of himself, but no military knowledge', and 'I do not consider he has really tried' to gain it. Pompey admitted to feeling

> very much disappointed about this man ... I have noticed, however, with great regret, that men who distinguish themselves frequently, if not of good education to begin with, fail to realise the value of book knowledge and are reluctant to make sustained effort to gain it.

One veteran, asked by Pompey about his pre-1914 background and shrewdly sensing the reason, replied straight-faced that before the war he was a swagman.

There was also the odd raised eyebrow about preferential treatment for Elliott's relatives. Pompey's cousin Charlie (the son of his uncle Robert Elliott) was the only English-born member of the 15th Brigade's machine-gun company to be commissioned, according to another Englishman in that unit who took a dim view of his own lack of promotion beyond sergeant and the anti-British tendencies that he felt Pompey displayed. By 1918, however, Charlie was no longer under Pompey's command. He proved 'a splendid officer', the brigadier reported, but had been reduced to 'a complete wreck' by the 1916-17 winter; 'rheumatism and sciatica have made an old man of him at 26'.

After that terrible winter Pompey had also been concerned about the precarious health of Eric Walker, brother of George Elliott's widow Lyn. At one stage it was feared he had consumption. Walker doggedly 'insisted on coming back', Elliott reported, but 'looked so ill that I would not let him go into the line'. In May 1917 Walker was about to move forward with his men to participate in the 15th Brigade's operation at Bullecourt when he was whisked away to a school at the last minute. Walker's ill-health would have proved fatal, Pompey believed, if he had not intervened. The officer who replaced Walker was killed in the battle.

Jack Prictor, husband of Kate's cousin Ina, enlisted in the Third Division, but Pompey arranged for him to switch across to the 15th Brigade. Asked about the transfer by one of his new comrades, Prictor claimed that he had simply applied for one. 'Come off it', his inquirer persisted, 'I couldn't get transferred to another company, let alone a different brigade'. When Prictor eventually admitted that he was related to the brigadier by marriage, there were confident predictions that he would soon find himself up for promotion. He did. Pompey sent him to the brigade school, then to England for officer training: 'Ina's Jack is a good signaller', Elliott told Kate, and 'I think he will do splendidly'.

Of course, being human, Elliott kept a close eye on his 'own', but he did not really treat them very differently. His desire to protect Eric Walker was partly influenced by the death of Eric's brother Ken; Pompey felt similarly protective towards non-relatives such as Lieutenant Bob Johnston, whose brother (like Ken Walker) had been one of the 7th Battalion officers killed at Gallipoli. It was the fact that Pompey knew something about Jack Prictor and Eric Walker before they came under his command—as distinct from men he did not know beforehand at all—that enabled him to assess them relatively quickly as potential officers. But they had to perform: 'I would not promote even my own brother' if he was not 'fit for the job'.

The case of Reg Avery typified Elliott's approach. Avery was a Charleville drover whose brother had married Pompey's sister. He was a Third Division NCO until Pompey arranged a transfer to the 59th Battalion, sent him to a school, and 'urged him to study hard and get a good report'. Although Reg thought 'he did all right' at the school, in fact he 'did very badly', the brigadier was told. 'If he cannot learn the work, it is no use promoting him', Elliott concluded, 'I've given him his chance'. There were no soft options. On 4 April 1918, during the fighting near Vaire, Avery was on a bicycle delivering a message from Elliott himself when he was killed. Reg's death convinced Jack Avery to return home to Australia. After his other brother was killed in France a year earlier, his mother 'nearly went out of her mind' with grief; he was worried about how she would react to the news about Reg, especially with her only remaining son liable to be sent into the battle zone. For thousands of Australians like her, this terrible war inflicted years of agony. It was a time of powerless waiting, inescapable tension, and overwhelming sorrow.

'I am perhaps a hard taskmaster, but I always try to be a just one', Pompey told Norman Marshall's mother. That he had no favourites when he detected any failure to meet his exacting standards was shown time and again. Visiting the 58th Battalion's advanced headquarters early one freezing winter's morning, he had to wait a few moments before Denehy, having been alerted to the brigadier's arrival, emerged from a dug-out looking flustered. 'Good morning Denehy, is this your first appearance today?' Pompey asked pointedly in front of the colonel's men. When he had to deal with serious offences by frequent wrongdoers, Pompey sometimes allowed them to expiate their sins by tackling dangerous assignments. He adopted this flexible approach at both Gallipoli and the Western Front.

At Gallipoli one morning a 7th Battalion rascal known as 'Scotty' was brought before him after souveniring the copious contents of a rum jar. Pompey had just returned from the front trenches, where a periscope he was looking through had been shattered by a nearby Turkish sniper ensconced in a fortified post. With his face and neck still smarting, Pompey decided to give Scotty a choice: court-martial and disgrace, or expiation and a recommendation for a bravery medal if he would crawl out that night and place an explosive device next to the sniper's nest. Scotty, full of alcohol-inspired bravado, was so keen to tackle this challenging task that he had to be restrained from setting forth immediately—any attempt in daylight would have been suicidal. Hours later, in mid-afternoon, Scotty was in a more sober state when he asked to be taken to a suitable vantage-point for a look at the sniper's post and surrounds. After a quick glimpse he was brought back to Pompey. 'Sir', he announced, 'I'll take the court-martial'. Pompey relished that story. The enjoyment he derived from such diverting moments helped to sustain him through the darker times.

Not everyone endorsed Elliott's methods. They could seem odd, if not eccentric, to outsiders unfamiliar with them, such as the member of Glasgow's staff who included disparaging references to Elliott in the unreliable account of Villers-Bretonneux he wrote decades afterwards. Some 15th Brigade officers felt harshly treated. Naturally, those keen to minimise friction sometimes found his tendency to call a spade a spade unhelpful. What was commendable decisiveness to his admirers could seem regrettable impulsiveness to others. Tivey thought Elliott was inclined to get too excited during a battle. Just before his men set off to carry out the Villers-Bretonneux counter-attack, Pompey rode up to give them a parting pep-talk; according to a 59th Battalion veteran, he promised to have them relieved before morning if they attained all their objectives. When this relief did not materialise, they realised that it might have become impossible for Pompey to keep his promise, but it was perhaps imprudent to give an assurance when his capacity to deliver was to a considerable extent out of his control.

Moreover, Pompey was convinced that it was essential to be able to evaluate subordinates accurately, and believed he did this pretty well—as indeed he did. But he was not infallible, as his underestimation of Lieutenant Moon VC confirmed. In addition, while keeping his officers on their toes, Elliott might have done more to show that he valued their efforts. Pompey regarded no-one in the 7th Battalion or 15th Brigade more favourably than Geoff McCrae (who admittedly lacked confidence in his own ability), yet McCrae had no idea how much his colonel appreciated him until he learned from his family back in Melbourne that Pompey had praised him glowingly in a letter to George McCrae.

Perhaps Elliott's greatest vindication in the context of his supersession was the overwhelming endorsement of his leadership by the men he led. Despite his eccentricities, his rough tongue and his rigorous standards, 'somehow they seem to know that I love even the worst of them'. As Bean wrote, with 'exuberant vitality he overworked them, strafed them, punished them; and yet they would do anything he asked of them'. Those who knew him best tended to have the utmost admiration for him. The mother of a 60th officer killed at Fromelles assured Kate in mid-1918 that 'many letters I have received from soldier friends ... say how loved your husband is'. Even after his death (long afterwards in some instances) Salmon, Schroder, Doyle, and others who had served on his staff all put their veneration on record, as did, among his colonels, Marshall, Stewart, Freeman, and Scanlan. Duigan described Pompey as 'absolutely the best General in the Australian Army'. According to Schroder, 'no greater soldier or gentleman ever lived'.

After Elliott became a brigadier, he was repeatedly assured by men he had previously led that they wished he was still their commander. This happened whenever he came across the 7th Battalion in France. And it was not just cheap flattery, either—some of them actually applied for a transfer to his brigade. So did a number of the light-horsemen temporarily attached to the 15th Brigade during its advanced guard operations; they wanted to become part of such a purposeful and proficient formation permanently. Even more telling was the number of wounded 7th Battalion officers who opted to rejoin Elliott when re-enlisting after being repatriated to Australia. Scanlan, Mason, Grills, and de Ravin were all familiar with Pompey and his methods, and all wanted to serve under him again. Even 'Birdie' Heron, whose fondness for drinking and skylarking had landed him in hot water with his colonel more frequently than any of Pompey's other original officers, joined the 15th Brigade after recuperating from his Gallipoli wounds, and persuaded his brother to do likewise.

Elliott's immediate superiors also rated him highly. He retained McCay's confidence as long as that unpopular general remained commander of Fifth Division. While the 15th Brigade was attached to the Third AIF Division, Monash lavishly praised the quality of Elliott's leadership. As for Hobbs, he clearly found Pompey a handful from time to time; the brigadier's volatility and forthrightness ensured that he would have been a difficult subordinate for anyone. However, after an awkward start while they were getting to know each other, Hobbs handled him pretty well, as Elliott increasingly appreciated. Hobbs certainly esteemed Pompey's capacity. He showed this not only by frequently choosing the 15th Brigade when there was a tough task to be allocated; he also told Birdwood that, as far as he was concerned, it would have been appropriate to give Elliott a division in 1918.

Pompey's aggrieved frame of mind was aggravated by the distribution of awards for Villers-Bretonneux. Having been informed by Hobbs that Birdwood wanted DSO submissions minimised, Elliott had confined himself to recommending the four colonels in his brigade most actively engaged in the operation. He was incensed to learn that not all of even this miserly quartet had been approved, yet more than a dozen DSOs were awarded to officers in Heneker's division. Watson missed out, Pompey fumed, despite obtaining 'the most valuable information' during the battle and sharing it with a brigadier in Heneker's division, General Coffin, who did not conceal from Watson his ire about being 'unable to obtain any information from his own battalions'. Coffin's battalions 'were utterly defeated, and he himself freely admitted that "but for the Australians the Bosche would have been firmly established in Villers-Bretonneux"', yet there was a DSO for Coffin but not for Watson.

Elliott took up the matter with White. It did seem anomalous, White agreed in an amiable reply, but he was powerless to intervene. He went on to deny a suggestion in Elliott's letter that he did not welcome 'strong and clear expression of honest opinion', and gave him some advice:

> I like you for your plain speaking. But as before I would caution you against extremes. Neither as children nor as grown up men can we run roughshod over our fellow creatures. And when we take a strong and fighting attitude we must—if we are going to achieve anything more than derision—be well balanced and sure of our ground ... whereas it may be honest always to say what one thinks, there are two objections to it: (1) the other person may be seriously damaged thereby (2) there is no certainty that the opinion expressed is the correct one.

This unsolicited advice was well targeted. In controversy Pompey sometimes undermined his argument (often in circumstances where he had a compelling case) by incorporating hearsay 'evidence' which turned out to be unreliable—in other words, by not being sufficiently sure of his ground. A typical example was his previous letter to White. He could convincingly claim to have been unjustly overlooked, but flying off the handle about being superseded by a British officer was hardly the best way to proceed when the response could predictably be made that Gellibrand was not, in fact, British.

White's advice did not deter Elliott from being characteristically frank in the full report he compiled on Villers-Bretonneux. The grossly inappropriate distribution of DSOs was, he declared, 'a further illustration of how unfairly the Australians are discriminated against in such matters'. He maintained that his brigade 'should have been permitted' to counter-attack early on 24 April, when 'it was quite evident that the 8th Divisional Staff had quite failed to cope with the situation and were in point of fact largely in ignorance of the situation'. Furthermore, the 'attack as finally ordered was misconceived': the operation should have been carried out by his brigade as he originally proposed, with the 13th Brigade, and any British units assisting, placed under his command.

Elliott's forthright report also referred to Birdwood's 'insulting' circular. 'For four years almost we have had to endure in silence albeit with writhing souls' British denigration of Australian indiscipline, when 'all they had to base it on was our men's lack of saluting and their free and independent manners'. Not only was this repeated criticism fallacious, he continued; considering the brazen British propensity to loot, it was blatantly hypocritical:

> One [British] Brigadier General who relieved me north of the Somme boasted in the presence of my Staff that they had eaten nothing but chicken, drunk nothing but champagne since the 2nd day of the Retreat. I said simply I don't permit looting here and he subsided.

After his controversial supersession and the suppression of his Polygon Wood report, Pompey decided to take no chances with this one. He handed it to Treloar himself.

Elliott's bitterness about the supersession grievance was so intense that he became resentful not only of those who made the decision to overlook him, but also of the promoted commanders who benefited from his rejection. Gellibrand and Glasgow, the men he felt had superseded him, became the main focus of his spleen. He seemed less perturbed (though irritation was occasionally discernible) about Rosenthal, a commander of prior seniority and similar style to himself. Pompey increasingly saw Gellibrand and Glasgow as rivals who had deprived him of the crowning accomplishment of his career. The unfairness of the situation from his perspective prompted him to compare their careers unfavourably with his and to draw conclusions that were in some instances (though not all) wayward. His distorted and sometimes distasteful assertions enabled his detractors to draw 'told-you-so' conclusions that he did lack judgment and therefore the decision to pass him over was correct. Pompey was his own worst enemy at times.

Gellibrand, Elliott alleged, had less experience both in front-line service and as a brigadier. This gap, according to Pompey, had been enlarged by Gellibrand's eyebrow-raising resignation from command of the 6th Brigade in 1917 and his ensuing four-month stint in England. Moreover, Gellibrand's advanced guard had been outperformed by Elliott's alongside in March 1917, with the Noreuil reverse a notable black mark. As for White's correction concerning Gellibrand's nationality, Pompey retorted that Gellibrand 'if not wholly British was well lacquered by his experience in the British Army'. (Gellibrand, for his part, had described Elliott in 1915 as 'bull headed and ultra Victorian', 'very gallant and despotic'.)

For Pompey, the obvious means of comparison with Glasgow was the famous counter-attack their brigades had just conducted together. Pompey became very touchy about suggestions made in contemporary accounts of the battle by Bean and Cutlack (and repeated ever since) that Glasgow's men had the harder task. In comparing the ground to be covered, for example, Pompey claimed that his brigade had 'by far' the more difficult assignment. Besides the multiple changes of direction, his men had more undulating terrain to contend with and more obstructive wire to get through. Furthermore, the 13th Brigade had more scope than the battle chronicles acknowledged for preliminary reconnaissance, which was undertaken by Pompey's men at his insistence with beneficial results. In particular, he would never have accepted at face value Heneker's claim that the British had dislodged the Germans from the nearby wood which became such a problem for the 13th Brigade, and Glasgow should not have done so either. Such assertions by Pompey were not without merit, but the adversarial tone he sometimes adopted in propounding them was regrettably unseemly.

By mid-1918 the AIF was in top form, full of confidence and well established as an outstanding combat force. There were several experienced and well-credentialled leaders who could consider themselves contenders for divisional vacancies. Rosenthal, Gellibrand, and Glasgow were not unreasonable choices once Elliott was ruled out by the selector-in-chief. If Elliott had not been deemed ineligible, however, his claims were at least as compelling as theirs, and he should have been well ahead of any other aspirant. Whether it was justifiable to disqualify Elliott from divisional command is debatable, but there can be no doubt about the impact of this setback. It was the greatest personal disappointment of his life.

CHAPTER EIGHTEEN

'As Usual My Boys Were ... Just Splendid':

Relentless offensive

JUNE–NOVEMBER 1918

A FORTNIGHT AFTER Elliott became aware of this crushing setback, he discovered that he had been awarded the CB in the King's Birthday honours for his role at Polygon Wood. It did not alleviate his acute disappointment, but there were gratifying reactions to the announcement. Not only did he receive letters from AIF generals including Monash, Hobbs, Rosenthal, and McNicoll; numerous admirers of lower rank congratulated him as well. 'All of us who know you are pleased', enthused a friend working at the AIF's London headquarters, 'I have not heard today of a more popular award with anyone than your CB'. Also sending a congratulatory letter from London was Captain Robinson, the capable and principled former Fifth Division intelligence officer who had approved Elliott's controversial Polygon Wood report before it was suppressed:

> It could not have been better deserved. The 'official' grounds for the distinction could be made convincing enough to all minds. But the thing which specially appeals to me, and I think too to all Aussies, are the unwritten yarns about Pompey Elliott which are bandied from mouth to mouth. You tell one of them yourself, and immediately someone answers with a better! And all together we find them among the most stimulating tonics and aids to winning the war that we know—from the ... hat story onwards. I would not

venture to write this if I did not thoroughly believe it, and thank you for it.

Elliott and his brigade returned to front-line duty in mid-June 1918. With his headquarters at Heilly, Pompey took over responsibility for the left half of the new sector allotted to the Fifth Division north of the Somme. 'Great deal of work to be done', he noted, his purposefulness undiminished. He had been away from home nearly four years, had known more than his share of tribulation and sorrow in that time, and his children were growing up without him. Moreover, he was also approaching his fortieth birthday, the kind of personal milestone that can sometimes prompt reflective reassessment. Even so, any wavering of his commitment was unthinkable. He had a passionate lifetime interest in soldiering, and this was the greatest war there had ever been. His sense of comradely identification with the men he was commanding remained fervent and profound (though it was frequently masked by the demanding demeanour he maintained to maximise their proficiency). And the principal war aim—stopping Germany, the main aggressor—was still far from fulfilled.

'We will win in the end', he told Kate in mid-June, 'but it will be a long time yet I fear'. As Elliott realised, the Germans had more divisions available for transfer from Russia to France to supplement the numerical advantage they already possessed over the combined forces of their adversaries. In March and April the British had narrowly averted disaster; a separate German offensive in May drove the French back no less than 32 miles, bringing the attackers within 50 miles of Paris. Elliott's brigade returned to something of a lull on the Somme front, but this had a calm-before-the-storm feeling about it in an atmosphere of continuing crisis. A renewed German onslaught somewhere soon seemed inevitable.

Meanwhile aggressive AIF skirmishing ensured that there was no respite for the enemy. With their confidence and resourcefulness higher than ever, the Australians repeatedly gained both ground and prisoners in spontaneous local exploits of remarkable initiative, skill, and tactical proficiency. Elliott's brigade was prominent in this well-recognised AIF phenomenon, which became known as 'peaceful penetration'. It was in fact the astonishing enterprise of Corporal Doug Sayers who, along with three 58th Battalion privates, brazenly and successfully attacked a patrol of 30 Germans in broad daylight on 5 April, which ushered in peaceful penetration on the Somme. At first Pompey found reports of such exploits hard to believe; when they were confirmed beyond doubt, he concluded that the enemy 'seems to have completely lost his punch'. The Australians had 'established a wonderful supremacy', he added:

> The Bosche ... is no match ... when it comes to personal combat. The Intelligence reports of these patrol encounters are joyful reading. I feel like going out myself for a rough and tumble, for the sport seems as harmless for us as chasing and rounding up barn door fowls.

The effectiveness of peaceful penetration had more than local significance. Ascertaining when and where the next German offensive would occur was a top priority; newly captured prisoners tended to be a fruitful source of information, and if these prisoners could be secured by peaceful penetration there was no need for the set-piece raids that were usually more costly and accordingly less popular. Peaceful penetration, however, suited some areas more than others. The sector the 15th Brigade entered in mid-June was relatively exposed; with scope for purposeful patrolling limited, raids would be necessary.

Elliott's fortieth birthday on 19 June engendered few pleasant memories. The Germans kept shelling the headquarters he and Tivey were sharing at Heilly chateau with a ferocity that eventually prompted Hobbs to insist on them moving further back. Furthermore, Elliott spent his birthday sick in bed. Like Hobbs and many others, Pompey was battling the unpleasant effects of an influenza epidemic in the AIF: 'it has made me as weak as a child', he told Kate, 'I can hardly hold the pen'. He was also concerned about a raid the 58th Battalion was going to carry out that night. Dissatisfied with Watson's arrangements, he suggested several alterations; but Watson felt that these changes might deprive the raiders of the advantage of surprise, and the debilitated brigadier did not press for them. Afterwards he wished he had insisted. The raiders were repulsed (despite inflicting more casualties than they sustained themselves) without managing to get into the German trenches or capture any prisoners.

In contrast, a raid by Scanlan's 59th Battalion three days later was a complete success. Five prisoners were captured, other Germans were killed, notification of the unit concerned reached corps headquarters in fifteen minutes, and the only Australian casualty was wounded by a retaliatory German bombardment. And early in July, after thorough preparations, the 58th made another attempt at the spot where it had been unable to penetrate on 20 June. This time it, too, was successful.

A few days later the 15th Brigade participated in Monash's first operation as commander of the Australian Corps. The importance of the battle of Hamel lay not so much in its scope or the magnitude of German losses in personnel and territory (though they were highly satisfactory). More significantly, this stunning triumph after months of anxiety and sometimes desperate defence highlighted the Germans' vulnerability to a powerful, well-planned assault and underlined Monash's capacity to organise one. Since 21 March the Germans had penetrated far, alarming British strategists and seeming at times within sight of victory; but their fundamental objectives were unfulfilled, and their great effort had taken its toll (as the success of peaceful penetration confirmed). Early on 4 July the Australians advanced about 2,000 yards, captured Hamel and the ridge beyond, and secured all their objectives in only 93 minutes. This notable feat was the biggest offensive success for the Anglo-French forces and their allies since the Germans had launched their onslaught on 21 March.

The contribution of the latest British tank was a highlight. Ever since Bullecourt the Australians had regarded this innovation with suspicion and hostility, but both the planning of tank operations and the performance of the tanks themselves were much better at Hamel. Even officers scarred by Bullecourt were full of praise for these more reliable and more manoeuvrable machines. The methods of tank–infantry co-operation which were successfully utilised with artillery and aircraft support at Hamel constituted a promising model for larger enterprises. Other features of Monash's plan included sophisticated artillery barrages, specially assigned aircraft to muffle the noise of approaching tanks, clever use of smoke, and the employment of planes and tanks to convey supplies to forward units. There were also a variety of co-ordinated feints and other measures to deceive the enemy.

The 15th Brigade undertook the main diversion. For some time Elliott had been advocating an advance of his brigade's front near Ville-sur-Ancre (about four miles north of Hamel), and this attack became part of the overall design. Pompey had envisaged it as a night operation, so that his men would be able to consolidate in their new line before morning and would be therefore less susceptible to German artillery fire from the Morlancourt heights to the south. He was unhappy about zero hour being shortly before dawn—to coincide with Monash's battle plan—because his men would be decidedly vulnerable to this shellfire while digging themselves in without the cover of darkness. His forceful protest to Hobbs produced additional protection in the form of a smoke screen. The aim was to seize the German trenches east of Ville from the Ancre to three-quarters of a mile south of the river, positions worth capturing not only for their intrinsic significance but also in order to provide a diversion to assist the main assault south of the Somme.

Elliott placed Scanlan in charge of organising the attack. It was to be carried out by two companies of his 59th and one from the 58th, and would be supported by artillery, trench mortars, and machine-guns (but no tanks), with a 60th company and another 58th platoon ready to help if needed. The attackers were able to scrutinise a model of the area to be blitzed, and also benefited from intensive practice after being withdrawn from front-line duty well before the assault. Captain Forbes Dawson, whose 58th company would be advancing on the far left alongside the Ancre, even arranged on his own initiative for his men to have four days' tuition in handling German machine-guns.

Having established an advanced brigade report centre under Captain Doyle, Elliott left Gollan in charge at brigade headquarters and went forward shortly before zero hour to monitor developments at 59th Battalion headquarters, where Scanlan would be directing the attack as it unfolded. The barrage descending at 3.10am was punctual and powerful. Early news from the right augured well. The 59th companies were soon reported to be consolidating on their objective and sending prisoners back.

On the left, however, Dawson's company had a tough fight, particularly the platoon nearest the Ancre. This platoon, under Lieutenant Ivo Thompson, was faced with a narrow approach across marshy ground as well as belts of wire and determined machine-gunners. Thompson handled the platoon superbly, spreading his men out and organising a series of successful assaults against these machine-gun posts, which enabled his men to attain their goal. They were consolidating there when another machine-gun opened up ahead. Thompson was in the process of arranging a further co-ordinated rush to deal with it when he was killed. His men hung on despite their losses, and

Dawson, covered in blood himself after a facial wound, was pleased to find that the other 58th platoons engaged had also reached their objectives. With most of their Lewis guns clogged with mud from the swampy marshland, Dawson's decision to ensure that his men were adept at using captured enemy machine-guns proved invaluable.

Meanwhile the 59th companies in the centre and right had also been engaged in tough fighting. At one stage Captain McDonald, in charge of the centre company, resorted to sending back a terse message by pigeon: 'SOS and reinforcements, Mac'. Eventually, though, the 59th men prevailed. The 15th Brigade had attained all its objectives, but the enemy, stung by this reverse, gave Pompey's men a torrid time after the fight with a prolonged burst of heavy shelling.

'My Brigade only had a small part', Elliott told Belle, 'but what they had to do they did magnificently'. The enterprise had succeeded as both an attack and a genuine feint—the 15th Brigade had significantly helped the main operation at Hamel, in conspicuous contrast to certain lamentable previous attempts at diversion, the fiasco of Fromelles in particular. Pompey was full of praise for Scanlan's arrangements and the way the attackers had comprehensively defeated an entrenched enemy force, despite being greatly outnumbered:

> The boys were splendid, particularly the 58th boys from Geelong under Captain Forbes Dawson. We did not know that there were three times as many Boches in their trenches as we had, but notwithstanding that we hunted them out and killed about 120 of them, captured 17 machine guns from them and 64 prisoners, whilst the rest bolted like rabbits.

While 15th Brigade casualties were appreciably fewer, Pompey was yet again saddened by the loss of outstanding officers. 'I lost three of the very finest officers I have ever had', he lamented. As so often happened, it was the bravest and best, like Lieutenant Thompson, who were taken. 'To my very great regret', Elliott wrote, 'Lieutenant Facey, 59th Battalion, a brilliant officer, was killed'. An athletic 31-year-old Mansfield farmer, Steve Facey had joined the 59th during the terrible 1916-17 winter, and so quickly distinguished himself that he was promoted from private to sergeant within a month. After Polygon Wood, where Facey captured several pillboxes almost single-handedly, acquiring a number of machine-guns and about 50 prisoners in the process, Elliott arranged for him to do officer training. He topped the course. Back with the 59th, Facey was given a key role at Ville. Again he was superb, leading his men to their objective in fine style, but was killed while marshalling them to repel a counter-attack. 'I have never heard such unanimous regret expressed throughout the Brigade as for the death of this officer', Pompey told Hobbs.

Two other first-rate lieutenants were also killed, Merv Knight and John Moore. Knight was one of the 4th Light Horse NCOs recruited by Pompey to fill officer vacancies in the brigade after Fromelles. He was widely admired: '[o]ne of the finest fellows we ever had and a great loss', wrote Doyle. Moore had joined the brigade in February 1917 and, like Facey, was rapidly promoted. Awarded the Military Medal at Bullecourt, Moore was sent by Elliott to an officers' school, where he did well. Now a lieutenant, he won the Military Cross for a remarkable exploit while leading a raid, and later received a bar to his MC for 'daring and dashing leadership' at Villers-Bretonneux. Moore 'had a most brilliant career in front of him', Pompey believed; 'utterly fearless' and 'a magnificent athlete', he had 'great physical strength' and a 'most winning personality'. When problems emerged with the Stokes mortars owing to inferior ammunition, and Pompey decided one of his best officers was needed to revitalise the 15th Brigade's battery, he chose Moore, who was vindicating this decision with inspiring leadership when he was struck by a German shell.

Arrangements had been made before the Ville attack for Elliott to have a month's leave. He certainly needed a rest. Although 'I have thrown off the influenza it has left me feeling distinctly stale', he told Kate before the fight:

> I shall be very glad to go on leave. It is now over 7 months since I was in England, and it has been a very anxious, trying time.

With the 15th Brigade soon to be withdrawn, he arranged with Hobbs to go on leave on 10 July.

In London Elliott had an enjoyable reunion with a pair of Ormond College luminaries, J.G. Latham and the deputy master 'Barney' Allen. Latham, as adviser to Australia's minister for the Navy, Joseph Cook, had travelled to England with Prime Minister Hughes, and Allen had arrived there as one of the 437 Ormond men who enlisted in the AIF (Pompey had presided when 21 of them, including George Elliott, attended a dinner for ex-Ormond members of the AIF at St Omer in August 1917). Latham had visited the AIF with Hughes and Cook just before Hamel. On his return to London he informed D.K. Picken (who had succeeded MacFarland as master of Ormond in 1915) that AIF morale was 'as high as possible', adding that 'the reputation which our fighting men have won for themselves and for Australia is almost beyond belief'. Latham also told Picken that he and Allen had recently 'spent a most pleasant evening' with Brigadier-General Elliott. 'Nobody could stand higher than Elliott in the estimation of his men', declared Latham. 'He has been doing great work, and has won a fine reputation as a fighting General'.

Soon afterwards Elliott travelled to Boston, Lincolnshire, for another reunion. This one was with his cousin Nellie (sister of Charlie Elliott), her husband, and their engaging young children—Alec, a precocious deep thinker, and Helen, who was exuberant and playful. 'The children are darlings', Elliott told Kate, and the regard was mutual. After meeting him earlier in the war, Alec and Helen had gravely informed their friends that 'Uncle Harold' was 'the most important man in the world—more important even than the King!'

A highlight of Elliott's leave was his visit to his Scottish in-laws. Kate's mother had fond memories of Ullapool in the highlands of north Scotland, and Elliott had been invited to stay by Jessie Campbell, Kate's second cousin. 'It is a lovely place right enough, but a terrible place to get to', he reported after a journey involving four trains, a meandering bus and extensive delays. The Campbells and their relations rolled out the red carpet. Jessie, awed by such an illustrious visitor, gave him a room with two beds in it so he could rest in one during the day without affecting the comfort of the other one he was to sleep in at night. She even proposed to serve him meals apart from the rest of the family until he demurred. And they 'will insist on calling me Sir, as if I don't get enough of that in France'. Elliott did his best to be unintimidating, and had an enjoyable time even though it rained for much of his stay. He was shown where Kate's father came from and where her mother was born, and met so many of Kate's relatives—including a 'dear old' Mrs Cameron 'just trembling with excitement because I knew something of her daughter' (a resident of Geelong)—that he asked Kate to send him a 'genealogical tree' showing where each of them fitted in, because it had become 'all mixed up in my head'.

Elliott had moved on from the Campbells to spend a few days with Milly Edwards at Bryn Oerog when he received an urgent summons to rejoin the 15th Brigade. He still had a week of his leave to go, but momentous developments were afoot. The Australians were about to spearhead an ambitious onslaught that could be crucial to the outcome of the whole war. Many participants at Hamel had complained that the swift success there had been insufficiently exploited; why call a halt after a limited advance and dig in to prepare for a severe response from the enemy artillery, when they could have penetrated much further and even captured those very German guns? This reaction, while understandable, overlooked the very real limitations of an advance on a narrow front.

But there was nothing limited or narrow about the undertaking Elliott was recalled to take part in early in August. The aim was to end the enemy threat to Amiens and its vital rail network once and for all. For the first time, all five AIF divisions would be involved together. Moreover, the Australians would be advancing alongside Canadians, which was also unprecedented. The enterprise was sure to benefit from the mutual affinity between these two armies and their confidence in each other's proficiency. And this time the objectives were undeniably expansive. South of the Somme the AIF was to penetrate the front east of Hamel and Villers-Bretonneux, and push forward over five miles. With complementary advances by the Canadians on their right and the British III Corps on the left, the attack frontage was no less than thirteen miles long.

Monash's planning was again meticulous and masterly. Successful Hamel innovations were again a feature. There were detailed arrangements for tank–infantry co-operation, with each tank assigned a particular role under a particular infantry commander. The Germans, as at Hamel, became accustomed to a regular early-morning barrage of mixed gas and smoke shells, so that when the onslaught began with a smoke screen without gas they would be disadvantaged by having their gas masks on when suddenly attacked in their trenches.

No Australian formation would be advancing further than Elliott's brigade. The AIF assault was divided into three phases. Two divisions were to attack side-by-side until they reached the first objective (the green line), where they would consolidate. Two other AIF divisions would then pass through them and press on to the second objective (the red line), with scope to exploit further ahead, if appropriate in the circumstances, to a third objective (the blue line). The 15th Brigade had been assigned the second and third objectives on the AIF's far right, where the blue line was furthest away; the Canadians would be on the right of Elliott's men, and Tivey's 8th Brigade on their left.

Preparations in the 15th Brigade proceeded methodically after the brigadier's hasty return, a process involving not just the usual conferences but also the distribution of a series of 'Preliminary Instructions' on particular topics. This enabled units to assimilate vital information gradually instead of having to resort—as they had too often previously—to a less effective last-minute cram when the operation order belatedly materialised from above. Monash's arrangements reflected his conclusion that

> the true role of the Infantry was not to expend itself upon heroic physical effort ... but, on the contrary, to advance under the maximum possible protection of the maximum possible array of mechanical resources, in the form of guns, machine guns, tanks, mortars and aeroplanes; to advance with as little impediment as possible; to be relieved as far as possible of the obligation to *fight* their way forward.

'I fully agree with that statement of principle', Elliott wrote when he later read it.

There was a palpable air of confidence in the AIF. The battle was clearly going to be a stroke of rare magnitude and an unusually well-orchestrated one. Peaceful penetration had repeatedly confirmed the Australians' ascendancy over the Germans. And having all AIF divisions assembled together at last was profoundly satisfying. It was unfortunate to lose part of his leave, but Elliott would have been more disappointed to miss this battle. Many in his brigade shared his anticipation that it could result in a red-letter day for the AIF. With all AIF divisions 'gathered together' for a really big assault, wrote Downing, this was a 'long hoped for' development that 'no adventurous soul could wish to miss'; there were 'high prospects of a sweeping and brilliant success'.

On 6 August Elliott's headquarters received from Monash a stirring message to be conveyed to 'soldiers of the Australian Army Corps'. They were about to 'engage in the largest and most important battle operation ever undertaken by the Corps'. It would be 'one of the most memorable of the whole war'. They would 'be supported by an exceptionally powerful artillery, and by tanks and aeroplanes on a scale never previously attempted'. By attaining their objectives they would 'inflict blows upon the enemy which will make him stagger', bring the conflict 'appreciably nearer' to completion, and win 'a glorious and decisive victory' that would not only 're-echo throughout the world' but 'live for ever in the history of our home land'.

The 15th Brigade benefited in particular from the innovative 'double leapfrog' manoeuvre designed by Monash. If Elliott's men (like other brigades assigned the most distant objectives) started, as usual, behind the formations engaged in the first phase, they would have so far to go that just the process of getting into position to begin their allotted task might well be enough to tire them out. Astutely anticipating this problem, Monash arranged for them to be bivouacked closer to the front line than the 7th Brigade, which was to pass through them and secure the first objective; they would then advance through the 7th Brigade on their way to the red line. Not only did this arrangement benefit Pompey's men by significantly shortening their approach march; it also provided them with a couple of days' rest before the battle in the familiar surroundings of Villers-Bretonneux. Elliott's temporary headquarters was a dug-out in the very path of his brigade's famous counter-attack. Being back there for another operation of the utmost significance was a good omen. Even conditions during the countdown to zero (4.20am) were 'very similar', the brigade diary recorded; 'the night was quite clear and calm', and the enemy unsuspecting.

The battle of Amiens (as it came to be known), on 8 August 1918, was a brilliant success for the 15th Brigade and the whole AIF. When Elliott's men left their bivouacs around 2.00am and moved forward towards their assembly positions, visibility was minimal owing to a thick mist as well as the darkness. Although this mist helped concealment and maximised surprise, officers in Denehy's 57th, leading the right of the brigade forward (with the 59th on their left), were unsure whether or not they were heading in the intended direction until they discerned through the veil the number 57 glowing prominently to guide them. This effect was produced by punctured holes in a petrol-tin lit from within by a candle and hoisted on to a pole, a deft touch that reinforced the impression that the organisation of this undertaking was first class.

Further confirmation was the tremendous barrage that descended at zero hour. The 7th Brigade moved off in its wake. Elliott's men had to wait on their tapes for an hour, but casualties were few; the enemy's response was 'feeble', Pompey noted. The artillery pounding the Germans was much more sophisticated than it had been even just two years earlier. Counter-battery techniques, in particular, proved devastatingly successful, all but silencing the German guns and playing a crucial role in the triumphant result.

At 5.20am the 15th Brigade advanced, guided by compass. The mist continued to cause directional uncertainty until it lifted at eight o'clock, revealing a breathtaking panorama—the whole enterprise was proceeding like clockwork. At 8.20am, right on time, Elliott's men began passing through the 7th Brigade. The red line was three miles ahead, and there would be no creeping barrage to guide them. Assistance would be provided by tanks, along with a few field artillery brigades that were being hurried forward. Resistance from German infantry was meagre, but the enemy artillery now became troublesome until the tanks supporting Elliott's men intervened. Bayonvillers, a village in the 15th Brigade's path, proved no obstacle. Scanlan's 59th skirted around it to the north and south in accordance with the brigadier's cherished envelopment methods; Watson's 58th, coming up behind, mopped up effectively. Pompey's leading battalions reached the red line shortly after ten o'clock.

The main impediment to their rapid progress was the difficulties experienced by the Canadian brigade alongside them; Elliott's men did their best to help. Nevertheless the 15th Brigade's momentum was so impressive and the enemy disarray so evident that Denehy and Scanlan decided to push on to the blue line straightaway, without even waiting for the tanks that had been allotted to help them in the third phase. The village of Harbonnières was a potential stumbling block, but the 59th Battalion, with other tanks making their presence felt, swiftly secured it. By eleven o'clock an Australian flag was fluttering from the Harbonnières church spire.

It was an exhilarating day. Not only was the 15th Brigade's achievement extraordinary after four years of mostly stagnant conflict; its success had been duplicated throughout the AIF. In seven hours the Australians had advanced seven miles, capturing no fewer than 7,925 prisoners and 173 guns, as well as vital documents and copious engineering materials. 'It was a splendid performance', Rawlinson enthused, 'as fine a feat of arms as any that even this war can produce'. AIF casualties, by Western Front standards, were relatively light; although any losses were begrudged, for once the gains seemed to justify the cost. As Downing observed, absent for the most part were 'the usual depressing concomitants of a major action—rain, tumbled waves of earth, enemy barrages, mutilation'—and 'it was more like a picnic than a battle'. For the Germans it was a shattering reverse. Their chief strategist described it as 'the black day of the German Army in the history of this war', a disaster demonstrating beyond doubt that victory for his side was no longer feasible.

Elliott was delighted. 'As usual my boys were ... just splendid', he told Kate. They had advanced further than any others, and captured 'a splendid haul of prisoners and guns'. 'Best of all', he enthused, there were 'very few casualties, not a single officer killed and not many men'. Many Australians sensed that Monash's painstaking planning had been crucial; as far as Pompey was concerned, the improved organisation since Birdwood's departure was no coincidence. 'As soon as we got out of his hands we did better than ever', he asserted. Elliott had been busy up forward for much of the day, especially when trying to overcome the difficulties on the right, which were caused mainly by the Canadians' slower progress; but everyone was weary—infantry, gunners and tank crews alike—and in a couple of localities he had to settle for only partial attainment of the blue line.

The main setback for the attackers on 8 August, however, occurred north of the Australians. There, General Butler's III British Corps was required to advance less than half the distance covered by the AIF but was unable to achieve its main task, the capture of Chipilly. Accordingly, the German guns ensconced there became, as Monash feared they would, 'the chief instrument of the enemy's resistance on the Australian front'. Astonishingly, an enterprising AIF patrol of two sergeants and four privates managed the following night to do what Butler's corps could not. The intrepid half dozen drove the Germans out of Chipilly, capturing hundreds of prisoners (assisted by British infantry advancing in their wake) and ending enemy harassment from that quarter. Butler, increasingly suffering from stress and insomnia, was replaced, to Pompey's unbridled satisfaction—he still felt that Butler had wrongly delayed the famous Villers-Bretonneux counter-attack and had been unjustifiably given credit for its success.

Outstanding planning had been integral to the triumph of 8 August, but the organisation of endeavours to exploit it was substandard. Rawlinson, Rosenthal, General Currie of the Canadians, and even Monash were all at fault. Elliott's contribution, in contrast, was highly creditable. The proposal eventually adopted was that Glasgow's First Division would have the main Australian role in a further co-ordinated advance with the Canadians. However, undistinguished administration resulted in Glasgow's division arriving much too late. With zero hour not far away and still no sign of the First Division, a Canadian brigade major appeared at Elliott's headquarters with an urgent plea for help. Could the 15th Brigade, he asked, move forward to protect the left flank of the Canadians as they advanced? Elliott was eager to help, but said that approval from Hobbs was necessary. Hobbs gave it. Gollan hurried away to the red line to inform the 60th and 58th Battalions (which had been in support the day before) that they were to leap-frog the 57th and 59th in the front line and attack.

Each battalion was on its way forward within 20 minutes of receiving the order. There was, unlike the previous day, no specific objective—the men just had to push on until the First Division materialised. Moreover, though the Canadians on the right and Tivey's brigade on the left were advancing with both a barrage and tanks to help them, Elliott's men had neither. Their task would not be easy, and they were far from fresh after their exertions the day before. Pompey was frantically busy with all the unexpected arrangements. The way he rounded in frustration on a hapless signaller when the only remaining line to any of his battalions was suddenly broken reflected his anxiety about this challenging improvised enterprise. Advancing on either side of Harbonnières, the 58th and 60th were shelled by several German batteries, but pressed on until intense machine-gun fire from a line of sunken huts prevented even gradual progress. In view of this hold-up, Pompey characteristically decided to go forward and assess the situation himself.

Not long after his arrival close to the front, a tank rolled across from the Canadian sector to offer assistance. Elliott, having quickly grasped what was required, bustled over to convey instructions. He was standing alongside it talking to the crew when he felt a sharp pain in his rump—a German bullet had smacked his left buttock. It was uncomfortably sore but not a serious wound, and he was contemptuous of suggestions that he should be evacuated to the rear for treatment. He did allow his own rear to be attended to, as long as it did not interfere with his direction of the fight. The upshot was an unforgettable spectacle—the brigadier perched on a prominent mound, surveying the battlefield intently and dictating messages uninhibitedly, with his trousers round his ankles and underlings fussing over his behind. Onlookers were amused by this further confirmation of his wholehearted commitment; there were also ribald remarks about the awesome amplitude of his posterior. According to Scanlan, seeing 'Pompey with his tailboard down having his wound dressed' was one of the sights of the war.

The unanticipated contribution of Elliott and his men on 9 August helped to make a success of that day's poorly co-ordinated exploitation of the breakthrough. The 58th and 60th Battalions eventually managed to overcome the resistance that held them up for two hours. Applying sustained pressure, the 58th advanced by alternate rushes under covering fire north of the line of sunken huts where German opposition was most determined, and succeeded in manoeuvring round behind these huts. Resistance began to waver and, as the 60th and 59th pressed forward, ended altogether. This line of huts proved to be an impressive divisional headquarters. Elliott came forward to take them over, acquiring valuable documents as well as trophies and equipment. In the afternoon Glasgow's First Division arrived at last, and passed through the 15th Brigade. To Downing, the 'fresh faces' of these newcomers 'contrasted' with the 'unshaven ... grimy and wan' visages of Pompey's weary men.

One of them, a young 60th Battalion Lewis-gunner, was struggling after a series of stressful front-line experiences, no sleep for 60 hours, concussion from a German shell burst and, worst of all, the discovery that his best mate had been killed. With the 15th Brigade withdrawn, he was trudging disconsolately back in a daze when he felt a comradely hand on his shoulder. It was Pompey. 'You've had a rough day, lad', said the general. Touched by this sensitivity, the youngster began to cry; the brigadier was sympathetic. After that encounter 'I really worshipped old Pompey', the Lewis-gunner confided decades later.

Elliott and his men had certainly earned a rest. Their performance on 9 August was, as Bean acknowledged, magnificent: the 15th Brigade had selflessly positioned itself to bear the brunt of 'a desperate effort of the enemy which otherwise would have been exerted upon the Canadian flank'. There was unstinting gratitude from the Canadian divisional commander, who knew Elliott had readily agreed to help although his men were tired and would be advancing without artillery support:

> It is difficult to express the appreciation which I, and all units under my command, have for the unselfish spirit in which this decision was made and for the very gallant co-operation which was thus given us.

Similarly, the commander of the Canadian brigade closest to the Australians acknowledged that he and his men owed 'a very great debt' to Elliott and the 15th Brigade for the 'very prompt and generous action' which 'enabled our attack to proceed in the initial stage and saved us numerous casualties'. He wrote to thank Elliott 'most heartily'. Pompey was magnanimous in reply. Although 'the same co-operation would have been proffered to any other troops similarly placed, it was a very great pleasure to be able to co-operate with the Canadians'. The 15th Brigade had 'long looked forward' to being 'placed side by side' with them, and 'the result of the recent operations has fully justified this wish'.

Pompey's contribution on 9 August was hardly the conduct of a commander who was unreliable as a team player. Moreover, his stipulation that assistance from his brigade was conditional upon approval from Hobbs contradicts those detractors who claimed he was too inclined to act independently of his superiors or the overall tactical situation. In fact, what happened on the afternoon of 9 August made Elliott's outstanding contribution seem even better. Having passed through the 15th Brigade, the stalwarts of the 7th Battalion (including some veterans he had commanded at Gallipoli) suffered severe losses as they advanced without support on their left—just as the Canadians would have that morning without Pompey's impromptu assistance—because Rosenthal's Second Division did not arrive forward until well after it was directed to do so.

Elliott's superiors, from Monash right up to Foch, were determined to maintain the pressure. The transformation since the months of desperate defence presented the promise of a substantial strategic gain at long last. With a weakened, war-weary enemy plagued by disorganisation and increasing demoralisation, a policy of relentless aggression might bring the ultimate reward of victory, and not just in the foreseeable future but quite soon, perhaps even before next winter. The challenge was to avoid being dazzled by this tantalising prospect into initiating inappropriate operations. Rash enterprises could still be punished by defenders of even mediocre strength and morale, and the most proficient attackers—the Australians in particular—were themselves under-strength numerically and anything but fresh. Meanwhile top-level German strategists, aware that winning the war was now beyond them, were desperately trying to infuse their forces with the steel to remain steadfast so they could negotiate peace on terms that were not devastatingly one-sided.

In these changed circumstances Haig issued a general order to announce the adoption of a new approach. The order reached Elliott's brigade on 23 August:

> To turn the present situation to account the most resolute offensive is everywhere desirable. Risks which a month ago would have been criminal to incur ought now to be incurred as a duty. It is no longer necessary to advance in regular lines and step by step. On the contrary each division should be given a distant objective which must be reached independently of its neighbour, and even if one's flank is thereby exposed for the time being ... The situation is most favourable. Let each one of us act energetically, and without hesitation push forward to our objective.

Two days later (as Gollan recorded in the brigade diary) Elliott reinforced this message in a personal address to his men:

> The Brigadier addressed each Battalion separately and thanked the men for their splendid work since coming to the Somme area in March last. This, he said, did not imply that the units had done nothing prior to coming to the Somme, but the past six months had been the most strenuous the Brigade and the whole AIF had experienced. All ranks had acquitted themselves with credit, and there was not the slightest doubt that but for the AIF the enemy would have occupied Amiens and there was no telling what would have happened then; probably the whole course of the war would have altered ... Now was the time to strike—while the enemy was reeling under the blows already given him. All men should realise that our efforts now would have a great effect on the termination of the war.

The fine line to be negotiated in trying to force the issue, now that the Germans were in a palpably bad way, while avoiding imprudent enterprises was underlined by a proposal involving the 15th Brigade in mid-August. Elliott's men had been given a key role on the Fifth Division's left in another large assault involving two AIF divisions and the Canadians. They had returned to the forward area and involved themselves in all the extensive preparations, all the deliberations, details, and discussions, only to be notified on the eve of the battle that it had been cancelled. This late change was initiated by Currie, who felt that the operation was unlikely to prove worthwhile even in the new environment now prevailing. The 15th Brigade was directed instead to revert to peaceful penetration.

Elliott's men gave the Germans no respite, and succeeded in pushing them back gradually. Pompey was particularly pleased with a 59th lieutenant whose patrol managed to capture the startled occupant of a German latrine. On 23 August the Australians again spearheaded a major assault supervised by Rawlinson, but Elliott's men were given a subordinate role assisting a fresher formation, Glasgow's division. Having played its part capably in another pronounced success, the 15th Brigade was withdrawn for another brief spell, which was especially welcome after a burst of hot weather. 'I never saw the war looking so promising for us', Elliott told Kate, 'but when the Bosche gets back on his old fortified Hindenburg line it may be a different tale'. As well as writing frequently to Kate, he was still writing chatty letters regularly to his children:

> I am living in a nice old house today laddie, but the shells have broken all the windows and two cheeky little swallows have come in and built their nest alongside a roof beam just over my table and hatched young ones there, and I didn't want to sack them so I had to have a board nailed on the beam under the nest to stop them making a mess of my table and papers, and the wee things didn't mind a bit and are up there now just as cheery and cheeky as anything and their mum and daddy are flying in and out all day long feeding them.

By 29 August the offensive that had begun three weeks earlier had brought the AIF to one of the Germans' strongest defensive positions at the Western Front. Péronne, the famous fortress now confronting the Australians, was protected not only by its massive ramparts and elevated south-eastern suburb of Flamicourt, by wooded hills to the east and further high ground to the south; even more daunting was the dominating height of Mont St Quentin a mile to the north, a formidable, sentinel-like bastion bereft of cover. Its occupants enjoyed commanding long-range observation to the north, south, and west. Yet another natural advantage for defenders here was the Somme itself. Fringed by numerous channels too deep to wade across and extensive marshland up to 1,000 yards wide, its canalised course curved in a sharp, almost right-angled bend near Péronne. Assisted by a tributary, the Somme further fortified the fortress by forming a moat around it. The beleaguered Germans had occupied Péronne and Mont St Quentin with specially chosen volunteers from five different divisions who were determined to resist the Australians. German strategists were counting on being able to hold their adversaries up in front of this exceptionally powerful stronghold for a considerable time—certainly long enough for them to make the mighty Hindenburg Line some fifteen miles further east, if in due course they had to fall back to it, virtually impregnable before winter.

The Fifth Division had returned to the front on 26 August under Monash's system of frequent rotation. Hobbs initially gave Tivey's 8th Brigade front-line responsibility with instructions to maintain the pressure. Late on 27 August Hobbs asked the 15th Brigade 'to reconnoitre forward with a view to leap-frogging through the 8th Brigade and carrying on the advance'. Next morning Elliott and Gollan borrowed a car from Fifth Division and scrutinised the front themselves. The 8th Brigade had succeeded in pushing back the enemy considerably, but Pompey was unimpressed by what he saw when he reached the forward area south of Péronne:

> The pursuit was being carried out with little energy ... I ... actually passed out into no-man's-land on the right and, finding there was no opposition, urged the Co[mpan]y Commander whom I met to push forward and so turn the flank of those holding up the advance on the left. He did so. There seemed to me a lack of intelligent leadership and the Co[mpan]y Commanders had not been fully instructed as to their work.

With the Germans on the back foot and the situation fluid, Pompey was typically ebullient. He was intent on ensuring there would be no respite for the enemy when his own men, then approaching the front in a long arduous march across the ravaged Somme battlefield of 1916, took over from the 8th Brigade.

On the morning of 29 August, with the 15th Brigade likely to relieve Tivey's men later that day, Pompey once again proceeded well forward. With him was Dave Doyle, who later reminisced about this memorable reconnaissance:

> General Elliott was absolutely fearless. He was a great believer in seeing things for himself and would go anywhere. He would plod along with a complete disregard of shellfire ... Accompanied by a member of his staff and a couple of signallers, Pompey set off to have a look at things. They went through the front line and down to the edge of the river. This in broad daylight. Coming back the small party was actually sniped at by a battery of whizzbangs—and the shooting was pretty good. Reaching a trench, the General found an old enemy dugout about fifty yards in advance of our front line. 'This will do for Brigade headquarters', said Pompey ... Probably on no other occasion during the war did a general establish his headquarters in *advance* of his front line.

Specific instructions materialised at midday. The 15th Brigade, Hobbs told Gollan, was to advance through Tivey's men, cross the Somme four miles south of Péronne and establish itself on the far side. Pompey was eager to oblige—even though it was by no means clear that all the Germans in the vicinity had retired across the Somme—and he summoned his battalion commanders to a conference at his remarkably advanced headquarters. There they were, Scanlan told Bean afterwards, 'away out in front without a digger in front of them'. As Bean wrote in the *Official History* long afterwards, they were perched 'high above the river ... standing on the old parapets with maps and field glasses', clearly visible to the Germans, as they 'planned the intended advance'.

A few hours later, with battalions already moving in accordance with these arrangements, came sudden news of a change of plan. Monash had decided to tackle Péronne and Mont St Quentin with a co-ordinated, flexible operation involving three AIF divisions the following morning; on the right the Fifth Division's role was to be undertaken by the 15th Brigade. But the order cancelling its relief of the 8th Brigade four miles south of Péronne did not arrive until after this changeover had commenced, and a dispatch rider who was sent to tell Elliott he was wanted at a divisional headquarters conference got lost. It was midnight by the time Pompey received this message.

Hurriedly returning from the front on horseback, he too missed a turn-off in the dark. It was 1.30am before he reached Hobbs's headquarters and received his instructions—to transfer his brigade north to the area west of Péronne occupied by Wisdom's 7th Brigade, to follow that formation when it crossed the Somme at dawn, and then to move through it and continue the advance. Elliott relayed this information to Gollan immediately by phone, sent his staff captain Clarrie Lay to Wisdom's headquarters, and snatched a few hours' badly needed sleep. Gollan's concern about the possibility of runners getting lost prompted him to deliver these important instructions to each of the battalion commanders personally. The brigadier commended him for showing 'great devotion to duty, as it was a very arduous and unpleasant task in the darkness and drizzling rain'.

Early next morning Elliott was on his way to his repositioned headquarters when he met Lay. Wisdom, Lay reported, had already decided that a crossing was impossible; even a relief, in Wisdom's opinion, would be inadvisable before nightfall. 'As it was very misty I disagreed', Elliott affirmed, but the reprieve was a blessing for his men. Some were very weary, having trudged forward to replace 8th Brigade units only to retrace their steps after the order cancelling the relief reached them. With the 15th Brigade now taking over the task of crossing the Somme in front of Péronne, all Pompey could do was to ensure that the relief of Wisdom's brigade began as soon as possible that evening. He directed that once his battalions were in position (the 57th, 58th, and 59th in the front line, in that order from right to left, and the 60th in reserve), they were 'to institute a vigorous system of patrols to probe the marshes fringing the river and canal, and endeavour to find crossing places'.

During that night and the following day, 31 August, Elliott's men tried to get across but were unsuccessful. They 'found every approach guarded by the enemy, and machine-gun fire was opened on every movement', Pompey noted. One patrol did manage to reach the far side at night, but the swampy expanse that then confronted them proved impenetrable. Another priority was to prevent the enemy from completing the destruction of any bridges still intact; Elliott was not convinced that the Germans had rendered all of them absolutely impassable.

Meanwhile an astonishing exploit on the 15th Brigade's left, the partial capture of Mont St Quentin by the 5th Brigade of Rosenthal's division, together with progress further north by Gellibrand's Third Division, prompted Monash to throw two additional brigades into the fray. At dawn on 1 September the 6th Brigade was to complete the seizure of Mont St Quentin, and Cam Stewart's 14th Brigade was given a most challenging task. Monash wanted it to deliver a left hook to the enemy by moving north and then east, crossing the Somme in the Second Division's area, before swinging around to attack Péronne from the north-west.

This was a complicated manoeuvre to organise at short notice. The 14th Brigade units had to cover a sizeable distance, and their multiple objectives included the staunching of enemy resistance not only between Péronne and Mont St Quentin but also within the fortress town itself and beyond. Elliott, familiar with the difficult ground the 14th Brigade would have to cover just to get into position, considered all this a tall order and said so at a conference called to discuss and refine the arrangements. Monash's aim was to exert maximum pressure on Péronne from the north; activity south-west of Péronne (where Pompey and his men were situated) was to be an adjunct only. But Elliott's concern about the immensity of the 14th Brigade's task was persuasive. Hobbs authorised him to persevere with the 15th Brigade's attempts to cross the Somme, with a view to providing whatever support was possible for Stewart's battalions. On his way back after the conference Elliott had some awkward moments when enemy gunners positioned on the heights opposite used their perfect observation to good effect.

Next morning the 14th Brigade's attack began auspiciously. At 7.30am Elliott was informed that Stewart's men had gained some sort of a foothold in Péronne. Immediately galvanised, the brigadier hastened forward, and located Scanlan and the acting commander of the 58th, Major Ferres (Watson was in England on leave). Both had their boots off, and neither seemed imbued with urgency. Pompey sought to alter this state of affairs, but Scanlan was unresponsive:

'Have you heard what the 14th Brigade's done? Are your men across the river?'

'We have taken all possible steps, General'.

Scanlan explained that patrols had been dispatched, and men would be sent across as soon as a viable crossing was located.

'But aren't they across there yet?'

'All possible steps are being taken'.

'Damn it, I'll take them over myself!'

With that Pompey headed off alone, down the slope to the canal, in full view of the Germans opposite. He made for a bridge that was reportedly destroyed and impassable:

> I found that the whole bridge had collapsed from the explosion, but that one of the steel girders had lodged across the canal in such a way that it was comparatively easy for an active infantryman to cross, and did so.

Clambering up the eastern bank, he found a useful vantage point, but a German machine-gun deterred him from lingering. Returning to the canal, he directed a 59th platoon posted near the bridge on the western side to come over. He 'waved his arm and bawled out to us to follow' him across, wrote one of the first to do so, who described Pompey's solo exploit as a 'not altogether unusual' feat for 'our famous Brigadier'.

After repositioning this platoon, Pompey hurried back across the broken bridge, intent on getting more of his brigade over as soon as possible. In his haste he trod on a loose beam and plunged spectacularly into the canal. It was 'very deep ... with steep sides', he found, and 'I had considerable difficulty scrambling out'. Scanlan and Ferres, having decided after the brigadier's hasty departure that they ought to go after him, laced up their boots and followed him down the slope, but German machine-gunners delayed their progress. They were taken aback when he panted up towards them, dripping wet. For the next few hours he once again became an arresting sight, directing developments with undiminished vim although trouserless. Doyle again:

> While his only pants were drying the Brigade Commander stalked about clad only in his shirt. The spectacle of his portly figure strutting on the parapet, looking through his field glasses and shouting out messages for transmission to Division, is unforgettable.

He was later told that divisional communications had been hampered because so many signallers were circulating the news that 'Pompey's fallen in the Somme'.

The 58th and 59th companies sent across the Somme after Pompey's dynamic and diverting intervention were unable to achieve much. He wanted them to attack Flamicourt in an envelopment manoeuvre: the 59th was to advance from the south, while the 58th proceeded to Péronne and utilised the 14th Brigade's progress there to launch a thrust towards Flamicourt from the west. But Flamicourt was a tough nut to crack. The railway station was a particular problem. It afforded excellent visibility for the resolute machine-gunners garrisoned there, and had been transformed by concrete and steel reinforcement into a virtual pillbox impervious to even direct hits from heavy guns. The 59th companies made some progress towards it, but the inaccessible marshland and the lack of available cover combined with the defenders at the station to bring them to a halt.

Meanwhile Ferres took his 58th companies and the battalion intelligence officer, 'Mick' Moon VC (who had recently rejoined the brigade), to the west of Péronne. They found Norman Marshall's 54th Battalion pinned down with no intention of attempting any further advance. The 58th companies, like their 59th counterparts, realised that their projected task was, for the time being at least, unfeasible. Elliott was notified that

> circumvented as they were by the ditch and marsh on either flank, and with every street leading northwards swept by machine-gun fire from the northern ramparts, which the enemy still held, it was impossible, despite every effort, to make any headway.

That evening, having transferred brigade headquarters further forward to a position with a marvellous view overlooking Péronne, Elliott reviewed the 15th Brigade's dispositions with Scanlan and Ferres, and was then notified that Hobbs had summoned him to a conference. A car was sent to collect him, but the driver could not locate his headquarters. After a lengthy delay Pompey decided to set off on foot, but 'having missed the track in the dark I had a very rough time of it getting over the old battlefield to the rendezvous'. By the time he arrived, frustrated and exhausted after wandering around for hours in 'a maze of tumbled trenches and barbed wire', it was after 2.00am and the conference was long over. Twice in four days a Fifth Division emissary had failed to find him; each time he had then lost his way trying to proceed alone to his destination.

When Hobbs told him what had been decided in his absence Pompey was appalled. As part of a renewed assault ordered by Monash to be carried out early next morning by the Second and Fifth Divisions, the 14th Brigade was to tackle the same objectives it had been previously unable to attain, and the 15th Brigade was to assist once again by advancing towards Péronne from the south. Elliott, however, had concluded that the previous day's attempts by his men had demonstrated the impossibility of accomplishing what his tired brigade was being asked to do, and he felt that the 14th Brigade was in a similar situation. He believed that since none of the other 'senior commanders concerned had made a personal reconnaissance of the ground' they 'were inevitably quite unaware of the difficulties involved'. The assessment he gave Hobbs was blunt:

> I felt obliged to tell the Divisional Commander that the task laid down was far too great for already exhausted men and that in setting it they were courting disaster. He replied that he had not wanted to do it but we must protect the flank of the other Division. [Nevertheless] if I was convinced my men were too exhausted for the task in front of them, he would put it before the Corps Commander [Monash]. I knew that I could barely reach my battalions in line as it was [and] if, as was almost certainly the case, the Corps Commander, who could know nothing of the ground…, ordered the matter to proceed I would never get the orders through in time, so having made my protest I decided I would carry on.

Since it was now too late to stop the operation, any notion of allowing the 14th Brigade to tackle such a daunting assignment unaided was unthinkable to Pompey. But how could his brigade help when its allotted task was, he believed, impracticable? No alternative method of assistance, he concluded after frantic evaluation, seemed more feasible. All he could come up with—'conceived', he later admitted, 'as a sort of forlorn hope' because he 'felt obliged to attempt the impossible'—was a proposal

> to defile my men in single file across the enemy's front ..., join in the fight for Peronne itself and later advance southwards. I was satisfied that unless something like that were done the 14th would be badly defeated, they had been allotted far too big a task for their strength, and although my own proposal seemed to me hairbrained ... there was this bare chance that the enemy would never dream that anyone would be mad enough to attempt it, and the occasion required desperate measures.

Hobbs reluctantly agreed. The previous night, he noted in his diary, he had been busy until 3.00am after a 'very difficult and trying day', but this situation was the most onerous he had ever known: 'I have been up against many trials, difficulties and problems in my life, but never have I had to face such an awful responsibility and danger'. Elliott, who wholeheartedly endorsed Monash's maxim that infantry should 'advance under the maximum possible protection of the maximum possible array of mechanical resources', felt that the 14th Brigade's task was a departure from this principle of such magnitude that it was difficult to justify. His forthright assessment reinforced Hobbs's misgivings, and Hobbs made sure that Monash knew the extent of the exhaustion in Fifth Division. Monash was aware that he was making severe demands on Hobbs and his division, but was ruthlessly determined to give the retreating enemy no respite, no time to make the defences stronger than they already were: 'I was compelled to harden my heart and to insist that it was imperative to recognise a great opportunity and to seize it unflinchingly'. The concern of Elliott and Hobbs about the task facing Stewart's men was to be validated by the casualty figures. Eight different AIF brigades were engaged at Péronne and Mont St Quentin; the 14th Brigade had nearly twice as many losses as any of the others.

Armed with Hobbs's consent to his audacious amendment, Elliott galloped back to his headquarters to organise its implementation. At 4.15am, with zero hour less than two hours away, he briefed his battalion commanders, carefully concealing his own misgivings about the desperate gamble. He decided to lend the 58th to his former colonel Norman Marshall, whose 54th Battalion had established itself in western Péronne and had been trying to clear the rest of the town. Two battalions, the 59th and 60th, were to follow the rest of the 14th Brigade around or through Péronne, while the 57th remained behind ready to advance if appropriate.

Ferres sent Moon away to get in touch with Marshall urgently. Moon had never run two miles harder, but when he reached 54th Battalion headquarters he found, to his amazement, that Marshall and the staff were sound asleep. From this legendary leader Moon was expecting to hear crisp instructions for the deployment of the donated 58th Battalion as well as appreciative thanks for his brigadier's admirable gesture (which Bean later described as 'almost unprecedented generosity'). Yet all he received from the drowsy colonel was a vague referral to the 56th Battalion, which was 'running the show'. Unbeknown to Moon, however, Marshall had managed to get hardly any sleep for three days, had no idea that the 58th Battalion had been allotted to him, and had mistakenly concluded that the 56th had taken over the main role in Péronne.

Meanwhile the 58th companies had reached Péronne and were proceeding along the main street when an enemy barrage caught them. About 40 men were hit, including Ferres himself and two other senior officers. Ferres lost a good deal of blood from a painful thigh wound, but managed to keep going despite limping badly. He was endeavouring to reorganise the battalion when Moon turned up with disconcerting news of the shemozzle concerning Marshall and the 54th. Ferres paused to reflect. He could either sit tight and wait for his superiors to sort out the mess and give him clear instructions, or he could attack on his own initiative immediately.

He decided to attack. The Germans defended fiercely, most notably a machine-gunner operating from a far upper window. But the attackers, led by 26-year-old Wimmera farmer Lieutenant Tom Slaughter, worked their way methodically from house to house, Lewis-gunners engaging the defending positions while their comrades manoeuvred round to the side and then charged: 'this method proved effective without exception', Ferres observed. Eventually even the elevated machine-gunner was toppled, along with his gun, into the street. It was a tough fight, but the 58th performed brilliantly and Péronne was conquered.

This was a marvellous achievement, but German resistance nearby

Above Charles Bean scrutinises an AIF advance, February 1917 *AWM E246*

Below Portrait photo taken at a professional studio, London *AWM H15596*

Above left This photograph of Kate and the children was a favourite of her husband's while he was separated from them during the war *AWM 2DRL 513/4*

Above right George Elliott

Below Darkie, with Jack Campbell in the saddle *AWM H15589*

Above Men of the 15th Brigade advancing near Warfusee-Abancourt on 8 August 1918, the day of the superb victory spearheaded by the Australians and Canadians that was described by the chief German strategist as 'the black day of the German Army in the history of this war' *AWM E2791*

Below At a captured German divisional headquarters, Harbonnières, 9 August 1918 *AWM E2855*

Above Inspecting a 15th Brigade parade with Captain Gollan (left) and General Hobbs (right) *AWM E3641*

Below Left Kate Elliott, to her husband's amusement, took a dim view of this published caricature by Bernie Bragg, a commercial artist who spent part of the war as a draughtsman at 15th Brigade headquarters

Below Right The general looking commanding *AWM H15595*

Above For his distinguished leadership of the Essendon boys, Elliott received from their parents and community supporters this special tribute

Right A memorial commemorating local enlisters in Victory Park Ascot Vale, unveiled by Elliott in April 1922; looking west towards a nearby street named after him

Below Close-up of memorial

Above After the war, the Australian War Memorial commissioned this painting by well-known portraitist Bill McInnes *AWM ART 3182*

Below 56 Prospect Hill Road, Camberwell

Above At Frankston with Ina Prictor's son Colin

Below Scouting enthusiast

Above Neil Elliott

Below Violet Elliott

had by no means ceased. The 59th and 60th Battalions had been pinned down, like the 14th Brigade units they were supporting, by machine-gun fire from St Denis Wood north of Péronne and from Mont St Quentin further north. 'Whole attack held up', Scanlan informed Elliott, after personally reconnoitring the most advanced positions; '14th Brigade report heavy casualties'. Even though the 58th was mopping up Péronne, Scanlan added, 'considerable artillery fire and a further advance along spur east of Mont St Quentin is essential for any further advance to be made' by the 59th and 60th (and the units with them). Tom Kerr, commanding the 60th while Layh was on leave, concurred. Elliott, accepting and endorsing this assessment, passed it on to Hobbs. Ferocious shellfire from the Germans as well as the lethal chatter of their machine-guns continued to speak volumes about their resolve to repel the Australians. The sustained bombardment endured by the 59th seemed even of Polygon Wood severity; to the hard-pressed 58th in Péronne itself (as Elliott later reported), 'the very foundations of the old city seemed to rock and sway as if in the throes of an earthquake'.

In the afternoon Hobbs directed Stewart to organise an advance eastwards towards St Denis Wood. Stewart did so, and a copy of these messages reached 15th Brigade headquarters. Once again Elliott reacted to an initiative from his superiors with abhorrence. It was precisely what he had strongly advised Hobbs not to authorise until the Germans overlooking that valley were removed. Pompey had 'no doubt' that the attackers would be 'utterly annihilated'. Convinced he had a better grasp of the situation than any other senior commander (thanks in particular to Scanlan's valiant inspection), he telephoned Hobbs to protest. If the proposed operation was undertaken despite his recommendation to the contrary, Pompey told Hobbs, he was prepared to help carry it out, but would resign the following day: 'I would no longer serve in the forces if men were wantonly sacrificed without proper reconnaissance and knowledge of the situation'. Hobbs, no doubt wondering when his tribulations in this organisational nightmare of a battle would end, responded by convening a divisional conference at Elliott's panoramic headquarters. Not only would the superb view assist their deliberations; Pompey's propensity to get lost while trying to find someone else's headquarters made it a good idea to have this one at his.

At 6.00pm Hobbs, Elliott, Stewart, Tivey, and their staffs began a thorough review of the situation. The upshot was vindication for

Pompey. It became apparent that Hobbs and Stewart, unlike Elliott, had been basing their decisions on faulty maps, which incorrectly situated the tactically vital feature of St Denis Wood. The operation opposed by Pompey was cancelled, the 14th Brigade was relieved, and a new policy was initiated. For the time being the aim was not to push the enemy hard, but to just keep in touch in order to discern any retirement quickly. Bean was no doubt aware of this controversial aspect of the battle (Pompey, of course, was characteristically frank about it in his report), but opted not to mention it in the *Official History*. It seems that no account by anyone else has referred to it either. While it is true that compiling a compressed account of the complicated fluctuations of this five-day battle was no easy task, a vehement protest involving a resignation threat by the most famous brigadier in the AIF—especially when the basis of that protest was vindicated—surely should have been mentioned in the *Official History*.

The main fighting in and around Péronne was over, but the 15th Brigade remained in the forward area for several days before being withdrawn. Elliott's men were engaged in consolidation and line-straightening, exploitation and pursuit. During these activities Pompey continued to make his invigorating presence felt, reconnoitring advanced positions to ensure that vigilant probing was maintained and no opportunity was missed.

Doyle accompanied him on some lively escapades. 'The General goes forward and I have a wild chase through Peronne after him', Doyle noted in his diary on 4 September, referring to their visit to 57th Battalion headquarters, despite vigorous enemy shellfire, because Pompey wanted to inspect front-line developments. At one stage the boyish exhilaration Elliott sometimes displayed under fire became evident as he spotted a boat, lowered his burly frame into it, and rowed about exuberantly with his reluctant intelligence officer while shells crashed into the water nearby. 'I hope they don't mistake us for a dreadnought and sink us', Pompey roared gleefully above the din. Hearing a cat meowing in distress, they rowed across at the brigadier's instigation to rescue it.

While relishing these high-spirited adventures, Pompey was well aware that extreme demands were being made on the stamina of not just Doyle but the whole brigade. On 3 September, Elliott noted, his men 'were too exhausted to do any patrolling and rested where they lay, too exhausted in most cases to go for their food'. Two days later he told Hobbs they were 'absolutely done ... and must be relieved'. Soon afterwards they were.

Once more Elliott and his men had been prominent in an outstanding accomplishment. Hobbs felt that it was as good as anything yet achieved by the AIF: 'how our men achieved the success they did is beyond me in the face of the difficulties they had to surmount', he wrote. Rawlinson described this triumph more than once as 'the finest single feat of the war'. He was not the only well-credentialled observer to think so. The Australians, although outnumbered and pushed close to the limit of their endurance, had overcome tenacious resistance from specially chosen defenders and driven the Germans out of a formidable bastion, which they had intended to retain for at least a month. And, yet again, there had been crucial contributions from the 15th Brigade and its tempestuous leader. Saluting these contributions on 7 September, Hobbs declared publicly that there was no better general in France than Elliott (and admitted privately that he had been right to protest against the operation that was cancelled five days earlier).

As usual after a big battle, Pompey obtained numerous personal narratives from 15th Brigade participants, and compiled an incisive report of his own. In this document he praised the 'excellent' artillery liaison, and commended the 'communications forward of brigade', which 'worked well', although contact with Fifth Division had been maintained less successfully. He again upheld the importance of personal reconnaissance by commanders: those 'unable or unwilling to do this must ... leave all initiative to the officer on the spot'. His report did not conceal his hostility to the proposed operations he had amended on 2 September. He also criticised Rosenthal's 'persistently exaggerated' claims of the Second Division's progress, which had exasperated him during the battle and, he felt, hindered the 14th and 15th Brigades' endeavours.

To Kate, Elliott emphasised the ferocity of the conflict and the gruelling impact on his brigade. It was five days of 'almost incessant fighting night and day', which 'raged with the utmost fury'. The combat was 'just about as terrible as it could be', he told Belle. After a supreme effort his valiant men had won another marvellous victory, but

> oh, Katie, the poor old Brigade! It would break your heart to see all that is left of them, the bravest wan, haggard and drawn, the others

> like men in a sleep walk almost ... For the first time in my life I am hoping we shall not be engaged until the men have a little rest. It was an awful experience.

The AIF was being stretched to the absolute limit. Numerically its battalions were woefully under-strength. Reinforcements were inadequate; the flow of recruits from Australia had slowed to a trickle. The AIF's outstanding proficiency in small-unit tactics compensated to some extent; the skilfulness and experienced professionalism that now supplemented the courage and dash Australian soldiers had shown ever since April 1915 was an important factor in their 1918 triumphs. But more and more was being asked of fewer and fewer. Monash was pushing the AIF hard because he felt that he could significantly shorten the war by doing so, but there were increasing signs that this policy was not without risk.

The culmination was a rebellious strike in the 15th Brigade. Early on 5 September, with Elliott's men looking forward to an overdue withdrawal, the 59th Battalion was ordered to pursue Germans retreating east of Péronne. Three platoons of B Company, together with a few men from A Company (about 60 in all), refused to budge. Scanlan spoke forcefully to these rebels, but they remained defiant. They were feeling too exhausted and too exploited, they told him. There had been no proper rest for far too long, and they were fed up with having to do more than their fair share just because the British were not up to it. At 7.15am Scanlan called at brigade headquarters and notified Elliott. Nonplussed and embarrassed, he then offered his resignation. Bean described this incident as 'the first recorded mutiny in the AIF', but his account in the *Official History* misdated it (a mistake which has prompted at least two historians to state incorrectly that the 59th was afflicted by two mutinies in September 1918).

Elliott's response to this challenging situation confirmed the quality of his leadership. He told Scanlan to go forward with the rest of the battalion, leaving the strikers where they were, and to forget about resigning. Pompey then sent Bob Salmon to ask the dissidents for a written statement outlining their grievances. The document they gave Salmon emphasised their exhaustion, overwork, and lack of relief. It also accused 'the Australian Higher Command' of failing to bring these circumstances sufficiently to its British superiors' attention, a neglect that had forced the rebels to act drastically as 'the only way they can impress the authorities of their needs'.

After studying this statement, Elliott went to the rebels and addressed them in compelling style. There was no blood-and-thunder bluff and bluster. He began by saying that he had carefully read their grievances. In some, he conceded, they had 'cause for complaint'; but the action they had taken was a dubious way to pursue redress. It amounted to a particularly serious crime for a soldier, more so than they probably realised, and a slur on the battalion, the brigade, and their gallant comrades who had fought and died alongside them. He himself was greatly saddened, not just in his capacity as their brigadier but because he had a special association with the 59th, having commanded its 'parent' battalion, the original 7th, in some of the AIF's most famous battles. Referring to a 1797 mutiny in the British navy by way of precedent, Pompey observed that genuine grievances had motivated those naval mutineers but the ringleaders were shot nonetheless. Urging the 59th dissidents to reconsider, he told them that he proposed to leave and return in half an hour. If, after reviewing their attitude, they still refused to go forward, he would have them sent to the rear; if, however, they agreed to come back to their unit, he was prepared to speak on their behalf when the incident was officially investigated because he believed they did not fully grasp the gravity of their action. The brigadier then left. When he returned 30 minutes later the rebels indicated that they wanted to rejoin the battalion.

This incident was a clear warning about the danger of pushing the AIF too hard. Elliott certainly heeded it. First and foremost was the obvious requirement to provide his men with the rest they so desperately needed. He was on the phone to Hobbs soon after Scanlan reported the trouble in the 59th (as Hobbs noted in his diary):

> Gen. Elliott rang me up at 7.30am and told me his men were absolutely done, fed up and on the verge of mutiny and must be relieved. I told him they would be tonight.

Elliott was similarly responsive concerning other grievances in the rebels' statement. Not enough food was reaching the forward area, the rebels claimed, and they were not getting a 'fair deal' from the battalion medical officer. Elliott appointed Doyle to inquire into the food complaint, and called for an immediate report from the 59th's doctor. Doyle's formal inquiry on 6 September concluded that the accusation about inadequate rations was, as Elliott put it, 'without any substantial foundation, but undoubtedly some grievances did exist' (he passed these on to Hobbs). The medical report was unequivocal:

> The men are one and all suffering from excessive fatigue, loss of sleep and nervous strain. In my opinion the limit of endurance has been reached for most of the men.

Elliott, pleased that his inclination to handle the rebels with kid gloves was supported by Hobbs and Monash, continued to do his utmost to avoid any repetition of the incident. He urged his battalion commanders to 'nurse the men at every opportunity'. They had to be 'rested as much as possible'. Pompey arranged for an instructional lecture to be given about the provision of rations to remove any misapprehensions on that score, and reminded his officers that there was plenty they could do to reduce tedium in the ranks by fostering an intelligent interest in military and non-military activities. Stimulating recreational pursuits should be another priority. The brigadier also instructed his battalion commanders to emphasise that everything possible was being done for the men, and to reaffirm that redoubled effort now might well produce 'a speedier termination of the war'. At the same time senior officers had to be 'on their guard against anyone who might take advantage of momentary discontent and exhaustion' to whip up further agitation.

Other Australians emulated B Company of the 59th in rebelling because they felt they were being unfairly overworked to compensate for conspicuous British inadequacy. A group of 119 men in the 1st Battalion refused to advance when directed to participate in an attack on the outer defences of the Hindenburg Line. But there were no further incidents of that kind in the 15th Brigade. However, later that month Elliott had to contend with an even larger bunch of strong-willed recalcitrants. Trouble arose this time in a different battalion over a different issue. The cause of the mutiny that erupted in the 60th Battalion late in September 1918 was the decision to disband it.

Disbandment had been on the cards for some time. In January 1918 Birdwood had foreshadowed to Defence minister Pearce that a reduction of one battalion per brigade was probably inevitable as a result of dwindling reinforcements (Britain and other combatant nations had already implemented such action). It was decided, partly because of the Australian government's reluctance to approve this unpalatable step, not to break any unit up unless this became unavoidable. The 36th and 52nd Battalions had been disbanded shortly after their gallant attacks at Villers-Bretonneux on 4 and 25 April respectively, and the 47th Battalion in the 12th Brigade had been dissolved as well. By August various other AIF units were significantly under-strength, and senior British strategists were insisting that it would be administratively inefficient not to disband more. But most Australians felt profoundly attached to their battalion, and Monash resisted the pressure. So long as the battalions each 'have 30 Lewis guns it doesn't very much matter what else they have', he maintained. Birdwood, however, was still GOC AIF, and he sided with his British superiors; Monash eventually had to yield.

Monash's acquiescence was influenced by the sudden authorisation of home leave for original Anzacs. Soldiers from some combatant nations had occasionally been able to go home on leave during the war, but the tyranny of distance had prevented their Australian counterparts from being allowed to do so. After four years away, that opportunity had now been obtained for the early enlisters by Prime Minister Hughes, who spent much of 1918 in England combatively engaged in a range of war-related matters. In September, during one of his visits to France, he met Elliott for the first time. The Prime Minister arrived very late at the brigade parade Pompey had organised especially for him (having not turned up at all when one was scheduled the previous day), stayed very briefly and, the brigadier felt, 'looked very absent-minded and had little to say'. (In fairness to Hughes, he did have a lot on his mind in mid-September.)

Pompey did not think much of Billy Hughes, and believed that the introduction of home leave for the originals was 'a big mistake'. These experienced men included many of the best leaders and trainers, and were the 'backbone' of the AIF. Pompey himself had been deprived of Layh, who accepted the offer of a place in the first batch of returning originals and departed on 14 September. With Denehy and Scanlan also eligible for leave, Pompey was concerned that he might lose three capable colonels in quick succession. Besides, this was no time for easing up or complacency—with the Germans 'more or less crippled', now was the time to finish them off. The decision 'shows the absolute folly of allowing politicians like Hughes to meddle with the Army', Pompey fulminated. 'If Mr Hughes had been in the pay of the Germans he could not have dealt us a more paralysing stroke'. Monash was also unimpressed with the Anzac leave initiative, which potentially affected over 6,000 Australians and made it harder to resist the pressure for further disbandments.

Each AIF brigade apart from the first four was to be reconstituted on a three battalion basis. With three units already disbanded, seven more battalions were to be broken up immediately, including one from the 15th Brigade. The 60th had always been the most vulnerable battalion in Elliott's brigade. At an early stage, instructions were circulated that in those AIF brigades containing battalions recruited entirely from one state, as the 15th Brigade was, 'as a general rule, and unless there are special reasons for the contrary, the fourth (or junior in numerical order) is to be eliminated'. In the aftermath of Villers-Bretonneux the 60th evidently only narrowly avoided the fate suffered by the 52nd, which had also lost heavily in that famous counter-attack on 24-25 April. On 14 May Elliott cabled a fervent plea home to his friend Duigan, who had commanded the 60th before succumbing to severe ill-health:

> AIF authorities decree 60th Battalion too weak [to] carry on ... no other reinforcements available. 60th Battalion fought hardest, penetrated farthest [into] enemy's ranks, killed most, lost most men [at] Villers-Bretonneux. For such a deed as this [the] French grant Croix de Guerre, the Germans the Iron Cross to their regiments, ensuring men immortal renown. Australia leaves hers to perish like sheep in drought time to please her Bolsheviks. Such regiments are not bred in a day ... In all Melbourne [are] there not a thousand volunteers to save this regiment created from its suburbs, blood of its blood, flesh of its flesh, bone of its bone, having won imperishable fame, from dissolution and the Brigade robbed of its right arm?

However, dispatch of this cable was blocked by Birdwood, who directed Hobbs to reprimand Elliott for what he described as its indiscreet wording and 'severe criticism of Military Authority'.

Four months later, when disbandment was decreed by Elliott's superiors, the earlier instructions applicable to same-state brigades were repeated, confirming the 60th's vulnerability. On 24 September Elliott was briefed about an imminent AIF assault on the Hindenburg Line and ordered to disband the 60th immediately. He decided to transfer the 60th into a combined and strengthened 59th Battalion, with the 60th becoming A and B Companies of the 59th, and the 'old' 59th comprising the new C and D Companies.

The rearrangement was to be formalised at a parade on 26 September. Beforehand Major Tom Kerr, the acting 60th commander, told Elliott that the men were upset about the battalion's dissolution, but he was not anticipating any of the rebelliousness already evident in other AIF battalions sentenced to disbandment. At the parade, however, few of the 60th men complied when Scanlan issued orders to them. Elliott, who was present (having assured Kerr he would speak to the men), was furious. One mutiny was more than enough. He rode up and gave them a piece of his mind in no uncertain terms.

'This nonsense must cease at once', Pompey thundered. He told the rebels he was surprised and pained to witness such defiance. If they were not going to obey lawful orders they would find themselves with a different brigadier, because he was not going to command a mob. In the AIF the death penalty could be imposed for desertion or mutiny. Where a large body of men mutinied, the ringleaders would be executed. If their identities could not be determined, then probably one in every ten would be shot. Pompey was so fired up, and expressed this threat with such menace, that some onlookers became convinced that he was prepared to shoot every tenth man himself there and then. 'We've got bullets too', remarked one of the rebels.

Changing tack, influenced perhaps by that pointed interjection, Elliott proceeded to explain why the disbandment decision had been taken. 'What's the use of keeping a full battalion staff with transport organised to administer a thousand men', he asked, merely 'to follow 200 men about the country?'

> It's no use blaming the AIF authorities ... Blame the politicians in Australia who, when we enlisted, promised to support us to the last man and the last shilling, [but failed to provide] the reinforcements to keep our splendid force going.

When asked months earlier to nominate the worst battalion in his brigade, Elliott continued, he had replied that there was 'no worst and no best'; in that situation, his superiors had directed, it was the last battalion that had to go. He read out the passionate cable he sent Duigan to avert the demise of the 60th, explaining that it had been suppressed. He concluded with an appeal to the dissidents' better judgment, urging them not to be influenced by outsiders, and said he would leave them for half an hour to enable them to reconsider their position. It was a memorable address, as the diary of one of the rebels attests:

> Col. Scanlan ... ordered slope arms—none budged. He then demanded it again—none stirred. Then old Pompey on his big black neddy fell on us like an avalanche. Man he was mad. If he'd had his revolver a few would have been shot very likely. He ... detailed the law dealing with mutiny. Then he dealt with the necessity of being broken up. Then he pleaded.

Leaving the rebels for half an hour after giving them plenty to think about had worked well with the 59th dissenters, who were ready to comply on his return, but the 60th recalcitrants were not convinced so easily. Not the slightest disrespect to the brigadier was intended, a number of spokesmen assured Elliott, but several concerns about the disbandment remained unresolved. 'It seems like deserting our dead', some said with tears in their eyes. So Pompey had further explaining to do. There was no foreseeable prospect of recruits or returning wounded rebuilding the battalion to its former strength; the identity and colours of the 60th would be retained to the extent possible—the training unit in England would now be known as the 60th Battalion, and ex-60th men would be able to retain their colour patches; the 59th was not a more appropriate battalion to disband, despite the recent refusal of some of its men to advance; and any rumour that the Australians would be transferred to Fifth Army so they could be squandered in gratification of Birdwood's latest ambitions was simply not true. These responses did the trick. Pompey handed the men back to Scanlan, and all four companies of the newly constituted 59th marched away together in fine style.

But it was a close call. In every other AIF battalion supposed to be disbanded in September 1918, the repugnance of the rank and file resulted in non-compliance. The intensity of feeling among the 60th men was no less; the difference was the calibre and influence of their brigadier. It was, as Bean recognised, 'a tribute to the unrivalled hold of Brig-Genl "Pompey" Elliott on the loyalty of his men' that the 60th Battalion only agreed to join the 59th 'after being addressed by this beloved stout-hearted Australian'.

The following day, however, there was a revival of the trouble. Overnight Pompey's men were visited by rebels from other battalions earmarked for dissolution; they reported that they had successfully prevented their units from being disbanded. These other dissidents, having maintained an independent existence under their own leaders (assisted by sympathetic comrades who donated or pilfered rations for them), had been given a reprieve—much to Elliott's disgust—and allowed to participate as reinstated battalions in the major operation about to be launched against the Hindenburg Line. In those circumstances renewed agitation in the 60th was predictable, and Elliott was not surprised when a deputation of 60th men asked to see him on 27 September.

He went over all the arguments again, adding that the rebels' apparent success in other battalions was illusory. All they had gained was a temporary reprieve; their battalions would still be disbanded after the attack, if necessary by denying them reinforcements so that they gradually withered ignominiously. He reminded his men that the 15th Brigade was about to go forward for an important operation; the Americans would be attacking initially, and the AIF had to support them and exploit their success. Any 60th men who were not prepared to help their comrades would be taken to the rear, locked up, and charged with mutiny. It was another challenging test of his leadership and influence, but his spirited appeal to his soldiers' loyalty and his blunt outline of the consequences of rebellion proved a persuasive combination. He was understandably proud:

> By using my influence to its utmost I managed to sway the men over the line, and they marched off in grand style. My Brigade is the only one in which the reorganisation was successfully accomplished.

Elliott was pleased to be in an operation involving the Americans. He and his men had developed an excellent rapport with a group of Americans attached to the 15th Brigade in June. In the 15th Brigade's sector there were three separate barriers in the Hindenburg Line system. They were, in the order Elliott's men would encounter them, the main Hindenburg line, the Le Catelet line, and the Beaurevoir line. The Americans' objective was situated beyond the Le Catelet line. Once they had consolidated there, the Australians (including the 15th Brigade) were to pass through them and undertake a more difficult open-warfare advance over two miles further past the Beaurevoir line.

However, as Elliott went forward on 29 September to follow his brigade's advance, leaving Gollan in charge at (rear) brigade headquarters, he noticed 'a great deal of confusion'. Numerous American stragglers, apparently leaderless, were backtracking. Elliott himself halted several of these groups and turned them round. 'Americans seem to be disorganised', he told Hobbs. Pompey's chagrin was intense as he realised the extent of the fiasco, which was largely attributable to the Americans' inexperience. (Afterwards he learned that the 15th Brigade lieutenants loaned by him to help these uninitiated allies with mopping-up and other front-line techniques had not carried out this important task because an American general had kept them at his headquarters to show him how to run the battle.) Moreover, Pompey found,

> the 59th lost heavily from surprise fire from flank and left rear as well as front, coming from trenches we had been informed had been captured already, and it was necessary to take steps to deal with them.

In fact, this battalion's commander had a narrow escape. Scanlan was leading the 59th through dense wire at the main Hindenburg line—with thick fog limiting visibility and the Americans' objective still two miles ahead—when he was startled by a warning shout. His adjacent adjutant had suddenly spotted a German 30 yards ahead who was taking aim at them. Scanlan immediately 'fell among the wire, tearing my hands and my trousers but saving my life', while the Lewis-gunners accompanying him quickly dealt with this German post. However, it was obvious that things had not gone according to plan. Far from it. On the 15th Brigade's left the Americans operating in front of Gellibrand's Third AIF Division had made even less progress (although on the right, where the British 46th Division performed brilliantly, the situation was more satisfactory). It was going to be up to the Australians to attain—

without the vital element of surprise or much artillery assistance—most of the American objectives as well as their own.

Once again Elliott and his brigade were equal to the challenge. The brigadier told his battalion commanders to organise an advance themselves as soon as possible, and to take the Americans forward in the process; the colonels were to tell him what they had decided, and he would arrange artillery support. Denehy and Watson decided to attack the Le Catelet line at 3.00pm. They arranged for their battalions (Scanlan's 59th was now in reserve) to be assisted by tanks and Americans, as well as the supporting barrage requested by Elliott. But this barrage proved to be disappointingly feeble, and the alerted Germans rained a lethal fire on the attackers. Nearly all the tanks were hit straightaway, no less than half the 58th men engaged soon became casualties, and the 57th suffered severe losses as well. Nevertheless, after ferocious fighting, the 15th Brigade established itself in the Le Catelet line. Next morning Elliott went forward to confer with Denehy, and became involved in the organisation of various subsidiary manoeuvres to consolidate his brigade's gains, but essentially the main focus on 30 September was on retrieving the much more serious situation on the left.

That night, however, Elliott was summoned to a conference, where he learned that an attack on a wide frontage was to be launched early the following morning. Arriving back at his own headquarters around midnight, he briefed his waiting battalion commanders about the operation. All three battalions in the 15th Brigade were to advance together, with Norman Marshall's 54th alongside the 59th.

A sharp ancillary barrage rendered enemy resistance to this attack much less formidable. Each of Elliott's battalions soon reported success. Pompey encouraged them to exploit beyond their assigned goals. When Denehy notified him that the 57th had reached its objective and could probably have gone further though the men were very tired, Pompey's reaction was characteristic: 'Damn it, if you can do it, do it now!' Hobbs was so encouraged by the reports of rapid progress reaching him that he urged Elliott's men to tackle the Beaurevoir line, the last of the three barriers in the Hindenburg system. However, like the Le Catelet line, it was strongly held—German resistance remained fierce at these main barriers though less determined between them—and this task was never really feasible for Pompey's exhausted, depleted units. That night the 15th Brigade was withdrawn, having completed (as Bean stated in the *Official History*) its 'exceedingly difficult task of confronting the Beaurevoir Line'.

That was the final battle for Elliott and his men. On 5 October, in fact, the last AIF brigade still engaged was withdrawn. The Australian Corps, having spearheaded the rupture of the mighty Hindenburg Line system, scored a prolonged rest as well as lavish praise from Rawlinson for its 'series of successes unsurpassed in this great war'. 'We are away back in peace country' where it 'seems like there is no war at all', Elliott wrote, but the carnage was never far from his thoughts. His brigade had done 'splendidly' in the Hindenburg Line battle, but it was 'another three days' dreadful fighting', he told Kate. Saddened once again by the casualties—which included over 30 officers in his brigade, and reduced it to the numerical strength of one and a half battalions—he was dismayed to find two of his 'old 7th boys' among the killed. They included George Elliott's friend and football team-mate Stan Neale, a fine officer 'who had been right through from the very beginning', had 'never had a scratch or been ill at all', and was about to depart for Australia on Anzac leave.

In a letter to J.F. Henderson Elliott described in admiring detail the extraordinary gallantry of 23-year-old Lieutenant Norman Dalgleish, one of his pre-war Essendon boys. Not only had Dalgleish kept going despite multiple wounds; he had also insisted—even after a shell fragment smashed into his head, inflicting terrible injuries and rendering him speechless—on informing his superiors personally (with a mixture of sign language, writing, and sketching, the paper scarred by blood pouring from his face) that his beleaguered company badly needed reinforcements. They arrived, thanks to his exceptional dedication, just in time. Conveyed to hospital, Dalgleish asked a nurse to help him compile gallantry commendations for two of his NCOs. That task completed, he collapsed and died. Touched by Pompey's stirring letter, Henderson read it to Dalgleish's father (who 'broke down completely and cried like a child', Henderson told Elliott), and gave it to the Melbourne *Herald*, where it was reproduced under arresting headlines: 'AS HIS LIFE-BLOOD FLOWS, OFFICER COMPLETES TASK: DUTY DONE WITH LAST BREATH'.

Pompey was also particularly affected by the recent death of one of his original 7th Battalion officers, Eric Connelly, who had re-enlisted after being sent home with a severe Gallipoli wound. Having shown impressive talent as a staff officer in the Third Division, Connelly had been fatally wounded by an aeroplane bomb dropped near his camp. He was a 'splendid fellow', Pompey wrote, and the wife he had married just before leaving Australia the second time was now on her way to England. 'Won't it be a dreadful shock to her on her arrival, away from home and friends and everything', he reflected.

Compared to the ubiquitous torment inflicted by this terrible war, another decoration was merely a pleasant distraction. Still, it was undeniably satisfying to be recognised with the French Croix de Guerre and a citation proclaiming that the 15th Brigade's 'brilliant results' were 'due in a very great measure to his personality, his strength of character, his initiative and his military talents'. The crushing devastation of the hopes and ideals of a generation was irreparable, but at least the conflict was hastening to its finale. Under sustained pressure the Germans kept retreating; their national cohesion rapidly disintegrated. Peace negotiations began, and an armistice ended the fighting on 11 November. At last it was all over.

CHAPTER NINETEEN

'Very Sad About Everything': Painful adjustment to peace

NOVEMBER 1918–JUNE 1919

IN LONDON, faraway Australia and elsewhere around the world, the outbreak of peace was greeted with jubilation and euphoria. Even staid people went berserk with relief. But the reaction in the AIF was generally more muted. The sense of satisfaction was swamped by sober reflection. Victory had come at a terrible price in Australian lives, and the prospect of civilian life seemed strange, daunting. Years of soldiering and strife had prompted many Australians to abandon their former aspirations of a safe return to a fulfilling post-war existence. Scotching such hopes as unrealistic, even unimaginable, amid the relentless slaughter, they had come to accept that they were probably doomed to share the fate of so many fallen comrades. Now, suddenly, they had a big adjustment to make. 'The feeling is bewildering', Charles Bean observed, 'one doesn't get used to peace in a day'.

Although 11 November was to become, for the rest of the century and beyond, a notable anniversary to commemorate the signing of the Armistice, it was just another day's training in the 15th Brigade. In fact, the Armistice was not even mentioned in the brigade diary, and Elliott's personal diary did not refer to it either. 'Musketry. Gas projector demonstration' was all he recorded on 11 November. However, to Milly Edwards he described the 'great rejoicing' of ecstatic French civilians, and he wrote buoyantly to Violet. 'Isn't this just splendid news we have now?' he enthused; 'soon I'll be coming back home to my little darlings'.

How soon was the big question. Organising the return of some 160,000 soldiers to Australia was a complex undertaking. There were a number of complicating factors. Most Australian soldiers had been away a long time, and wanted to get home as soon as possible; there was intense competition for the limited available shipping, and obtaining the necessary vessels was difficult; the AIF was expected to be represented in an army of occupation in Germany; Prime Minister Hughes was wary of unemployment problems in Australia if too many soldiers were sent home too quickly; and, after the biggest war there had ever been, the transition to peacetime conditions involved such immense upheaval that organising anything substantial was bound to be difficult. For some time, while various issues affecting the repatriation of the AIF were worked through, Elliott had no idea when he might get home. 'No one knows when apparently', he told Kate. But from what he could ascertain, he wrote in mid-December, peace would not be finalised until 'at least May ... and it will be 9 or 12 months after that before we all get away from here'.

However, the demobilisation and repatriation of the AIF became another organisational feather in Monash's cap. After Hughes placed him in charge, Monash applied his masterly administrative proficiency to this challenging task with distinct success. Appropriate criteria were established to determine which men were entitled to return sooner rather than later; the requisite ships were prised from the British authorities; and it was eventually resolved, after some confusing toing and froing, that there would be no AIF participation in the army of occupation in Germany. Thanks to Monash's outstanding organisation and the skilful leadership of commanders closer to the men, including Elliott, the AIF did not experience the serious unrest that plagued the forces of some other countries during this difficult period. By the end of 1918 Pompey was beginning to realise that he might be home much sooner than he had pessimistically predicted.

Oddly, the Armistice actually postponed his reunion with Kate. His persistent efforts to persuade her to come to England, as other AIF wives (including his sister Violet Avery) had done, had finally paid dividends. Kate planned to leave soon after Christmas; Belle would look after young Violet and Neil. Elliott was thrilled. 'Oh Darling, I am counting the days till you come to me', 'I can hardly go to sleep at night for thinking of it'. When he first saw her again, he warned, he might burst into tears. But the Armistice was a spanner in the works: 'with a very sad heart I have sent ... a cable telling you that it is now inadvisable to come'.

Elliott's chagrin was all the greater because he needed his 'sunshine lady' more than ever. Since the Armistice he had been in the grip of a pronounced morale plummet. The fighting from March to October had been almost continuous; he had been sustained through those arduous and stressful months by his unswerving focus and single-minded commitment to the ultimate goal of victory. With that supreme objective attained, a big letdown had materialised in its wake. His purposefulness and motivation had vanished, leaving a void that was filled neither by satisfaction with the war's victorious conclusion nor by his post-Armistice activities. There was too much waiting and uncertainty, too much time to think and brood.

His surroundings were no help. Late in November Elliott and his brigade were transferred to Favril, 25 miles east of Bellicourt. Pompey was unimpressed. 'We are still in the same place and a very damp, dull old place it is', he was reporting within a week. A December shift to Dourlers, near the Belgian border, brought no improvement. 'It's a melancholy country in the winter, with dripping skies and hardly a green leaf showing'; the meagre ration of daylight began to disappear soon after three o'clock, and there was 'unending drizzle for days'.

At a deeper level Elliott was troubled by guilt. The aspect of the war he had found most difficult was having to order men into situations that put their lives at risk. Some, inevitably, had died; yet he was still alive. Most AIF veterans, having seen so many of their comrades perish, had not expected to survive; when they found that they had, many felt guilty as well as relieved. This sentiment was more prevalent among front-line soldiers than brigadiers, but Elliott felt it acutely—no brigadier was a more front-line commander than Pompey, and he identified strongly with his men. His survival was one of the minor miracles of the war.

Remarkable escapes had continued right to the end. On 29 September he went forward with his newly appointed intelligence officer to scrutinise developments in the Hindenburg Line battle. They were ahead of the advancing 15th Brigade when a shell hit the intelligence officer, who was right beside Elliott. Pompey, yet again, escaped unscathed, and proceeded further forward undeterred. It was universally recognised that he would never send a man anywhere he was not prepared to go himself. During the war he proved this time and time again; afterwards the men he led confirmed it time and time again.

Still, he had somehow managed to survive when so many fine men had not. Among them were the Henderson brothers and Jimmy Johnston in the early days at Gallipoli; Norman Greig at German Officers' Trench; Ken Walker at Steele's Post; Noel Edwards and Harry Webb at Lone Pine; Geoff McCrae and Tom Elliott and all the others at Fromelles; Jimmy Topp at Bullecourt; Herb Dickinson and John Turnour at Polygon Wood; Dick Simpson at Villers-Bretonneux; Steve Facey and Merv Knight at Hamel; and Stan Neale and Norman Dalgleish at the end. This was not to mention his own relatives, George Elliott and Jack Campbell. With 'Death as an ever present companion', Pompey informed Latham in September, 'we have lost so many good companions that it seems but a step over the border to join them'. Two months later, after the Armistice, he assured Charles Denehy's wife of his

> love and gratitude towards all the gallant boys who have died for us in the ranks of the Brigade. It has been an inspiration to live with them. One might well wish to have died with them.

Similarly, to Belle:

> I don't think that in civilian life one realizes how gradually we come over here to regard death almost with contempt. There were so many of our pals gone before that it seemed little more than a step in the darkness to join them.

Elliott's frame of mind was not helped by a conference he attended at Corps headquarters on repatriation arrangements. Among the commanders present was Birdwood, exuding as usual what Elliott described as 'a pretended affability that he imagines deceives us'. But when Birdwood noticed the 60th Battalion colours Elliott had been wearing on his sleeve since that unit's disbandment—a considerate gesture appreciated by 60th men—the veneer of feigned bonhomie vanished in an instant, and Elliott found himself on the receiving end of an extraordinary full-blown tantrum. Birdwood began to 'chatter and jibber' at the miniature colour patch 'like a demented monkey' (another Pompey account described the AIF chief spitting like a cornered cat):

> 'What is that you are wearing? … How dare you, sir, wear colours which are not authorised? … Quite wrong, a brigadier favouring one of his battalions.'
>
> 'Sir, I am not showing preference to one battalion over another. That battalion no longer exists. It is a tribute to the dead. I put in an application to wear it at the time the dissolution was carried out, and have had no reply.'
>
> 'You'll get a reply all right.'

With that, Elliott recorded, Birdwood flounced 'out of the room, calling Generals Monash and Hobbs to follow him, for all the world like a cock wren and his harem'.

What happened while they were outside Elliott did not know. But he concluded that Monash must have spoken to Birdwood 'very tersely' about the way Elliott had handled the 60th's disbandment, because when Birdwood reappeared he had transformed himself into the acme of affability:

> he came back and fairly slobbered over me. He wanted to thank me for getting the dissolution carried out so smoothly which he was informed was done using the weight of my personal influence with the men, and that he was informed also that this made possible the carrying out of the dissolution of other units in the force, and so forth. I told him it was mainly due to my officers. 'Oh no', he said, 'I am sure it was due a great deal to your personal influence and your inculcation of a brigade feeling in your brigade'. The little worm omitted to mention that he was one of the greatest obstacles to the formation of a brigade spirit in the beginning.

Moreover, Pompey alleged, Birdwood had been careful not to jeopardise his prestige within the AIF by addressing the men himself on the subject of disbandment.

This incident reinforced Elliott's rancour. He had already told Kate he would not be following her advice to keep his bitter criticism of the AIF chief to himself: 'I don't care who hears my opinion of General Birdwood or repeats it'. In fact, he threatened, he was going to express his condemnation publicly in due course. It was 'the greatest possible misfortune for the Australian[s] … that they were ever placed under his command'. Pompey suspected—correctly, and perceptively early—that Birdwood's ultimate ambition was to become governor-general of Australia. 'General Monash is worth a dozen of him as a soldier', Elliott told Belle, 'and as a man there is no comparison at all'.

Pompey was predictably irate about some of the decisions announced at the conference where the Birdwood tantrum occurred. He was, of course, incensed that Birdwood was to continue as GOC AIF—or, as he and certain others saw it, had managed to cling to the Australians. With Monash now Director-General of Repatriation and Demobilisation, and Hobbs chosen to succeed him as the Australian Corps commander, Pompey was also infuriated to learn that the vacated command of the Fifth Division had been given to Tivey. Aspersions previously cast on Tivey within the 15th Brigade—in particular, the jibe that he made a habit of keeping his 8th Brigade out of the fighting whenever he could—were revived in earnest:

> I am very dissatisfied. No one here has the slightest confidence in Tivey as a leader, and I think everyone said when they heard of it 'Thank God the war is over'. They all know it is because Birdwood has a spite against me for standing up to him for the boys' sake.

Elliott's burning resentment about being overlooked for divisional vacancies resurfaced with a vengeance:

> Passed very restless night ... Birdwood's supersession of me by Gellibrand and Glasgow keeps recurring to me with stinging force and gives me no rest. I must bring this feeling to a head by demanding to have placed before me in black and white what my alleged crime has been and when the punishment for same is going to end.

The following afternoon Elliott raised the matter with Hobbs, who promised to discuss it with Birdwood at the next opportunity. He did. As Hobbs told Pompey afterwards, Birdwood claimed that there was nothing against Elliott except certain episodes of 'irrational conduct', and asked Hobbs if he was prepared to recommend Elliott for promotion to divisional command; Hobbs replied that he was. 'Not likely to do me much good now', Pompey concluded.

When Haig's official dispatch concerning the famous Villers-Bretonneux counter-attack was published, Elliott was irked by its implication that the task of Glasgow's brigade south of the town had been more difficult than his own brigade's assignment to the north. Pompey sent a forceful correction to Treloar at the Australian War Records Section, contending that this perception had been influenced by Birdwood, who had already decided to supersede him by promoting Glasgow (and Gellibrand). The contrasting treatment he had received in awards for the Villers-Bretonneux triumph was no coincidence, Pompey assured Treloar. Whereas the French had awarded him the Croix de Guerre and a citation of lavish praise, he had received from the British—with Birdwood ultimately in charge of honours and awards to the AIF—nothing at all, even though a copy of his operation orders had been requested by British staff officers and acclaimed at British military schools.

The supersession grievance was not his only gnawing concern. The prospect of being reunited with his wife and children was marvellous, but he was increasingly perturbed about his capacity to provide for them amid post-war uncertainty, disruption, and probable unemployment because, he feared, his professional reputation had been tarnished:

> with all the trouble I will have to face as soon as I arrive it will be as hard as any battlefield or rather far worse, for I would rather go on facing the Germans here for 20 years than face those people Roberts has cheated of their money.

He had not heard for some time from those handling his affairs, and realised that they might be reporting as infrequently as possible, professionally at least, because whenever they did the fees they would be charging him would accumulate further. But he became alarmed when Kate mentioned that she had recently endorsed several cheques at his lawyer's request. For over a week he remained 'very much upset about this matter', worried that these amounts may have comprised expenses that he might end up having to pay, until it suddenly occurred to him as he tossed and turned with Christmas Day about to dawn that they concerned something altogether different, and there was no need for anxiety. Still, acute feelings of shame and disgrace about the Roberts defalcation continued to haunt him. The thought of having to deal with its consequences on his return filled him with dread: 'I am shrinking from it like a child from a scorching fire, but it must be faced'.

Reports reaching him of family friction were another concern. The central figure was his temperamental sister Flory. When Elliott heard that she and Lyn were not getting on, he instinctively sided with his sister-in-law. He then discovered that his mother was finding Flory so obnoxious that she had decided to move to Brisbane with Violet and the other Averys in order to get away from her. Learning of this distasteful quarrelling straight after losing Stan Neale and other fine officers and men in the Hindenburg Line battle 'seemed just about the last straw' to Elliott. He sent Flory a blistering letter. 'I never want her near my house again', he told Belle. 'She'd be turning Katie and the children against me next with that poisonous tongue of hers'. Later, when he became obsessed about the impact of the Roberts defalcation on his professional future, his revived anxiety was redoubled by his conviction that Flory was more than capable of maliciously aggravating the situation if she had any inkling of it. He felt extremely vulnerable:

> She would ruin me with anyone at all if she could, and I only wish some one would get her away out of Melbourne before I get back there. I never want to see her again.

Other factors contributed to his severe post-Armistice plummet. It was 'very sad' to see 'the old battalions dwindling down' as drafts of homeward bound veterans departed. He was still receiving distressing letters from relatives of 15th Brigade soldiers who had been killed. And the advent of the Spanish influenza pandemic was a chilling development. Its fatalities included officers in his brigade and a nephew of Milly Edwards, who succumbed when convalescing after a slight wound. Reports of its virulence in Melbourne were alarming. Then, on top of everything else, came the unsettling spectacle of 'a thick clot of blood' in his urine.

All this had reduced him to a sorry state:

> At times I get fearful fits of depression when I can see nothing but misery for us all, and I wake up sometimes in the night with a shock and my heart feels as if it is on fire and every nerve aches because I can see no way out anywhere, and no promise of getting on with the weight of debt over me.

With his slumber frequently disrupted, he felt 'constantly dull and sleepy and tired' in the daytime, unable to shrug off a lethargic 'good for nothing feeling' despite various endeavours to get a good night's sleep. 'I have tried sitting quietly reading, and walking until I am tired out, but it does not seem to make any real difference'.

Late in January he crossed the Channel for a month's leave in England. He was feeling 'very homesick and miserable and depressed', he told Kate, and longed to be able to 'rest my head in your lap and feel your fingers over my eyes and hair ... to soothe away my troubles'. Elliott spent much of his leave at Bryn Oerog with Milly Edwards, who considerately organised a series of outings to keep him occupied, without managing to ameliorate his depression.

He was feeling more past his prime than ever:

> I fear you shall find me greatly changed, dear, very much older. Do you remember having to hunt for grey hairs in my head? I think the difficulty soon will be to find the black ones.

Like many AIF survivors, he was beginning to realise that his best years were behind him. 'I have been through a lot of things, dearie, and am not what I once was' after 'four years of war and disappointment'. But it was more than just a sharpened sense of middle age or anti-climactic past-his-best malaise. Pompey was being tormented by bouts of severe depression—'fits of the blues' he called them. They were 'terrible, almost more than I can bear'. He tried to 'cheer up', but felt essentially powerless to avoid or resist them. His English leave made no difference. 'I am very sad about everything', he wrote after returning to Dourlers.

Not everything, of course, caused him anguish. Kate was unflaggingly supportive; her responses to his melancholy letters soothed his torment. He was pleased to learn that his children reacted excitedly to news of the Armistice, realising it would expedite his return. And the telegram he received from Kate in March stating that the household had escaped the Spanish flu was a great relief. So, too, was the all-clear he received about the blood in his urine. The doctor he consulted found no sign of disease or inflammation, and concluded that the most likely cause was 'worry and weakness' as 'I am very much run down'.

Another boost for his morale was the reunion dinner for past and present 15th Brigade officers held at his headquarters on 3 January. This function was a great success. The Dourlers chateau was decorated with the colours of the brigade units (the red and white of the 60th Battalion being especially prominent), and various trophies were displayed. Officers present included former battalion commanders Cam Stewart, Charles Mason, and Neil Freeman. With Pompey presiding, Denehy moved a toast to the brigade in fine style. 'To toast the brigade', Denehy began, was 'to toast our brigadier, for the name of General Elliott would forever be associated with the 15th Brigade'. Denehy recalled the brigade's inauspicious start as an assortment of disparate remnants and recruits; it was the brigadier who had unified them into a cohesive formation. The first great test was the infamous desert march, 'a well-nigh impossible task' which should never have been attempted. It 'was accomplished ... only by the dominating personality of the brigadier'. Denehy went on to salute the 'spirit of unity' within the 15th Brigade that had produced its superb record at the Western Front, and referred to the notable contribution its officers had made elsewhere:

> We gave General Stewart and Major Cameron to the 14th Brigade, and the 14th got four VCs. (Applause.) We gave [Colonel] Freeman to the 8th Brigade, and their brigadier got promotion. (Applause and laughter.) The toast was drunk with enthusiasm. So spontaneous and demonstrative was its reception that it was several minutes before General Elliott could make himself heard when he rose to reply.

The brigadier thanked everyone present for the loyalty to himself and the brigade encapsulated in Denehy's speech, reminisced about shaping raw material into cohesive AIF units, and expressed the hope that everyone would soon be home to enjoy the peace that their efforts had done so much to precipitate. Another feature of the evening was music (with fervent renditions of 'Auld Lang Syne' a highlight), and there were speeches by Scanlan, Freeman, and Mason. Responding to Scanlan's toast to 'Old Comrades', Stewart said he was delighted to be back at such a happy reunion. Although he now commanded another brigade, he still felt he belonged to the 15th Brigade.

Even more memorable than this gathering of his officers was a unique tribute Elliott was given by his men. Its genesis was his decision to call a brigade parade, ostensibly to present certain medals that had been awarded and not yet received, but mainly for another reason. As he announced to the men paraded before him, this was probably the last time they would be able to assemble as a brigade because of the increasing flow of departures. Accordingly, he wanted to take the opportunity to express to the brigade as a whole his heartfelt thanks. He had set high soldiering standards, but the 15th Brigade had attained them, even during the most severe trials. Because he had insisted on high standards for decorations, everyone with an award in the 15th Brigade knew that it had been genuinely earned. He had scrutinised every recommendation himself, and 'honour was awarded only when honour was due—there was no eyewash'. As for the decorations he was wearing himself, he regarded them merely as souvenirs won for him by the officers and men of the brigade. It was sad to see the 15th Brigade 'gradually dwindling away', but he wanted to extend his best wishes to everyone about to go home. The parade broke up, and Pompey returned to his paperwork.

That afternoon, to his astonishment, the whole brigade marched back to the chateau. After the morning parade the sentiment had spread that a gesture of tribute to the brigadier was called for, particularly in view of the brigade's limited future. It was a voluntary demonstration, but practically everyone participated. The first Pompey knew of it was when the battalions marched into the chateau grounds at 3.00pm, preceded by their bands and colours. As each company skirted the chateau its commander demanded three cheers for the brigadier, which were lustily given. This cheering brought Pompey outside, where he stood on the front steps with a lump in his throat, acknowledging each company as it passed. The battalions then formed up together, and executed a ceremonial manoeuvre as the bands played the brigade's marching music.

Gollan described it as a 'never-to-be-forgotten' experience. Emotions were stirred, the weather for once was splendid, and there 'could not have been a more picturesque setting' with the 'beautiful surroundings of the chateau' blending superbly with the bands and regimental flags. At the end of the manoeuvre, Denehy (as the senior battalion commander present) called for three more cheers for the brigadier from everyone. Those cheers were heard a very long way away. Denehy and the other leaders then explained to Pompey that the men wanted to demonstrate their feelings for him. They had the utmost confidence in him, and knew that wherever he sent them he was always ready to go himself.

This marvellous tribute was, of course, a profoundly gratifying fillip for Pompey, especially considering his struggle with depression. It was hard to respond adequately to such an unexpected and moving demonstration, he began. The main thing he wanted to say to supplement his morning remarks was to 'have faith in yourselves as Australians and in your land of Australia'. When he was forming the 7th Battalion in 1914, he recalled, English officers were available and seeking appointments, but he had refused to accept any officer without experience in the Australian military forces. 'This is an Australian battalion and will be officered by Australians', he had insisted. During the war the AIF had repeatedly shown that Australians could match it with anyone:

> It has been the fashion in Australia to decry our own, but the men of the AIF will alter this when they return. You men have equalled the English Guards with their strict discipline; you have fought against the pick of the German Army, the Prussian Guard and the Wurtembergers; you have competed on the rifle range with the French Chasseurs Alpins—all with the same result. Think of these things when you go home. Have pride in yourself and in your country and determine, relying on yourself, to make your country the best to live in and die for ... When we came to the Somme in March last year it seemed that there was nothing left for us to do but just to die in our tracks in trying to stop the rush. But when we met the Germans in a really determined manner they did not have a chance with us at all ... I thank you for your spontaneous token of respect. I am proud to think that for over three years I have served with you, and have at times had to punish you, and yet I hold your respect. It is a great thing, and I thank you for this demonstration of your loyalty and your devotion.

On 26 March the 15th Brigade ceased to exist as a distinct formation. Early in April Elliott took over command of the combined residue of the 8th Brigade and his own. Now based at the unprepossessing Belgian mining town of Charleroi, he was asked to recommend a site for the proposed Fifth Division memorial at Polygon Wood. Visiting Hobbs to discuss this and other matters, Elliott had a conversation with another commander who happened to be at Australian Corps headquarters, the Commander-in-Chief himself. Haig told Pompey that it had been essential to keep hammering away at Ypres in 1917 because the French army had been gravely weakened by mutiny, a fallacious and historically significant claim—the record of this conversation in Elliott's diary demonstrates that Haig was propagating this deception much earlier than realised by even historians who have denounced him for it. Elliott also had a private quest at Polygon Wood:

> I got to see poor Geordie's grave. The cross is still standing, but has a shrapnel bullet through one arm of it which has splintered it ... The cemetery where Geordie is buried is being done up.

The following day he journeyed to another battlefield of grim memory, Fromelles. It was still a forbidding place, especially for AIF visitors; Charles Bean, spending Armistice Day there, found it full of the remains of Australians killed in July 1916. Elliott's inspection of the German positions uncovered another harrowing dimension:

> [A] church ... had been turned into a solid cube of concrete, except for a stair so narrow that only with difficulty could a normally built man ascend it. At its head near the ridge pole it terminated in a loophole for an observer, who with a telescope could, with perfect safety to himself, count every sentry in our lines. He also had an extensive view across our back areas, and could at once detect any preparation for attack. A more unsuitable site from which to launch a well-advertised attack could hardly have been found on the Western Front.

There was also the sad task of relinquishing Darkie. After their long association Elliott would have liked to bring him home to Australia, but the cost was prohibitive and he had to be sold in London instead. Before reluctantly parting with him, Pompey arranged for a leather label to be tied around Darkie's neck with a note outlining his war service and asking the purchaser to look after him well. Subsequently Elliott was delighted to receive a letter of assurance from his new English owner that he was being treated kindly.

Late in April Elliott concluded his duties in France, and crossed to London just in time for the celebratory march past the King by Dominion soldiers on 3 May. Pompey declined to participate himself, being 'not at all keen on these show jobs', and aware that if he did march he would be installed at the last minute to lead the Fifth Division column, a role that had been given to his friend Stewart (who may have been looking forward to it). But he did go along to Buckingham Palace to have a look. Securing a good seat in the front row near Haig, Hamilton, Rawlinson, and the King, Elliott felt 'our boys ... looked very well' as they marched proudly past.

With his own departure for Australia now imminent, he began a busy round of farewells. In the longish letters he sent the children he was about to rejoin there was perhaps a sense that he was consciously preparing himself to resume a direct fatherhood role. He told Violet that he was delighted her music was progressing so well that she would be able to play hymns for him when he returned; he encouraged Neil to strive to emulate his sister's scholastic commitment, regretting that he had been unable to 'be near you and advise you' like other fathers. Even as the war ended he was still giving Belle the same refrain he had sent ever since leaving Australia: 'Send me lots of stories of the wee people soon, I am never tired of hearing of them'. As for his own frame of mind, Kate's soothing letters had helped, but

> I am still feeling a good deal run down, dearie. I expect it is the Australian sun and your own dear smile and presence that I really need to buck me up and put me right. At times I feel very tired, listless and helpless—nervous breakdown due to war strain. Hundreds of officers have completely broken down in that way and are complete invalids ... I believe it is the worry of the business more than the war that has brought it on.

By mid-May he was on his way home. The *Orontes* left Devonport on 16 May with Elliott allocated a congenially situated cabin alongside his old friend Brigadier-General Bennett. The generals were given a break from official duties; during the voyage the officer in charge was Colonel Ferres, and the adjutant and quartermaster were 15th Brigade lieutenants. Shipboard administration was impressive. The *Orontes* population (which included a contingent of nurses and AIF wives) had a variety of activities to choose from. For the first few days seasickness was widespread; but within a week the sea was calm, the weather fine, and deck quoits and cricket were all the rage. Empire Day, 24 May, was marked with a special program of events, including a concert, a dinner, and a lecture by Elliott on the origin and history of the commemoration.

On 6 June the *Orontes* arrived at Durban for a two-day stay. Leave was granted to explore ashore, and 'the people of Durban could not have been more hospitable'. Choppy seas revived seasickness on the 11th, but not for long. Wireless contact was established with Australia on 17 June.

The *Orontes* reached Adelaide on 26 June. South and West Australians disembarked, and Elliott set foot on Australian soil for the first time in over four and a half years. That Thursday was also special for another reason—it was Kate's birthday. He sent her a telegram: 'Expect arrive Melbourne Saturday, can you arrange carrier baggage, happy returns love Elliott'. The message she sent him was full of anticipation: 'Counting the days till you arrive, will meet you, fondest love Katie'.

It was just after midday on 28 June when the *Orontes* reached Port Phillip Heads. Quarantine authorities came on board to check everyone's temperature; medical checks had been scrupulously regular throughout the voyage, and the all-clear was duly given. By the time the *Orontes* reached Port Melbourne it was getting dark, and the disembarkation officer ruled that the returning men would have to stay on board until morning, although they were only 200 yards away from the pier and their waiting loved ones. This was insensitive bureaucratic inflexibility at its worst. Pompey got hold of a boat and went ashore, and his forthright representations did the trick: the preposterous decision was countermanded, and disembarkation began. At last Elliott found himself able to do what he had rehearsed over and over in his imagination. With a racing heart, he proceeded towards the welcoming embrace awaiting him.

CHAPTER TWENTY

'No Obligation at All to the National Party': Into parliament

JUNE 1919–JULY 1920

A PROFOUND READJUSTMENT was in store for Elliott. This was inevitable in view of his long absence, the severe cumulative strain of his experiences, the switch he would be making from soldier to solicitor, the chasm between army life and suburban domesticity, and the exponential development of the tiny toddlers he had left in 1914. Less obvious, but no less significant, was the fact that civilian life itself was going to be very different. Not only had Australia been transformed during the divisive war years; he himself had become a public figure. In August 1914 Harold Elliott was unknown to the general populace (apart, perhaps, from Essendon citizens interested in military affairs); five years later he was returning as the colourful and controversial General Pompey Elliott, a household name to tens of thousands of soldiers and their families, and one of the most renowned identities in the whole AIF. His imminent arrival on the *Orontes* generated lengthy profiles in the press and extensive excerpts from Fred Cutlack's vivid portrait saluting the vibrant brigadier 'of big burly build', 'immense' jaw, and 'tuft of iron grey hair' sticking up 'permanently on end with sheer energy'. He received numerous personal greetings on his return. Among them was a poignant letter from the mother of 'a brave son' who had served under him in the 58th Battalion but was 'now in heaven':

> Welcome, welcome back to dear Australia ... I cannot face any welcome homes now that my dear one will never return, but my heart is with all the brave ones who fought ... They are going to give you a great welcome ... I wish I could face it, but I am not brave enough. Yours, a proud but sorrowing mother.

The magnitude of the adjustment Elliott had to make was immediately apparent. After a tender reunion at the pier, he and Kate were on their way home in the car she had booked when they were stopped at an intersection near central Melbourne by a crowd of Pompey admirers. This special reception had been planned for the afternoon, but it was five hours later and well and truly dark by the time the brigadier's vehicle materialised. Nevertheless hundreds of enthusiasts were still waiting to greet him. Amid fervent cheering, Elliott was presented with an address of welcome. He responded appreciatively. A reporter described him as 'robust and cheerful' but not overly talkative; hardly a surprise—all he wanted, of course, was to get home, especially at that hour. He confined himself to saying, in response to journalists' questions, that Australia's soldiers had performed outstandingly, demobilisation under Monash was progressing well, and he had certain ideas about the post-war organisation of Australia's defence forces which he would submit later at an appropriate juncture.

This reception was the first of a series of welcome-home functions. Elliott was feted by Essendonians at their town hall on 24 July, where the returning hero was regaled with songs, poetry, and a performance by a ventriloquist and his partner Tommy the Nut. 'Unfortunately', the local paper reported, 'persistent encores dragged out the first half of the programme'. After being presented with another illuminated address praising his leadership and gallantry, Elliott echoed its commendation of his wife and mother (both present at the function) when he began his reply with a warm tribute to them as part of a collective salute to

> all those mothers, sisters and wives who so loyally gave their dear ones, and through the long years of the war worked for them, prayed for them and waited heroically for them to come back.

He then proceeded to outline the exceptional deeds of individual Essendon soldiers, including Cedric Permezel, Harry Webb, Bill Scurry, and Norman Dalgleish. Elliott was also guest of honour at a 'Welcome Home and Presentation of Address' arranged by the 15th Brigade Association in collaboration with the Boer War veterans' organisation. Over 400 soldiers gathered at Melbourne Town Hall to acclaim him. There were also various receptions for certain categories of returned soldiers, such as the function honouring Melbourne University graduates, also at Melbourne Town Hall, where distinguished guests included the Governor-General, the Premier of Victoria, and Generals McCay and Legge.

Another such function attended by Elliott was particularly memorable. Footscray council organised a special welcome home to the returned men of their municipality. On 9 August 593 soldiers, accompanied by bands and carloads of incapacitated comrades, marched through the streets of Footscray to the drill hall for a civic dinner. The hall was 'lavishly embellished' with decorations, coloured lights, 'flags, flowers and foliage'; the atmosphere was already vibrant when General Elliott arrived to take his seat at the top table. His appearance, reported the Footscray *Independent*,

> was the signal for tumultuous cheering from the 'Diggers'. Never was a leader more beloved by his men than is this gallant soldier ... He appeared to know the name of every man in the ranks, and had a word and a hearty grip of the hand for each ... Nearly every soldier handed up his menu card to be autographed by 'Pompey', and for nearly an hour the general was kept busy writing his name.

'There was a hush throughout the building' as the mayor referred poignantly to Footscray's dead, but when he concluded his speech of welcome by calling on General Elliott to address the gathering there was pandemonium. The diggers greeted him with 'a hurricane of cheers', dozens rushing the platform to shake his hand; then, all standing, they launched with gusto into 'For He's a Jolly Good Fellow'. It was several minutes before this wonderful ovation subsided. Eventually, with difficulty, order was restored sufficiently to enable him to speak. In a wide-ranging address Pompey recalled his visit to the hall five years earlier to enrol the recruits who became the E Company originals of the 7th Battalion, and emphasised how pleased he was to see so many of them again. He reminisced about the Gallipoli landing, Lone Pine, and Fromelles before urging the Footscray diggers to tackle peacetime problems with the same commitment and cohesion they had shown in the AIF:

> [M]ake the name of Australia as respected in the time of peace as you made it respected in war. It can be done if we make the start precisely in the same way as in the old battalion. You started to make your battalion and your brigade the best in the AIF. Start right now and make your district the best in the State ... Make your city the best suburb of Melbourne. You can do it if you make up your minds. (Great cheering.)

With Elliott's reputation and influence among the men of the AIF so evident, his significance as a public figure was accentuated by the widespread perception that the returned soldiers were going to be a force to be reckoned with in post-war Australia. The possibility that they might not placidly revert to competitive, acquisitive civilian life was generating considerable apprehension and, in some quarters, profound anxiety. Most alarmed were the conservatives, now politically ascendant under the Nationalist Party banner following the seismic ALP schism of 1916-17. For these Nationalists, the prospect of unsettled warriors involving themselves alongside radical agitators in disruptive behaviour—perhaps even violent unrest—was nightmarish. If, however, the returned soldiers could be so harnessed or conditioned that most of them supported the Nationalists most of the time, they could prove an invaluable asset both socially and politically.

Influential conservatives were pulling out all stops to engineer the kind of soldiers' transition they wanted. Various groups had emerged to represent ex-servicemen and their interests, but the federal Nationalist government had made a crucial deal with the most conservative of these organisations, the Returned Sailors' and Soldiers' Imperial League of Australia (RSSILA). By anointing the League with 'official' status, the government endowed it with invaluable patronage and significantly disadvantaged rival associations. In return, the League's leaders privately assured senior Nationalists that they would strive to minimise disruption by returned soldiers, and 'avoid tactics which might embarrass the government'. Elliott's potential role in this process of guiding the returned men along desirable paths had been recognised six months earlier, when he was still in France, by the ex-Essendon mayor J.F. Henderson:

> Some one is needed to help direct the energies of the returned soldiers organisations, and I know of no one who appears to have such a hold on the affections of the men as you have, or whose advice they would be more likely to accept. The soldiers will of course be in a position to rule this country for some years to come if their energies are consolidated.

Within a month of Elliott's return he found himself in the front line of these activities. Before July 1919 there had been a number of disturbing events involving returned soldiers—mutinous shipboard incidents, a major riot in Adelaide, mayhem in Brisbane streets. When the Nationalist Premier of West Australia led strikebreaking labour to Fremantle to smash a wharf labourers' strike in May 1919, the willingness of returned soldiers aboard a passing troopship to aid the strikers was a particularly alarming development for the authorities. But until mid-1919 the most significant incidents of this kind had occurred outside Victoria. In July, however, there was serious trouble in Melbourne.

On Saturday 19 July there was a victory march through the city as the signing of peace was celebrated around Australia and beyond. About 7,000 soldiers and sailors participated, divided into eleven groups, with Elliott commanding one of them. The third anniversary of Fromelles—perhaps the greatest disaster the AIF ever experienced—was a peculiar day to celebrate victory, but there were plenty of onlookers and the mood was joyous. Afterwards, however, high spirits led to boisterousness, rebelliousness, and arrests. Some soldiers, resentful of what they considered excessive police heavy-handedness, decided to raid Victoria Barracks. In the ensuing skirmish one of the raiders was killed.

An urgent meeting of the RSSILA on the following Monday, 21 July, authorised the dispatch of a deputation forthwith to the Police Commissioner. He agreed to investigate the returned soldiers' grievances. When this deputation reported back to another spirited RSSILA meeting, majority sentiment was strongly in favour of pursuing immediate redress rather than being fobbed off by the prospect of some inquiry. An estimated 3,000 demonstrators then marched to police headquarters. When the Police Commissioner refused to budge, they proceeded to Parliament House to submit their grievances directly to the Premier, H.S.W. Lawson. Cabinet was sitting at the time, but they burst in anyway and demanded the dismissal of an especially loathed senior constable, the release of soldiers arrested during the weekend, and an end to the wielding of police batons against returned servicemen. Lawson urged the intruders to listen to reason and to uphold law and order, but the leading dissidents refused to be mollified unless he acceded to their demands straightaway. Amid extraordinary scenes of escalating disorder, the Premier's office was ransacked and an inkstand was hurled at Lawson, striking him heavily on the head. A police contingent was summoned to disperse the insurgents; after performing a baton charge, they succeeded in doing so. Later a violent melee erupted outside police headquarters, which resulted in protesters and policemen being hospitalised. There were further clashes the following day.

This sequence of events, in particular the culminating violence against the head of an elected government, seemed to embody the conservatives' worst nightmares about rampaging returned soldiers. Similar unruliness in Brisbane could be characterised as well-intentioned attempts to deal with dastardly 'Bolsheviks' and their 'disloyalist' acolytes who had infiltrated the state Labor government, but in Melbourne there was a Nationalist premier with a sore head and an intense grievance with the RSSILA after a demonstration under its auspices had resulted in intruders assaulting him in his own office. Corrective intervention was clearly necessary.

A mass meeting of returned soldiers was convened in the Domain on 23 July. Thousands attended. They heard a selection of the best-known Melbourne-based AIF leaders provide a series of pep-talks on the need to curb disorderliness. Elliott was one of the speakers; they also included his old friends and fellow AIF brigadiers Smith and Bennett, together with the state commandant, General 'Digger' Brand. The gathering was chaired by the recently elected national president of the RSSILA, Gil Dyett, who had served briefly under Elliott at Gallipoli. On 6 August 1915 Dyett had shared a last meal with two other Bendigo-born lieutenants in the 7th Battalion who, like him, did not expect to be alive after the imminent offensive; 'Curly' Symons survived and won the VC at Lone Pine, Noel Edwards was killed and perhaps deserved that decoration as well, and Dyett was so severely wounded in the battle that he was reverently covered with a blanket on Anzac beach prior to burial. Pompey had not seen Dyett for four years until July 1919. Now here they were together at this important gathering, stepping up onto an improvised platform to proclaim their abhorrence of disorderliness.

When it was Elliott's turn to speak he was again given a tremendous reception. 'I want to say a few words about our conduct ... in this city', he began, associating himself directly with his audience right from the outset. The men of the AIF had enlisted voluntarily to overcome a brand of tyranny that aspired to world domination, he pointed out, yet a proportion of returned men were now associating themselves misguidedly with forces of disorder tainted by not dissimilar tyranny. Attempting to coerce an elected government with threats and violence was unjustifiable. Australia was a proud and free democracy, where rich and poor were equal before the law; its soldiers should appreciate and be prepared to uphold this democratic system of government. There was no place for unconstitutional methods; if they did not like what a particular government was doing, their remedy was to vote against it on election day. He urged soldiers to show restraint, while empathising with their frustration that

> some, through no fault of their own, are out of employment and suffering hardship ... First and foremost we must unite to defend the government of the State and maintain order. It is essential that we should not mix ourselves up in disturbances in the city. In the battles we fought in together it was possible that there were many Germans who were opposed utterly to German militarism and despotism, but it was impossible for us to discriminate in a bayonet charge. If only through motives of curiosity you join in the crowds in the city, it is equally impossible for those guarding the city to discriminate in carrying out their duty.

If, Elliott continued, some returned soldiers were being led so astray that they were threatening violence unless they were given what they wanted,

> then, boys, I have to tell you that I myself would be one of the first to volunteer to stand as a guard to protect property and protect the government. I value your good opinion and respect ...
>
> Interjector: You've got that, Pompey! (Laughter and cheers.)
>
> ... But if my country calls in this matter, then I will serve even at the risk of sacrificing your friendship and respect.
>
> Interjector: You can't lose that! (Cheers.)

The ensuing decline in unruliness by returned soldiers in Melbourne indicates that this meeting was influential. After addresses by six generals, three colonels, two captains, and a corporal, Dyett called on all present to raise an arm if they supported the maintenance of law and order. The unanimous response was trumpeted by the press. In the *Age* it was proclaimed as a 'TRIUMPH FOR LAW AND ORDER', and the *Argus* account was headlined 'UPHOLDING THE LAW: SOLDIERS WILL AID: EMPHATIC DECLARATION'. It was on the same day these reports appeared that Elliott was feted in the evening at Essendon Town Hall, where his speech included some observations about the returned soldiers' adjustment to civilian life. Intriguingly, the report of his comments on this pivotal issue in the local paper was reproduced when its Footscray equivalent described his address to the returned men of that municipality sixteen days later. The identical accounts in the *Essendon Gazette* and *Footscray Advertiser* stated that Brigadier-General Elliott

> made an appeal to everybody to be patient with men who had gone through so much. Government help could, after all, be only temporary, and if all the returned men were to be absorbed into ordinary life the task would rest largely with the private employer. "No one could be more down on lawlessness, even among these men, than I am", he said. "We must, at all costs, maintain respect for law and order. Given that, we must make all possible allowances for these men, and try to realise how much they have done for us". (Applause.)

The word-for-word duplication, extending even to punctuation and concluding applause, was surely no coincidence. At the very least it suggests that Elliott was acutely aware that the right message should be given to both returned men and civilians, and that he was prepared to ensure it was (from his wartime dealings with Australian correspondents Charles Bean, Keith Murdoch, and Fred Cutlack he might well have acquired some journalistic and publicity savvy). Whether he was acting of his own volition or at the instigation of others intent on quelling the dangerous restlessness of returned servicemen—establishment figures, perhaps, with influence in government, the military, the press, or conceivably all three—is hard to gauge.

What was clear, however, within a month of Elliott's return, was that civilian life for him was going to be very different from pre-war days. He was not the only one who had to make a sizeable adjustment; his public prominence involved a big change for Kate as well. The main thing from her perspective was that he had managed to return home safely. As he became increasingly in demand on a variety of fronts, she remained the same accepting, unassuming, supportive 'sunshine lady' she had always been. Adjusting to his frequent absences owing to welcome-home functions, meetings, and various other events and engagements was relatively straightforward for her, after having had to cope with his complete absence for nearly five years. Belle remained in the household after her brother-in-law's return, and continued to be an influential presence in it. The residence he came home to was located in the eastern suburb of Surrey Hills, a rented house at the eastern end of Prospect Hill Road.

Elliott's most pressing personal concern since the Armistice, his future as a lawyer, was resolved satisfactorily soon after his return. A long-established Melbourne firm of solicitors, Lynch and MacDonald, had lost its senior partner when Hector MacDonald died in October 1917 (William Lynch, the founder of the firm, had died in 1901). The sole surviving partner, MacDonald's son (also named Hector), carried on the practice, and in 1919 invited Elliott to join him. Partnership of a well-known, well-credentialled firm was just what Pompey was after, and he moved into an office at 360 Collins Street, the prestigious address of the renamed concern now known as Lynch, MacDonald and Elliott. His new partner's brother, artist James MacDonald, had been severely wounded at Gallipoli and was to become a controversial art critic.

Pompey's anxiety about being tainted by his former partner's disgrace proved unfounded. He was fanatical about his professional integrity. Even the slightest hint of an unwarranted blot on his reputation, especially his financial probity, was intolerable. But there was no lingering slur to endure. The cause of his rupture with Glen Roberts was not widely known, and of course no-one aware of the circumstances could rationally blame Elliott in the slightest. In fact, far from being ostracised because of his former partner's dishonesty, Elliott's exalted reputation after his wartime accomplishments made him an attractive proposition for solicitors on the lookout for a partner. As Hector MacDonald realised, Elliott would bring valuable prestige to his firm as well as additional clients. Other offers accepted by Elliott confirmed that his concern about his reputation was groundless. With impeccable credentials a pre-requisite, he was invited to become a director of the National Trustees Executors and Agency Company Limited, a graduates' representative on the Ormond College Council, and a member of the Victorian Law Institute's Council.

Elliott's obsessive worrying about the impact on his own financial circumstances of Glen Roberts' defalcation also subsided once he became properly aware of the situation. The contribution of his ex-partner's wife, Katie Roberts, had been crucial. Both she and her son Eric retained the utmost regard for Elliott, and were determined that he would not be financially disadvantaged by Glen's disgrace. Eric, having joined the Australian Flying Corps after Elliott thwarted his intention to join the 7th Battalion because it would be 'like taking my own son', had seen Elliott occasionally during the war, and continued to do so subsequently. Reminiscing over 60 years later after a distinguished flying career which saw him reach the rank of wing commander, Eric was adamant that he and his mother had ensured that Pompey suffered no financial detriment at all as a result of the defalcation. Glen Roberts resumed as a lawyer, entering a partnership with another solicitor who eventually became a victim just like Elliott; Eric, then overseas, returned to find that he had to extricate his father from yet more financial embarrassment. After this episode he and his brothers insisted that Glen was never to practise again. At no stage, according to Eric, was there any contact between his father and Elliott after the war.

Someone who *was* in frequent contact with Elliott after the war was Charles Bean. Having made a research trip to Gallipoli after the Armistice, Bean had arrived back in Australia to embark on his magisterial history of the AIF. He was intent on writing a different kind of military history. Instead of the traditional focus on the highest commanders' conceptions and dispatches, Bean had decided to concentrate on the action at the sharp end. Ascertaining and describing what front-line soldiers did would enable him to produce fresh, compelling history. This approach also appealed to him as an excellent way of ensuring that the AIF's superb contribution was honoured and remembered. It would be a new type of history, then, for a special story, and the nationalistic idealism that inspired him and the determined persistence that sustained him enabled Bean to carry this vast project through to completion, even though his method involved the absorption of a dauntingly vast array of information.

In September 1919 Bean called at Elliott's Melbourne office. He wanted to discuss Elliott's daring encounter in a Gallipoli tunnel in July 1915 that exemplified the truism (repeated by his men forever afterwards) that Pompey would never send anyone where he was not prepared to go himself. It was typical of Bean's diligence and commitment to novel military history from a front-line perspective that his notes of this conversation were extensively detailed; it was typical of Elliott's keen interest in the subject matter that after seeing the historian he looked up the coverage of that incident in his diary, and sent Bean a three-page letter elaborating on the information he had provided in his office. That same month Elliott received from Wieck, then commanding a military school at Liverpool, New South Wales, the detailed reminiscences he had asked his former brigade major to provide concerning the advanced guard operations they had supervised together in March 1917.

For the rest of his life Elliott's penetrating scrutiny of the progressive documentation of the AIF's history never wavered. He became a frequent supplier of information and material to Bean, whose dedication, thoroughness, and integrity he admired (as did everyone who knew the AIF correspondent-turned-historian well). Elliott's intense interest in Bean's work was shaped by his lifelong fascination with military history, his familiarity with the leading actors in Bean's great story, and his personal involvement in many of the engagements featured in it. Also influential, of course, was his yearning for vindication in relation to deeply felt grievances.

Bean's admirable idealism was embodied in his tract entitled *In Your Hands Australians*. This short but passionate book urged its readers to live up to the ideals of the AIF by reproducing them in peacetime in order to make Australia a better place. Education and the need to guide Australian youth along the right lines was a prominent theme of *In Your Hands Australians*, as was another Bean initiative, the 'Young Australia Force'. Bean's aim was to inspire Australian children with a strong spirit of nationalistic idealism, inherited from the AIF, in a movement devoid of militaristic, political or sectarian overtones.

Letters inviting support for the establishment of this Young Australia Force were sent to influential AIF identities in each state, including Elliott. The suggestion that the scheme could be launched by Birdwood during his forthcoming tour of Australia received, not surprisingly, a frosty response from Pompey, who objected to this aspect of the proposal in a characteristically candid letter to Bean. The scheme failed to prosper, not as a result of Elliott's antipathy to Birdwood, but because the Boy Scouts Association saw it as a threat and successfully lobbied both the Governor-General and Birdwood to withdraw their support. Bean, bitterly disappointed that his heart-and-soul commitment to a worthy ideal had been stymied, maintained that the Young Australia movement, unlike the Scouts, would be open to girls as well as boys, was non-militaristic in character, and was uniquely Australian rather than something initiated in England and reproduced elsewhere. Still, if the essence of his proposed organisation—its inspiration, appeal, and pulse—was, as he envisaged, fervent national pride and idealism, it was perfectly appropriate for Elliott to affirm that an Australian (Monash, for example) should be launching it rather than Birdwood.

Elliott's significance as a public figure was consolidated by the announcement on 29 October that he would be a Nationalist candidate in the imminent federal election. During the war the Nationalists had presented themselves assiduously as the natural party of allegiance for the men of the AIF and Australians at home who had someone precious in the trenches. These endeavours were successful enough to make the maintenance of this allegiance a top priority for the Nationalists, who endorsed well-known AIF identities for the Senate in four states.

An obvious potential candidate for them to approach was Brigadier-General Elliott CB, CMG, DSO, DCM, Croix de Guerre, Order of St Anne (Russia), who had been repeatedly mentioned in dispatches. First and foremost he was tremendously popular. By placing him at the top of their Senate ticket, the Nationalists could expect to reinforce their existing support and attract additional electors who otherwise would not necessarily vote Nationalist. Furthermore, Elliott had demonstrated his capacity to influence the men of the AIF, both during the war and afterwards (especially at the important July meeting in the Domain), with a virtuosity admired by those conservative powerbrokers who were apprehensive about the unruly tendencies of returned soldiers. Moreover, his distinguished scholastic record demonstrated that he was equipped to be much more than a vote-getter on polling day; he could make a genuine contribution as a law-maker through his ability to scrutinise parliamentary legislation effectively.

Of the available prospective candidates who could be used by Victorian Nationalists to secure the AIF constituency in their state,

Elliott stood out clearly. Monash had misgivings not only about aligning himself with the Nationalists but with the political process as a whole. He also had an awkward relationship, characterised by mutual wariness and friction, with Prime Minister Hughes, who feared him as a potential rival for national leadership. Besides, Monash did not return to Australia until the election was over. The most famous Victorian AIF identity besides Monash and Elliott was Albert Jacka, the first Australian to win the VC in the Great War; but he was shy and, in addition, disagreed with the Nationalists' advocacy of conscription (according to his father, a Labor activist). Elliott's friend Bennett was invited by Hughes to stand for the Senate in New South Wales (having moved there since his return), but declined.

Elliott, on the other hand, was willing to have a crack at politics. His decision to stand was primarily prompted not by overtures from senior Nationalist strategists—in fact at one stage he declined a personal approach from Prime Minister Hughes—but by persistent entreaties from returned soldiers. 'We won't be looked after properly unless you get in there and straighten things out for us poor buggers, general' was the gist of numerous appeals he received. It was the cumulative impact of these requests that was decisive.

The idea of being a representative of returned soldiers appealed to Pompey, who retained a strong sense of comradeship, loyalty, and obligation to the men he had commanded. They had served him well during the war; he felt impelled to keep doing whatever he could for them in peacetime. For the rest of his life he was burdened by unceasing requests from ex-servicemen seeking assistance with various problems relating to post-war adjustment; always responsive, he did what he could to help. (Even before returning home Pompey had urged his men to be wary of affirming that they were 100 per cent fit, and to accept whatever pension entitlements they were offered.) As a member of federal parliament, Elliott reasoned, he would be better able to look after returned soldiers and their interests.

Moreover, as someone with strong views about certain issues which did not relate particularly to ex-servicemen, he felt he could make a contribution in a more general political context. And, following the offer to join Hector MacDonald's firm, accepting the invitation to stand for parliament would further assuage the profound insecurity about his post-war future that had tormented him during the immediate post-Armistice period. The £600 parliamentary salary would help to allay his concern about his financial circumstances as well.

Two months earlier Elliott had touched on the subject of politics in the course of his speech at the celebrated civic dinner for Footscray's returned men, asserting (according to the Footscray *Independent*) that he 'never was a politician, and never would be'. He elaborated a few days later in a letter to a 7th Battalion original, Dan Toohey:

> In regard to my remark about Parliament I said that I had declined to be a 'Party' Candidate. Both parties want you to bind yourself body and soul to some platform or other, and then they proceed to go into details which often pan out unexpectedly and by signing the platform you are precluded from any form of criticism of the platform. This will never suit me at all, and if any one wants me to stand for Parliament they must have sufficient confidence in me as an honest man to trust me to run straight without binding me or attempting to bind me body and soul.

The Nationalists evidently decided that Pompey's popularity was such a sure-fire vote-winner that they ought to utilise and benefit from it on polling day, despite the risk that his independent inclinations might cause problems afterwards. For his part, Elliott detected no fundamental personal incompatibility with the Nationalist platform that would prevent him from giving the party his broad support.

He was an instinctive conservative. Like many others who overcome unpropitious origins and attain conspicuous accomplishment through determination, drive, and self-discipline, Elliott tended to believe that others could emulate his success if they emulated his dedication (a perception that conveniently ignored the impact of the Londonderry golden hole). It was not for governments to nurse the improvident with a generosity the state or nation could not afford, especially if one held—as Pompey did—an essentially pessimistic view about human nature and the community's collective capacity to achieve good works. Elliott's insecurity about his own financial circumstances was mirrored by his hostility to unsound governmental finance. He had first-hand experience of the dreadful 1890s depression in Victoria, which had demonstrated the disastrous potential consequences of imprudent administration.

During the war he had predicted that the immediate post-war

period would be a daunting challenge for governments. It would involve considerable dislocation, upheaval, and readjustment, and the public funds available to ameliorate these unsettled conditions would be limited after the immense expenditure and debt accumulated during the war. To Pompey, the returned soldiers would clearly be the most deserving of the various claimants pursuing a share of the public purse, but in the circumstances there would be precious little the government could afford or be expected to do even for them.

Elliott was a committed conservative, then, but whether he was temperamentally suited to politics was another matter. Although he had been persuaded to stand by the numerous requests he received from returned soldiers, some of the men he commanded felt that the forthrightness and uncompromising candour he had displayed as a military commander would prove incompatible with the slippery deviousness of political combat. 'For God's sake don't go into Parliament', one pleaded. 'It is no place for an honest man'.

It was not as if the idea of standing for parliament was a novel proposition for Elliott. From time to time, even before returning home, he had acknowledged that politics was a post-war possibility for him. Early in 1917 he was being urged to consider standing for parliament: 'they said the Returned Soldiers' vote alone would put me in', he told Kate. He laughed off the idea at that stage, but a letter he sent Belle immediately after the Armistice indicated that he was considering standing for Ballarat. While he had 'received good encouragement' in AIF circles, his primary motivation was the decidedly hostile impression he had formed of the wartime activities of the sitting Labor member, D.C. McGrath, who had campaigned actively against conscription within the AIF. 'I regard it as a disgrace to Ballarat that she should be represented in the national Parliament by such a man', he fumed. However, senior Nationalist tacticians evidently preferred to maximise the fruits of Elliott's popularity by endorsing him as a statewide Senate candidate rather than confining him to a particular lower house electorate; and from his own perspective, winning a Senate seat would be easier than dislodging a sitting Labor member of the House of Representatives (MHR). All the same, he was particularly looking forward to making his presence felt in Ballarat during the campaign.

There was perhaps another motivation influencing Elliott's decision to stand. Decades later a friend of his, returned soldier and parliamentary official Frank Green, recalled an intriguing conversation in which Elliott said he had entered parliament to support an alternative to Hughes as prime minister. It is certainly plausible that Elliott preferred someone else to Hughes; as far as Pompey was concerned, Hughes was forever tainted by his Labor origins. In his wartime correspondence Elliott had been as scathing about Hughes as he had been about anti-conscriptionists such as Archbishop Mannix and the ALP leader chosen after the party's great 1916-17 rupture, Frank Tudor. Also significant was the fact that Elliott had rejected an approach from Hughes, but had been more responsive to the overtures of another Nationalist powerbroker, W.A. Watt, who was, unlike Hughes, a Victorian with no ALP background. Watt had been premier in Elliott's home state for two years before transferring to federal politics; in that sphere he became Treasurer and, in Hughes's absence, acting prime minister for sixteen months. A close friendship developed between Elliott and Watt. While Hughes was away, Watt had organised a deal with one of the organisations behind the emerging political force that was to become known as the Country Party; this involved its representative withdrawing from the Flinders by-election in May 1918—thereby ensuring the election of the Nationalist candidate, S.M. Bruce—in exchange for an undertaking from Watt that preferential voting would be introduced before the next federal election.

According to Frank Green, Elliott later recalled that he had agreed to stand for the Senate partly to increase the proportion of Nationalist MPs in favour of replacing Hughes as leader and prime minister. Pompey added, Green claimed, that the successor he and others had in mind was Bruce. Green's memory of this conversation decades later, long after Elliott's death, may not have been accurate. Elliott may well have been keen to see Hughes replaced, but it is unlikely that he and others were envisaging Bruce as the most appropriate and probable successor to Hughes as early as October 1919. Bruce was a political novice when he won Flinders, and had spent most of the ensuing months overseas. A more likely alternative Nationalist leader to Hughes towards the end of 1919 was a prominent minister whose dislike of Hughes had by this time become intense—Watt himself.

The bitter divisiveness that had convulsed Australia during the war made a lively election campaign in 1919 inevitable, but the Nationalists held all the aces politically. Labor's devastating wartime rupture had left the party in disarray. In 1915 Labor had been in government federally and in five of the six states; now, only four years later, the exact opposite was the case—the party was in opposition federally and in five of the six states. Tudor was decent and likeable, but troubled by ill-health. He was no match for his wily, mercurial former chief, Prime Minister Hughes, who had led a capable and experienced ex-ALP contingent into a merger with the conservatives. The only Labor leader who had proved more than a match for Hughes since the split, talented Queensland Premier T.J. Ryan, was in the process of transferring to federal politics. He was appointed campaign director for the 1919 election, handed a safe Sydney seat, and expected to take over the leadership in the not-too-distant future.

Discrediting Ryan was the paramount campaign objective as far as Labor's opponents were concerned. Another priority for the Nationalists was to emphasise their party's claim to exclusive affinity with the AIF. Accordingly, the military credentials of Labor MPs who had enlisted—those in federal parliament included McGrath, A.T. Ozanne and 'Gunner' Yates—were belittled and besmirched at every opportunity. Also prominent in the campaign were certain home front issues that had exacerbated the searing divisiveness occasioned by the conscription referenda and heightened sectarianism. The relentless tension that afflicted so many families with someone in the trenches was intensified by economic hardship arising from severe inflation (the cost of food had almost doubled during the war) and the failure of wage increases to keep pace with soaring prices. Such grievances produced an outcry about 'profiteering', and contributed to unprecedented industrial unrest: the amount of working days lost in 1919 remained the highest in any year for over half a century.

In his policy speech Hughes contended that his government's vigorous prosecution of the war had been in the national interest, opposed by post-split Labor, and ultimately vindicated. He proposed to encourage local industry by overhauling and strengthening tariffs, and promised to tackle profiteering by establishing a royal commission and holding a referendum seeking enhanced powers for the national government. Labor, in turn, promised to increase pensions, tax the rich more heavily, and introduce a national health scheme; the AIF constituency was wooed with the promise of generous repatriation benefits, including free housing for life for incapacitated returned soldiers and the widows and children of deceased servicemen.

Another prominent political issue was preference in employment for returned soldiers. The Hughes government claimed to have already fulfilled its commitment to this policy (which had featured in wartime recruiting campaigns), particularly in relation to public service employment. But the RSSILA contended that so many employers were evading their obligations that the principle was being honoured more in the breach than the observance.

Elliott was personally and publicly involved in the preference issue himself as the federal election campaign was getting under way. The Melbourne City Council's solicitor having died, the council decided in October to appoint a well-known firm of lawyers to take over its legal work. But none of this firm's senior solicitors was a returned soldier, and preference activists were soon up in arms: this was a semi-public position with a lucrative salary of £250, ex-AIF lawyers could do the work satisfactorily, and it was precisely the kind of appointment where the preference principle should apply if it meant anything at all. RSSILA pressure, protest meetings, and the airing of discontent in the press culminated in a deputation to the council, which agreed to reconsider its decision at its quarterly meeting on 10 November. A letter was submitted to that meeting from Hector MacDonald confirming that Elliott had become a partner in his firm. After considerable discussion the council agreed to rescind its previous appointment, and a ballot was held to determine whether Elliott or two other ex-AIF applicants would become the city solicitor. Pompey won the ballot easily.

Later that same day, however, Elliott was less successful when he turned to electioneering. He had meetings in familiar territory, the suburbs of Newmarket and Moonee Ponds. The Newmarket meeting was so rowdy that Pompey struggled to make himself heard as his numerous supporters in the Essendon district tried to drown out Labor devotees intent on giving him a hard time. There was much less disruption at Moonee Ponds, where he declared himself in favour of the foreshadowed new tariff, and advocated more industrial co-operation to reduce industrial unrest. Devising appropriate policies to help returned soldiers readjust was not easy, he asserted, but 'the Prime Minister has made an honest attempt to grasp the situation ...' (Interjection: 'He was never honest in his life!' Cheers and dissent.) Elliott ploughed on resolutely, of course—determination might have been his middle name—but it was clear that he was confronted by a steep learning curve.

Even at an overwhelmingly supportive meeting like Moonee Ponds there would be hostile interjectors to deal with. He did what he could to improve his platform skills, and became more comfortable and effective as the campaign progressed; but as a political spruiker he was more workmanlike than rapier-like, persistent rather than adroit.

After his challenging ordeal at Newmarket, Elliott was, for the rest of the campaign, usually accompanied by another Nationalist speaker, often a Queenslander imported to discredit Ryan. On 12 November he and Nationalist MHR George Maxwell addressed a joint meeting at Prahran. Pompey then had a daunting engagement at Richmond, Tudor's home turf and a traditional Labor stronghold; he withdrew owing to ill-health, which was just as well—the *Richmond Guardian* described the meeting as 'disorderly from beginning to end'. Elliott was still ill the following week, when he was scheduled to tour south-east Victoria. At Leongatha his replacement apologised to all the returned soldiers of the district who had come to hear Pompey, but his doctor had forbidden him to attend. Within 48 hours, however, the patient had recovered sufficiently to address a meeting at Korumburra. Two days later he transferred his attentions to the west of the state, beginning at Geelong (where he scored a good write-up by none other than Roy Gollan, his former brigade major, who had returned to the *Geelong Advertiser*). He spent the rest of the campaign outside Melbourne; Kate travelled with him.

To help with organisational details, Elliott engaged as his 'secretary' the 15th Brigade's VC winner, 'Mick' Moon. Like many ex-comrades, Moon was unemployed and finding the adjustment to civilian life difficult. Moon appreciated this offer of a job, while sensing that Pompey had concluded that travelling around with a VC winner would do his campaigning no harm. And so it proved—they had rapturous receptions throughout country Victoria. In some centres, as well as the political meeting Elliott was there to address, a separate function was arranged just to welcome them. Perhaps never in the entire history of Portland, gushed its local paper, had 'two more distinguished persons visited the town'. Shops were closed, the main streets were decorated with bunting and flags, the waiting crowd cheered loudly when their car arrived, and the local schoolchildren 'showed no small amount of excitement at viewing for themselves the idol of most young people's worship—a real Victoria Cross winner, and a Brigadier-General whose name is a household one with them all'. At these functions Pompey met up with numerous men who had served under him, reunions that were relished on both sides. Another feature of these functions was the surprised reactions of civic office-bearers when this beefy, red-cheeked, 'man of action' brigadier they had heard so much about politely declined a beer—he was an unlikely looking teetotaller. When Bean described Pompey's post-war appearance, he highlighted 'that sturdy figure, the bluff red cheeks, almost without a line, the twinkling, knowing eyes, the confident smile ... that iron grip of a handshake [and] that decisive voice'.

The content of the campaign speeches Elliott delivered while travelling around Victoria with Moon and Kate did not vary much. He tended to begin with a plug for his Nationalist Senate colleagues, wool expert Frank Guthrie and talented ex-Labor renegade Ted Russell, before pointing out, apropos of his own candidature, that he was a political novice and only standing because he had been repeatedly pressed to do so. The Nationalists, keen to endorse for the Senate a representative of returned soldiers, had insisted that he was the best available Victorian. Whether or not that was correct, he added modestly, that was what they were saying, and it was to their credit that they were prepared—unlike any other party—to endorse someone specifically for the soldiers. He had not, however, committed himself to toe some party line willy-nilly:

> I am under no obligation at all to the National Party, rather the other way. I have signed no platform, nor been asked to sign one. I am therefore free to advocate or oppose whatever measures I deem fit.

All the same, Elliott praised the Nationalist government's record and commended its main policies for the future, associating himself firmly with its stance in four spheres he characterised as fundamental. He and the Nationalists, he affirmed, were in favour of national cohesion, and against disunity and 'class hatred'; in favour of constitutional government, and against revolution and Bolshevism; in favour of conciliation and arbitration, and against strikes and disruption; and in favour of imperial unity and patriotism, and against disloyalty. Hughes and his government had much to be proud of, Elliott reiterated at meeting after meeting. Organising and maintaining the AIF, capably protecting Australia's primary produce (wool, wheat, butter, metals) amid wartime upheaval in international markets, vigorously safeguarding Australia's national security at the Versailles peace conference—these were all,

Pompey contended, outstanding achievements.

Elliott left anti-Ryan propaganda largely to others, but participated wholeheartedly in the Nationalists' attacks on Labor's credentials concerning the AIF constituency. As well as regularly denouncing McGrath, Ozanne, and other ALP diggers in his campaigning, Pompey associated himself with a shabby stunt involving a poem written during the Boer War by a former Labor MP, J.K. McDougall. The Nationalists distortedly trumpeted McDougall's satirical anti-war adaptation of a Kipling battle-hymn of Empire, concealing its Boer War origins and context, and pretended that it represented contemporary ALP policy. McDougall was not even a candidate in 1919—he was living near Ararat with his young family, working his farm—but that did not stop Hughes and other Nationalist candidates demonising him. At Horsham on 4 December, for example, Elliott recited the most controversial portion of McDougall's poem. It was the rowdiest part of his whole speech. Amid uproar, he claimed not only that this verse embodied official Labor policy, but also that he particularly resented the aspersions McDougall cast on fallen Australian soldiers because his own brother and brother-in-law were among them. Hughes and other Nationalists campaigned in similar vein. The conservative press, the *Argus* in particular, fanned rancour rankly with inflammatory reports of angry meetings of ex-servicemen, including the Essendon branch of the RSSILA.

This unsavoury campaigning led to a sensational culmination. Two nights after Elliott's Horsham speech McDougall was assaulted and kidnapped, then tarred and feathered. He was lured away from his isolated farmhouse by a request for assistance with car trouble before being waylaid by numerous assailants in the dark. Labor spokesmen were furious. McGrath accused Hughes of inciting the incident, and warned that if there was any more violence perpetrated against Labor individuals the labour movement would retaliate with force. There was further indignation when the *Argus* published a detailed account of the incident, which was so remarkably informative that it invited suspicion about the paper's complicity. When half a dozen returned soldiers (including three officers) were arrested in due course, it became evident that the enterprise had been a combined initiative of returned soldiers from Essendon and Ararat. Among the ringleaders was an ex-officer who had driven himself and others up from Essendon, knocked on McDougall's door, and told the *Argus* all about it afterwards. One of Pompey's original 'Essendon boys', he had performed so superbly as a young lance-corporal at the Anzac landing, taking over the leadership of the depleted 7th Battalion machine-gun section after all his superiors had been put out of action, that he became one of the first Australians to receive the DCM at Gallipoli.

It was three days after the McDougall incident, with polling day four days ahead, when Elliott's roving electioneering brought him to Ballarat. The campaign temperature there was particularly high. McGrath, the local Labor MHR, had coupled his angry response to the tarring and feathering of McDougall with a sensational retort to a platform utterance by W.K. Bolton, a sitting Nationalist senator. Bolton had commanded the Ballarat-based 8th AIF Battalion and served as the inaugural RSSILA president before being replaced by Dyett amid criticism that he was too deferential to the government. Campaigning in support of E.T.J. Kerby—who had served under him in the 8th Battalion and was McGrath's Nationalist opponent in Ballarat—Bolton had publicly compared McGrath's AIF service unflatteringly with Kerby's. Stung by this remark and still fuming about the assault on McDougall, McGrath went after Bolton with a vengeance.

At a public meeting called to reveal 'hidden facts about Gallipoli' relating to Senator Bolton, McGrath revealed that Bolton had sought his assistance after returning to Australia in 1915, having left Gallipoli early in the campaign in the wake of the disastrous charge at Krithia (where Bolton had been promoted to acting brigadier when McCay was hit). According to McGrath, Bolton was feeling unappreciated and underemployed following his early return, and was critical of the capacity and courage of McCay and the 6th Battalion commander, McNicoll (both severely wounded at Krithia). McGrath went into bat for Bolton with the AIF authorities as requested by the colonel, but received a disconcerting reply to the effect that Bolton's record with the AIF was undistinguished and he was no longer wanted.

Having revealed all this to the special Ballarat meeting on 7 December 1919, McGrath asserted that he, unlike Bolton, had no tickets on himself as a soldier. He had enlisted at the age of 43 to do what he could to make a contribution, having had no previous military training, and he had not intended to descend to personal allegations about individuals' AIF service. If, however, Bolton was going to pose as a gallant commander and then sneer at McGrath's soldiering, it was time to reveal the truth. McGrath's allegations were not without substance.

Bolton's early return from Gallipoli was not unrelated to adverse impressions his superiors had formed about the 54-year-old colonel's capacity to provide energetic and inspiring leadership. However, Bolton was able to repudiate McGrath's damning revelations in December 1919 by citing a supportive letter from Birdwood which gave the impression that Bolton's early return was solely due to ill-health.

Elliott involved himself in this venomous controversy by launching a counter-attack against McGrath. On the day after reporting Bolton's repudiation of McGrath's allegations, the *Ballarat Star* published an anti-McGrath blast from Pompey. 'Mr McGrath knows nothing of war, and in particular knows nothing of the AIF', Pompey declared. He was only in the AIF 'for a short time' while he had 'a safe and cushy job' in London at its Horseferry Road headquarters. Elliott then alleged that McGrath had pulled strings to look after his son:

> This young man enlisted and proceeded to England at the Government expense ... On arrival there Mr McGrath, having apparently in the meantime looked up the lad's birth certificate and discovered that he was under age, objected to allowing him to go to France, and the boy was returned home. Mr McGrath then used all his influence to have his son sent to Duntroon school as an officer, apparently on the ground that he had been on active service.

McGrath's response was to reaffirm his allegations about Bolton, and to foreshadow a defamation writ against Elliott. He had neither avoided Western Front service himself, he insisted, nor had he arranged to have his son sent home. That son had in fact served in France (including at the battle of Fromelles) before going home to Australia in 1917 under the impression that he was, like other under-age AIF youths, being given a furlough before returning to the Western Front when older. Instead he arrived home to find the Nationalists claiming that his father had insisted on his discharge, the same furphy Pompey was propagating in 1919. Meanwhile McGrath senior, who was keen to get to the front, felt convinced that devious influences were preventing him from doing so, in order to enable the Nationalists to sneer that he had done no real soldiering. He did eventually manage to cross to France for some perilous experiences, but his political opponents repeatedly claimed that he had performed no front-line service.

Pompey's resentment of McGrath was genuinely deep, but the elaborate Nationalist endeavours to discredit the Labor MPs who had enlisted are among the most murky and sordid episodes in Australian political history. And Elliott was aligning himself with some unlikely allies in this controversy. Not only had he been contemptuous of Bolton's early return to Australia at the time; the Nationalist candidate for Ballarat Pompey was doing his utmost to assist, the 8th Battalion officer he was sharing platforms with to help unseat McGrath, was none other than the same Captain Kerby he had paraded and humiliated at Gallipoli for casting aspersions on his own 7th Battalion. McGrath had dropped a bombshell into the campaign with his allegations about Bolton, but if he had been aware of Pompey's scathing 1915 criticism of both Bolton and Kerby he would have had even more sensational revelations to divulge.

The election results were very satisfying for Elliott. The Nationalists were returned to office, he topped the Senate poll himself in Victoria, and McGrath lost in Ballarat by one vote. As the top Senate candidate on the Nationalist how-to-vote card, Elliott's success at a time when Labor was in disarray was hardly a surprise, but it was gratifying all the same to record more than twice the votes attained by any other Victorian Senate candidate. 'Of course I voted you first', enthused an admirer, 'and it looks as if everyone in Victoria did the same'. Among numerous messages of congratulation Elliott received, the most notable was a postcard from a group of Gippsland returned soldiers who sent it simply to 'Pompey' without, except for that single word, specifying any name or address. Thanks to an enterprising postal clerk who endorsed it 'Try Brigadier-General "Pompey" Elliott, Melbourne', the postcard reached its intended recipient. More than 14,000 Victorians who gave him their number one vote gave their second vote to a non-Nationalist candidate. Not even the emergence of the country political organisations as a national force (eleven country candidates won seats in the House of Representatives) deprived the Hughes government of a working majority in both houses. Labor won only a third of the lower house seats and only one of the nineteen vacancies in the Senate.

When Elliott had time to take stock early in 1920, he was able to reflect that his first half-year back home had gone quite well, certainly better than he had feared in his black moods of foreboding about his post-war prospects. He had extricated himself from Roberts satisfactorily and joined an established solicitors' practice as a partner; his awesome popularity, confirmed at a series of welcome-home functions, had resulted in his election to federal parliament with a resounding personal endorsement; and further distinctions, professional and personal, had also come his way. His reintroduction to family life had been highly satisfactory as well. Kate was not intrinsically interested in politics at all, but she had devotedly accompanied her husband on the campaign trail (even though he was so busy and preoccupied with electioneering that he sometimes forgot where he had arranged to meet her). Before the campaign Elliott had been reunited with his brother when he and Kate went up to Tocumwal and stayed with Rod and Liz, the sister-in-law Harold had never met. Belle took Violet and Neil there for the Christmas holidays while Harold opted to unwind with Kate in Melbourne after his electioneering exertions.

Even with the election decided, though, he still had too much on his plate for a prolonged rest. Monash's return to Australia was a notable event. Elliott was among numerous dignitaries assembled at the pier when the 'boss digger' landed in Melbourne; he attended some of the various functions in Monash's honour, including a civic reception at Melbourne Town Hall. In January 1920 Birdwood arrived in Melbourne as part of a national tour marked by extraordinary fanfare, publicity and red carpet treatment. Swank and formality were hardly Pompey's cup of tea, especially to acclaim Birdwood of all people, but he swallowed his resentment and endured the charade. He and Kate donned their glad rags for the Governor-General's dinner party and, a week later, afternoon tea at General Chauvel's; Elliott, like other senior AIF generals, also attended a grand dinner at Parliament House. Birdwood's tour, like the visits of Lord Jellicoe previously and the Prince of Wales later on, were intended by their imperial-minded instigators to enhance cohesive pro-British sentiment in Australia after such a divisive and traumatic war.

At least, now the election was over, Elliott did not have daily political gatherings to address. But there were frequent meetings in connection with his various other commitments, and numerous AIF-related requests ranging from memorial unveilings to the foreword he wrote for a book of impressive anecdotal reminiscences, *To The Last Ridge*, by 'Jimmy' Downing of the 57th Battalion. 'I have read this little book with deep interest', Elliott's foreword began. He considered that Downing's vivid description of 'the thoughts and sensations of the soldier in battle' should be 'welcomed as a valuable addition to our literature'; his accounts of Fromelles, the 1916-17 Somme winter, Polygon Wood, and Villers-Bretonneux 'are, in my opinion, by far the truest and best I have read'. As well as 'commending this book to the public', Pompey's wide-ranging foreword praised Monash's custom of issuing orders well in advance so that they could be properly explained and understood, and pointedly contrasted this with Birdwood's approach: 'Under our previous commander this was not the case'. Downing was thrilled: he 'had scarcely dared hope' for such a glowing and influential endorsement.

He was not the only 15th Brigade soldier to appreciate the brigadier's post-war comradeship. Captain J.D. Schroder, who had spent much of the war at brigade headquarters, returned to Australia after Elliott:

> as the 'Ypiranga' pulled into the pier at Melbourne I could see a familiar figure on the wharf waiting to meet me. Yes it was Pompey. He never forgot his officers or men, and on the way to Menzies [Hotel] where he took me to lunch we must have been stopped twenty times by diggers who wanted to shake his hand and tell him where they had served under him.

In February 1920 verdicts acceptable to Elliott were delivered in two court cases arising from the election campaign. At Ararat the culprits in the tarring and feathering of McDougall (including the ringleader who had served under Pompey) were, in effect, flogged with a damp lettuce. The partisan judge was openly scornful about the charge of grievous bodily harm, decreed that a gaol sentence was out of the question, and imposed a paltry fine for the lesser offence of common assault. On the following day a Supreme Court judge dismissed the libel action brought against Elliott concerning his allegations against the McGraths. Six weeks later this verdict was confirmed on appeal by the full court, which comprised the chief justice (and former prominent conservative politician) W.H. Irvine and two notable Ormond identities known to Elliott. There was, however, better news for McGrath when a hearing in a different jurisdiction upheld his claim that electoral irregularities had tainted Kerby's knife-edge victory in Ballarat; it was accordingly declared void, and a by-election became necessary. At that by-election, in July 1920, McGrath defeated Kerby and regained his seat. That same month Elliott made his parliamentary debut in the Senate.

CHAPTER TWENTY-ONE

'A Special Desk in This Chamber' for the War Historian:

Period of 'Elliott's exuberance'

JULY 1920–1921

ELLIOTT, LIKE ALL new senators elected in 1919, did not become entitled to sit in the Senate until July 1920. He had been absent and uninvolved, therefore, when legislation authorising a controversial increase in MPs' salaries was whipped through both houses in May, a raise that boosted his parliamentary income from £600 to £1000. His inaugural contribution to parliamentary debate occurred on 28 July. It was not a traditional maiden speech in the sense of a wide-ranging formal declaration of his political philosophy and priorities, but some brief observations concerning a bill dealing with organisational changes to the public service.

Right from the outset Elliott lived up to his pre-election assertions about his political independence. In only his second Senate speech he called on the government to 'revise drastically' some of its proposals to overhaul public service administration. He also supported amendments initiated by other senators, and showed ingenuity and tenacity in moving some of his own (one was eventually accepted by the government). His legal expertise and drafting flair were also soon illustrated when his amendment extending the provisions of the war service homes legislation, to the benefit of returned soldiers, was accepted by the minister for Repatriation, Senator E.D. Millen, in August.

Pompey's independent approach became even more evident in October when the topic of expenditure on Canberra was debated in the

Senate. With federal parliament continuing to sit in Melbourne until the national capital was established, it was hardly surprising that Victorian senators in 1920 were less enthusiastic than their New South Wales counterparts about pushing on with the development of Canberra. On 1 October Elliott's Victorian colleague Frank Guthrie objected to £150,000 being spent on temporary buildings for 'a bush capital', denouncing this budget item as 'reeking of extravagance' when Australia's war expenditure had resulted in an 'enormous' foreign debt (£656 million) and the government was supposedly being frugal. Amid testy exchanges Elliott vehemently supported Guthrie. 'When we were invited to support the Ministry at the recent elections', Pompey declared, 'one of the main planks in their platform was that the strictest economy would be observed'. When New South Wales Nationalists (particularly H.E. Pratten, a prominent Sydney manufacturer who entered parliament in 1917) asserted that development of Canberra had also been party policy at election time, Elliott and Guthrie disagreed. 'So far as I am aware that matter was never mentioned', Elliott contended.

> Senator Pratten: Did not the honourable senator say that he agreed with the Prime Minister and with the policy of the National Party?
>
> Senator Elliott: I do not know what Senator Pratten signed, but I certainly signed no platform whatever ... I gave a general support to the policy of the Ministry, but I did not support any expenditure upon Canberra. In fact, I feel so strongly upon this matter that I have no desire to sit behind the Ministry if they are going to incur this expenditure. I would rather form a party of my own.
>
> Senator Guthrie: We shall join the Country Party.
>
> Senator Elliott: I again express my profound dissatisfaction with the general policy of the Government in this regard.

Elliott did not proceed to form a party of his own, but he did rapidly establish a reputation for outspokenness in parliament. The composition of the Senate fostered an independent approach. Likeable ALP veteran 'Jupp' Gardiner, a 53-year-old former rugby champion who tipped the scales at eighteen stone, was Labor's solitary senator, and Elliott was not the only Nationalist senator to conclude that this circumstance imposed a greater responsibility on them to scrutinise government measures carefully. Pompey's individualistic instincts were soon evident. He was particularly critical of the government when he considered it was not doing enough to reduce spending. During his first few months in the Senate he aired his disapproval of excessive expenditure in a number of spheres besides Canberra's development. While he remained devoted to returned soldiers and continued to be a dedicated advocate for their cause, he felt instinctively protective of those he described as 'the middle classes, the people who get it in the neck every time'. And, though sometimes flummoxed by procedural intricacies in the Senate, he was soon using parliament effectively as a forum for raising issues in order to expedite desirable outcomes.

Meanwhile he continued to be busy outside parliament with a host of AIF-related activities. With structures to commemorate the AIF being erected all round Australia, Pompey was in high demand as an unveiler. Dignitaries doing the honours on such occasions tended to concentrate on abstract concepts—honour and glory, gallantry and valour, duty and sacrifice. Elliott spoke that language too, but his unveiling speeches were more effective than most because of his anecdotal style; rather than laboriously pontificating in general terms about those concepts, Pompey told vivid stories to exemplify them. When he unveiled an honour roll at crowded St. John's church in Camberwell, for example, he admitted that he was unfamiliar with most of the individuals named on it; but he said he knew the kind of things they had done, and proceeded to describe particular Australian deeds at Gallipoli and the Western Front.

While this approach was well received whenever Elliott officiated at such ceremonies, it was especially appreciated when he was able to go into detail about the individuals being commemorated. When he laid the foundation stone of a war memorial church in Essendon, he talked about what the Essendon boys did at the landing. When he journeyed to the Euroa district to unveil a striking monument at Strathbogie, he described how those famous local identities Fred Tubb and Alex Burton had won the VC at Lone Pine. His audiences were enthralled. People flocked from miles around to attend the Strathbogie ceremony in October 1920; there had been no larger gathering in the town's entire history.

Elliott's connection with these commemorative structures was not confined to unveilings. He involved himself in fund-raising activities to help pay for them, such as his well-attended lecture on modern battle which substantially assisted the construction of a memorial hall at Camberwell. This lecture was illustrated with official AIF slides and film footage. The friendship of mutual regard and trust forged during the war between Elliott and J.L. Treloar continued into peacetime. Treloar, now the dedicated and diligent director of the Australian War Museum (later to become the Australian War Memorial), readily acquiesced when Pompey asked if he could borrow slides and film for his lecture; Elliott, in turn, was responsive when Treloar asked him to donate to the museum. Among the items he relinquished were the boots he was wearing when wounded at the Gallipoli landing, the hole made by the bullet that hit his ankle still clearly visible. Pompey was also involved when a proposal gathered momentum in Melbourne to cement Australia's connection with Villers-Bretonneux through a financial contribution to the French town's post-war restoration. In October 1920 he told a public meeting convened to discuss this proposal that the French regarded the AIF's recapture of Villers-Bretonneux as the turning point of the war; a committee was formed to pursue this initiative, with Elliott as a vice-president.

There was one commemorative involvement he did distance himself from, however. It concerned his old school. Nowhere was Pompey a more celebrated hero than at Ballarat College. He was given a rapturous reception when he presented the prizes at speech night, and again when he attended the annual collegians' reunion. On both occasions he was greeted with a standing ovation, cheers, and 'For He's a Jolly Good Fellow'. A student present at that speech night recalled long afterwards Elliott's imposing stature—immense chest and shoulders in particular—and the impression he conveyed of dynamic physical strength. At the ex-collegians' gathering Pompey was acclaimed as 'the greatest son the college ever had', 'a man whose name had rung through the whole British Empire'. He was elected president of their association, and it was proposed that a memorial hall should be constructed and named after him. Elliott told the meeting that he supported the concept of a memorial hall, but was not keen on having his name associated with it: 'I'm not dead yet', he explained.

He was as fond of Ballarat as it was of him. In 1920 Bean contacted him to ask which town, suburb, or district he would like to be associated with in the AIF official history. The answer was Ballarat. Although he had not lived there for decades, 'I ... have regarded myself always as belonging to the Ballarat district' and 'have a great liking' for it.

In mid-1920 Elliott's prestige and reputation as an authority on the

AIF landed him in a bitter sectarian controversy. On 3 July a theatrical play about the war, 'Advance Australia', was performed at Bendigo to raise funds for a Catholic convent carnival. Its anti-British sentiments, particularly evident in its depiction of the battle of Fromelles, offended 'loyalists', and a furore erupted. There were angry demonstrations and protest meetings. Discrediting the play was not a straightforward matter, as its author and producer, Father J.J. Kennedy, had not only been at Fromelles himself—as the (Catholic) chaplain of the 53rd AIF Battalion—but had been awarded the DSO for conspicuous gallantry in caring for the wounded there. Strident objectors to the play invited their local MP, Prime Minister Hughes, to address a protest meeting on 9 July, but he was too busy; when General Elliott signified his willingness to speak, the *Argus* reported that 'satisfaction was expressed' in Bendigo.

The meeting was crowded and rowdy. Pompey provided a long and detailed account of the battle, and insisted that a theme in the play which loyalists found particularly offensive—that the British had let the Australians down as usual—was factually misconceived. Whenever Elliott sensed that pro-Irish Catholics were taking on pro-British Protestants he instinctively aligned himself with the latter; also, throughout the 1920s he vigilantly scrutinised the way AIF history was being documented. Even so, considering Pompey's real views about British generalship and staff work at Fromelles, this was a peculiar intervention. Its timing, just before the Ballarat by-election contested by the Labor identity he abhorred more than any other, D.C. McGrath, was surely no coincidence. Kennedy and his supporters had no doubt that the agitation surrounding the play was a deliberate attempt by Nationalist manipulators to fuel sectarianism in the last week of the campaign in Ballarat. If so, the tactic failed—McGrath won the by-election.

Elliott's AIF-related activities were not confined to commemorative monuments and attempts to influence how the history of the war was being written. Providing practical assistance to the men who had returned from the war was also a big priority. Striving to improve their lot was a constant preoccupation. Besides doing his utmost in parliament for them collectively and—where particular grievances were brought to his notice—individually, he wrote numerous references. One to survive from this period concerned Corporal Frank South of the 60th Battalion. Armed with Elliott's recommendation praising his 'excellent service' during three years in the 15th Brigade, South succeeded in getting the position he was after. But Pompey's references did not always do the trick. Despite his 'very strong' letter of support, the quest of his old friend McNicoll to become administrator of the mandated territory of New Guinea was unsuccessful.

In February 1921 Elliott's supersession grievance was reignited when divisional commands in Australia's post-war defence scheme were announced. With seven appointments to be made (there were five infantry and two Light Horse divisions in the reorganised peacetime force), and his supersession wound of 1918 still raw, it was a stinging personal rebuff for Pompey to find himself overlooked when Gellibrand, Glasgow, Rosenthal, and Tivey were all among the selected seven. The other three chosen were Hobbs, 'Digger' Brand, and a well-known New South Wales Light Horse commander who was also assistant minister for Defence, Sir Granville Ryrie. Elliott's chagrin at missing out resulted not only from his conviction that he was entitled to one of these commands on merit; he had also received what he interpreted as an inside tip that he could expect to get one.

His 'informant' was Digger Brand. After the mid-1918 appointments that had so affronted Pompey, Brand had been earmarked as next in line for an AIF divisional command (unbeknown to Elliott, who had far superior claims). No such vacancy had arisen and, after the Armistice, Brand became state commandant in Victoria. In that capacity Brand had been at the pier to meet Elliott when the *Orontes* arrived in June 1919, and had been one of Pompey's fellow speakers at the influential returned soldiers meeting in the Domain the following month. He had later approached Pompey for advice in connection with peacetime command appointments: if Elliott were given a division in the post-war force, who would he recommend as prospective brigade commanders in Victoria? While providing the assessment Brand requested, Elliott remarked that Brand's letter was the first intimation he had received of the potential offer of a divisional command; Brand replied that Pompey's claims could hardly be overlooked.

Since that exchange Elliott had been awaiting developments with wary expectancy. In August 1920 when Gellibrand, having returned to Tasmania, accepted an invitation to become Victoria's Chief Commissioner of Police, he was quoted as admitting that his decision to accept this interstate position had been influenced by a foreshadowed appointment in the new defence force. Elliott even made this reported remark the subject of a question without notice in the Senate: 'I have no knowledge of any employment of a military character being offered to Sir John Gellibrand', Pearce replied. (In fact, Brudenell White, with adroit behind-the-scenes manoeuvring, had engineered the offer of the police commissionership because he wanted Gellibrand to be available to command a Victorian-based division.) On 8 February 1921 it was announced that Gellibrand (and Brand) had each been given a division, and Elliott discovered that his most heartfelt ambition had eluded him once again.

He was, of course, furious. He immediately fired off a protest letter, declaring himself unavailable for a brigade command in the peacetime force (as a Victorian brigadier, his immediate superior would have been either Glasgow or Gellibrand). He also contended that this repetition of his 1918 supersession warranted a personal investigation by Senator Pearce into 'why I have been deemed unfit for promotion'. This letter was referred to the highest military tribunal in Australia, the Military Board; Pearce, as Defence minister, was its president. Accepting Elliott's withdrawal of his services with regret, the Military Board ruled that his latest claim to have been superseded was misconceived. Moreover, the board 'reluctantly' concluded (in a formal minute endorsed by Pearce) that 'the substance and tone of General Elliott's statement of his grievance show him to be lacking in the restraint and judgment necessary for high command'. Elliott was informed that the board (including the minister) found his representations unsustainable. Pompey persisted:

> As I have been thus superseded by the Military Board without any crime or fault imputed to me, or any opportunity to answer any accusation made against me ... I must respectfully request that the matter be made the subject of an enquiry by a Supreme Court Judge or other independent Commissioner on the lines mentioned in my former letter so that I may be informed wherein I have failed to win the favour of the Military Board or other authority.

Predictably, the Military Board confirmed its previous ruling. Elliott was notified that neither the regulations nor 'the custom of the service entitles an officer to demand an enquiry'. Furthermore, the investigation of 'a purely military matter' by a senior judge or equivalent would set a most undesirable precedent. It 'would have far reaching effects and militate against the very foundations of military discipline'. Besides,

Elliott had 'no reasonable grounds for considering himself aggrieved'.

Pearce signed his formal endorsement of this Military Board verdict on 5 April. The following day, when federal parliament resumed after its lengthy summer break, Senator Millen announced that the session then beginning would be primarily devoted to overhauling the tariff; other government initiatives would be meagre. It seemed that a staid, torpid parliamentary term lay ahead, but Pompey Elliott was in such an aggrieved frame of mind that he single-handedly torpedoed these expectations.

Warming up with some critical remarks about the Air Defence Bill, Elliott declared that there was 'absolutely no necessity' for an expansive and expensive peacetime air force, which had evidently been advocated by 'certain highly-placed officers' in order to secure remunerative positions for themselves. If, however, such a measure was going to be introduced, tighter provisions were needed to prevent inappropriately rapid promotion for certain officers who possessed social influence. By way of illustration, he contrasted the treatment of Street and Scanlan (without naming them) during the war, describing his frustration when his repeated attempts to have Street replaced as his brigade major were thwarted until this wealthy 'social butterfly' who 'could not sleep in anything rougher than silk pyjamas at ten guineas a suit' made a grave mistake at a critical time in April 1918. Whereas Street had been sent to Staff College at Cambridge, the officer Pompey wanted as his brigade major and recommended for an advanced training course, Scanlan, who was more talented but without influence, was sidelined at Salisbury Plain until Pompey rescued him. Another shortcoming of the Air Defence Bill, according to Pompey, was its failure to ensure that officers with grievances were able to seek redress: 'I know from bitter experience during the recent war ... that threats and duress were applied to prevent an officer exercising his statutory right of appeal to the Minister'. Accordingly, he would be introducing an amendment to enable an aggrieved individual to sue for damages in the civil courts in such circumstances.

The following week Elliott moved into top gear. His vehicle was an amending Defence Bill; while merely 'a machinery measure' to Millen, it was teeming with dangerous flaws in Pompey's estimation. Uppermost in his 'very grave and serious objections' to the bill was its incorporation of the British Army Act into Australia's peacetime defence administration. He also became animated about the issue of 'redress of grievances'. After a terse exchange with Pearce, who denied Elliott's claim that the right of appeal to the Defence minister no longer existed, Pompey proceeded to dissect the Military Board. This time he named names. Brudenell White had 'washed his hands of the Australian forces' when he accompanied Birdwood to the Fifth Army in 1918; of the other board members, only Elliott's old friend General Forsyth had distinguished himself in the field during the war, and because his health broke down soon after the AIF's arrival at the Western Front he was unaware of developments after 1916. No member of the Military Board except White, therefore, was competent to judge the comparative suitability of Australia's generals for higher command, a state of affairs that was demonstrably unsatisfactory and also unnecessary:

> Senator Elliott: We have here General Monash, who commanded the Australian forces in France with the utmost success, and [who excited] the admiration of the whole world. He has not been admitted to the Board—
>
> Senator Pearce: But he was consulted about the divisional appointments.
>
> Senator Elliott: Since the Minister has raised that question, I have the best authority for saying that, although General Monash has been consulted upon numerous occasions, upon no occasion has his recommendation been followed.
>
> Senator Pearce: The honourable senator is wrong there. I have the signature of General Monash to his recommendations, and I can produce it.

This was unsettling. Elliott had nurtured all along the conviction that Monash held him in high regard and would have treated him differently. But it was, in fact, Pearce who was mistaken, not Elliott. Monash had been privately consulted about these appointments, but was annoyed that his views (especially his strong objections to giving Gellibrand a division) evidently 'carried no weight'; the 'reference of the matter to me was more or less a farce', he concluded. Pompey foreshadowed the same type of amendment he had proposed in his response to the Air Defence Bill, a provision enabling an aggrieved member of the force who had been improperly dissuaded from appealing to the Defence minister to sue in the civil courts for damages. In this speech he decided to draw on his personal experience to underline the need for such an amendment. Headlines resulted.

'I am reluctant to bring in anything of a personal nature', he said, 'but I want to show the Senate that I have had bitter experience of this sort of thing'. What followed was a graphic account of the desperate defence of March 1918, when his brigade was flung into a series of alarming situations, on more than one occasion having to march all night. He described how the tremendous exertions of his men were hampered at a critical stage by the unauthorised occupation of Hedauville by a detachment of British 'fugitives', who were obviously prepared to stay where they were and leave the fighting to others until Pompey took vigorous action to evict them. Quoting freely from his report to Hobbs about this incident, Elliott told the Senate that the staff officer in charge of these British renegades had protested to his superiors about Elliott's forceful intervention:

> Three weeks later General Hobbs called to see me. He said, 'I want to speak to you privately', and took me out into the garden. He then said to me, 'General, I have instructions to tell you that while you are in the Australian Imperial Force you will receive no further promotion by reason of your conduct to the [British] officers'. When he said that, I turned away rather dumbfounded, and he struck me on the back and said, 'I have got to tell you that, but by God you were right'. It turned out that this staff officer was the son of a Duke, and put the acid on General Birdwood for my conduct, and you see the result.

Shortly afterwards, Elliott continued, he discovered that he had been superseded by Gellibrand. He had protested to Brudenell White, raising the prospect of an appeal to the Defence minister; Pompey then read out White's reply threatening to send him straight back to Australia if he resorted to 'political influence'. The conclusion was clear. 'There was absolutely nothing against me on the score of capacity to command or lead', he contended. Yet if he had opted to exercise his undoubted right of appeal he would have been sent home in disgrace. The impact of these stunning disclosures was intensified because awareness of such contentious developments was minimal (censorship during the war was rigorous).

Pompey then analysed the recent appointments in the post-war force. He claimed that he had again been superseded by Gellibrand, he had again tried to exercise his right of appeal, and White had again stood in his way. Since White was the only member of the Military Board really in a position to evaluate the comparative abilities of the generals concerned, it was as if 'I have appealed from him to himself', and the result was predictable. Elliott concluded this sensational speech by announcing that the defects he had highlighted would no longer affect him personally: 'I am so sick of the whole business that … I shall no longer serve in the Citizen Forces of the Commonwealth under the present heads'.

With numerous high-ranking AIF personalities in the Senate, the reaction to Elliott's speech promised to be as riveting as his remarkable revelations. Strong support from a non-AIF quarter came from Senator Pratten: he had 'never been an admirer of General Birdwood', who was 'a lime lighter'. From 'Fighting Charlie' Cox, a Light Horse brigadier from New South Wales, on the other hand, came vacuous disapproval, not for the last time during a controversy involving Elliott. A more discerning contribution came from Brigadier-General E.A. Drake-Brockman, a Western Australian senator. Referring to Elliott as 'my gallant and distinguished friend', Drake-Brockman said he had shown 'the same courage that he was so celebrated for in the field' in raising 'a matter which concerns himself very closely in order to illustrate what he considers a great defect in our present system'. While declining to discuss 'the merits or otherwise' of Pompey's supersession complaint ('I know nothing more about it than he has told us here'), and proclaiming himself an ardent admirer of both White and Birdwood, Drake-Brockman said that Elliott's point about 'appealing from Caesar to Caesar' was compelling.

Pearce, the following speaker, admitted that he was 'very much impressed' by Drake-Brockman's remarks on that aspect, but not at all by Pompey's wartime recollections: 'I deprecate discussion on the personal matters that Senator Elliott has brought forward'. The Defence minister said that he had no idea what had transpired in private discussions between Generals White, Hobbs, and Elliott in 1918; making an issue of it three years later was pointless as well as undesirable. With scores of soldiers feeling disgruntled about some wartime incident or another, an inquiry into Elliott's grievance would set a precedent and open the floodgates. Moreover, any retrospective re-evaluation of command appointments was simply impracticable—some of the necessary witnesses were dead, and others were either overseas or scattered around Australia. As for himself, Pearce continued, he had not been in a position during the war to exercise an informed veto on appointments made overseas, and he had assured both Bridges and Birdwood beforehand that he would not be interfering. He had in fact benefited from a tip Bridges had given him years earlier, when he was inexperienced and unfamiliar with defence matters, that he should read a well-known book on the American Civil War, Henderson on Stonewall Jackson. This authoritative work, Pearce added, contained 'a very good lesson for politicians' about the disastrous consequences of meddling in such matters.

Six days later Elliott launched a counter-attack, instigating a special debate in the Senate on the 'uncontrolled power' Pearce had allowed Birdwood during the war. Pompey's acute sense of grievance spawned intense resentment whenever he was embroiled in a dispute and other individuals involved did not see things his way. When overlooked in 1918 he had blamed Birdwood and White, vented his spleen on them, and looked to others (Monash, Pearce) to put things right. When he missed out on a division again in 1921 and his protest to the Military Board was dismissed, he impugned the credentials of board members and looked to Pearce to overrule them. When Pearce confirmed in the Senate that he had approved both the 1918 and 1921 appointments and was unmoved by Elliott's indignant protests, Pompey went gunning for him.

On 27 April 1921 Pearce tried to have the Pompey-initiated debate about Birdwood's power disallowed, but was unsuccessful. Elliott embarked on an analysis of the Civil War and Henderson on Stonewall Jackson, intending to demonstrate the inappropriateness of the conclusion Pearce said he had drawn from that book. He also sought to link the unfettered power ceded by Pearce to the denial of his right to appeal in 1918. Pearce parried this thrust easily enough: the admission that he felt unable to overturn AIF command appointments in no way signified that he had authorised Birdwood or White to suspend any AIF officer's right of appeal. Moreover, while 'General Elliott would have us believe that he had been superseded owing to a bias against him', there were actually other generals more senior to Elliott (McNicoll and Tivey) who were also passed over—and did not protest—when Gellibrand and Glasgow were promoted. Besides, White's letter of May 1918 was more 'kindly advice' than menacing threat. Pearce cited its praise of Elliott's undoubted 'courage' and 'ability', quoted White's qualifying stricture that 'you mar it by not keeping your judgment under complete control', and added a pointed observation of his own: 'Senator Elliott is falling into the same error in Australia'.

Next day the Senate resumed debate on the Defence Bill, and Pompey was back on the warpath. Moving an amendment granting 'additional rights' to superseded officers, he embarked on another caustic exposé of Western Front controversies. Pearce tried to rein Elliott in, accusing him of 'indulging in his reminiscences' and claiming that his amendment was out of order, but the Senate Chairman overruled him. This Pompey diatribe was all the more dramatic because the central figure in it was Albert Jacka, Australia's first VC winner in the Great War and a legendary soldier. Although he shunned publicity himself, Jacka's awesome front-line prowess was so renowned that he was one of the three most famous AIF identities in post-war Australia (the other two being Monash and Elliott himself). Time after time Jacka had been superseded in the 14th Battalion, Pompey told the Senate, even though he 'repeatedly distinguished himself' as a brilliant tactician and 'the bravest of the brave':

> He led dozens of desperate charges, he was worshipped by his men, and notwithstanding this, officers were repeatedly placed over him. The position became so critical that men in Jacka's battalion refused to go into action unless under his command. Honourable senators may think that is an astonishing statement; but it is an absolute fact.

Why was Jacka subjected to 'such a cruel embargo'? According to Pompey, it was because of his bitter reaction to the fiasco of First Bullecourt. Tanks proved a great success in 1918 when Monash ensured that they went into action 'fully protected'—he 'even had aeroplanes buzzing up and down above to confuse the enemy'. But they had been a disastrous failure at Bullecourt in April 1917 because Birdwood and White had sent them forward without protection at a time 'when the ground was white with snow, so that every tank stood out' starkly. These tanks were supposed to be supporting the advancing AIF infantry, but nearly all of them failed:

> One of them suddenly blundered into a sunken road in which the members of the 14th Victorian Battalion were waiting to attack. The man in charge [of the tank] was so utterly panic-stricken that he turned his guns on our own men, and at a range of 5 or 10 yards killed at least thirty. It was said at the time that if the men had had a tin-opener they would have murdered the man who was responsible; but he was inside the tank.

About 70 per cent of the Australians engaged at First Bullecourt became casualties there; more than 600 were in the 14th Battalion. After the battle Jacka, as battalion intelligence officer, compiled a frank and understandably scathing report about the tanks which, Pompey alleged, was suppressed by Birdwood and became a watershed for Jacka: from then on he did not get a fair go.

Elliott qualified these astounding revelations with a caveat. They were largely based on statements to him by various 14th Battalion members, notably Jacka himself and the widely esteemed commander of the battalion at Bullecourt, Colonel Peck (who came into closer contact with Elliott later in the war as Hobbs's chief-of-staff). 'I cannot, of course, vouch for their absolute accuracy', Pompey pointed out, 'as I had no means of investigating them'.

His revelations were challenged straightaway in the Senate by Drake-Brockman, who was in charge of the 16th Battalion alongside Jacka's unit at First Bullecourt before becoming commander of the 4th Brigade, which included both these battalions. Drake-Brockman conceded that the tanks were 'rottenly officered' in April 1917, and their 'complete failure' at Bullecourt justified the 'very strong protest' submitted by Jacka. However, he distanced himself from Elliott's criticism of Birdwood and White, and insisted that Jacka was in no way penalised because of his Bullecourt report. This could not have happened, Drake-Brockman told the Senate, because Jacka's report was never forwarded. Both it and the equivalent review by his 16th Battalion counterpart were so controversial that Peck and Drake-Brockman decided to adopt them as their own rather than hide behind the commendable frankness of their subordinates.

This sophistry did not vitiate the essential validity of Elliott's allegations. The damning report written by Jacka had, in fact, been forwarded. Although countersigned by Peck and Drake-Brockman, its real author's identity had been obvious. And it was true that Jacka did not receive the promotion and decorations his leadership and battle deeds deserved. His admirers claimed that he performed at least one VC-winning exploit at the Western Front on top of the VC he won at Gallipoli. Bean and others regarded what he did at Pozières as the most outstanding individual feat by any Australian in the whole war. It was also correct that Jacka's Pompey-like tendency to criticise his superiors bluntly was the main reason for his under-recognition. Elliott may not have realised, however, that probably a bigger culprit than either Birdwood or White in this unfair treatment was Brand, whose inept handling of Jacka—a difficult subordinate, admittedly—demonstrated the inappropriateness of preferring him to Elliott as a divisional commander.

That same day Pompey aired more startling revelations in the Senate when he referred to a letter he had received from his old friend McNicoll, now the principal of a school at Goulburn. McNicoll, writing to congratulate Elliott for exposing dissatisfaction with the Birdwood–White regime, recalled his own aggrieved protests about Gellibrand in 1918, and claimed that the rejection of his application for the New Guinea post despite 'the very strong letters of yourself and Monash' indicated that he was still paying a price for them:

> I have never recovered from having stood up for a decent thing ... There are many other matters which we know of mutually and which one does not care to write about, and I'm sure I'm not alone in my feeling of satisfaction and gratitude to you for the action you have taken in raising a protest.

McNicoll might well have been taken aback to find such a letter quoted by its recipient in parliament (and cited accordingly in the press); but Pompey was all steamed up, and the letter was irresistible ammunition to refute Pearce's assertion that other AIF generals did not object when they were bypassed in 1918. Not only had Tivey been furious, as 'his batman told my batman', Elliott declared, but McNicoll's letter was incontrovertible proof that Pearce's claim was 'absolutely false'.

As Pompey quoted its contents and elaborated on them, he once again had his fellow senators on the edge of their seats. He vividly described how McNicoll, his 'oldest friend in military and civil life', had recovered from a near-fatal wound at Gallipoli to become a senior brigadier under Monash at the Western Front, before being leapfrogged in the promotion stakes by Gellibrand in mid-1918. Unlike Elliott, McNicoll then had Gellibrand as his immediate superior, and they were soon at loggerheads, as Elliott underlined with this excerpt from McNicoll's letter:

> I don't know whether I told you that in June 1918, after he [Gellibrand] had been appointed to the 3rd Div[ision] he treated me so abominably that I asked to be relieved of my command and returned to Aust[ralia].

However, a detailed appraisal of this damaging rift by Gellibrand's biographer decades later concluded that the root of the conflict was not Gellibrand's manner (as Monash claimed, siding with McNicoll) but the conduct of McNicoll, who was 'downright insubordinate and disloyal', incompetent as well, and 'an unwanted and unwarranted burden on Gellibrand'.

In response to Pompey's revelations Pearce reiterated his distaste for Elliott's preoccupation with personal grievances. The relevance to the Senate debate of what General Tivey's batman had said to General Elliott's batman was 'beyond my comprehension', he remarked. Furthermore, the changes Pompey was advocating would produce 'hopeless confusion' and 'chaos'. Elliott disputed this angrily—'I do not ever remember hearing such a travesty of facts'—and counter-attacked with more recriminations. He let fly with a highly jaundiced blast about preferential treatment for Gellibrand and an astonishing outburst about an unspecified AIF officer:

> In France one of the biggest 'duds' I know of commanded a regiment of Light Horse, and he was stationed in a village behind the lines for the whole period of the war. During practically the whole of that time he was there he was intoxicated, and the villagers in pity and contempt named him 'Le Toujours Zig-Zag', by which they meant that he was always drunk ... He returned to Australia and is now in command of the troops in Tasmania.

In view of these 'extraordinary statements', Senator Gardiner observed,

> whoever is engaged in writing up the history of the war should be supplied with a special desk in this chamber and should be given a special invitation to be in regular attendance in the Senate, because matters of the greatest interest to them may crop up here at any time.

A week later Pearce told the Senate he had a statement to make in response to allegations by Senator Elliott. The officer Pompey had traduced as Toujours Zig-Zag was Colonel Dudley White, brother of Brudenell White; his 'charge of drunkenness in France' had been investigated, and was 'entirely unfounded'. A pre-war accident, which partially paralysed Colonel White for some time, had bequeathed 'lameness' and a 'slight speech impediment' as permanent legacies, but 'throughout his war service this officer was of temperate habits'. This statement was presented as a verdict of the Military Board. Perhaps it was (although Pearce received it from Brudenell White personally) but, whatever its origins, it demonstrated that Pompey, not for the first time, had jumped in without checking his information sufficiently. Although he maintained that Colonel White's 'incompetence in command' was notorious 'in the whole AIF', the upshot was tantamount to an embarrassing own goal.

Elliott did not heed the lesson. A few hours later, during the resumed Senate debate on the Defence Bill, he returned to the supersession issue and Jacka's treatment. He had not fully investigated Jacka's case before raising it in the Senate previously, he admitted, but had now done so, and was even 'prepared to lay before the Senate statutory declarations on the subject ... to clear up the matter and to give the public an opportunity to learn the real facts of the case.' Pearce unleashed an impatient rejoinder: 'I should be busy for the next fifty years if I followed up all these tarradiddles.' Maintaining that Jacka had been unfairly treated when inferior officers were imported into the 14th Battalion and placed over him, Pompey launched into a pungent analysis of their deficiencies. One of them had left Australia with the Third Division:

> General Monash tried him in two places, as a brigade-major and as a battalion commander, and he had to be kicked out of both [yet] General Birdwood ... after Bullecourt ... insisted on this man taking command of the 14th Battalion over Captain Jacka's head ...

> At Polygon Wood [he] disappeared for two days, and during three days Captain Jacka ran the whole show. The colonel, in disappearing, took his telephone instruments with him, and Jacka had to beg, borrow or steal telephone instruments, make a new headquarters, and continue the action.

There was also the 'Polish Jew' who 'was put in command of the battalion although he could not speak English'. While he was with the 14th this 'unfortunate illiterate' (who 'could not write his own orders')

> never by any chance went near the front line. Whenever an action was imminent he developed synovitis ... I do not know where he came from originally, but the position became so bad at last that headquarters could not stand him and fired him.

Pompey's denunciation of the colonel who absented himself at Polygon Wood was factually based, but he was taken to task for his criticism of the other 14th Battalion commander. Drake-Brockman was soon on his feet to set the record straight about Eliezer Margolin:

> He was my second in command in France ... I have never served with a more gallant gentleman. Perhaps it was unfortunate that subsequently he was sent to the command of the 14th Battalion, because it is quite true that his method of speech was not quite orthodox. But this 'illiterate' Jew, as he has been termed, could not only speak English well though with a slight foreign accent, but he could also speak French, German, Russian, Hebrew and the Arabic languages fluently.

According to Drake-Brockman, Margolin was unable to go forward because he twisted his knee when he fell into a Messines shell hole:

> Of course he could not get up to the front line. How could he with his knee swollen to about four or five times its normal size? I saw it myself ... I know that Senator Elliott has not deliberately misinformed the Senate with regard to this matter. But he did not know all the facts. I do.

Senator George Henderson, another Western Australian who knew Margolin personally, hastened to corroborate Drake-Brockman. Henderson sang Margolin's praises effusively—'there was never a more loyal or more courageous gentleman'—and contended that

> if Senator Elliott's statements generally, in connexion with all other matters upon which he has spoken in this chamber, are as far removed from the facts as his comments concerning [Margolin], then his every word ought to be discounted and discountenanced by the Senate.

Elliott was clearly nettled by Henderson's stinging reflection on his credibility. His strained attempts to defend himself only made matters worse. The protest he made about being subjected to a 'personal attack' by Henderson sounded hypocritical as well as hollow. His plea that he had been relying on information given to him in good faith, which he was unable to test by examining the informants on oath, invited the predictable rejoinder that he should be more careful about using such information to malign innocent individuals in their absence. While maintaining that transferring 'a foreigner, a stranger, to take over the command of a battalion from a man of the type of Captain Jacka' had been a grave mistake, he conceded that if the men who understandably resented this had inadvertently misled him about Margolin 'I am sorry that I was led into error'.

The manner of Pompey's attacks on both Margolin and Brudenell White's brother exposed the fundamental flaw White himself had pinpointed in mid-1918—Elliott's tendency in controversy to shoot himself in the foot by using inadequately checked ammunition. The egg on Pompey's face concerning Margolin detracted from the validity of his allegation about the other colonel who disappeared at Polygon Wood, and undermined his argument about Jacka's unfair treatment in the 14th Battalion. Drake-Brockman, who had been closer to the 14th Battalion action than Elliott, had already challenged some of his assertions about Jacka; it was imprudent, if not peculiar, for Pompey not to check with Drake-Brockman before firing off his anti-Margolin broadside. The crowning humiliation for Elliott was the intervention of another influential authority who publicly aligned himself with

Margolin's defenders. In a letter to the *Argus* the soldier Elliott admired above all others, Sir John Monash (who was also Australia's most prominent living Jew), wrote that the characterisation of Margolin as 'an illiterate Polish Jew' was 'lamentable' and 'ridiculous'; Margolin was 'a gallant, cultured gentleman, of fine physique and engaging personality, ardently loyal to Australian soldiers and ideals'.

After reading Monash's published letter, Pompey sent one of his own to the *Age*. Some of 'my friends ... disapprove of my actions', he acknowledged. But he had decided, with his eyes open, to raise his own case publicly as the best way of exposing the deficiencies of the system on behalf of numerous others who also had grievances:

> I knew quite well that I should be outraging the military tradition and so-called custom of the service, that my motives would be misunderstood and my actions maligned, but I owe something to the boys who served under me, and they have ever said that I would never ask them to do something which I would not do myself.

As for Margolin, Elliott had not identified that officer by name in parliament until others did so, and he resented the assertion in Monash's letter that he had acted 'without knowledge or inquiry'. Having

> never met the officer in my life ... I investigated the complaint made to me in the presence of a representative of the "Sun" newspaper for several hours, and examined a number of witnesses.

Whatever Margolin's defenders said about his character, and whether the criticisms of him by 14th Battalion men that Pompey had aired in the Senate were unduly harsh or not, the main point, Elliott insisted, was that Margolin had been a conspicuous failure as commander of that unit, and should never have been installed over Jacka in the first place. This was all very well, but if someone else had publicly denigrated Elliott as he had disparaged Margolin and Dudley White, his outrage would have been apoplectic.

On the next Senate sitting day, 11 May, there was more drama when debate resumed on the Defence Bill. After a number of senators, including Elliott, had discussed the Australian government's refusal to yield to insistent British pressure and authorise the death penalty in the AIF (a contentious issue during the war), Pearce pulled a rabbit out of the hat. Evidently annoyed by Pompey's recalcitrance—especially his success in spearheading resistance to the incorporation of the British Army Act into Australia's post-war defence organisation—Pearce announced that a document retrieved from AIF records confirmed that an Australian commander had ordered 'men to be shot in a certain eventuality'. The Defence minister then proceeded to read out Elliott's Villers-Bretonneux order (countermanded by Hobbs) that retreating British soldiers were 'to be rallied and re-formed' as the 15th Brigade advanced through them, 'and on any hesitation to be shot'. Pearce, capitalising on his ambush, declared that Elliott's repeated call for a strengthened appeal mechanism for aggrieved commanders 'certainly comes with a very bad grace' from someone who issued such an order. 'General Elliott was not then prepared to give even a trial'; it was 'shoot first and give a trial afterwards'.

Pompey defended himself with a spirited account of that 'extremely critical time' when the British 'started to stream back in utter rout'. He had to 'take the most drastic steps to stop the panic' because 'there was every possibility of a general rout'. That situation was exceptional, he insisted, and there was 'no analogy' between it and his advocacy of an appeal mechanism. Other senators denounced Pearce's retaliatory manoeuvre:

> Senator Foster: You must have been pretty badly rattled last week to have had that raked up.
>
> Senator Pearce: Senator Elliott is so fond of reminiscences that I thought I would give him a dose of his own medicine.
>
> Senator Gardiner: I think it redounds to his credit ... [B]ecause Senator Elliott has been criticising somewhat severely the Bill which the Minister is handling, he has taken this opportunity of getting a little of his own back, and in what I consider a very discreditable way ... To say that there is an analogy between an officer faced, not only with disaster to his own troops, but disaster to the whole of the Allied Forces, is ridiculous in the extreme ... My heart fills with pride to think that we had an Australian officer who, in the face of overwhelming disaster, had sufficient pluck, courage and determination to do what Senator Elliott did, and I am sure that sentiment will ring from one end of Australia to the other.

The continuing controversy over Elliott's sensational revelations was not confined to the Senate. His speeches were, of course, prominently featured in the newspapers. 'AMAZING AIF DISCLOSURES: Differences Between Generals' blared the *Age* above its lengthy report of one of his parliamentary outbursts. Another tirade was reproduced in the Sydney *Sun* under arresting quadruple headlines—'DUKE'S SON AND AUSTRALIAN GENERAL: Secret of Great War Revealed: Aussies Halted in Sodden Fields: Social Influence Stops Promotion'.

Others entered the fray, notably Elliott's old Labor foe D.C. McGrath. In the House of Representatives on 12 May McGrath accused Elliott of being 'utterly inconsistent'. He contrasted Elliott's reaction to Father Kennedy's play ten months earlier, when the general had publicly denied that British soldiers ran away, with his assertion in the Senate on 11 May (after Pearce divulged his countermanded Villers-Bretonneux order) that they did. Pompey's immediate response, a letter to the *Argus* published on 14 May, emphasised the difference between the battle of Fromelles (the subject of Kennedy's play) and the defence on the Somme nearly two years later. At Fromelles, he insisted, the British 'did not run away, but advanced gallantly and lost heavily'; their 'failure was largely due to the faulty tactics of their commanders'. Maybe, but when he went on to contend that Kennedy's play 'was utterly false in its suggestion that the British ran away or in any manner let us down in a discreditable manner' this was irreconcilable with his own scathing criticism of the British 184th Brigade's 'shameful betrayal' of half the 58th AIF Battalion.

McGrath would have had Elliott on toast had he been aware of it. Politics, military history, and personal grievance were a murky mixture; Pompey's counter-attacking instincts were luring him into deep water. In the *Argus* letter he distanced himself from aspersions on the British infantry generally (as distinct from certain staff officers and commanders), and even made the bald declaration that the British Fifth Army 'was deliberately sacrificed by Sir Douglas Haig' in 1918. Moreover, not even in March 1918 could it validly be said (as a character in Kennedy's play had claimed) 'that the Australians had been always let down', an observation hardly consistent with Elliott's wartime perception that his own brigade was let down substantially by a neighbouring British formation in each of its most important engagements at the Western Front.

For the rest of May Elliott and McGrath went round for round in the pages of the *Argus*. McGrath reiterated that Elliott had been 'plainly inconsistent': the anti-Kennedy protesters were fired up because the play alleged that the British had run away and let Australians down, not because Kennedy had wrongly attributed this state of affairs to July 1916 instead of March and April 1918. Pompey countered by denying McGrath's allegation that he had accused any British soldier of cowardice at Fromelles, the Somme, or anywhere else. All he had said, he claimed, was that

> under certain circumstances certain officers, so specifying them that no innocent person could be injured, were guilty of misconduct, and these in almost every instance were officers appointed through social or other interest to posts for which they were quite unfitted.

Why, he had not even accused McGrath of cowardice, he continued, a gratuitous shaft that McGrath predictably resented, even though the *Argus* refrained from publishing Pompey's elaboration (presumably for legal reasons, since McGrath had sued earlier in similar circumstances).

That same month Elliott was also prominent, and in combative mode, in the columns of the *Age*. On 14 May the newspaper published an article by a British visitor who felt Australia had emerged from the war with a bad case of

> excessive national self-esteem ... detected in numerous speeches which seem to suggest that the Australians won the war. Even though such speeches are usually made by irresponsible persons, they create an unpleasant impression in Europe.

Pompey, identifying himself as one of the main offenders in this British critic's eyes, was incensed by the thrust of the article and its condescending tone. Dissemination of such supercilious sentiments, after what he and other Australians had experienced during the war, was like 'waving a red rag at a bull', he admitted in his searing rejoinder in the *Age* a fortnight later.

This 4,500-word outburst was an extraordinary effusion. No more powerful assertion of Australian nationalism in the context of the Great

War has ever been published. Elliott's virulent analysis encompassed Fromelles, First Bullecourt, Polygon Wood, Villers-Bretonneux, and the offensive of 8 August 1918. He also covered such inveterate hobby-horses as unwarranted British slurs about AIF indiscipline; Birdwood's 1918 circular urging the AIF not to belittle the British; the chasm between Monash and Birdwood in capacity, character, and performance; what happened when Pompey acted on the post-Fromelles tip he received from General Feilding about how to avoid complying with an ill-conceived order; and much, much more. It all culminated in a fervent peroration:

> Australians have come to the conclusion, from bitter experience, that never more will they entrust the Australian soldiers' lives to the control of irresponsible British officers, who, for the sake of their own personal ambition or selfish glorification, are willing to break every rule, regulation or act devised for the safety, comfort and well-being of the despised, but necessary, animal, the private soldier.

When Elliott's *Age* tirade was criticised in a *Bulletin* article headed 'Anti-British Propaganda' on 9 June, the upshot was another spirited exchange in the press. While the *Bulletin* endorsed the sturdy nationalism reflected in Pompey's criticism of the inadequate generalship which had 'uselessly sacrificed' Australian lives 'in hopeless attacks on impregnable positions', the famous weekly felt he should have left it at that:

> Unfortunately, in his impetuosity, the Brigadier went on to make wounding comparisons and descended to personal attacks ... His animus against Birdwood peeps out in every paragraph ... The fact is that wherever his personal prejudices come into play his judgments are of small value. This is illustrated, not only by the obsession which causes him to see red when Birdwood's name is mentioned, but by the unprovoked attack on Margolin, an indiscretion for which he was very properly rebuked by Monash and ... Drake-Brockman ... There is still a great deal that Australia can usefully learn about the war, but the effect of these 'revelations' is more harmful than helpful. An honest man in a temper who has somehow persuaded himself that in airing his private grudges he is doing his country a service is always a painful spectacle.

Touché, but Pompey was undeterred. His forthright reply, published in the *Bulletin* a fortnight later, slated Birdwood as 'a mere painted lath of a soldier' who 'was utterly incapable of understanding the simplest tactical problems'. He again emphasised that the real issue with Margolin was not his character, but his failure as a battalion commander and the injustice of installing him over Jacka. And once more Pompey scorned the alleged black mark against him, the notion that

> though my courage and capacity were undoubted, I had failed to keep my judgment under perfect control. In other words, I had failed to do the kow-tow act with sufficient humility.

The *Bulletin* was more measured in its response, praising Elliott's 'splendid' role in preventing the incorporation of the British Army Act into Australia's defence administration, while maintaining that

> men in General Elliott's position should not let their feelings run away with their judgment when discussing the war. Individual soldiers (Jacka, for instance) may be championed without the depreciation of others (such as Margolin), for that sort of thing leaves a bitter taste in the mouth ... Hasty generalisations and injurious comparisons can only produce anger and bitterness of spirit.

The *Bulletin* published only a fraction of Pompey's forceful epistle. He was evidently so stung by what the famous periodical said about him on 9 June that he sent a counter-attacking rant to other publications as well as the *Bulletin*. On 25 June a short-lived Melbourne weekly, the *Midnight Sun*, announced that in response to the *Bulletin*'s 'Anti-British Propaganda' critique of Elliott's effusion in the *Age* (which had 'created a considerable stir'), Elliott had 'furnished us with a complete statement, which we regret being unable to publish in full'. What the *Midnight Sun* was able to find room for not only coincided with sentiments attributed to Elliott in the *Bulletin* on 23 June. It also comprised excerpts of the staggering diatribe—28 typed pages—he sent on 17 June to the Sydney *Sun* (which apparently did not publish any of it). All three pieces were similar, if not practically identical: each contained, for example, Pompey's distinctive refusal 'to do the kow-tow act with sufficient humility'.

Through these trenchant newspaper contributions Elliott continued to maintain his rage publicly after the Senate commenced a mid-year recess in mid-May. He also used other means. His robust criticisms of Pearce's administration in a lecture entitled 'The Defence of Australia' indirectly revived the supersession controversy. When Pearce retaliated by claiming that Elliott was embittered because he had been anticipating a divisional command, Elliott countered that he had good reason to expect one because he had been given an informed—and implicitly official—tip to that effect from Brand.

This startling allegation inspired another protracted run for Pompey's supersession in the Senate and the press. The official file on the matter was called for and examined; it contained no such letter from Brand. Elliott said it was incomplete. Pearce sent urgent telegrams to Brand to elicit his version of events. All Brand had done, came the reply, was to ask (as state commandant) who Elliott would recommend—presuming he was given a division himself—as prospective brigade commanders. Elliott had written some comments on Brand's letter and returned it, and Brand had then destroyed it because it was essentially personal. Pompey, on the other hand, alleged that Brand had, in effect, given him a provisional offer; he had replied that he wanted to see the government's defence policy before he committed himself. When he then found himself overlooked upon the announcement of the appointments, the reason was obvious: it was 'because I was not prepared to swallow anything before me without criticism'. The debate was predictably inconclusive. There was no evidence besides the conflicting recollections of the two individuals involved. But when Brand admitted to telling Elliott in a conversation or separate personal letter that his claims to a division could hardly be denied, some observers regarded this admission as tantamount to corroboration of Pompey's version of events.

Reactions to Elliott's agitation were mixed. For the individuals he was attacking, it was of course distinctly unpleasant to be the subject of unwelcome headlines. 'Inwardly much distressed at Elliott's attacks, mainly owing to their injustice and intemperance', Brudenell White acknowledged in his diary. It was also in a terse diary note that Gellibrand alluded to his discomfort. 'Period of Elliott's exuberance', he wrote. Birdwood, then in India, 'felt sorely tempted to reply' to Elliott's 'onslaughts', but contented himself with sending Bean a self-serving version of the controversies animating Pompey. Bean replied with his own assessment:

> I too have been very sorry that Elliott has taken the action of which we have read so much of late, but I always regarded it as certain that some grievance would be raised by him. I have a great admiration for the old chap ... He was undoubtedly one of the great characters of the AIF, complex, and in many ways one of the most interesting.

A remarkable letter Elliott received from a senior minister in the Queensland Labor government, J.A. Fihelly, underlined the bizarre political ramifications of his 'exuberance' that were already evident in the Senate, where Pompey was supported by Gardiner in his frequent clashes with Pearce. Fihelly's notorious pro-Irish outspokenness had made him the bête noire of Australia's ultra loyalists. Acknowledging that he and Elliott were poles apart politically, Fihelly wanted nevertheless to commend Pompey's penetrating portrait of Birdwood in the *Bulletin*, which was spot on from what he had observed as acting premier during Birdwood's 1920 visit to Queensland:

> Probably we (you and I) would disagree upon most matters but your summing-up of Birdwood is ... excellent ... He is just a drawing-room Johnny ... a posturer addicted to society tittle-tattle and small talk.

At functions in Brisbane, Fihelly continued, Birdwood would prattle on

> with unbelievable drivel. His comment on our Australian officers was also tactless and free, and, incidentally, very unfair. He is just one of those conceited grown up puppies who imagines that the Australian forces were made for his benefit ... I think you summed him up well.

Elliott claimed that he had retained the support of most returned soldiers—both officers and rank and file—and 'the great middle party of moderate Australian opinion is with me heart and soul'. It was certainly true that the misgivings of some observers about Elliott's outbursts were countered by the undiminished admiration of many of those he commanded. One wrote to inform Pompey that he and others were 'seething with ... indignation on your behalf' after 'these revelations of yours (hitherto unknown)' about the 'deplorable' supersession:

> On behalf of others I wish to congratulate you Sir on the splendid fight you are now making, and maintaining your prestige through the press—also the able way in which you helped to eject the Army Act recently.

An officer who had served under him advised the *Midnight Sun* that

> a more straightforward or conscientious man it would be impossible to find ... He does not understand the truth-twisting methods of the present-day politician. And because his principles will not allow him to conform to the tactics of the crowd he finds himself being tripped up at every step ... But if there was another war tomorrow and 'Pompey' Elliott called for volunteers to form a division, he would get enough for two, while many of the Brass hats would be lucky if they got a platoon.

'Stick to it Pompey and you will win through yet', encouraged '3 old Pals' from the 58th Battalion. And from another 15th Brigade veteran Elliott received a letter commending his 'noble stand', which, he was assured, was a big talking point in returned soldier circles. This admiring correspondent concluded with reminders of two of the most stirring incidents the 15th Brigade had experienced—Pompey's response to the disbandment mutiny, and the spontaneous tribute his men gave him in January 1919:

> When I recall to mind the breaking up of the 60th Bn I see you addressing the boys who feel the "Breaking Up". I try to picture you standing up and addressing the "House" in the same way. Some would say Bluff, but those who know you, know well that it is only the pleadings of a strong man for that which is *Just* and *Right*.
>
> In conclusion, Dear General, I would just like to say that if at any time you feel that the odds are against you in the House, think of the day when ... to a man the Battalions marched voluntar[il]y to your Billet and gave you a token of their respect, and I feel sure this memory will urge you on to *Success*.
>
> Trusting you are in good health, I am honoured at being
> One of your Diggers

CHAPTER TWENTY-TWO

'Finest and Most Authoritative Advocate' for Returned Soldiers:

The aftermath of war

1921 - 1925

AT NO STAGE during the rest of his parliamentary career did Elliott recapture the prominence he acquired during his campaign about his supersession. On issues of concern to him he continued to be a force to be reckoned with, but higher political honours never looked like coming his way. His 1921 speeches on the Defence Bill left him with a political reputation as an erratic maverick, and he realistically accepted that his forthrightness, independent streak, and uncompromising temperament were incompatible with the front bench.

While Elliott was airing his own perspective on AIF controversies in the Senate, he was wondering what Bean would make of them in the official history. Having someone of Bean's integrity and industry tackling the AIF story was welcome, but it was a huge undertaking, very different from his everyday journalism. Whether he would be able to handle the daunting combination of large themes, sweeping span, numerous narrative threads, complex analysis, and difficult verdicts on controversial individuals (Elliott very much included) remained to be seen.

Bean had decided to tackle this momentous project by writing six large and immensely detailed volumes himself, two covering Gallipoli and four on the Western Front. In addition, he would be editing other ancillary ones—eventually amounting to eight—dealing with naval, air, and medical aspects of the war, as well as developments in New Guinea, Palestine, and the Australian home front; he was also to annotate a separate volume of photographs. In November 1921, having vetted the final proofs of his first volume, which covered the prelude to the AIF's involvement in Turkey together with the Gallipoli landing itself, Bean wrote to Elliott about the dramatic event he was planning to start Volume II with, the charge at Krithia. Bean felt that he needed to find out more about what had happened to the 7th Battalion there. Many of its officers had been hit and, partly as a result, information in the war diary was meagre. Although Bean knew Pompey's wounded ankle had prevented him from being at Krithia himself, the historian wondered if he could suggest which ex-7th officer to approach for more details.

Elliott's immediate response was to send off a five-page letter packed with valuable help for the historian. It was a remarkably knowledgeable document from someone who had not been at Krithia, underlining his intense interest both in the individuals who had fought under him and in the AIF historical record. Pompey outlined what had happened to the various 7th officers hit during the famous charge, suggested who would be the most worthwhile survivors to contact and how to locate them, and provided some insightful observations of his own about Krithia. Recalling the condemnation of Bean's role in the pre-landing controversy over AIF misbehaviour in Egypt, Elliott affirmed that this unpopularity 'was absolutely obliterated by … your own good work at Krithia and attention and service to the wounded'. Moreover, the

> general impression I gained from officers and men was that the whole scheme of the advance was an impossible one and should never have been attempted, and the feeling of hostility which is pronounced in this State against General McCay has its origin in the blame attributed to him, as I believe quite unjustifiably, by reason of his association with two tragic blunders of someone [else] in authority at Krithia and [Fromelles].

'I … shall await with great interest your account of that battle', Pompey told Bean.

It was shortly afterwards that Elliott read Volume I of the AIF history, which had just been published to wide acclaim. He found that Bean had given him a special introduction into the narrative, as befitted one of the most celebrated characters in the whole force:

> Elliott was a heavily-built man of bull-headed pugnacity, but with some of the simplicity and buoyancy of a child. He placed in the old principles of drill and field tactics a simple faith which was very largely justified. He cherished a boy-like admiration for the great soldiers of history and a simple ambition to imitate them. Outspoken, impulsive, excitable, "straight" as a ruled line, intensely headstrong, he worked his men perhaps harder than any commander in the force ... but they loved him from the first.

There followed a version of the notorious hat story, a tribute to the 7th Battalion's prowess which 'cannot be fully appreciated without an understanding of the leader ... affectionately nicknamed "Pompey" Elliott' and, later on, a compelling account of his exertions at the Gallipoli landing before he was wounded.

Elliott joined the queue of enthusiasts writing to compliment Bean on his first volume, but supplemented his congratulations with a query about the attribution of the adjective 'headstrong' to himself:

> I would be glad to know on some occasion when you are not too busy of any incidents in my life upon which you base this judgment. I am not at present saying you are wrong or right, but I certainly am not aware of any incident at which you were personally present and directly observed such characteristics. I am therefore somewhat curious to know who was your informant and the nature of your information and whether you verified it with your usual care.

That Pompey's concern about Bean's closeness to Brudenell White was behind this request became clear when he went on to tell the historian what General Walker had said to him about the Lone Pine awards. Pompey informed Bean that Walker had been so amazed to find Elliott's name omitted from the published list after he had placed the 7th Battalion commander at the very top of his recommendations that he had left his hospital bed to make a special visit to the Gallipoli Commander-in-Chief in an attempt to rectify this injustice. Walker had even sought out Pompey himself later to apologise for what he called the most outrageous ill-treatment he knew of in 30 years of soldiering. From a conversation between Layh and a highly placed friend at

Birdwood's headquarters, Major Tom Griffiths, Pompey had since learned, he told Bean, that his name had indeed been deleted from Walker's list: 'Your C.O. is not popular here', Griffiths had remarked to Layh. With Lone Pine to be covered in the *Official History* volume that Bean was then working on, Elliott sought to connect his omission from Walker's list to his later supersession:

> Do you know the reason why I was continually superseded in the field? ... Yet was there ever an occasion [when] my men failed to achieve everything asked of them and even more? White now says there is nothing against my courage or capacity, yet I lack some indefinite quality unfitting me for command ... was it the absence of this indefinite quality which caused the removal of my name from General Walker's list?

In reply Bean thanked Elliott for his congratulations, and handled his awkward query with an admirable blend of tact and frankness. That superb label 'straight as a ruled line' fitted Bean as aptly as Pompey. Bean told Elliott he was reluctant to engage in

> any such long drawn-out post-mortem as I fear would be involved if I were to fulfil your request, and I therefore do not propose to answer it unless you absolutely force me to do so. Of course if you care to ask me sometime when I see you, and are really anxious to press the matter, I will tell you frankly, in a friendly talk, the basis of my judgement.
>
> In regard to your being passed over in promotion, I know nothing of the facts except what has been recently published in the press. Concerning the matter of honours which you mention, surely Elliott, you are too big a man to be one of those who complain that decorations are not bestowed upon them. Personally, I would rather pick up cigarettes in the street than myself raise a finger to reach for any decoration or honour of my own initiative. Surely it is enough that your name is honoured by the people and that you will go down to posterity, undoubtedly, as one of the big Australian figures of the war; I would strongly urge you to leave it at that.

Pompey was stung by Bean's forthright advice. Concerning the assessment of him as 'headstrong', he accepted Bean's suggested deferral. But he was keen to elaborate on the awards issue:

> [in] regard to the further questions that you raise as to *desiring to complain that decorations are not bestowed upon me* I would say that so far as they themselves are concerned no one desires them less than myself, but where one has evidence of bias and deliberate injustice in one direction the fact of their non bestowal is valuable corroborative evidence in the same direction. As I thought that in the main you had derived your knowledge of my character whatever it may be from the same source, I merely asked whether you had taken the same precautions in regard to checking your information as I know you did in other matters.

Elliott's enquiry about Bean's biographical portrait of him may have been untoward, but his concern about White's influence on the historian was understandable. The publication of the first volume of the *Official History* was a revelation. Bean had a marvellous story to tell, of course, but he was chronicling it superbly. With his innovative emphasis on what individual front-line soldiers actually did underpinned by his painstaking research and exceptional command of detail, the quality of this initial volume indicated that Bean was likely to produce a history of the conflict at least as good as any equivalent being compiled anywhere. His paramount motivation was simply to ensure that his history did justice to the men of the AIF and their deeds: it was 'the only memorial which could be worthy of them', he declared in a preface. He remained unflaggingly dedicated to this self-imposed 'duty'. For Elliott, who was longing to see the story of Australia's war—and, of course, his own part in it—told well, Bean's emergence as a first-rate historian was very gratifying. But his satisfaction was qualified by nagging misgivings about Bean's closeness to White. With the Australian *Official History* proving to be a work of such quality, it was all the more galling to suspect that its assessments of controversies involving him might be unduly influenced by Bean's friendship with the senior staff officer he had crossed swords with in many of those episodes.

Pompey was right to be concerned. Bean had a fervent, starry-eyed admiration for White, precisely the kind of boyish hero-worship that the historian had ascribed to Pompey when describing his regard for legendary commanders of the past. It was the combination of White's charm, capacity, and quiet commitment that appealed to Bean. As official war correspondent, Bean had been so impressed by White's magisterial supervision of the AIF in all its significant facets, by his unswerving dedication to the cause, and—at least as important—by the self-effacing, undemonstrative way he went about it that Bean spearheaded an unsuccessful agitation to have White rather than Monash elevated to the command of the Australian Corps. For Bean, White came to epitomise the notion of selfless devoted service to an ideal; it was because White refused to assert himself with ambitious self-promotion in 1918 that Bean resolved (even against White's explicit wishes) to lobby for him.

The contrast with Elliott's agitation in the Senate over his supersession could not have been more stark. Egocentric fulminating day after day in the national parliament about perceived injustice to oneself was, to both Bean and White, unthinkable and abhorrent; Bean's repugnance was unconcealed in his letter to Pompey on the subject. Like White, Bean was temperamentally poles apart from Elliott, but the historian warmly esteemed Pompey both as one of the AIF's outstanding leaders and as a marvellous character in the monumental story that was to occupy him for another two decades. When Elliott clashed with White, however, Bean tended to side with his hero.

Moreover, while Bean generally guarded his independence as AIF historian zealously, he routinely sent draft chapters to White for review before publication. White, understandably annoyed by Pompey's tirades against him in parliament and the press (and not being as nobly selfless as Bean imagined), sometimes used this opportunity to recommend alterations less favourable to Elliott. His manipulation of Bean's analysis in the *Official History* of Pompey's suppressed Polygon Wood report was not the only blatant example of this tendency. When vetting some other draft chapters, White made the gratuitous observation that 'Elliott had not greatly proved himself' at Gallipoli, an assertion so wide of the mark as to be implausibly artless. White's enduring resentment of Elliott's public diatribes was also evident when Bean consulted him, as the historian frequently did, seeking assistance with research queries.

During the second half of 1921 the dominant issue in the Senate was the tariff. The government wanted to change—in nearly all instances, raise—the rates imposed on particular goods, and also to establish new procedures to administer tariff policy in the future. Several bills were involved. Elliott had recently converted to protectionism after being an ardent free trader. The logic of free trade was unassailable in theory, he declared in the Senate, but in practice so many countries adopted a self-interested protectionist policy that it would be imprudent for Australia not to do likewise. With the zeal of the convert he consistently aligned himself during interminable tariff debates with manufacturers and Victoria's traditional adherence to the protectionist cause. Whether it was beer or malted milk, corsets or chamois leather, explosives or porcelain insulators, Pompey wanted the local product protected.

In November 1921 Elliott returned to Ballarat to deliver a lecture about the war. He was replicating for his old school what he did at Camberwell—giving a talk on modern battle, principally based on the events of 8 August 1918, as a fund-raiser to assist the construction of a memorial hall. As at Camberwell, Pompey illustrated his address with photographs and film footage borrowed from Treloar's museum. The lecture was well attended and financially successful, and was reviewed appreciatively by both Ballarat newspapers. 'I wish I could have heard it', Treloar assured him afterwards.

Ballarat College representatives praised Elliott's wholehearted and generous support of the school. Their gratitude was appropriate. Besides donating his services as a lecturer, Pompey had assigned his accumulated war gratuity and other funds, over £500 in all, to establish a scholarship and prize in memory of his brother. The scholarship, worth £20 annually, was to be awarded to sons of soldier fathers who were unable to provide for their children's education after becoming casualties during the war. Rhodes-like principles were to determine the recipient of the Captain G.S. Elliott Prize: personality, character, and leadership were to be important attributes, and sporting proficiency was to be taken into account as well as scholastic distinction. There was also provision for a possible studentship to assist a Ballarat Collegian proceeding to the University of Melbourne.

The scholarship proved to be a life-changing boon for a number of recipients. The unpromising horizons of Percy Beames, the raw son of an unemployed ex-37th Battalion battler, were transformed when he was offered an Elliott scholarship. After his brilliant feats for cricket and football teams of Ballarat College had brought him to the attention of

Melbourne talent scouts, he went on to represent Victoria at both sports, and to write about them for decades in the *Age*.

Elliott also continued to be actively involved in the affairs of Ormond College. He was on the committee handling fund-raising for the substantial building extensions which had for some time been the most important item on the college council's agenda. The new development was officially opened by the Governor of Victoria at an impressive ceremony on 23 May 1922. With the Old Ormond Students' Association chairman, Elliott's old friend J.G. Latham, unable to attend, Elliott agreed to speak in his stead. He emphasised how splendid it was to have the esteemed initial master, Sir John MacFarland, present at the inauguration of the new library named after him.

Pompey also officiated at a more solemn ceremony later that year when he unveiled a brass plaque commemorating those from Ormond who had fallen. George Elliott was named on it, of course, along with such renowned and lamented identities as Murdoch Mackay and Mervyn Higgins, and also officers killed while serving in the 15th Brigade—John Sterling at Fromelles, and Wilfred Beaver at Polygon Wood. George was among the ex-Ormond residents also honoured with an individual plaque mounted in the room they used to occupy.

Elliott continued to be sought after as an unveiler. An invitation to unveil an honour board at his birthplace was a particularly welcome request. On 12 November 1921 he assured the overflow crowd at Charlton that it was good for Australians to remind themselves through the erection of honour boards and other memorials that their own men had performed feats of outstanding valour and chivalry, as inspiring as the finest deeds recorded in centuries of military history. Pompey then proceeded to authenticate this claim in characteristic style with a series of vividly described examples—Private McArthur, in the leading 7th Battalion boat at the Gallipoli landing, continuing to row despite being fatally wounded; Corporals Harry Webb and Fred Wright, killed while catching Turkish bombs to hurl them back; the 7th Battalion's quartet of VC winners at Lone Pine; Lieutenant Stewart Smith, in agony with a shattered leg at Fromelles and barely able to crawl, yet refusing to call for stretcher-bearers because others needed them more; and Sergeant Colclough's intrepid intervention at Polygon Wood.

'No matter where you search for noble deeds in the annals of no matter what nation's armies, you will find them paralleled by the deeds of our own boys', Elliott reiterated. He had 'told these stories in the hope that the traditions of self-sacrifice would be perpetuated by this school board'. Regrettably, they were living in 'a materialistic age' when 'the measure of success' was 'the amount of money that a man could pile up in his lifetime'. In contrast, the men of the AIF had been prepared to risk their lives in order to achieve collective success. Emulating that spirit in peacetime was the key to Australia consolidating as a 'free and mighty nation' and 'sailing safely' through whatever 'great troubles' lay ahead. Pompey's stirring speech was the highlight of a ceremony that 'will live long in the memory', the local paper reported.

He spoke in similar vein at numerous unveilings. A week later, when he travelled to Ballarat to deliver his fund-raising lecture in aid of the memorial hall to be constructed at his old school, he officiated at no fewer than three memorial ceremonies that weekend. On Friday 18 November he formally opened the Avoca Memorial Rotunda, and 24 hours later he was in action again at the unveiling of the Clunes memorial; a large crowd attended each ceremony. From Clunes he proceeded to Ballarat for the lecture that evening, and the following afternoon he did the honours when the Neil Street church commemorated its diamond jubilee by unveiling a memorial to 32 congregation members who had not survived their war service (including Les Blick, a 7th Battalion officer killed at the landing). The previous month Elliott had journeyed to Mornington to speak at the opening of an unusual memorial: a sizeable residence had been purchased, renovated, and transformed into accommodation for homeless and destitute children by relatives of Andrew Kerr, a 57th Battalion sergeant killed at Fromelles, as a lasting tribute to him. Not long before, Elliott had ventured out to Lilydale to enlighten another large crowd about McArthur, Smith, Colclough, and the 7th Battalion's exploits at Lone Pine while unveiling an impressive honour board erected in tribute to the 492 men who had enlisted from that shire.

Pompey was also busy around Anzac Day 1922, which he spent at the northern Victoria town of Kyabram. From the time he arrived on Saturday 22 April he was well looked after by local returned soldiers. On Sunday he accompanied them to nearby Stanhope and Girgarre to meet soldier settlers from these districts; the wisdom of settling returned soldiers with limited agricultural experience on farms of varying viability was not universally accepted, and Elliott was keen to learn how these men were going. There was an Anzac commemorative service in Kyabram on Sunday night. The following evening, Anzac eve, Elliott gave a talk on Villers-Bretonneux; the local paper observed that his 'famous' war lectures had been 'delivered ... with much success in various parts of the Commonwealth'. Then, on Anzac Day itself, after addressing a service attended by 250 people at nearby Tongala, Pompey returned to Kyabram, where a bigger crowd assembled to watch him present medals to a dozen returned soldiers (including one of his 7th Battalion originals), and unveil the Kyabram memorial. Afterwards, at a social gathering in his honour arranged by the returned soldiers, he gave them an entertaining account of amusing wartime incidents.

Four days later he was back in Melbourne to officiate at the Oakleigh Sailors' and Soldiers' Memorial Institute, laying a memorial stone before 1,500 onlookers and declaring the institute formally open. The next day he was in action once more, unveiling a memorial column at Victory Park in Ascot Vale. Soon afterwards he was off again, this time to tell the citizens of Morwell about McArthur, Smith, and Colclough while doing the honours at the soldiers' memorial there.

When he was not travelling his home base was still Prospect Hill Road, Camberwell, but he and the family had moved to a different house in that street. They were now residing further west in an area of unequivocally middle-class ambience not far from Burke Road. The brick residence built for the Elliotts at 56 Prospect Hill Road—which remained Pompey's home for the rest of his life—was spacious and functional without the slightest hint of grandeur or pretentiousness. The overwhelming impression from the front of the house was reddish robustness, with terracotta tiles on the steeply sloping roof complementing its wide, symmetrical red-brick frontage. Anyone noticing the giant letter box on the way in would have correctly concluded that someone living there received a great deal of mail. Visitors entered via an arched recess in the brickwork, with stained glass above and beside the front door, into an entrance hall separating the feature front spaces of lounge and dining room. Further in, the main bedroom was to the left, and had east windows to catch the morning sun. Generally, however, light was not a feature, an impression reinforced by the extensive use of dark timber for doors, architraves, skirtings, shelves, and mantlepieces; this was particularly prominent in Pompey's den, with its floor-to-ceiling bookshelves dominating one wall. A distinctly nippy house in winter, even at the height of summer it remained pleasantly cool.

Making the most of the outdoors was a big priority for the whole family, Harold very much included. The naturalist instincts that had so pleased his mother when he was young were again to the fore as magnificent gardens took shape at 56 Prospect Hill Road and the vacant block the family owned and enjoyed alongside. The array of trees nurtured by the numerous returned soldiers Pompey employed as gardeners during the 1920s included silver birches, rhododendrons, magnolias, flowering gums, and fruit-bearing varieties that supplied the Elliotts with oranges, plums, cherries, and guavas. There was also a flawlessly maintained croquet-standard lawn, a rose garden, an asparagus bed, rockeries, and a bird bath. It was a superb haven, relished by all the Elliotts. On a fine spring day, with the garden in bloom and teeming with birds, it was idyllic. One acquaintance was given a guided tour and never forgot it:

> General Elliott loved the simple things of life. To walk with him round his garden was an education, not only in the habits of Australian plants, but in the simple joy of being alive. In the bush of his beloved homeland he was really at home. The trees and the flowers were his friends.

It was a residence for an extended family, home not just for Harold Elliott's wife and children but his sister-in-law and mother-in-law as well. Belle continued to be the main domestic organiser of the household; capable and practical, she still answered to 'Dear' and generally kept the children on a tight leash. Kate, more deferential and less assertive than her sister, remained Harold's 'sunshine lady', ever loyal and supportive; with Harold often away, she appreciated Belle's contribution. Visitors like Violet's schoolfriends felt that Belle was strict and admirably efficient, while Kate was a delicate, sweet-natured, less worldly soul. One family friend remembered Kate as 'charming' and 'like a little Dresden doll'.

Belle's assistance also came in handy when Kate was expected to partner her husband at various functions. Some were particularly memorable. On 8 August 1921 she accompanied him to a dinner organised by Monash to commemorate the third anniversary of the decisive

Western Front offensive. Two years later Senator and Mrs Elliott jointly (and generously) hosted the main social function of the Old Ormond Students' Association (Elliott was its president in 1923), an 'At Home' at Menzies Hotel that was attended by over a hundred guests.

Mary Campbell lived at 56 Prospect Hill Road with her daughters. Never the same after her 1917 stroke, she was sometimes reduced to a semi-invalid's existence, but enjoyed pottering about in the garden when she felt up to it. The house was in fact in her name. One of the repatriation initiatives of the Hughes government was the provision of housing via the War Service Homes scheme. As the mother of an AIF soldier killed in action, Mary was as entitled to benefit from the scheme as her son-in-law; as a back-bench member of the government that had introduced the scheme, Pompey presumably concluded that it would be more appropriate for her to be the War Service Homes beneficiary. However, he provided the bulk of the capital; the finance obtained under the War Service Homes scheme was only a small part of the overall cost. Mary died early in 1923, aged 82.

Violet's school was Fintona, a private Presbyterian girls' grammar situated in nearby Burke Road. Founded in 1896 by Annie Hughston, a gifted teacher who was still actively involved while Violet was there, Fintona flourished under her progressive guidance. The school environment suited Violet, and she soon made her mark; within a year of joining Fintona she was captain of her class. Striving purposefully to make the most of an intellectual endowment that was serviceable rather than outstanding, she delighted her father by sometimes managing to come top of her class. She mixed well with her peers, her popularity unhampered by a lack of sporting prowess (though she was an enthusiastic swimmer). It was her distinctive manner, a quiet maturity beyond her years, that most impressed her teachers.

The boundless love and support Elliott gave his children, so obvious in his wartime letters, was very evident to Violet's friends during the 1920s. He followed her progress at Fintona appreciatively, occasionally involving himself prominently. A notable example was his stirring address at a Fintona Anzac Day service held at Camberwell's Trinity Presbyterian Church. A strong bond between ten-year-old Violet and her father was already apparent; when he addressed the whole school she felt proud yet self-conscious. His customary rendition of a series of stories about the deeds of individual Australians went down well. It 'was most inspiring', reported the *Fintonian*. 'He gave us example after example of the patriotism, courage and self-sacrifice of our Anzacs'. Also speaking at that service, as he did on many notable Fintona occasions, was the Trinity church minister Patrick Murdoch, father of Keith, the renowned newspaperman who knew Pompey well. Patrick's enduring commitment to Fintona had been consolidated by the marriage of his younger brother Walter to Annie Hughston's sister.

The Murdochs also had connections with the school that the Elliotts sent Neil to in 1920, Camberwell Grammar (also handily located in Burke Road). Walter Murdoch, a brilliant student who was to become a well-known writer, and his nephew Keith were both, a dozen years apart, dux of Camberwell Grammar. Neil Elliott began well at his new school —like Violet, he was noticeably self-contained and self-reliant from an early age—and he was dux of his class in both 1921 and 1924. But Camberwell Grammar was not thriving like Fintona, and tended to lose students to more prestigious alternatives, Scotch College in particular.

On school holidays Violet and Neil were often to be found at the beach. The family now had a car, an asset Belle had fantasised about acquiring during the war. Harold still commuted to work by public transport, frequently presenting his office staff with produce from his splendid garden (and sometimes absentmindedly leaving belongings on the train). The car was used primarily for social outings and longer trips to the country or the beach. Pompey liked socialising with wartime comrades. One he often caught up with was Bert Layh, who lived not far away from the Elliotts with his family. Pompey enjoyed these outings, and it was important to him that others did, too. 'Is everyone happy?' he would ask before they all set off. Brother Rod was still farming productively at Tocumwal, where Violet and Neil had stayed during at least one Christmas break since the war, but the usual holiday destination for the family was Frankston, where Elliott had an interest in land at Oliver's Hill.

He liked seeing children enjoying themselves at the beach. Noticing a youngster one summer's day struggling to improvise a boat out of a bit of wood with a scrap of paper for a sail, he was moved to unearth a model yacht he had played with himself at a similar age, and to present it to this delighted stranger. When Kate's cousin Ina Prictor and her toddler Colin accompanied the Elliotts to Frankston shortly after the war, Harold took Colin to the beach while the cousins had a chat. 'Does it matter if he gets a bit damp?' Harold asked Ina. 'Oh, no', Ina replied, presuming all Colin would be having was a gentle splash in the shallows. Sixty years later she chuckled as she recalled the sequel: 'A bit damp—he was saturated up to the shoulders!'

This domestic serenity was suddenly threatened by an international crisis. On 17 September 1922, a Sunday, Australians learned that Britain had given an ultimatum to the resurgent Turkish forces who were, under their legendary Gallipoli commander, Mustafa Kemal, overturning the crushing treaty inflicted on their nation following its surrender in 1918; having just trounced the Greeks at Smyrna, they were now confronted by a weak British post at Chanak. The message from the British government to the rampaging Turks was clear: so far, and no further. To reinforce this blunt ultimatum, Prime Minister Lloyd George and Colonial Secretary Churchill sought to involve the Dominions, inviting them to send contingents. Australia was pointedly reminded that the security of Anzac graves at Gallipoli was at stake. Many Australians wondered with grim foreboding whether they were in for a chilling replay of August 1914. As in 1914, the crisis had arrived out of the blue. As in 1914, the dispute in question seemed of obscure geographic and strategic relevance to Australia. And, as in 1914, the British government appeared to take Australia's support and willingness to participate for granted. Prime Minister Hughes, who first learned about this sudden Chanak crisis and the expectation of Australian military involvement from the Sunday newspapers, was furious, and vented his spleen in a blistering cable to Lloyd George.

Publicly, however, the Hughes government supported Britain's stand. This response was not surprising, since such potent triggers of Australian sentiment as the British connection and the Anzac ethos were both involved. In contrast, the ALP, under its new leader Matthew Charlton (Tudor and Ryan had both recently died), upheld publicly the views that Hughes expressed privately in his scathing cable to Lloyd George. In stark contrast to the jubilant euphoria of August 1914, the mood was sombre: 'the position is undoubtedly grave', observed Senator Millen.

Elliott supported the government unequivocally. It was, he declared in the Senate,

> [no] mere local quarrel between the Turks and the Greeks in which we have been asked to assist. If that were all, we could allow them to

> fight it out. When a bush fire starts in the back country the settlers in the adjoining territory do not wait until it reaches their holdings before they attempt to render assistance, but immediately start for the scene and help in subduing it. In this instance we have ... been asked ... to associate ourselves with Great Britain in an endeavour to avoid a conflict. The recent Great War sprang from an insignificant cause—the murder of a prince in Serbia. But what did it lead to? ... It is the possible result which has to be considered.

To refute the charge that government supporters were obnoxious warmongers, Elliott provided a gruesome glimpse of what he had experienced at Lone Pine, and recalled the deaths of his brother and brother-in-law in quick succession on the battlefields of Ypres.

> Do we support the Government because we love those things? No. We abhor them with every fibre of our being, and yet we must face a renewal of those things with what nerve we can muster. In my own case ... I would regard it as an absolute calamity if I were to be taken away from my business affairs again, because, after an absence of five years, I have been laboriously endeavouring to put things into some sort of order. And yet if the Government call upon us for our assistance once more, what can any of us who served in any sort of official position in the recent war do but place our services for what they are worth at the disposal of the Government? Would we do this with any feelings of joy? ... I speak tonight with very mixed feelings indeed, but in the great hope that no call will be necessary ... Nevertheless I must support the Government, and I ask the people of Australia to join with me in supporting the Prime Minister.

Fortunately the call did not come. War was averted, primarily because of the resourcefulness of the British commander at Chanak, General Harington. His adroitness came as no surprise to Elliott, who had encountered no abler British staff officer during the Great War. The Turks were apparently deterred in part by the prospect of having to take on the Anzacs again. Elliott, like other Nationalists, had cited this deterrence factor when explaining his support of the Hughes government's response. Although the crisis did not escalate into war, the British government's imprudent handling of the situation was instrumental in its downfall a few weeks later. Churchill and several other ministers lost office, and Lloyd George was never prime minister again.

With a federal election imminent in Australia, it was possible that Britain might not be the only nation with a new prime minister in the wake of the Chanak crisis. Elliott's campaigning in 1922 was minimal—the parliamentary term of senators elected in 1919 did not expire until the election due in 1925. Polling day was on 16 December. The results shocked the Nationalists. No fewer than five of Hughes's ministers lost their seats, including Walter Massy Greene; he was unexpectedly defeated by a 27-year-old Country Party candidate, Roland Green, who cleverly turned his loss of a leg during the war to advantage by campaigning on the slogan 'Vote for the Green Without an E'. Green's triumph exemplified his party's success. The Country Party had captured the balance of power, with 14 members in the House of Representatives compared to 26 Nationalists and Labor's 29 MHRs. There was also a separate contingent of non-Labor anti-Hughes MPs, five in all, including the new member for Kooyong, Elliott's old friend Latham. And Elliott would be operating in a different Senate environment, too. Gardiner had represented Labor on his own for much of the previous three years, but during the next parliament eleven ALP senators would join him.

For nearly two months after the 1922 election there was a vacuum in Australia's national government due to a political stalemate. The Country Party, led by Dr Earle Page, was determined to use its numbers in parliament to remove Hughes and form a coalition with the Nationalists. Protracted negotiations ensued. Nationalist MPs discussed the situation in lively and lengthy party meetings. Hughes had his critics in his own party, but the senators elected in 1919 tended not to be among them; some observers concluded that because of their minimal participation in the recent campaign they did not fully appreciate the strong anti-Hughes mood in the electorate. During this period, Elliott maintained afterwards, his 'strong feelings of loyalty to Mr Hughes, who was in effect declared "black" by the Country Party', induced him to react without initial enthusiasm to the formation of the Bruce–Page coalition government after Hughes ultimately accepted the inevitable and resigned.

Prime Minister Bruce was a complete contrast to Hughes in background and style. He preferred to be referred to as S.M. rather than Stanley Melbourne (Stan was sacrilegiously unthinkable). A successful businessman before entering parliament, Bruce was born to the purple.

He cloaked his political ambitiousness by cultivating a languidly refined air of lofty imperturbability, which contrasted starkly with his predecessor's capriciousness, raucousness, combativeness, and chaotic administrative ways. Bruce had a different policy emphasis, too, although this was not immediately apparent. On his first appearance in the House of Representatives as prime minister, Bruce admitted that his new ministry had not decided how to proceed on almost any issue of substance. He kept parliamentary sittings unusually brief in 1923 and headed to London for that year's Imperial Conference, where he summarised his government's priorities as 'men, money and markets'. Essentially Bruce was intent on enhancing Australia's economic development with an integrated approach involving increased immigration, foreign capital inflow, and trade opportunities.

Something Bruce did make clear right from the outset was that Australia's national security would be his government's highest single priority. That this objective, along with men, money and markets, had to be pursued in a British imperial context was axiomatic to the new Prime Minister, and spawned his emphatic resolve to attend the Imperial Conference. The agreed principles of imperial defence ratified at the conference included an acknowledgment of Australia's 'deep interest' in the construction of a naval base at Singapore; it became widely accepted that such a base would constitute the mainstay of Australian post-war security.

Elliott continued to expound assertively on defence policy. He repeatedly affirmed that encouraging Britain to fortify Singapore was fundamental to Australia's national security. Furthermore,

> I say deliberately that the time has arrived for Australia to stipulate that, as a condition for its co-operation in Empire wars, its men shall be commanded by their own officers exclusively, and that British officers shall exercise no jurisdiction whatever over them.

To underline the necessity for this contentious requirement, he went on to deliver another pungent denunciation of what happened at Fromelles. Before the Imperial Conference Elliott also publicly recommended that Bruce should ask Monash to accompany him to London as an adviser on defence matters, and to assist him afterwards in implementing whatever scheme of defence the conference decided to adopt. In post-war Australia

Monash had been conspicuously neglected in policy-making circles and on ceremonial occasions. Elliott publicly deplored this neglect, and attended the stirring tribute dinner in Monash's honour organised by the RSSILA on Anzac Day 1924.

When it came to analysing Labor's defence policy, however, Elliott aligned himself unambiguously with the vehement criticism forthcoming from Pearce and other Nationalist hardliners. The pre-1914 compulsory military training scheme, a Labor initiative, had proved 'of incalculable advantage' when the AIF was created, Elliott acknowledged in July 1923. If the ALP had retained its pre-war attitude to defence and remained united during the war, the party 'would have been so firmly established in power' that its 'position would have been unassailable ... for a very long time'. Instead, he asserted, Labor was abdicating its defence responsibilities by advocating a 'hollow' policy that was 'a delusion and a sham'. Moreover, the lamentable continuing hostility to compulsory military training from Labor activists was making its administration much harder for the authorities. It was standard Nationalist rhetoric to claim that pre-war Labor was retrospectively acceptable but post-war Labor was not. As ALP luminaries retorted, Labor's opponents had condemned pre-war Labor measures when they were introduced just as vehemently as their Nationalist equivalents were now criticising Labor policies in the 1920s.

But Elliott continued to react to government announcements and legislation with forthright independence. As he admitted in the Senate, 'I have on some occasions been a severe critic of the Government'. He opposed the decision to do without a separate ministry for repatriation. When a substantial rift developed between the RSSILA and Prime Minister Bruce over controversial government appointments that contravened the principle of preference to returned soldiers, Pompey sided with the League and publicly criticised the appointments. And he often initiated amendments to government bills in the Senate. His skilful draftsmanship was increasingly recognised; when he came up with an adroit solution to a seemingly intractable problem late in 1922, Pearce, the government's influential leader in the Senate, thanked him warmly for his 'brilliant suggestion'. Now that Pompey had stopped castigating Pearce publicly as one of the culprits in connection with his supersession grievance, they were getting on much better. In 1924 Elliott became aide-de-camp to the Governor-General, Lord Forster.

In April 1923 Elliott responded to a congenial request for help. Charles Bean, beavering away on Lone Pine for his second volume of the Australian *Official History*, had found that his material concerning the 7th Battalion's role in that battle was meagre: would Pompey be able to supplement it? He would indeed. His prompt, detailed reply—just like the response he had provided in 1921 when Bean had made an equivalent approach about Krithia—contained useful information about both the battle itself and those 7th Battalion survivors who would be most likely to be worth contacting for their own perspectives (and how to get in touch with them). For more than a month Bean and Elliott exchanged frequent letters (and sketch-maps) about Lone Pine—the historian grappling with the exceptionally complex task of reconstructing what happened in that labyrinth, the commander ever-ready to inundate him with lengthy reminiscences and suggestions (sometimes elaborating for page after page just to help Bean fathom the precise location of a particular trench). '[My] Lone Pine file is becoming one of enormous dimensions', Bean observed.

The fruits of his toil (and Pompey's enthusiastic assistance) were there for all to see when Volume II was published. Authoritative, accessible, and extraordinarily detailed, it covered the Gallipoli campaign from Krithia to the evacuation in compelling style. Some of the most dramatic episodes in that crowded story featured Elliott and the 7th Battalion. Notable examples included Pompey's celebrated duel in the tunnel near German Officers' Trench, the ensuing raid led by Lieutenant Greig (Bean's narrative of this desperate diversion was enriched by the account he obtained from the Turkish officer in charge of the defence at German Officers'), and all the drama of Lone Pine itself, including such vivid vignettes as Pompey's parting words to Symons: 'I don't expect to see you again, but we must not lose that post'. Elliott was not the only participant to be impressed: 'I ... find an improvement even on the excellence of the first volume', he complimented Bean.

Pompey continued to be a magnet for disgruntled ex-soldiers with a grievance, and Warrant Officer J.R. Allen was one of many who contacted him. An experienced instructor in the Light Horse, Allen had been dismissed in 1922 at the behest of his divisional commander, General Tivey. Allen felt that his discharge was unjustified, and had unfairly deprived him of a pension into the bargain. He convinced Elliott that he had been unjustly treated; Tivey's involvement presumably influenced Pompey to take the matter further. On 12 July 1923 he rose in the Senate and moved that a select committee be appointed to inquire into the issue. Pearce, on behalf of the government, claimed that any such inquiry would be inadvisable because it would open the floodgates (just as he had when Pompey was up in arms about his own supersession). All the Nationalist generals in the Senate besides Elliott—Cox, Drake-Brockman, Glasgow, and W.G. Thompson (a Queensland brigadier elected in 1922)—agreed with Pearce. However, Labor senators supported Elliott's motion, and enough Nationalists sided with him to produce a Senate majority in favour of establishing a select committee.

The committee began its inquiry on 7 August. It was conducted by the seven senators Elliott had nominated (five Nationalists, including Glasgow, Thompson and himself, together with Labor's Jim Ogden and Allan McDougall); Pompey was chairman. A dozen witnesses appeared before the inquiry. Elliott's penetrating questions produced frosty exchanges with Tivey; Pompey probed the appropriateness of Tivey's harsh treatment of Allen, and Tivey stiffly insisted that he knew (and, without saying so explicitly, knew better than this cross-examiner who coveted his job) where his responsibilities as a divisional commander began and ended. With examination of the available witnesses completed, Elliott compiled a draft report which concluded that Allen had been unfairly treated. However, to his chagrin, the rest of the committee except McDougall agreed with Glasgow's assessment that Tivey's action had been justified. After submitting a minority report on behalf of himself and McDougall, Pompey publicly attacked the majority finding as a 'calamity', prompting predictable retorts about sour grapes since he had chosen and chaired the committee himself. Pompey, sticking to his guns, divulged that he had deliberately included on the committee senators 'who were strongly opposed to my views' (Glasgow was clearly one) in order to constitute a balanced jury and to 'strengthen' its finding accordingly. But what was the point of a well-credentialled jury if you did not accept its verdict, challenged a Nationalist senator. Juries sometimes make mistakes, Elliott replied.

Elliott also found himself in a minority when he became involved in a more important investigation, a royal commission formed to inquire into allegations that the regulation of Australian coastal shipping under the Navigation Act was having a detrimental effect on trade and national development. The commission was chaired by J.H. Prowse, a Country Party backbencher from Western Australia and a persistent critic of the Navigation Act, which had been introduced by a pre-war Labor government to protect the working conditions of Australian seamen. Its other members besides Elliott were Tasmanian MHR A.C. Seabrook and Senator W. L. Duncan, both Nationalists, and a Labor trio comprising Frank Anstey, Senator C.S. McHugh, and 'Gunner' Yates. The commission toiled and travelled industriously: there were hearings in each state, 95 sittings altogether, and 139 witnesses testified.

After all this work the commissioners disagreed. Prowse and Seabrook, both from less-populated outlying states where complaints about the Navigation Act had been particularly aggrieved, advocated complete repeal of its coastal trade provisions in order to allow foreign vessels open slather. The Labor threesome, however, maintained that there was nothing fundamentally wrong with the legislation; many of its alleged shortcomings had not been substantiated by the commission, and those that had could be fixed by proper administration. Positioned between these two extremes were Elliott and Duncan: they agreed with Prowse and Seabrook that the coastal trade provisions should be repealed but, instead of agreeing to hands-off deregulation, proposed as their remedy a significant tariff adjustment.

The secretary of this royal commission was parliamentary official Frank Green, a Tasmanian-born returned soldier who had befriended Elliott and sometimes accompanied him to Frankston. During the commission's visit to Hobart Green took him to the Military Club, where Pompey asked for cider. Someone spiked it. Amid the uproarious sequel Pompey told his favourite wartime anecdote, the one about the amorous Egyptian donkey whose ear had to be twisted, which Green considered 'the funniest AIF story I ever heard'—no mean accolade from someone renowned as a Rabelaisian raconteur himself. Next morning Pompey was seedy with an unaccustomed hangover, and Green shepherded him to the exclusive Tasmanian Club to recuperate. The only member present as they entered happened to be Green's friend Gellibrand, who greeted Green, conspicuously ignored Elliott, and walked out. 'Pompey offered no comment', Green observed, but the animosity fuelled by his supersession crusade was obvious.

Friction with another AIF general may well have been instrumental in Elliott's withdrawal from the Navigation Act inquiry. He resigned as the commission was about to embark upon the second part of its deliberations, an evaluation of the legislation's impact on Papua and New Guinea. This assignment would involve close liaison with the Administrator of New Guinea, Brigadier-General Wisdom. The decidedly dim view Pompey had formed of Wisdom during the war had been reinforced by what he had heard of New Guinea administration since Wisdom's appointment to that post in preference to the friend he had recommended, McNicoll.

In November 1923 the traditional Melbourne Cup festivities were scarred by serious civil unrest. With chronic problems plaguing Victoria's underfunded police force, the accumulated grievances of its members had intensified; but the Chief Commissioner of Police, Alexander Nicholson, was out of his depth, and the conservative state government did nothing (Nicholson's immediate predecessor, General Gellibrand, had resigned when it refused to endorse measures to alleviate these problems). When a relatively small group of discontented Melbourne constables refused to parade for duty, Nicholson and the government reacted with such inept tactlessness that half the metropolitan police joined the strike. Eventually 635 constables, together with a solitary senior constable, became involved—more than a third of the whole state-wide force. On 2 November, the Friday before Cup Day, disorder ensued on Melbourne streets. Policemen who remained on duty, refusing to align themselves with the strikers, were jeered and harassed; some were assaulted. Order was eventually restored after police reinforcements were hastily transferred from the country.

The authorities' response to these disturbing developments included the formation of a committee of prominent citizens. Elliott was invited to join it. This committee met on Saturday morning, 3 November, at the office of the Chief Secretary (and future premier), Dr S.S. Argyle. Among those in attendance with Elliott were Monash, Nicholson, Premier Lawson, and Attorney-General Sir Arthur Robinson. Monash's prodigious prestige guaranteed him a leadership role. Elliott was assigned the important task of organising the supplementary force of special constables being enrolled at Melbourne Town Hall.

Within hours this function became critical as opportunist looting and violence escalated into unprecedented lawlessness. Riotous mobs rampaged through the city. Bottles doubled as weapons and missiles. Plate-glass windows fronting most of the biggest stores were successively and exultantly smashed, and pilferers poured in to filch or grapple for the spoils. Trams were halted, a scared horse bolted, shots were fired; there were brawls and deaths, and hundreds were hospitalised. This blot on Melbourne's civic pride was deplored in the *Age* as a 'cyclone of anarchy', and in the *Argus* as a 'Bolshevik Orgy'. To Attorney-General Robinson it was a repugnant reminder of 'what a thin crust there is between ordered society and revolution'.

Amid this mayhem and tumult the Town Hall became a hive of activity. An urgent government message was screened at picture theatres calling on returned soldiers to enrol as special constables under General Pompey Elliott in order to inhibit further looting. Hundreds of ex-soldiers flocked to the Town Hall.

> 'Here we are again, General', said a volunteer who led a party of 15 men. He saluted General Elliott and added 'We are ready and willing for another stunt under you'.
>
> 'Where's Pompey? Is this his GHQ?' asked another ex-soldier arrival. 'Anywhere with Pompey', he continued to a neighbour. Meanwhile Senator Elliott, with a felt hat resting at a digger-like angle on his head, directed, organised and distributed his 'specials'.

His wartime officers were prominent in the special force; Layh, Denehy, Watson, and Conder all had senior positions. Some of the police strikers had also served under Pompey, including several 7th Battalion originals. None were ever re-employed in the force.

Elliott was at the forefront of strenuous endeavours to prevent any recurrence of the sweeping havoc of that notorious Saturday. As Monash acknowledged, 'undoubtedly his presence and personal influence during those hectic hours did much to restore a semblance of security'. At the Town Hall on Sunday (when his wartime superior, Sir James McCay, became involved in the emergency arrangements) Pompey was characteristically purposeful and resolute. 'The people can rely upon the sternest possible measures against a repetition of last night's disgraceful scenes', he assured a journalist. Although sporadic incidents continued to cause concern and the atmosphere remained tense (anxious vigilance was maintained for days), the sense of crisis gradually eased. On Monday, with the situation under overall control, the citizens' committee met again in the morning. After the meeting Elliott said he would like to be released so he could participate in Queensland hearings of the Navigation Act Royal Commission. Monash thanked him for his valuable contribution, and Elliott headed north.

The train journey gave him time to brood, and he decided to divulge the real reason for his unostentatious withdrawal. The result was a startling communication to Attorney-General Robinson. In this letter, written from a Sydney hotel, Elliott complained about McCay's intervention. It was particularly inappropriate, Elliott contended, when the government's public appeal (evidently authorised by Robinson) had specifically used his name and no-one else's in urging returned soldiers to enrol as special constables. It was an implicit reflection on the way he was superintending these specials when on 'Monday morning, to my astonishment, without even the courtesy of a direction from yourself to me, General McCay took over the direction of affairs out of my hands'. This unwarranted development was dangerous as well as discourteous, since 'a great many of the men who were willing to serve with the utmost zeal under my direction were by no means happy to do so under Sir James, and I had to use my personal influence to ensure their continuance, for a time at least, in the duties they had undertaken'. Moreover, 'since I have been so superseded … this absolutely precludes me from offering my services to the State in future in any capacity, as I cannot afford to be under the slightest accusation of inefficiency'. Robinson, understandably perturbed, sent this letter to his old friend Monash, and asked for advice about how to respond to it.

'If anyone is to blame in this matter, it is myself and no one else', Monash assured Robinson, 'certainly not you, and not McCay'. Monash explained developments from his perspective. He had initially arranged for Elliott to organise the specials then being enrolled into squads, which would operate as reinforcements to the regular police force as and when requested by Nicholson. When Nicholson, evidently overwhelmed, 'did nothing whatever' even after the most serious looting, Monash decided late on Saturday night to establish a separate structure in view of the police chief's 'paralysis':

> I therefore got hold of Elliott and instructed him to commence the organization of a Headquarters and a fighting and feeding staff, on military lines … Overnight I thought things over, and came to the conclusion that the trouble might develop on such serious lines as

> to be beyond Elliott's capacity and experience. He is a splendid leader, but has no idea of organization. Very early on Sunday, Nov. 4th, McCay asked by telephone if he could help. I told him to meet me at the Town Hall, which he did. He said he didn't want to 'butt in', but was available. Knowing that I would be engaged all day at Cabinet, and feeling that I could rely *entirely* on McCay but not on Elliott, I sought the latter, and in McCay's presence asked Elliott if he was prepared to take orders from McCay, and he at once *and cheerfully* said that he was ... Elliott's place in [the reshaped] organization was to be that of 'outside' commander, acting under McCay's staff arrangements, and this job he did excellently well during the rest of that Sunday.

On Monday morning, Monash continued, Elliott said he wanted to travel north to resume his work on the royal commission. He seemed to leave

> with no disturbed feeling. The grievances now expressed in his unfortunate letter appear to me to rest upon an entirely false basis. All AIF leaders were trained to defer habitually, in any situation, to the senior man on the spot. The fact that Elliott happened to be the AIF senior within my reach on Saturday evening gave him no moral right to claim that the instructions which I then gave him debarred me from placing him subsequently under the orders of any other senior officers ... who might become available later.

The best way to respond to Elliott's letter, Monash advised Robinson, would be to 'disclaim ... any knowledge of the circumstances' and 'leave it to me to try and bring Elliott to see the matter in the right light'. Robinson complied. 'I know nothing of the circumstances under which, as you state, the direction of affairs was taken out of your hands', Robinson lied in the brazen letter he sent Elliott immediately after receiving Monash's version of events.

'Some of Elliott's statements are not accurate, others are not justified', Monash had pronounced in his letter to Robinson. But that assessment applied more to Monash's letter than to Pompey's. The assertion that Elliott had 'no idea of organization' was preposterous. The 15th Brigade could hardly have become such an outstandingly formidable formation if its commander had been an inadequate organiser. Monash, a peerless administrator himself, would not have been the first to be misled by Pompey's outward appearance. His tendency to personify an archetypally volatile man of action understandably prompted some observers to categorise him as an impulsive fire-eater of limited sophistication, someone who was the very antithesis of a painstaking administrator methodically ticking off agenda items in precise order, Monash-style. Bean's first impressions of Elliott were along those lines, until he realised that administration in the 15th Brigade was first-rate and at times inspired—he was astonished to discover that Pompey had arranged for his front-line men to receive three hot meals a day during the terrible winter of 1916-17. Monash also claimed that during the police strike Elliott had breached a golden rule in the AIF that leaders should 'defer habitually, in any situation, to the senior man on the spot'. Yet that is precisely what Pompey did on that Sunday morning, as Monash's own letter confirms.

Later Elliott realised he had been usurped by McCay, and resented it. Withdrawing from the organisation of the specials may well have been an overreaction; but after being overlooked in both 1918 and 1921, and railing bitterly against his supersession in each instance, he was ultrasensitive to such slights. Significantly, his protest letter to Robinson claimed that he had been 'superseded' on this occasion as well. Monash, surprised and embarrassed by the letter his friend Robinson had received about a contretemps he had created (as he admitted himself), extravagantly exaggerated the extent of his misgivings about Elliott's administrative capacity in order to justify supplanting him with McCay. But the fact that he had misgivings at all was significant. Pompey's conviction that he would have fared differently if Monash had controlled the 1918 and 1921 appointments may not have been well-founded.

The returned soldiers who flocked to the Town Hall to serve again under Pompey relished the revived camaraderie that was one of the few positives of their war experience. Their transition to peacetime conditions had not been straightforward. Most were relieved (if not amazed) to have survived, thrilled to get back home, and keen to forget the ghastliness of front-line combat. But many did not adjust satisfactorily to civilian life, finding it humdrum and anti-climactic; its acquisitive individualism alienated those who missed the comradeship that had sustained them amid the horror and squalor of the battlefield. That brotherhood of mutual regard and interdependence, flourishing most intensely in those terrifying times when they were well and truly on the edge was, for numerous ex-diggers, a sublime sentiment and the main redeeming feature of their terrible torture in the trenches. But to comprehend it, to appreciate it, you had to be there. Understanding was impossible otherwise. There would forever be, they were realising, an unbridgeable chasm between those who had been there and those who had not.

What happened to Ellis 'Teena' Stones epitomised the difficulties of post-war adjustment. A 7th Battalion original, Stones was a trained sniper who never fired a shot in action. One of the Essendon boys who suffered terribly at the landing, he was incapacitated with a crippling leg wound; his best mate Bill Elliott was killed, along with many others, in the ill-fated first boat. Eventually Stones was rescued and conveyed (like Colonel Elliott) to hospital at Heliopolis, where his leg was about to be amputated until a last-minute intervention by a doctor from Ascot Vale who knew him. Greatly inconvenienced and in permanent pain, he endured a series of operations as well as headaches, nerves, and nightmares about the events of 25 April 1915. Although pleased to be home, he sadly missed the Essendon mates he had gone away with. He married Bill Elliott's sweetheart, and tried to resume his pre-war occupation, limping about as a carpenter–builder; but his sore leg was not up to it, and he eventually collapsed. He suffered a complete breakdown, compounded by the death from meningitis of his young son. While he was to recover and ultimately become one of Australia's finest landscape designers, at the end of 1923 Ellis Stones was in a bad way, a shadow of his former decisive, gregarious self.

For some who returned from the war with conspicuous scars, physical and/or emotional, readjustment was well nigh impossible. Stewart Smith, the officer who featured in the stories Pompey told at unveiling ceremonies for his remarkable selflessness in refusing stretcher-bearer assistance because he thought others were in greater need, died as a result of his wounds a few years after returning to Australia. Besides men like Smith who did not survive long after their return, other tragic cases among the thousands who served under Elliott included a proportion who returned with emotional scars that were severe as well as permanent. Some of these unfortunates were institutionalised due to psychological trauma. Pompey was greatly saddened by their plight.

Even soldiers who appeared relatively unscathed on their return found civilian life challenging. Captain Moon VC, unsettled and battling a delayed nervous reaction to his wartime experiences, left Australia after his stint as Elliott's 1919 campaign secretary, and spent the next few years working at a Malayan rubber plantation. Many others were similarly affected; unsettled behaviour was rife. A particularly distressing example, aired by Elliott in the Senate, concerned a 7th Battalion original who had enlisted as an 18-year-old and 'by almost miraculous good luck served from the beginning to the end of the war without getting a scratch'; he survived the Gallipoli landing, the Krithia charge, Lone Pine, and all the rest. The 'strain which the war imposed on the nerves of a young fellow like that', Pompey continued, was dramatically revealed after the war when he found his wife's childbirth agony unbearable. He became 'worked up to such a pitch of worry and excitement that he went out of the house, walked into a dam and drowned himself'.

Readjustment to civilian life was especially difficult for thousands of returned men who endured terrible hardships on unpropitious soldier settlement blocks. Enthusiastic advocates of the idea of turning soldiers into farmers had overridden pessimists familiar with similar settlement schemes; even applicants who would clearly be handicapped as farmers owing to their severe war wounds were accepted. While some soldiers managed to succeed, most struggled against the combined difficulties of escalating debt, infertile blocks and grinding toil. By the mid-1920s in Victoria (where there were more soldier settlers than in any other state) dozens each week were giving up, simply abandoning their blocks.

Many of Elliott's men gave the scheme a go. Among them was Bert Heighway, one of the 7th Battalion lieutenants who had been hit as the ill-fated boatloads of Essendon boys rowed themselves towards Fishermen's Hut. Heighway's enduring admiration for his colonel prompted him to call a thoroughfare adjoining his property 'Pompey Lane', which eventually became its official name. Elliott himself endorsed soldier settlement wholeheartedly. He provided references in support of applicants, and maintained a keen interest in how the settlers were faring. While sympathetic to individuals who were not prospering, he was consistently optimistic about the scheme overall. 'It is a wonderful record', he enthused in mid-1923; some settlers 'have made extraordinary progress' and 'are delighted at having had the opportunity of their lives'.

When returned soldiers did manage to attain distinction after the war, their achievements were especially appreciated by admiring wartime comrades who were painfully realising that their best years were behind them. They knew how much of their own drive and zest had been irretrievably lost at the war, and sensed what other Anzacs had overcome to accomplish significant post-war achievements. Among the men under Elliott's command who returned after sturdy AIF service to play League football was Ivor Warne-Smith, a brilliant champion who won the Brownlow Medal twice in the 1920s. Jim Phillips entertained audiences in an altogether different way; an amusing mimic, with bird calls a specialty, he performed professionally at the Tivoli as 'Pompey's canary'. Especially inspirational to their former comrades were Albert Coates and Vern Mullin. Coates was displaying the determination and resourcefulness that were to underpin his illustrious career, achieving brilliant results in his medical studies despite spending evenings on night shift at the Melbourne GPO. Mullin, one of the ill-fated 7th Battalion reinforcements who arrived at Gallipoli just before Lone Pine, returned home blind. Undeterred, he became not only an accomplished switchboard operator at the Repatriation department, but a fine gardener and—of all things—a prize-winning stamp-collector as well.

Former 7ths were also remarkably conspicuous in the collective organisation of returned servicemen. Gil Dyett was in the early years of a stint as national RSSILA president that was to last until 1946. George 'Gunner' Holland, a 7th Battalion original (like his brother, who had been killed alongside him at Krithia) was also prominent in the organisation, becoming Victorian president during the 1920s and retaining this position for 21 years. Elliott himself was a notable contributor to the League. President of its Camberwell branch in 1919, he redrafted the national RSSILA constitution, and assisted the organisation in numerous other ways. Pompey became such an influential advocate for returned soldiers in the national parliament and the public domain generally that a Tasmanian senator described him as their 'finest and most authoritative advocate of all'.

RSSILA membership declined in the early 1920s. With many ex-soldiers increasingly preoccupied with civilian priorities, only 7 per cent of the returned men in Elliott's home state were members in 1924. There was also a widespread perception that RSSILA leaders were too inclined to align themselves with the conservative end of the political spectrum. Thousands of working-class diggers were alienated by the League's firm advocacy of preference to returned soldiers rather than unionists.

It was not only those men who returned broken in body, soul or both who found post-war life dispiriting. Thousands of bereaved families could not get over their crushing loss. Geoff McCrae's parents kept his bedroom as a personal shrine, his officers' cap on the pillow; even in 1922 his father was still asking Elliott to clarify esoteric details about Geoff's AIF career, which had ended at Fromelles over six years earlier. For too many Australians, the 1920s resembled an unending funeral. Elliott's own relatives were affected. His sister-in-law, George's widow Lyn, could not come to terms with her bereavement. She openly resented the return of other soldiers. Her bitterness often surfaced if she noticed an AIF father out with his offspring when she was strolling with little Jacquelyn: 'See, *their* father didn't get killed at the war like *yours* did', she would say. Kate and Belle found Lyn's erratic tendencies alienating, but Elliott urged them to be tolerant. 'Even if we don't like Lyn', he cautioned, 'we must see that Geordie's wee bairnie does not suffer, because he died for us'. To enable Jacquelyn to be 'properly educated', Elliott and his brother Rod agreed to supplement the widow's pension Lyn received. Their combined contributions more than doubled it.

Pompey Elliott did whatever he could to help men who had served under him and their families. Some he employed himself on various tasks at Frankston or on gardening work at Prospect Hill Road. (At one stage even sweet-natured Kate felt moved to utter a mild protest: 'Does the garden really have to be dug up *every* day?') Long after Elliott's death veterans were expressing gratitude for jobs he had organised in difficult times that gave them secure employment for decades. Moreover, as a member of the board of management of the Melbourne Hospital, he was on the selection committee that gave Albert Coates his first job as a doctor.

But it was not just employment that he provided or organised—he was indefatigably helpful in all sorts of ways. It was remarkable, a Pompey admirer testified,

> how much of his time—time that he could very ill spare—was bestowed in acting as the (unpaid) guide, philosopher and friend of innumerable returned soldiers who found their way to his office, always ready to listen to grievances and wrongs, always ready to give

> not only advice, but personal help and intervention according to the demands of individual cases.

By personal intervention he managed to alleviate the tragic circumstances of the childbirth-related suicide case, explaining directly to the minister in charge of repatriation, Sir Neville Howse, precisely 'what that boy had been through', particularly at Lone Pine where he had been in charge of a desperately defended post, and how those experiences had produced 'such an effect on his nerves that he could not face his wife's agony as a sane man would'. The result was gratifying: Howse responded to Elliott's compelling submission by granting a pension to cover both the widow and her baby.

One day in Collins Street Elliott chanced upon Clarrie Wignell, who had been the 16-year-old 'baby' of Fred Tubb's Euroa contingent of 7th Battalion originals. After introductory greetings the conversation went something like this:

> 'I doubt you'd remember me.'
>
> 'Come off it, I remember everyone in that first thousand. But you've got me tossed, there were two of you Wignell brothers and I'm not sure which one you are.'
>
> 'I'm Clarrie, number 20 on the battalion roll. My brother was number 19.'
>
> 'I see. Where are you going now?'
>
> 'Solicitor. Legal problem.'
>
> 'Well if you want to come to me it wouldn't cost you anything.'

It was indeed Pompey's custom to provide free legal aid to men he had commanded, and his recall of them was as good as he claimed. One evening during a country trip his car became so badly bogged that local assistance was sought. The rescue party happened to include an original 7th, who wondered if he could perhaps discern a familiar figure in the dark. 'Aren't you General Elliott?' he asked hesitantly. 'Yes, and you're Jim Milroy' came the immediate rejoinder, as Pompey correctly identified the inquirer despite the murk.

Another Pompey contribution to the returned soldier cause was his significant role in the emergence of Anzac Day as a prominent annual commemoration. Relentless RSSILA lobbying to have 25 April proclaimed a public holiday had been resisted by business representatives concerned about the loss of a day's trading, but Anzac Day activists had a breakthrough when the 1923 premiers' conference carried a resolution that 25 April should be commemorated as Australia's national day. This was gratifying, but only a stepping stone towards the objective of enacted legislation; to maintain the pressure, the RSSILA decided to organise a special remembrance on 25 April 1925. On Anzac Day 1921, the same month the AIF officially ceased to exist, Pompey had participated in a sizeable and successful commemoration in Melbourne (a march through the city and a memorial service at the MCG); but for the next three years the activities the League organised to mark the day did not include a march. As long as business and government remained opposed to a holiday, whenever 25 April was a weekday most employed ex-soldiers would be unable or unwilling to participate.

Anzac Day enthusiasts also had to contend with a mixture of sentiments related to the war's aftermath. Some Australians had been so scarred by either the turmoil and torment of the trenches or the tumultuous home front that they found remembrance of the war years unbearable. Others felt that it was time the returned men concentrated on civilian endeavours and put the war behind them. Disagreements about the most suitable observance of Anzac Day did not help either. Nevertheless, in 1925, shortly before the tenth anniversary of the Gallipoli landing, the League decided to take advantage of Anzac Day falling on a Saturday that year by initiating another national commemoration in Melbourne. In charge of its organisation was Pompey Elliott.

There was very little time to put it all together, but the arrangements were admirable and the publicity effective. The march was to start at 10.00am and proceed along Swanston, Bourke, and Spring Streets to the Exhibition Building, where Prime Minister Bruce and Governor-General Forster were to speak at a commemoration service. Traffic through some city streets was closed during the procession; so were the pubs. There were exhortations beforehand from Anzac luminaries, including Pompey. 'Let us be united on this day of remembrance', he urged:

> Let us forget all differences of creed and all party strife, and remember that on us lies the fate of Australia just as surely in these days of peace as in those great days of the war—the day of Anzac, the day of Amiens, the night of Villers-Bretonneux.

Elliott also utilised a publicity opportunity provided by Keith Murdoch's Melbourne *Herald* to write a stirring panegyric to the AIF. This was just like one of his speeches at memorial unveilings, a detailed description of exceptional individual deeds by men who had served under him. He highlighted Norman Greig at German Officers' Trench, the renowned VC trio at Lone Pine (Tubb, Burton, and Dunstan) and their assistants, Corporals Webb and Wright (who died, Pompey wrote, while catching Turkish bombs 'like fieldsmen at cricket and hurling them back'). At the Western Front he singled out Lieutenants Turnour at Polygon Wood, Moon at Bullecourt, and Dalgleish in the 15th Brigade's last battle. Such examples of what Australians actually did, Pompey enthused, should 'rouse in us a white-hot pride in the almost impossible feats' they accomplished.

The day itself went off very well. At least 5,000 marched (the RSSILA estimate was over 6,000, with 2,000 more returned soldiers lining the route). A large crowd watched reverently as the marchers filed past with Monash in the lead; Elliott was delighted to be able to ensure on this occasion the kind of prominence Monash should have had at other equivalent events. The service at the Exhibition Building was 'very inspiring', wrote C.J. Dennis, who listened to it on the wireless and was 'much affected'; the Governor-General, in particular, delivered a fine speech. A distinctive sentence predictably gratified Elliott:

> On the third anniversary of Anzac Day, at Villers-Bretonneux, Australian soldiers saved the day—maybe saved the war—by a feat of arms so brilliant, so valuable, as to be unsurpassed in the long story of the war. (Loud applause.)

It was a busy weekend for Pompey. As well as representing the Governor-General at a service at St. Patrick's Cathedral that morning, Elliott formally opened a substantial new memorial hall at South Melbourne in the afternoon at a ceremony attended by almost 2,000 onlookers. Then on Sunday he addressed a morning service at St Mark's Camberwell (where there were dignitaries galore), and also spoke at a memorial service in the afternoon at Coburg Town Hall. The success of the main commemoration on 25 April 1925 was instrumental, just as the League had hoped, in securing a public holiday. The Victorian government legislated to this effect a few months later, and this crucial goal in the entrenchment of Anzac Day's special place in the calendar had been achieved.

While these Anzac Day commitments were keeping Elliott busy and prominent, he had to put up with notoriety of a much less welcome kind concerning an incident at Frankston. This episode originated in a dispute about ownership of the land at Oliver's Hill that the Elliotts used when staying at Frankston. Elliott had acquired his interest in this property from an officer he had served with in the Victorian Bushmen's contingent during the Boer War, Major Michael O'Farrell. As Elliott knew, O'Farrell had originally fenced it at a time when ownership of the land was obscure. Under the law of adverse possession, the continued absence of any apparent owner for fifteen years would enable Elliott to claim that it belonged to him. If an owner or owners materialised in the meantime, Elliott had in mind negotiating to buy them out. During the 1920s ostensible owners did materialise, the Wilson family of Footscray (consisting of Charles, a blacksmith in his sixties, his wife Jane and their son Bert), who tenaciously claimed a valid entitlement—intriguingly, also on the basis of adverse possession. Not only did they resist Elliott's offers to buy them out; they erected their own fences to substantiate their claim. In 1924 Elliott sued the Wilsons for trespass. The Wilsons' defence was undermined by trouble with their solicitors. The lawyer they eventually hired after discarding alternatives, well-known Labor identity Maurice Blackburn, advised them to settle rather than pursue a costly court case with an uncertain outcome. A compromise was agreed, with the land in question being divided between the Wilsons and the Elliotts.

Far from settling the dispute, this resolution only exacerbated it, as the Wilsons maintained that Blackburn had negotiated the compromise without their authorisation. The friction escalated. There were confrontations between rival caretakers, and claims and counterclaims of fence destruction and other infringements. The culmination was a skirmish involving the leading protagonists on Easter Saturday 1925. Elliott had arranged for an additional residence to be erected on the land that had been confirmed as his under the 1924 agreement with the Wilsons. On 11 April Charles and Bert Wilson, the aggrieved father and son toting crowbar and axe, menacingly intent on destroying this partly constructed dwelling, approached the men Elliott had engaged as builders and told them to clear out. Bert Wilson reinforced this edict by biffing one of them. Someone sounded a bell (which

Elliott had evidently instructed them to ring if any trouble developed). The burly brigadier burst onto the scene, and immediately flattened Bert. When the elder Wilson attempted to aid his son he found himself accommodated, too. The police were called, and another court case ensued. The Wilsons hardly had a leg to stand on legally, and this time they accepted Blackburn's advice. They tendered a formal apology to Elliott, and accepted £400 from him to compensate them for relinquishing their claim to the land in dispute and the 'improvements' they had made to it (less £14 reimbursement for the damage they had inflicted on his property).

This trifling personal kerfuffle became of more than minimal significance when *Truth* newspaper trumpeted it in characteristically vivid style. Adopting amusing alliterative allusions as almost always, *Truth* gave the story the full multiple-headline treatment—'GENERAL "POMPEY" ELLIOTT IN FIERCE FRANKSTON FISTICUFFS: AUSTRALIAN WAR HERO "OVER THE TOP" AGAIN: ROUGH AND TUMBLE IN THE FRANKSTON HILLS: CITY COUNCIL'S SOLICITOR SITS ON OPPONENT', and so on. At Oliver's Hill on this balmy sunny Saturday, according to the dispatch filed 'by *Truth's* war correspondent', 'the spectacular sweep of the sparkling bay could be seen in its exquisite entirety, scintillating and solacing'; 'perfect peace' prevailed as the 'hills wore their most handsome habiliments, and a halo of haze hung over habitations'. However, the 'hour of Zero was at hand', and the 'hefty and heavy' military celebrity known as Pompey was 'prepared to go over the top once more'. When the Wilsons initiated the fracas

> a cow-bell rang long and loudly. That was the signal for the Brigadier-General to climb the parapet. Down pounded 'Pompey'. Young Wilson was standing with axe in hand at the embryo mansion. Elliott allegedly rushed at him and grappled. The next instant 'Pompey' executed something of a 'flying mare' in the undergrowth … and pinned his opponent to the ground. Wilson was [unable] to rid himself of the 16 stone or so of military rank.

After the constabulary arrived, *Truth* surmised that 'Pompey … must have felt his spine sparkle' when directed to accompany the Wilsons to the police station, even though he was convinced that he was completely in the right.

The Wilsons gave *Truth* a full account of their side of the story, but Elliott declined to go on the record for the notorious scandal sheet other than to cite the consensual 1924 settlement that rendered their conduct indefensible. Because the Wilsons were more informative, their version of the dispute dominated *Truth's* analysis of the background to the Easter Saturday incident. An explanatory letter setting the record straight from Pompey's perspective was sent to the paper, but was evidently ignored.

Political combat was lively in 1925, too—it was an election year. Industrial unrest was the dominant issue. The Bruce–Page government was increasingly irritated by the recalcitrance of the Seamen's Union, which was thumbing its nose at the arbitration process under the militant leadership of Tom Walsh (who had associated himself prominently with the Communist Party) and Jacob Johnson. In 1925 the coalition decided that enough was enough. It rushed punitive measures through parliament, sabotaging the union's influence by allowing the coastal trade provisions of the Navigation Act to be suspended, and dealing with Walsh and Johnson personally by an Immigration Act amendment authorising the deportation of foreign-born individuals involved in major industrial disputes. (Walsh was Irish-born, but had been an Australian resident for over 30 years; Johnson's birthplace was Sweden, but he too had lived much of his life in Australia.) Implementation of this deportation initiative was resisted by the Labor Premier of New South Wales, J.T. Lang, who refused to allow the police in his state to co-operate. The Bruce–Page government responded with legislation to establish its own uniformed force.

During the lively parliamentary debates on these measures Senator Elliott made it clear that he firmly supported this vigorous action. The changes to the Navigation Act were consistent, he asserted, with the royal commission report that he and Senator Duncan had submitted in 1924. Amid escalating acrimony Labor's Charlton challenged the Prime Minister to go to the people. Bruce shrewdly acquiesced (an election was due soon anyway), and the stage was set for one of those law-and-order, 'kicking the Communist can' campaigns that were to become very familiar in Australian politics.

An effective Senate campaign was an acknowledged priority for the government. The senators whose terms were expiring (including Elliott) were nearly all Nationalists; with 22 vacancies to be decided,

Labor only had to win seven to secure a majority in the next Senate. To maximise campaign cohesion, the coalition had negotiated an electoral pact: the four Senate vacancies in Victoria would be contested by three endorsed Nationalists and a candidate from the Country Party (a prominent Bendigo identity, David Andrew). Elliott had decided to stand again. He felt that he was discharging his parliamentary responsibilities competently and making a difference for returned soldiers. His Nationalist colleagues were to be Senator Guthrie (as in 1919) and party president William Plain. They were each given a portion of rural Victoria to concentrate on during the campaign. Elliott's allotted region was the north-west of the state; he spent only four days electioneering in Melbourne during more than five weeks on the campaign trail.

Once Elliott had signalled his willingness to stand again, his popularity and repute ensured his endorsement by Nationalist power-brokers despite the independent streak that had intermittently perturbed them. This widespread esteem was a feature of a perceptive *Punch* profile of him in August 1925. 'Brigadier-General ("Pompey") Elliott was perhaps the best-known and best-liked member of the AIF', it began; 'he is certainly one of the best-remembered'. Once-famous VC winners were now 'dimming memories', Birdwood was 'recalled with little real enthusiasm when … recalled at all', and 'thousands of ex-diggers … would not recognise … Brudenell White if they met him in the street'. Yet 'everyone who has had anything to do with soldiering knows all about "Pompey" Elliott, and speaks of him with affection'. During the war he was 'extravagantly brave'. A 'terrific worker', he 'toiled incessantly' whenever his men were on front-line duty, and spent much of his leave visiting the wounded in hospital. He established himself as 'the most distinguished Brigadier in the AIF'. But he should have risen higher:

> It was not that he lacked the ability to command a division, or even a larger formation. He had been a student of the art of war since boyhood; he was young as senior officers go, and his mental equipment was of the best. His handicap was that he was always ready to stand up for his men against Army H.Q. when he came to the conclusion that the latter was in the wrong … He was written down as fractious, irresponsible and even insubordinate; a good fighting soldier but lacking in suavity; a useful man in the line but a difficult one to get on with out of it. His officers and men loved

> him for the very qualities which made him objectionable to the higher command, but that was no particular good to his career. With a more deferential manner, and five or six thousand superfluous deaths on his soul, he might have celebrated the Armistice as a Major-General and a K.B.E.

His time in politics had been 'rather like his army career'. Once again his attributes might have been expected to equip him for high honours. Not only did he have first-rate 'intellectual qualifications' and abundant experience as a lawyer to commend him:

> He speaks well. Standing over six feet in his socks and weighing some seventeen stone, he has a most impressive presence. His character is impeccable. He was a great athlete in his day ... and he still retains that genuine interest in all classes of sport which so endears an M.P. to the electors ... But nothing is surer than that he will do no better for himself in Parliament than he did in the army. With all his shining mental and moral gifts, he lacks one that is almost essential to success in politics—the capacity to be humble and pliant in the presence of his Party bosses.

Elliott concentrated on two main themes in the campaign. Having presented himself as a returned soldiers' candidate in 1919, he felt impelled to stress what the government had done for them. The war gratuity promised in 1919 had been delivered; so had 'liberal' war pensions, preference in employment and war service homes. He qualified his customary enthusiasm about soldier settlement by emphasising that while the federal government had provided funding for the scheme that had enabled 34,995 ex-soldiers (including 10,565 Victorians) to participate, any administrative 'defects and blunders' were a state responsibility. They were certainly not attributable to the federal government, which had spent over £150 million altogether in meeting its obligations to Australia's returned men. It was an 'incomparable' record, Pompey claimed, exceeded by no other nation. Elliott covered other topics (the government's record on postal, telephone, and road improvements in country areas, for example), consistently endorsed his fellow candidates on the coalition's Senate ticket in Victoria, and also countered various issues raised by the opposition. But his other main electioneering theme was the issue at the heart of the campaign. 'Do you prefer constitutional government or mob rule?' he asked audiences in successive speeches at St Arnaud, Birchip, Charlton, Donald, and Hopetoun. Unions were 'permeated by the Communist virus'. Walsh and Johnson were 'as deadly to the society' as 'cancer is to the human frame'.

On Thursday 15 October Elliott's travels around northern Victoria with Kate (and an ex-AIF officer acting as his secretary-publicist) brought them to Mildura. During their four-day stay at the Grand Hotel he had a series of engagements. Once again he gave the contrast between constitutional government and mob rule a recurrent airing. There was 'no side-stepping that plain question', least of all from him as he delivered his standard campaign address at Mildura, Merbein, and Red Cliffs.

At the completion of the third of these speeches, at Red Cliffs on Saturday morning, he found that a surprise had been planned for him. The meeting chairman, G.C. Green (who had eloped with the sister of up-and-coming barrister Robert Menzies) announced that he had a 'very pleasing duty to perform on behalf of ex-members of the 7th Battalion' who were represented among local soldier settlers. Green went on to recount how Pompey had castigated one of his men for appearing on parade in Egypt without a hat, scorned the unfortunate's explanation that it had been stolen, and soon afterwards found he had been deprived of his own. After ten years it was time the hat was returned, said Green, pulling an old crumpled one out of his pocket and presenting it to Elliott. The recipient joined in the universal laughter, and said he was 'touched' by the gesture. He was reluctant to 'spoil a good story', he added amiably, before gently correcting Green's version. (So renowned was the hat story that its 'return' was reported in Melbourne and Sydney newspapers, prompting Treloar, who sensed its potential as a notable exhibit at the Australian War Memorial, to ask Elliott if he would be prepared to donate it. 'I would be delighted', replied Elliott, but 'beware of the leg-pull'—that 'pitiful wreck' was, 'I strongly suspect', not 'the real thing'.)

Later that Saturday Elliott returned to Mildura, where he was guest of honour at a memorable RSSILA social. The struggling soldier settlers packed up their troubles in their old kitbags, and enjoyed a jovial evening of spirited singing and reminiscing. They saluted Pompey with three cheers, 'For He's a Jolly Good Fellow', and genuine gratitude for his keen interest in their cause.

On election day, 14 November 1925, the government had a comfortable victory. Labor went backwards. In the House of Representatives the ALP lost seven seats, and the coalition emerged with a sizeable majority; in the Senate Labor did not win a single seat in any state. It was a sweeping vindication of the coalition's cohesive campaign. Once again Elliott was the first senator elected in Victoria, and the returned soldiers' 'finest and most authoritative advocate of all' was back in federal parliament for another six-year term.

CHAPTER TWENTY-THREE

'We Feel It Was Long Overdue': Major-General at last

1925–1929

PROMINENT AMONG THE tasks confronting the re-elected Bruce–Page government was the transfer of federal parliament to Canberra. Elliott had consistently opposed this move. In 1920 he had denounced expenditure on Canberra's development in one of his earliest Senate pronouncements, and in 1923 he proposed in a formal motion that the transfer of parliament from his home city to the bush capital should be delayed. However, the Bruce–Page government authorised the accelerated construction of a new parliament house in Canberra, and in May 1926 the Prime Minister announced that it would be opened twelve months later.

After visiting Canberra himself in mid-1926, Elliott became a vigorous critic of its leasehold system of land tenure. The Federal Capital Commission tightly regulated all aspects of Canberra's development, including the allocation of land. Its chairman, J.H. Butters, told Elliott during his visit that business blocks at Civic (in central Canberra) were being released on a strictly controlled basis. All sites so far offered had been taken, so there were none presently available; there would be another auction in due course, and aspiring purchasers would be able to bid for a site then if they wished. On 21 July 1926 Elliott rose in the Senate to condemn this state of affairs. There was plenty of suitable land available, he pointed out, yet a prospective purchaser could only acquire a business block by outlaying a hefty premium to someone who was sitting on a still-vacant site; rampant speculation was impeding Canberra's progress. A Nationalist colleague (who, being from New South Wales, had a much more positive attitude to the federal capital than most Victorian MPs) contrasted Elliott's previous speeches denigrating Canberra 'as a wilderness where no one with any sense would desire to go' with his frustration at being unable to get land for himself now he had seen how impressive it really was. Elliott insisted that more land should be made available, and his persistent criticism of the 'altogether too autocratic' commission culminated in a sharp exchange with the new minister for Home and Territories, Glasgow.

Elliott was interested in purchasing a business site for himself. Besides sensing that it would prove worthwhile as an investment, he wanted to set up a branch of his legal firm in Canberra. He and Hector MacDonald were no longer partners; Elliott had established his own practice. Thanks in particular to his continuing remunerative position as the Melbourne City Council's solicitor, H.E. Elliott & Co was doing well; the firm occupied part of the fifth floor at 94-98 Queen Street, paying an annual rent of £660. His living-legend status awed new employees, but around the office he was a friendly, fatherly figure who regularly presented staff with fruit from his splendid garden. The 'city solicitor' (as Elliott was widely known in legal circles) had a high profile in the profession. In 1926 he was vice-president of the Law Institute of Victoria, and serving on most of its executive committees.

But his plans to set up an office in Canberra were frustrated by the unavailability of land. He realised that if he wanted a business site he had no alternative but to negotiate with existing leaseholders. The premiums many of them were demanding (through their agents) he considered outrageous. Eventually he struck a deal with two Sydney sisters who had acquired four adjoining blocks; he bought them for £1,100. Elliott's resentment at such exorbitant prices was unleashed when parliament resumed after its summer break in March 1927. He refrained from referring to his own transaction, but lashed out at the commission's land policy, describing it as 'profiteering' so flagrant that it was tantamount to the worst excesses of the 1890s land boomers: 'a continuance of this policy will cripple the progress of the capital'.

Elliott followed his inspection of Canberra with another interesting trip when he returned to his birthplace for the 1926 'Back to Charlton' festivities. Planning for the celebrations had been under way for a year.

Organising committees in Charlton and Melbourne co-ordinated arrangements; Elliott was president of the Melbourne group. On 16 October a special train containing 460 'Comebacks' arrived at lavishly decorated Charlton station to a rapturous welcome from the town's entire population. The celebrations during the next few days included a reunion dinner, a concert, a picnic, a 'back to school' function and sporting events. Speeches from Charlton's most famous son were, of course, unavoidable. Elliott thanked all concerned for 'the opportunity of visiting the scenes of his boyhood', which had been a 'great pleasure'; there had been so much progress that he 'hardly recognised the old place'.

The memorable 'Back to Charlton' celebrations were surpassed by the formal opening of parliament in Canberra. On 9 May 1927 an array of dignitaries headed by the Duke of York, the future king of England, assembled on a sunny windless morning for the grand ceremony. Senator and Kate Elliott were among the official guests, and there were thousands of uninvited onlookers. The Elliotts were impressed by the ceremony, which featured trumpet fanfares and a 21-gun salute; Dame Nellie Melba sang the national anthem, and an air force squadron roared overhead. The speeches stressed Australia's progress since federation and the AIF's contribution in the Great War. Though Australia's gallant fallen 'have passed into the Great Beyond they are still speaking to those who choose to listen', said the Duke of York; 'if Australia listens to the voices of the noble army of the dead ... the glorious destiny of this country will be assured for all time'. Anzac was still omnipotent even a near-decade after the Armistice. At the conclusion of this special one-day sitting the government adjourned parliament for months, pleading the impossibility of normal arrangements while the administrative machinery of government was being transferred to Canberra.

The long parliamentary adjournment did not prevent Elliott from continuing his campaign to change land policy in the capital territory. Eight days after the big Canberra ceremony he raised the issue with Latham, his old Ormond friend who had become Attorney-General in Bruce's cabinet. Now that Elliott was a leaseholder himself (he had acquired a residential site at Red Hill as well as his four adjoining blocks at Civic), a continuation of current land policy would suit him financially, he assured Latham, but 'from a National point of view' it was objectionable. This was the start of a sizeable correspondence, as Elliott kept submitting his accumulating grievances with the commission to Latham, bypassing various ministers for Home and Territories (Glasgow had been moved after less than a year in that portfolio, and he had a series of short-lived successors).

Elliott insisted that too few blocks were being made available, which played into the hands of speculators. Furthermore, this reprehensible speculation was being orchestrated by some of the commission's own employees, who were profiting from their inside knowledge. '[T]he whole thing to my mind bears a suspicious resemblance to graft', he asserted. And once a leaseholder had acquired a lease at an extortionate price, that leaseholder then had to contend with undue interference from the commission when erecting a building and trying to arrange a sub-lease. The family company Elliott had set up with his brother Rod had invested almost £10,000 to construct a building at Civic without any return for months, because a prospective tenant he was negotiating with about a sub-lease (which was to cover the whole building apart from an office for H.E. Elliott & Co) pulled out as a direct result, he alleged, of the commission's culpable interference and imprecise requirements. Heading the Canberra branch of his law firm was Eric Hart. Son of a 7th Battalion officer who had served under Pompey at Gallipoli, Hart was probably the first solicitor to practise in Canberra.

In March 1928 the Joint Committee of Public Accounts began an inquiry into housing and building costs in Canberra. Elliott appeared as a witness. Most of his evidence covered the now-familiar criticisms of the commission's land administration. The 'buildings erected by me in the Civic Centre have been idle since Christmas', he lamented, and 'there appears to be no reasonable prospect of letting them'. Elliott also revealed that the commission had prevented him from disposing of three leases he did not really want (he had initially sought only one business block, but the Sydney sisters who eventually sold out to him had insisted that they would only sell if he purchased all four). When Butters, also testifying to the Joint Committee inquiry, denied that the commission had prevented Elliott from disposing of these unwanted three sites, Elliott was incensed. Butters 'went remarkably close to committing perjury', he told the Senate. Eventually Elliott managed to find a tenant. It was the government itself that 'came to the rescue' (as he put it), leasing vacant space in his building for departmental offices. All the same, he admitted,

> I am sick and tired of trying to carry on under the conditions that prevail here. I would gladly hand over the whole of the buildings in which I am interested if I could get my money back.

Hostilities escalated further when Elliott refused to pay commission levies for kerbing, guttering, and footpath construction. Such charges were neither fair nor lawful, he insisted, and invited the commission to sue. While maintaining that he was a true 'friend of the Territory', he blasted Butters at every opportunity in the Senate and called for the abolition of the commission. He even warned Latham that if the commission did not change its ways he would consider withdrawing his support from the government. In an attempt to smooth things over, the hard-pressed Attorney-General organised a meeting with himself, Elliott and the then minister for Home and Territories, Sir Neville Howse. Pompey appreciated Latham's efforts, but would not be mollified. 'It's all unjust and I'm going to fight', he vowed. After the meeting Latham briefed the Prime Minister. He told Bruce that a High Court hearing was looming and the dispute was a serious problem:

> I am strongly of opinion that an injustice is being done to Senator Elliott and that he is not being treated reasonably. When I say this I do not mean that I think that Senator Elliott is reasonable in everything that he demands or says, but ... Senator Elliott has real grievances which I consider ought to be removed by amendments of ordinances where necessary. I regard this as an example of the errors which are gravely interfering with the happiness of Canberra.

Judgment in the commission's High Court action against Elliott's company was delivered late in 1929. Elliott was successful, though on a legal technicality.

Pompey was sticking to his guns about Canberra, but had withdrawn his objection to serving in the defence force. It was the resignation from the army of Brudenell White (to become chairman of the Public Service Board) that paved the way for Elliott's return. White's successor as Chief of the General Staff was Sir Harry Chauvel, the renowned AIF Light Horse commander. The divisional commanders appointed in 1921 had agreed to a maximum term of five years. This restriction had been imposed to keep the promotion channels open, so talented leaders would have an incentive to stay in the force and a supply of experienced senior officers could be accumulated. It was Elliott's resentment at being overlooked in 1921 that had prompted him to resign in the first place; it was the expiry of the five-year terms of those appointed in 1921 that made his return straightforward. In March 1926 a number of new appointments were announced. Among them was Elliott, chosen to command the 15th (Victorian) Brigade.

This appointment, with all its obvious Western Front associations, was particularly welcome to Pompey, and he reverted to active command with characteristic wholeheartedness. Always keen to instil esprit de corps and pride in a unit's heritage, he assured his men at the end of their camp in March 1927 that he 'was satisfied ... they would worthily uphold the traditions' of the 15th AIF Brigade. When he presented a trophy to the 60th Battalion for being the most successful unit in the brigade at rifle-shooting, he said 'the spirit of the old 60th' lived on; he provided a special medal of his own for the best individual shooter. Later that year, when a divisional vacancy materialised, he was chosen to fill it. He became Major-General Elliott, commander of the Third (Victorian) Division. This was a gratifying development, of course, after his desolation when such a promotion did not come his way in 1918 and 1921. It had eventuated, he told Bean, simply because General Chauvel 'removed the embargo placed upon my promotion by General White'.

Also pleasing to Elliott was the way the commemoration of Australia's role in the Great War was progressing. Memorials were still being erected across the nation; Pompey continued to be a popular choice to unveil Victorian ones. Construction of more prominent commemorative structures, however, was being delayed. Progress with the projected Australian War Memorial in Canberra had been minimal, and the main Melbourne monument, the Shrine of Remembrance, looked like being scuttled altogether until Monash (supported by Elliott and others) spearheaded a counter-offensive that eventually thwarted the Shrine's opponents. These delays were disappointing; but Bean was continuing to produce an outstanding chronicle of Australia's contribution in the war, and the annual Anzac Day commemoration was growing exponentially. In 1926, with Monash in charge as president of the Anzac Day Commemoration Council and the crucial RSSILA objective of a public holiday at last achieved, some 12,000 veterans marched (about twice the previous year's turnout) despite heavy rain.

The following year was a triumph. Monash pulled out all stops when he learned that the Duke of York would be in Melbourne on Anzac Day. Wartime subordinates of Elliott were given important roles: Cam Stewart was 'commander' (chief marshal), Charlie Watson was his 'chief staff officer', and Roy Gollan attended deftly to publicity. On Monday 25 April 1927 about 30,000 marched, and there were no fewer than half a million onlookers. Probably no bigger crowd had ever assembled in Australia.

The Duke of York's presence and the public holiday were significant, but other factors were also influential. In the immediate aftermath of the war most Australians, returned soldiers and civilians alike, did not want to dwell on a conflict that had been so painful. The soldiers had experienced unimaginable horrors on the battlefield, and their wives and mothers had endured years of tension so agonising that the mere glimpse of a clergyman walking along their street could make them shriek with terror because he might be delivering the message they dreaded above all else. While such a searing catastrophe was impossible to forget, many Australians understandably wanted to put it behind them as much as they could. But adjusting to peace after such a prolonged and devastating conflict had not been easy, as Elliott himself acknowledged in an article published in the Melbourne *Herald* on Anzac Day 1928. 'For some time after peace was declared', he wrote, Australians had 'lived in a whirlpool, trying to adjust our ideas, so forcibly wrenched to war's purposes, to the arts of peace'.

By the later 1920s, however, a decade had elapsed, providing distance and context. The war could be seen in better perspective, reviewed with some detachment. Increasingly, returned soldiers seemed prepared to acknowledge that it had been an obviously pivotal part of their lives, and reuniting with the men they had experienced it with was something more and more of them wanted to do. These tendencies should not be overestimated—many scarred veterans kept insisting that they wanted nothing to do with war commemoration. But even those who abhorred what they went through at Gallipoli or the Western Front, even those who resented the war's savage impact on themselves individually and on their doomed generation collectively, and even those who disapproved of the conservative political hue of the RSSILA, were likely to feel increasingly drawn to catch up with men they had shared their war experience with and to march in honour of comrades who had not survived it. Commemorative rituals such as Anzac Day were important for the grieving bereaved, too. The graves were too far away for all but a tiny minority to visit; without that traditional tangible focus for grief, ceremonies on Anzac Day and at memorial unveilings became a kind of substitute.

On Anzac Day in 1928 Elliott was in Bendigo. Many 7th Battalion men had enlisted there before serving under him. At the request of the Bendigo RSSILA president, Pompey led the march through that city, and was the main speaker at the commemorative ceremony afterwards. When he stepped forward to speak, he was greeted with a stirring ovation; shouts of 'Good old Pompey!' and 'Where's your hat, Pompey?' were also heard. 'I have at other times spoken of outstanding heroes, men of iron nerve and incredible daring', he observed, but this time he wanted to focus on 'men who just did their bit, who never received a decoration, were never mentioned in dispatches, and never honoured by any individual recognition'. To provide a vivid description of the front-line horrors they had endured, he proceeded to recite graphic extracts from Downing's *To the Last Ridge*. It was an extraordinary speech. Neither before nor since, surely, has there ever been a more frank portrayal of the Western Front at a formal Anzac Day address. It ended with a tribute to comrades who had not returned:

> These men who died amidst these scenes are with us still. They are near to us in spirit. Our memory is full of them.

The genuineness of these concluding sentiments was immediately demonstrated when Pompey mingled with spectators after the ceremony. With a big crowd in attendance, he 'met many mothers and relatives of boys in the old 7th', and his remarkable recall of individuals, considering thousands served under him, was again evident. He spoke to numerous parents of ex-7ths, the *Bendigo Advertiser* reported, and 'his memory is so good that in almost every case he remembered the Digger quite well'. This personal remembrance, so impressive even thirteen years after the landing, was especially appreciated by relatives of deceased Anzacs.

As Anzac Day flourished in the later 1920s, there was an equivalent surge in popularity of unit reunions. The battalion Elliott commanded at Gallipoli was a typical example. A 7th Battalion Association was established soon after the war, but did not prosper. In 1921 a function was organised in honour of one of the most admired officers in the battalion, Hec Bastin, who had served throughout the war in the 7th and was returning home after being in India since the Armistice; the event had to be cancelled because of lack of interest. Shortly afterwards the association folded. In 1925 a special meeting was called to revive it. The convenor was Bill Jamieson, a 29-year-old bank officer with creative instincts and considerable determination. A humble foot-slogger during the war, Jamieson became the indefatigable, ultra-efficient secretary of the association and, remaining in that role for six decades, was chiefly responsible for ensuring that there was no more vibrant and cohesive veterans' unit in Victoria than the 7th Battalion Association. At the 1925 meeting he convened, held on 3 August, a proposal to organise a get-together on the evening before the traditional Show Week public holiday (when country Victorians regularly travelled to Melbourne) was supported with 'the utmost enthusiasm', Jamieson noted in the minutes. He ensured that the function was publicised in the *Age*, the *Argus* and the *Herald*.

Pompey Elliott was one of 177 ex-7ths who gathered at the Ambassador's in Swanston Street on 23 September 1925. He was elected president of the association, and gave what the *Age* described as 'a rousing speech'. As Jamieson recorded, Pompey

> was greeted with loud applause, and feelingly spoke of the war record of the Battalion, of the traditions it had set and the history it had so materially helped to make, of the Government's assistance to returned soldiers in general. He concluded with the hope that our association would grow and flourish ... and, in feeling terms of appreciation, accepted on its behalf three floral tributes sent by the parents of deceased comrades. [Most of the] rest of the night was given to reminiscences. Everything went with a swing from start to finish, when the happy gathering broke up with a singing of Auld Lang Syne and the determination to make next year's function a still greater success.

It was. With Show Week Wednesday locked in as the regular date, '240 members mustered' on 22 September 1926 'to live again snatches of the life that has made so marked an impression on them', Jamieson recorded. Colonel Scanlan proposed a toast to 'our famous President, which was enthusiastically received'. There was such 'tremendous enthusiasm' at these revived reunions, in fact, that at the first three of them the scheduled formalities could not be carried through because 'high-spirited reminiscing and jollification had taken a complete hold of the gathering'. They were raucous, boozy affairs. It was not that poignant memories were unacknowledged. 'Fallen comrades' were honoured with a toast, the Last Post and a minute's silence; George Henderson attended to mix with the men his sons had briefly led before being killed in the first fortnight at Gallipoli. But boisterous reminiscing soon swamped the sombre overtones.

Jamieson maximised the association's cohesion by producing *Despatches*, an admirable annual publication full of stylishly expressed news about the activities of the association collectively and its members individually. When a 7th veteran was chosen to play for a country team against the touring English cricketers, this feat was reported in *Despatches* with a clever twist: 'George Ogilvie upholds the sporting traditions of the Battalion. He played for Bendigo against the English XI, and as always with the Seventh was sent in first.' Congratulating Elliott for his promotion to Major-General, *Despatches* frankly expressed the reaction of association members: 'We know it was well merited—we feel it was long overdue'. And Jamieson kept exhorting ex-7ths to make their association second to none. According to the 1928 *Despatches*, the 7th Battalion had achieved the biggest unit representation (700) in the 1927 Anzac Day march, but he was still not satisfied. 'Help us to beat that this year', he urged.

Elliott was delighted by the vibrancy of the reincarnated 7th Battalion Association. He remained its president, although he was rarely able to participate in committee discussions: his 'extremely busy life exempted him from attendance at our meetings'. Some officers felt awkward about catching up with men they had once commanded, but Pompey enjoyed reunions. He genuinely wanted to know how they were going—whether someone who needed a job had found one, whether another's dispute about a pension entitlement had been sorted out, whether Ellis Stones's leg was any less troublesome. A 7th veteran, asked decades later for recollections of Pompey at reunions, replied that he would shake hands all round, 'seemed to know everyone', and assured each and all that 'if there was anything he could do to help he would'.

He enjoyed reminiscing and swapping anecdotes, too, such as the story about the donkey that needed its ear tweaked. Another favourite concerned Birdwood's approach to a grimy Anzac at Gallipoli who was doing his best to wash himself with a meagre mess-tin of tightly rationed water. 'Hello', greeted the general, 'having a bath, my man?' The digger, unaware who was addressing him, snorted contemptuously: 'What do you take me for, a bloody canary?' Of course, Elliott featured prominently in many stories himself. There was the one about Harold Schuldt's crooked finger, damaged by the impromptu uppercut he resorted to when Pompey directed him to silence a drunkard who was being uninhibitedly vocal, within earshot of the Turks, about the top-secret plan to evacuate Gallipoli. And, inevitably, the story about Pompey's hat kept circulating in various versions—it was probably the best-known AIF anecdote of all.

But it was not just at battalion reunions that Elliott enjoyed catching up with wartime comrades like Bill Scurry. One of Pompey's pre-war 'Essendon boys', Scurry had arrived at Gallipoli just before the evacuation and devised the famous drip-rifle that helped the Anzacs escape. At the Western Front Elliott had been delighted with Scurry's 'splendid work' after selecting him to head the 15th Brigade Light Trench Mortar Battery: he was 'the best and most enthusiastic officer in my brigade'. However, to the brigadier's dismay, Scurry was severely wounded in 1916. During the 1920s Scurry's wounds became increasingly troublesome, but his attractive geniality and optimistic outlook were unaffected. When Pompey took the Elliotts on one of those country outings he liked to Silvan, where Scurry was an orchardist, the strong mutual regard of these ex-AIF officers was very evident. Their families became close, too. After Scurry's wounds forced him to stop work at the orchard, he lived with his wife (an ex-AIF nurse) and their four daughters at a house on Elliott's Frankston land for a while. Scurry's toddler twins enjoyed playing with Pompey, whose expansive girth provided ample scope for both to bounce on his stomach simultaneously. Violet Elliott called the drip-rifle inventor 'Uncle Bill', and became lifelong friends with the Scurrys.

Elliott and Jamieson did their utmost to help ex-7ths who were struggling, particularly those afflicted with psychological trauma. One sufferer had been on the initial 7th Battalion Association committee before being institutionalised later in the 1920s. When Jamieson wrote to inform Elliott about another 7th original in November 1928, Pompey replied immediately:

> Many thanks for your letter ... I had heard that poor Lennon had been committed to Mont Park. His mother and sister have consulted me at various times over their troubles but I was not aware of his domestic history. I shall write to the second Mrs Lennon and ask her to call and see me with a view to giving her all the assistance that is possible.

For troubled veterans unable to catch up with former comrades, long-term hospital residents in particular, Elliott agreed to provide an informal radio talk featuring some of the stories these ex-diggers would have heard at the reunions they could not attend. While a rendition on radio 'tends possibly to cramp one's style in detailing the exact words used by a digger', he began, 'I shall do my best'. What followed was a tribute to the nurses whose devoted care of wounded Australian soldiers during the war was continuing still, and an entertaining series of anecdotes. The celebrated hat and donkey stories were prominent, along with an account of the work of Percy Carne, Wally Fisher, and the 7th Battalion snipers, and an amusing airing of 'Scotty' Campbell's choice of court-martial in preference to a risky encounter with a Turkish sniper.

There was another annual reunion that Elliott attended regularly in the later 1920s, the commemorative dinner of senior commanders that Monash hosted each year to mark the anniversary of the decisive offensive that began on 8 August 1918. Monash took great pains to make the event a special occasion, and succeeded. Guests raved about his potent punch, which fuelled spirited singing and reminiscing. When deciding seating arrangements at the dinner table, the host took into account Elliott's sporadic friction with certain other AIF leaders (although his customary geniality on social occasions made turbulent exchanges unlikely), but Pompey was involved in a significant conversation at the 1927 gathering. Elliott himself left no record of it, but Brudenell White did in a brief note about Monash's 'jolly party' in his diary. 'Had to sit beside Elliott part of the time and we had a reconciliation', White wrote, 'but not before I had told him what I thought of him'.

What Elliott thought of a British appraisal of the Anzac landing became a controversial issue shortly afterwards. In October 1927

Australian newspapers claimed that a draft version of the British Official History contained such damning aspersions on the AIF's performance on 25 April 1915 that Bean had convened a committee of influential AIF identities, including General Elliott, in order to have these outrageous and offensive distortions corrected. Blaring headlines underlined the enduring power of Anzac. 'VILEST LIBEL OF THE WAR', raged the Sydney *Daily Guardian*. 'SLUR ON ANZACS', thundered the Melbourne *Sun*, 'Ill-Trained, Ill-Led, Is The Charge: Famous Generals Will Meet To Refute Canard'. In fact, although Bean was striving—with eventual success—to have the references to excessive AIF straggling deleted, there was no such committee.

Elliott was intensely curious about Bean's next volume, which would begin the Australian *Official History*'s coverage of the Western Front, and he felt impelled to ensure that the historian was fully informed about the 15th Brigade's contribution there. In August 1927 he sent Bean a collection of documents about the battle of Péronne, reviewed several Western Front controversies from his perspective (the advanced guard operations of March 1917 and the Villers-Bretonneux counterattack, in particular), and asked Bean what the next volume would cover. Bean replied that it would take the AIF story from the Gallipoli evacuation to February 1917, and would be ready for the publisher in a few months. Pompey encouraged the historian not to be distracted by the allegations of excessive delay that were being made. 'It would be a very great pity indeed to spoil the accuracy and completeness of the work' by cutting corners in response to uninformed criticism, he assured Bean.

A year later, though it would clearly be a good while yet before Bean reached April 1918, Elliott forwarded another submission about Villers-Bretonneux. By arrangement with a bookseller, Pompey acquired the latest books on the Great War as soon as they became available; he had recently read *The Remaking of Modern Armies* by B.H. Liddell Hart, an emerging military historian who was building a reputation in Britain and beyond as an innovative commentator. Not only did Liddell Hart's new book state that the Villers-Bretonneux counter-attack was 'designed by General Butler', the III Corps commander; its author went on to accuse an unnamed AIF brigadier of altering his objective 'according to his own ideas instead of complying' with superiors' orders. The regrettable sequel was 'an object-lesson in what may be termed the discipline of leadership'. As if that was not enough to raise Elliott's hackles, on 15 September 1928 the *Argus* published excerpts from a book on Rawlinson which quoted that general's praise of Butler's skilful planning of the brilliant counter-attack. A few days later Elliott received a letter from Bob Salmon:

> Did you read the extracts from General Rawlinson's Life which were published in Saturday's Argus? It was news to me that anyone but yourself conceived the method of attack of Villers Bretonneux. If my memory serves me aright you outlined to me on the morning of the capture by the Huns the method which should be adopted for recapture. You desired to put these plans into execution before the Huns had time to settle down. Your ideas were communicated to Division who delayed the attack but adopted the plan. Apart from this error of credit I thought the extracts quite unworthy and futile. It shatters your belief in history when you read of events, which were enacted within your memory, being misconstrued by one who should be an undoubted authority.

Shortly after receiving Salmon's letter, Elliott wrote to Treloar to say how 'concerned' he was about Liddell Hart's interpretation of Villers-Bretonneux. 'Certainly I never departed from the objectives given me by the Higher Command', Pompey insisted. In response to the annoying assertions that Butler had designed the operation, he enclosed Salmon's letter and contended that perusal of the 15th Brigade's reports and diaries 'which you hold will in the clearest possible manner refute' any idea that the originator of the famous counter-attack could have been anyone other than himself. It 'was based on my recollection of the Battle of Cannae' in 216 BC when Hannibal routed the Romans in a 'famous victory which was the most complete I would imagine in History. The same manoeuvre was successfully carried out in a precisely similar manner by Condé at the battle of Rocroy in 1643 and partially by Cromwell at Naseby' (1645), he added, and the idea would have worked even better at Villers-Bretonneux if he had been in charge and able to carry it out his way, with Glasgow temporarily under his command. Pompey urged Treloar to attach this reassertion of the 'true facts' to the report of the battle he had compiled at the time, and to send both to Bean in due course.

Treloar sent Elliott's letter on to Bean straightaway. Bean was sceptical about the purported link between Villers-Bretonneux and Cannae, and felt protective of Glasgow, who was one of his most admired AIF leaders, if not on the same exalted pedestal as White. While detailed examination of all this would have to wait until Volume V, Bean's provisional assessment was that 'Elliott's claim' to have been the real architect of the counterattack 'may be correct, but it should not be accepted without complete verification, as, fine old chap that he is', his 'whole outlook' had been profoundly affected by being overlooked in 1918, and his preoccupation with that rejection 'amounts almost to a mania'.

Another concern of Elliott's was that the victory ultimately won in 1918 at such terrible cost was being undermined in the war's aftermath by international trade patterns. He was not the only prominent Australian to take a dim view of the way the United States seemed intent on making the most of Britain's post-war financial discomfort. America was only in a position to do so, he declared, because for much of the war it 'refused to help France and the other countries allied with Great Britain in their desperate need'. Although Pompey could be vitriolic about individual British officers or units whose performance he assessed as substandard (or if they claimed credit when he felt they were unentitled), when it was a case of Britain (and its Empire) against any other great power, he was instinctively pro-British. He was certainly an ardent nationalist, prone to citing British deficiencies in order to highlight contrasting AIF attributes or accomplishments; but fundamentally he retained the dual loyalty exemplified in the phrase 'independent Australian Britons' that was soon to be popularised by historian Keith Hancock.

On 4 August 1927, the thirteenth anniversary of the outbreak of the war, Elliott chaired the inaugural meeting of the Pendulum Club, an organisation formed to 'consolidate the victory of our troops in the Great War' by boosting 'the reciprocal development of trade between Australia and the Mother Country'. The idea was to 'keep the Pendulum of Reciprocity swinging from Australia to Britain and back'. About 300 enthusiasts turned up to register their concern and support the aims of this new movement, which was spearheaded by a number of prominent citizens besides Elliott (Monash was vice-president). Charles Noad, an officer in Elliott's 15th AIF Brigade, was another Pendulum activist; it seems he was the movement's secretary and organiser, and the editor of its magazine, *Pendulum*. In a speech to the inaugural meeting Elliott deplored the proliferation of inferior American films in Australia as part of the phenomenon that was to become known as American cultural imperialism.

Elliott promoted Pendulum objectives assiduously. He personally funded prizes for the best essays written by Ballarat College students (as adjudicated by an Ormond history and economics lecturer) in answer to the question 'How do I serve the Empire by buying Empire goods?' As guest speaker at the Bendigo RSSILA's commemorative dinner on the tenth anniversary of the Armistice, Elliott urged his audience to 'go out of their way to support British trade and British manufacturers'. If Australians 'took as many of Britain's products as possible, Britain could absorb all [our] products'. It was 'a policy of mutual benefit', he explained. When Sir Granville Ryrie, the former AIF general and Nationalist minister who had become Australia's High Commissioner in London, was quoted in the press as having denigrated British cars, Pompey fired off a vigorous telegram to Latham:

> Agents British cars here strongly protest statement allegedly made Sir Granville Ryrie published Sunday Times Sydney ... derogatory British cars. Have written fully Prime Minister. Letter should be delivered this morning. Those concerned desire Cabinet take immediate action.

Violet Elliott was continuing to progress well at Fintona. She certainly impressed Beatrice Chilvers, who taught at the school throughout the 1920s (and for more than three subsequent decades), and clearly remembered Violet more than half a century after her last year at Fintona. Violet was tall, and attractive in both appearance and manner, Beatrice Chilvers recalled; she mixed well with her peers, and possessed 'unmistakeable fibre' and maturity:

> It was not that she was old for her age, but she had a most marked quiet dignity—any adult would have been struck by it ... Not strikingly academic, she was highly intelligent and in charge of herself as few are as schoolgirls ... She was reserved—if she had problems she wouldn't be likely to tell you about them. The fact that I can remember as much of Violet after all this time is [confirmation of her special qualities, because] I can remember very little about only a couple of her contemporaries.

Violet's obvious integrity and strong facial resemblance to her father prompted assessments that she was more like him than Kate, but people who knew the Elliotts well were beginning to realise that Violet in fact embodied the best attributes of both her parents. A schoolfriend recalled Violet's fascination with flowers and trees—she once said she 'didn't need to go to church because God was in the trees'—and her affinity for English. She was familiar with a great deal of poetry and could write a good essay. When her class had to produce a composition entitled 'If I Had a Bicycle', none responded better than Violet. Her essay so impressed her father that he bought her one as a surprise (and then became concerned about her safety because she loved it so much she rode it everywhere, including to school).

In 1926 Violet sat for her first public examination. The Intermediate examination was intended to be suitable for sixteen-year-olds, but Violet was fifteen when she tackled it. Her preference for humanities subjects was already apparent. Shunning physics and chemistry, arithmetic and geometry (and drawing and Latin), she sat for English, French, botany, history, music, geography, and algebra, and passed all but the last two. She had therefore secured five of the six passes she needed for her Intermediate Certificate. Algebra continued to be a struggle, but her perseverance eventually paid off. While grappling with the intricacies of Intermediate algebra again in 1927, Violet tackled her strong suits—English, French, and botany—at Leaving level, and passed all three. She was thinking about following her father into the law. Popular among her peers and liked by her teachers, she became one of eight school prefects in 1928 and chaired the committee responsible for producing the *Fintonian*. Its May 1928 issue contained an impressive editorial about the evolution of aviation as well as a poem by Violet, possibly inspired by the superb garden setting at 56 Prospect Hill Road. Pompey followed her progress devotedly. His association with Fintona remained close. He addressed the whole school at its 1925 speech night, and remained a hero to many Fintona students; Violet's botany teacher even became a family friend. An announcement at the final school assembly for 1928 made him prouder than ever: the following year Violet would be head prefect of Fintona.

Elliott also had a close association with his son's school. Neil's parents had transferred him from Camberwell Grammar to Scotch College. In prestige Camberwell Grammar was not a patch on Scotch.

One of the leading private schools in Australia, Scotch was a bastion of traditional Presbyterian orthodoxy, where boys were encouraged and exhorted to strive and achieve; it had close links to an institution with similar values that Pompey knew well, Ormond College. Critics condemned Scotch as an exam factory that inculcated superiority and smugness, conformity and complacent conservatism. Devotees pointed to its polished products, those distinguished 'Old Boys' whose accomplishments added lustre to their former school. Elliott had known some of them well in the AIF; the most famous Old Scotch Collegian of all was Sir John Monash.

Neil Elliott was placed in Monash House after he started at Scotch as a twelve-year-old in 1925. He soon found that he had inherited his father's nickname; throughout his years at Scotch he was known as 'Young Pompey'. This was hardly surprising—his father was such a household name that at schools all over Victoria in the 1920s boys surnamed Elliott were liable to be known as Pompey. Neil was developing into a sturdy, self-reliant enthusiast of outdoors pursuits. He could make friends well enough, but had an essentially reserved temperament. His satisfactory scholastic results were a product of hard work more than a first-rate intellect. Photography was an absorbing hobby, and he was a dedicated rower, but he enjoyed camping, hiking, and 'adventure' most of all. When Scotch started its own Scout troop, Neil became a keen participant.

His father wholeheartedly supported Neil's involvement with the Scouts. To Pompey, the aims and ideals of the Scout movement were admirable; he encouraged Neil's participation to the hilt. Sometimes father and son went hiking together. Neil became a patrol leader in 1928. An early priority for the Scotch Scouts was to get hold of some land for a bush headquarters. To help pave the way financially, they organised a Hobbies Exhibition which raised £40; in the Australian Stamps category Neil's collection was awarded first prize. But it was hard to find land near Melbourne that was available, within their means, and with accessible water.

Eventually, at a memorable parents' meeting in 1928, General Elliott offered to donate part of the bushland he owned at Chum Creek near Healesville. The scouts and their parents arranged to meet at the property weeks later to inspect it, but that October Saturday proved to be one of the wettest ever recorded. Nevertheless a band of hardy souls led by the general himself tramped around in torrential rain; the visitors liked what they saw, and his offer was gratefully accepted. Five acres were formally transferred from Belle (who was, as with the Frankston property, the legal owner) to a group of trustees. The Scotch Scouts were soon using their new headquarters for camps, and discussing whether to devote the £40 they had raised to the construction of a hut.

Not since the climactic 1918 battles had Elliott been so busy. The multitudinous demands on his time were relentless. Being a senator who treated his parliamentary responsibilities seriously while the principal of a law firm and the commander of a division would have stretched anyone, but that was only the start. Pompey was active in numerous other spheres. In 1927, in addition to accepting the inaugural presidency of the Pendulum Club, he became president of the Law Institute of Victoria. He was still a member of the board of management of the Melbourne Hospital, and a director of the National Trustees Executors and Agency Company. As well as involving himself at Fintona and Scotch, he continued to be an influential identity at the colleges that were significant in his own education. At Ballarat College, where a succession of students were benefiting from his generous endowments, he became a member of the school council in 1926. And he remained on both the Ormond College council and the committee of the Old Ormond Students' Association throughout the 1920s; when financial difficulties threatened the publication and distribution of the Ormond magazine the *Chronicle*, he came to the rescue by announcing he would provide the shortfall himself.

Military activities took up much of his time, as they had for most of his adult life. On many a Saturday he was to be found at the Williamstown rifle range scrutinising the shooting. In September 1928 he and Kate hosted what the *Age* described as the Third Division's 'brilliant ball', where there was 'a wealth of splendid colour'. He was still in high demand as guest speaker at returned soldier gatherings. There were, in particular, the various ex-AIF reunions around Anzac Day and Show Week. He tried to attend them all—not just the 7th Battalion functions, but get-togethers of 15th Brigade units as well. In 1928 the annual reunions of the 57th and 59th Battalions were held on the same evening; he was guest of honour at each function, and managed to attend both. At the 58th reunion the following night he found everyone else attired in special paper hats. His had mysteriously disappeared, and he was presented with a 'replacement' inscribed with the words 'Pompey's hat. Not to be pinched'.

Moreover, Elliott's public renown made him a target for journalists hunting for quotable quotes. This occurred most often on issues affecting returned soldiers or in response to the latest British 'revelations' concerning the AIF. But he was not only approached in connection with military concerns. He was, for example, one of the 'business men of wider outlook' prepared to publicly endorse a proposed foundation to assist scholarly publications in Australia: 'the whole country benefits from the work of these writers', Pompey testified. Elliott also kept a shrewd eye on the value of properties he had acquired; in 1928 he sold part of his Frankston land, and at the instigation of his brother-in-law, Queenslander John Avery, had a small flutter in a speculative oil-exploration venture at Roma. He somehow found the time to keep in touch with Milly Edwards and other British relatives he had met during the war; he sent them primary produce, publications (including *Pendulum*), shares in his Canberra building company, and newsy letters covering current events, his children's latest doings, and his own wide-ranging activities. One of his English cousins could not imagine how he managed it all: 'Does a 24 hour day suffice or have you a secret means of expanding them over there'?

Invitations to unveil memorials continued to accumulate. What the AIF did in the war was 'getting to be an old story now', Elliott said at a ceremony near Creswick in December 1927, but it was worth reaffirming that the inspirational deeds their countrymen had performed were second to none in all recorded history. 'Nothing had occurred in any war that the Australians had not matched', he reiterated, before confronting with characteristic candour the toughest question of all (especially for bereaved relatives)—had all the horror and slaughter, the terrible waste, the deaths of 60,000 of Australia's finest, been worthwhile? Yes, indeed it had, he insisted, to keep Australia secure. 'No one who had not seen war could understand what it meant', and in 1918 the Germans had been perilously close to a victory that would have had catastrophic implications for the future of Australia and Australians.

But of all the demands on Elliott, the pressure he felt most acutely stemmed from the constant requests he received to help struggling returned soldiers. To Charles Noad, the former 15th Brigade officer who saw Elliott often in the later 1920s when they were both prime movers in the Pendulum Club, Pompey seemed increasingly burdened by the post-war troubles of men who had served under him. Ina Prictor, who stayed at Prospect Hill Road when visiting Melbourne, was struck by the frequency of the phone calls Elliott received from returned soldiers seeking assistance. One morning she accompanied him into the city as he commuted to the office; when they had found seats together on the train he began thinking about the day ahead, and became so immersed in what he had to do that he forgot she was there. It was not that he was rude—he was, in fact, considerate and genial. It was, she realised, simply a result of having so much on his plate. Like Noad, she had no doubt that the ordeals many returned soldiers were enduring was his greatest concern.

Even when Elliott's multifarious activities were clustered in Melbourne (apart from a commitment in rural Victoria now and again) it was difficult to find time for them all. After the transfer of federal parliament to Canberra it became harder still. His absentmindedness on trains was also evident during the long trips to and from the national capital; on several occasions he managed to alight without his briefcase (he was so well known and liked that it was always handed in). In September 1928, to enable him to attend an engagement in his home city, he was flown from Canberra to Melbourne. It was apparently his first plane trip, and he found it fascinating; he had already publicised the advisability of senior commanders, as recommended by the War Office in London, familiarising themselves with aerial reconnaissance.

As he did in Melbourne, Pompey bustled about purposefully in Canberra. One day in Parliament House he was hurrying across King's Hall towards the Senate chamber when he slipped on the polished jarrah surface and executed such a spectacular slide on his back that he ended up entering the chamber in arrestingly horizontal style, feet first. This amusing incident led to a less zealous polishing regime. Reduced cleaning costs at Parliament House enabled newspapers to announce that '"Pompey" Elliott's Slip May Save Australia Money'.

The government Elliott continued to support (while reserving the right to criticise it and vote against it on some issues, Canberra land administration in particular) was a government of limited horizons. Prime Minister Bruce, whose deceptively languid manner masked a steely resolve—he dominated his government and his party—had a narrow view of his government's role. A 'country was best governed' when it 'was governed least', he said. The economy was the 'be all and end all'. Bruce saw himself essentially as its managing director; men, money, and markets were important objectives to pursue, but management of the economy on sound business principles was crucial. Businessmen like himself—provided they were successful—were, in Bruce's eyes, paragons of civic virtue. He even displayed a much-discussed tendency to deal with troublesome policy issues by setting up a board or commission of inquiry headed by a businessman. It is true that he was inconsistent, and occasionally intervened to fetter the operations of private enterprise when it suited his political objectives, sometimes incurring the wrath of his more forthright and independently inclined backbenchers, such as Pompey Elliott, in the process.

But certainly never before, and perhaps not since, has there been an Australian government more single-minded about serving the needs of business. Under the Bruce–Page government unemployment was regarded as undesirable because of its adverse implications for the overall economy rather than the suffering of the individuals directly affected. Welfare and culture were shamefully neglected, income tax was almost halved, and the Prime Minister's aloof detachment from the reality of widespread poverty in Australia was confirmed by his assertion that life was far too easy.

Industrial relations dominated a series of election campaigns during the 1920s. In 1925 the contentious legislation the Bruce–Page government had introduced just before going to the people had much to do with its election victory, but when its amendment to the Immigration Act was invalidated by the High Court soon afterwards, Bruce and his new Attorney-General, Latham, had to go back to the drawing board. With Australia's foreign debt rising and the Prime Minister continuing to be preoccupied with boosting business efficiency and taking vigorous action against strike leaders, the result was a renewed resolve to cut the cost of labour. The government acted on a variety of fronts to achieve reductions in both workers' pay and industrial disputes. Amendments to the Arbitration Act clearly signalled the government's intentions on wages, and draconian measures were introduced to deal with recalcitrant strikers.

Bitter disputes ensued. In August 1928 an Arbitration Court judge handed down a deliberately provocative award affecting the maritime transport industry; his aim, he told Latham, was to incite the wharf labourers into a strike that would ultimately result in the excision of 'unreasonably militant' elements from their union. Resistance from the Waterside Workers' Federation was predictably fierce. With a federal election imminent, the government rushed a repressive Transport Workers Act through parliament; among wharfies it was loathed as the 'Dog Collar Act'. The coalition retained office at the election, but its campaign emphasis on industrial relations proved less effective than it had in 1925. While the government remained unassailably dominant in the Senate, its majority in the House of Representatives was significantly reduced.

In 1929 substantial disputes escalated in other industries. As with the wharf labourers, a bitter strike among timber workers was sparked by an award imposed by another Arbitration Court judge responsive to the government's desire to slash wages and conditions. This decision, by a reactionary judge who had been appointed by Bruce and Latham, was condemned by the Australian Council of Trade Unions as 'the most iniquitous award ever proposed by any Arbitration Court in Australia', and the timber workers refused to accept it. For speaking out in support of their defiance, E.J. Holloway, secretary of the Melbourne Trades Hall Council, was prosecuted and fined. Meanwhile a searing dispute was convulsing the New South Wales coalfields. The employers proceeded there without any Arbitration Court imprimatur, and simply told the miners that they would be sacked unless they accepted reduced wages and conditions. The most notorious proprietor, wealthy colliery owner John Brown, told miners that they would either have to capitulate or eat grass. The workers bitterly resented what they saw as an orchestrated offensive against them, aided and abetted by the Bruce–Page government. Resistance was committed and effective, particularly in the timber workers' dispute, and it consolidated opposition to the coalition.

The Prime Minister became increasingly frustrated. He sensed that Australia's economic situation and his government's popularity were both in serious decline, and he felt that the arbitration system was 'becoming a farce'. Bruce prepared a surprise for the May 1929 Premiers Conference. He decided to announce that the system of overlapping state and federal awards was proving unworkable: as a result, unless the states were prepared to relinquish their industrial relations powers so this troublesome issue could be handled properly on a national basis, his government would remove itself from the arbitration arena. This abdication proposal was 'certainly drastic', Bruce admitted.

Because such a stark and sudden reversal of government policy would obviously be a bombshell, he decided to give Nationalist backbenchers some warning beforehand. Telegrams were sent to dozens of MPs, including Pompey Elliott: 'Government is proposing to States that either they immediately give full powers to Commonwealth or ... Commonwealth repeals its industrial legislation'. It was immediately clear that there was no prospect of the premiers ceding their powers; accordingly, Bruce affirmed, his government would be withdrawing from the arbitration process almost entirely. There was uproar in response to these startling developments, but Elliott replied to Bruce's notification with an unequivocal telegram: 'Will support your policy industrial legislation to limit. H.E. Elliott'.

CHAPTER TWENTY-FOUR

'The Injustice ... Has Actually Colored All My Post War Life': Disintegration

1929-MARCH 1931

WHILE ELLIOTT STRONGLY supported Bruce's bombshell, not all his Nationalist colleagues did. Hughes, sensing an opportunity to pursue revenge for his removal from the prime ministership six years earlier, moved in parliament that such a drastic turnaround in government policy should not be implemented without prior endorsement from the people. Bruce responded that if this unpalatable motion was carried he would regard it as a vote of no-confidence in his government. With the stakes unambiguously high, Hughes harvested discontented Nationalists. Other issues besides the arbitration somersault were preoccupying these Nationalist dissidents. Bruce and Latham had withdrawn the prosecution launched against John Brown for initiating a lockout; this decision prompted predictable and damaging accusations that under this government there was one law for the rich and another for the poor. The imposition of an entertainment tax was also contentious; Elliott, like all federal MPs, was inundated with 'propaganda' (as he called it) from activists hostile to this new tax. Hughes's skilful manoeuvring paid handsome dividends. His motion was narrowly carried on 10 September, parliament was dissolved, and another election followed a month later.

Elliott agreed to speak at Caulfield Town Hall on 30 September in support of the Nationalist MHR for Balaclava, T.W. White. This was the same Tom White who had been Elliott's fierce antagonist in that cringingly petty affair, the smoke-night saga of 1913. Since then White had distinguished himself during the war as a gallant pilot and a daring escaper from the Turks, and had written a vivid account of his experiences, *Guests of the Unspeakable.* He and Elliott had long ago resolved their pre-war differences, and Pompey was happy to support his campaign.

But their association was once again scarred by a bizarre episode. At the end of Elliott's speech questions were invited from the audience, and an old man at the back of the hall responded. Varying versions of his query were reported, but it was something like this: 'If you lose the election, are you going to take off your coat and do a hard day's work for once instead of wasting money?' The question touched a raw nerve. Elliott leapt from the stage, strode down the aisle towards the questioner and, amid a mounting chorus of boos, remonstrated with him, evidently trying to eject him, before being dissuaded. When order was restored, Pompey admitted that he had taken the question as a personal and unwarranted barb, having toiled for long hours from an early age on his family's struggling farm at Charlton.

White managed to retain Balaclava in spite of Elliott's assistance, but many coalition colleagues lost their seats. It was a Labor landslide. Even Prime Minister Bruce lost his seat, defeated by the union leader his government had prosecuted, E.J. Holloway. For the first time in his decade-long political career, Elliott had to adjust to being in opposition.

Another development of immense significance to Elliott in 1929 was the publication of Volume III of the Australian *Official History.* Bean's comprehensive research and readable style was again evident as he covered the AIF in 1916 in just under 1,000 pages of impressively detailed narrative that featured the post-Gallipoli expansion of the AIF, its involvement in the Somme offensive, and the dreadful winter that followed. There was no more enthusiastic or appreciative reader of Bean's work and no more penetrating critic of it than Pompey Elliott, and he lost no time in giving the historian a frank preliminary assessment:

> I have just read through a first time your third Volume. It is a story of unrelieved tragedy throughout but I think you have got most of the main facts relating to the fighting correct. On the whole, however, it does appear to me that you have strained your conscience in the endeavour to let the Higher Commands down as lightly as possible.

The 1916 episode of overriding importance to Elliott was, of course, the disaster of Fromelles. Having read and reflected a great deal about that battle, he was already convinced that Haking was the main culprit. The revelation in Volume III that Haking had been implicated in a similar fiasco—the Boar's Head operation—a few weeks earlier was stunning confirmation to Elliott of both Haking's culpability and Bean's exceptional diligence and skill in distilling the essential facts after sifting through a vast array of information. However, Elliott felt that Bean was less convincing in the deductions he drew from those facts. On Fromelles, for example, he felt that Bean should have been more critical of Haking, and he challenged the historian's conclusion that the result of the battle was more attributable to the failure of the supporting bombardment than the width of no-man's-land.

Pompey also disputed Bean's suggestion that Brudenell White had disapproved of the unjustifiable attacks attempted towards the end of the Somme offensive. He asserted that when he (Elliott) had made a vigorous protest about a proposed advance in impossible conditions at Flers, White had dismissed his misgivings 'as due to failure of nerves'. In fact, concluded Elliott, White 'was in no way opposed to the policy of these attacks at the time'. And it was odd, Elliott continued, that such a long and detailed volume did not feature that protest of his, which had 'surely' been a significant development. Elliott had briefed Bean about it in 1927. (The historian sometimes aired his irritation when AIF officers declined to assist his research by divulging their firsthand knowledge of a particular engagement, yet later had the effrontery to criticise alleged inaccuracies in the *Official History* account of that very engagement. This was not something Bean could ever say about Pompey, who inundated him with material throughout the 1920s.)

Bean's reply to Elliott contained more than a hint of weary resignation about the impossibility of satisfying everyone:

> I have to thank you for your letter. Like everything else that you write, it will have full consideration when the several matters to which it relates are being studied. I have an enormous mass of material, and all I can do is to endeavour to arrive at a fair judgment and leave it at that, for criticism or otherwise, as readers think fit.

The only specific query from Pompey that Bean responded to was the *History*'s non-reference to the 15th Brigade's stint at Flers:

> the sole reason why the tour was not mentioned was that no active fighting occurred in it, and the conditions of the line had already been described ... It was a difficult job to compress the winter fighting into two chapters.

The historian's brief reply prompted Pompey to elaborate on his initial response to Volume III. Having now read the whole volume a second time, he was at pains to reiterate his admiration for Bean's capacity to unearth the key facts and to tell the story so well, despite the difficulties imposed by the need for compression and the magnitude of the task. 'Many thanks for your letter', he began:

> I certainly realize your difficulties and appreciate your patience and industry in dealing with such an enormous mass of material. That will be your monument—this accurate condensation of the mass of evidence. I accept your assurance that the 15th Brigade tour of duty in the line was omitted because of lack of space—I feared indeed that its records had been sunk 'like the Lusitania' without leaving a trace.

He enclosed extracts from his diary to emphasise the significance of what had happened at Flers before stating his main reservation about the *Official History*: 'Where you cease to deal with the facts and proceed to inferences from facts it does appear that you are inviting severe criticism'. Pompey's ensuing review of numerous incidents and engagements, four times longer even than his initial nine-page letter about Volume III, was fervent and candid:

> Hobbs, a gunner, had mighty little idea of infantry tactics. Birdwood had none that I could ever discern; White knew the theory ... but because the enemy had one flank in the sea and the other in Switzerland and thus presented no chance for cavalry to ride round his outer flanks he fell back on frontal attacks as the only thing left, and the same idea seemed to be common to the whole British staff.

It was, as Elliott realised, Bean's veneration of White that skewed his conclusions and had much to do with the *Official History*'s analytical shortcomings. (White was 'a man I worshipped', Bean was to admit after learning of his hero's death in 1940. 'I could never believe he was wrong in anything, and indeed I never found him so'.) Pompey's respect and regard for the historian was considerable, but he characteristically did not shy away from frank and direct criticism, accusing Bean of writing about White more like an 'advocate' than 'the impartial judge' he should be:

> You have I think allowed yourself to succumb entirely to White's exceptionally charming manner which is undeniable, and proceeded to paint him entirely as he would wish to be presented to the Jury of his countrymen ... You have also I think consciously or unconsciously permitted yourself to absorb without full examination his point of view upon [a range of subjects].

But Elliott's genuine appreciation of the virtues of Bean's history was evident in the conclusion to his lengthy letter:

> You are doing such wonderful work ... that I admire so much that I hate even to seem to cavil at any part of it. Go right ahead elicit the whole truth and set it down fearlessly as you are doing. No one is bound to accept your deductions if they prove wrong. It is the facts after all that we really want. All else will come out in the wash.

A feature of Bean's third volume that did please Elliott was its treatment of McCay, his immediate superior in 1916. McCay's wide-spread unpopularity stemmed from his aloof, abrasive personality and his association with three notorious AIF episodes—the Krithia charge, the desert march, and the Fromelles disaster. Having long felt that McCay had been unfairly blamed for these fiascos, Elliott was 'delighted' by Bean's exoneration of McCay in Volume III. The historian was unequivocal:

> The case of McCay may indeed stand as a classic example in Australia of the gross injustice of such popular verdicts, he having been loaded with the blame for three costly undertakings ... for none of which was he, in fact, any more responsible than the humblest private in his force.

This issue was a feature of two appraisals in the *Bulletin* on 8 May 1929 that were among the earliest published responses to Bean's new volume. A review headed 'A Year of Horror' praised Bean's 'admirably clear and simple style', but suggested that his exoneration of McCay was unjustified; Bean's 'natural amiability' was a 'weakness' in a historian because it deprived him of 'the capacity for indignation'. The same *Bulletin* issue also included a separate article entitled 'Was General McCay to Blame?' by a contributor calling himself 'Miltiades', who likewise felt that Bean had not substantiated his exoneration of McCay.

These *Bulletin* articles constituted 'the first sign' that Elliott had noticed of 'operations under Birdwood' being seen 'in their true perspective', and he felt impelled to respond. He sent two articles to the *Bulletin* under a pseudonym of his own, 'Xenophon'. 'I desire to remain strictly anonymous', he emphasised in a covering letter, 'because having already suffered sufficiently from my habit of free criticism, I do not wish to again come into conflict with military authority', especially now 'General Chauvel has been able on White's departure from Army Headquarters to lift the ban against my further employment'.

On 22 May 1929 the *Bulletin* published a response to Miltiades from Xenophon. Confronting the question 'Was General McCay to Blame?' directly, Xenophon answered with an emphatic no—not for Krithia, not for the desert march, and not for Fromelles either. In the *Official History*'s account of Krithia, Xenophon asserted, 'McCay is rightly absolved from all blame'. Such blame properly rested with 'General Weston Hunter' (the double-barrelled surname was back-to-front in the article Elliott submitted, and the error was uncorrected in the published version in the *Bulletin*), although Hamilton 'cannot escape responsibility altogether'. Concerning Fromelles,

> Bean has disclosed sufficient evidence to finally establish that McCay was not to blame for the order to attack. He might have made some protest, it is true. But ... if, as Bean states, [Birdwood and White] were throughout opposed to the attack, they cannot escape from the damning circumstances that they allowed this hopeless thing to proceed without protest ... [H]eavy responsibility lies on Haking, who afterwards attempted to throw the blame upon the infantry ... Haig's action in the matter was weak. He appears to

> have been far too easily satisfied by Haking, particularly as the latter was already known as more or less of a failure.

As for the desert march, Xenophon pronounced, 'there is no longer any doubt that … General McCay was not to blame for ordering it'. Having protested against the direction to march his brigade across the desert, 'McCay had done all that was possible to an officer of his rank' (though whether 'his protest against it was vigorous enough is another matter'). In all this the identity of Xenophon was obscure, but Pompey could not resist a revealing insertion about himself. While analysing the desert march controversy Xenophon included a compelling account of the vigorous action taken by 'Elliott' to obtain the water his men desperately needed. 'Elliott from that day never received any further promotion in the AIF', Xenophon continued, 'although senior to others who superseded him in France'.

Elliott's other contribution as Xenophon, a response to the *Bulletin* review of Bean's Volume III, appeared in the following issue of the famous weekly. There had been an inappropriate focus on McCay's role in the lead-up to Fromelles, Xenophon contended, when the neglect of Birdwood and White to intervene was much more reprehensible. As for the *Bulletin* reviewer's charge that Bean was insufficiently indignant about

> that year of horror—his job surely is to elicit and record the truth and leave the indignation to be registered by his readers and the Government. That duty he has tried hard to discharge, but circumstances have been too strong for him. [During the war, as official correspondent, he] represented Birdwood as the Soul of Anzac and White as the divinely-gifted staff officer whose lynx-eyed vigilance foresaw every difficulty, anticipated every obstacle … Later Bean was made official historian … How can he pull aside the curtain and display the clay feet of these colossi that he has so painfully built up? … It would seem like treachery to his friends to reveal all. So he has attempted to steer a middle course—to put down the facts, but to camouflage the awkward ones discreetly or pass them gently by.
>
> His estimates of some officers are particularly suspect. They are colored far too deeply by his associations. Legge is an able man, but

> something was lacking; Monash has a brilliant brain, but is no fighting man; Leane the bravest of the brave, but disobeyed orders on the battlefield; Elliott valiant but rash, and with a childlike faith in obsolete rules of tactics. When all is said, there will remain, apparently, but one flawless constellation in Bean's universe—the glorious Birdwood-White Combine.

The only notable Australian commanders to be treated differently by Bean, according to Xenophon, were Gellibrand and Glasgow, whose 'virtues are carefully extolled' in the *Official History*. Both pre-war comrades of White, they were 'the only prominent commanders who have so far escaped sneer or censure'. Xenophon also directly accused Birdwood and White of ordering 'as is well known ... on more than one occasion ... the destruction of original reports, messages and orders', which made it harder for Bean to ascertain 'the full truth'. This controversial allegation was, however, toned down in the published version in the *Bulletin*, which included the allegation that destruction of records had occurred, but deleted the forthright assertion that it was Birdwood and White who had ordered it. A concluding flourish from Xenophon, however, appeared in the *Bulletin* essentially intact:

> Bean's succeeding volumes will undoubtedly form most interesting reading and will be eagerly awaited. Whether they can be the last word on the subject is another question.

Debate in the *Bulletin* continued. 'T.T.T.' claimed that 'Fromelles was not the impossibility it is now alleged to have been', and the 'idea that a soldier can protest against an order from a superior is something new'; while a few AIF commanders may have had a crack at it, 'never under any circumstances did they extend the right to their subordinates'. Again Pompey sent a rejoinder to the *Bulletin*, this time styling himself 'X.X.X.'. He dismissed the suggestion that Fromelles was anything but 'impregnable', and maintained that a commander's right to protest was 'by no means new'. Protesting in the AIF was 'difficult', however, because 'Birdwood expected to be treated by every subordinate as the captain of the football XV of an English public school expects to be treated by his fag'. Allowing an occasional right to protest encouraged 'originality, enterprise and initiative', and was not, as alleged by T.T.T., 'hostile to discipline'. Moreover, each 'time a commander protests he puts his reputation at stake'; he would soon lose it if his concerns proved repeatedly unwarranted.

> But the resolute protest of a brave and capable subordinate ... against what he honestly considers an impossible attack, especially when it is known that he has personally reconnoitred the position and bases his opinion on the knowledge thus gained against his superior who has not had that opportunity, may cause the latter to think deeply before he will overrule his subordinate. Undoubtedly the superior has the right to the final say and the subordinate must in the last resort obey. In view, however, of the fact that the recorded protest may arise to damn him in the future, such an action may act as a powerful deterrent against a hasty and ill-considered determination to attack.

T.T.T. had another go, again disputing the right to protest and the impregnability of Fromelles. In a further reply, published in the *Bulletin* on 7 August, Elliott (writing once more as X.X.X.) accused T.T.T. of not reading Bean's Volume III and being ignorant about Fromelles; he also cited a British corps commander's 'most emphatic protest' against the continuation of the Somme offensive in November 1916. Another contributor, '927', contended (in a further substantiation of McCay's blamelessness) that incompetent organisation below divisional level contributed substantially to the Fromelles disaster; operational details were bandied about within earshot of 'half the civilian population', and bombs were sent forward without detonators. Pompey rebutted 927 firmly, too, this time using the pseudonym '303', and reiterated that chief culpability was not attributable to anyone in the AIF: the 'slaughter of the 15th Brigade occurred almost wholly in No Man's Land long before they could use a bomb'. The entire *Bulletin* debate lasted three months.

Pompey was hardly a detached commentator, of course, but his criticisms of Bean's work were compelling. Haking was indeed chiefly responsible for Fromelles, and Bean could well have criticised him more vigorously in Volume III. Moreover, it was, to say the least, peculiar that the official history of the AIF prominently quoted the 'strong protest' of a British general commanding a separate corps undertaking a separate operation, while referring to the forceful protest of a famous AIF general in a similar context in a way that was, in comparison, understated and not couched as a protest. Might Bean's wording, Pompey wondered, be not entirely unrelated to the reflection on the historian's hero implicit in his protest?

Elliott had a good case concerning his initial colonels, too. During Bean's dedicated roving throughout the AIF as official correspondent he had repeatedly observed the clear connection between a unit's performance and the calibre of its leadership; time and again he had noticed it and noted it in his diary. That perception would presumably have predisposed Bean to write approvingly in Volume III about Elliott's endeavours to replace three of the four battalion commanders Birdwood and White had given him upon the formation of the 15th Brigade. However, Pompey felt that Bean had let White off lightly once again in his coverage of this issue. The historian had stressed Elliott's 'precipitancy' and 'headstrong' pursuit of his unwanted commanders' removal, and had also drawn the soft conclusion that it was merely 'at least arguable' that the AIF's overall efficiency would have been enhanced if appointments by Birdwood and White that Bean clearly regarded as unsuitable—including the three commanders Pompey objected to—had never been made. Later in 1929, when Bean tried to reassure an aggrieved widow that the portrayal of her husband (a 52nd Battalion captain) in Volume III as someone whose outspokenness had retarded his promotion was 'intended' as 'a noble tribute', he went on to assert that 'no one can peruse these volumes without realising that the writer's sympathy is on the side of the outspoken man every time'. The treatment of Pompey Elliott in the *Official History* does not substantiate Bean's claim.

While Volume III confirmed for Elliott the limitations of Bean's history as far as his personal interests were concerned, he recognised that Australia was fortunate to have an official chronicler of the utmost dedication and decency who was writing innovative military history of a higher quality than had ever been produced anywhere. Elliott and Bean remained on good terms and in close contact: later in 1929 they corresponded extensively about the advanced-guard operations commanded by Elliott in March 1917 to be featured in Bean's next volume. Pompey kept hankering for ultimate vindication from Bean. 'Now that you have elicited the truth in regard to General McCay, I am looking forward to your clearing me from the stigma placed upon me by being superseded in the field', he reiterated. He even revived the query he had raised in 1922 about Bean's portrayal of him in Volume I:

> I am waiting until you are at the end of your History to hear your evidence as to my being 'rash and headstrong'. I am hopeful that as you go along you will discover that, so far from these traits characterising me, I was often compelled to imperil my own career in order to prevent rash or ill-considered action in others senior to me.

A perfect example, he contended, was the controversy concerning the three unsuitable colonels initially allotted to him in March 1916. However, while Elliott kept hoping against hope for an ultimately favourable verdict from Bean, he reluctantly accepted after reading Volume III that the vindication he desired was unlikely to materialise in the *Official History*. This unfulfilled yearning was increasingly gnawing at him, undermining his peace of mind. He decided to pursue other avenues of redress.

On 13 June 1929 Elliott wrote to Hobbs. His wartime supersession was still rankling, he declared frankly, and he wanted to clarify why Birdwood and White had overlooked him in 1918:

> I would be greatly obliged if you could ... set out as far as it was officially or unofficially revealed to you just wherein my supposed offences lay. I propose to file your reply together with a copy of this letter with Major Treloar the Director of the War Museum so that it may be available upon research to any historian of the future who may be interested in the matter. I am of opinion that Captain Bean from his long association with Corps Headquarters has become so saturated with their particular point of view that I cannot hope for an impartial Verdict from that source.

For Hobbs in faraway Western Australia this was an unexpected and difficult request. His main response was predictable: he did not know precisely why Birdwood had rejected Elliott in 1918. While Hobbs did not deny that 'your impulsiveness and want of tact on more than one occasion caused me serious concern and trouble', his letter was full of praise for Elliott's 'courage and capacity' as a 'gallant able' leader whose 'untiring energy initiative and determination' and devotion to the welfare of his men had won him their 'respect and affection' to a remarkable degree. Hobbs assured Elliott that 'few men I know have more cause for pride and satisfaction' about their war service, and 'you have no cause to worry about your record and reputation as a soldier'.

But Pompey would not be deterred, and pressed Hobbs again:

> The injustice of the position as I conceive it has actually colored all my post war life ... Such an obsession I recognise is not good medicine and I desire to have the thing set at rest. Possibly I may be quite mistaken in my ideas on the subject, nevertheless I repeat I am determined to have it stated in black and white just in what my disqualification lay.

Hobbs, truly perplexed now, did his utmost to soothe Elliott's great hurt. 'Please remember that I have never been a bar to your promotion and if you make enquiries you will find that few of your friends have been more loyal to you or have spoken better of you than I have'. Moreover, 'I really am deeply concerned that you should worry yourself unnecessarily in connection with the past'.

In September 1929 Elliott turned to McCay. Expressing his satisfaction with the sweeping exoneration of McCay in the *Official History* after the 'unjust blame' he had endured—'I doubt if anyone else would have borne it so philosophically and ... I have often urged Bean to be sure to do what he has now done'—Pompey went on to ask for a formal appraisal of his war service from McCay as his immediate superior. McCay obliged:

> Throughout all his service under me, even in such trying circumstances as the Battle of Fromelles, I found him loyal, capable and efficient and the exhibitor of great personal courage. Both in training and in action he fulfilled all my expectations of him.

Elliott even wrote to London in search of a testimonial from Plumer, the 72-year-old former army commander, asking him to confirm the glowing praise he had lavished on the 15th Brigade in 1917 for its contribution at Polygon Wood.

Elliott also approached Monash. 'I have never been able to ascertain just what General Birdwood found fault with in me', he wrote, asking Monash to 'let me know whether General Birdwood ever imparted to you this secret offence of mine'. Once again he stated his intention of placing 'these letters in the War Museum so that my family may have an answer to any charge of incompetence brought after my death'. Monash, like Hobbs, was concerned about Elliott's frame of mind, and compiled a sensitive and carefully worded reply:

> Your letter ... perturbed me, because I felt sorry to think that you were still worrying about real or fancied wrongs of the war days, and that you were concerned about your personal reputation. Many of us felt similar grievances at one time or another, but most of us have forgotten about them. I know that I have ... What actuated General Birdwood in making the selections I cannot possibly say, for I do not know. That he actually did withhold promotion from you because of some 'secret offence' I regard as out of the question. I never heard then, or at any time since, any whisper reflecting upon your capacity or fitness for the command of a Division; and I could scarcely have failed to hear of it.
>
> I have myself felt that the affection and confidence of the men of the AIF was worth a great deal more to me than any empty honors. This same affection and confidence you have enjoyed in rich measure, and no one can question that it was well deserved. After all, you commanded a celebrated Brigade during the period of its greatest successes. There were only four men on the Western Front (the Commanders of your Division, Corps and Army and the C.-in-C. himself) who were competent to give you any order. Is it not a great thing to have lived to play such a role in the greatest war in History? Then why worry as to the verdict of posterity upon so brilliant and soldierly a career?

However, not even such a considerate, generous, and supportive letter from the AIF general Elliott admired above all others could assuage his supersession fixation.

Also profoundly unsettling for Elliott was Australia's calamitous economic depression. A heavy budget deficit and a balance of payments crisis had left Australia acutely vulnerable to external economic forces. In

1929 access to British loan finance underpinning Australia's development was tightened, and the New York Stock Exchange dramatically collapsed. Unemployment in Australia increased sharply, leading to widespread misery, insecurity, and anxiety. To Elliott, it was not just that the Great Depression was a phenomenon of catastrophic magnitude with appalling consequences for most Australians, struggling returned soldiers in particular. The primary responsibility for orchestrating Australia's response to this crisis rested with an inexperienced Labor government imbued with ideas and values that were repugnant to him.

The new government's capacity to deal with the economic crisis was hampered by the opposition's overwhelming supremacy in the Senate. The landslide that brought Labor to office under Jim Scullin had occurred at an election for the House of Representatives only. There had since been intermittent speculation that Labor might capitalise on its electoral momentum by forcing a double dissolution in order to boost its representation in the Senate. Within two months of the election Elliott felt moved to 'protest' against threats and intimidation about the fate of the Senate if it proved obdurate: 'I have always maintained that it is my privilege to oppose any legislation with which I do not agree', he declared, citing as examples his hostility to the 1921 Defence Bill and aspects of Canberra administration. Influential opposition senators, Pearce in particular, were keen to avoid an early confrontation with the government while Labor retained the popularity that had brought it to office, but Elliott expressed himself very differently. The Senate electoral process was 'equally as democratic' as the lower house's, he insisted, and opposition senators were 'entitled to influence legislation to the full extent of our authority'. The Scullin government had 'attained power' by pulling off 'the most colossal confidence trick in history', which 'combined the skill of the go-getter with the craft of the pick-pocket'.

Elliott quickly established himself as one of the government's most implacable opponents. Not long after the election he made an issue of a colourful ALP senator's acquisition of the nickname 'Digger'. Pompey ridiculed this step, reciting in the Senate the Registrar-General's document that formalised J.P. Dunn's decision to 'hereby ... absolutely adopt and assume the additional Christian name of "Digger"', and suggesting that Dunn 'could not have been too sure of his right to share in the glory attached to that name, so he took out patent rights for it'. Dunn retorted that he had served under Elliott's command, was as entitled to 'Digger' as Elliott was to 'Pompey', and proceeded to describe his former brigadier as 'bombastic' and 'stupid'. In April 1930, when *Smith's Weekly* published allegations of impropriety involving senior ministers and a John Wren mining venture in New Guinea, Elliott took it upon himself to raise the imputations in the Senate in order to publicise them further; Dunn and Attorney-General J.J. Daly accused Elliott of blatant muckraking.

Another strident Pompey tirade was described by Daly as 'a vile outburst' that 'accused' the government of 'almost every conceivable political crime'. Pompey's old foe McGrath asked retaliatory questions in the House of Representatives on successive days about Elliott's property interests in Canberra, pointedly suggesting that the government should be terminating its leases with his company as soon as possible. Elliott evidently expressed his resentment to McGrath, who responded with a stinging letter:

> You have no regard for the feelings of other men—yet you never miss an opportunity to assail others; but you are very sensitive to any disparaging reference to yourself. With reference to your Canberra property, you omit to mention that if it had not been for the action of the late Government, whom you no doubt mourn, in leasing your tenantless premises, they would still be tenantless, and your lamentations would no doubt be louder.

Pompey tore the letter up furiously.

One of the Scullin government's most controversial early decisions was the replacement of the longstanding compulsory military training scheme by a voluntary system. Elliott denounced this decision vehemently and repeatedly. Not only had the Scullin government 'filched from us our defence system'; it was undermining the sustained efforts of officers like himself who were battling uphill to make the new scheme work. It was exasperating and disheartening, he told Jamieson:

> The prospect of getting an efficient force seems so impossible under present conditions that I am seriously thinking of resigning from the Forces and if I were not in Parliament I would do so, but as many people would regard it merely as a political move on my part, I would not accomplish much.

He decided instead to publicise his concern about Australia's inadequate defence preparedness in the Melbourne *Herald*, deploring the skewed priorities of Australians who 'seem to regard defence as entirely a matter to be left to Providence' while finding 'the latest Test match scores of absorbing interest' (Don Bradman's record-breaking feats during the 1930 tour of England had commenced).

Scullin's Defence minister, 'Texas' Green, fed up with Elliott's persistent criticism, hit back. Since Major-General Elliott was being 'paid £250 a year for his services to the Defence Department', Green retorted, he was guilty of 'either a lamentable ignorance in regard to the responsibilities of his position' or a deliberate intention to sabotage the voluntary training scheme. While the new system overall was 'proving a success', the minister claimed, Elliott's 'propaganda' had contributed to the unsatisfactory enlistments under the new system in Victoria, and 'I would be justified ... in declining to recommend his reappointment' as a divisional commander.

Pompey predictably counter-attacked. He had been assiduous in striving to make a success of the new scheme, he maintained, and the Victorian figures in fact proved it. The 'total percentage of enlistments for the divisional area under my charge is the highest in the State', he contended, despite the handicap of three safe Labor seats where recruiting was minimal. 'Although urgent and repeated requests' had been made to senior government ministers who represented these electorates

> to address meetings in their constituencies in support of recruiting, they and supporters of the Government have invariably refused to do so. In this matter, of course, they are absolutely consistent; they do not want a defence system. [T]he failure of voluntary enlistment, so far as it has failed in Victoria, is due largely to the misfortune that great and populous constituencies are represented by gentlemen who make it their boast that under no circumstances would they take up arms.

When Attorney-General Daly retorted that in view of Elliott's repeated assertions that Labor's defence scheme was 'dishonest ... hypocritical and a farce' he could not honourably retain a position in it worth £250 a year, the result was another Pompey outburst. In a lengthy and intensely personal response Elliott analysed comparative recruitment statistics, cited repeatedly rejected requests to Scullin government ministers for assistance with recruiting activities, listed numerous trophies won by Third Division units (to confirm his efficiency as a commander), and detailed his out-of-pocket expenditure to emphasise that the £250 was not really income but reimbursement of accumulated diverse expenses associated with his command. There were also aspersions from Pompey on McGrath's war service, and yet another airing of the supersession grievance:

> I have endeavoured by all the means in my power to have that matter investigated, but so far I have failed. I have, not, however, given up hope. History is being written and it is revealing a great deal.

A good example of recently revealed history, he told the Senate, was his own attempt to prevent the disaster of Fromelles. He followed up with a vivid account of his protest at Flers:

> Precisely the same position then arose as has now arisen. On that occasion I perceived that an impossible task was being attempted. I opposed the course suggested with all my power, and today I am opposing a policy that I believe to be equally disastrous. Narrow-minded bitterness has been aroused against me, as it was then. I was regarded as an obstructionist as I am now. I was then as unperturbed by the consequences as I now am. I shall not resign ... and shall continue to do my duty to the public of this country as I see it, again regardless of the consequences.

As the economic crisis became increasingly grave and the Scullin government became increasingly divided over how to go about alleviating it, Elliott remained steadfastly committed to traditional measures. He believed that

> the people should be given as much liberty and freedom as possible to adjust themselves to the difficult state of affairs today, and ... every possible economy both public and private should be practised in order to provide the necessary capital to carry on and restore or increase the production of commodities.

In other words, it was essential to 'reduce the cost of production' in order 'to increase our exports'. He had no time for radical or unorthodox measures. Proposals to assist the desperate plight of Australian wheat growers with such measures as compulsory wheat pools and a guaranteed price appealed to some Nationalist senators, but cut no ice with him:

> Many honourable senators ... appear to have forgotten the anti-socialist principles for which they stand. They seem to think that the Commonwealth Bank has a vast store of gold and notes which can be looted for the purpose of providing a guaranteed price for wheat.

When the Senate voted to disallow the Wheat Marketing Bill, there was uproar in the bush. Growers had responded to official encouragement to produce more wheat in Australia's hour of need; they felt that those senators who voted down the bill had flagrantly welshed on a clear commitment. Resentment was intense. One branch of the Victorian Wheatgrowers' Association condemned Elliott in no uncertain terms:

> We have unanimously decided that you are hopelessly out of touch with the real interests of Australian wheatgrowers, and furthermore we desire to express our definite intention of supporting ... new candidates for the Senate. You shall not represent us again.

Not even Pompey's popularity in Charlton prevented a gathering of local wheat growers from unanimously endorsing a motion that 'this meeting ... strongly condemns the action' of Senator Elliott. During his political career Elliott was usually responsive on issues affecting the interests of returned soldiers or his home state; he tended, in fact, to be suspicious of government expenditure unrelated to these principal constituencies. In this instance he perhaps underestimated the strength of feeling among Victorian wheat growers.

On 8 March 1930 there was a ceremony at the Chum Creek property Elliott had donated to the Scotch College scouts in appreciation of the fine contribution that scouting had made to Neil's development. It was the formal opening of Elliott Lodge, the newly constructed hut named after him; Pompey was among the speakers. Neil was progressing well at Scotch. He distinguished himself as a rower, narrowly missing selection in the senior crew, and in 1930, his final year at school, he was Senior Probationer. His sister had already left her school days behind. Violet had crowned her Fintona years—and delighted her father—by returning as head prefect in 1929; in September he arranged for Violet and three of her school friends to make their début at the grand Third Division ball. The following year Violet began a diploma at Emily McPherson College.

Pompey was still tremendously busy. He continued to be in extraordinary demand as a speaker at functions involving returned soldiers. 'There is only one "Pompey" Elliott', the RSSILA felt obliged to remind members in its magazine. He did the honours at memorial unveilings at Numurkah, Gre Gre, Tongala, and Ararat; he was 'Australia's foremost unveiler', Jamieson claimed in *Despatches.* To ease his workload Elliott restructured his legal practice, joining forces with a new partner, W.H. 'Jimmy' Downing, the former 15th Brigade NCO whose vivid war memoir *To the Last Ridge* he had supported a decade earlier by providing an influential foreword.

Elliott's focus on the way AIF history and his own place in it were being recorded remained as keen as ever. He was progressively consigning his own war records to Treloar for deposit in the Australian War Memorial. Pompey often sent Bean historical snippets he came across which he thought might interest the historian. When it was reported that the Scullin government had leaned on Bean to expedite completion of the AIF history as an economy measure, Elliott aired his strong disapproval in parliament.

He further contributed to the chronicling of the AIF's history by writing articles himself for the magazine *Reveille.* In 1930 he contributed profiles of Bill Scurry and John Turnour, who had both served under him at Gallipoli before becoming officers in the 15th Brigade; a rebuttal of the allegation in Robert Graves's memoir *Goodbye to All That* that Australians had murdered German prisoners when capturing Morlancourt (Pompey insisted that the AIF had never taken Morlancourt); and an article reproducing and endorsing the scathing report by Jacka VC on the tanks' performance at Bullecourt which had resulted, according to Pompey, in Jacka being 'systematically ignored both in regard to decorations and promotions' even though his 'report bears all the marks of genius'.

Elliott was also very involved in the compilation of a history of the 7th Battalion. Eventually published in 1933, its chapters on Gallipoli relied heavily on his contribution. He also lectured on AIF history. Addressing the Constitutional Club in 1929, he described the Gallipoli campaign as a 'mess' that had no real chance of success, and condemned Winston Churchill as an 'amateur adviser' whose ill-informed advocacy of the proposal to invade Turkey had overridden the contrary and more considered pre-war appraisals of professional defence experts.

Pompey's most famous lecture was the penetrating exposé of Fromelles that he delivered to the Canberra RSSILA in July 1930. It owed a great deal to Bean's work, as Pompey acknowledged both in the lecture itself and in an appreciative letter to the historian. In style, however, it was very different from the *Official History*. Full of forthright assertions and compelling conclusions, it was the kind of account that Elliott felt Bean should have written after ascertaining the essential facts so capably. 'I propose to outline the course of events … and endeavour to show what errors were made and who was responsible for them', he began. The disaster stemmed directly from 'shocking generalship'. The operation was 'a wretched, hybrid scheme, which might well be termed a "tactical abortion"'; 'the methods actually chosen seem to have been the worst possible'.

Amid this appalling ineptitude, Pompey pinpointed ten basic errors and proceeded to catalogue them pungently. For example, he cited his post-Armistice discovery of a nearby church with visibility so splendid that a single German observer

> with a telescope could, with perfect safety to himself, count every sentry in our lines. He had also an extensive view across our back areas, and could at once detect any preparation for attack. A more unsuitable site from which to launch a well-advertised attack could hardly have been found on the western front.

Haking, Pompey concluded, 'wished to risk all for a spectacular success that would put himself into the limelight', and had to 'take the chief blame for the debacle', although 'the weakness displayed' by his superiors, including Haig, had also contributed.

> The whole operation was so incredibly blundered from beginning to end that it is almost incomprehensible how the British Staff, who were responsible for it, could have consisted of trained professional soldiers of considerable reputation and experience, and why, in view of the outcome of this extraordinary adventure, any of them were retained in active command.

No more incisive analysis of Fromelles had been seen or heard anywhere. The lecture, not surprisingly, made headlines, and not only in Australia. 'Bungled Battle: General Critic of Generals' proclaimed the London *News-Chronicle* above its account of Elliott's 'remarkable attack'. Underneath was Haking's blustering denial of these 'charges', which he dismissed as 'preposterous'. The *Age* described the lecture as an 'amazing outburst', sparking a spirited rejoinder from the lecturer:

> The address in question consisted, as I announced at its outset, almost entirely of literal extracts from vol III of the official history by C.E.W. Bean, with assurances from me as a participant as to their truth ... Surely ... one ought to be able to quote to a gathering of returned soldiers ... facts such as have been revealed by history, without one's remarks being made to appear as a general and reckless personal attack made without foundation [and] characterised as an "amazing outburst".

The substantial interest in his lecture resulted in a repeat performance, which he delivered to the United Service Institute in Melbourne. It was also printed as a booklet; copies were sent to London (unbeknown to Elliott) for evaluation by the War Office and Liddell Hart. Pompey's accumulated writings about the AIF (both published and unpublished) remain more significant to the recording of its history than those of any of his contemporaries except Bean.

Elliott's prominence as a forceful and authoritative analyst of AIF history reinforced his remarkable reputation. To thousands of the men he commanded—and their families—Pompey was an inspiring figure. Successful in a range of pursuits, publicly prominent, famous for jaw-jutting fearlessness and charismatic leadership, unswerving determination and incorruptible integrity, he nevertheless remained down-to-earth and approachable. There was nothing aloof or pretentious about him. Many of his men revered him, and revelled in the reflected glory of being one of Pompey's boys.

> When the name of Pompey Elliott is mentioned, the most war weary soldier straightens his back and clutches an invisible rifle, the dull eyes gleam, and in the glamour of the 'greatest Brigadier ever' there is not a man left of the Fifteenth Brigade who does not feel a thrill of honest pride. And [if] he calls to war again ... for the veterans who yet remain, there is not one who walks who will not run to follow him.

But not even this exceptional veneration could prevent Elliott's fixation about the supersession from continuing to eat away at him. Much of the material he was depositing in the Australian War Memorial related to it. In mid-1930 he even raised the issue directly with White. Perhaps he was encouraged by their 'reconciliation' of sorts at Monash's commemorative dinner in August 1927, but it was an astonishing move to resort to after relentlessly denigrating White in relation to this issue ever since 1918. It was also revealingly symptomatic of the torment and desperation plaguing him. The approach amazed White. 'Extraordinary letter from Genl Elliott', he noted in his diary. In a brief reply White avoided the issue:

> I do not think that any good purpose can be served now by a discussion as to the basis upon which General Birdwood made his selections for promotion, even if such a discussion were proper, and I refrain therefore from any comment.

Pompey tried again: 'I enclose herewith pro forma schedules upon which you could I think probably base your reply without in the least degree contravening any canon or convention of conduct military or otherwise'. Once again White was startled—'Another strange letter from Genl Elliott'—and once again he refused to be drawn: 'In all kindness may I say in reply that I have nothing to add to what I previously wrote you'.

Shortly afterwards Bean and White corresponded about Elliott. Pompey had just sent Bean a copy of Jacka's report on the tanks at Bullecourt, claiming once again that Jacka's promotion had been blocked because of the robust criticism in the report. 'The very idea is perfectly absurd', White replied after Bean sent him Elliott's letter and Jacka's report (although Jacka's Pompey-like outspokenness had indeed impeded his promotion). White in turn sent Bean his own recent correspondence with Pompey, contended that Elliott's 'mental balance' had 'been disturbed', and in effect lobbied Bean to disregard anything Elliott told him:

> no doubt you will conclude, as I have concluded, that he has become obsessed with the promotion idea which to some extent has affected his reason. I am inclined to think that his methods will very soon discount the value of anything that he says or writes, and it is better perhaps to let him bring about his own ruin than to enter [into controversy] with him.

The following month White excused himself from Monash's annual 8 August dinner, pleading a non-existent prior engagement, even though he had been (like Elliott) a regular attender and enjoyed the gatherings immensely. The unavoidable conclusion is that he wanted to avoid Elliott.

It was only six days after White dismissed 'the value of anything that he says or writes' that Elliott delivered his illuminatingly trenchant lecture on Fromelles. Even so, White's assessment of Elliott's frame of mind was correct. Pompey was really struggling. His preoccupation with the supersession issue, which Monash and Hobbs described as deeply concerning and Bean likened to a 'mania', had become, as both White and Elliott himself recognised, an 'obsession'. Elliott acknowledged that 'the injustice ... has actually colored all my post war life'. It was clear to Labor senators that he had an obsessive personality, especially when he became embarrassingly hypersensitive about the slightest slight affecting his reputation, whether it occurred in parliament, in the press, or on the hustings at Caulfield Town Hall.

But it was not just the supersession. Australia was shaken to the core by the Great Depression. Unemployment soared. At its peak probably half the workforce had to make do without full-time work. Bankruptcies climbed, snaring even the well-to-do and the notable (including Rosenthal, the distinguished architect–soldier who had been given one of the AIF divisional commands Elliott thought he should have secured in 1918). Solicitors suicided. Misery was rife, together with a harrowing fear of upheaval; it seemed to many Australians that the whole system was about to crumble. 'There lay over Melbourne, as over all Australia, a mass hopelessness that touched everyone, even those who felt secure', recalled writer Alan Marshall. 'It was impossible to escape being affected'. That the Scullin government, flailing around in desperate but unsuccessful efforts to alleviate the widespread misery, was flirting with measures that were not just unorthodox but profoundly disturbing to someone of Elliott's conservative outlook further aggravated his unease. Amid this palpable insecurity, fears of left-wing unrest and even violent revolution gained momentum, prompting the formation or activation of secret armies to resist such eventualities. While plenty of like-minded ex-AIF officers involved themselves in these shadowy activities, there seems no definite evidence that Elliott did.

The Depression, of course, was the last thing returned soldiers needed. Coping with the aftermath of the war was difficult enough for most of them; the impact of another havoc-wreaking phenomenon was devastating. With unemployment soaring to calamitous levels, distress widespread, and rumours circulating that war pensions would be reduced as an economy measure, Elliott was inundated with pleas for assistance. 'I am at my wits end at the present time in finding an opening for the man who gets out of a job', Elliott admitted to Jamieson. It was as if the Depression was undermining all his dedicated efforts on behalf of his 'poor boys', and he was powerless to prevent it. Many of them were suffering from the legacy that was to become known as post-traumatic stress syndrome.

This affliction was causing Elliott health problems of his own. He, too, was plagued by nightmares and ghastly flashbacks, when he not only relived front-line horrors he had repeatedly witnessed as the AIF's most famous fighting general; even more distressing was the memory of all those times he had been obliged to order subordinates to undertake perilous assignments. Elliott felt increasingly tormented by the deaths of the many fine men who had lost their lives in such enterprises, although he was convinced that no alternative was open to him at the time. 'No other aspect of his war service affected him so deeply', observed his friend Rowan Macneil, the Scotch College chaplain.

Other ailments were troubling Elliott as well. His blood pressure was disturbingly high, he now had diabetes and, on top of everything else, he sustained a severe head injury while horse-riding. Some who knew about this accident wondered whether it had resulted in permanent impairment.

In the end it all became overwhelming, too much to bear. Elliott was no stranger to severe depression. This was especially so during the war, when he had much to be depressed about. Indeed, it was perhaps a family tendency (his sister had suicided and his niece later did). This time, though, he plumbed the depths as never before.

There was perhaps an early sign that Elliott was far from well in August 1930 when he unveiled the main Ararat memorial, and broke down and wept during his speech. But it was not until early 1931 that his ill-health became publicly known. The Senate did not break for its summer recess until a week before Christmas, and Elliott was an active participant in parliament right up until this adjournment; staff at his law firm had 'no inkling at all that he was disturbed or upset', a typist recalled long afterwards. On 16 February 1931, however, the Melbourne *Sun* announced that General Elliott had been admitted to the Alfred Hospital after 'a sudden collapse' and 'a severe breakdown'. Similar reports soon followed in the other Melbourne dailies.

What these reports were alluding to was attempted suicide. Arriving home from his city office on 5 February, he handed Belle the children's insurance policies together with some share certificates, and said she might 'need the money'. Belle did not go to bed that night until after midnight, and then lay awake, concerned about her brother-in-law's frame of mind (the fact that he had altered his will the day before would have made her even more worried if she had known). She heard him get up, walk into the kitchen, and close the door. Silence followed. Thoroughly alarmed now, Belle woke Violet and Neil, and together they went into the kitchen. Confronting them was a shocking spectacle. The general was sitting in front of the oven, which was turned on and open but not lit; the gas was reeking, and he was semi-conscious. They had arrived just in time. Violet turned off the gas, and they helped him out of the kitchen. When he had properly revived they all went back to bed.

In the morning Harold headed off to work as normal, and the rest of the family tried to come to terms with the incident. It was extremely difficult. They were so accustomed to his strength, vigour, and determination that it was hard to accept that such an incongruous, nightmarish incident had really happened. It was so out of character. Working out how to respond was not easy, especially in view of the stigma associated with suicide in that era and Elliott's paramount concern about his reputation. They decided to get in touch with Rod Elliott, who agreed to come down from Tocumwal straightaway. He stayed at Prospect Hill Road with the family, and helped keep an eye on his troubled brother. Nothing untoward happened while Rod was there, but he had a farm to run and naturally could not stay indefinitely; after a week he returned home. Harold, Belle thought, seemed relieved when Rod left. Shortly afterwards he disappeared into the toilet with a pyjama cord in hand; when Neil followed him in, he hurried out immediately. Belle summoned a doctor, and requested hospitalisation in order to prevent suicide. An ambulance was called, and Elliott was conveyed to the Alfred Hospital.

He remained there almost a month. Initially there were daily bulletins in the press about his progress. Whereas at first 'his condition caused anxiety', he was soon 'making good progress' and 'able to receive visitors'. Among them was the 7th Battalion's Gallipoli chaplain, who found Elliott 'very depressed and unhappy'. The manager of the Alfred, Peter Eller, knew Pompey well; an original 6th Battalion officer, Eller had sailed away to war in the same troopship. He ensured that Pompey had a prolonged stay at the Alfred with the best possible treatment.

With Eller satisfied his famous patient was much better, Elliott was allowed home in March. But he was still deeply troubled. His supersession obsession, post-traumatic stress, diabetes, and high blood pressure were all still unabatedly potent; so, too, was the sad plight of too many of his 'poor boys'. And the palpable atmosphere of national crisis was more intense than ever. Many Australians with views and values similar to Elliott's feared that the whole fabric of society was teetering on the brink of collapse. On 6 March a wild rumour of communist-inspired insurrection swept across rural Victoria, prompting vigilant mobilisation in numerous districts by doughty secret army stalwarts. Five days earlier another prominent Melbourne solicitor had suicided.

At this profoundly unsettling time Elliott was being tormented by delusions relating to his integrity. He became terribly concerned about investment advice he had given to clients, even though he had always been impeccably prudent in such matters. Moreover, he was dreadfully worried about his own financial position, even though there was no cause for concern that anyone else could discern. It was appalling, he kept saying, to have to face this disastrous financial crisis after what he had been through during the war; the damage to his reputation if he went broke would be unbearable. Elliott's own great depression was intensified by the economic Great Depression. Belle heard him say he was 'done' and did not want to live. He told his 81-year-old mother he felt so awful he wished he had never been born. His friend and former political colleague W.A. Watt tackled Elliott's worries directly, asking his permission to go through all his financial records. Watt examined them comprehensively at Elliott's city office, confirmed there was nothing to worry about, and hurried back to Camberwell to reassure him. But Elliott was too unhinged for this news to provide more than fleeting comfort.

By now a psychiatrist had been contacted. Dr J.F. Williams, a leading specialist (and son-in-law of a Nationalist Party powerbroker), saw Elliott at Prospect Hill Road. They discussed Elliott's physical symptoms, his worries, and the oven incident. Williams diagnosed a 'definite form of nervous disorder', reinforced Watt's assurances about the finances, and recommended hospitalisation for observation and treatment. 'I did not consider', he said later, 'that he was sufficiently disordered mentally to require certification as insane'.

Williams organised immediate admission to a private hospital in Malvern. Upon his arrival the senior nurse's curiosity about this 52-year-old Harold Elliott she was admitting was irresistible. 'Are you *Pompey* Elliott?' she asked; he laughed his assent. When Williams called later that day, at 7.00pm on 22 March, Elliott was in bed, 'apparently cheerful and reconciled to his stay', although he doubted whether he would be able to pay for it. Williams reiterated that there was no need for concern on that score. He told the hospital staff to keep Elliott in bed (no toilet or bathroom trips), and to be alert for suicide attempts. After Williams left, when the sedative he prescribed was being administered, Pompey's anguish overflowed: 'Oh, nurse, why can't you give me something so I'll sleep for ever?' The staff did keep him in bed, and checked him periodically during the night. But he outwitted them with resourcefulness born of desperation, having realised the potential of something they had overlooked—his shaving gear. He was checked at two o'clock and three o'clock, but when a nurse looked in at him at 4.25am she found blood everywhere. A razor blade was embedded in a deep gash near his left elbow; the peace and release he craved had come swiftly. All Pompey Elliott's battles and worries were over.

CHAPTER TWENTY-FIVE

'Thousands of Diggers Will Truly Mourn for Pompey': Afterwards

MARCH 1931 -

THE EXTENSIVE PRESS coverage of Elliott's death included no mention of suicide. There were discreetly vague references to 'nervous strain', a 'brief illness', and 'high blood pressure'; some newspapers reported the cause of death as 'haemorrhage while undergoing treatment in a private hospital'. Swamping these evasive reports was a torrent of tributes. Among the first to pay their respects publicly were Cam Stewart, Senator Pearce, Prime Minister Scullin, and representatives of numerous returned soldiers' associations. The *West Australian* approached Hobbs. 'I find it difficult to express my sorrow and regret' at the loss of 'a very dear friend', Hobbs replied. 'He was indeed a gallant and brilliant leader' of 'remarkable initiative and determination', who 'knew no fear and was ready always to engage in the most desperate enterprise'. Lengthy obituaries dipped into the plentiful fund of Pompey stories. The *Argus* quoted Bean's memorable character sketch in the *Official History* ('Outspoken, impulsive, excitable, straight as a ruled line'), the *Sydney Morning Herald* revived Cutlack's vivid 1918 portrait. 'Probably no other officer of the AIF is the subject of so many anecdotes and reminiscences', concluded the *Argus* obituarist.

On Tuesday 24 March the national parliament adjourned in Elliott's honour. Latham, now Opposition Leader, said it had been his 'privilege' to know Elliott well for over three decades:

> He was a fearless man, of remarkable resolution and tenacity of purpose. Above all, he was, throughout his career, a man of unswerving loyalties. His achievements should be an inspiration to all Australians.

In the Senate there were generous tributes from Glasgow and other coalition colleagues. Elliott's 'friendly nature' was emphasised by Labor senators; 'some of us may not have agreed with him politically', said one, but 'we always knew that with him the political fight was over as soon as we left the chamber'. Senator Payne, a Tasmanian Nationalist, described Elliott as

> one of nature's gentlemen, who had always consideration for the feelings of others ... I can say, with all sincerity, that no man whom I have ever met in a public capacity appealed to me more than he did.

Another Tasmanian Nationalist, Senator Sampson, an ex-AIF officer and a good friend of Elliott's, praised his 'abounding generosity' to returned soldiers in a heartfelt speech. It may be tempting to discount the sincerity of lavish tributes as inevitable when MPs go on the record about a just-deceased colleague, but Sampson was even more fervent in private. 'My heart is sore and I am sad', he told Jane Sampson,

> for this morning a wire from Sir George Pearce told us that Pompey Elliott had 'gone west'. To us, his soldier comrades, it is a great blow and I feel sadly at a loss. He was a rare character, direct and absolutely fearless, clean minded, warm hearted, generous to a fault. In this Senate he was one of the few we have, whom nothing could turn from the right and straight way—true as steel and just as hard when it came to a fight. Those long years of war, when he drove himself by sheer will power, often when physically and mentally tired out, have told their tale and ... towards the end he was an old and desperately tired man, worn out ... Thousands of diggers will truly mourn for Pompey, they respected him oh so highly as well as loved him, for he was never one to spare himself or forget an officer's duty—the care of his men ... Pompey is at rest —his spirit still lives and will while men of the AIF remain.

The funeral on 25 March, with full military honours, was an extraordinary event. After a brief ceremony at 56 Prospect Hill Road, the coffin was placed on a gun carriage draped with the Union Jack and the general's cap, sword and medals, and then conveyed to Burwood Cemetery four miles away. There was a sizeable military escort in full dress with regimental bands. It was a sombre journey. The bands played Handel's 'Dead March in Saul' and Chopin's 'Funeral March'. Large crowds had assembled beforehand (though it was a workday morning); thousands followed the cortege, or lined the route to the cemetery. Bystanders sobbed as the coffin passed.

One of the youngest onlookers, three-year-old George McKaige, was with his father, a 7th Battalion original who would say proudly, when asked about his war service, 'I was with Pompey Elliott'. This funeral, and the fervent emotion it aroused in his father and others, remained one of George's earliest memories: 'I can still see the plumed horses and the cortege going by', he said 63 years later. Those following the gun carriage not only included former members of the 15th Brigade and 7th Battalion (a blinded veteran among them); former prime minister S.M. Bruce marched as just another returned soldier. A roll of muffled drums ushered the gun carriage into the cemetery. There was a moving service at the packed graveside, and a thirteen-gun salute from a nearby artillery battery. 'The boom of the guns had hardly died away, and the blue smoke hung about the hillside still, when the notes of the Last Post ... rang out', reported the *Herald*; those notes, Jamieson wrote, 'never sounded so poignant'.

'I have just returned from his funeral and I have never seen a greater tribute paid to a man', Bruce assured Kate; 'it must be some comfort to you to see the universal regard, esteem and even affection in which he was held'. The former prime minister was not the only Pompey admirer to write to Kate after attending the funeral. Another was MacFarland, the former Ormond College master: 'The funeral today was a wonderful display of the affectionate regard of all sections of the community, and did honour both to our citizens and his memory'. Kate also received a letter from one of Harold's old colleagues in the pre-war militia:

> About 25 years ago we were Lieutenants together in the old 5th Regiment and I have watched and admired his glorious career since, a career covered with honours which compare with the

greatest men in the British Empire. Of the lot I believe he valued his DCM as the most precious, but added to these the CB, CMG, DSO, BA, LLM, Major-General and Senator, and it is doubtful if any man has risen to greater eminence purely off his own bravery and efforts. But added to all this and perhaps worth more than all, to you, and to me as his friend was an extraordinarily kindly and gentle nature unspoiled in any way by his honours and position, still exactly the same clean wholesome outlook on life as he had 25 years ago. That to me was his greatness. That phrase of [Bean's] 'straight as a ruled line' was his life's motto, and I know he never deviated from it one iota ... After this marvellous experience today of the love of countless numbers of men of all conditions creeds and callings of life you may well be proud.

Tributes paid at a meeting of Collingwood Council, a Labor stronghold hardly compatible with Pompey's political outlook, underlined how comprehensive this admiration was. One councillor, a trooper with Elliott in the Boer War, described Pompey as one of the finest men he had ever known; another councillor, who had served under him in the Great War, had no doubt he was the greatest soldier in the whole AIF. Bean dashed off a superb obituary for *Reveille*:

So Pompey Elliott is gone! No more shall we meet in Collins Street or at Canberra that sturdy figure, the bluff red cheeks, almost without a line, the twinkling, knowing eyes, the confident smile. No more we shall feel that iron grip of a handshake, or catch that decisive voice. The old soldier has laid down his arms. The stalwart figure has gone ... we can picture Pompey going round the turns of that long road that we all must travel some day, with his head high, his senses alert, his strong chin set. It is not the first time that he has gone out alone into Nomansland. We know this about Pompey: he goes out as a soldier, utterly unafraid ... What a brigade he made of the 15th! ... In his exuberant vitality he overworked them, strafed them, punished them; and yet they would do anything he asked of them ... [H]istory will do him an injustice if it does not hand him down to posterity as—with very few peers—one of the outstanding and most lovable characters of the AIF.

A few weeks later, amid the press coverage of Anzac Day, was this salute:

> At the last Anzac reunion attended by the late General 'Pompey' Elliott a Digger appealed to him for help, saying grimly that he was 'down and out'. At the general's call a sum was subscribed, and the Digger was fitted out with a pie stall. Out at the Shrine at the dawn muster yesterday he did a roaring trade. Sold out, and with a pocketful of money, he left the ground blessing the name of 'Pompey' Elliott.

Tributes from institutions and organisations were numerous. From the Law Institute and Melbourne City Council came salutes to his work as a solicitor. The Melbourne Hospital praised his longstanding contribution as a member of its board of management. His role at Ormond College was acknowledged in similar terms, and Ballarat College was particularly glowing:

> No more loyal son of the college ever lived ... he has left behind him an enduring memory, and an example of work, of determination, and of loyalty, which will be as beacon light to his fellow-collegians, to ourselves, and to the collegians of the days that are yet to be.

At a school function shortly after his death the main speaker, an officer in the 15th AIF Brigade, described Elliott as the college's 'noblest son' and 'probably the most outstanding personality in the AIF'. Students who had noticed this 'quiet, kindly man' on his frequent visits to the school after the war 'could have no conception of his extraordinary force and driving power as a commander of a fighting unit'; they should strive to be, like him, 'as straight as a ruled line'. He was also extolled as an example to follow at a special service 'in thanksgiving for, and commemoration of, the life and influence of Senator Major-General Harold Edward Elliott' at Trinity Presbyterian Church, Camberwell, four days after his funeral.

The next day there was a coroner's inquest into the cause of death. After hearing evidence from the police and hospital staff together with Belle, Watt, and Dr Williams, the coroner formally concluded that Elliott had died from a self-inflicted wound while 'temporarily insane'.

That Belle represented the immediate family at the inquest was no surprise; she had long been the dominant female presence in the practical affairs of the household. Moreover, Kate was struggling to come to terms with it all. Having unquestioningly accepted the appropriateness of a traditional supportive role as the wife of a vigorous and busy celebrity, content to be his 'sunshine lady', she was not only overwhelmed and mystified by the way her world had been turned upside down; she was dismayed that all her loving support and desperate endeavours to ease his worries had in the end proved in vain. The children, of course, were also devastated. Too hurt and embarrassed to discuss their pain with friends, 20-year-old Violet and 18-year-old Neil carried their tragic burden largely unaided.

Their anguish was intensified by a newspaper. *Smith's Weekly* was lively, iconoclastic, and a self-proclaimed champion of returned soldiers and their interests. More than once *Smith's* had expressed itself as a fervent Pompey admirer, and in the wake of his death published another glowing profile headed 'VALE "POMPEY" ELLIOTT, HERO OF VILLERS BRET'. On 18 April, however, *Smith's* revealed, in sensational style, the 'secret' of the real cause of death:

> A camouflage thrown over the events that led up to the fatal sequel made it appear that the great soldier had died from natural causes as the result of a haemorrhage [but] there was no reason why the circumstances of his passing should have been withheld. Certainly there was no moral stigma in the fact of a man, holding an office of trust and jealously anxious to safeguard his professional honour at a time when the reputation of solicitors was being assailed from all quarters, taking the short road out of life during a mental lapse in which he was under the delusion that the affairs of his clients had suffered shipwreck.

Using the official inquest report, this dramatic exposé quoted the testimony of Belle, Dr Williams, and the hospital nurses to demonstrate the pitiful 'state of the unfortunate soldier–lawyer's mind'. While the article included graphic details about his death and previous suicide attempts, the overall tone was admiring and sympathetic. Senior identities at *Smith's* maintained that they had published these revelations with the best of intentions, and there was nothing untoward about revealing the sad truth: 'despairing, unbalanced, perhaps, by some legacy of his campaigns, he found himself driven to the act which closed so tragically a famous fighting career'.

But they completely misjudged their readership. Returned soldiers were appalled. Men who had served under Pompey were livid. To them, these revelations a week before Anzac Day represented crass, sordid journalism at its worst. Violent retribution against *Smith's Weekly* was proposed. Agitators were intent on smashing windows at its Melbourne office; some zealots wanted to set fire to it. A band of militants did in fact assemble there in a threatening manner; serious trouble was narrowly averted. A retaliatory article in the *Terang Express* exemplified the widespread fury. It described the *Smith's* exclusive as 'low and vicious' journalism, 'a pitiless exploitation of a dead war hero for pecuniary gain', by a 'contemptible' newspaper that purported to be a caring advocate for returned soldiers yet preferred 'sensationalism' and 'bad taste' to proper consideration for 'bereaved relatives' of a 'dead hero'. Pompey's men maintained their rage against *Smith's Weekly* for years. Long afterwards 'Jimmy' Downing became immediately animated when he noticed his son had a copy of the newspaper:

> If you want to waste your money you can buy that paper. If you want to waste your time you can read it. But don't bring it into this house!

This intense hostility to *Smith's Weekly* was further confirmation of Elliott's enduring esteem in the eyes of his men. It also underlined the jolting impact of his death, especially the manner of it. At a time of such pervasive misery and pessimism, the sudden discovery that their idol, the leader they admired above all others for his bravery and determination, had found it all too hard was a devastatingly bitter pill to swallow. Some refused to digest it at all, finding it simply unthinkable. Some did not find out themselves for years—not everyone perused *Smith's Weekly* (or the *Terang Express*)—and, when they finally discovered the truth, found it incomprehensible. Some found it profoundly disappointing that an inspiring leader of such renowned courage had resorted to such distressingly drastic action. A few were even unhinged by it. Bert Layh, a captain under Pompey at Gallipoli and a 15th Brigade colonel in France, was so disturbed after returning home following the funeral that his wife felt it necessary to lock his children in their bedrooms because he was threatening to kill them.

A proposal for a permanent memorial to Elliott soon gained momentum. It was decided to finance the construction of a headstone over his grave. Fund-raising was difficult, naturally, in the worst of the Great Depression, but the 7th Battalion Association was indefatigable, the RSSILA and various 15th Brigade unit associations involved themselves, and the necessary £200 was eventually collected. The memorial comprised a stone column featuring a sculpted portrait of Elliott; underneath was an inscription listing his decorations, degrees, and commands, and saluting him as a 'valiant soldier, a great citizen, an upright man'. It was unveiled at another moving Burwood Cemetery ceremony by the youngest 7th Battalion original (and Victorian RSSILA president), 'Gunner' Holland, on 24 April 1932.

Elliott's estate was valued at just under £18,000. This amount, together with his parliamentary salary and earnings as a solicitor as well as revenue from various other sources, reinforced how distorted were his concerns about his own financial position, as distinct from the other worries that contributed to his suicide. But it was clear to Kate, Belle, and the children that without his regular income major changes were unavoidable. They moved to a smaller house in Hawthorn, disposing of 56 Prospect Hill Road and the Frankston property. Violet took up nursing, not because of any pronounced vocational impulse but because it seemed a financially prudent move in the family's altered circumstances. Neil landed a position at Kodak; he had been a photography enthusiast for years, and Kodak had connections with Scotch College. Belle stayed on with the family following the move to Hawthorn, and was needed more than ever after Kate was skittled by a motorbike when alighting from a tram. She was seriously injured, and there was no way back after this second crushing blow; Kate was a reclusive semi-invalid for the rest of her life.

Until 1934 Neil combined part-time work as a chemist at Kodak with a science course at the University of Melbourne, and crammed into his spare time as many outdoors pursuits as possible. He enjoyed hiking and rowing, and was active in both the scout movement and the militia, where he was a capable machine-gun sergeant. After getting undistinguished results, he discontinued the science course in 1934. He became a full-time film processor at Kodak, and the following year applied for a position as a cadet administrative officer in New Guinea. Testimonials testified to his 'initiative, endurance, leadership, love of outdoor life' and suitability 'in any position where character counts'. One referee urged the adjudicators not to 'judge him by his manner' because he was 'shy with strangers'. Only those who knew him well could properly discern the 'concentrated power' within—he was really 'a replica of his father'. Another referee contacted the Territories minister (Pearce) directly, to emphasise that not only did 'young Elliott' have an 'outstanding' record; appointing him would be an 'instalment by way of repayment of the debt which Australia owes to his father'.

His application successful, Neil left for New Guinea in February 1936. He established himself as a respected and resourceful patrol officer; extensions of his service were approved by other ministers who knew his father well, T.W. White and W.M. Hughes. During home leave his relationship with an ex-Fintona friend blossomed, and they became engaged. In July 1939, with developments in Europe foreshadowing the ghastly prospect of another world war, Violet and Belle were visited at the Parkville flat they were now sharing—Kate had died, aged 63, seven months earlier—by a sombre stranger who notified them on behalf of the government that Neil had been killed. The government released a statement, and the press pounced: 'NATIVES KILL MELBOURNE MAN: AIF GENERAL'S SON DIES IN ATTACK ON NEW GUINEA PATROL', proclaimed the *Sun*.

It was one of Neil Elliott's police assistants who had sparked the skirmish, rebuking and assaulting a woman who refused to comply with his order to clean up the village. The local headman, who was the woman's father, took umbrage, and launched a mutinous retribution that caught Neil and his staff unawares. The headman confronted Neil, attacking him with a knife, but he managed to get hold of his nearby revolver and shoot this assailant. However, he did not notice two of the headman's brothers, who each flung a spear accurately—one penetrated his stomach, the other his chest. Wrenching these spears out himself, Neil ignored his wounds while he and his staff concentrated on quelling the uprising. When one of his police assistants was speared in the shoulder, Neil even extracted this spear head with his teeth. After it was all over, Neil collapsed. He died soon afterwards. In due course the perpetrators were caught, tried, and executed. Meanwhile Australia's Administrator in New Guinea, McNicoll—now installed in the position he had unsuccessfully sought nearly two decades earlier with the strong support of Neil's father—confidentially notified the government 'with regret' that the excessively authoritarian style Neil had sometimes displayed as a patrol officer might have partly provoked the clash. There was no hint of this in the Australian press coverage of the incident, which concentrated on Neil's Pompey-like bravery and resourcefulness in a tight corner. He 'acted in accordance with the high standard of courage and devotion to duty which his father set', Treloar assured Violet.

The shock of her brother's violent death was yet another terrible blow for Violet. Her closest friends, nursing colleagues especially, wished that she felt more able to open up and unburden herself about her troubles. Like many others, they admired Violet's special qualities. Upright and decent, sensitive and compassionate, she gave help where it was needed unstintingly; she was fun-loving and down to earth, but there was (as one of her closest friends put it) 'an aura about her which anyone who had anything to do with her never forgot'. Employees of Holeproof Pty Ltd, where she pioneered industrial nursing, acclaimed her contribution. So did soldiers who met her during her nursing service in the Second World War after having served under her father in the Great War. (Pompey's influence lived on through those of his men who held senior commands in World War II; most modelled themselves on him. 'Wish Pompey was still around' was the gist of many a heartfelt sentiment in the dark days of 1942.)

After the war Violet returned to Holeproof. She became prominent in the development of industrial nursing in Australia, chairing its professional association and addressing international conferences. She continued to provide remarkably generous help to relatives and others in need, particularly her troubled cousin Jacquelyn (George's daughter, who suicided in 1963). In 1962 she retired from Holeproof because Belle was ailing and needed full-time care. Presented with a gift of £500 from the company in appreciation for decades of outstanding service, she opted to use it not for herself but to establish a course for industrial nurses. In her spare time she taught herself to type, and embarked on a history of her profession in Australia. Maximising awareness of her father's career was another priority. She spent months combing through his papers with a view to depositing collections in national repositories, the Australian War Memorial in particular. Although severely afflicted with scleroderma, a serious and painful disease, she managed to complete both these projects before her death in 1971.

Despite Violet's efforts her father has been largely overlooked by posterity. Presumably the manner of his death played its part—suicide, in that era especially, was acutely confronting and, for someone with Pompey's reputation, incongruous. Admittedly, an Elliott Memorial Lodge was founded in 1947, streets have been named after him in Melbourne and Canberra, there are Elliott Gardens at Charlton, and Ballarat College has an Elliott House; other commemorative gestures have included a wattle tree at the Hawthorn Tea Gardens, and a variety of gladiolus featuring 'rose pink petals ... richly splashed with lemon and wine red' that was dubbed 'General Elliott'. Since 1992 there has also been an annual commemoration at his graveside; returned soldiers, their relatives and representatives of Ballarat College have attended this ceremony on 23 March each year. By and large, however, the living legend faded into obscurity. His men, of course, never forgot him. More than half a century after his death, surviving members of the 7th Battalion and the 15th Brigade were dwindling, but he was still in their thoughts, their conversations, even their dreams. Among the wider public, though, awareness of him was meagre. An Australian as famous, inspirational, and historically significant as Pompey Elliott deserves to be better remembered.

BIBLIOGRAPHY AND NOTES

Abbreviations Used

ADB *Australian Dictionary of Biography* (with appropriate volume number)
ADMS Assistant Director of Medical Services
AWM Australian War Memorial, Canberra
BC Belle Campbell
Bde Brigade
Bn Battalion
BR Battle Report (in AWM 4)
Coy Company
CPD Commonwealth Parliamentary Debates
D Diary
Div Division
ECT East Charlton Tribune (from 1927 known as Charlton Tribune)
EP Elliott papers, AWM
EP (SLV) Elliott papers, SLV
fn footnote
15 BD 15 Brigade Diary, AWM 4
GM Geoff McCrae (thereby distinguishing references to him from citations mentioning his father, George McCrae)
HE Harold Elliott
HE D Harold Elliott Diary
HE to BC Harold Elliott to Belle Campbell
HE to KE Harold Elliott to Kate Elliott
inf information (provided to Ross McMullin by …)
IWM Imperial War Museum
JT John Treloar
KE Kate Elliott
McCP McCrae papers, AWM
ME Emily (Milly) Edwards
NAA National Archives of Australia
NAM National Army Museum, London
n.d. no date
NLA National Library of Australia, Canberra
OH Official History of Australia in the War of 1914-18 (with appropriate volume number)
PRO Public Record Office, London
PROV Public Record Office, Victoria
SLV State Library of Victoria
SMH Sydney Morning Herald
UMA University of Melbourne Archives
V/Bret Villers-Bretonneux

Select Bibliography

The main source for this biography has been Elliott's papers at the Australian War Memorial. Deposited in instalments, the papers have been accessioned in four different collections (1DRL 264, 2DRL 513, 3DRL 3297, 3DRL 3856). The classification of his papers (and other AWM collections) has altered since I first looked at them; I've tried to cite all such references in their reclassified formats, but it's possible that a small number may be cited in their former guises. There is also a small collection of Elliott papers at the State Library of Victoria.

Elliott's diaries of the Great War are in five volumes, 2DRL 513/2-6. His original 1914-1919 letters to his wife and children are located in two sequences in the Elliott papers, 2DRL 513/7-9 and 3DRL 3297/2-12; typed copies of these letters are to be found in 2DRL 513/24-30, but edited alterations have been made to them. Original 1915-1919 letters from Elliott to Belle Campbell, his sister-in-law, are in a separate sequence, 2DRL 513/10-12. Another batch of original letters to a relative, his 1916-1919 correspondence to his cousin Milly Edwards, is to be found in 3DRL 3856/2. There are numerous references to each of these sources in the endnotes; I have outlined the DRL locations here instead of mentioning them over and over again in the notes.

Another important source has been the papers of Charles Bean, also deposited in the AWM in instalments and reclassified as collection AWM 38.

Primary Sources

Manuscripts

Australian National University Survey of War Memorials, AWM.
A. Bazley papers, AWM.
C. Bean papers, AWM.
E. Beddington, 'My Life', Hertfordshire County Council Archives.
W. Birdwood papers, AWM.
R.H.K. Butler papers, IWM.
J. Campbell papers, AWM.
P. Carne papers, privately held.
G. Christie-Miller papers, IWM.

A. Coates papers, SLV.
A. Court papers, privately held.
C. Denehy papers, privately held.
K. Doig papers, SLV.
J. Edmonds papers, University of London.
Edwards family papers, Talbot Museum.
H. Elliott papers, AWM.
H. Elliott papers, SLV.
G.R. Freeman papers, privately held.
P. Game papers, IWM.
J. Gellibrand papers, AWM.
D. Haig papers, PRO.
Henderson family papers, privately held.
J.J.T. Hobbs papers, AWM.
Kent Hughes family papers, privately held.
J. Latham papers, NLA.
P. Ledward papers, IWM.
B. Liddell Hart papers, University of London.
K. Mackay papers, privately held.
McCombe family papers, privately held.
G. McCrae papers, AWM.
I. Marsh papers, NLA.
J. Monash papers, NLA.
E. Need papers, privately held.
J. North papers, University of London.
G. Pearce papers, AWM.
H. Rawlinson papers, IWM and NAM.
J. Richardson papers, AWM.
7th Battalion Association papers, AWM.
N. Smyth papers, privately held.
E. Tivey papers, AWM.
F. Tubb papers, privately held.
Walker family papers, SLV.
C.V. Watson papers, privately held.
D. Whinfield papers, privately held.
C.B.B. White papers, NLA.
T. White papers, privately held.
H. Wilson papers, IWM.

Commonwealth Parliamentary Debates
I read every speech Elliott made in the Senate during his parliamentary career (1920-1931).

Official Records, AWM
AWM 4 AIF official unit diaries
AWM 25 Files created by AIF units
AWM 26 AIF operations files
AWM 27 AWM subject files
AWM 38 C. Bean papers
AWM 43 AIF biographical and other research files
AWM 44 Official History drafts
AWM 93 AWM registry files
AWM 140 AIF biographical cards
AWM 183 AIF biographical forms
AWM 252 AWM subject files

Official Records, PRO
CAB 45 Correspondence re Official History drafts
WO 95 British unit war diaries
WO 158 British unit war diaries
WO 256 D. Haig papers

Official Records, PROV
VPRS 24 Inquest deposition files
VPRS 30 Criminal trial briefs
VPRS 251 Register of inwards correspondence, Attorney-General's department
VPRS 626 Land selection files
VPRS 640 Primary school correspondence files
VPRS 795 School building files
VPRS 7556 Admission warrants of patients to Yarra Bend

Official Records, National Archives of Australia
CRS A518/1 New Guinea staff
CRS A6273/1 Canberra administration: Senator H.E. Elliott's appeal against kerbing and guttering charges
CRS B2455 AIF personnel dossiers
CRS B4747/1 Army militia records, attestation documents
MP 84/1 Defence department correspondence files

University of Melbourne Archives
Examination results
Ormond College records

Ballarat College Archives
Council minutes
Register of enrolments

Fintona archives
Examinations register

Secondary Sources

Books

E. Andrews, *The Anzac Illusion* (Melbourne, 1993)
C. Aspinall-Oglander, *Military Operations: Gallipoli vols 1 & 2* (London, 1929 & 1932)
C. Bean, *Official History of Australia in the War of 1914-18 vols 1–6* (Sydney, 1921-42)
——, *Gallipoli Mission* (Canberra, 1948)
——, *Two Men I Knew* (Sydney, 1957)
——, *Anzac to Amiens* (Canberra, 1968)
F. Brennan, *Canberra in Crisis* (Canberra, 1971)
G. Cadzow, *Charlton in the Vale of the Avoca* (Charlton, 1988)
E. Childers (ed), *The Times History of the War in South Africa 1899-1902 vol. 5* (London, 1907)
R. Corfield, *Hold Hard, Cobbers vol. 1 1912-1930* (Melbourne, 1992)
——, *Don't Forget Me, Cobber* (Melbourne, 2000)
C. Coulthard-Clark, *No Australian Need Apply: The Troubled Career of Lieutenant-General Gordon Legge* (Sydney, 1988)
F. Cutlack (ed), *War Letters of General Monash* (Sydney, 1934)
A. Dean & E. Gutteridge, *The Seventh Battalion AIF* (Melbourne, 1933)
S. Dewar, 'Having a Lively Time': Australians at Gallipoli in 1915 (Melbourne, 1990)
T. Dingle, *Settling* (Sydney, 1984)
W. Downing, *To the Last Ridge* (Melbourne, 1920)
J. Dunn, *The War the Infantry Knew* (London, 1989)
J. Edmonds, *Military Operations: France and Belgium 1918 vols 1, 2, 4 & 5* (London, 1935-47)
——, *Military Operations: France and Belgium 1917 vol. 2* (London, 1948)
A. Ellis, *The Story of the Fifth Australian Division* (London, 1920)
C. Falls, *Military Operations: France and Belgium 1917 vol. 1* (London, 1940)
B. Gammage, *The Broken Years* (Canberra, 1974)
W. & W. Gherardin (eds), *The Volunteer* (Melbourne, 1995)
I. Grant, *Jacka VC* (Melbourne, 1989)
F. Green, *Servant of the House* (Melbourne, 1969)
P. Griffith, *Battle Tactics of the Western Front* (New Haven & London, 1994)
P. Hocking, *Twice a Digger* (Melbourne, 1995)
C. Hughes & B. Graham (eds), *A Handbook of Australian Government and Politics* (Canberra, 1968)
K. Inglis, *Sacred Places* (Melbourne, 1998)
H. Knyvett, *Over There with the Australians* (London, 1918)

A. Latreille, *The Natural Garden* (Melbourne, 1990)
N. Lytton, *The Press and the General Staff* (London, 1920)
S. Macintyre (ed), *Ormond College Centenary Essays* (Melbourne, 1984)
S. Macintyre, *The Oxford History of Australia vol. 4 1901-1942* (Melbourne, 1986)
R. McMullin, *Will Dyson: Cartoonist, Etcher and Australia's Finest War Artist* (Sydney, 1984)
——, *The Light on the Hill: The Australian Labor Party 1891-1991* (Melbourne, 1991)
W. Mein, *History of Ballarat College 1864-1964* (Ballarat, 1964)
M. Middlebrook, *The Kaiser's Battle* (London, 1983)
W. Miles, *Military Operations: France and Belgium 1916 vol. 2* (London, 1938)
J. Monash, *The Australian Victories in France in 1918* (Melbourne, 1923)
B. Nairn & G. Serle (eds), *Australian Dictionary of Biography vols 7–10* (Melbourne, 1979-86)
T. Pakenham, *The Boer War* (London, 1979)
P. Pedersen, *Monash as Military Commander* (Melbourne, 1985)
G. Powell, *Plumer* (London, 1990)
R. Prior & T. Wilson, *Command on the Western Front: The Military Career of Sir Henry Rawlinson* (Oxford, 1992)
——, *Passchendaele: The Untold Story* (New Haven & London, 1996)
F. Richards, *Old Soldiers Never Die* (Sydney, 1933)
J. Ritchie (ed), *Australian Dictionary of Biography vols 12–15* (Melbourne, 1990-2000)
J. Robertson, *Anzac and Empire* (Melbourne, 1990)
P. Sadler, *The Paladin* (Melbourne, 2000)
G. Sawer, *Australian Federal Politics and Law 1901-1929* (Melbourne, 1956)
G. Serle, *John Monash: A Biography* (Melbourne, 1982)
G. Serle (ed), *Australian Dictionary of Biography vol. 11* (Melbourne, 1988)
A. Sprake, *Londonderry: The Golden Hole* (Perth, 1991)
A. Thomson, *Anzac Memories: Living with the Legend* (Melbourne, 1994)
A. Wildavsky & D. Carboch, *Studies in Australian Politics* (Melbourne, 1958)
D. Winter, *25 April 1915* (Brisbane, 1994)
G. Witton, *Scapegoats of the Empire* (Melbourne, 1907)

Theses

M. Chamberlain, *Victoria at War 1899-1902* (MA thesis, University of Melbourne, 1977)
D. Chambers, *A History of Ormond College 1881-1945* (MA thesis, University of Melbourne, 1966)
A. Moore, *'Send Lawyers, Guns and Money!' A Study of Conservative*

Paramilitary Organisations in New South Wales 1930-1932, Background and Sequel 1917-1952' (PhD thesis, La Trobe University, 1982)
D. Potts, *A Study of Three Nationalists in the Bruce–Page Government of 1923-29* (MA thesis, University of Melbourne, 1972)

Periodicals

Despatches 1925-1992 (not paginated until 1964)
Duckboard (various issues)
Fintonian 1915-1940
Reveille (various issues)
Scotch Collegian 1914-1940

Newspapers

I consulted numerous newspapers at the SLV for various periods, principally the *Argus*, *Age*, *SMH*, *ECT*, and *Ballarat Courier*. I utilised many others, far too many to list here, when Elliott visited a particular locality on electioneering duty or to unveil a memorial. The holdings of both the *Herald* library and the AWM were also useful.

Notes

Chapter One [pp 1–19]

1-5 Main source for Elliott's ancestors is inf Jan McCombe. Immigrants' troubles in rough seas: R. Broome, *Arriving* (Sydney, 1984), p. 70.

7 Selectors everywhere: *St Arnaud Mercury* 24.6.1874, quoted in R. Falla (ed), *Knocking About* (Donald, 1976), p. 15. Fearful gale: *St Arnaud Mercury* 15.9.1875, quoted in Falla (ed), p. 47.

8-9 Unforeseen expenses: T. Janverin to Minister for Lands 28.10.1875, VPRS 626/2171/553, PROV. Janverin's request: T. Janverin to Minister for Lands 24.4.1878, VPRS 626/2177/884, PROV. Elliott seeking extension: T. Elliott to Secretary for Lands 9.9.1878, VPRS 626/2171/553, PROV. Low yield: T. Janverin to Minister for Lands 23.12.1880, VPRS 626/2177/884, PROV.

10-11 Request for a school: J. Postich & others to W. O'Callaghan MP 12.4.1881, VPRS 795/1476, PROV. Rock Tank's inadequate accommodation: J. Sadler to Secretary, Education Department 30.4.1888, VPRS 640/1692, PROV. Intellectual poverty: R. Selleck, *Frank Tate* (Melbourne, 1982), p. 82.

11 Harold a keen student: *ECT* 25.3.1931. Awkward bush shyness: HE to KE 27.7.1917.

12-14 Robert's accident: VPRS 7556/P1/4670, PROV. False pretences and arson: VPRS 30/742 & VPRS 7556/P1/4670, PROV; *Bendigo Advertiser* 15.10.1886. Snakebite: *ECT* 19.1.1889, *Charlton Independent* 18.1.1889. Rampage: *ECT* 23.2.1889, *Charlton Independent* 26.2.1889. Escape: *Police Gazette (Vic)* 20.11.1889, p. 380.

15-17 Wheat industry in crisis: T. Dingle, *Settling* (Sydney, 1984), p. 111. Kimberley goldfields unsettling: *ECT* 26.6.1886. Breaches of Education Act: *ECT* 27.3.1886, 26.6.1886, 28.6.1890.

17-18 Dundas Hills: *Ballarat Star* 19.2.1895. Helen fuming: *Donald Times* 10.7.1894. Payment impossible: H. Elliott to Secretary for Lands 29.3.1894, VPRS 626/2177/884, PROV.

18-19 Effusive announcement: *West Australian* 3.7.1894. Confusion re discoverer's identity: *West Australian* 3.7.1894, *Argus* 3.7.1894, *Avoca Mail and Pyrenees District Advertiser* 6.7.1894, *Avoca Free Press and Farmers and Miners Journal* 4.7.1894, *Donald Times* 10.7.1894.

Chapter Two [pp 20–32]

21 Ballarat: W. Bate, *Lucky City* (Melbourne, 1978), p. 180 ('howling wilderness'), pp. 225-6 ('city of statues').

22-3 Nell: VPRS 24/1894/1404, PROV; *Ballarat Courier* 19-21.11.94.

23-6 Ballarat College rules: Prospectus, 1907. Garbutt's priorities: Prospectus, 1907 & Bate, p. 236. Newton Wanliss on Garbutt: W. Mein, *History of Ballarat College 1864-1964* (Ballarat, 1964), p. 37. Sturt Street: A.G. Austin (ed), *The Webbs' Australian Diary 1898* (Melbourne, 1965), p. 91. Harold's results: *Ballarat Courier* 13.12.1895, 11.12.1896, 17.12.1897. Garbutt's tribute: *Ballarat Courier* 18.12.1897. 'Jumbo': inf Lorraine Paddle.

27-8 Ormond generally: S. Macintyre (ed), *Ormond College Centenary Essays* (Melbourne, 1984); D. Chambers, A History of Ormond College 1881-1945 (MA thesis, University of Melbourne, 1966). Stodgy food: P.A. Jacobs, *A Lawyer Tells* (Melbourne, 1949), p. 22. MacFarland: Macintyre, *Ormond Essays*, pp. 48-9.

29-32 Elliott's academic results: UMA. University Officers Corps: *Alma Mater* April 1898, p. 31. Reading Henderson on Stonewall Jackson: *CPD* 27.4.1921, p. 7729. Students' Club: Minutes 30.5.1898, 6.3.1899, 5.3.1900, UMA.

Chapter Three [pp 33–54]

34-5 Hughes analogy: F. Crowley (ed), *A Documentary History of Australia: Colonial Australia 1875-1900* (Melbourne, 1980), p. 571. Condescension: *Alma Mater* September 1899.

35 Tremearne on enlisters' motives: A.J.N. Tremearne, *Some Austral-African Notes and Anecdotes* (London, 1913), pp. 2-3. Stirring farewell: Tremearne, p. 7.

36-8 Riding test: G. Witton, *Scapegoats of the Empire* (Melbourne, 1907), p. 2. Langwarrin: *Argus* 17 & 30.4.1900; M. Chamberlain, Victoria at War 1899-1902 (MA thesis, University of Melbourne, 1977), pp. 90-2. Departure of Bushmen: *Argus* 2.5.1900.

38 Voyage: Witton, pp. 8-10; E. Tivey to M. Tivey 20 & 25.5.1900, Tivey papers 3DRL 3058/2, AWM.

39-40 Journey to Bamboo Creek: E. Tivey to M. Tivey 22.6.1900, 3DRL 3058/2. Bamboo Creek: Witton, p. 20. To Umtali: E. Tivey to M. Tivey 22.6.1900, 3DRL 3058/2. Unsettling night noises: Witton, p. 24.

41-2 Clash with sergeant-major: *CPD* 5.5.1921 p. 8091. Queen's death: E. Tivey to M. Tivey 23.1.1901, 3DRL 3058/2.

42-3 Pursuing de Wet: HE D Feb 1901, EP 3DRL 3297/1; E. Tivey to M. Tivey 10, 19 & 25.2.1901, 3DRL 3058/2; G. Powell, *Plumer* (London, 1990), pp. 77-80; E. Childers (ed), *The Times History of the War in South Africa 1899-1902* vol. 5 (London, 1907), pp. 135-57.

44-5 Notable exploit: varying accounts include *Argus* 10 & 30.4.1901, 17.5.1901; *Age* 10.4.1931; *Times* 24.3.1931; HE to G. McCrae 16.4.1917, McCP; R.L. Wallace, *The Australians at the Boer War* (Canberra, 1976), p. 308.

45 Elliott commended: *Argus* 8, 26 & 28.3.1901. Cable from Ormond: Ormond College Students' Club records, UMA.

46-7 Victorians have no idea: E. Tivey to M. Tivey 3.3.1901, 3DRL 3058/2. No rest: E. Tivey to M. Tivey 22.5.1901, 3DRL 3058/2. Engagement, 12 May: HE Boer War diary 12.5.1901, EP 3DRL 3297/1; E. Tivey D 12.5.1901, 3DRL 3058/1; *Historical Record of the Victorian Imperial Bushmen*, EP 1DRL 264/1A. Inclement weather: Tivey D 13.5.1901, 3DRL 3058/1; F.G. Purcell letter 10.6.1901, Purcell papers, PR 88/121, AWM.

47-8 Wallace's praise: J. Stirling, *The Colonials in South Africa 1899-1902* (London, 1907), p. 428.

48-9 Return voyage: HE to C. Bean 10.6.1929, EP 1DRL 264/1B; K. Mackay to Colonel Cooper 16.8.1901, EP 2DRL 513/13. Welcome home: *Age* & *Argus* 13.7.1901.

49-51 British not superior: *Age* 28.5.1921. Discipline in the Guards: *CPD* 5.5.1921, p. 8097. Learning from Guards NCOs, & ex-British sergeant and cheeky bugler: HE lecture notes, EP 2DRL 513/1. Glowing praise 30 years later: *Age* 26.3.1931.

51-2 *Britannic* and Victorians: *Argus* 26.8.1901; B. Hayes, *Hull Down* (London, 1925), pp. 131-3. Elliott on Witton: *CPD* 11.5.1921, p. 8246.

53 Testimonials: K. Mackay to Colonel Cooper 16.8.1901, EP 2DRL 513/13; N.W. Kelly to HE 21.8.1901, EP 1DRL 264/1A; J. Garbutt to HE 16.11.1901, EP 2DRL 513/43; J.R. Cairns to HE 18.11.1901, EP 2DRL 513/13; J. MacFarland statement 5.11.1901, EP 2DRL 513/13.

53-4 No railway, road or bridge: M. O'Farrell to 'Ned' 12.9.1901, O'Farrell papers, NAM. Border Scouts: Stirling, pp. 249-51. Birkbeck cable, & Kitchener telegram: EP 2DRL 513/13.

Chapter Four [pp 55–77]

55-60 Academic results: UMA. Harrison Moore: B. Nairn & G. Serle (eds), *ADB* vol. 10 (Melbourne, 1986), p. 574. Hancock's praise: K. Hancock, *Country and Calling* (London, 1954), p. 70. Not supremely brilliant: *Duckboard*, 1.5.1931. Evening debate at city cafe: Law Students' Society records, University of Melbourne. Honours: University of Melbourne examinations, 1906. Testimonial: EP 2DRL 513/13.

61 University footballers different: L. Sandercock & I. Turner, *Up Where Cazaly* (London, 1982), p. 260. First glimpse of Violet: HE to V. Elliott 16.5.1918.

62-3 No non-military holidays: *CPD* 20.8.1924, p. 3325. Kipling: HE to K. Roberts 31.12.1916, EP 3DRL 3297/14. Excellent officer: MP 84/1, 430/2/3 & 430/2/39, NAA (Victorian branch). World going mad: J. Mordike, *An Army for a Nation* (Sydney, 1992), p. 221.

64-70 Lecture on discipline: EP 2DRL 513/1. Native-born taunted: HE to C. Chomley 25.4.1918, Marsh papers, NLA. Pep-talk at officers' training school: *Essendon Gazette* 17.7.1913. Matters of conscience: HE to KE 27.7.1918.

70-3 Smoke night saga: T. White papers (made available by Judith Harley); *Herald* 10.5.1913. Military fete: *Essendon Gazette* 2.4.1914; *Argus* 30.3.1914.

75 'Do it again': inf Alec Burns.

Chapter Five [pp 78–107]

78 'Look here Mac': *CPD* 28.4.1921, p. 7829.

81-2 Tubb to Euroa enlisters: C. Wignell, interviewed by Murray Hamilton 10.7.1979 (transcript made available by Murray Hamilton). Clarrie Wignell: inf C. Wignell.

82 March to Broadmeadows: A.W. Keown, *Forward with the Fifth* (Melbourne, 1921), p. 18. First impressions: A. Dean & E. Gutteridge, *The Seventh Battalion AIF* (Melbourne, 1933), p. 8. Ironsides comparison: HE to 7 Bn, February 1916, EP 2DRL 513/35.

83-4 Soaked: GM to A. McCrae 21.9.1914, McCP. 'One learns exactly': HE to K. Roberts 17.3.1917, EP 3DRL 3297/14. E Coy exuberance: J. Lack, *A History of Footscray* (Footscray, 1991), p. 211. No hyphens: H.F. O'Neill D, 7 Bn Assn papers, PR 87/215, AWM.

85-6 Inexperience undetectable: *CPD* 24.11.1920, p. 6886. Lunch with Elliott: C. Kent Hughes to G. Kent Hughes 2.9.1914, Kent Hughes papers (made available by Lady Kent Hughes).

86-8 Footscray send-off: Lack, pp. 211-12. Essendon function: *Essendon Gazette* 10.9.1914. Parade through Melbourne: *Argus* 26.9.1914. Horse batmen: *Despatches* 1937. Tired of Broadmeadows: W. Kent Hughes, 'The Departure',

Kent Hughes papers. 'Goodbye now': HE to KE 18.10.1914.
88-90 Dog-boxes: GM to A. McCrae 18.10.1914, McCP. Sardines: W. Kent Hughes, 'The Departure', Kent Hughes papers. Disbelieve rumours: EP 2DRL 513/44. 'Very fine sight': HE D 1.11.1914. No marital regrets: HE to KE 11.11.1914. Ibuki: HE to KE 11.11.1914. 'Emden beached and done for': *OH* vol. 1, p. 106. Happy family: GM to 'everyone' 25.10.1914, McCP. Colombo: HE to KE 23.11.1914. Perspiration: W. Kent Hughes to G. Kent Hughes 14.11.1914, Kent Hughes papers; GM to 'everyone' 25.10.1914, McCP. 'Scarlet runners': E. Pinder to C. Bean 4.4.1960, AWM 38 3DRL 6673/46.
90-2 To Egypt: HE to KE 1.12.1914. Intense affection: HE to KE 1 & 3.12.1914. 'Very interesting journey': HE D 6.12.1914. A 'considerable stay': HE D 7.12.1914. To Cairo with Layh: HE D 8.12.1914.
92-4 Hygiene: HE to KE 10 & 13.12.1914; HE to BC 13.1.1915; HE D 7.12.1914. Thieves and cheats: HE to KE 13.12.1914. Prostitution: HE to KE 22.2.1915. 'Stupendous Scene of Stoush': Dean & Gutteridge, p. 12.
94-5 Cairo ceremony: HE D 20.12.1914, HE to KE 21.12.1914. Reid's speech: O'Neill D; C.B.L. Lock, *The Fighting Tenth* (Adelaide, 1936), pp. 312-13. March past: F. Tubb D 30.12.1914 (made available by Murray Hamilton).
95-7 'Training was hard': O'Neill D. Little news: HE to KE 10.1.1915. Marching song: O'Neill D. 'Pompey has been working us': A. Latreille, *The Natural Garden* (Melbourne, 1990), p. 8. 'Pompey the bastard': *Illustrated Tasmanian Mail* 21.8.1929. My ideal soldier: R. Taylor to HE 2.3.1916, EP 2DRL 513/14. Knows how to make soldiers: B. Elliott to H. Stones 9.1.1915 (made available by Anne Latreille). Lubke: HE to KE 31.1.1915.
97 Knees knocking: HE to KE 18.3.1915. 'Captain Weddell': *Despatches* 1952. 'Captain McKenna': *Despatches* 1956. Signallers' dread: O'Neill D.
98-100 Hat story: *Mufti* March 1954, pp. 26-7; O'Neill D; *Despatches* 1967, p. 12. 'Twist his ear': HE, Recollections, PR 87/215, AWM.
101 First impression of Birdwood: HE to KE 31.1.1915. Disagreement over tactical exercise: HE to JT 25.5.1918, EP 2DRL 513/46.
101-2 Urgent summons: HE to KE 2.2.1915. Firing line at daylight: HE to KE 13.2.1915. 'Damn it, man': *Despatches* 1947. 'By God Denehy': *Despatches* 1940, 1947. Bootless sergeant: *Despatches* 1937.
103-5 McCrae incensed: GM to H. McCrae 26 & 28.2.1915, McCP. In they go: J. Gellibrand to W. Gellibrand 8 & 14.3.1915, Gellibrand papers 3DRL 6541/2, AWM. 'It is just scandalous': HE to KE 4.1.1915. Sending wasters home: HE to KE 29.2.1915. Wonderful behaviour overall: HE to KE 13.2.1915. Bean's despatch a great pity: HE to KE 7.3.1915. Boer War veterans angry: HE to JT 25.5.1918, EP 2DRL 513/46. Requesting statistical analysis, no objection from McCay, but disallowed: HE to J. McCay 7.3.1915, J. McCay to W. Bridges 7.3.1915 & J. Gellibrand to J. McCay n.d. [March 1915], Gellibrand papers 3DRL 1473/104 AWM. Bridges opposed to Bean addressing meeting: Bean D 9.3.1915, 3DRL 606/2, p. 57. 'I was summoned': HE to JT 25.5.1918, EP 2DRL 513/46.
105-6 Stand up for my boys: HE to KE 14.3.1915. Misconduct minimal, Essendon boys in splendid health: HE to J.F. Henderson 18.3.1915, EP 2DRL 513/44.
106 Hot as hell: GM to H. McCrae 28.2.1915, McCP. Sucking pebbles: GM to G., A. & H. McCrae 13.3.1915, McCP. Sick of sand and dust: HE to KE 25.3.1915.
106-7 Hamilton's praise: HE to KE 3.4.1915. Elliott pleased: A. Court to mother 2.4.1915, Court papers (made available by Jim Court). Delighted to be leaving: HE to KE 4.4.1915.

Chapter Six [pp 108–134]

109 Satisfied with officers: HE to BC 22.4.1915. Blick splendid: HE to KE 19.5.1915. Good pals: HE to BC 22.4.1915.

110-13 Exceedingly dangerous: HE to KE 22.4.1915. Wonderfully interesting trip: HE to KE 13.4.1915. Duty paramount: HE to KE 19.12.1914. Reading letters over and over: HE to KE 18.3.1915. Watching and waiting: HE to KE 23.2.1915.

113-14 Bennett reflective: *SMH* 25.4.1939. A. Henderson's letter, 24.4.1915: 1DRL 339, AWM.

115-22 Main source is HE D; Elliott described the landing in a detailed separate diary entry, which is referred to hereafter as HE D (Landing). It is located at the start of the second volume of his 1914-1919 diaries, viz 2DRL 513/3.

117 'Keep your bum down': inf E. Marshall. Machine-gun fire: D. Winter, *25 April 1915* (Brisbane, 1994), p. 173.

119 Sinclair-Maclagan pessimistic: *OH* vol. 1, p. 222; C. Bean, *Two Men I Knew* (Sydney, 1957), p. 53.

121-2 Henderson's message: *OH* vol. 1, p. 372; HE D (Landing). Howse scathing: J. Robertson, *Anzac and Empire* (Sydney, 1990), p. 197. Murder: M. Tyquin, *Neville Howse* (Melbourne, 1999), p. 162.

123 Illness: HE to KE 7.5.1915.

123 Pre-war advice: *Essendon Gazette* 17.7.1913. Wignell on the Landing: unattributed newscutting, 7 Bn Assn papers, PR 87/215, AWM.

123-4 McCay: Winter, p. 166; HE D (Landing).

124 Objective too difficult: HE D (Landing). Elliott proud: HE to KE 13.5.1915; HE to G. Henderson 11.5.1915, *Argus* 24.6.1915; HE to J.F. Henderson n.d., *Essendon Gazette* 24.6.1915.

125-8 McArthur, & Elliott lyrical: HE to C. Chomley nd [1918], Marsh papers, NLA. Stones: E. Stones letter 16.5.1915 (made available by Anne Latreille). Heighway smelling burning paint: *Age* 12.6.1915.

128-9 'I wonder': HE to KE 13.5.1915. Stones cable: Latreille, p. 16. Cables re Elliott: Defence Dept to KE 30.4.1915 & HE to G. Roberts 2.5.1915, EP 2DRL 513/44. Like Sandringham: HE to KE 3.5.1915. No finer feat: *Argus* 8.5.1915.

129-32 Hunter-Weston: R. James, *Gallipoli* (London, 1965), p. 210 ('self-important and vain'); S. Robbins, 'The Right Way to Play the Game': The Ethos of the British High Command in the First World War', *Imperial War Museum Review* 6 (1991), p. 41 (latrines inspections); J. North to C. Carrington 30.4.1917, North papers, Liddell Hart Centre for Military Archives, University of London ('off his head'). Shovels like umbrellas: C. Bean, *Anzac to Amiens* (Canberra, 1968), p. 124. Should have been shot: O'Neill D. Elliott's response to news of Krithia: HE to KE 17.5.1915.

132-4 Grills: S. Grills D 9.5.1915, 7 Bn Assn papers, PR 87/215, AWM. Hunter on no beg pardons: *Ballarat Courier* 7.9.1914. Elliott on Hendersons: HE to KE 19.5.1915. McCrae: GM to G., A. & H. McCrae 2.5.1915, 2.6.1915, McCP. Elder Henderson brother: Hancock, *Country and Calling*, p. 54. 'What will be the end': HE to KE 23.5.1915. Condolence letter to Hendersons: HE to G.G. Henderson 25.6.1915 (made available by Dr Margaret Henderson).

Chapter Seven [pp 135–166]

135-7 Elliott's return: Grills D 4.6.1915. Not many left, & Anzac transformed: HE to KE 7.6.1915.

138-41 'It is very hot': HE to KE 28.6.1915. 'We rushed': HE to KE 7.6.1915. 'You would laugh', & 'At this moment': HE to KE 14.6.1915. Close shaves: GM to G., A. & H. McCrae 12.6.1915, McCP; HE to KE 28.6.1915; *Despatches* 1932. Elliott swimming: HE to KE 26.8.1915.

141-2 Elliott's snipers installed: HE to KE 28.6.1915. Until the last gleam: *Reveille* 31.3.1930, p. 7. Carne finding it very hot: P. Carne D 3.7.1915 (made available by Allan Box).

143-4 Bombardments at Steele's: HE to KE 7.7.1915. Carne's shaken nerves: Carne D 6.7.1915.

144-7 Tunnel encounter: HE to JT 25.5.1918, EP 2DRL 513/46; HE to KE 12.7.1915; *OH* vol. 2, pp. 333-4; HE to Bean 20.9.1919 & 'Fighting in Tunnels at G.O.T.', AWM 38 3DRL 8042/29. Elliott's justification: HE to JT 25.5.1918, EP 2DRL 513/46. 'My boy': G. Pennefather to KE 10.10.1915, EP 2DRL 513/15.

147-50 Greig's attack: HE D 13.7.1915; *OH* vol. 2, pp. 337-40. Tubb's initiation: Tubb D 10-13.7.1915. Elliott devastated: HE to KE 12.7.1915. 'It is terrible', & 'For myself': HE to KE 21.7.1915.

150-1 Cracking the whip: Tubb D 20-21.7.1915, HE D 25-28.7.1915. Untrained reinforcements: Grills D 31.5.1915; *OH* vol. 2, pp. 411-12; HE to KE 28.6.1915; Tubb D 4.7.1915.

151-2 Identifying with the 7th: HE to J. Latham 26.7.1915, Latham papers 1009/1/141, NLA; HE to J. Richardson 26.7.1915, Richardson papers 3DRL 3328, AWM. Kerby: HE D 20, 26.7.1915; Tubb D 26-29.7.1915.

152 Elliott's realisation: HE to KE 21.7.1915. Grills' departure: Grills D 13-21.7.1915.

153 Bean detects a mood change: *OH* vol. 2, pp. 426-7. Elliott hoping for the best: HE to Richardson 26.7.1915, 3DRL 3328, AWM.

154-5 Johnston's Jolly operation: HE to Richardson 25.1.1916, 3DRL 3328, AWM; *OH* vol. 2, p. 496. Address to 6th Reinforcements: *Despatches* 1957, 1958; Tubb D 5.8.1915.

155-6 Dyett, Edwards and Symons: *ADB* vols. 8 & 12; R. McMullin, 'Bendigo's Original Anzac', *Wartime* 8 (Summer 1999), pp. 34-5; *Bendigo Advertiser* 22.3.1916; *Bendigo Independent* 13.1.1916.

156-7 Elliott on 1st Brigade: HE to KE 8.8.1915. 'We were saved': HE to Richardson 25.1.1916, 3DRL 3328, AWM. Like an underground city: HE to KE 8.8.1915.

157-9 7 Bn at Lone Pine: HE BR; 7 Bn D; HE D; Tubb D 6-10.8.1915; HE to KE August 1915; HE to Richardson 25.1.1916, 3DRL 3328, AWM; *OH* vol. 2, pp. 553-63.

159-60 Splashed with blood and brains: HE to C.B.B. White 30.5.1930, EP 2DRL 513/46. Allocating meagre resources: HE to KE 26.8.1915. Dealing with unsettled recruits: HE to KE 14.8.1915.

160-3 Number 1 Post: HE to KE 8.8.1915, *OH* vol. 2, pp. 557, 561-3. Tubb's post: Tubb D 10.8.1915, *OH* vol. 2, pp. 560-1. Edwards: *Bendigo Advertiser* cutting n.d. [1917], Edwards papers, Talbot Museum.

163-4 Walker: HE BR, pp. 13-14; HE to Richardson 25.1.1916, 3DRL 3328, AWM. 'Hang on boys': *Despatches* 1968, p. 53. Most desperate battle: HE to KE 14.8.1915. Would swap the glory: HE to KE 8.8.1915. D Coy losses: *Bendigo Advertiser* 22.3.1916. 5 Bn assistant: T. Murphy interview, SLV. Tubb thrilled: Tubb D 10.8.1915.

164-5 Elliott's difficult task: HE BR, p. 14. Dunstan: *Independent Monthly* July 1989; K.

Dunstan, *No Brains At All* (Melbourne, 1990), pp. 67-70. Webb: HE to KE 8.8.1915; HE BR, p. 12. Graphic glimpse: HE to Richardson 25.1.1916, 3DRL 3328, AWM.

166 'The dead still lay': HE to KE 14.8.1915. Watching Turks scatter: HE to KE 18.8.1915. Elliott not conned: *Despatches* 1946. Elliott's high standards and standing: HE to KE 26.8.1915. Ill: HE D 26-28.8.1915; HE to KE 15.9.1915.

Chapter Eight [pp 167–198]

167-8 Pleurisy: HE to KE 15 & 19.9.1915. 'Most beautiful place': HE D 24.9.1915. No endurance: HE to KE 6.10.1915.

168-9 Gateshead fortnight: HE to KE 12.10.1915, 7.11.1915; HE to ME 15.10.1915, McCombe papers. A terrible rush: HE to KE 6.11.1915. Piles: HE to KE 19.10.1915. 'I have the feeling' & 'ordinary sort of person': HE to BC 21.11.1915.

169-70 Pinder critical: E. Pinder to Bean 4.4.1960, AWM 38 3DRL 6673/46. Unjust and unreasonable: Tubb D 21.7.1915.

170-1 Delighted about VCs, 'more than any slab': HE to KE 12.11.1915. 'When I think', 'Your old man' & 'I told them': HE to KE 16.11.1915. Ken Walker: HE to KE 1.10.1915.

171 Missing Kate: HE to KE 12 & 16.11.1915. Letters an inspiration: HE to KE 18.8.1915.

173 Evacuation bombshell HE to KE 12.12.1915; Robertson, p. 182. Scurry, Lawrence and drip-rifle: R. McMullin, 'Escape from Gallipoli', *Wartime* 12 (Summer 2000), pp. 28-31.

175-6 Disappointed he could not 'stick it out': HE to KE 26.12.1915. Cause of ankle injury: inf W. Carter, B. Lawrence. Same old ward: HE to KE 26.12.1915. Amazed by success: HE to Richardson 25.1.1916, 3DRL 3328, AWM. Recovery slow: HE to KE 2.1.1916; HE to Richardson 25.1.1916, 3DRL 3328, AWM.

177-8 Stiff penalty: *Despatches* 1947. Lawrence disciplined: inf B. Lawrence. Sad and weary: HE to KE 7.2.1916. Annoyed by unfairness: HE to G. McCrae 26.1.1916, McCP. Reliving Lone Pine: HE to KE 27.1.1916, 2.2.1916. Easily riled: HE to KE 7.2.1916.

178-80 Symons and the King: HE to KE 2.2.1916. Farewell message: *Despatches* 1966, p. 31.

180-1 Initially ill-at-ease: HE to KE 18.2.1916; HE to BC 19.2.1916. English staff: HE to KE 25.2.1916. British officers' changed attitude: HE to KE 16.1.1916. Pleasing transfer to 15 Bde: HE to KE 8.3.1916.

182-8 Looking to White for support: HE D 9.3.1916; HE to White 12.3.1916, EP 3DRL 3297/14. Not forthcoming: White to HE 11[=12].3.1916, EP 3DRL 3297/14. Legge's response: Legge to HE 12.3.1916, EP 3DRL 3297/14. Elliott's livid rejoinder: HE to White 14.3.1916, EP 3DRL 3297/14. Elliott on Birdwood: HE to KE 14.4.1916. Birdwood letter to Pearce 24.3.1916, Birdwood papers, 3 DRL 3376, AWM; Elliott on Irving: HE to KE 2 & 14.4.1916. Prince of Wales: HE D 22.3.1916. Spirited talk with White: HE D 22.3.1916; HE to KE 24.3.1916. Wieck splendid: HE to KE 17.4.1916. Reluctant acceptance: HE D 22.3.1916.

188-9 McCay unpopular: HE to KE 20.3.1916. Initial briefing: Birdwood to Pearce 24.3.1916, 3 DRL 3376, AWM. Elliott summoned: HE D 23.3.1916.

189-90 'I was awakened' & 'not even a wart': J. Schroder in AWM 38 3DRL 606/276.

'Send them back!': unattributed newscutting, McCombe papers. Walker's visit: HE D 20.3.1916, HE to KE 24.3.1916. McCrae on freemasonry: GM to G. McCrae 5.3.1916, McCP. 4,000 'lives rest on my judgment': HE to KE 14.4.1916.

192-4 Drawing pistol: HE to KE 14.4.1916. 'Who lit that?': inf H. O'Brien. Protest re water: *Bulletin* 22.5.1929. Sympathising with Irving: HE to KE 2.5.1916.

194-5 Wright: R. Taylor to HE 2.3.1916 & 27.5.1916, EP 2DRL 513/14.

195 Bit of a lecture: K. Roberts to HE 12.4.1916, EP 2DRL 513/14. Elliott touched: HE to KE 18.5.1916.

195-7 Brigade's pleasing progress: HE to KE 11.5.1916. 'I am gradually', & Morrow excellent: HE to KE 8.5.1916. McCrae a favourite: HE to G. McCrae 26.1.1916, McCP. 'People tell me': HE to KE 6.6.1916. Old fossils, & Field's illness: HE to KE 18.5.1916; HE D 20.5.1916.

197 Blick: HE to KE 20.4.1916; *Argus* 25.4.1916. Children: HE to KE 3.6.1916, 8.5.1916, & 29.5.1916.

198 Accolades: HE to KE 6.6.1916 (McCay); HE to KE 5.6.1916 (Wagstaff). Davies ill: HE to KE 21.6.1916.

Chapter Nine [pp 199–235]

199-203 Elliott impressed, Steenbecque & communication with Madame Brunet: HE to KE 3.7.1916. Madame Brunet excited, & strict edict re conduct: HE to KE 5.7.1916. Terrific bombardment: HE to KE 3.7.1916. Wieck & Legge: HE to KE 24.7.1916, 11.5.1916. Tivey: Birdwood to Pearce 3.7.1916, 3DRL 3376, AWM.

205-6 Haking claiming attackers' success inevitable: R. Haking, *Company Training* (London, 1913), p. 103. Game on Haking: P. Game to G. Game 20.12.1915 & 3.2.1916, Game papers, IWM. Haking keen on Aubers Ridge: E.C. Jepp to J. Edmonds 13.3.1937, CAB 45/134, PRO. Boar's Head: N. Lytton, *The Press and the General Staff* (London, 1920), p. 42; WO 95/2563, PRO.

208-9 McCay too eager: HE to BC 26.8.1916. Artillery inadequate: P. Landon to Edmonds 2.4.1937, CAB 45/135, PRO; W. Greene to Edmonds 13.5.1937, CAB 45/134, PRO.

209-11 Carter: G. Christie-Miller memoirs pp. 163, 174, 190, IWM. Conversation with Howard: AWM 38 3DRL 6673/954, p. 7. Haking adamant: *OH* vol. 3, p. 347. Elliott's misgivings: HE D 17.7.1916.

212-13 'My poor boys': HE to KE 18.7.1916. Slackness in 58th: HE D 18.7.1916. Jackson: HE to G. McCrae 6.5.1918, McCP. Tom Elliott's transfer reversed: HE to BC 17.12.1916.

213 'I am writing this': HE to KE 19.7.1916. McCrae's letter is in McCP. Tom Elliott's letter: 3DRL 2872, AWM.

216-17 'Boys, you won't find': *OH* vol. 3, p. 362. Haking's assurance: memorandum 16.7.1916, WO 95/881, PRO. Mapless artillery commander: WO 95/165, PRO.

217-21 Messages sent by Elliott & the communication from 184 Bde are in 15 BD. Doyle: R. Corfield, *Hold Hard, Cobbers* vol. 1, 1912-1930 (Melbourne, 1992), p. 34. Greyhounds on the leash: *OH* vol. 3, pp. 394-5. Splendid dash: *OH* vol. 3, p. 395. McCay's 9.25 message: 5 Div D. No further use: *OH* vol. 3, p. 398. Criss-crossed lattice of death: W. Downing, *To the Last Ridge* (Melbourne, 1920), pp. 24-6.

222-5 A thousand butcher-shops: H. Knyvett, *Over There with the Australians* (London, 1918), p. 155. Everything red: Downing, p. 30. Doyle: Corfield, p.

34. An hour's hard work: Downing, p. 29. Heart-rending spectacle: *OH* vol. 3, p. 437. A 'tremendous length': AWM 38 3DRL 606/123, pp. 19-20. Legge's messages to Elliott are in 15 BD. Schroder accompanying Elliott, & Pompey's tears: AWM 38 3DRL 606/276; inf A. Ebdon. Smith, & rescuers 'out under fire six times': *Strathbogie: A Souvenir of the District Soldiers' Memorial*. Truce: R. Corfield, *Don't Forget Me Cobber* (Melbourne, 2000), pp. 260-70, 452-63. Marshall and Knuckey: inf B. Knuckey. Fraser's account: letter dated 31.7.1916, 1DRL 300, AWM.

226-7 Unprepared little shows: *OH* vol. 3, p. 443. 'Poor old Tivey': AWM 38 3DRL 606/52, pp. 18-20. British communique: *OH* vol. 3, p. 446. Bean flabbergasted: AWM 38 3DRL 606/52, pp. 22-3. 'Our men … are disgusted': *SMH* 27.9.1916. 'We may deceive': *OH* vol. 3, p. 443.

227-8 Haking's conclusion: Haking to C.C. Monro 24 & 26.7.1916, WO 95/881, PRO. Bean's view: *OH* vol. 3, p. 445. Abominable libel: W. Greene to J. Edmonds 13.5.1937, CAB 45/134, PRO. Fatuous bluster: Haking to McCay 20.7.1916, WO 95/881, PRO.

229-31 'The battle is over': HE to KE 20.7.1916. 'God knows why': HE to ME 23.7.1916. McCrae: HE to G. McCrae 21 & 23.7.1916, McCP.

231-2 No unworthy names: HE to KE 29.4.1916. Poulter: Corfield, p. 45. McCrae: CRS B2455, NAA (ACT branch). Hutchinson: 1DRL 371, AWM; HE to JT 25.5.1918, EP 2DRL 513/46. Tom Elliott: 3DRL 2872, AWM.

232-4 'I can honestly say': HE to BC 13.8.1916. 'General McCay said': HE to KE 31.7.1916. Generals sacked, & sympathy for Pope: HE to BC 13.8.1916. Bean on 58 Bn attack: *OH* vol. 3, p. 394. 'I am very sad': HE to BC 26.7.1916. 'They were great pals': HE to KE 1.8.1916. Magnificent young officers: HE to G. Ellingsen 26.7.1916 (made available by Bruce Ellingsen & Weston Bate).

Chapter Ten [pp 236–264]

237-8 Elliott melancholy: HE to KE 20 & 22.8.1916, 18.9.1916. Scurry: *Reveille* 1.12.1932; HE to KE 20.8.1916; *ADB* vol. 11, pp. 557-8; HE to BC 11.9.1916.

238-9 Doyle wounded: HE to BC 11.9.1916. 'This morning': HE to M. Campbell 13.9.1916, EP 2DRL 513/10. Fantasy: HE to KE 26.8.1916. Very sad: HE to KE 16.9.1916. Egypt seeming long ago: HE to KE 13.8.1916. Russian decoration: HE to KE 16 & 18.9.1916.

240 Hospital visits, 'looking … dilapidated' & daunting cost of new uniform: HE to KE 11.10.1916. Kerr ashamed: T. Kerr D 21-23.8.1916 (made available by Margaret Wood).

241-3 Montauban: 15 BD (Wieck) & HE D 22.10.1916. Roar of guns: HE to KE 24.10.1916. 'Everything is desolation': HE D 24.10.1916. Darkie struggling: HE to BC 28.10.1916. Wretched in the extreme: HE D 29.10.1916. Downing lamenting the torment: Downing, pp. 31-6, 48. Elliott compassionate: HE to KE 2.11.1916; HE D 30.10.1916. Sopping wet: HE to KE 2.11.1916. Mud, mud, mud: HE to KE 14.11.1916. One vast bog: 15 BD 19.11.1916.

244-5 Protest vindicated: HE to KE 9.11.1916. Conscription: HE to KE 2 & 9.11.1916, 24.10.1916; HE to BC 17.12.1916.

246-7 'Well, boys': *Despatches* 1939. Ball: HE to BC 17.12.1916; *ADB* vol. 7, p. 160.

247-8 Talk with Feilding: *Age* 28.5.1921; AWM 27, 172/10. Guards 'at liberty to postpone': WO 95/1221, PRO. 'I reported this conversation': HE to JT 25.5.1918, EP 2DRL 513/46.

249 Forward with Knyvett: HE D 22.11.1916; HE to KE 2.12.1916; Knyvett, pp. 223-5.

250-1 Dreadfully cold and frosty: HE to KE 2.12.1916. At wits' end: HE to KE 27.11.1916; HE to BC 17.12.1916. Hot-box contrivance: HE to KE 16.12.1916. Distressingly powerless: HE to KE 16.12.1916. Worst sector: D. McCarthy, *Gallipoli to the Somme: The Story of C.E.W. Bean* (Sydney, 1983), p. 264.

251-2 Near miss with Greenway: HE to KE 16.12.1916. Disrupted sleep: HE to BC 17.12.1916.

252-3 Elliott pessimistic: HE to KE 8.12.1916. Tanks: HE to KE 16.9.1916 & 24.11.1916, HE to BC 17.12.1916. Sombre about McCrae and others: HE to K. Roberts 31.12.1916, EP 3DRL 3297/14. 'I can assure you': HE to G. McCrae 9.11.1916, McCP.

253-7 Like Sandringham: *Argus* 9.6.1915. Cherishing Kate's letters: HE to KE 2.11.1916. Swearing: HE to KE 27.3.1916, 14.4.1916, 1 & 13.8.1916. 'You would not think': HE to KE 28.10.1916. Violet's first letter: HE D 27.9.1916. Higher pedestal: HE to BC 3.5.1918. 'Since I wrote': HE to N. Elliott 27.12.1916. Neil to Duntroon: HE to BC 27.8.1916. Dealing with bullies: HE to N. Elliott 10.9.1916. Story about Dida: HE to KE 27.8.1916, 27.9.1916. Best little fairy lady: HE to V. Elliott 30.11.1916.

258-9 McCay: HE to G.G. Henderson 17.3.1917, Henderson papers (made available by Dr Margaret Henderson); HE to BC 21.1.1917; McCay to HE 17.1.1917, EP 1DRL 264/1B. Initially unimpressed with Hobbs: HE to KE 8.1.1917. Defiant re Davies: HE to KE 18.1.1917. Denehy: HE D 19.12.1916. Trickey: Corfield, p. 65; HE to KE 16.12.1916.

260-3 Huge wedding cake: HE to KE 20.1.1917. Elliott ill: HE to KE 16 & 26.12.1916. Everything frozen: K. Doig to L. Grant 31.1.1917, Doig papers, SLV. Icy feet in bed & conceding to doctors: HE to KE 2.2.1917. Testing icy shell-holes, & Salmon orchestrating fireworks: HE D 23.1.1917; AWM 38 3DRL 606/276. Handling unwelcome visitors: HE to KE 12.2.1917.

263-4 Hobbs worrying: HE D 13.2.1917. Elliott given leave: HE to KE 17.2.1917; HE D 16.2.1917. Duigan: J. Duigan to KE 7.3.1917, EP 2DRL 513/20.

Chapter Eleven [pp 265–281]

265-6 Elliott cautioning: HE to KE 2.3.1917. Repugnance: HE to BC 9.4.1917.

267-9 Envelopment: HE to Bean 10.6.1929, EP 1DRL 264/1B; HE to Bean 29.8.1927, AWM 38 3DRL 606/260. Wieck observing nervousness: Wieck to Bean 7.10.1929, AWM 38 3DRL 606/26. Delsaux Farm, & unimpressed British officer: HE to Bean 1.8.1929, AWM 38 3DRL 606/260. Praising Wieck: HE to KE 24.7.1916. Walker's experiences: E. Walker D 19.3.1917, SLV.

269-71 Concern re right flank: HE to 5 Div 6.40am 20.3.1917, 15 BD & 5 Div D. Bertincourt clear: Layh to HE 10.25am 20.3.1917, 15 BD. 59th platoon will remain: HE to 5 Div 9.30am 21.3.1917, 15 BD. Napoleonic ideas: HE to Bean 29.8.1927 & 2.8.1929, AWM 38 3DRL 606/260. Elliott 'amusing': AWM 38 3DRL 606/276. 'Always a weak spot': Wieck to HE 5.9.1919, EP 2DRL 514/42B. Constant anxiety: AWM 38 3DRL 1722/21.

271-2 Frustratingly fettered: 5 Div to HE 11.10am & 9.35pm 21.3.1917, 5 Div D. Fret, fume and swear: HE to BC 9.4.1917.

272-6 Wieck's account is in AWM 38 3DRL 606/260. Scanlan's corroboration: AWM 38 3DRL 606/276. The messages between 15 Bde and 5 Div are in AWM 4.

Missed opportunity: HE D 23.3.1917. Elliott's postwar assessment: HE to Bean 1 & 2.8.1929 & 29.8.1927, AWM 38 3DRL 606/260; HE to Bean 14.9.1929, EP 2DRL 513/46. Gough's biographer: A.H. Farrar-Hockley, *Goughie* (London, 1975), p. 204.

277 Beaumetz, 24 March: HE to Bean 1.8.1929, AWM 38 3DRL 606/260.

278 Bean on Lagnicourt: *OH* vol. 4, p. 201. Communication execrable: 27 Bn D.

280 'Retire be buggered': Wieck to HE 5.9.1919, EP 2DRL 513/42B; Wieck to Bean 7.10.1929, AWM 38 3DRL 606/260.

280-1 'My word Katie': HE to KE 28.3.1917. 'We finished up': HE to KE 29.3.1917. Literally unconquerable: HE to G. McCrae 16.4.1917, McCP.

Chapter Twelve [pp 282–299]

282-3 Elliott pessimistic about Hindenburg Line: HE to KE 7.4.1917. The 'best time': Doig to L. Grant 26.4.1917, Doig papers, SLV. Swanking feed: HE to KE 25.4.1917. Peaceful rest: HE to KE 29.4.1917; HE to BC 3.5.1917. Weather: Doig to L. Grant 2.5.1917, Doig papers, SLV.

283-4 Close shave: HE D 8.5.1917. Graphic description: Downing, pp. 75-7.

285-7 Strongpoints bristling: HE to R. Elliott 14.5.1917, EP 2DRL 513/41. Elliott on Cumming: HE D 11.5.1917. Denehy's worship: HE to KE 21.7.1917. Information was provided by a 58 Bn officer who did not want to be identified. Pelton's letter: F. Breed (ed), *From France with Love* (Donald, 1995), pp. 182-3. Midnight conference: C. Denehy to G. Topp 7.10.1917, Topp papers 1DRL 583, AWM.

287-9 German bombardment: HE to R. Elliott 14.5.1917, EP 2DRL 513/41; HE to BC 15.5.1917; Hobbs D 11.5.1917, PR 82/153/3, AWM; Downing, pp. 74-5. Stokes Mortars: HE to R. Elliott 14.5.1917, EP 2DRL 513/41. 'Come on boys' & 'My word': E.J. Dillon statement, Denehy papers (made available by Mrs M. Denehy). German officer: HE to R. Elliott 14.5.1917, EP 2DRL 513/41. Boys magnificent: HE to KE 14.5.1917, HE to BC 15.5.1917. Doig proud: Doig to L. Grant 15.5.1917, Doig papers, SLV. Pelton & Topp gallant: HE to R. Elliott 14.5.1917, EP 2DRL 513/41. Moon exceptional: HE to KE 14 & 16.5.1917.

289-90 Wonderful sight: P. Freyberg, *Bernard Freyberg VC* (London, 1991), p. 105. Pompey's strong reaction: HE to JT 25.5.1918, EP 2DRL 513/46.

290 Tired out, concerned about Layh, & sleeping in: HE to KE 16.6.1917.

290-1 Warmer weather: Wieck in 15 BD 31.5.1917, HE to KE 7.6.1917. Lacking confidence in Hobbs: HE to KE 7.4.1917. Bean on Hobbs: AWM 38 3DRL 606/82, p. 37. Elliott preferring McCay: HE to KE 15.4.1917.

291-3 Not wanting Street: HE D 22.7.1917; *CPD* 13.4.1921, p. 7378. Phoney as an eel: HE to BC 21.7.1917. Too 'weary and worn for words': HE to KE 5.8.1917. Street's start: HE D 25.7.1917.

293-5 DSO: HE to KE 21.7.1917. No end in sight: HE to BC 24.8.1917. No 'push or go left': HE to KE 27.7.1917. Debt reduction: HE to KE 19.8.1917. Not Eric: inf E. Roberts. First impression of Stillman: HE to KE 20.9.1916. Stillman promising: HE to K. Roberts 17.3.1917, EP 3DRL 3297/14. Conversation embarrassing Stillman: P. Hocking, *Twice a Digger* (Melbourne, 1995), pp. 28-9. Aram: J. Aram to Mrs Ostberg 20.7.1917 & 1.8.1917, Aram papers, PR 84/87, AWM. 'Hullo Pompey': H.R. Williams, *Comrades of the Great Adventure* (Sydney, 1935), pp. 194-5.

296-7 'Fancy Katie': HE to KE 7.4.1917. Willing to 'give it a fly', & Doyle on Marshall:

Reveille 31.12.1931. Acting the goat: HE to KE 14.7.1917. Denehy 'coming on excellently', Mason doing 'very well', & fortunate with bn commanders: HE to KE 6.7.1917.

297-8 Disciplining Legge: HE to BC 9.4.1917. Legge different now: HE to KE 30.8.1917.

298-9 Boys looking splendid: HE to KE 21.7.1917. 'Dear wee chap': HE to KE 6.7.1917. Codicil: EP 2DRL 513/43. So 'tired and worn out', & 'great and terrible battle': HE to KE 5.8.1917.

Chapter Thirteen [pp 300–346]

301 Artillery, trench mortars better: HE to KE 17.2.1917. Monash on bite and hold: G. Serle, *John Monash: A Biography* (Melbourne, 1982), p. 292.

302-3 Elliott on Plumer: HE to KE 8.9.1917. On Harington: HE to Bean 10.6.1929, EP 1DRL 264/1B. Exchange with Noad: inf C. Noad. Plumer pleased: HE to KE 8.9.1917.

304-5 Guns booming: HE to BC 19.9.1917. Glorious advance: HE to BC 20.9.1917.

307 Headquarters unsuitable: HE BR, p. 2. With great success: HE BR, p. 1.

310-16 Hourly more precarious: H. Boyd BR, p. 4. Hooge crater dangerous: C. Stewart BR, p. 1, C. Mason BR, p. 2. Hobbs not suicidal: Hobbs D 25.9.1917, PR 82/153/3, AWM. Elliott's reassurance: AWM 38 3DRL 606/239, p. 13. Confidence in Marshall: *OH* vol. 4, p. 802. Very serious: Stillman BR. Marshall's assessment: HE BR, pp. 8-9. Harington remembering: T. Harington, *Plumer of Messines* (London, 1935), p. 116. Boyd admiring Marshall's grasp: Boyd BR, p. 7. Beaver: Marshall BR, p. 2. Downing on 57th's experience: Downing, pp. 82-6. Dickinson's advice: inf C. Noad. Elliott to Stewart: 57 Bn D.

317-20 Utmost anxiety, 'not a single' & 'Division insists': HE BR, p. 10. Exchange with Mason: AWM 38 3DRL 606/181, p. 6. Without a hitch: AWM 183/33 (Mason). 'The last man': HE BR, p. 14. Wood to Heriot-Maitland: 33 Div D, WO 95/2406, PRO. McDonald's message, & instructing Stewart: HE BR, p. 14.

320-3 Barrage like Gippsland bushfire: *OH* vol. 4, p. 813. Toll unequivocal, 'Whatever justification' & 'Push on at once': HE BR, p. 17. Joint message: 5 Div D. Obscure on right: HE BR, p. 19. 'The barrage continued': Downing, pp. 89-91. Stewart's report: HE BR, p. 19.

324-5 Dunn: Introduction by Keith Simpson to reissued J. Dunn, *The War the Infantry Knew* (London, 1989). Cameron House: HE BR, p. 20. Richards: F. Richards, *Old Soldiers Never Die* (Sydney, 1933), pp. 220, 223-6. Writing interrupted: Dunn, p. 398.

326-9 Wood to Heriot-Maitland: 33 Div D, WO 95/2406, PRO. Plumer's proposal approved: WO 158/208, PRO. Contradictory information: 15 BD. Elliott's challenge: inf B. Bragg. Schroder on 'Pomp' going forward: AWM 38 3DRL 606/276. Richards marvelling: Richards, p. 226. Dunn stunned: Dunn pp. 346, 401. Battlefield chaos: HE to KE 2.10.1917. 'I arranged with Marshall': HE D 26.9.1917. Retaliatory bombardment heavy: G. Laing BR, p. 2.

329-31 Bean on Elliott: *OH* vol. 4, p. 832. News of George's death: HE to G.G. Henderson 18.10.1917 (made available by Dr Margaret Henderson). Man in a trance: HE D 28.9.1917. Never nearer death: Doig to L. Grant 30.9.1917 & 19.10.1917, Doig papers, SLV. Street on casualties: 15 BD 28.9.1917.

323-3 All quotes from 'Poor old Geordie' to gladly welcoming a shell are from HE to

KE 2.10.1917.

333-5 At home with the dead, & Passchendaele: HE to G. McCrae 13 & 19.10.1917 & 8.1.1918, McCP. Too heartsore to write much: HE to KE 3.10.1917. 'My dear little laddie': HE to N. Elliott 3.10.1917.

335-6 Critical of Street: HE BR, p. 16; HE D 10.10.1917; HE to KE 11.10.1917. Another narrow escape: HE to KE 11.10.1917; HE D 11 & 17.10.1917.

336-7 Awards for Polygon Wood, & Stillman splendid: HE to KE 22.10.1917. 'That pleased me': Hocking, pp. 51-2.

337-8 Jack cheery: J. Campbell to KE 23.9.1917, Campbell papers, 2DRL 34, AWM. Elliott unprepared: F.L. Wright to M. Campbell 28.10.1917, Campbell papers, 2DRL 34, AWM. More melancholy tidings: HE to KE 28.10.1917. Facial rash: HE D 24.10.1917.

339-40 'On my return': HE to editor *Sun* (Syd) 17.6.1921, EP 2DRL 513/42B. 'You probably know': Birdwood to Bean 25.8.1921, AWM 38 3DRL 6673/352. Hobbs's view: Hobbs D 31.10.1917, PR 82/153/3, AWM.

340-4 HE BR: delay re boundary & orders too late, p. 1; 'I would respectfully', p. 2; best judge, p. 24. Flagrant exaggeration: Birdwood to Bean 25.8.1921, AWM 38 3DRL 6673/352. Middlesex: HE BR, pp. 5-7. Critical of 98 Brigade: HE BR, pp. 8-10, 14-15, 18-19. Well-credentialled historians: R. Prior & T. Wilson, *Passchendaele: The Untold Story* (New Haven & London, 1996), p. 211 fn 19. 'Preliminary Instructions': no. 11, 24.9.1917, 5 Div D. HE BR: resorting to borrowed bn, p. 18; belated arrival yet valuable assistance, p. 1; Toll & Purser, p. 13; failure to advance, p. 9; Welch, p. 23; Stokes mortars invaluable, p. 24.

344-5 Bean on Elliott's report: *OH* vol. 4, p. 832 fn 140. Early draft: AWM 44 4/21 part 5. Testy sentence: HE BR, p. 15. White's intervention: White to Bean 17.6.1932, AWM 38 3DRL 6673/258. Birdwood's view: Birdwood to Bean 25.8.1921, AWM 38 3DRL 6673/352.

Chapter Fourteen [pp 347–359]

347-8 Praise for Layh: HE to KE 11.11.1917. Blisters inflamed: HE to KE 11.11.1917, HE to BC 11.11.1917. Startling appearance: HE D 15.11.1917. Real bushranger: HE to KE 16.11.1917. So run down: HE to KE 11.11.1917. Not a kick: HE to KE 16.11.1917.

348-9 Elliott on Birdwood: HE to KE 30.8.1917, 26.2.1918. Tell me all: HE to KE 22.6.1917. Mind made up: HE to G.G. Henderson 16.1.1918 (made available by Dr Margaret Henderson). 'I told the boys': HE to KE 7.1.1918.

350 Depressed: HE to BC 26.2.1918; HE to Richardson 15.1.1918, 3DRL 3328; HE to KE 31.12.1917.

350 Appalled by referendum result: HE to KE 10.2.1918, 18.1.1918, 26.3.1918, 3.3.1918, 26.2.1918, 18.1.1918; letter to Henderson is in EP 2DRL 513/43.

351 Awful time ahead: HE to BC 19.1.1918, HE to KE 24.12.1917. French and British weakened: HE to G.G. Henderson 16.1.1918; HE to Richardson 15.1.1918, 3DRL 3328.

351-2 Anxiety about legal practice: HE to KE 10.2.1918, 7.1.1918, 24.12.1917, 22.10.1917. Apology: K. Roberts to KE 21.2.1918, EP 2DRL 513/43. Elliott grateful: HE to KE 22.11.1917. Great relief: HE to KE 17.4.1918.

352-5 'I wish I knew': HE to KE 24.12.1917. Touching condolence: HE to KE 26.11.1917. Very sad time: HE to KE 11.11.1917. Desolate laddie: HE to KE 7.1.1918. Like his daddy too: HE to ME 30.4.1918. Faces unchanged: HE to N.

Elliott 24.12.1917. Praying properly: HE to ME 18.3.1918. Astonished and elated by Violet: HE to V. Elliott 17.3.1918 & 19.4.1918.

355-6 Weather not bad: HE to KE 10.2.1918. Snow crystals sparkling: HE to KE 24.12.1917. Lovely place to rest: HE to KE 27.1.1918. Things pretty quiet: HE to BC 26.2.1918. 'I always begrudge': HE to KE 13.2.1918. Shrieks drowning barrage: HE to KE 5.3.1918.

356-8 On Mason, Freeman, Stewart, Layh & Marshall: HE to KE 18.1.1918, 10.2.1918, 22.3.1918. Young men with old faces: I. Chapman, *Iven G. Mackay* (Melbourne, 1975), p. 96.

358-9 British unreliable: HE to KE 27.1.1918. Frank memorandum: AWM 27 304/11. Ready for anything: HE to KE 26.2.1918. Shakespearian flourish: HE to ME 14.2.1918.

Chapter Fifteen [pp 360–384]

360-1 Intensifying shellfire, & offensive welcomed: HE D 19-21.3.1918. Bean delighted: *OH* vol. 5, p. 113; AWM 38 3DRL 606/102, pp. 14-18. Crisis: *OH* vol. 5, p. 115. Crushing tension: V. Brittain, *Testament of Youth* (London, 1979), p. 411.

361-3 Exciting times ahead: HE D 23.3.1918. 'What will happen': Hobbs D 27.3.1918, PR 82/153/3, AWM. Awful situation, & morale admirable: HE to KE 26.3.1918. Pensive journey: Downing, p. 110. Train hit: J.A. Stevens D 27.3.1918, SLV. Inspecting outposts, & praise for Doyle: HE D 28.3.1918. Doyle reciprocating: Corfield, p. 120.

364 'Vive l'Australie!' & 'Fini retreat': *OH* vol. 5, p. 177. 'Pas necessaire maintenant': *OH* vol. 5, p. 120. Outstanding morale: HE to KE 26.3.1918. Elliott's damning impressions: HE D 27-28.3.1918.

365-7 Hedauville episode: HE D 29.3.1918; *CPD* 21.4.1921, p. 7559; HE to Hobbs 25.5.1918, EP 2DRL 513/46.

367-8 Covering Amiens vital: Haig D 26.3.1918, WO 256/30, PRO. Sickening confirmation: Hobbs D 29.3.1918, PR 82/153/3, AWM.

368-9 March to Corbie: HE D 29-30.3.1918; *OH* vol. 5, p. 525; E. Need unpublished memoir (made available by Joan Scott), pp. 186-91; Downing, p. 112; G.R. Freeman D 29-30.3.1918 (made available by Bill Freeman); *CPD* 22.8.1923, pp. 3272-3.

369-71 Cracking the whip: HE D 30.3.1918. Diverting incident: AWM 38 3DRL 606/276.

372 14 Div: M. Middlebrook, *The Kaiser's Battle* (London, 1983), pp. 326-7; Haig D 29.3.1918, WO 256/30, PRO; HE D 2.4.1918.

372-4 Looting in Corbie, & 'I have read': HE to ME 22.4.1918. General Craufurd, & no test case: HE to Treloar 25.5.1918, EP 2DRL 513/46. No trouble afterwards: HE to KE 11.4.1918. 'That yarn has spread': HE to BC 19.4.1918. Hat story still circulating: HE to KE 17.4.1918.

374-7 German breakthrough: HE D 4.4.1918. In 'great gloom': *OH* vol. 5, p. 332. Absolute readiness: 15 BD 4.4.1918. Elliott to Ferres: *OH* vol. 5, p. 327. Cavalry magnificent: HE D 4.4.1918. Urgent business elsewhere: HE to KE 18.4.1918. Marvellously meagre casualties: HE to ME 12.4.1918. Rawlinson's assessment: Rawlinson to H. Wilson 5.4.1918, Rawlinson papers, NAM. Bean's appraisal: *OH* vol. 5, p. 328. Edmonds misleading: Bean to Edmonds 17.9.1935, AWM 38 3DRL 7953/30. 14 Div unreliable & commander useless: Edmonds to Bean 2.10.1935, AWM 38 3DRL 7953/30. The 'absolute limit': J. Monash to V. Monash 4.4.1918, Monash papers, NLA. 15 Bde superb: Monash to Hobbs 5.4.1918, Monash papers, NLA. Praise from cavalry: L.E.W. Harman to HE

6.4.1918, EP 2DRL 513/15.

377-8 Sayers exploit: HE to KE 18.4.1918, HE to BC 19.4.1918. Corbie headquarters: HE to KE 11.4.1918; HE to BC 11 & 19.4.1918; HE to ME 12.4.1918 & 1.5.1918.

379-81 'Hamel untenable': HE D 6.4.1918; *OH* vol. 5, p. 527. Pompey livid: HE to JT 25.5.1918, EP 2DRL 513/46; *CPD* 13.4.1921 p. 7378. No luxury for Tivey: HE to KE 11.4.1918. Cable: EP 2DRL 513/21. Proud of AIF, praise for 58 Bn, Hedauville encounter: HE to KE 17 & 18.4.1918.

381-2 Elliott on the British: HE to ME 12 & 19.4.1918 & 4.5.1918. Machine-gunners grateful: C.H. Reid to HE 9.4.1918, AWM 38 3DRL 606/261.

382-4 Backs to the wall: *OH* vol. 5, p. 437. Situation bad indeed, new Cromwell needed, & fervent morale booster: HE to ME 19.4.1918. Forthright edict: HE memorandum 15.4.1918, WO 95/3641, PRO.

Chapter Sixteen [pp 385–423]

385-7 Marshall: HE to KE 18.4.1918; HE D 21.4.1918; Doig to L. Grant 29.4.1918 & 2.5.1918, Doig papers, SLV. Helping 'old CO', & 'greater efficiency': 15 BD 21.4.1918. Praising Denehy: HE to M. Denehy 24.11.1918 (made available by Mrs J.F. Timberlake); HE to JT n.d. [24.9.1928], EP 2DRL 513/40.

387-9 Sound military principle: *OH* vol. 5, p. 535. Heneker: P.A. Ledward memoirs p. 43, IWM. Rawlinson's perceptions: Rawlinson to C. Wigram 27.3.1918, to Wilson 17.4.1918 & to Lord Derby 11.4.1918, Rawlinson papers, NAM.

389-91 Bois l'Abbé vital, & Hobbs rejecting Elliott's suggestion: HE BR, p. 2. Elliott's Aubigny report: HE to 5 Div 24.4.1918, 15 BD.

392-8 British retirement predictable: HE BR, p. 3. 'He replied "Yes"': HE BR, pp. 4-5. Hobbs's qualified assent: Hobbs to HE 8.40 & 8.50am 24.4.1918, 5 Div D. 'Get in touch': HE to 57-60 Bns 9.05am 24.4.1918, 15 BD. 'Your troops have retired': Hobbs to 8 Div 8.59am 24.4.1918, 5 Div D. Heneker unforthcoming: Hobbs to Birdwood 9.32am 24.4.1918, 5 Div D. Hobbs instructing Elliott: Hobbs to HE 9.55am 24.4.1918, 15 BD. Pompey's compliance: HE to 57-60 Bns 10.00am 24.4.1918, 15 BD. Plain as a pikestaff: HE to ME 1.5.1918. Watson informative: Report centre to HE 2.25pm 24.4.1918, 15 BD; HE BR, p. 13. Christian: HE BR, p. 8. Pompey remonstrating: Need, p. 207.

398 Harrowing ordeal: Ledward memoirs p. 73, IWM. Terrifying iron pill-box, & monster's nose appearing: *OH* vol. 5, pp. 552, 554.

399 Elliott justifying controversial order: HE to JT 25.5.1918, EP 2DRL 513/46; HE BR, p. 9; *CPD* 11.5.1921, p. 8255. Bean unconvinced: *OH* vol. 5, p. 550.

400 Rawlinson summoning 13 Bde: *OH* vol. 5, p. 568. Children: Rawlinson to Wilson 24.4.1918, Rawlinson papers, NAM.

400-1 Butler advising Heneker: Butler to Heneker 10.50am 24.4.1918, III Corps D, WO 95/678, PRO. Butler urging co-operation: Butler-Hobbs conversation 11.23am 24.4.1918, 5 Div D. Hobbs's assistance ignored: Hobbs to Bean 30.7.1936, AWM 38 3DRL 6673/350. Hobbs obliging: Hobbs to Heneker 11.57am 24.4.1918, 5 Div D. White on Beddington: E. Beddington, 'My Life', Hertfordshire County Council Archives, p. 179. Recollection unclear: WO 95/435, PRO. Rawlinson instilling urgency: III Corps D, WO 95/678, PRO. 'We *must* get it back': Rawlinson to Wilson 24.4.1918, Rawlinson papers, NAM. Plaintive protest: Heneker to III Corps 12.40pm 24.4.1918, III Corps D, WO 95/678, PRO.

403 A.C. White unequivocal, & 'bloody lucky': A.C. White to Bean 27.4.1936,

AWM 38 3DRL 6673/519.

404-5 Shepherding job: HE to JT n.d. [24.9.1928], EP 2DRL 513/40. Plenty of stew: Need, p. 208. Delay baffling: J. McKenna, 'The Australian Night Attack on Villers-Bretonneux', p. 2 (made available by John McKenna). Nerves shredded: D. Whinfield D 24.4.1918 (made available by Ken Hubbard).

406-7 Bean & others pessimistic: AWM 38 3DRL 606/108, pp. 23-4; Downing, p. 132; Need, p. 208. *British–Australasian*: HE to C. Chomley 25.4.1918 & 7.5.1918, Marsh papers, NLA. Monash: Serle, p. 363.

408-9 Straining at the leash, & 'blood run cold': J. Scanlan BR, p. 1. Calm easy voice: *OH* vol. 5, p. 602. Throat jab: HE to G. McCrae 6.5.1918, McCP.

409-11 Elliott only guessing: HE BR, p. 18. Flexible instructions: HE to Denehy 3.20am 25.4.1918, 15 BD. Sadlier: *OH* vol. 5, p. 583. 'I never departed': HE to JT n.d. [24.9.1928], EP 2DRL 513/40. Heneker's HQ: A.C. White to Bean 27.4.1936, AWM 38 3DRL 6673/519.

413 A 'hairbrained suggestion': Hobbs-HE conversation 8.10am 26.4.1918, 5 Div D; HE to JT 7.7.1918, 15 BD.

414-15 Bean on casualties: *OH* vol. 5, p. 637. Elliott gassed: HE to KE 28.4.1918; HE D 26.4.1918. Lavish praise: HE to KE 28.4.1918.

416-7 Aubigny retraction: HE to ME 30.4.1918; HE to Bean 10.6.1929, EP 1DRL 264/1B; HE to JT 25.5.1918 & HE to Hobbs 30.4.1918, 2DRL 513/46. Shelled while writing: HE to ME 30.4.1918.

418-21 Butler credited: Fourth Army to GHQ 3.50pm 25.4.1918, III Corps D, WO 95/678, PRO; Haig D 24.4.1918, PRO. Pompey livid: HE to KE 5.5.1918; AWM 38 3DRL 606/108, p. 60; HE to G. McCrae 6.5.1918, McCP. Heneker: 8 Div report pp. 6, 8, PRO. Hobbs claiming credit: Hobbs D 27.4.1918, PR 82/153/3, AWM. Numerous conversations: III Corps report p. 12, Butler papers, IWM. Hobbs reminiscing: Hobbs to Bean 30.7.1936, AWM 38 3DRL 6673/350. Planned by III Corps: Fourth Army to GHQ 3.50pm 25.4.1918, III Corps D, WO 95/678, PRO. Bean singling out Elliott: *OH* vol. 5, pp. 638-9.

422-3 Praise: *OH* vol. 5, p. 638; F. Cutlack (ed), *War Letters of General Monash* (Sydney, 1934), p. 238; *Reveille* 1.8.1936; Ledward memoirs, p. 78, IWM; Lytton, pp. 163-4; H. Essame, *The Battle for Europe 1918* (London, 1972), p. 3; R. McMullin, *Will Dyson: Cartoonist, Etcher and Australia's Finest War Artist* (Sydney, 1984), pp. 162-3.

Chapter Seventeen [pp 424–453]

424-5 Cutlack's portrait: EP 2DRL 513/43. Joy-ride, & spoiling the shrubbery: HE to KE 12.5.1918, HE D 11.5.1918.

426 Experience valuable: Birdwood to Pearce 13.5.1918, AWM 27 361/10. Lost our Trumper: AWM 38 3DRL 1722/30.

427-30 Hasty protest: HE D 21.5.1918. Spirited reply: White to HE 22.5.1918, EP 2DRL 513/46. Elliott upset: HE D 22.5.1918. Heated discussion: HE to KE 24.5.1918. Melbourne meeting: J. Marshall to HE 28.3.1918, EP 1DRL 264/1B. Embittered: HE to JT 3.6.1918, EP 2DRL 513/46. Bow and scrape: AWM 38 3DRL 606/276. Conned by deception: HE to Bean 10.6.1929, EP 1DRL 264/1B.

431-6 'The complaint against me': HE to JT 25.5.1918, EP 2DRL 513/46. Condemning Birdwood circular: *Age* 28.5.1921; HE to ME 4.5.1918; HE to JT 25.5.1918, EP 2DRL 513/46. Criticisms not universal: HE to editor *Sun* (Syd) 17.6.1921, EP 2DRL 513/42B. Birdwood squirming: HE BR (V/Bret), p. 10.

Shameless lies: HE to JT 25.5.1918, EP 2DRL 513/46; HE BR (V/Bret), p. 9. Transformed perceptions: AWM 27 357/12. Smuggled to me: JT to A. Bazley 24.2.1932, 3DRL 6673/258.

436-8 Convincing demolition: HE to Hobbs 25.5.1918, EP 2DRL 513/46. Delighted by departure, & White under the thumb: HE to KE 1.6.1918; HE D 29.5.1918. Preferring Monash, & solitary misgiving: HE to KE 1.6.1918; HE to BC 7.7.1918. Hobbs consoling: *CPD* 21.4.1921, p. 7560.

438-40 McCay's protest: McCay to H. Walker 15.6.1915, AWM 25 789/4. Brand's 'representation': Birdwood to Pearce 24.3.1916, 3DRL 3376, AWM. Formal advice: V. Sellheim to Secretary, Defence department 21.5.1918, AWM 27 361/10. Glasgow & Rosenthal: Birdwood to Pearce 7.5.1918, 3DRL 3376, AWM. So 'entirely wanting': Birdwood to Bean 25.8.1921, AWM 38 3DRL 6673/352.

440-2 Monash supportive: Monash to HE 16.9.1929, EP 1DRL 264/1B. Lagnicourt: *OH* vol. 4, p. 201. Born soldier: AWM 38 3DRL 606/276.

443 Zeal and ability: HE BR (V/Bret), p. 5. Chestnut Troop: Chestnut Troop D 29.4.1918, WO 95/455, PRO; *OH* vol. 5, p. 675.

444-7 Magnificent instrument: *OH* vol. 5, p. 524. Fight 'to the end': HE to Hobbs 30.4.1918, 5 Div D. 15 Bde school: Hobbs D 10.7.1918, PR 82/153/4, AWM. No obligation: HE to ME 4.5.1918. 'You've got men's lives': inf C. Noad. Brockfield: HE to 5 Div 23.4.1918, 15 BD; AIF Admin HQ London to AIF HQ France 18.4.1918, 15 BD. Swagman: *Despatches* 1968, p. 30. Charlie Elliott: HE to KE 20.8.1916; HE to G. McCrae 13.10.1917, McCP. Eric Walker: HE to BC 12.10.1917. Jack Prictor: inf A. Dineen; HE to KE 8 & 15.6.1918. Had to perform: HE to KE 1.3.1916. Reg Avery: HE to KE 27.7.1917, 30.8.1917, 8.9.1917. Mother's grief: HE to ME 30.4.1918.

448-9 Hard but just: HE to J. Marshall 1.1.1917, EP 3DRL 3297/14. 'Good morning Denehy': inf A. Dineen. Scotty: PR 87/215, AWM. Love even the worst: HE to KE 1.6.1918. Bean's tribute: *Reveille* 31.3.1931, p. 32. How loved: M. Plowman to KE 4.6.1918, EP 2DRL 513/15. Absolutely the best: J. Duigan to KE 7.3.1917, EP 2DRL 513/20. No greater: AWM 38 3DRL 606/276.

450-3 Coffin cf Watson: HE to JT 7.7.1918, 15 BD. White's reply: White to HE 13.6.1918, EP 2DRL 513/46. Characteristically frank: HE BR (V/Bret), pp. 9-10, 25-7. Gellibrand's nationality: HE to JT 25.5.1918, EP 2DRL 513/46. Gellibrand on Elliott: 3DRL 1473/36, AWM. By far: HE to JT 10.11.1918, AWM 252 A158.

Chapter Eighteen [pp 454–495]

454-6 Congratulations: J. Anderson to HE 3.6.1918 & F. Robinson to HE 6.6.1918, EP 2DRL 513/16. Work to do: HE D 16.6.1918. 'We will win in the end': HE to KE 15.6.1918. Enemy's lost punch: HE to ME 22.4.1918. Flu: HE to KE 21.6.1918.

459-60 McDonald's communication was noted in 15 BD list of messages. Elliott on Ville operation: HE to BC 7.7.1918; HE to KE 8.7.1918. Facey: HE D 4.7.1918; HE to Hobbs 9.7.1918, 15 BD. Knight: Corfield, p. 158. Moore: HE to Hobbs 9.7.1918, 15 BD.

460-1 Rest needed: HE to KE 26 & 28.6.1918. Latham's perceptions: Latham to D. Picken 16.7.1918, Latham papers 1009/1/455-56, NLA. Alec and Helen: HE to KE 15.7.1918, EP 2DRL 513/43; N. Peaston to HE 11.1.1917, EP 2DRL 513/14. At Ullapool: HE to KE 21 & 27.7.1918.

463-6 True role: J. Monash, *The Australian Victories in France in 1918* (Melbourne, 1923), p. 104. 'I fully agree': AWM 38 3DRL 606/266. Downing optimistic: Downing, p. 141. Monash's message: 15 BD. Conditions similar: 15 BD 7.8.1918. Feeble response: HE D 8.8.1918. Splendid performance: Rawlinson to Aust'n Corps 16.8.1918, 15 BD. Downing's observation: Downing, p. 148. Black day: P. Pedersen, *Monash as Military Commander* (Melbourne, 1985), p. 247. 'As usual', & no coincidence: HE to KE 11.8.1918. Chief instrument: Pedersen, p. 245.

468-9 Tailboard down: AWM 38 3DRL 606/276. Contrasting First Div faces: Downing, p. 155. Rough day: K. Mackay memoirs, pp. 10-11; inf K. Mackay. Bean's praise & Canadians' gratitude: *OH* vol. 6, p. 629; 6 Canadian Bde BR, p. 5, 15 BD; A.H. Bell to HE 14.8.1918, 15 BD. Pompey magnanimous: HE to A.H. Bell 17.8.1918, 15 BD.

470-1 Haig outlining new approach: *OH* vol. 6, p. 761. Elliott's address: 15 BD 25.8.1918. Never so promising: HE to KE 28.8.1918. Cheeky swallows: HE to N. Elliott 23.8.1918.

472-4 Elliott's reconnaissance, & advanced HQ: HE D 28.8.1918; AWM 38 3DRL 606/276 & 214, p. 64; *OH* vol. 6, p. 786. Gollan commended: HE D 29.8.1918. At variance with Wisdom, & vigorous patrolling: HE D 30.8.1918. Unable to cross: HE D 31.8.1918.

475-7 Elliott galvanised: AWM 38 3DRL 606/213, p. 16; HE D 1.9.1918. Bawled to us: E. Whiteside (ed), *A Valley in France* (Melbourne, 1999), p. 165. Canal deep: HE D 1.9.1918. Unforgettable spectacle: AWM 38 3DRL 606/276. Communications hampered: *OH* vol. 6, p. 851 fn 55.

477-81 58 Bn companies stymied: HE BR, para 9 (copy perused is unpaginated). Very rough time: HE D 1.9.1918, 28.8.1918. Other commanders uninformed: HE BR, para 12. Blunt assessment: HE D 1.9.1918. Forlorn hope: AWM 38 3DRL 606/266; HE BR, para 12; HE to Bean 10.6.1929, EP 1DRL 264/1B. Most onerous: Hobbs D 31.8.1918 & 1.9.1918, PR 82/153/4, AWM. Monash's maxim, & 'I was compelled': Monash, pp. 104, 209. Remarkable generosity, & Marshall to Moon: *OH* vol. 6, p. 865. Effective method: H. Ferres BR, p. 2. 'Whole attack held up': Scanlan to HE 9.55am 2.9.1918, HE BR, para 14. Like an earthquake: HE BR, para 18. Annihilation inevitable: HE BR, para 21. Resignation threat: HE D 1.9.1918.

482-4 Lively escapades: Corfield, p. 186; AWM 38 3DRL 606/203, p. 30. Elliott's men exhausted: HE D 3.9.1918; Hobbs D 5.9.1918, PR 82/153/4, AWM. Beyond me: Hobbs D 6.9.1918, PR 82/153/4, AWM. Rawlinson's praise: *OH* vol. 6, p. 873 fn 1. Ferocious and gruelling: HE to KE 6.9.1918; HE to BC 8.9.1918.

484-7 First recorded mutiny: *OH* vol. 6, p. 875. Rebels' statement: 15 BD. Cause for complaint: 15 BD 5.9.1918. On the phone: Hobbs D 5.9.1918, PR 82/153/4, AWM. Doyle's conclusion: HE D 6.9.1918. Medical report: H.S. McLelland to ADMS 5 Div 5.9.1918, AWM 26/573/4. Elliott to bn commanders: 15 BD 7.9.1918; 15 Bde Circular Memorandum Sept 1918, 15 BD. Monash resisting: Pedersen, p. 277.

487-91 Hughes distracted: HE D 14.9.1918. Elliott against home leave: HE to KE 23.9.1918. Instructions circulated: 5 Div to 15 Bde 19.9.1918, 15 BD. 'AIF authorities decree': HE to H. Duigan 14.5.1918, 15 BD. Elliott reprimanded: T. Dodds to Hobbs 29.5.1918, 15 BD. Elliott furious: 15 BD 26.9.1918. 'We've got bullets': inf E. Rowe. Like an avalanche: Whinfield D 26.9.1918. Like 'deserting our dead': HE to editor *Sun* (Syd) 17.6.1921, EP 2DRL 513/42B. Bean's conclusion: *OH* vol. 6, p. 939. Understandably proud: HE D 27.9.1918.

492-4 Confusion, & Americans disorganised: HE D 29.9.1918; HE to Hobbs 12 noon 29.9.1918, 15 BD. 59 Bn lost heavily: HE D 29.9.1918. Scanlan: Scanlan BR, p. 1. 'Damn it': *OH* vol. 6, p. 1011. Exceedingly difficult: *OH* vol. 6, p. 1013.

494-5 Successes unsurpassed: Rawlinson to Aust'n Corps 14.10.1918, 15 BD. Peace country: HE to BC 18.10.1918. Dreadful fighting, & Neale: HE to KE 3.10.1918. Dalgleish: J.F. Henderson to HE 15.1.1919, EP 2DRL 513/43; *Herald* 7.1.1919. Connelly: HE to BC 18.10.1918. French citation: AWM 38 3DRL 606/261.

Chapter Nineteen [pp 496–510]

496-7 Peace bewildering: AWM 38 3DRL 606/117, p. 80. Elliott's reaction: HE D 11.11.1918; HE to V. Elliott 12.11.1918; HE to ME 11.11.1918. 'No one knows': HE to KE 4 & 15.12.1918.

497-8 Counting the days: HE to KE 19 & 31.10.1918. Now inadvisable: HE to KE 26.12.1918.

498-9 Surroundings no help: HE to KE 4, 10 & 13.12.1918. So many dead: HE to Latham 13.9.1918, 1009/1/503, NLA; HE to M. Denehy 24.11.1918 (made available by Mrs J.F. Timberlake); HE to BC 15.11.1918.

499-501 Pretended affability: HE to KE 5.1.1919. Birdwood's tantrum: HE D 26.11.1918; HE to editor *Sun* (Syd) 17.6.1921, EP 2DRL 513/42B. 'I don't care': HE to KE 31.10.1918. Compared to Monash: HE to BC 6.11.1918. Aspersions on Tivey: HE to KE 15.12.1918. Burning resentment: HE D 15.12.1918. Hobbs to Elliott: HE D 10.1.1919.

502-4 Concern about Roberts defalcation: HE to KE 5.1.1919, 25.12.1918, 5.3.1919. Flory: HE to BC 19.2.1919 & 6.11.1918; HE to KE 5.1.1919. Bns dwindling: HE to KE 5.1.1919. Blood clot: HE to KE 14.3.1919. Fearful depression: HE to KE 22.2.1919. Lethargy: HE to BC 19.2.1919. Soothing needed: HE to KE 4.2.1919, 24.1.1919. Past his prime: HE to KE 20.3.1919, 7.2.1919, 5.1.1919. Blues: HE to KE 5.4.1919, 20.3.1919, 5.3.1919. Worry and weakness: HE to KE 14 & 20.3.1919.

505-7 Reunion dinner: 15 BD 3.1.1919. Brigade tribute: 15 BD 21.1.1919.

508-10 'Geordie's grave': HE to KE 5.4.1919. Church: AWM 38 3DRL 6673/954, p. 6. London march: HE to KE 3 & 5.5.1919. Children: HE to N. Elliott 19.4.1919; HE to BC 6.11.1918. Still run down: HE to KE 30.4.1919. Durban: AWM 7 item 9. Telegrams: EP 2DRL 513/21.

Chapter Twenty [pp 511–536]

511-14 Cutlack's portrait: EP 2DRL 513/43. 'Welcome, welcome': A. McKenzie to HE 26.6.1919, EP 2DRL 513/43. Robust and cheerful: *Age* 30.6.1919. Essendon function: *Essendon Gazette* 31.7.1919; *Argus* 25.7.1919. Footscray function: *Footscray Advertiser* 16.8.1919; Footscray *Independent* 16.8.1919.

514-15 Crucial deal: M. Lake, *The Limits of Hope* (Melbourne, 1987), p. 211; R. McMullin, *The Light on the Hill: The Australian Labor Party 1891-1991* (Melbourne, 1991), pp. 117-18. 'Some one is needed': J.F. Henderson to HE 15.1.1919, EP 2DRL 513/43.

517-18 Domain gathering: *Age*, *Argus* 24.7.1919. Identical accounts: *Essendon Gazette* 31.7.1919; *Footscray Advertiser* 16.8.1919.

520-2 Like own son: inf Eric Roberts. Young Australia Force: AWM 38 3DRL 6673/432.

523-5 The 'us poor buggers' sentence is the way the gist of these requests was described to me by an observer who heard plenty of them and did not wish to be identified. Never a politician: Footscray *Independent* 16.8.1919. Body and soul: HE to D. Toohey 22.8.1919 (made available by Eileen Barrett). 'For God's sake': *CPD* 28.4.1921, p. 7835. Urged in 1917 to consider parliament: HE to KE 4.5.1917. Anti-McGrath: HE to BC 15.11.1918.

256-7 Green's account is in his *Servant of the House* (Melbourne, 1969), p. 37. Political background to 1919 election: McMullin, *The Light on the Hill*, chapter 5.

528-30 Moonee Ponds: *Age* 11.11.1919; *Essendon Gazette* 13.11.1919. Disorderliness: *Richmond Guardian* 22.11.1919. Portland: *Portland Guardian* 4.12.1919. Bean's description: *Reveille* 31.3.1931. No obligation, & 'class hatred': *Camperdown Chronicle* 27.11.1919; *Ballarat Star* 10.12.1919.

531 McDougall: *Horsham Times* 9.12.1919; T. King, 'The Tarring and Feathering of J.K. McDougall', *Labour History* 45 (November 1983), pp. 54-67.

532-3 Hidden Gallipoli facts: *Ballarat Star* 8.12.1919. Anti-McGrath blast: *Ballarat Star* 11.12.1919.

534-6 'Of course': R. Harris to HE 19.12.1919, EP 2DRL 513/18. Postcard: EP 2DRL 513/44. Foreword: Downing, pp. 7-11. Downing thrilled: Downing to HE 24.2.1920, EP 2DRL 513/18. Schroder: AWM 38 3DRL 606/276.

Chapter Twenty-one [pp 537–564]

537-9 Second speech: *CPD* 29.7.1920, p. 3065. Canberra: *CPD* 1.10.1920, pp. 5229-34. In the neck: *CPD* 29.7.1920, p. 3064.

540 Ballarat: *Ballarat Star* 17.12.1919; *Ballarat Courier* & *Ballarat Star* 3.5.1920; inf G. Clarke; HE to Bean 20.7.1920, AWM 43.

541-2 Satisfaction in Bendigo: *Argus* 8.7.1920. Rowdy meeting: *Bendigo Advertiser* 10.7.1920. References: HE to F. South 10.8.1920 (made available by Frank South); McNicoll to HE 25.4.1921, EP 2DRL 513/46.

543-4 Pearce's denial: *CPD* 1.9.1920, p. 4001. Elliott's protest letter (10.2.1921), the Military Board minute, Elliott repeating his request for an inquiry (15.3.1921) and the Board's confirmation of its refusal are all in EP 2DRL 513/46.

544-8 Air Defence Bill: *CPD* 13.4.1921, pp. 7376-8. Top gear: *CPD* 21.4.1921, pp. 7552-62. Monash annoyed: Monash to J. Bruche 25.2.1921, Monash papers box 78 folder 543, NLA. Pratten: *CPD* 21.4.1921, p. 7573. Drake-Brockman: *CPD* 21.4.1921, p. 7580. Pearce: *CPD* 21.4.1921, pp. 7590, 7585.

548-53 Six days later: *CPD* 27.4.1921, pp. 7727, 7734. Warpath: *CPD* 28.4.1921, pp. 7825-9. Drake-Brockman: *CPD* 28.4.1921, p. 7832. Quoting McNicoll: *CPD* 28.4.1921, pp. 7829-30; McNicoll to HE 25.4.1921, EP 2DRL 513/46. Detailed appraisal: P. Sadler, *The Paladin* (Melbourne, 2000), pp. 163-6. Pearce's distaste, & Elliott's anger: *CPD* 28.4.1921, pp. 7834-5. Astonishing outburst: *CPD* 28.4.1921, p. 7837. Special desk: *CPD* 28.4.1921, pp. 7839, 7846.

553-7 Pearce's statement: *CPD* 5.5.1921, p. 7955. Notorious incompetence: HE to W. Massey Greene 24.2.1922, EP 2DRL 513/46. Jacka again: *CPD* 5.5.1921, pp. 8098-9. Drake-Brockman & Henderson: *CPD* 5.5.1921, pp. 8101-3. Elliott nettled: *CPD* 5.5.1921, pp. 8103-4. Monash on Margolin: *Argus* 7.5.1921. Elliott's letter: *Age* 9.5.1921. Pearce's rabbit & Elliott's defence: *CPD* 11.5.1921, pp.

8252-5. Foster & Gardiner: *CPD* 11.5.1921, pp. 8253-6.

558-62 Headlines: *Age* 29.4.1921; *Sun* (Syd) 30.4.1921. McGrath: *CPD* 12.5.1921, p. 8407. Elliott's response: *Argus* 14.5.1921. Shameful betrayal: HE to JT 25.5.1918, EP 2DRL 513/46. Round for round: *Argus* 18, 21, 26, & 31.5.1921. Excessive national self-esteem: *Age* 14.5.1921. Searing rejoinder: *Age* 28.5.1921. Painful spectacle: *Bulletin* 9.6.1921. Elliott forthright, & measured response: *Bulletin* 23.6.1921. Rant: *Bulletin* & *Midnight Sun* 25.6.1921; HE to *Sun* (Syd) 17.6.1921, EP 2DRL 513/42B. Elliott's lecture, & 'not prepared to swallow': *Age* 4.8.1921.

562-4 White 'distressed': White D 29.4.1921, NLA. 'Elliott's exuberance': Gellibrand D 28.4.1921, 3DRL 1473/14. Birdwood–Bean correspondence: AWM 38 3DRL 6673/352. Unbelievable drivel: Fihelly to HE 27.6.1921, EP 2DRL 513/44. Heart and soul: HE to editor *Sun* (Syd) 17.6.1921, EP 2DRL 513/42B. The letters Elliott received from admirers are in EP 2DRL 513/46. Truth-twisting methods: *Midnight Sun* n.d. [1921], AWM newscuttings.

Chapter Twenty-two [pp 565–604]

566-70 Krithia: HE to Bean 1.12.1921, AWM 38 3DRL 8042/14. Special introduction: *OH* vol. 1, pp. 133-4. Querying headstrong: HE to Bean 9.3.1922, AWM 38 3DRL 6673/468. Reply: Bean to HE 16.3.1922, AWM 38 3DRL 6673/505. 'As you suggest': HE to Bean 20.3.1922, AWM 38 3DRL 6673/468. Only memorial worthy: *OH* vol. 1, p. xxx. Gratuitous observation: White to Bean 20.3.1926, AWM 38 3DRL 606/256.

571-4 'I wish': JT to HE 28.11.1921, AWM 93 3.2.144. Stirring speech: *ECT* 16.11.1921. Famous lectures: *Kyabram Free Press* 21.4.1922.

575-8 Garden enthusiast: *Despatches* 1932. Kate: inf E. Marshall. Most inspiring: *Fintonian* July 1921, p. 12. 'Is everyone happy?': inf B. Harris. Colin saturated: inf I. Prictor.

578-82 Sombre mood: *CPD* 20.9.1922, p. 2396. Elliott unequivocal: *CPD* 20.9.1922, pp. 2426-8. 'Without an E': G. Souter, *Acts of Parliament* (Melbourne, 1988), p. 193. Strong loyalty: *Duckboard* 1.6.1929. 'Men, money and markets': S. Macintyre, *The Oxford History of Australia* vol. 4 1901-1942 (Melbourne, 1986), p. 201. Deep interest: P. Hasluck, *Australia in the War of 1939-1945: The Government and the People 1939-1941* (Canberra, 1952), p. 17. 'I say deliberately': *CPD* 9.8.1923, p. 2369. On ALP defence policy: *CPD* 11.7.1923, pp. 890-1 & 9.9.1925, pp. 2307-8. Severe critic: *CPD* 17.8.1922, p. 1437. Brilliant suggestion: *CPD* 10.10.1922, p. 3419.

583 Big Lone Pine file: Bean to HE 7.6.1923, AWM 38 3DRL 8042/20. 'I don't expect': *OH* vol. 2, p. 562. Complimenting Bean: HE to Bean 2.7.1925, AWM 38 3DRL 606/256.

583-5 Allen inquiry: *CPD* 22.8.1923, pp. 3307-8. Funniest AIF story, & Tasmanian Club sequel: F. Green to A. Bazley 20.9.1966 & 4.4.1965, Bazley papers 3DRL 3520/81, AWM.

587-9 Lawlessness deplored: *Age* 6.11.1923; A. Moore, *The Secret Army and the Premier* (Sydney, 1989), p. 48; C. Massingham, 'When Police Strike: The Victorian Police Strike of 1923' in K. Milte, *Police in Australia* (Sydney, 1977), p. 289. 'Anywhere with Pompey': *Age* 5.11.1923. Monash's acknowledgment: Monash to A. Robinson 6.11.1923, Monash papers, folder 587, NLA. 'The people can rely': *Herald* 4.11.1923. Elliott's startling letter to Robinson is in

Monash papers NLA, as is Monash's reply to Robinson (folder 587). Robinson lying: A. Robinson to HE 9.11.1923, EP 2DRL 513/19.

591-5 Stones: Latreille, pp. 13-23. Distressing drowning: *CPD* 11.3.1926, p. 1521. Soldier settlement enthusiast: *CPD* 11.7.1923, p. 894 & 14.8.1923, p. 2669. Finest advocate: *CPD* 9.12.1921, p. 14205. Lyn's bitterness: inf R. Headley & P. McCombe. Urging tolerance: HE to BC 15.11.1918. Jacqui's education: *CPD* 2.7.1930, p. 3548. Mild protest: inf I. Prictor. Guide, philosopher and friend: *Duckboard* 1.5.1931. Childbirth-suicide tragedy: *CPD* 11.3.1926, p. 1521. Collins Street encounter: inf C. Wignell. Jim Milroy: PR 87/215, AWM.

596-7 'Let us be united': *Herald* 24.4.1925. Stirring panegyric: *Herald* 25.4.1925. C.J. Dennis: *Punch* 21.5.1925. Gratifying sentence: *Herald* 25.4.1925, *Age* 27.4.1925.

598-604 Frankston skirmish: *Truth* 18.4.1925. Perceptive profile: *Punch* 6.8.1925. Campaigning: *Bendigo Advertiser* 8.10.1925; *St Arnaud Mercury* 14.10.1925; *Birchip Advertiser* 16.10.1925; *Donald Times* 16.10.1925; *Sunraysia Daily* 16, 17 & 19.10.1925. Hat's return reported: *Herald* 20.10.1925; *Guardian* 20.10.1925. Beware leg-pull: HE to JT 23.12.1925, AWM 93 419/31/2. Memorable social: *Sunraysia Daily* 19.10.1925. Finest advocate: *CPD* 9.12.1921, p. 14205.

Chapter Twenty-three [pp 605–628]

606-9 Elliott on Canberra: *CPD* 21.7.1926, p. 4390, 8.7.1926, p. 3906, 12.8.926, pp. 5333-6, 5342-4. Profiteering: *CPD* 22.3.1927, pp. 820, 833. Back to Charlton: *ECT* 20.10.1926. Dead still speaking: *CPD* 9.5.1927, p. 3. Sizeable correspondence: Latham papers, series 41, NLA. Idle since Christmas: F. Brennan, *Canberra in Crisis* (Canberra, 1971), pp. 120-1. Close to perjury, & 'sick and tired': *CPD* 20.9.1928, pp. 6972, 6964. To the rescue: HE to Latham 15.8.1928, Latham papers 1009/41/402, NLA. Friend of Territory: *CPD* 6.10.1927, p. 262. 'It's all unjust': notes of interview 22.9.1928, Latham papers 1009/41/419, NLA. Serious problem: Latham to S.M. Bruce 12.12.1928, Latham papers 1009/41/448, NLA.

610-12 Stressing units' heritage: *Argus* 7.3.1927. Embargo removed: HE to Bean 15.5.1929, AWM 38 3DRL 606/261. In a whirlpool: *Herald* 25.4.1928. Bendigo: *Bendigo Advertiser* 26.4.1928.

613-16 Assn minutes: PR 87/215, AWM. Rousing speech: *Age* 24.9.1925. Clever twist: *Despatches* 1929. Congratulating Elliott, & 'Help us': *Despatches* 1928. Extremely busy life: 7 Bn Assn minutes 23.10.1929, PR 87/215, AWM. Pompey at reunions: inf J. Bignell. Bloody canary: *Smith's Weekly* 4.4.1931. Scurry: HE to KE 20.8.1916; *ADB* vol. 11. Poor Lennon: HE to Jamieson 14.11.1928, PR 87/215, AWM. Radio talk: PR 87/215, AWM.

616-19 Jolly party: C.B.B.White D 8.8.1927, NLA. Blaring headlines: *Sun* (Melb) 7.10.1927; A. Thomson, '"The Vilest Libel of the War"? Imperial Politics and the Official Histories of Gallipoli', *Australian Historical Studies* 101 (Oct 1993). Very great pity: HE to Bean 23.9.1927, AWM 38 3DRL 7953/7. The Villers-Bretonneux assessments in Liddell Hart's *The Remaking of Modern Armies* (London, 1927) are on pp. 303-4. 'Did you read': R. Salmon to HE 18.9.1928, AWM 93 419/31/2. Elliott 'concerned': HE to JT n.d. [24.9.1928], EP 2DRL 513/40. Bean's provisional assessment: note 4.10.1928, AWM 38 3DRL 606/273.

619-20 America's refusal to help, & Pendulum Club: *Pendulum* 25.10.1927. Dual loyalty: K. Hancock, *Australia* (London, 1930). Essay competition: *Minervan* December 1928. Anniversary dinner: unidentified newscutting, Herald library. Criticism of Ryrie: HE to Latham 20.6.1928, Latham papers 1009/41/395, NLA.

620-2 Chilvers remembering: inf B. Chilvers. God in trees, & bicycle essay: inf J. Robison. 'Young Pompey': inf B. Lewis & A. Lyne.

623-5 Brilliant ball: *Age* 15.9.1928. 58 Bn reunion: *Herald* 28.9.1928. Endorsing scholarly publications: *Herald* 7.7.1924. Cousin baffled: N. Peaston to HE 19.1.1929, EP 2DRL 513/20. Old story now: *Ballarat Courier* 19.12.1927. Spectacular slide: unattributed newscutting, McCombe papers.

625-8 Bruce's narrow view: D. Potts, A Study of Three Nationalists in the Bruce–Page Government of 1923-29 (MA thesis, University of Melbourne, 1972), p. 144; McMullin, *The Light on the Hill*, p. 130. Deliberately provocative: Macintyre, *Oxford History*, pp. 244-5. Most iniquitous: D. Carboch, 'The Fall of the Bruce-Page Government' in A. Wildavsky & D. Carboch, *Studies in Australian Politics* (Melbourne, 1958), p. 129. Bruce's bombshell: Bruce to J. Hunter 25.5.1929, 1009/39/37, NLA. Telegrams to MPs: Latham papers 1009/39/33, NLA. Unequivocal support: HE to Bruce 29.5.1929, Latham papers series 39, NLA.

Chapter Twenty-four [pp 629–655]

629-30 Propaganda: *CPD* 4.9.1929, p. 498. Bizarre episode: *Age*, *SMH* & *Herald* (Melb) 1.10.1929.

630-1 Elliott-Bean correspondence re *OH* vol. 3: HE to Bean 15.5.1929, Bean to HE 21.5.1929 & HE to Bean 10.6.1929, EP 1DRL 264/1B. Bean worshipping White: letter to his mother quoted in a letter by his brother J. Bean 25.8.1940, White papers carton 4, NLA (seen in 2000 as part of recently acquired material prior to sorting).

633-8 Bean unequivocal: *OH* vol. 3, p. 447. Early published appraisals: *Bulletin* 8.5.1929. Elliott impelled to respond, & covering letter: HE to *Bulletin* 14.5.1929, AWM 27 172/10. Xenophon articles: *Bulletin* 22 & 29.5.1929. The pre-edited versions are in AWM 27 172/10. T.T.T., X.X.X., 927 & 303: *Bulletin* 5, 19 & 26.6.1929, 10.7.1929, 7.8.1929. British protest: *OH* vol. 3, p. 903. Bean on unwanted colonels: *OH* vol. 3, p. 47, 52. Aggrieved widow: Bean to Mrs H. Littler 22.10.1929, AWM 38 3DRL 7953/4.

638-41 Pompey hankering: HE to Bean 15.5.1929, EP 1DRL 264/1B. Elliott–Hobbs correspondence: HE to Hobbs 13.6.1929 & 23.7.1929, Hobbs to HE 8.7.1929, 14.8.1929 & 20.9.1929, EP 2DRL 513/46. Turning to McCay: HE to McCay 9.9.1929 & McCay statement 13.9.1929, EP 2DRL 513/46. Approach to Monash: HE to Monash 1.9.1929, EP 2DRL 513/46; Monash to HE 16.9.1929, EP 1DRL 264/1B.

642-5 Elliott on senators' rights: *CPD* 11.12.1929, pp. 975-9. 'Digger' Dunn: *CPD* 21.11.1929, p. 65 & 13.12.1929, p. 1293. Vile outburst: *CPD* 9.4.1930, pp. 991-3. Stinging letter: McGrath to HE 31.7.1930, EP 2DRL 513/20. Defence system filched: *CPD* 11.12.1929, p. 979. Exasperating and disheartening: HE to Jamieson 10.5.1930, PR 87/215, AWM. Cricket more compelling: *Herald* 21.6.1930. Green's retort: *CPD* 24.6.1930, pp. 3097-9. Pompey's counterattack: *CPD* 25.6.1930, p. 3193. Daly's challenge: *CPD* 25.6.1930, p. 3199. Intensely personal reply: *CPD* 2.7.1930, pp. 3544-50.

645-6 Against unorthodox measures: *CPD* 22.5.1930, p. 2016, 11.12.1929, p. 976 &

17.12.1930, p. 1608. 'We have unanimously': *SMH* 19.8.1930. Condemned in Charlton: *Charlton Tribune* 16.7.1930.

647-50 Only one Pompey: *Duckboard* 1.5.1930, p. 40. Foremost unveiler: *Despatches* 1930. Elliott's *Reveille* articles appeared in its issues of February, April, June & October 1930. Constitutional Club: *Age*, *Argus* & *SMH* 23.4.1929. Fromelles lecture: AWM 38 3DRL 6673/954. 'Bungled Battle': *News-Chronicle* 18.7.1930. Amazing outburst: *Age* 18.7.1930. Spirited rejoinder: *Age* 21.7.1930. 'When the name': *Duckboard* January 1924, p. 5.

650-1 Reconciliation: C.B.B. White D 8.8.1927, NLA. Approaching White: HE to White 30.5.1930 & 6.6.1930, EP 2DRL 513/46. White startled & evasive: C.B.B. White D 2 & 10.6.1930, NLA; White to HE 3 & 10.6.1930, EP 2DRL 513/46. 'The very idea': White to Bean 11.7.1930, AWM 38 3DRL 606/247.

651-3 Supersession obsession: Bean's note 4.10.1928, AWM 38 3DRL 606/273; HE to Hobbs 23.7.1929, EP 2DRL 513/46. Mass hopelessness: A. Sharpe, *Nostalgia Australia* (Sydney, 1975), p. 131. At wits end: HE to Jamieson 10.5.1930, PR 87/215, AWM. 'No other aspect': *Despatches* 1932. No inkling: inf J.M. Coldrey. Newspapers: *Sun* (Melb) 16.2.1931; *Age*, *Argus*, *Herald* 17.2.1931.

653-5 Oven incident: VPRS 24/1193/333 (1931), PROV. Daily bulletins: *Sun*, *Age*, *Argus*, *Herald* 17.2.1931. Chaplain: *Despatches* 1932. Severely depressed, & last hours: VPRS 24/1193/333 (1931), PROV; *Smith's Weekly* 18.4.1931.

Chapter Twenty-five [pp 656–666]

656-7 Discreetly vague: *Herald* 23.3.1931, *Age* 24.3.1931, *Labor Daily* 24.3.1931. Hobbs: *West Australian* 24.3.1931. 'Probably no other': *Argus* 24.3.1931. Latham: *CPD* 24.3.1931, pp. 511-12. Labor senators, & Payne & Sampson: *CPD* 25.3.1931, pp. 560, 562. 'My heart is sore': B. Sampson to J. Sampson 23.3.1931, EP SLV.

658-9 Funeral: *Argus* 26.3.1931, *Herald* 25.3.1931, inf G. McKaige. Jamieson: *Despatches* 1932. The letters to Kate from Bruce, MacFarland & the militia colleague, C. Nelson, are all 25.3.1931, EP SLV.

659-60 Bean's obituary: *Reveille* 31.3.1931. Anzac Day tribute: unattributed newscutting, McCombe papers. 'No more loyal': *Despatches* 1932. School function: *Ballarat Courier* 4.5.1931. Thanksgiving service: PR 87/215, AWM.

660-3 Inquest: VPRS 24/1193/333 (1931), PROV. Glowing profile: *Smith's Weekly* 4.4.1931. Exposé: *Smith's Weekly* 18.4.1931. Retaliation: *Terang Express* 17.4.1931. 'If you want': W. Downing's introduction to his father's reissued book *To the Last Ridge* (Sydney, 1998), p. xii. Memorial: personal inspection.

664-5 Neil and New Guinea: CRS A518/1 852/1/552, Australian Archives (ACT branch); *Sun* (Melb) 5.7.1939; JT to V. Elliott 20.9.1939, AWM 93 12/4/59.

665-6 Violet's 'aura': inf J. Smithers. Heartfelt sentiment: see e.g. N. Denehy to V. Elliott 10.4.1942, McCombe papers. Gladiolus: unattributed newscutting, McCombe papers.

Acknowledgments

During my progress on this book many people gave me information about Elliott. I remain very grateful for this valuable assistance, but unfortunately it is not possible to mention all of them here.

I first became interested in Pompey Elliott many years ago. Subsequently, while working on another project, a knee injury prevented me from sitting at a desk; on crutches for a month, I spent much of my convalescence propped on a couch, ringing up veterans who had served under Pompey and others who had known him. When I later decided to embark on a biography, the information derived from those conversations proved immensely useful. After I made a start, my research at times had to give way to other projects and activities. For this and other reasons I completed this project a good while after I first began contemplating it.

Along the way my research and writing was assisted by funding from the Literature Board of the Australia Council, the Australian War Memorial, the Army History Research Grants Scheme, and Arts Victoria (the Victorian Ministry for the Arts). Also beneficial to this project was a National Library Fellowship, which I was able to utilise for research on Pompey as well as the centenary history of the Australian Labor Party I was then beginning.

I am grateful to Henry Rosenbloom of Scribe Publications for publishing the book, and the organisations providing publication subsidies—the University of Melbourne, which provided a publications grant (initiated by the Department of History), the Department of Veterans' Affairs (through its Local Commemorative Activities Fund), and the Australian Academy of the Humanities.

I thank Catherine Magree for her editing contribution and Chandra Jayasuriya for drawing the maps and designing the family tree.

The Australian War Memorial (AWM) provided almost half the photographs. Most of the rest came from Pompey Elliott's great-niece Jan McCombe, whose notable contribution also included expertise on the genealogy of her ancestors.

For assistance with nearly all the non-AWM illustrations I'm indebted to the skills and obliging responsiveness of Melbourne photographer Ross Genat. For making individual photographs available I also thank Marjorie Wieck, Barbara Blomfield, Ina Prictor, and Sarah Martin of Ormond College.

Many others have provided assistance and encouragement during the years I have been engaged on this book. They include the staffs of the Australian War Memorial (in particular, Peter Stanley, Ian Smith, and Ian Affleck), the National Library of Australia (especially Graeme Powell), the State Library of Victoria, the National Archives of Australia, the *Australian Dictionary of Biography*, the University of Melbourne Archives, the Melbourne Cricket Club Library, the Imperial War Museum, and the Public Record Office in London and its namesake in Victoria; those helpful school archives officers Lorraine Paddle (Ballarat College), Dick Briggs (Scotch College, where I was also aided by Paul Mishura), and Alison Adams (Fintona); Grace Cadzow at Charlton; the late Poppy McCombe and Rosemary Headley; the late Bill Jamieson, Bruce Burrows, and the 7th Battalion Association; Lambis Englezos, Robin Corfield, and the Friends of the 15th Brigade; the late Jan Bassett; Michael Piggott; Stuart Macintyre; Ken Inglis; Bill Gammage; David Day; David Horner; the late Lloyd Robson; John Lack; Robin Prior; Michael McKernan; Peter Sadler; Garrie Hutchinson; Denis Winter; Elizabeth Wood-Ellem; Alec Hill; Lenore Frost; the late Kath Emms; Betty Emms; Bruce McMullin; Lesley McMullin; Ruth Naumann; and Sandra Zarbo.

In particular, I thank Joan Monti, David McMullin, and Kate McMullin for supportiveness and tolerance. My apologies to anyone who should be mentioned here and has been inadvertently omitted.

INDEX